THIS GAME
OF BLOOD AND IRON

The Reverend Richard Griffiths, August 1915

THIS GAME
OF BLOOD AND IRON

**LETTERS HOME FROM THE
REVEREND RICHARD GRIFFITHS,
CHAPLAIN TO THE FORCES**

VOL 1 – 1914–1916, FRANCE

Transcribed and collated by
Diana Heywood

*for Janyce & Derek
with my very best
wishes
Diana Heywood*

BROWN
DOG
BOOKS

Published under licence by Brown Dog Books and
The Self-Publishing Partnership, 7 Green Park Station, Bath BA1 1JB

 www.selfpublishingpartnership.co.uk

ISBN 978-1-78545-225-3

Cover design by Diana Heywood

Internal design by Jenny Watson Design

Printed and bound by CPI Group (UK) Ltd, Croydon CR0 4YY

CONTENTS

INTRODUCTION

My grandfather, the Reverend Richard Griffiths, wrote home almost every day from the front line in France, sometimes only a line or two as he was writing by the light of a candle, with gun fire and shells all around after a fearful day tending the wounded and helping the dying. The sentences are often short and staccato as were many of the lives he prayed over and buried. I think what carried him through was his unshakable and certain belief that those who gave their lives were going to a far, far better place "where pain and suffering was no more". Many of his letters contain domestic matters as to the running of the Parish in his absence and these I have, in the greater part, left out.

My grandparents lived with my mother, my brother and me from 1946 (when I was eight) until they died. My mother, Agatha Faith was their youngest daughter. I adored both my grandparents, but my grandfather was really special. He was a feisty little Welshman with an endless fund of stories and jokes to amuse a little girl. He would come up to my bedroom after his supper where I had been pinching myself to keep awake, stand in the doorway and tell me endless tales, much to my mother's horror as I should have been asleep by then. We used to play dominoes together (at which I cheated and he knew but never said!) and an early form of scrabble called Lexicon. He took so long to find the ultimate word that I was armed with a pencil and paper to draw on to stave off boredom – he always won!

He would sit in his extremely untidy bed/sitting room at the top of the house surrounded by old books mostly in Greek and Latin. He bought me the first printing of the Lion the Witch and the Wardrobe in 1957 and also took out a subscription for the Eagle comic for me as it had religious stories on the back page. In return, I used to send him the Latin crossword out of my textbook from school. The house always seemed to be full of visiting bishops, and if he heard a Jehovah's Witness or similar at the front door, he was down the stairs in a flash and would engage them in lengthy arguments on the Bible, which he knew in more detail than they did.

He was endlessly patient and loving to me, probably a demanding and tiresome child, and I never ever remember being told off by either of my grandparents, but was surrounded by their undemanding love. I often wonder how my grandfather, having been through the Boer War and the First World War, coped with the sorrow of his much-loved youngest daughters' loss when her husband of three years (my father) was reported missing, presumed dead, in 1940 after the Battle of Dunkirk. His body was never found and we do not know how, where or when he died, and one remembers the countless men that my grandfather had buried and prayed over – it must have been very hard.

When my grandfather died in 1952, this moving tribute was paid to him by the Rector of Kingston, "Your dear husband always seemed to me to portray what is best and most loved in the Ministry of the Church of England. The Minister who is a beloved pastor to his people. He had the culture, gentleness, sound judgement and Christian dignity which is rarely combined in our Ministry these days. He never grew old. Of course his body did, but never the man himself; he lived always in the present and the future, not in the past. This is remarkable and showed that his constant walk with his Lord was always fresh and vital. Few men I have met have had the freshness and Christian courtesy and love which he showed always".

He was an amazing man who never spoke of the War or his other sorrows, made sure that his two daughters were educated to the same high degree as his son and was always kind, clever and loving – on the day he died he was not going to linger in bed, but made his son carry him downstairs for breakfast, as always.

These tributes of thanks are to my beloved Grandfather, and to my Grandmother who kept all his letters – and the haste with which the envelopes were torn open in an age when letter-openers were always used is a very poignant reminder of her anxiety; to my uncle, Eric Griffiths, who kept everything, and eventually passed it all on to me; to Col. Norman Davies OBE who checked and corrected all the military points; to W.L.R. without whose urging I might never have embarked upon this undertaking; to Concord Cameras in Cirencester who enhanced many of the old photographs; to Busy Fingers also in Cirencester who scanned the photographs. But most of all my complete gratitude and thanks to my two children, Benedict and Rosalind, without whom this 'opus Magnus' would never have got off the ground. Rosie has edited the entire work and Ben has researched over 900 footnotes. I am hugely grateful, my Grandfather would have been so proud of them – as am I.

Diana Heywood, 2017

Richard and his wife Margaret

Reverend Richard David Griffiths

1867   *Born May 24th, 1867, Pontypridd, Son of Griffith Griffiths, of Rye Park House, Rixton. Educated at King's School, Gloucester*

1888   *St Aidan's Theological College, Birkenhead, where he passed out First Class with prizes for Hebrew, literature and Missionary essays and the reading prize.*

1890   *Ordained Deacon, Ripponden in Yorkshire, ordained priest in 1891.*

1892–93   *Assistant chaplain at Holy Trinity, Nice, France.*

1893   *Curate at Holy Trinity, Cambridge, student at Corpus Christi College.*

1896   *B.A. in Theology 2nd class, with star for Church History, M.A. in 1902.*

1897   *Domestic Secretary and Examining Chaplain to the Archbishop of Sydney, William Saumarez-Smith, lecturer in Church History at Moore Theological College, Sydney.*

1900–02   *Travelled in America, acting Chaplain to the Forces in South Africa (2nd Boer War 1899 – 1902) receiving the Queens Medal with 3 clasps.*

1903   *9th July married Margaret eldest daughter (of six) of William Saumarez-Smith.*

Four children: Eric (William Sydney) (b.1904 – d.1996), Margaret (Joyce) (b.1906 – d.1946), Hope (d. in infancy), Agatha (Faith) (b.1911 – d.1997).

1903–10   *Chaplain to the Mission to Seamen, Rochester, Medway. Built the Mission Church and Institute at a cost of £4000.*

1910–20   *Vicar of All Saints, West Farleigh, Kent.*

1914–16   *Chaplain in France to 24th Ambulance Brigade, 8th Division serving in the battles of Neuve Chapelle, Aubers Ridge, the Somme and at no.12 Casualty Clearing Station. He received the 1914 Star, Victory medal and European War Medal, mentioned in dispatches.*

1917   *Joined the Navy as Chaplain with the North Channel Patrol of Minesweepers, Port of Larne, NI. Served in HMS Thetis and HMS Vigorous and was specially thanked by the Admiralty.*

1920   *Appointed to the living at Darley Dale, Derbyshire.*

1938   *Retired, Hope Lodge, Manor Road, Littleover, Derby.*

1952   *Died, 39 Liverpool Road, Kingston, Surrey.*

"... and some there be that have no memorial ...
and are become as though they have never been born.
But these were merciful men ... with their seed shall continually
remain a good inheritance and their children are within the covenant ...
their seed shall remain for ever and their glory not be blotted out.
Their bodies are buried in peace ... but their name liveth for evermore"

Ecclesiasticus 44:12

Thursday, June 4th 1914, Kent

My Darling,

Now I am in the new world! My things have just gone into the tent and I have had tea with two of the officers. A high wind is blowing and rattling the canvases everywhere. Fortunately this Mess place is a wooden hut – roomy and not uncomfortable, in fact, fairly luxurious. The young officers are inclined to grumble – they are a small number, have heavy duties and it is not so cheerful doing them with fewer fellows – strugglers as it is when there are more people to help. I do not know either of them. The intention was a good one, to place a West Kent clergyman[1] with Kentish officers, but lacking in information, for they are young and all rather inexperienced and are mainly from East Kent. I was in their military Battalion for a little while at Kroonstad however, so that makes a little common ground[2]. They are so far Lt. Davison and Lt. Glyn (son of a KC), Capt. Friend, Lt. Cronk[3] and that, I think, is all! No doubt the interest will grow in time.

Your letter has not appeared yet. Perhaps it has gone to the other end of the Garrison! All in good time, I came up soon after lunch today. Rev. Deane Oliver[4] is very nice – a kind, unselfish man, very evangelical with much of the Irish temper about him, quick and hot with his dependents. 'On the edge' of being censorious and caught with the Army spirit of requiring things to be as "they must be or I'll know the reason why!" Not that he thinks that way towards me, but it is his way of looking at and speaking of everything. He is becoming a 'settled' bachelor, and it is just as well he should – it would be difficult now for him to become an adaptable married man! Nor, if he ever had children, would they find him able to be very companionable with their growing years. So I hope he will not think of marrying.

---

1 Rev. **Richard David Griffiths** (RDG) (b.1867 – d.1952) was the vicar of All Saints, **West Farleigh** in Kent, 4 miles west of Maidstone from 1910 – 1920. The letters home are written to his wife, **Margaret Saumarez-Smith** (b.1872 – d.1953), and children **Eric William Sydney** (b.1902 – d.1996), **Margaret Joyce** (b.1906 – d.1949) and **Agatha Faith** (b.1911 – d.1997).

2 **Kroonstad** is the third-largest town in the Free State province of South Africa. Kroonstad was established in 1855 by the Irish pioneer Joseph Orpen, and was the first town founded after the independence.

3 2nd Lieut. **William Guy Cronk** (3rd Battalion E. Kent Regt.), 1st Lieut. **Richard Spenser Glyn** (1st Battalion E. Kent Regt., son of Louis Edmund Glyn KC). Both attached to 1st Battalion King's Royal Rifle Corps. Capt. **George Burton Taddy Friend**, 6th Battalion, E. Kent Regt. 2nd Leiut. **Louis James Davison**, E. Kent Regt.
   Lt. Cronk was killed on 26th October 1914 (aged 21), Lt. Glyn was killed on 20th October 1914 (aged 22). Capt. Friend was killed on 27th July 1915 (aged 35).

4 Reverend **Richard John Deane Oliver** (b.1863 – d.1942). Son of Sir Richard Charles Deane Oliver and Katherine Hawtayne, Co.Cork. Trinity College, Dublin. Listed as Chaplain 4th Class, Captain in Territorial List of 1890, during WW1 he was mentioned in dispatches three times, gaining the rank of Assistant Chaplain-General, 1915 –1920 in the service of the Eastern Command. He was the Chaplain in 1924 at St. Maxine. He was the Anglican Chaplain from 1924 – 1925 at Capri and 1925 – 1929 at Grasse, France. As RDG correctly points out, he never married.

West Farleigh Vicarage, Maidstone, Kent

The wind is rather cold now. I must just go and see my tent and see again if your letter has come. If not, this will be closed and go.

Much love my darling, and to Miss baby – a kiss from Daddy

Thursday June 18th 1914 c/o 3rd Buffs[5] (for the last time this year), Shorncliffe Camp[6]

Odd! At the time of writing it is not clear that I am at liberty to quit Camp. No 'authority' appears to have been received at the Brigade Office closing my tenure, or appointing my successor! The 'officials' are perturbed. Horan[7] is coming, and I am going, if we were strictly Army people I suppose I should be liable to arrest for quitting duty without leave! And Horan would be subject to pains and penalties for taking on himself my office, to which he has not been assigned! It happened through Deane Oliver being away in Switzerland, and Anderson, his junior, now in charge by reason of his tenure, is a 'juggins' – literally a 'juggins[8]'.

However Horan comes tomorrow, and unless something tremendous happens I shall return by the 7.7 at Teston Halt, 'bag and baggage[9]'. What my postcard, sent

---

5   **3/4 Battalion, East Kent Regiment,** 'The Buffs'. RDG was attached as Territorial Army Reserve.
6   **Shorncliffe Army Camp** is a large military camp near Cheriton in Kent. The camp was established in 1794, extended in 1796 and 1806. Shorncliffe was used as a staging post for troops destined for the Western Front during WW1.
7   Rev **Frederick Seymour Horan** (b.1870 – d.1956)
8   A fool; someone very credulous or easily fooled.
9   **Teston Crossing Halt** was situated on what is now the Medway Valley Line, south of

2

Postcard of Shorncliffe Camp

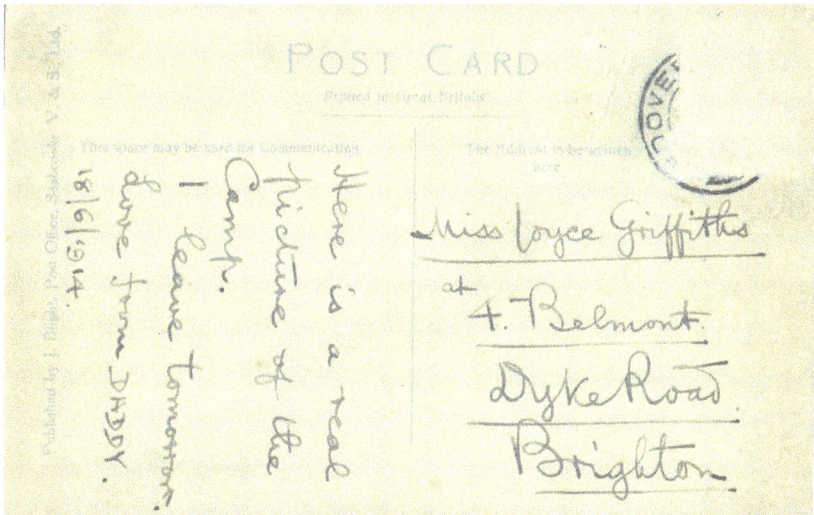

'Here is a real picture of the Camp.
I leave tomorrow.
Love from DADDY.
18/6/1914'

earlier today was meant to say was, that failing Horan's being allowed to carry on here, I would remain here over Sunday, take the duty in order to comply with the regulations, and Horan will come up to West Farleigh, and occupy my bed and take the Sunday service! If a telegram comes to that effect (hardly likely, but if it does) you will understand.

I have just been over to Dover to see the new work and the station. We also saw the Ostend boat going out with but a few passengers. The station will be a fine place when it is finished[10]. Lizzie and Harry are very comfortable in their quiet way[11]. The former is getting fatter and in danger of being vulgar, but Harry is a clever good-tempered sort, very keen on his work and capable at it. Now that the time has come, I find that I am sorry to be leaving the camp. The interest has been great all through, and with improved acquaintance with various people, grows absorbing. The enclosed pictures speak a little. The end officer of the five whose names are on the back, the one to the left, has had a sad year. His wife was killed in a motor accident in February, both her legs being torn – she lingered for 3 months. Then a son at Christ Church, Oxford, behaved foolishly, and then some speculation went wrong and about £30.000 disappeared and he has come to camp to try and work it off.

Thursday August 27th 1914[12] (The Chaplain's House, Warley[13]), Essex
You got home alright, I hope, and found nothing vanished, out of place, broken, soiled or over-used in any way – nothing?

A poor sick soldier called for my attention late last night. They are lonely drift-wood some of them – he is young, and weak with rheumatic fever. I hope he will be better soon.

It has been a day of settling up, after a very short time! And many kind expressions of regret have been made – so unexpected and there will be much to do tomorrow if my relief comes before I depart. What a lot of red tape there is in the Army! The

Maidstone, and served Teston and West Farleigh. It opened in September 1909 and closed in November 1959.
10 **Dover Marine/Dover Western Docks.** Situated on Admiralty Pier for connection to ships, this was constructed on an expanded pier by SECR, finished in 1914, began to be used on 2nd February 1915 but was not available for public use until 18th January 1919; in the meantime it had been renamed *Dover Marine* on 5th December 1918. It was a large terminus with four platforms covered by a full roof.
11 RDG's sister Lizzie and Henry, an engineer, of Deal, Kent.
12 Archduke Franz Ferdinand was assassinated on 28th June 1914, and Britain declared war on Germany on 4th August 1914. After his service in the second Boer War in Southern Africa, RDG was part of the Territorial Army reserve. Hence his presence at Shorncliffe in June 1914, and his presence in the formation of the 2nd Army, preparing to move to France in support of the BEF.
13 **Warley:** suburb of Brentwood in Essex, situated to the south of the town, and from 1842 East India Company's barracks. The area and men were absorbed into the British Army after the Indian Mutiny in 1857, and in 1861 the barracks was bought by the War Office.

price of so splendid an organisation no doubt. It is splendid how you can get even paper fasteners and tin-tacks within 50 miles of a battle field.

I am sorry about the money and I hope you managed alright, perhaps I suppose with Day's help[14]. Unfortunately one has to pay out some things for the Army. I hope they will pay back! At least for the journey's hitherward.

I have been to see Great Warley[15] Church this afternoon in the next Parish, beyond a common with a pond, and great fat geese wandering about. The Church was built in 1902 regardless of cost[16]. Small, but remarkable, with the font shielded by 2 bronze angel figures placed like the Cherubim. The pulpit fronted with a huge, flat bronze cross with some kind of azure stone inlaid. The chancel is an apse, of hammered bright steel, and an oil-painting in the side aisle – much to describe. I also peeped into the Roman Catholic Church[17], where there is a pathetic figure of the Crucified Saviour near the door – very moving.

Saturday September 26th 1914, Dover

It is 7.00 p.m. and I have only just arrived at Lizzies', finding everything in Dover quiet and subdued with an air of tense attention and sense of duty. The harbour is full of naval craft, all with steam up ready for anything. The train was very late, and what with the late arrival and the difficulties about Sunday journeying, I am fair (entre nous) to bide quiet, and join up as I am told to do on Monday at Hythe[18]. If the Government were liberal with travelling facilities to Home Chaplains, I should come upon them and go forward for some effort tomorrow – but literally, I cannot afford it, for a problematical usefulness, and that not being in the 'official' programme here I am, and Harry and Lizzie are most kind in saying 'be quiet here till Monday.' After the rush of things, this will be pleasant. Well, it is a high price we are paying, you and I, to a sense of duty and I pray blessings may come of it. God will assurdly in His mercy accept the offering in the name of the Great Exemplar. We shall put our hearts into 'Give peace, O Lord! Give peace again[19]' – and how we can enter into the feelings of so many thousands whom this wicked Teutonic lawlessness has called to suffer. Let God now prove His righteousness.

---

14   **Day** was **Agatha Faith's** nanny.
15   **Great Warley**: a village in the Brentwood borough of Essex.
16   **St. Mary the Virgin** is the parish church for Great Warley, noted for its unique art nouveau interior, designed by Sir William Reynolds-Stephens. Built in 1902 and consecrated in 1904, the church is Grade I listed. The architect was Charles Harrison Townsend.
17   **Holy Cross and All Saints Roman Catholic Church**, Warley, Brentwood, 1881. Architect; FW Tasker. Built as a mission church for the RC soldiers of Warley barracks and donated by Countess Tasker.
18   **Hythe** is a small coastal market town on the edge of Romney Marsh, in the District of Shepway on the south coast of Kent. The 8th Division assembly point for embarkation at Folkestone/ Dover.
19   Hymn. *O God of Love, O King of Peace*, Henry Baker 1861.

I find I have left my 'orders' behind after all and my little Church calendar – you may possibly find time to post them here before Church time tomorrow, Sunday morning, in one of the big envelopes from a pigeon-hole in my desk? But do not bother if it rushes you, I will chance reporting myself without them.

Sunday September 27th 1914, Dover

Thank you for the 'orders' – it was quick of you to find them and think of their importance. It was a rush and it will be a comfort to settle down rather to the 'one thing' of army work and you to the 'one thing' of abiding by the children.

I have felt all justified in waiting here today. It would have been an ill-fitting 'squeezing in to' things at Hythe, with nobody knowing who was who and nothing prepared, and there would have been the cost of the hotel, and my experience is that the Army accommodation, especially at this strained time without a days' notice, would have scarcely been available.

A nice quick service at St James[20]', and a helpful 'word' from the vicar on "Jesus said unto her…… Weep not[21]." Tears are caused by bereavement, suffering, pain, poverty and sin. Christ bears for us, and will take away many of the causes. Do not overwork with the house things. I think Mr and Mrs Fawns will understand[22]. Particularly do not bother about the loose books and papers in the study too much.

Tomorrow I want to ask to have 3 or 4 small things sent on, including the shirt in which the acceptable links were. There are some officers from the East Surreys down here, whether moving or holding the Garrison I could not ascertain[23]. Such wonderful weather here! 3 aeroplanes flew over going to the continent.

A nice letter from Mrs Harmer – I must write to the Bishop when I get into quarters[24].

---

20 **St James' Church** in Sandgate was built in the 11th century and restored in the 19th century. On 19th March 1916, a seaplane dropped bombs which fell nearby; pieces of the bomb caused damage to the roof, restored in 1931. Damaged again in WW2, it was demolished in 1951.

21 **Luke 7:13** 'And when the Lord saw her, he had compassion on her, and said unto her, Weep not.'

22 Rev. **Cecil Anderson Fawns** (b.1864 – d.?) Chaplain of St Cuthbert's Gateshead 1895 – 1900, Holy Trinity, Launceston, Tasmania 1901–1903, Chaplain to the Bishop of Tasmania 1903–4, Rector of All Saints, Hobart, Tasmania 1911–1913. Locum of West Farleigh; Margaret would have been preparing the rectory for his arrival.

23 1st Battalion E Surreys were already in France with the BEF. 2nd Battalion arrived in France in January 1915.

24 **Mary Dorothy Somers-Cocks (Harmer)** (b.1857 – d.1949). Bishop **John Reginald Harmer** (b.1857 – d.1944). Educated at Eton College and King's College, Cambridge. Ordained priest in 1884, he was a curate at Monkwearmouth before becoming Vice-Principal of the Clergy Training School in Cambridge. From 1892, he was Dean of Corpus Christi College, Cambridge, then the Bishop of Adelaide from 1895. In 1905, he was translated back to England when he was elected Bishop of Rochester in July 1905 and served for a quarter of a century before his retirement in 1930.

Monday September 28th 1914, Sandgate, Kent[25]

My Darling,

The 'roughing it' has begun. This is the Woodford Temperance Hotel, and I am not sure that the blankets have been washed all this season. I am writing in the bedroom, the window of which overlooks the middle roof upon which the washing that IS done is hung out – I do not think that I shall stay here many days! Tomorrow will decide, I hope, the arrangements possible for a longer period. There is some doubt about the movements round Hythe.

Tuesday September 29th 1914, Sandgate.

Your two letters, via Lizzie, have come this evening – quite a little feast.

I hope that you will go over to see the little boy[26] tomorrow, and that he will be able to be philosophical about the leave-taking.

It may be that I shall be moved rather nearer to Dover in charge of about 8000 men who are to be quartered in huts. 8000!! I shall be thankful to get into quarters as at present in the Hotel I have to go past the dining room to get to the bath!! Two flights of stairs and past the Scullery on a chilly morning. Miss Brownlow and the Misses Margary, whom you will remember at the Soldiers Home in Chatham, are staying here. Miss Brownlow's father has died and her brother, and her brother-in-law was reported wounded and missing, but from what a wounded Corporal of his who has returned said, they think there is no hope whatever of his being alive. Where if it were not for the 'Everlasting Arms[27]', should we all be at a time like this?

I hope that Mr. Fawns is feeling at home – let him, by all means, have as many of our damsons as he likes if he does not mind paying say 3d a half pound for the picking towards Philpott's wages, rather than go outside of the place and pay 1/-[28]

Soldiers everywhere! I talk to everyone I can – they are ALL the Chaplains' flock. There is a scathing article in this week's Church Times about the shortage of Chaplains and the bias in the choice of them.

Wednesday September 30th 1914, Sandgate

The weather certainly is wonderful and we had some tea this afternoon outside the Soldiers' Institute up in Shorncliffe camp, in the open air! We made a round of

---

25   London Gazette, 20th October 1914. 'ARMY CHAPLAINS' DEPARTMENT. The undermentioned are to be Temporary Chaplains to the Forces, 4th Class…Dated 28th September 1914…The Reverend Richard Griffiths.' Chaplain 4th Class would have given him the rank of Captain.

26   His son **Eric W S Griffiths**, b.1902

27   Hymn: *Leaning on the Everlasting Arms*, 1887, with music by Anthony J. Showalter and lyrics by Showalter and Elisha Hoffman.

28   **Herbert** and **Mary Philpott**, of 3, Clarence Cottages, West Farleigh, Maidstone, gardners and ground managers for the Vicarage.

the Club centres this afternoon – 3 in Folkstone, 2 at Shorncliffe, 1 at Hythe, 1 in Sandgate, and 1 to be started at Saltwood.

About things to be sent on – better let be for a day or two. It is yet uncertain where I may be located and Hythe will practically be deserted in a few days! Only about 800 men 'occupy' there from time to time for musketry. But the red address-book I should like to have some time – it is a lettered one and did repose in a right-hand pigeon-hole of the study bookcase. I hope to write more later – it is getting cold for men in tents.

Thursday October 1st 1914, Sandgate

(While I think of it, do not put CF[29] after my name yet. D. Oliver is tremendously excited over this war. Rather egotistical, with 16 000 troops committed to him, and very full of his own importance. So until I am gazetted again to the appointment to come, whatever it is to be, better put nothing.)

I am glad that the cow and calf are gone – Philpott will now be on his mettle with the other one. If Mr Fawns finds it does not answer, we must sell it later on, perhaps nearer the Christmas Market. The main question will be the feed – do you think they will need a boy, with just one cow? Philpott is paid 3/- a week extra, above his £1.1.4p per week for his care of it. He had a boy to help him only when I took on the second cow, and I took on a boy when we had extra people in the house, on account of extra knives and boots etc, to clean.

It has been very bothering and inconvenient this uncertainty about the camping out of troops, and now it is no more clear what I shall be doing. I have written a report to the Chaplain General[30] viz. that Hythe camp is only about 800 strong, and the tents are all empty for 3 days this week, troops being billeted in houses for just that time. And he will hear that the Sandling Camp[31] will be another month in forming. As it is I am lending a hand at Shorncliffe Camp as well, and talking to soldiers anywhere

---

29 **Chaplain to the Forces.** Chaplains are the only British Army officers who do not carry standard officer ranks. They are officially designated Chaplain to the Forces (CF) (e.g. "The Reverend John Smith CF"). They do, however, have grades which equate to the standard ranks and wear the insignia of the equivalent rank. Chaplain-General (CG) = Major-General:
Deputy Chaplain-General (DCG) = Brigadier:
Chaplain to the Forces 1st Class (CF1) = Colonel:
Chaplain to the Forces 2nd Class (CF2) = Lieutenant-Colonel:
Chaplain to the Forces 3rd Class (CF3) = Major:
Chaplain to the Forces 4th Class (CF4) = Captain.
The senior Church of England Chaplain is ranked within the church hierarchy as an Archdeacon. The Senior Roman Catholic Chaplain (usually a CF1) is normally ranked as a Monsignor. Since RDG was a Territorial Army appointment from his service in the Boer War, he was potentially a lesser service than a regular army chaplain.

30 The Rt Rev. **John Taylor Smith**, KCB, CVO, DD (b.1860 – d.1938) was the Anglican Bishop of Sierra Leone at the end of the 19th century and Chaplain General to the Forces 1901–1925. He was Honorary Chaplain to Queen Victoria from 1896 to 1901.

31 **West Sandling**, a few miles north of of Hythe.

and everywhere, and as 9 out of every 10 people you meet are such, it is not far to go for one's work!

I spent this morning with the machine guns, and part of the afternoon looking for lodgings in case I remain at Hythe for much longer, should more troops come here. This evening I was up on the plain among 1000s of men – it is getting cold for them at night now. They manage by sharing blankets – 2 blankets a man, and so put one under them, and sleep two men under 3 blankets. It is alright if you can find a congenial bed-fellow! They are of every description these Kitchener's recruits, business men, public school boys, clerks, waggoners, labourers, all massed together, 'herded' literally as the CG said[32].

I am so sorry to be separated from my 'kit' – (I have lived in one collar!) and my portmanteau all this week, and one pair of socks. I bought 2 pairs of socks tonight.

Now I must go 'soldiering'. A Dulwich[33] boy who enlisted among the Field Artillery fell into a low class tent, with a sergeant of vulgar and rough spirit, and had a most miserable time. We have got his Major to agree to trying to get him transferred to a Public School Corps, and the Major has been most kind in taking trouble about it.

Friday October 2nd 1914, Sandgate

I nearly lost the two letters this morning. The maid said there were none, on two separate occasions of my calling – and they were reposing on a table under some papers in Deane Oliver's dining room. Luckily I called to see him after dinner! I am wondering how this place will work out. The Camp is empty till tomorrow night and according to the regulations men ought not to be under canvas after the 30th September. But apart from my little camp, there are soldiers on the hill in their 1000s, and my little camp will be all empty by the 15th. Meanwhile the men come down in small detachments from all the country round to fire off their musketry, and I see them

---

32 On 5th August 1914, the day after Britain declared war on Germany, Field-Marshal Lord **Horatio Herbert Kitchener, 1st Earl Kitchener,** (b.1850 – d.1916) – a national hero of the Sudan and South African campaigns – accepted the vacant post of Secretary of State for War. Kitchener was one of the few leading British soldiers or statesmen to predict a long and costly war and to foresee that the existing British Expeditionary Force of six infantry divisions and four cavalry brigades would be far too small to play an influential part in a major European conflict. He therefore decided to raise, by traditional voluntary means, a series of 'New Armies', each duplicating the original BEF. His first appeal for volunteers was issued on 7th August. He also permitted the part-time Territorial Force – originally intended primarily for home defence – to expand and to volunteer for active service overseas. After a relatively slow start, there was a sudden surge in recruiting in late August and early September 1914. In all, 478 893 men joined the army between 4th August and 12th September, including 33 204 on 3rd September alone – the highest daily total of the war and more than the average *annual* intake in the years immediately before 1914. Throughout his diaries RDG shows unadulterated loyalty to the leadership of the Secretary of State for War; as a veteran of the Boer War, he, like other South African veterans admired Kitchener deeply.

33 **Dulwich College,** South London. As has been said the Western Front was a microcosm of the British class system in all its complexity.

MESSAGE FROM LORD KITCHENER.

You are ordered abroad as a soldier of the King to help our French comrades against the invasion of a common Enemy. You have to perform a task which will need your courage, your energy, your patience. Remember that the honour of the British Army depends on your individual conduct. It will be your duty not only to set an example of discipline and perfect steadiness under fire but also to maintain the most friendly relations with those whom you are helping in this struggle. The operations in which you are engaged will, for the most part, take place in a friendly country, and you can do your own country no better service than in showing yourself in France and Belgium in the true character of a British soldier.

Be invariably courteous, considerate and kind. Never do anything likely to injure or destroy property, and always look upon looting as a disgraceful act. You are sure to meet with a welcome, and to be trusted; your conduct must justify that welcome and that trust. Your duty cannot be done unless your health is sound. So keep constantly on your guard against any excesses. In this new experience you may find temptations both in wine and women. You must entirely resist both temptations, and, while treating all women with perfect courtesy, you should avoid any intimacy.

Do your duty bravely.

Fear God.

Honour the King.

KITCHENER.

Field-Marshal.

Lord Kitchener's guidance to troops, issued August 1914

there by the dozen. The talks I have are most fascinating – one man this morning followed me up to get a word with me. "The first person who took care of me when I was wounded" he said "was a clergyman" (that was in the other War) and he described how the clergyman gave him brandy and water and propped his head behind a rock to shelter him from further fire, and how the Sergeant-Major begged the clergyman to go back out of the fire, least he should get hit and be killed unnecessarily. Today a great crowd of National Reserves[34] were down here doing their firing. They were splendid in the quiet seriousness of going about their work – rather proud and pleased with themselves in a quiet way. They love chatting – one group after another waiting for me to come over to them, and when I had finished a chat with one group, a man involuntarily said "Thank you, Sir." I pity the Germans who come in the track of these reserves as the number of bull's eyes was really remarkable, the white ball going up in one target after another like clockwork[35]. The Colonel himself was struck by it and I could see how pleased he was – that is 'seasoned' English soldiering. One man, in discussing the War and the cause of it said "God always reckons up with men sooner or later. As a man sows, so shall he reap. It will be so with the Germans." They thought the German Emperor[36] was mad, a mixture of religious and war mania.

I will write about the motorcycle later – I shall not need it down here this next fortnight. When we get into the winter camp of huts on the hill, 4½ miles away, I shall probably be glad of it. But, everything is most uncertain.

---

34   The **National Reserve** was a register of trained officers and men who had no further obligation for military service. Its purpose was to enable an increase in military resources in the event of imminent national danger. The register was maintained by the County Associations that also organised the Territorial Force and they would frame their own rules for organising the reserve within their area. The National Reserve was a register maintained by Territorial Force County Associations. Registration was voluntary but complex rules of eligibility applied. Its strength at 1st October 1913 was 215 000 of all ranks. In October 1914, the National Reserve was formed into *Protection Companies*, which were attached to existing TF battalions, for the guarding of railways and other vulnerable points in Britain. That November, all Class I and II men were ordered to present themselves for enlistment.

35   British Army training emphasised rapid marksmanship and the average British soldier was able to hit a man-sized target fifteen times a minute, at a range of 300 yards (270 m) with his Lee-Enfield .303 rifle. This ability to generate a high volume of accurate rifle-fire played an important role in the BEF's battles of 1914.

36   **Wilhelm II** (*Frederick William Victor Albert of Prussia*; b.1859 – d.1941) was the last German Emperor (*Kaiser*) and King of Prussia, ruling the German Empire and the Kingdom of Prussia from 15th June 1888 to 9th November 1918. He was the eldest grandson of the British Queen Victoria and related to many monarchs and princes of Europe, three notable contemporary relations being his first cousins King George V of the United Kingdom, founder of the House of Windsor, Marie of Romania, Queen consort of Romania and the Czarina Alix of Hesse, consort of his second cousin Tsar Nicholas II of the House of Romanov. Crowned in 1888, he dismissed the Chancellor, Otto von Bismarck, in 1890 and launched Germany on a bellicose "New Course" in foreign affairs that culminated in his support for Austria-Hungary in the crisis of July 1914 that led to WW1.

Saturday October 3rd 1914, Sandgate (at Eastry Vicarage. 5.30 pm)[37]

My Darling,

Another nice letter from you – it seems years since I came away, but it is only a week. War's vicissitudes have sent me a long way today. The Vicar of Eastry was besieged by some 1000s of Territorials and others last week, and as my camp at Hythe was only filling up last night and unready for ministration, I came over here today. 7.am Holy Communion at Shorncliffe first, with 11 men present, then a rail journey through Dover here to Sandgate, and a cab drive starting at a quarter to 9 and reaching here at 10.30.

The troops have thinned down immensely. A big section of them at the other end of the parish were formed up for 10.30am Parade taken by Mr Stather Hunt (of Holy Trinity, Tunbridge Wells)[38] who is chaplain to the 10th Kents, and about whose presence someone ought to have been aware! So that at church there were just about 40 soldiers, and as it was a continuation of the Parish Harvest Festival, I was asked to preach *ad rem*, and did so! I spoke to the children in the afternoon and have just been round chatting with the men in the Y.M.C.A. tent. There is to be a second Harvest sermon in the church this evening, followed by an address in the Y.M.C.A. tent, and I shall then hope to get away alive! There is a lot of amateur soldiering about, and we all talk after the military manner nowadays.

Some further movements are on – a section of the Naval Brigade (Royal Naval Reserve men) are being sent over to Dunkirk this morning. The Vicar is a depressed kind of a man and has taken fresh alarm at this, and the War is making him quite ill. The youngest son – a Cambridge man – joined as a recruit and is now in Malta. The mother is very sad[39].

No letter from you today of course, as I have not been near Deane Oliver's – two tomorrow perhaps.

These are stirring times down here, soldiering everywhere, and almost every man so wistfully glad to be talked to by 'the Minister.' It is good to feel how definite a need is being met. The great plan at this moment is providing Institutes – soldiers swarm everywhere of an evening, and they MUST have wholesome places to go to – otherwise, what else?

---

37 **Eastry** is a village situated just off the A256 approximately 2 miles from Sandwich, 9 miles from Dover and 12 miles from Canterbury.

38 Canon **David James Stather-Hunt** (b.1856 – d.?), Vicar of Holy Trinity, Tunbridge Wells, Chaplain to the Forces, 2nd Class.

39 Rev. **C. E. Meeres** of St Mary The Virgin, Eastry. His son, Lance Corporal **Henry William Hugh Meeres** (b.1880) (sometimes Meers), educated Jesus College, Cambs, enlisted in the 2 Bn The London Regiment (Royal Fusiliers), which was dispatched to Valletta, Malta on 4th September 1914. On 2nd January, they sailed for Marsailles and joined the 17th Brigade of the 6th Division in February. Henry Meeres was killed in action 19th March 1915. Husband of Mrs. **E. Meeres**, Eastry Vicarage, Eastry.

Yes, please! All the wearable collars there are, also the wearable hat with the leather kind of lining, and the brown leggings – are they left behind? I have offered Deane Oliver to try and raise one Institute and a temporary Church for the camp to which I may be posted at a cost of £180 to £250. 10 000 men, they now say, will be here for the winter quarters – men always coming and going, away in a hollow of the hills, and the Government provides no church at all. They will, however, peg out a site of ground, and let us have two old shells of buildings, wooden with corrugated roof at a nominal price (£175) and we will remove, set up and furnish, etc. I am making those two things my quest for the next week or two, although we ought to have £500 – a good round sum to pray and appeal for, and we will trust it will come soon.

I think now I shall remain in Sandgate for the next week and perhaps longer – the Hythe Camp is so very fluctuating, and I can be better employed it seems, with one foot still in Shorncliffe camp.

My love to little Miss Baby[40], much love dearest one from your Warrior Husband.

Monday Oct 5th 1914 (at Woodford House, Sandgate)

This address will be safe for the next three days, I will not answer for it beyond, as I may move into Hythe. It depends upon the movement of troops. I much hope I shall go up into the new wooden Camp now forming and so be right among the men – how they do swarm!

You got my letter from Eastry? The evening service was a very crowded one, and a great many soldiers came, and the service went well. After 10 minutes for supper, I went on to the Y.M.C.A. tent which was also crowded full of men – there things did not go with quite the same smoothness of spirit: I mean they were having a kind of semi-sacred concert and I had to sandwich my address in after a recitation about a blacksmith who dies of a dog bite, a wholesome story of manliness and self-sacrifice, but the atmosphere did not seem quite there. However, I got in some pious sentiments and an exhortation, and we know the labour is not in vain in the Lord! It was late by the time I got back, just on bed time.

Today, down to the camp at the Range, and some very nice talks with the men, who really are very responsive and accessible – all straining at the leash to get out to Berlin. A pair of brother, twins, from business, quite nice and earnest and another man who is an employee of Lord Northcliffe's[41], who "attends church every Sunday of his life" and one of the workers tells us of another who has not missed Holy Communion every Sunday for three years. The rest of the day getting from one point to another, and writing letters asking for £375 (plus £50 for Church fittings) for the Church

---

40   **Agatha Faith** (b. December 1911)

41   **Alfred Charles William Harmsworth, 1st Viscount Northcliffe** (b.1865 – d.1922), newspaper and publishing magnate. As owner of the *Daily Mail* and the *Daily Mirror*, he exercised vast influence over British popular opinion.

and Institute in the huge winter camp. There is not much time to do it as the men are expected to move in by November 1st. I think Miss Willett[42] will provide the other institute, as her idea of housing needy dependents of soldiers and sailors has found no acceptance anywhere. That would mean her being able to donate quite £180, which would build and furnish the wooden place we have in mind. All the clubs here round the Shorncliffe neighbourhood, 7 in number, swarm with men every night to over-flowing, and as the dark winter nights come on, they will do so more, and that new camp is to be in a region dreary to a degree.

Two letters from you today, Saturday's and Sunday's– I dare say Aunt Mai[43] will get over the shock and value us all the more on our return.

Tuesday October 6th 1914, Sandgate

My plans seem to get vaguer. The War Office have sent Deane Oliver another man and he has taken on three Irishman on his own account, and if they get their expenses, they will be lucky! I have not got my early August ones yet (I mean their day pay of course). He has rather an impulsive Irish way with him – if he wants a thing he WILL have it and fights for it with the Chaplain General to whom, I am sorry to find, he is not much attached and against whom he speaks rather too recklessly. He was an only son and his mother was for many years a widow. Yet he is so good when he is good, and devoted.

Hythe is dwindling, with the expected 8000 becoming less than 800 – so it will be clear that I shall not remain attached there long. As it is I am living in a Temperance Hotel and Deane Oliver seems to think that as I am on the list of 'abroad', it is better not to regard me as going to be in charge of the Sandling Camp – so I keep a foot in Hythe, and turn round to help Shorncliffe and elsewhere as the occasion made by the unresting re-distribution of troops arises. While at the same time I am raising the Church and the 2nd Sandling Club, Miss Willett has agreed to provide the first, instead of the Home for needy dependents of Soldiers. If the Kentish churchwoman is able to respond after her manner, it will not take long. Clubs here there MUST be, or the men will become insane, if not wicked.

Three public school boys today, and an undergraduate from Magdalene College

---

42 **Florence Mary Ann Willett**, (b.1884 – d.1957), wife of developer Wiliam Henry Willett of Chiselhurst, promoter of British Summer Time.

43 Aunt Mai: Mary Campbell Smith Foster (b.1839 – d.1927). The daughter of Rev. Richard Snowdon Smith (b.1809 – d.1906), a Prebendary of Chichester Cathedral, fellow of Gonville & Caius College, formerly of All Soul's Brighton, and father of RDG's wife's father, Archbishop William Saumarez Smith. Aunt Mai's mother was Ann Robin of Jersey (from whence the name 'Saumarez' originates). Her husband was Ebenezer Bird Foster (b.1838 – d.1908), principal of commercial bank Foster & Sons, of Trinity St., Cambs and owner of Anstey Hall, Trumpington, Cambs. Anstey Hall was a major estate, and E. B. Foster was a wealthy man, which accounts, even after his death, for Aunt Mai's generosity in terms of items – Jaeger blankets, overcoats, billiard tables, trench lights – provided by her for RDG at the Front.

Cambridge, among the new Tommies this morning! Two aeroplanes flew over going towards France, though the wind was strong. Stringent rules now about no lights towards the sea. The same at Brighton?[44]

Wednesday October 7th 1914, Sandgate

The parcel of lantern slides and the camera arrived duly today – it ran a risk of being lost, as just now the Chaplain's House is inundated with parcels of comforts for the troops. In case of any other parcels I think I must give another address, as the lumping together of parcels is rather haphazard. I was very glad to get your postcard at mid-day. You <u>say</u> you had to change "at Erith" – I do not believe that is true, my dear Megaline. Erith is near Woolwich, and if you wandered as far out in that direction, all I can say is, dear lady, you deserved to have to change. Of course what you do mean is <u>Eridge</u> – I know you see – ah ha! I am so glad dear Baby was good, people often say how like her dear –Fa– Mother she is so what can you expect?

It has been a very full day here and a very interesting one. One day, early last month, I saw at a carriage window on Paddock Wood station[45] a little Belgian boy looking out, and I chatted with him. I asked him if he was not content to be in England and there was NO doubt in his reply. He had just come from the battle of Charlroi[46]. This morning, two little boys were looking at the machine-gun exercise at Hythe – one of them was that same little boy! He is en route for Paris, starting on Saturday.

You may remember my talking of Capt. J.P. Benson of the East Surreys – he is in the picture of the group with a 4:7 gun being brought down a hill near Paardekop. They told me in the 3rd Battalion in June that he had given up his commission and was at a Theological College reading for Holy Orders. It was surprising as in the Paardekop[47] days he was a little argumentative against religion – who can tell? I saw in the papers last month that he had rejoined as Captain and was with the Expeditionary Force and I see in this morning's Times that he has died of wounds[48] – such are the realities

---

44   Margaret's Aunt Alice lived in Brighton, married to the Rev C H Griffiths.

45   The South Eastern Railway opened a line from Redhill to Ashford and on to Dover in 1842. The village of Paddock Wood developed quickly around the station, which took the name **Paddock Wood** in 1844 when the branch line to Maidstone West was opened.

46   The **Battle of Charleroi** or the **Battle of the Sambre** was fought on 21st August 1914, between French and German forces and was part of the Battle of the Frontiers. The French were planning an attack across the Sambre River, when the Germans launched an attack of their own. The Germans were victorious.

47   Horsehead Pass, W. Cape, S. Africa. RDG was there in the Second Boer War.

48   Capt. **John Penrice Benson**, (b.1877 – d.1914), 1st Bn East Surrey Regiment, killed Battle of Mons, 23rd August 1914. *""C" and "D" Companies under Major Doughty were ordered to proceed at once to the canal to reinforce the 1st East Surrey Regiment and as these two companies marched through Haine they came under the enemy's artillery fire. On arrival at the canal, Major Doughty reported to Lieutenant-Colonel Longley, commanding 1st East Surrey Regiment, who ordered two platoons ("C"*

of this dreadful War.

Miss Willett will undertake one of the institutes at the new Saltwood[49] camp and finance it all necessary to make it a going concern, and *entre nous* kind Lady Pearce has given £60 towards the Camp Church – things are moving! It has now been decided that there must be 3 Institutes, as the length of the camp has been extended and at the end of the longer bit dividing the camp, there is a deep valley which will be practically impassable in winter.

A most important leader in the Times today about such provision for Kitchener's Army as we are working at – you must read it – also about urgent women's work. I motored over today to Saltwood with Mrs Dainty, deputed by Mrs Archbp. Davison[50], to work up such women's help as the article hints.

Thursday October 8th 1914, Sandgate
My darling,
A telegram from the Chaplain General[51] asks today can I be "ready at an early date for the Front. Wire reply." I replied "Yes. At any hour, kit all in hand. Griffiths, Hythe." So it looks as if this indefiniteness will now shortly be ended and the more advanced works be begun. I dare say a week or ten days interval will be given to avoid what will be one day called 'an unholy scramble' and then I go to where I really think I can be of better service. I will keep you in touch about every step – now and again it may be by telegram, so you will not be suprised. If possible, I should go up to London for the day to get one or two final things for the Kit – to lessen it rather than to increase it – and perhaps we might meet there? If I do not manage that, I will leave my unnecessary luggage at Lizzie's, together with my gold pencil, medals and gold watch, none of which are the kind of things to take on active service. If in this world of uncertainties, anything should happen to me, of course everything I possess goes to you and the chicks. There is not much. About business things – the Motor Bicycle I will lend to Littlewood, who would like to know how to ride it, would find it useful for his work, and would be content to keep it in going order for the use of it – he may also like to buy it. I have sent you one cheque for Drye and Page

---

Company under Captain Hepworth) to push across the canal and reinforce Captain Benson's (1st East Surrey Regiment) company holding the bridgehead. At this point there was some sharp fighting, Captain Benson and a number of his men being killed" War Diary, The Suffolk Regiment 1914–27. He joined E. Surrey Regiment in 1898; served in S. African War, wounded, 1899–1901; Adjutant, 1902; Capt. 1905. Son of Judge William Denman Benson and Jane Benson; husband of Laura Annette Benson.

49 **Saltwood**, Kent is located immediately to the north of Hythe on the high land looking over the Romney Marsh.

50 **Edith Murdoch Tait**, Baroness Davison of Lambeth, (b.1858 – d.1936), daughter of Archibald Campbell Tait, Archbishop of Canterbury, married Archbishop of Canterbury Randall Davison in 1878.

51 **Taylor-Smith's** rank was Major General. He oversaw the expansion of the chaplaincy service from around 120 chaplains in 1914 to almost 3500 in 1918.

of £4.7.7, you got that no doubt. I will write two others and will also send you half a dozen blank cheques, signed. You could then draw £10 a month for yourself and the babies. I might not be able to get cheques to you for some months and letters are uncertain things. In that case, you could draw <u>one</u> cheque for £50 or so, <u>after</u> Christmas as there will be enough in the bank to meet it by then as I have asked Arnold, Day and Tuff of Rochester to pay my tithe straight into my account at the London County and Westminster Bank, Rochester. If the Fawns do not find the one cow answers, let her be sold by advertisement if some neighbour or other does not care to buy her. That will reduce Philpott's wage by about 2/6 a week, but it is only fair the Fawns should have the advantage of the cow if they provide her winter feed. She will sell best in the spring.

Friday October 9th 1914, Sandgate

It really was rather alarming – for want of a little patience (he is a hot-headed Irishman) Deane Oliver hustled all the parcels off to the other end of the Garrison. They have been coming in briskly with comforts for the troops, and rather than sort them out or have them sorted out at his house, Deane Oliver peremptorily sent them all to the Ordinance Store. There they were by the 100s – and my parcel got there too!! I just managed to rescue it this evening but it had been opened. Fortunately (in this connection) a parcel of D.O.'s own containing some new gloves etc. got away there too, and so a different plan is now in operation!

Nothing has moved much today and no further word from the War Office – so I expect it means short notice when the time comes. My Hythe soldier Doctor went off at a days' notice! Judging from the notice they implied they would give me I shall not go before Thursday or Friday of next week and perhaps even later than that. The Chaplain General is very wise about these things.

If Baby is a strain on you too much, why not get in a day girl? After all 'il faut vivre', though the French judge added 'I do not see the necessity!'[52]

Saturday October 10th 1914, Sandgate

My Darling,

Events have moved rapidly as they have been doing often in the latter part of this amazing year. The orders are to join at Winchester on Monday and I am posted to the 8th Division[53]. I propose leaving here on Monday morning by the 9.30 train,

---

52 A common aphorism referencing a French tale: 'Once upon a time a thief put forward the plea of necessity "Mais, il faut vivre!" But the judge quietly and pertinently replied, "Je ne vois pas la necessitt.", and sentenced him to death'. Often used in justification of Victorian Necessarism or Individualism; all actions have consequences.

53 The **8th Division** was formed in England during October 1914 by the bringing together of regular army units, which had been stationed at various points around the British Empire. The Division moved to France in November 1914, a badly-needed reinforcement to the BEF.

arriving at Charing Cross at 11.51 and going at once to see the Chaplain General at his request, then doing a little necessary extra shopping for kit – e.g. a coat, (British Warm[54],) a forage cap, some pyjamas, a kit bag and also a service uniform of lighter khaki for more knock-about work. The Misses Warde's knife, fork and spoon were not in my parcel, perhaps they have been lost in the tumble? I am sorry as they would prove useful I hear. I am glad we have got all business matters so much in hand. There is nothing now outstanding. I will bring the cheque book on Monday – have this letter with you that nothing be forgotten. I want to leave with you my gold watch and chain, my gold pencil case and the medals, as we shall undoubtedly meet. Now that you can sign my cheques, I feel pretty safe about business matters. From abroad letters to you may come irregularly, and from you to me. But I believe postal communication, except of course, on long marches, is very good[55]. At the same time, I think the authorities do not encourage correspondence very much.

I expect to go by the 4.50 train, unless I learn from the W.O. that it might be earlier, in which case it will be the 2.55 from Waterloo – not much time in that case! We can have dinner at the Army and Navy Stores[56] where some purchasing can be done.

Monday October 12th 1914 (in the train), London
My Darling,
I hope you have not been exhausted by a trying day – rest all you can.

The train did pop off!! The Colonel who got into the same carriage and who is also joining the 8th Division, thinks we will not move off for a week, so we can exchange

some more letters. We will take every development as it comes 'One step enough

---

54   **A greatcoat**: The main characteristic of this overcoat was its heavy taupe *Melton* cloth. The name derives from the small town of Melton Mowbray. The cloth, which was first mentioned in 1823, is a tightly-woven woollen fabric that is heavy milled and weighs at least 34oz. It has a short, raised nap, which provides it with a fleece-like, non-lustrous texture. In 1914, the Scottish company Crombie switched to war-time production and manufactured about 10% of all greatcoats for British officers. At that time, the term *British Warm* was born, and to this day, the heavy Melton fabric is often referred to as *Crombie Fleece*.

55   The **Army Postal Service**: Responsible for army mails in all theatres of war, the APS (APO) not only handled mails between Britain and the forces abroad but coordinated communications between units at the front. With the onset of trench warfare, all mails bound for troops on the Western Front were sorted at the London Home Depot by the end of 1914. Covering five acres of Regents Park, this was said to be the largest wooden structure in the world. During the war the Home Depot handled 2 billion letters and 114 million parcels. In France, the APS established base depots at Le Havre, Boulogne and Calais and mail was carried with munitions on supply trains to the front. Trench warfare meant that British positions at the front remained fairly static and this enabled a comprehensive network of lorries and carts to develop for written communications and parcels between units at the front.

56   The **Army & Navy Co-operative Society**, formed in 1871 by a group of army and navy officers. The intention was to supply 'articles of domestic consumption and general use to its members at the lowest remunerative rates'. The store opened in February 1872.

for me[57]' God knows, God cares and He is our heavenly Father who loves us with a perfect love – a real love which makes no mistakes. He holds the key to all unknown, and we are glad – thus we rest in the Lord and plod on.

What an afternoon in the Stores and how much easier with that envelope behind us to back us up. It is annoying about the knife, fork and spoon and the leggings. However, the latter were rather old and I doubted if they would do except for rough work and indeed they were rather small for my expanding limbs! The Chaplain General in bidding me farewell, placed both his hands on my head and prayed a blessing.

THE GEORGE HOTEL, WINCHESTER[58]. I went out to the camp and reported myself – no tent prepared, so with the advice of the Colonel on duty, I came back into Winchester and am putting up here for the night. A little bit of Aunt Mai's goodness fits me into a room here instead of having to hunt the town at half past seven at night for a lodging. So we do not move off today or tomorrow, and I can write to you again for perhaps some days, though of course you will not know where to write to me. I know one thing – I am to be attached to the 24th Ambulance[59]. That is the way for Chaplains – the 24th Ambulance, and to them I stick. Colonel Hayes, the Colonel on the train[60], thinks this 8th Division is not complete. My experience of a moving off like this, is that they give you notice a day or two ahead. The work of Chaplains is thus, just now, speaking to everyone in Khaki, and gathering in good thoughts[61].

Tuesday October 13th 1914, Hursley[62]

I write notes at intervals. They will be scrappy. You will not mind.

---

57 Hymn: *Lead Kindly Light:* "Lead, kindly Light, amid th'encircling gloom; lead thou me on! The night is dark, and I am far from home; lead thou me on! Keep thou my feet; I do not ask to see the distant scene – one step enough for me". Text: John Henry Newman, 1801–1890, Music: John B. Dykes, 1823–1876

58 **George Hotel, High Street** at the junction with Jewry Street, demolished 1957. A 'hotel' had stood on the site since 15th century.

59 **8th Division, 24th (1st Wessex) Field Ambulance.** The first and second 24th (Wessex) Field Ambulances were Territorial Battalions and the man at the head of each Battalion was not only a high ranking-officer such as a Lieutenant-Colonel, he would have been at least a Doctor of Medicine. His 2/IC would have been a Captain or Major who was a Bachelor of Medicine. An 'ambulance' was literally the unit that would ferry, by hand, wounded men, often under fire, from the front to a casualty clearing station where their care could begin.

60 Lieut. Col. **Robert Hall Hayes** (b.1867 – d.1946) the 2nd Battalion (the 77th Foot) Middlesex Regiment. Went out to Western Front with 8th Division, 23rd Infantry Brigade.

61 A **Field Ambulance** (FA) is the name used by the British Army and the armies of other Commonwealth nations to describe a mobile medical unit that treats wounded soldiers very close to the combat zone. In the British military medical system that developed during the First World War, the FAs formed an intermediate level in the casualty evacuation chain that stretched from the Regimental Aid Posts near the front line and the Casualty Clearing Stations located outside the range of the enemy's artillery.

62 **Hursley Camp. Hursley** is a village and civil parish in Hampshire located roughly mid-way between Romsey and Winchester on the A3090. Hursley Park, with **Hursley House** was the assembly camp for the 8th Division in 1914. Hursley House is an 18th-century Queen Anne style mansion, now an IBM campus.

Colonel Hayes thinks it will take some days to complete the 8th Division, but they are moving horses and much of the baggage at night[63], so night movements may take place at any moment. Privately I shall be glad when you get to Edge. The German aircraft are dying to begin to 'hit' England I think, and they will try bombing if they can. It will be easier in quiet country districts than in the big towns.

I see that the Times is taking up the need for Soldiers' Clubs, and this is partly on account of a letter I wrote to the Editor, urging him to give the movement a push forward and not to omit to tell of the strenuous work done by the Army Chaplain's Department. This I felt was only just, as Deane Oliver, for example, has really worked like a horse in getting things going. The Editor replied to my letter very courteously and appreciatively, saying that he would follow it up, so that our £250 raised in a fortnight was time well spent[64].

---

63   The British **8th Division** was a Regular Army division that was formed by combining battalions, both British and native troops, returning from outposts in the British Empire at the outbreak of the First World War. It thus took longer to assemble than the BEF, already in France.

64   "**The Social Welfare of Recruits**:
The more obvious troubles attending the abnormal conditions at home created by the war have been removed or are in process of removal, but others reveal themselves by degrees and call for attention. It must be expected. Extraordinary circumstances produce unforeseen results, and among them some are sure to be undesirable. When once they are recognised, common sense, patience, and a certain degree of firmness will suffice to deal with them; but these are needed, and it is wise to apply them as soon as any mischief makes its appearance. Among the abnormal conditions peculiar to the moment is the concentration of very large numbers of young men in camps necessitated by the creation of a new army upon a great scale in the shortest possible time. When recruiting became really active various evils immediately made themselves apparent, the machinery for dealing with them was overwhelmed by sheer numbers, and the resources proved inadequate to provide them with proper accommodation, clothing, and other necessaries. These material defects have been or are being made good, but others are becoming apparent. These young men are suddenly removed from their homes, their work, their ordinary interests; and their whole course of life, and are plunged into a strange and entirely novel environment, in which everything is changed. Their occupations, their daily routine, and their companions are all new. They lack what they are accustomed to, and find themselves surrounded by other things to which they are not used. Such a change is trying to anyone's moral equilibrium, and allowance ought to be made for it. An adjustment of circumstances is needed. The problem differs from that presented by ordinary recruits in many ways. The number to be looked after is enormously larger, while there are fewer non-commissioned officers to look after them, and many of these past the age when they can impress younger men with the physical superiority which is sometimes essential to the maintenance of authority. Then many of the new recruits belong to a superior class, accustomed to various recreations and refinements, such as the means of writing and reading, which are lacking. There is nothing to replace the pursuits with which they are accustomed to occupy their leisure. They have money to spend, and are more than usually exposed to the temptations which the inevitable crowd of undesirable camp followers press upon them without restraint. These things need attention, and reform seems to be indicated in two directions – one positive and the other negative. More means should be provided for recreation in the evenings. We believe there are no bands in these camps; they might be supplied. Reading and writing rooms might also be supplied. The Young Men's Christian Association did valuable work in this direction for the Territorials at the beginning of the war, but we do not know if they have been able to do anything for the training camps. On the negative side the temptations of drink and women need to be removed or restrained with a firm hand, and the military authorities should be given the necessary power. They should have the same sort of power to deal with the diseased prostitutes who swarm about these camps as that entrusted to the authorities of our collegiate universities.

I have just seen a Staff Officer who thinks that they cannot possibly be ready for a week – if they are pushed they will do it quicker, and they may well be pushed. But there is the information now, for what it is worth. Do not think of us therefore as 'across the water' until we disappear! <u>In Camp. Important.</u> The address is for the present Rev.Richard Griffiths C.F. (C of E)

24th Field Ambulance
8th Division
Hursley Camp. Winchester

Later it will be Rev. Richard Griffiths C.F. (C of E)

24th Field Ambulance
8th Division Expeditionary Force.

I will write or wire the day the first address ceases. This may be 3 or 4 days hence or it may be a fortnight, nobody knows. When my letters cease you will guess that we are on the move.

It is very interesting – the men are very accessible. You will like to know the disposition of things and the organization of a Division[65]. On the hills, well sheltered, are the General and his staff. On the brow of a hill are the Field Artillery, and along the valley, the Devons, the Middlesex, the Scottish Rifles and some Highland Light Infantry. On one side of the valley, the Ambulance Corps, and here the 24th Field Ambulance. I am living with the Commanding Officer Colonel Pickard – a nice man[66], keen and good and a teetotaler I think. The Mess are nice also, the names of whom I will

---

As for drink when the Russian forces have given up vodka, the French have renounced absinthe, and our own in the field are setting an example of sobriety, the recruits who aspire to follow them can well consent to have the present over-abundant and abused facilities for drink curtailed. The same national evil has cropped up in another quarter in connexion with the war. We have recently published several letters drawing attention to the growth of drinking among women in receipt of separation allowances. This is no new thing; it always occurs on similar occasions, and is perfectly intelligible. Many wives of soldiers are placed in the position of having less to do and more to spend than when their husbands are at home; and the general atmosphere of war interest, in which they feel that they play a personal and particular part, guides their steps to the place where the war can be most socially discussed – the public house. Our correspondents speak of the demoralising influence of these conditions, and we fear the charge is only too well founded. The result of an inquiry carried out in every borough in London has been furnished to us by an experienced correspondent occupying a responsible position. It is too long to publish, but the answers form one continuous list of complaints of increased drinking and drunkenness in every part of London. The regular accompaniments of neglected homes and children are not lacking. It is difficult to say what can be done to stop this very serious evil, but a further curtailment of the hours of opening for public houses might make some difference. The suggestion that some mothers whose children have free meals would drink less if the meals were withheld has been made, and is worth consideration; but it would need great discretion and precise knowledge of the circumstances for its beneficial application".
The Times, Editorial 7th October 1914.

65 More information on the 8th Division can be found here http://1914-1918.net/8div.htm
66 Col. Dr. **Ransom Pickard**, MD. (b.1868 – d.1959). 24th (1st Wessex) Field Ambulance, the Royal Army Medical Corps. Noted opthamologist, resident of Exeter and Mayor in 1927.

mention later, but in one Mess is the Rev. Watson, a Baptist Congregational who comes originally from Melbourne and knows Sydney[67].

Next to us, lies the 25th Field Ambulance with a Major in command and Chaplains Canon Tyrwhitt (C of E)[68] and Father Knapp (RC)[69]. Next to them lie the 26th Field Ambulance, with Chaplains Father Conran[70] (C of E) of the Cowley Fathers and another non-conformist chaplain who has not yet arrived. I had a walk this afternoon with Father Conran who is a nice Christian-minded man and we agreed that we should get on! My soldier servant is Peter Wait, a Scotchman[71].

Wednesday October 14th 1914, Hursley

Another letter is possible, and I now hear the probability that I can write till Monday, and Air letters till Monday morning – at least it is worth trying and hoping for. Preparations go on briskly. The country, anxious to see more and more strength in the field, would be rejoiced to see the zeal and enthusiasm and energy with which things are pushing forward. Nearly all night long motors are rushing along the roads, and of course all day too – horse transporters, motor lorries, cavalcades of horses and men huge wagons laden, happily, with blankets as well as other provisions for the men – it is a wonderful organisation, the British Army!

Today we had a ride out with my Field Ambulance[72], with me falling into my place

---

67 Rev **Ernest Lodge Watson** (b.1878 – d.1951) appointed as a Temporary Chaplain to the Forces 4th Class on 12 October 1914. Watson was the first Baptist commissioned chaplain. Before coming to Britain, he was pastor of Melbourne Baptist Church. Watson trained at Victoria Baptist College, Victoria.

68 Rev. Hon. **Leonard Francis Tyrwhitt**, M.A., M.V.O, O.B.E. (b.1863 – d.1921) was Rector of St Mary's, Rolleston (1907–21), Chaplain to the King (1901–21), Canon of Windsor (1910–21) and Chaplain to the Forces (1914–21). His epitaph reads: "Not slothful in business, Fervent in spirit, Serving the Lord". He used a large Union Flag as an altar cloth and, on his safe return hung it in the Sanctuary in St. Mary's.

69 Father **Simon Stock Knapp**, DSO MC. (b.1858 – d.1917). Attached to 1st Battalion Irish Guards at 3rd Ypres. Died of wounds 1st August 1917. Knapp also was a RC padre in the Boer War with General Allenby.

70 Rev. **Marcell William Townend Conran**. (b.1868 – d.?) A former curate of Barton on Humber, Conran served as a chaplain officer at the front, receiving the DCM (Chaplain 4th Class). From 1891, a member Society of St John the Evangelist (SSJE), Cowley Brotherhood. He appears to have survived the war.

71 Pvte **Peter Waite**, Highland Light Infantry. He survived the war. **Batman**; the official term used by the British Army in WW1 was Soldier-Servant. Every officer was assigned a servant, usually chosen by himself from among his men. Batman was usually seen as a desirable position. The soldier was exempted from more onerous duties and often got better rations and other favours from his officer. Senior officers' batmen usually received fast promotion to lance-corporal rank, with many becoming corporals and even sergeants.

72 A **Field Ambulance** (FA) is the name used by the British Army and the armies of other Commonwealth nations to describe a mobile medical unit that treats wounded soldiers very close to the combat zone. In the British military medical system that developed during the First World War, the FAs formed an intermediate level in the casualty evacuation chain that stretched from the Regimental Aid Posts near the front line and the Casualty Clearing Stations located outside the range of the enemy's artillery. FAs were often assigned to the brigades of a division.

Peter Waite

Richard's Chaplain to the Forces badge

as we shall march, and where we shall be in time of action, and I am with the Colonel and at 'A' section[73]. We deployed as for a huge battlefield, and really you might fancy that you were out for a country ride, so vast are the operations – some little peeps here and there of troops, and that is all.

I have just had a conference with the other Chaplains about our plan of campaign for Sunday and I have discovered that Canon Tyrwhitt is the Canon of Windsor! – Chaplain to the King! Chaplain to King Edward M.V.O. etc., etc. He is bright and keen and nicely companionable.

Rain, rain, nearly every day.[74] My love to the Aunts – Aunts Mai's help has been most valuable.

October 15th 1914, Hursley

Your letter came, and dear little Eric's. I am glad he thought of saying that he would pray – and the enclosed copying pencil, plain pencil and an india rubber.

I shall write home again of course, before we move. I would have done so today, but time is full enough. If we had been moving Tuesday I should have fired off then (been interrupted) and the tent is occupied with inoculations at the present time. Only one tent for all things at present. Is the Balaclava helmet ready? It would be safer to arrive if sent before we go. Miss Warde's canteen has been invaluable. Another ride out today, getting used to horseback.

Take care and rest a lot, darling.

Friday October 16th 1914, Hursley

I am sorry about Baby[75] – I hope better weather will mean better health for her – and I am so sorry about your teeth. Need you have them out just yet? Could you not train your body to wait say, three weeks or so till Baby is more the thing? If one can manage to get just one thing at a time to tackle, so much the better.

No marching orders yet, but a full day looking round in preparation for Sunday, and a ride into Winchester to see about some more kit – it is astonishing how many little

---

73 The Field Ambulance was divided into 3 Sections. In turn, those Sections had Stretcher Bearer and Tented subsections. The Field Ambulance was composed of 10 officers and 224 men. A **Section:** 65 men: 1 Lieutenant-Colonel, in command of the Ambulance and A Section; 1 Captain or Lieutenant in command of Stretcher Bearer subsection; 1 Sergeant and 1 Corporal; 1 Bugler; 3 Privates (wagon orderlies) and 36 Privates (bearers); Captain or Lieutenant in command of Tent subsection; 1 Quartermaster, 1 Sergeant-Major, 2 Sergeants, 2 Corporals; 15 Privates (including a cook, a washerman and 2 orderlies).

74 1914–15 is second-wettest winter on record with 423 mm for December, January and February. The wettest is 2013/2014.

75 **Agatha Faith** (b. December 21st 1911).

'R.G. on a winter's morn'

Another view of a very distinguished officer. U no oo'

things come up as necessary. A pair of spurs now, not very expensive, but wanted for a field officer's use as well as appearance.

Poor Watson, the Congregational Chaplain, and Father Conran have suffered unnecessary inconveniences, the former in fact has been ill and the latter slightly so, for want of even proper bedding. Too desperate!

Various dates are still mentioned for going – Monday by some, Wednesday by others, the last week in October by others. They are waiting still for some materials, though the traction engines and motor lorries go puffing up and down the road unceasingly. I met this morning on the road someone from Rochester, Mr and Mrs........I forget their names for the moment, motor-tricycling through from Wales. She was the daughter of Dr Breness 'Guide of Knowledge' – you remember them, she large and masterful-looking, he dutiful and less in proportion than she.

Some of the officers' wives came to tea this afternoon – they are resolute in keeping close as long as they can. They have come from Plymouth and Exeter, and one has taken a room in a cottage in the village as a mess room, and the other wife came out on an ambulance waggon. They brought some cakes with them for tea, and some cream! The Colonel[76] is about 53 and his wife, Mrs. Pickard, looks about 30. Doctor Captain Duncan's[77] lady is very pleasant, and Transport Officer Lieut. Squire has a nice partner also[78]. The other officers are Major Sayers R.A.M.C[79], Lieuts. Stuart, Burgess and Perry[80], all R.A.M.C. and a cheerful party[81].

Saturday October 17th 1914, Hursley

Life grows harder as the days go on, I mean that the conditions become gradually less 'civilised' and kit is reduced to a minimum. You will pray that all these men may be kept gentle, humane and courteous, and that I may too. I shall be sending one portmanteau on to you. I am sure that Aunt Alice will not mind finding storage room for it at 4 Belmont, and of course, her honesty is unimpeachable!

---

76 Col. Dr. **Ransom Pickard**, MD. He was 46; a year younger than RDG! RDG will reference him throughout his posting to 24th Ambulance, as the Colonel, noting his connection to Devonshire and his skill and expertise operating on eyes.

77 Maj. **Thomas Duncan** MD (b.1861 – d.1921) 24th (1st Wessex) Field Ambulance, the Royal Army Medical Corps. Husband of **Isabella Duncan**. Born in Auchtermuchty.

78 Lieut **EF Squire**, 1st Wessex, 24th Ambulance.

79 Maj **EWF Sayers**, RAMC.

80 Lieut **William Howard Edin Stewart** RAMC, Dr. St Thomas Hosp. London and graduate of Gonville & Caius, Cambs. Lieut **Robert Burgess** RAMC, Dr. London Hosp. London. Lieut **George Perry** RAMC.

81 **The Royal Army Medical Corps** (RAMC) is a specialist corps in the British Army which provides medical services to all British Army personnel and their families in war and in peace. Together with the Royal Army Veterinary Corps, the Royal Army Dental Corps and Queen Alexandra's Royal Army Nursing Corps, the RAMC forms the British Army's essential Army Medical Services.

The living is rough and we are indeed reduced to our primitive humanity. There is all uncertainty and of course leave is only given day by day and there is NO night leave. We shall be sent off undoubtedly by night, and then the great task begins. The love of God, darling, and from Him the love of man, carries through, and perfect love casts out fear. Then in the cloud of a great mystery, the mystery of iniquity and the cloud of danger, and for us all, sometime sooner or later, the cloud of the experience of death, and they feared as they entered into the cloud. But perfect love casteth out fear[82]. You have faced death in your own body 4 times in the passing forward of the gift of a new life, and love has won through.[83] So must it be with a hard and dangerous endeavour for the souls and well-being of many brethren – Love must win through and over all. Pray that it may be so, as we are striving for the very existence of our Nation – for honour – for truth – for liberty – for righteousness. Not a man, woman or child in England but must take their share, and the successful end depends, humanly speaking upon that. When we are where God wants us to be, where we think we ought to be, doing what we believe to be right, the rest may be safely left to Him

Smooth let it be, or rough,
It will still be the best.
Winding or straight it leads
Right onwards to His rest.[84]

Peace, perfect peace, with loved ones far away. In Jesus' keeping we are safe, and so are they[85]. Troops still keep coming in – we shall be a huge multitude when we move.

Goodnight my beloved, God bless and keep you all, your loving Ritchie.

Sunday October 18th 1914, Hursley

I am so sorry about the teeth, it must be a trying time for you in so many ways. Perhaps it is a useful distraction to have this in the midst of all. Anyhow you are in surroundings where teeth trials are, now, perculiarly understood and undoubtedly sympathised with – you will never have another tooth pulled out! And each day you will be getting better

It has been a beautiful day, and an encouraging one. We had Holy Communion at 7am with 11 men present and at 'my' parade at 10am there were over 1200 men! They sang well and the whole service was over in 23 minutes! We have such a nice General – he speaks to you as "Yes, old man" or "Yes we will, old chap"! He is General Holland[86],

---

82   1 John 4:18 'There is no fear in love; but perfect love casteth out fear: because fear hath torment. He that feareth is not made perfect in love.'
83   Margaret gave birth to four children: Eric, Joyce, Hope and Agatha (Faith). Hope died in infancy.
84   **Psalm. 9.10** Knowing and Trusting.
85   Hymn. *Peace, Perfect Peace*. Edward Bickerseth, 1875
86   Lieutenant General **Sir Arthur Edward Aveling Holland**, KCB, KCMG, DSO, MVO (b.1862 – d.1927) was a British Army officer and Conservative and Unionist politician. Holland was commissioned into the Royal Artillery in 1880. He served in the Second Boer War and then

and this afternoon 4 officer's wives came to lunch and tea and the daughter and son of one, and the two little boys of another – such a happy party.

Dates are still variously discussed. Some say off Wednesday next, others <u>not this month!</u> They are waiting for ammunition (I do not know how far that is confidential). Nerve strain is getting to many of them, we all need the peace that alone the mercy and grace of God gives. He has said "I have loved thee with an everlasting love[87]" and "nought shall pluck us out of His Hand[88]". And naught shall separate us from His love.

Monday October 19th 1914, Hursley

Behold me – a chilly tent, the falling night, my camp bed, a walking stick with a bit of candle stuck in it, standing upright on the ground and this tablet on my knee. Around, a portmanteau half-open, a small hand-bag, a communion bag, a piece of canvas with the canteen things on it, the large portmanteau half open acting as a wardrobe, another piece of canvas viz. a tent-peg bag on which rests the kit-bag, sponge and dressing case, the rubber bath and a little wooden improvised table on which to wash – also a bucket filled with very cold water. In the tent next to mine the Colonel[89] is chatting with his lady who is much younger than he is, half his age perhaps and he is about 54. In a tent the other side the Transport Officer[90] is also talking with his lady – he had rather a bad kick from a horse yesterday - and the Quartermaster talking to his lady and two little boys of 9 and 4. In the row of tents behind I hear some joking among the men over the letters which have just come. Many of the men have gone off to Winchester 4 miles away, walking or seizing a lift from any kind of vehicle – hawkers' carts, traction engines, empty motor lorries, ammunition carts etc. – it is a marvellous highway of traffic.

We have not moved yet you see. I think it may be a fortnight yet, sometimes, or Wednesday or Thursday next. Everything is so secret and we so are glad of it. We only know, superficially, things do not seem very much prepared eg. the Indian troops are still in their khaki, but things can be done so quickly in this marvellous organisation, you can be surprised at little.

I have been into Winchester today about more kit – a knife, fork and spoon, the others not having turned up, and Deane Oliver not having written as he promised. I did not, however, succeed in getting all! A strap for the watch, and a look at a khaki

---

became Assistant Military Secretary to the Governor and Commander-in-Chief of Malta in 1903 before holding a similar role at the War Office from 1910. In 1912 he was appointed Commandant of the Royal Military Academy, Woolwich. He served in World War I becoming **Commander Royal Artillery for 8th Division** in which capacity he took part in the Battle of Neuve Chapelle in March 1915.

87 **Jeremiah 31:3** 'The Lord hath appeared of old unto me, saying, Yea, I have loved thee with an everlasting love: therefore with loving kindness have I drawn thee.'

88 **John 10:28** 'And I give unto them eternal life; and they shall never perish, neither shall any *man* pluck them out of my hand.'

89 Colonel **Ransom Pickard**, MD.

90 Lt. **Squire**.

cardigan with which also I did not find myself able to be suited! I am so sorry about the gums – sulphide calcium ½ grain every 2 hours if the swelling continues. Each day, I hope, you will get better.

We had a nice evening service yesterday, voluntary, the Camp being nearly empty as the men have gone on leave into the town, so we were a small party only 6 all told! I called on the Senior Chaplain, Winchester, today, Norman Lee[91], who is very hurt not to be sent to the front - and very grumbly. I went over the Cathedral – it is very interesting, the sarcophagi containing the bones of Saxon Kings being specially impressive.

The Commander-in-Chief came round the camp this afternoon – which may mean nothing in particular[92].

Tuesday October 20th 1914, Hursley

Still nothing but manoeuvres. The appearances tonight are that we do not get off certainly before Sunday next. Men who wish are taking 48 hours leave tonight, and the other half will be entitled to do the same. What a system it is! Everybody is getting very impatient, and that includes not least the Chaplains!

Dear little Baby – in 9 cases out of 10 when there are contretemps, look for the physical. It is not all, but it is behind much. Health is that state in which it is a pleasure to think, to feel, and to be. I hope the Misses' Wardes' parcel will turn up this time! Dear old Deane Oliver might, 1) not have lost it, and 2) not have got it found. He is rather an excitable Irishman rushing from one thing to another, and often not finishing anything. He telegraphed last weekend he is writing – he promised me certain expenses, and assured me the Army pay for the first fortnight of the war would go duely through. None of these promises have as yet been fulfilled! Will they be? Nous verrons.

I have just been to see the Vicar of Hursley, a nice keen man[93]. Two soldiers came to me wanting to be married in a hurry, so I passed them on to him. They will have to get licenses which will cost them £1 each! As they were pressed for time he advanced them each the £1 that they might telegraph these and then to their fair demoiselles!

---

91 Rev. **Frederick Bethune Norman** (Norman-Lee) (b.1874 – d.1921).
92 General Sir **Francis John Davies** KCB KCMG KCVO (b.1864 – d. 1948) Commissioned into the Worcestershire Militia in 1881. He transferred to the Grenadier Guards in 1884 becoming Adjutant to the 2 Bn Grenadier Guards in 1893. In 1897 he was posted to South Africa where he became DAAG for the Cape of Good Hope in 1897. He served in the Second Boer War as DAAG responsible for Intelligence at Army Headquarters. He returned to the UK in 1902 and became Deputy Assistant Quartermaster General at the War Office in 1902 and Assistant Director of Military Operations in 1904. He was made GOC 1 (Guards) Brigade in 1909 and then Director of Staff Duties at the War Office in 1913. He was appointed GOC 8th Division in 1914 and Military Secretary in 1916. After the War he was appointed General Officer Commanding-in-Chief for Scottish Command in 1919, retiring in 1923.
93 Rev. **Josiah Robert Husband**, vicar of Hursley.

He is trusting them implicitly and I feel sure it will come out alright. One said he had been engaged to his young lady since she was 14. Hursley Church was built and opened by Keble, and he himself was vicar here for some years[94], and of course many of his poems were written here.

This morning we all had our photographs taken, first as a group of officers, and then as a unit with all the men.

PS Is General Holland a friend of your family?

'*Officers 24th Field Ambulance*
**Bottom row: RDG, Mj Sayers, Lt Col Picard, Mj Duncan, Rev W Molloy*'

Wednesday, October 21st 1914, Hursley

Rather a scramble for letter writing tonight. No lamp in the Mess tent and I am being 'accommodated' in the Office Marquee with all the bustle of busy eventide going on round. Yours has just come – I am sorry about the teeth and the bruised face[95]. What a mystery this life of pain and warfare is – we shall understand better by and by.

---

94 The theologian and poet John Keble was appointed Vicar of Hursley in 1835, rebuilt All Saints church in 1848, and remained there until his death in 1866. Keble was Professor of Poetry at Oxford University from 1831 to 1841, and was the originator and subsequently one of the leaders of the Oxford Movement. Keble College, Oxford was founded in his memory. Keble is buried at All Saint's Church, Hursley.

95 RDG wrote to his wife Margaret every day, at times the letters were purely domestic – how to pay the bills and organise the finances and the Parish. Margaret had been 45 when 'baby' (Agatha Faith) was born. Margaret had lost another daughter – Hope – a year earlier. RDG was very concerned for her health and did not want her to travel to Winchester to visit him.

"Not now but in the coming years
It may be in that better land
We'll know the meaning of our tears
Ah! Then some day we'll understand."

We expect now not to go before Friday week, and all signs point that way, except an emergency arise. We are ready to go at 8 hours notice any time. I do not think, especially in your present upset state of health, it would be advisable for you to come over to Winchester. It is difficult from this end as well – and many things might intervene.

An excitement today in the shape of 21 brand-new Motor Ambulances! most convenient and comparatively comfortable[96]. They will be a boon and compare nobly with the old-fashioned, and now, lumbering horse ambulances – splendid.

I discover among my men today an Oxford MA! Jesus College, Oxford and Wycliffe Hall. He, and a King's College London man, make an interesting pair. We have dentists, school teachers, business men, clerks, houseboys, farmers and many varieties. Some of the Regiments from India we understand, cannot land for some reason. The Antwerp refugees used up a crowd of transport[97].

Thursday, October 22nd 1914, Hursley

We have had a route march today, testing the new Ambulance cars. They did well. The men liked being run home the 6 miles without walking! Especially as it rained in torrents for the earlier part of the day. There is a rumour today we may be kept back and sent to the East Coast in anticipation of a possible attempt at invasion. But I do not think there is much in it. Germany will not invade England - I do not think it possible. The nearest attempt, anyhow, would be next spring – in West Equinoxtial gales Zeppelins would hardly get far and I do not think they will try without their assistance[98]. Besides they are driven back north – all the signs seem favourable.

---

96   'Napier' 15 cwt. Ambulance made by D. Napier and Son Ltd., which had an excellent reputation for quality and reliability.

97   The **Siege of Antwerp**: After the invasion of Belgium in August 1914, German troops besieged the garrison of the Belgian army in Antwerp. The Belgian garrison had no hope of victory without relief and despite the arrival of the Royal Naval Division beginning on 3rd October, the Germans penetrated the outer ring of forts. When the German advance began to compress a corridor from the west of the city through which the Belgians at Antwerp had maintained contact with unoccupied Belgium, the Belgian field army withdrew westwards towards the coast. On 9th October, the remaining garrison surrendered, and the Germans occupied the city.

98   **Invasion literature** is a literary genre most notable between 1871 and WW1. The genre first became recognisable starting in Britain in 1871 with *The Battle of Dorking*, a fictional account of an invasion of England by Germany. This short story was so popular it started a literary craze for tales that aroused imaginations and anxieties about hypothetical invasions by foreign powers, and by 1914 the genre had amassed a corpus of over 400 books, many best-sellers, and a world-wide audience. The genre was influential in Britain in shaping politics, national policies and popular perceptions in the years leading up to WW1.

Friday October 23rd 1914, Hursley

It is pretty clear now we shall not march before the end of next week. The fact of men going on leave decides that. The 'leaves' cannot be worked off until about Tuesday, and there are, quite likely, other odd ones also entitled. So everyone is making up their minds for so long. Though of course, anything might happen, as with the Naval Brigade who went away at 7 or 8 hours notice[99].

Your letter came today at mid-day. The postal congestion here must be something enormous, and everywhere's a little disorganised. No word about the other knife, fork and spoon and the leggings – and no letter from Deane Oliver, though he promised one, and indeed ought to send one in a business way.

Pouring rain yesterday – very unpleasant in camp, slop slop! but refreshing today. New saddles today for the Chaplains – two horses dead, this weather rather tries them, but the motor ambulances are a great boon.

Saturday October 24th 1914, Hursley

We have had a 'puddly' day, trudging over the hills to the Infantry camps to arrange about Sunday and all the time ankle-deep in mud. I found a man bleeding and unconscious by the road-side, his horse having thrown him and then rolled on him. I galloped off for a doctor and found on returning that a R.A.M.C. Sergeant had come along and was binding him up – first aid. He had by then recovered consciousness, but his clothes were torn and he looked a pitiable sight rolled over in the mud – there have been a number of casualties like that.

The rumour is that we go off Thursday – or Wednesday! – no one knows. A Divisional 'route' march has been ordered for then, and that is how they have sent off one or two Divisions. They have started off for a route march, and have not returned and no one has known they have gone, and they did not know they would not return to the Camp. Other say that the 'off' is on the 10th of November.

Sunday October 25th 1914, Hursley

(I have cut my thumb with a razor so cannot write quite the copperplate hand you must by this time have grown to admire!)

It has been a somewhat dismal Sunday outwardly, joy and peace within. But the Camp is less cheerful in a ceaseless mizzle, nor can people do things so briskly, and feet drag with the heaviness of things. I had a mile ride this morning to the Artillery Camp for H.C. in

---

99   The **Royal Naval Division** – later designated the 63rd (Royal Naval) Division – was formed in WW1 to make use of surplus reserves of the Royal Navy who were not required at sea. It included two naval brigades and a brigade of Royal Marines, and fought in the defence of Antwerp in 1914, Gallipoli in 1915, and the Somme in 1916.

theY.M.C.A.[100] tent with only one soldier present and three civilian workers in the Tent. The parade service in this Camp at 10. am was not so bad, with about 450 people present. I think one or two of the doctors are materialists – they did not look happy but others, the majority, are good, keen and serious-minded men[101] , and a pleasure to deal with.

The Major in this Mess, Major Sayers[102] seems nice. His son, a boy from Epsom College is spending a weekend in camp with his father – roughing it rather but enjoying it as a boy of 15 would.

I spoke on St James 1:12 "Blessed is the man that endureth trial" etc.[103] There is a glow of patriotism in the hearts of all men alive just now. By and bye trials will come and the romance will wear off a little. Some days will come when it will seem out of sight – then shall we be tested. We are wise at a service like this to let our hearts realise our entire need of God and His grace, thus storing up grace to help in time of need. There will come the trials that only the grace of God can carry us through. But that grace can do anything, and so we will have ready in our minds the thought "He giveth more Grace"[104]. I hope a blessing went out, but the rain began to splutter and the service had to be hurried to a close.

Conran[105] is a nice fellow, very gentle, thoughtful and loving and lovable, but Tyrwhitt is a little loud and pushful. The big Canon! M.V.O.[106] Canon of Windsor, Chaplain

---

100 **The Young Men's Christian Association** (YMCA) Within ten days of the declaration of war, the YMCA had established 250 soldier's recreation centres, providing a cup of tea, sandwiches or other refreshments, and reading materials. Many of these centres were at or near railway stations or other places where large numbers of troops would be passing. In November 1914, the first YMCA contingent went to France and organised similar centres at Le Havre. Later, they were also in operation at Rouen, Boulogne, Dieppe, Etaples and Calais (the principal army bases), Abbeville, Dunkirk, Abancourt (railway junction), Paris and Marseilles. Eventually there were numerous such centres in each of the places mentioned, and another three hundred along the lines of communication. Vast quantities of refreshments were served out to troops on the move: for example, one centre at a railway siding at Etaples served more than 200 000 cups of cocoa each month.

101 The German materialist and atheist anthropologist Ludwig Feuerbach would signal a new turn in materialism through his book, *The Essence of Christianity* (1841), which provided a humanist account of religion as the outward projection of man's inward nature. Feuerbach's materialism would later heavily influence Karl Marx.

102 Maj. Dr. **Alexander Ward Fortescue Sayres** MD (b.1867 – d.1917). Attended St Thomas's Hospital; Lieutenant-Colonel in January 1916, in command of 21st Wessex Field Ambulance; mentioned in despatches. Severely wounded by a shell in the trenches on 17th July 1917 and died of his wounds on 10th October 1917. Youngest son of the Rev. Edward Sayres, of Cold Ashton Rectory, Glos.; husband of Bertha Sayres, of 4, Marlborough Terrace, Bovey Tracey, Devon. His son was **Richard John Sayres**, who attended Epsom College 1911–16 (born 1899), and would be 2nd Lt. in the Royal Garrison Artillery in 1918, and Temp. Major in the Burma Regiment 1939–45.

103 **James 1:12** 'Blessed *is* the man that endureth temptation: for when he is tried, he shall receive the crown of life, which the Lord hath promised to them that love him.'

104 **James 4:6**: 'But he giveth more grace. Wherefore he saith, God resisteth the proud, but giveth grace unto the humble.'

105 Father Conran, Canon Tyrwhitt. See letter October 13th, 1914.

106 The **Royal Victorian Order** is a dynastic order of knighthood recognising distinguished

to King Edward VII, Chaplain to George V, etc., etc. We had, i.e., I had to pull him up a little.

There is a big Infantry Camp on the hill. The great assembly place, the Artillery camp and this one are smaller. We had arranged that each chaplain should take each camp in turn, and thus get known among ALL the men of the Division, as we do not know in the march who may be thrown with whom or where or when. In spite of this, Tyrwhitt assigned himself the largest camp again a second Sunday and we two were to 'find' ourselves elsewhere. He was really not quite gracious when I suggested Conran's going to that camp, and although Conran acknowledged to me that he felt it was not right to depart from the original plan without a word of explanation, he was very glad when I put the point, and he pressed it home himself with some refreshing emphasis. How human! And at a time like this, when we are in the midst of life and death! I let the Canon know that we deferred to his Canonship naturally and did not let him know that Norman Lee (who is Senior Canon to the Forces for the Winchester Command) had explained to me how I am the senior of the three of us by Army etiquette, being both in longer service and being earlier gazette! What does it matter?!

The order has been given to us to shed our extra kit tomorrow. One more sign of the times! Tomorrow, if I can, I will work out a code by which I can say things to you which it is not necessary that the Censor should read. I understand letters will go through to you alright, but will be subject to delays of two to three days. The printed postcards will go through straight away and parcels and letters from you will come through promptly. Thank you – at present food stuffs do not signify much – we live roughly enough, but we get supplies of Devonshire cream, 2 days last week! This being the 1st Wessex Ambulance – all Devonshire men. The 2nd and 3rd Wessex (25th and 26th Ambulance) are also Devon and Cornish men.

The Regiments – in the Division are the 2 Devons, 2 Middlesex, 2 East Lancs., 2 Worcester, 2 Scottish Rifles, 2 Notts and Derby, 1 Northampton Yeomanry, 2 Lincoln Royal Field Artillery, Royal Garrison Artillery, Royal Horse Artillery, some Royal Engineers and the Motor Cycle Corps, etc. I will try and get all the names of the Generals and chief Officers. You will then be able to see what is happening if any mention is made of Regiments in the papers – there is a directory of the Division, but it is not easy to get hold of a copy[107].

---

personal service to the order's Sovereign, currently the reigning monarch of the Commonwealth realms, any members of their family, or any viceroy. Founded in 1896 by Queen Victoria.

107 **The order of battle of the 8th Division, November 1914:**

23rd Infantry Brigade: 2nd Bn, the Devonshire Regiment; 2nd Bn, the West Yorkshire Regt; 2nd Bn, the Scottish Rifles; 2nd Bn, the Middlesex Regt.

24th Infantry Brigade: 1st Bn, the Worcestershire Regt; 2nd Bn, the East Lancashire Regt; 1st Bn, the Sherwood Foresters; 2nd Bn, the Northamptonshire Regt; 1/5th Bn, the Black Watch

25th Infantry Brigade: 2nd Bn, the Lincolnshire Regt; 2nd Bn, the Royal Berkshire Regt; 1st Bn, the Royal Irish Rifles; 2nd Bn, the Rifle Brigade; 1/13th Bn, the London Regt

Divisional Troops: 8th Divisional Train ASC; 15th Mobile Veterinary Section AVC; 8th

From across the water, I think soft biscuits and that kind of thing may be very acceptable – but we will wait and see. Lifebuoy Soap! Yes! One cake about once a month – in camp life it is invaluable!

Monday October 26th 1914, Winchester

My darling,

Thank you for yours and the peppermints, any little alleviations like that are very pleasant.

I write this in Winchester whither we have come to get final bits of kit i.e. 2 winter undervests and a pair of waterproof boots – the pair I have are like paper! Moral – one has to pay for cheapness. Next week is the latest rumour, and that we are for Belgium, but others still think that we are in reserve for a possible invasion of the East coast. Anyway, we are the next fighting Division. A great service last night with the tent packed, driven in by the rain and the men standing wedged together – all so hearty and inspiring.

Tuesday October 27th 1914, Hursley

My own darling,

I am so glad that the face operations are now at an end – those splintered jaw cases are common enough, but it does not make them any easier to bear[108].

We had a practice pack this morning and it was well one did, as it was found that my new saddle, one that I had not used before, was too small for the horse! It is such a business anything done away from this camp and every day we are all occupied with active service preparations and instructions. Our entraining instructions are very full and minute and our place in the Divisional marching has to be known and learned. We are told about our relationship to the Armies of the Allies, and an illustrated book has been given to us, each one describing the ranks and distinctions of the other armies – doctors, officers and the like. There is so much to know. A letter from Kitchener today, expressing approval of the advances made in completing the establishment, and saying that he would not send us off until we are fully prepared, if he could help it. This we were told, was read at a meeting of the Generals and Colonels commanding. There are four Generals, the head one being General Davies

---

Divisional Motor Ambulance Workshop; 1/1st Northamptonshire Yeomanry (mounted); 8th Company, Army Cyclist Corps **Divisional Artillery:** 5th Brigade, RHA; 23rd Brigade, RFA; 45th Brigade, RFA; 8th Divisional Ammunition Column RFA

Royal Engineers: 2nd Field Company, 15th Field Company, 1st (Home Counties) Field Company, 8th Divisional Signals Company.

Royal Army Medical Corps: 24th (1st Wessex) Field Ambulance, 25th (2nd Wessex) Field Ambulance, 26th (3rd Wessex) Field Ambulance

108 Margaret, having had four children at quite an advanced age, had had to have all her teeth removed.

of the Grenadiers Guards[109], and the others being Brigadier-General Lowry Cole[110], Brigadier-General Adam[111], and Brigadier-General Holland[112].

Camp life is very troublesome at times – we are short of light tonight, and all camp chairs have been packed off so we sit on boxes and stuffed sacks! It is all on the move! Fortunately, I have gleaned from one of the Generals that on the other side, there is likely to be more of billeting. I am going to try and get a recreation tent to go with the Division (£180). There is nothing but that between the men cooped up in their tents – and the mud.

Wednesday October 28th 1914, Hursley

Things have improved a little tonight. The Motor Ambulance have a portable workshop, and it can make a degree of electric light, and a burner is fixed to the Mess tent, and by its light, I write this!

An interesting discovery – the driver of the Lieutenant in command of the Motor Ambulances is in private life chauffeur to the Bishop of Chichester[113]! I had a lift into Winchester this afternoon to send my spare portmanteau to Sophie (– it has gone!) and the talk with the chauffeur brought that fact out. He was in the Grenadier Guards in the Boer War and is now attached to the 24th Field Artillery. By the by, on our identification labels each person has his name, office and religion attached to him, printed on a little round disc.

About your letters – I do not want to lose them! They are happily accumulating, but they weigh our baggage by pounds, and I begin to think the best plan will be to return them to you from time to time for safe custody? It is cold at night sleeping

---

109 General **Sir Francis John Davies** (b.1864 – d.1948). He transferred to the Grenadier Guards in 1884 becoming Adjutant to the 2 Bn Grenadier Guards in 1893. In 1914, he was **General Officer Commanding 8th Division.**
110 Brigadier General **Arthur Willoughby George Lowry Cole**. (b.1866 – d.1915) Brigadier General, General Staff, **commanding the 25th Infantry Brigade**. Formerly Royal Welch Fusiliers. Died of wounds, Battle of Aubers Ridge, May 9th, 1915. See footnote 295.
111 Brigadier General **Frederick Archibald Adam**, GOC 23rd Infantry Brigade. On 28th October 1914, he was replaced by Brigadier General **Sir Reginald John Pinney**, (b.1863 – d.1943), GOC 23rd Brigade October 1914 – June 1915. 24th Infantry Brigade: Brigadier-General **Frederick Charles Carter** (b.1858 – d. 1931). He was commissioned in the 5th Foot in 1878. He saw active service with his battalion in the Afghan War (1878–80) and was later District Staff Officer/DAAG Bengal. He transferred to the Royal Berkshire Regiment in 1894, seeing more action in the Hazara Expeditions (1888–1891) and the Lushai expedition (1889). Carter became CO 1st Battalion Royal Berkshire Regiment in 1899. He was on half-pay for more than three years (April 1903–August 1906) before being appointed Brigadier-General Commanding a Sub-District, SA, until April 1909. On his return from South Africa he was given command of 16th Brigade in Ireland. When this appointment expired in May 1912 he retired from the army, reactivated in September 1914 as GOC 24th Brigade. After the fiasco of Neuve Chapelle (10–12 March 1915), Carter resigned, sick, and was replaced by Brigadier General **Reginald Stuart Oxley.**
112 See October 18th, 1914. Holland was **Commander Royal Artillery, 8th Division.**
113 Charles John Ridgeway (b.1841 – d.1927) was the **Bishop of Chichester** from 1908 to 1919.

in a tent, but directly one gets between the blankets – one snuggles up! A big thanks for that extra Jaeger one[114].

Thursday October 29th 1914, Hursley

Today has been much disorganized and we shall hardly get it right before we go. A Divisional route march took place. We packed everything up just as if we were going abroad – not a fork or strap was left in the camp which we might require on active service. Every single person in the camp fell in, and about 10,000 or 15,000 men marched off in a huge column over the hill. Within 3 miles of Southampton, we turned and marched back here again across country, much to the disappointment of most people, and so here we are, making our beds and arranging an evening meal in the old camping ground. It is excellent practice, and as the weather has been admirable, it was not unpleasant.

Breakfast at 6.30am, and everything up in the Baggage waggons by 9 am, and the march began at 9.30. All the villagers turned out and cheered, and one lady remarked that she had been standing where she was for 3 hours looking at the men going past. Some people had arranged seats along their garden walls! It was a great sight – South Africa days all over again, only the columns were longer. You saw lines of khaki men in front of you and behind you as far as your vision could travel and everybody is impatient to be off. But the practice march was necessary and showed the deficiencies – saddlery, harness, rugs, that kind of thing in short supply and you cannot ride a horse if you are short of a saddle girth or a bridle! It is marvellous how many hundreds of people you see as you journey like this, and of all the hundreds as it happens that you see, not one single face you knew. They waved flags and the people cheered, and the flighty girls shook hands with the soldiers and asked them for buttons. One dear little girl, not unlike Joyce[115], stood diligently waving her Union Jack at the front gate and I told her she was like the 'Rule Britannia', and she was very pleased to be spoken to by an officer on horseback!

Mercifully the portable workshop, which marched with us, has been able to get into 'position' 5 minutes after its return and has pumped up electricity for the Mess tent since darkness fell. Darkness in Camp is a most trying experience, so these moonlight nights are very pleasant. My work in Camp in June may have been of use. Two of the young officers with us there in yester-days, killed. One of them R.S. Glyn from Rochester Diocese, a bright young barrister, who was the first to greet me in the

---

114 **Jaeger** was established by British businessman LRS Tomlin as 'Dr Jaeger's Sanitary Woollen System Co Ltd' in 1884, capitalising on a craze for wool-jersey long johns inspired by the theories of German scientist Dr Gustav Jaeger. Jaeger's writings about the value of wearing animal fibres (not cotton) next to the skin had attracted fans including George Bernard Shaw. Jaeger began creating wool suits, and by the start of WW1 it had cut its associations with Germany and become a British brand.
115 RDG's eldest daughter.

Shorncliffe Camp that time[116] – so many of the young ones gone, Benson[117], Francis Pemberton[118], Glyn and so on.

November 1914[119] First letter from France, la Gorgue

Heavy shell firing all night – not very much sleep. Shells pretty close. A German plane over the village, dropping black puffs of smoke to show the range, being shelled by our own guns – white puffs. The Artillery roaring near, now rumbling in the distance both day and night. It is very pathetic to hear the villagers asking all the time the one main theme. "How is it going? There is no danger now? The Germans will not come back?"

We are surrounded by ruins and desolation. Mud-soaked refugees, old men, old women - mothers with babies in arms, babies in prams all plod patiently along these flat country roads. The nights are taken up with searching for wounded, attending to them and sending them down country. Such wounds! And such patience! and the pathos of the talk of the men, delirious with pain and cold.

Constant rattle of musketry late tonight. Such sights! mud and hair and cloths in clots. A poor man with the top of his forehead blown away by a bullet and unconscious, dying in the shed there. I prayed over him for his friends. 56 sick and wounded in our little hospital today. The way it is arranged here that near the firing line a doctor or two are waiting to dress wounds. They pass on the cases by car and wagon to a mile or so back. There they are cleared into a Field Hospital; mostly they are kept there one night and then passed down country to another hospital, and so on. We are next to the firing line; each night our doctors go out searching for wounded. How awful is this unceasing thunder of destruction and this constant stream of mutilation and death. When comes the promised time?

I find myself greatly in request as interpreter[120]. Hour after hour, in fact, I am so employed by one officer or another, in ascertaining the way, in getting supplies, in

---

116 Lieut. **Richard Spenser Glyn** was killed on 20th October 1914, aged 22.
117 Capt. **John Penrice Benson** (b.1877 – d.1914), 1st Bn East Surrey Regiment. Son of Judge William Denman Benson and Jane Benson; husband of Laura Annette Benson. He had served in the Boer War but had left the Army in early 1914 to train for the priesthood. He was recalled to the East Surrey Regiment in August 1914. Benson was wounded in a skirmish before the Battle of Mons on August 23th and taken prisoner. He died the following evening in the village school and was buried in the Hautrage Military Cemetery
118 Capt. **Francis Percy Campbell Pemberton** (b.1885 – d.1914). 2nd Life Guards, "C" Sqdn. Killed at Moreslde, Belgium on 19th October 1914. Only son of Canon and Mrs. T Percy Pemberton, of Trumpington Hall, Cambridge; husband of Winifred Mary Colegate (formerly Pemberton), of 16, Prince's Gardens, London. Educated at Malvern and Trinity College, Cambridge.
119 War Diary, 24th Field Ambulance (WO 95/1703/1). After a march from Hursley to Southampton, 24th Ambulance embarked November 5th, landed Le Havre November 6th. They entrained on 11th November to Veille Chateau, Merville then marched to their base at La Gorgue, November 15th. "Billeted in a small farm, dressing station in an inn, adjoining cottage."
120 RDG lived in France 1892–3 as Assistant Chaplain at Holy Trinity Anglican church, Nice.

*'The moat and bridge entrance to the Farm.
Grande Marais, Nr. Estaires, La Gorgue'*

'The Farm. Grande Marais, Nr. Estaires, La Gorgue'

establishing relationships with the villagers and in cheering the latter up when they come appealing for news of the conflict and for help in various ways. I have for the next day or two got a hall for the men, in the village near by – the Parish priest has lent me an old school hall. It will cost about 2 francs a day for cleaning and so on, and another 2 francs for coal and light. We may be here two or three days, it may be longer, but there is snow on the ground two inches thick, and the men have nowhere to go. I shall venture on a few day's expenses and trust for the future. That is what is wanted, a fund, to use as opportunities crop up. I have also been able to obtain four tubs, and by buying some coal have provided hot baths for men and officers – the first bath some of them had had for 3 weeks or more. You can smell the unhealthiness of some of the men's clothes. They are thankful – in the trenches they get swathed in mud and come back from the firing line like earth-dwelling animals.

I am going on with this little effort. I am now billeted in a house – the proprieter (a land-owner pretty well off) and his daughter are reduced to living in the kitchen and two wing bedrooms. The dining room and other bedrooms were smashed with shell fire 3 weeks ago, and the drawing room is smothered with debris and dust. Watson (the Baptist Minister) is in another small bedroom above.

Frozen feet, this is the difficulty now with the men. For nearly a month now not one of us has known what it is to have dry boots. For myself, I have been saved by being able to get dry socks, though day after day they have been wet again in an hour or two and soaking wet by night. What it would have been like not to change I dare not think, and besides I have bought at different places seven pairs of socks of different kinds – soldiers have only two pairs! Now we have them coming away from the trenches by the dozen with frozen feet – feet literally mortifying with the damp cold (this is a clay, flat country). It is pitiable to see those blue and white puff balls that numbers of feet have become. 150 men from this regiment alone today with agued feet[121]. I have got my church room going – I can get a stove in it, it will not be too far for a number of the men to come, and so at least at the stove they can dry their socks. Mud and damp has now changed to snow 3 inches thick, and the roads are glassy ice.

It will cost about 5/- a day, and if we are here only a week it will be worth it. When the men come back after 3 or 9 or 19 days in trenches they are given a day or two or a week of change, and then, 2 or 3 miles back, my Church room comes in. I have fixed up with the old French caretaker who is not afraid to remain in the shelled neighbourhood. It will be nice to see it going.

---

121 **Trench foot** is a medical condition caused by prolonged exposure of the feet to damp, unsanitary and cold conditions. Feet become numb, affected by erythrosis (turning red) or cyanosis (turning blue) because of poor vascular supply. Feet begin to have a decaying odour due to the early stages of necrosis. Feet may also begin to swell. Advanced trench foot often involves blisters and open sores, which lead to fungal infections. If left untreated, trench foot usually results in gangrene and the need for amputation. If trench foot is treated properly, complete recovery is normal, though it is marked by severe short-term pain when feeling returns. The condition is named for the conditions in the trenches in WW1.

Very cold, with 19 degrees of frost in the trenches. The men are falling in tens and twenties from frozen feet. I buried a man shot in the head – had to see about the grave myself and help lay him out and tie him up in his blanket with my own hands. We are crowded out with frozen and agued men. My little church room is going, 3 miles from the firing line and at least the men can thaw their feet there. I am going on in faith for £1 a week expenses until we move on, and I pay 1 franc a day for wood to heat the water for the baths in an old wash-house. So many of the houses here are shelled or burnt – it is a scene of utter desolation. We live in a village of ruins, and yet we can buy supplies – luckily some milk and butter.

Sunday November 15th 1914, La Gorgue

Sunday night shells began to drop round busily. I got up and looked and they seemed to be pretty near, but what was to be done? If you're hit, you're hit, if not, you cannot do anything. So I sought sleep again and woke up only once or twice when a shell dropped specially near, 3 fields off. We found this morning two houses struck, two men killed and a third wounded[122].

A most interesting Sunday with Holy Communion at 8 with 21 present and at 11 a crowded service, 200 present. At 11.45 a deeply thrilling service in a farm behind the firing line with about 50 men and officers who go back, after 3 days, to the trenches tonight. THEY ARE SPLENDID. Just after service one of our aeroplanes returned over our heads followed by a blaze of German shells – we were amazed that none of the shell stuff fell on us, too high up I suppose.

Lord Roberts[123] was 100 yds from us with some Hindus the evening before he died, and the Prince of Wales came to see our lines 3 days ago. The club is answering – after 3 days in the trenches they come back to the village to buy bread, coated with mud and shivering with cold, and I can offer them a fire to dry their socks by, and a table to write their letters on, and in the twilight, a light to see by. So it is money well spent and I shall go on as long as we can buy coal and wood. All we want is more men from England.

Thursday November 26th 1914, La Gorgue

… you will have heard of our arrival behind the firing lines, and the house with the gas stove which the next night proved to be in the line of shell firing. Two houses 100 yds away along the same road have since been smashed to pieces by shells, and 60 yds away there is a big hole in the road made by a shell which is big enough to put

---

122 Lance Corporal **W Dyer** and Private **P Fogerty**, 1 Bn Connaught Rangers. Both died 15th November 1914, both buried La Gorgue Communal Cemetery.

123 Lord Roberts died of pneumonia at St Omer, France, on 14th November 1914 while visiting Indian troops. After lying in state in Westminster Hall (one of two non-Royals to do so during the 20th century, the other being Sir Winston Churchill), he was given a state funeral and was then buried in St. Paul's Cathedral.

'Our staff in winter garb. Back row from left to right: Lt. Maunder,
Rev E.L. Watson, Lt. Squire, Lt. Burgess, Lt. Perry, Lt. Murphy,
Capt. Stewart, Lt. Price. Front Row, from left to right: Lt. Meynell, Rev. Griffiths,
Maj. Sayres, Col. Pickard, Maj. Duncan, Rev. W. Molloy.'

Bobby[124] in. Four spies were captured in the village yesterday. It is they, they say, who have been assisting in guiding the shell fire. Only two cases of wounded last night – and a thaw has set in and frost bite has stopped[125]. A number of the feet will have to be amputated, all of us now wear two pairs of socks at a time … such doings! And such heroism! One man was picked up yesterday – he had been twitted by his companions for timidity. "I will show you" he said "If I am afraid". He climbed out of the trench, in the dark, crept along to a German trench, fired right down into it, tore back, fell to the ground and crawled homewards. Just as he was reaching his own trench again, a bullet got him in the head. He was conscious, but it is a question if he will live.

A town about the size of Stroud[126] was shelled on Sunday, Monday and Tuesday week. Yesterday there was not an inhabitant left in the place. The front of the church is blown off – the clock has fallen into the front porch. You ride down empty streets. The shop doors are open. There are all the things on the counters and shelves, cottons, boots, hats, scales. In a restaurant, the plates are all set out on the tables, and an unfinished meal is on one of them. A cat sat airing itself in an open shop doorway –

---

124 His daughter Joyce's pony.
125 War Diary, 24th Field Ambulance (WO 95/1703/1) 20th November: 'Large no, (about 30) of frostbite today. Frost after much wet & about 5 days in trenches'. 24th November: 'Frost ceased. Have many more cases of swollen feet.' The diary was written by the OC 24th Ambulance, Colonel Ransom Pickard.
126 La Gorgue.

no one comes to attend to it ... In one street, a man with two women has come back to get some bedding. He is glad to have someone to tell in passionate grief, though tearless "these three shops are my property. They are all smashed about with shells. And he adds, pointing to a village further on "ten houses of mine over there have been burnt." No one has dared to attempt to thieve. No soldiers going through, or the sentries posted at various ends of the town, may take anything. The punishment for looting is as much as 15 years penal servitude.

Advent Sunday, November 30th 1914, La Gorgue[127]

An encouraging day with 13 communicants, and a good morning service. Then on at the gallop – the men only out of the trenches at 7am, so the Colonel pleaded no service, but I was able to address two groups and then on again at the gallop. The General, his ADC, the Colonel, about 19 officers and about 60 men in the loft of a barn away from observation. A German aeroplane was being bombarded about a mile away, and was being prevented from observing the regiment that I was with by one of our own aeroplanes flying to and fro across our firing line. The shell explosions now and again made our roof thump, what a scene! I preached a few words on the great Advent. A gallop back, three quarters of an hour, galloping most of the way past ruined farms and cottages. A late short lunch and then a rest ... tea, and then a service in hospital, very hearty and touching, and a crowded service in our Church room. The men's singing is grand. (That Church Room is answering – I do not know what we shall do if my funds spin out) 3 officers present. We are delighted to find tonight, by Lord Kitchener's speech in the House of Lords, that 'nothing has been more striking in the whole campaign than the arrival of the 8th Division at the critical moment for the defeat of the Prussian Guard'[128] – though we did not know much about it!

Thursday December 3rd 1914, Estaires

Monday and Tuesday have been very special days. Monday I paid my first pastoral visit right into the trenches. In South Africa[129] there was nothing quite like it. There the firing was more in the open and over wide areas. Here some of the trenches are within 30 yds of the German trenches and on Monday I came within 180 yds. A very kind Adjutant agreed to conduct me along the line. The present firing line is

---

127 From 30th November, the 24th Ambulance station was at Pension des Demoiselles, Estaires.
128 The **Battle of the Marne** fought from 5–12th September 1914. It resulted in an Allied victory against the German Army under Chief of Staff Helmut von Moltke. The battle was the culmination of the German advance into France and pursuit of the Allied armies, which followed the Battle of the Frontiers in August, which had reached the outskirts of Paris. The counter-attack of six French field armies and the BEF along the Marne River forced the German Army to abandon its push on Paris and retreat north-east, leading to the "Race to the Sea" and setting the stage for four years of trench warfare on the Western Front. The Battle of the Marne was an immense strategic victory for the Allies, wrecking Germany's bid for a swift victory over France and forcing it into a drawn-out two-front war.
129 During the 2nd Boer War in which RDG had served as a chaplain.

*'Taking the names and addresses of Madame of the Grande Marais and her visitors –
by a distinguished visitor: for the purpose of sending them copies of their picture.'*

The farm girl on the right. Madame and her two visitors bargaining over a pig.'

about 2½ miles from here, though the nearest trenches are about a ½ mile. About 6 o'clock I started out, glad that it was a blustery clouded night. Two Red Cross officers accompanied me for part of the way, the rest I tramped on alone, passing 2 sentries on the way, and what is always so weird in these parts, a provision column winding its way in remarkable silence (for horses and wagons) and with no lights. The officer had arranged a spot half a mile behind the firing line for our rendezvous. We duly met, and preceded by a man with a loaded rifle in case we met stray Germans, we walked forward in single file. Soon the stray bullets began to fly around, hitting the ground in the fields near, or the walls of a deserted cottage and so on. Turning to the right we came to a white thatched cottage in which the officers live and sleep by day, most of the fighting being done at night. Nearing the cottage, we made a little dash, because a sharp shooter had marked the cottage, and was blazing away in the dark at it. The Colonel and Major had just got up – it was now about 7.15 p.m. Great silence everywhere – people walking about quiet and serious, and there we chatted for about half an hour.

The Colonel and Major had both been in S. Africa and we had all of us been over some same ground. Then to my surprise they brought in dinner – a roasted chicken, very tough (they are common on these deserted farms), potatoes, cabbage, rice, bread and butter and tea, not bad. Then an orderly brought in some rifle grenades they are trying, and the detonators[130]. We started about 9.30 – out past the sharp shooters bullets again (all too high up), across a field and among some trees, the air all the time cracking with bullets, then past a belt of trees which was good cover. We were now about 700 yds from the German trench. Past a burnt-out cattle shed near which a shot bullock lay dead. We had to be careful to avoid huge shell holes in the clayey turf. Then through still more trees fortunately, and the bullets sail high up. Then a dash into the ditch, and we were at the end of the trench. Just as we got there two loud claps of thunder sounded at our right – there was a swish and a sing above, then another and the night lit up red for a moment. They were our own guns shelling the German trenches. Their firing ceased for some minutes after, and we were told our shells had landed well on their trench. It was very close and one can appreciate how it has happened once or twice that a shell falling short has injured some of our own people instead of the enemy.

It was a relief to be down in the trench. We were deep down. The parapets are high above one's head. Men step up onto a ledge to reach the loop-holes – and there they stood, hundreds of them, yard after yard of this winding tortuous ditch (for the

---

130 Britain entered WW1 without any rifle grenades, so Hales Pattern No2 hand-thrown grenades were hastily adapted. The Rifle Grenade variant of the No 2 came in two forms, 7mm and 8mm. The 7mm model was produced for Mexico and is designed to fit into the M95 Mauser rifle used by the Mexican Army, while the 8mm model was designed to be used in the Lebel Rifle. The 7mm variant was used by the British as a temporary rifle grenade until others, such as the Hales rifle grenade, were developed; hence its other name, The Mexican Pattern.

trenches are not dug straight but zigzag to prevent enfilading), each at his vigil waiting for something to shoot. They fire at where the rifle shots come from. Now and again they see a flash and fire at its whereabouts, but short as the distance is, it is practically impossible to see anyone. I looked out through a number of loop-holes ... all the time the fusillade kept going. Now and again a machine gun would rattle at us, or ours at them, and the din and rattle became considerable. Then as you walked from one post to another you caught the strong smell of smoke from a wood or coke fire. Since the piercing cold weather, they have rigged up old biscuit tins as braziers, and these do something to alleviate the intense cold and to reduce the dampness of the feet. But it is all open to the sky, and the mud is more than ankle deep in places. Here and there a little cave is dug into the bank, where a man whose turn it is for a relief spell can turn in for a quiet rest, or where in case of shelling everyone can find shelter. And so we walked on from one man to another for nearly a mile. We left newspapers with each company officer and in one case we sat quite a long time in an officers' dugout while he boiled some water and made us a cup of delicious hot coffee!

Then we came to a part that was at a convenient angle not far from the German trench, about 200 yds. Here the Major chose to fire his first rifle grenade and one officer fired a flare pistol. This silently fires away a ball of light, which we could see carried as far as the German wire entanglement. While it remained still ablaze, the officer firing the rifle grenade could see where to aim. Soon it came to midnight and I thought it was time to move so I left them at their rifle-grenading and the kind officer came with me again. We walked back from where we were in the trench through another zigzag trench at right-angles to it for about 50 yds, then along the bottom of a ditch, shots cracking over us all the time, then along a line of willow trees which I used a little as shelter, then we doubled back along a track in the direction of the cottage. A horse lay dead on a grass plot and the moonlight was now nearly as clear as day. For a good distance we were shielded away on our left by the dark outline of a low hedge but all the while bullets were whistling and snapping over us. And then we came to a long open stretch of about 30 yds. Here it seemed to us that we had been seen, for a regular hailstorm of shots rattled round us. We walked quietly on – a run would have drawn fire. We talked of many things. The officer spoke of the rightness of our cause, and we agreed that it was that which kept a man 'peaceful' as he remarked, "whatever happens". And with the noise round us and the sense of the big gunfire with us, I remembered and quoted the verse from the poem in the Times:

Not for passion or for Power
Clean of hand and calm of soul
England in this awful hour
Bids her battle thunders roll![131]

---

131 **James Rhoades**, *Sonnet for England*, The Times, August 21st, 1914. Rhoades was an English poet, mystic, translator and author (b.1841 – d.1923).

I think we talked to keep each other going ... when we got past the open stretch the fusillade subsided, but hot shooting still followed us, the bullets all, luckily for us, still high. Near the cottage again, there seemed quite a little breeze of them. It was now very late, and the Colonel very kindly offered the use of the headquarters bicycle and I was thankful enough for it – I passed the first sentry all right as he was under a tree, and shouted out his challenge vigorously, and I shouted my reply "Chaplain Griffiths" no less vigorously and with no delay that I knew of! The other sentry half a mile further on was sheltering from the wind and the moonlight behind a wall, and I did not at first notice him, nor did he see me. Anyhow, I thought it safer to shout out "Goodnight sentry" His reply, with a broad provincial accent, was "Here, stop. Who are you?" (Very loudly) "Come back". So I stopped and said "You didn't challenge, you know. Chaplain Griffiths, you see I am, so that's all right" And he peered into my face and said "Oh yes sir, that's all right". Then I said, "now you can help me back on my bicycle" and so he kindly did. But all the while he had his rifle slung on his arm, and I said "You'll be careful won't you? I don't want any of that in me" He replied "No sir, but you would have had it if you hadn't stopped." You can imagine I slept when I turned in soon after 2 a.m! The Colonel's goodnight was "I'm glad you haven't been killed".

The next day following, the King of England[132] himself came up to our village[133]! The reserves lined the road way (i.e. the men out of the trenches for their three days). Our R.A.M.C. helped and I was placed at the end of our line with the Colonel. The King returned our salute as he did to all the officers. Through being at the end of the line, I missed one thing. When the King stopped at the other end of the line, the Chaplains near there with other officers were presented to him – better luck next time! The Prince of Wales chauffeured his father's car and with him was Major Wigram[134]. With the King was President Poincare[135] – behind

---

132 George V (**George Frederick Ernest Albert**, b.1865 – d.1936) was King of the United Kingdom and the British Dominions, and Emperor of India, from 6th May 1910 until his death.

133 Chateau Dermont, Merville. 1st December 1914. *Merville, 1 December 1914* (Sub-title: The meeting of King George V and President Poincaré of France at the British Headquarters at Merville, France, on 1 December 1914). Herbert Arnould Olivier, 1916, Government Art Collection. Merville is 3 miles E of La Gorgue.

134 Maj. Sir **Clive Wigram**, 1st Baron Wigram. GCB, GCVO, CSI, PC (b.1873 – d.1960), was a British soldier and court official. He was Private Secretary to the Sovereign from 1931 to 1936.

135 **Raymond Poincaré** (b.1860 – d.1934) was a French statesman who served three times as Prime Minister, and as President from 1913 to 1920. He was a conservative leader, primarily committed to political and social stability. In 1902, he co-founded the Democratic Republican Alliance, the most important centre-right party under the Third Republic, becoming Prime Minister in 1912 and President in 1913. He was noted for his strongly anti-German attitudes, and twice visited Russia to maintain strategic ties. At the peace conference, he favoured re-occupation of the Rhineland, which he was able to carry out in 1923 as Prime Minister.

General Joffre[136] and General French[137] and then some Hindu generals[138] and so on, about nine cars altogether. I had a little fun notwithstanding. Directly the King had gone, I got the driver of one of our motor ambulances to try a side track and head the cars off so that now, being unofficial, I might try some snapshots, and we were very successful. We found His Majesty at the General's billet with all sorts of people round him, and being a chaplain, I was allowed to move in and out of the group freely. By this means, though the light was very poor, I got half a dozen fairly close pictures. Only one other camera was at work, that of a French Marquis on Joffre's staff[139]. When he saw mine, he sidled up to me and said slyly "If you get some good ones, will you let me have a copy? I will give you some of mine!" and we agreed. "But you know" he whispered "it is forbidden!" But now, near the door a row of men were drawn up dressed in the new goatskin coats, with those improvised straw and sacking feet protectors. The King was rather amused at them, and the point is that when he caught sight of the French officer's camera, he sent him a special message asking that a photograph of the men might be taken! There upon, a third camera came out belonging to a young Lord Rothschild[140]. Later on I met the King a third time as he returned from the next village, so it was quite a full afternoon ...

---

136 Marshal **Joseph Jacques Césaire Joffre**, GCB, OM (b.1852 – d.1931). He is most known for regrouping the retreating allied armies to defeat the Germans at the strategically decisive First Battle of the Marne in 1914. His popularity led to his nickname *Papa Joffre*.

137 Field Marshal **John Denton Pinkstone French, 1st Earl of Ypres**, KP, GCB, OM, GCVO, KCMG, ADC, PC (b.1852 – d.1925), known as **The Viscount French** between 1916 and 1922, was an Anglo-Irish officer in the British Army. He distinguished himself commanding the Cavalry Division during the Second Boer War, became Chief of the Imperial General Staff in 1912 but resigned over the Curragh Mutiny, and then served as the first Commander-in-Chief of the British Expeditionary Force for the first two years of World War I before serving as Commander-in-Chief, Home Forces, then becoming Lord Lieutenant of Ireland in 1918, a position which he held throughout much of the Irish War of Independence.

138 General Maharaja Sir **Ganga Singh**, GCSI, GCIE, GCVO, GCStJ, GBE, KCB (b.1880 – d.1943), was the ruling Maharaja of the princely state of Bikaner (in present-day Rajasthan) from 1888 to 1943. He is widely remembered as a modern reformist visionary, and he was also the only "non-white" member of the British Imperial War Cabinet during WW1. For military training, he was sent to Deoli in 1898 and attached to the 42nd Deoli Regiment. During WW1, he commanded the Bikaner Camel Corps which served in France, Egypt and Palestine. Lieutenant-General Maharaja Sri Sir **Pratap Singh** Sahib Bahadur of Idar, GCB, GCSI, GCVO (b.1845 – d.1922) was a career British Indian Army officer, Maharaja of the princely state of Idar (Gujarat) and heir to Ahmednagar from 1902 to 1911, when he abdicated in favour of his adopted son. Despite his age, Sir Pratap commanded his regiments heroically during WW1 from 1914–1915 and in the Palestine Mandate at Haifa and Aleppo. He was promoted to Lieutenant-General in 1916.

139 **Duke of Albufera**: The title of Duke of Albufera and Empire refers to the Albufera, a lagoon located 6 miles South of Valencia in Spain, bordering the Mediterranean, with which it communicates. Created by Napleoen in 1812, RDG would have met the 3rd Duke **Raoul Napleoen Suchet** (b.1845 – d.1925).

140 Sir **Philip Albert Gustave David Sassoon**, 3rd Baronet, PC, GBE, CMG (b.1888 – d.1939), was a British politician, art collector and social host, entertaining many celebrity guests at his homes, Port Lympne Mansion, Kent, and Trent Park, Hertfordshire. He was Private Secretary to Field Marshal Sir Douglas Haig from 1915–1918. He was a cousin of the war poet Siegfried Sassoon.

'A Field Service. Bodyguard of HM George V – and of M. Poincare, President of the French Republic – on the occasion of their visit 'to the Front' – December 1914. (Taken by the Marquis of Albufera – one of General Joffre's staff: copy presented to RG).'

Please thank your cousin warmly for the help towards the Club Room Fund. Headquarters staff proposed to me a second room near the other village this morning – a disused cinema. Conran may like to try and work it. If so, we will be thankful for all the help we can get – though as we pay no rent our expenses are very reasonable. I shall try and get notepaper and envelopes and writing materials to give out to the men – lighting is however our main difficulty.

Saturday December 5th 1914, Estaires

We move again Monday morning we hear, only a short distance away and chiefly because there are better buildings in which to bestow the patients – the latter are fortunately not so much of the casualty kind as of the weather-bitten, though the latter with their frozen feet are of a very unpleasant character. Fighting is much quieter, and the impression prevails that the Germans have given up this end, for the time being, in order to resist invasion from the East. It would be a bitter pill to them to have a foreigner place foot on their soil.

"He lay like a warrior taking his rest"[141]. That is how one case we brought in last night struck me. The good regimental doctor carried him out of the trench on his back. The

---

141 "No useless coffin enclosed his breast, Not in sheet or in shroud we wound him; But he lay like a warrior taking his rest With his martial cloak around him": *The Burial of Sir John Moore after Corunna 1814* by Charles Wolfe, b.1791 – d.1823.

49

man was wounded in the head – so often it is the head or the hand, so close is the firing and so little the chance given just through the little loop-holes[142]. The doctor then ran along in the moonlight to where we were waiting with a motor ambulance behind a farm cottage. There the man could be laid on a stretcher and sent back to our field hospital in the car with, mercifully, lightning speed. The flare of an acetylene lamp, the quiet orderlies round. The skilful keen doctor, and the man lying there. The grim bullet wound in the centre of the forehead coming out beyond the crown of the head – and he lay there, his face fresh looking and placid, one foot crossed over the other, his hands folded like some crusader on a church monument. The brain was touched and the man quite unconscious. He slept on peacefully as a child while the doctor dressed the wound, put on the fresh bandages and prepared him for sending him on down-country to the next hospital. A finely built man – the head cases are wonderful – they do not say he has not the chance of recovery. Another head case – struck in almost the same manner, raved and struggled greatly – a different nature? Yet another slept on as the first one did, like a little child. Once or twice he sighed and moaned a little. On the third morning not having wakened at all and without moving hand or foot, I stood by him and prayed with him, hoping his soul joined in and thought of those who loved him – someone loves him we may be sure – then we carried him across to the little village graveyard and laid him like Pilgrim, to rest in the Chamber whose windows look towards the rising sun, and the name of that Chamber is 'Peace'[143].

We expect to get orders tomorrow. Rain every day, soaking soil often frozen, which extends the sore feet cases, and we are going to where there will be accommodation for keeping the men on a few days in the hope of mending them up quickly to return to their duty. If they go on down country, nobody knows when they may be returned to their regiments, and those frozen feet if taken in good time, may be healed up in a week or so. Many more have been incapacitated by their feet than by bullets lately, which is annoying.

The Church room has justified itself more and more. 46 communicants this morning – 4 officers including a staff officer. I am thankful I thought about it. We must keep something like it going everywhere if possible – an old barn or even a disused cattle shed. I think we must keep this place going, by riding over if possible, though that will be difficult – we must see. Over 180 at Morning Prayer and this evening quite 200 were present including 4 officers. It is a great thing being able to provide the building. Later we may be able to run a concert and I am trying to think how to evoke contributions from the men, though thinking of all that they are going through,

---

142 Until the issuing of the Brodie Helmet in April 1916, British soldiers relied on a simple cloth cap for head protection, and lethal head wounds were a serious problem. The first country to issue steel helmet was France in mid 1915.

143 Pvte **Bert Sampson** Lincolnshire Regiment 2nd Bn, died 5th December 1914. *The Pilgrim's Progress from This World to That Which Is to Come; Delivered under the Similitude of a Dream* is a Christian allegory written by John Bunyan and published in February, 1678. It is regarded as one of the most significant works of religious English literature.

RDG in the trenches

the roughing it and the sacrifices, I hesitate a little to go for what can be got out of them. When the men are out in the trenches, they can come for an hour or two in the day time into the neighbouring villages, walking perhaps a mile or two to get here. I am going to try to get writing materials for them – they are pretty well supplied with tobacco. The woollens are coming along well, although socks will not easily be beyond men's needs, as after much wear they cannot easily be mended, the wet and the mud tending to spoil them in addition to the wear, and it is so difficult to dry things. This is a flat and dreadfully slushy country.

Such impressive services besides those in the building today, with first and second Reserves towards the firing line – in barns, out of sight of possible aeroplanes. Each Sunday so far happens to have been clear, and an aeroplane was seen reconnoitering along our front. The General does not wish it to be a regular practice for Chaplains to visit the trenches, though he will not forbid an occasional visit.

Tuesday December 8th 1914, Estaires

I met a Mr. Stanley today. He has given two or three Red Cross cars, and he himself assists in the running of them. He is well-to-do and has land in Queensland. He knew your father, and although of a different school of churchmanship admired him greatly, said "he had such a large heart!" Then I said I was married to you. Then he said he knew another clergyman who had married another Miss Saumarez-Smith – Will S[144] and he said "he is a promising fellow"!

Friday December 11th 1914, Estaires

By the time you get this events will have moved. But just where we are there is somewhat just now to cause alarm – we are on what is called the 'edge of circumstance'. On one side, as we gather, the enemy is retiring, on the other they are gathering for a fierce attack and our position is between the two places. Last night there was a terrific fusillade. Tonight all is still, and cannonading has ceased for 2 or 3 days. Some think the quietude is ominous, others hope that it means their having had to clear away to repel the Russians. Then there is that mysterious message, that General Joffre has a surprise for us for Christmas – that may mean anything large or anything trivial. As in the rest of this remarkable year, we must 'wait and see'.

It has been very nice. I told you that after each burial of our soldiers, someone had gone to the new grave and planted a small tree on it. I found out the kind soul and paid him a visit to thank him in the name of the Chaplain and the men's friends. Then I asked him to write his full name and address in my pocket book, pour souvenir. He wrote this – "R.d'Hallain, notaire a …………….au nom de toute la municipalite de la ville, a promis de faire orner toute les tombes des soldats francais et allies dans terrain reserve du cimetiere de la ville, et il s'est fait l'entreprete de tout la population en affirmant qu'elle irait priere sur les tombes de ces heroes."[145]

Your letter, after the appearance of yours to the 'Times' has just arrived. The result is excellent and justified both of us in our endeavours. The room in the village has to be closed for the present as we have moved on here. But when reinforcements follow on behind us, as we hope they may, it will be delightful to be able to pass on this plan to any chaplain coming with them. Meanwhile we are spending £2 or £3 on fitting out the disused Cinema Hall for a church. Some men of the C.E.M.S are doing the work and apart from necessary payment to a carpenter for structural work and some cheap material for draping, we shall need little outlay – we get the Hall free. Conran is delighted that we have now a central place instead of having to use a ward in the Temporary hospital. We may move any day, that is everybody's hope, but if it is only for certain week-days and one or two Sundays, Conran and I agree that the pound or two spent will be worth the while, and if we should still be here for Christmas, there is the opportunity of giving the relief men, in their day or two out of the trenches, a chance to turn their thoughts from the incessant snarl of musketry and the paddling in rain and mud. In the place we are now in, the baths idea has been

---

144 **Dorothy Saumarez-Smith** (b.1881) married William Stevenson.

145 "… speaking for the entire local Council of the Town Hall we have promised to honour and decorate all the tombstones of French and allied soldiers in the selected area of the town's Churchyard, and (he) has made himself the interpreter for the entire population, stating positively that they will go and pray on the tombs of these heroes."

admirably run by some Sisters of Charity as far as the officers are concerned, and some public bathing tanks have been organised for the troops, the comfort of which can be imagined. The men march there in detachments and the smiles and fun you see among them as they march back speak for themselves.

Rumours accumulate about there being a big move. We are determined to think that it is a move forward, but the suspense is curious, and in any case, move forward notwithstanding, death and pain must come among us inevitably. As I write tonight the crackle of musketry is very heavy over the fields, but their cannons have been silent for four days now. But what a post that was! How much goodness this war is bringing out.

Saturday December 12th 1914, Estaires

Help is forthcoming briskly and I begin to see it becoming something to cope with. If I can, tomorrow I shall begin to enlist the help of members of the C.E.M.S.[146], in acknowledging and working things out. It appears that the Daily Mail as well as the Evening News has taken up the cause, and things are arriving by each post so much so that we shall need a baggage wagon to take them all! How real is the sympathy all round that comes out of these doings. We have been hard at work all yesterday and today fitting out the little temporary church in this next place, and it looks quite nice. Some of the men are asking if it can be made a club as well, so that must be considered. At the same time rumours of our moving on are become more insistent.

I passed the Prince of Wales[147] again this morning, twice. They tell me he has now the rank of Captain. He was smoking away briskly[148]. We have put up a larger card intimating that we have in the given place a Temporary Military Church and I overheard the Staff Officer accompanying the Prince quoting that intimation to him so that if I can get word with him, I shall ask him to come and join in prayer – if we do not move on.

---

146 The CEMS (Church of England Men's Society) was formed in 1899 by Archbishop Frederick Temple by the amalgamation of the Church of England's Young Men's Society, the Young Men's Friendly Society and the Men's Help Society. It was intended to be educational, social and representative of the Church of England whilst also adapting to local circumstances.

147 Edward VIII (**Edward Albert Christian George Andrew Patrick David**; later the **Duke of Windsor**; b. 1894 – d.1972) was King from 20th January 1936 until his abdication on 11th December 1936. Commissioned in the Grenadier Guards, but when his battalion was posted overseas he found himself transferred to the 3rd battalion, which was to remain in England. He protested to George V, only to be told that Kitchener did not mind if the young prince was killed on the front line, but he could not risk his being captured and used as a hostage. His protests at being left behind won him a transfer to the staff of the BEF's commander in France and he spent the rest of the war as a roving morale-raiser and collector of intelligence.

148 The Duke of Windsor would die of smoking-related throat cancer.

Sunday December 13th 1914, Estaires

The Military Church has been well used – 27 communicants at 8 am, 17 officers, 1 staff officer and about 100 men at 10.30 am, a General, 3 staff officers and about 120 men at 6.30 p.m. and at 7.15 p.m. about 300. The situation is in a little back alley. If we are here next Sunday its position will be better known. We have announced daily communion at 7.30 am and Evening service Friday at 6.30. But tomorrow, Tuesday or Wednesday we may move on. I shall leave the Club Room in charge of the Cure of the parish, and give him a sum for the expenses, and get him to work it for the soldiers who follow on in conjunction with the Chaplain who will accompany them (that is unless I get in touch directly with the Chaplain concerned). I was going to close it, but the help your letters speak about changes my mind, and the men go on finding the next place out. So let it march – and I shall be able now for the rest of the winter to systematise wherever we go as far as possible. The help is certainly most generous. I do hope that it will keep coming on, as we can use any amount of help at one or the other of the bases.

Trench work is frightfully exhausting and it is not exhilarating. They take it without 'grousing' too, in a remarkable way. You should see the ragged sight the men present when they come out on relief – dishevelled, unshaven, and caked with mud. They do not appear to care about anything, but talk to them and the eye lights up – the spirit is there and the grumbling soldier of peace time is unknown. How splendid it is! As I overtook a cavalcade of them this morning, men and horses splashed to the eyes with mud, trotting cheerfully back from watering to the gun parks, I must say I could only look on in admiration – they are splendid.

Here is a story just brought in by a Colonel about one of his men. The man was shot in the right lung. He fell, and then jumped up again, saw what had happened, clapped his hand to his side and turned to his neighbour and said "which side's the heart, mate?" "Left, of course" "That's alright then!" Some great move is on we think. Our hospital has sent out every single patient, either in preparation for another fight, or for our moving to attack.

I saw a long procession of intercession in this little town today. It was nearly half a mile long and it seemed as if every man, woman and child in the place were in it and they carried a statue of the Blessed Virgin and banners, and chanted as they went. There was real prayer in it.

There is all the excitement of a big move – but nobody knows anything. Three or four more parcels of socks have arrived and they will be very welcome. But if anybody asks you about sending them will you say 'not before the beginning of the new Year', as the parcel post at Christmas will be very heavy.

I heard a good story this afternoon. A lady in Berlin wrote to the wife of one of our colonels. The letter gave a description of life in Berlin that was all 'couleur de rose'. At the end of the letter the writer said "I should keep the stamp on this letter as some day hence it may be valuable". The lady who received the letter steamed the stamp off, and underneath it was written a message "the real truth, this place is in the depth of gloom."

Tuesday, December 15th 1914, Estaires

We are expecting some hot fighting very soon but I must not say where. If the letters get fewer you will know, and if I stop writing for a bit you will let it be known in the family that it is due to pressure. Such a sad case – a terrible shrapnel wound[149]. The operation was a most skilful one, but the dear lad died, ten minutes after it, concious to the last and talking to me coherently about "home" and "pain".

The Fund must go on. Before the end of the winter we shall have used all of it – we are over 30,000 men. I have been talking with the Brigade Staff (one or two of them) and shall be seeing the General tomorrow. They suggest hot coffee in the trenches and cocoa for a change. It will be worth it. Then I have had a little deputation from the town, some godly men, who would like a place for devotional times together. I think it will be in the temporary Church, which means warmth and light, and by a little adaptability, another warming and drying centre. There is a strange lull in the proceedings again today. No firing tonight and no casualties we hope. A patrol taken yesterday – one prisoner, 3 killed. Everybody is wondering what next – we may move and we may not! Meanwhile we are getting up a football match[150] and a concert and filling the interval with giving out dry socks and cigarettes.

With the former in view, I rode along our front this afternoon to see the Chaplain of the next Ambulance Brigade, who will muster a team to meet ours. They are in a village about 3 miles away and as you ride you see many things. Hundreds of soldiers, dozens of horses, plenty of mud knee-deep, with, out in the fields, bare-looking enough, old men and boys and women working the land, loading wagons, driving horses. A frightened looking woman stops us to ask, as our trenches have been so quiet, "Are we going back? Are the Germans coming?" and she shows us the arm of her 15 year old daughter still in a sling, which was injured by a German shell. Roofs and walls are smashed – here a whole set of farm buildings, house included, is a heap of ruins and ashes. Each row of cottages of any pretension, has its little brick shrine to the Christ or the Blessed Virgin, as has each farm house. Some of the shrines are poorly tawdry, childish figures of a praying priest or a jubilant little cherub protrude themselves from the side wall in front of the Crucifix. Each farm

---

149 **Shrapnel** is named after Major-General **Henry Shrapnel** (b.1761– d.1842), a British artillery officer, whose experiments, initially conducted in his own time and at his own expense, culminated in the design and development of a new type of artillery shell. **Shrapnel shells** were anti-personnel artillery munitions, which carried a large number of individual bullets close to the target and then ejected them to allow them to continue along the shell's trajectory and strike the target individually. They relied almost entirely on the shell's velocity for their lethality.

150 In October 1915 Rev. **H. C. Hargreaves** requested a donation of 'football outfits &c for the 24th Ambulance' from Everton Football Club. Hargreaves was RDG's replacement at 24th Ambulance after his transfer to the 20th Infantry Base Dept at Etaples in September 1915.

A dog cart

has its dog wheel, and now and again you meet a dog in a cart, either drawing a cart suited to its size alone, or harnessed under a hand cart pushed by hand. The church in this neighbouring village, has like others, been gutted.

Can you let it be known that we are rather 'under sufferance' about the number and length of the letters we write? We depend on the good graces somewhat of our Censor. Fortunately he is sympathetic towards a wife, being married himself.

Friday, December 18th 1914, Estaires

A battle at last[151]! All our strength is drawn up behind the firing line, and the big guns are lighting up the night sky and making a great noise. The darkness is deep and there is a drizzle of cold rain with a fairly driving, whistling wind. Our little town is almost deserted of soldiers – we are attacking, I understand, and trying to get hold of a thin line of men holding a section of trenches. By the time you get this, if you get it soon, you will probably have known as much about it as we do, or more. 10p.m. The battle so far has gone our way – the firing has gone on and on away from us. I rode out to back behind the lines – a strange ride and a weird sight in the wild dark night. Once, a German searchlight flashed right across my path, and they have illuminant shells which swing a ball of light through the night sky, lighting up everything around us. The noise was something terrific and the flashes of bursting shells are, in contrast to the deep darkness, for the moment dazzling! But I think we

---

151 **Battle of Givenchy** (December 18th – December 22nd, 1914) was a battle fought during WW1 as part of the First Battle of Champagne, that saw an initially advancing British force face strong opposition and counter-attack from a solidly entrenched German force around the village of Givenchy.

must be breaking through. No German cannon have replied and our own have gone gradually silent. I expect there must be a retreat on their side. Now we must await the accounts of those who have gone out to collect the wounded. There have been so many letters to write that I have not gone with them – everything is packed up ready to retire in case things went against us, the horse ready saddled in his stable. I have just had a report that we have carried the first line of trenches. I shall turn in and they will call me in case any very serious casualty comes in.

Saturday, December 19th 1914, Estaires

The battle last night – today the aftermath. It is a horrible thing – people who can talk glibly of the 'romance of war' ought to be put first into the firing line and then into the hospital. We carried a trench last night and today we hear it is re-taken – 23 prisoners, 49 by another account. Probably there are two lots: one is described as composed of ragged people, some dressed in discarded English khaki, an older man of over 70 and a lad of 16 or 17. The others including an officer, a well set up lot, very well fed and comfortable looking … but what scenes here!! The poor lad I buried yesterday shot through the nose and out through the ear – the Major with the battered skull – the livid, grey, pinched face of the man whose neck and chest were clawed through by a lump of shrapnel. Tonight again a roar of artillery and the dark rain-swept sky lit up with the wide sweeps of shell flames – it is the awful fury of man's wrath. We can only say 'be ye angry and sin not[152]' would that the sun need not go down upon it.

The editor of the Church Times has written kindly twice about the Fund and I have replied suggesting that what we do not use for coaling needs etc., now in the harder fighting area may come into use for Recreation Huts and the like at the Base. The Y.M.C.A. are already going in for work of that kind. I think that we of the Church of England (and the Chaplains Department) ought not to lag behind in these things. The point will be that more chaplains and some honorary workers must come out here and so with this idea in view, I think I shall not stop the contributions yet. So many are ready to give liberally, and others give a wide range (margin) of purpose. I think they will not mind a balance being available for such a purpose, and we have yet to see the first three months of the New Year through.

Sunday, December 20th 1914, Estaires

Three officers are with us having meals today, one of whom I knew in South Africa. The back of his hand is gashed, his right temple is cut with a grazing wound, and his cap got another grazing wound on the left side. His fellow officer is shot in the arm but will sit up cheerfully to meals. Downstairs the Major of both of them is at close grips with death – tonight there is a sign of renewed force after 24 hours – strange this weighing of a life in the balance.

---

152 Ephesians 4:26-27 'Be ye angry, and sin not: let not the sun go down upon your wrath.'

'The back of our hospital'

This morning was a broken one – had it not been for the temporary Church it would have been a blank Sunday. As it is we did have at 8 am seven communicants, at 10.30 about 40 men, a General and 5 officers, and this evening at 6.30 over a hundred men with about 8 officers. My Brigade General could not arrange any other services here today, but he advised my trying one farm as a venue, at the same time saying that as it was the centre of Friday night's fighting it might be dangerous, and so I must proceed with caution and take things as I found them.

It was a beautiful morning and the horse was in excellent spirits. An officer who had been at the service accompanied me part of the way. As we rode along, the other General who had been at the service, overtook us and as he passed leaned over and said cautiously "We are just going to try and take these lines". I thought I would ride on but the other officer had to turn off, so I rode on alone. By and bye the usual Sunday morning scene took place. One of our aeroplanes, high up in the clear blue sky, was circled round with bursting shells — little white rosebuds of smoke that blossomed out into full flowers, and then vanished. They did seem to get very near him today and I felt bound to exclaim "a brave man that!"

Then by and bye I was overtaken by General no. 2, who had been to see no. 1. He now said "they tell me that the manoeuvre is off", and so I rode on. At the given farm, surely enough the men were all fully armed, crowded under shelter out of sight. It was evidently no time for a service, and the Colonel, a nice man, felt the same, but the morning was well spent. Then came a little excitement – the ominous hiss and 'sing' of an aeroplane fairly low down, the maltese crosses on it quite visible showing it to be a German plane. It circled round us – the men were all forbidden to show a nose. Then one of our aeroplanes came near, then a second one of ours. It circled close to the German one and we expected a duel. It passed on however, and the German one, finishing his circle round our billet, received a tremendous cannonading. The first percussion sounded so close that some thought it was a German shell but it was our own, so that was alright. It had the effect however of so frightening my horse, which was tethered nearby, that he careered round and finally fell flat on his side in the deep mud. He was caked with it, and the saddle and the khaki cassock strapped to the saddle, inside which was my surplice! Thus we had to stay, everybody in hiding, till at last the aeroplane sailed off. Then after rubbing it down as well as possible in the time, I mounted the muddy saddle and lost no time in getting further down the line. Mud everywhere, and if you are at all in a hurry as today, you get splashed up to the waist more or less. That was Sunday morning! It seems likely we shall not move from this neighbourhood at all events before Christmas, so I hope the temporary church will come in well for keeping that.

Wednesday, December 23rd 1914, Estaires

Everybody will be glad to know that the Generals have arranged for all the men to have a periodical bath. The 'tub' side of my little scheme has therefore been superseded, and the idea was taken up apparently simultaneously – but the drying of socks must go on. There is such a difficulty in drying anything.

Four days in the open with a gash right through the thigh! He has just had his leg off and wonders what has become of it? But the spirit of these men is wonderful and grumbling is practically unknown. The Fund at work. A man down with dysentery – milk must be got. My little knowledge of French helps me to know from where it can be bought and I get it.

An officer is here, for the moment really broken down. One temple wounded, his cap on the other temple grazed, his hand grazed. His fellow captain is with him with an injured hand, and his Major is lying dead behind the hanging blanket at the end of the hall. His subaltern was shot through the eye and is left dead in the German trench which they had been trying to capture[153]. The whole of this officer's company was on his hands, being hand-bombed by the Germans at only a few dozen yards distance, and the description he gives of those two hours was that they were in an inferno. The reaction came when he got in here – his Major killed, his subaltern killed, his fellow captain wounded, many dead, many wounded. His nerve gave at last for a few moments and his jaw trembled and his eyes gleamed. A fine man that, he owned that he felt it all and the only thing to do with a man in that state is to make him stay in his blankets and try to sleep. He had not slept for three nights and days. I get eggs for him, the knowledge of French comes in again and I get milk. A field ambulance is not provided with a diet scale, it is all rough and ready and so the Fund comes in.

---

153 Lieutenant **Alexander Dewar**, Royal Engineers. Major **Reginald Garrett Cooper-King** (b.1879 – d.1914) 2 Bn West Yorkshire Regiment (Prince of Wales's Own), Son of Lt. Col. Charles Cooper-King and Harriet Cooper-King, of Camberley, Surrey. Both died 21st December 1914, buried at Estaires Communal Cemetery. See March 15th, 1919.

Thursday, December 24th 1914, Estaires[154]

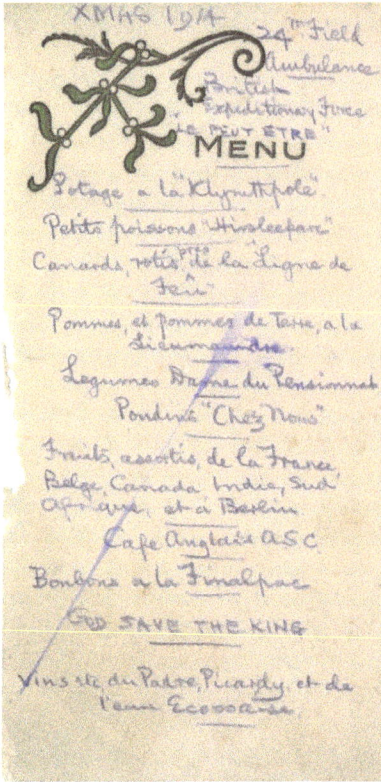

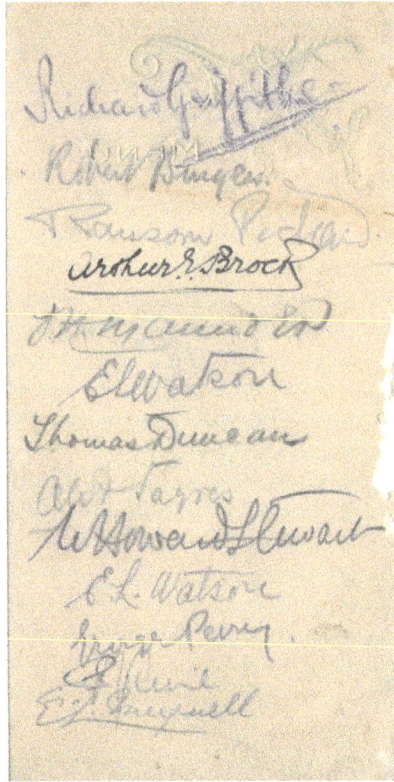

XMAS 1914 24th Field Ambulance British Expeditionary Force
"Le PEUT ETRE" MENU
Officers' signatures on the reverse

Friday, December 25th 1914, Estaires

Christmastide has kept me very busy with the temporary Church being a real joy. In addition to the services behind the firing line, in the disused cinema we held H.C. at 7 am with about 65 present, H.C. after Morning Prayer at 10.30 about 60 present, and two Generals among them at which Conran gave a straight, manly address. I was unable to have a set service behind the firing line as all the men were mustering to change in and out of the trenches, and the Communion kept us late into the morning.

There was Evening Service at 4 p.m. and we feared whether or not anyone would be there but there must have been over 70 – and how they do sing at these services!

---

154 Xmas 1914 Day Menu for the officers of 24th Ambulance, written in RDG's own hand. Signed on the reverse: Richard Griffiths, Robert Burgess, Ransom Pickard, Arthur S Brock, ?, E L Watson, Thomas Duncan, E W F Sayres, W Howard, E Stewart, E L Watson, George Perry, E F Squire, E L Meynell.

Goudge[155] (an additional chaplain) took this service and confessed himself surprised to find so many present, and spoke very nicely about trust in God. I was in the congregation, and as the men round me sang away to the fullness of their powers 'Hark the herald angels sing'[156] – out of the trenches only the day before, plastered with mud some of them, one or two with big tears in their clothes – as they sang away like that I am afraid my eyes got a little dim. Any one of them might be brought in tonight with one of those ugly gashes in his head, cold and stiff. Each morning my first visit has to be to that dark corner near the staircase, behind the hanging blankets.

We buried 3 on Christmas Eve – late – with just enough daylight left to feel what we were doing, the pale moon shining down on us, a red glow fading in the darkening sky and an icy wind blowing on the freezing mud. The 'Last Post' on the bugles (the soldier's goodnight) over those three sombre, blanket-wrapped forms in their shallow graves – and the interminable rumble of the artillery away at the end of the long road, make one feel sadly in the gloom of this sin-saddened world. There is a wail in the last few notes of the 'Last Post' under these circumstances – in ordinary times it is meant to be a gentle sending off to sleep to the tired man[157].

Then at the end of the day – Christmas Day, our 'Church' furniture was reverently removed by our C.E.M.S. men and our Church became a concert hall. By 6 o'clock it was filled, by 6.30 it was packed with men for the concert, and a very good concert it was. We hired a piano from an anxious householder, and we got hot coffee, bread and butter and some strange, not very palatable, French cakes and warmed the men up and a really joyful Christmas evening was spent by everybody. One man recited "And then you'll be a man, my son[158]" by Kipling really very nicely. It was a good concert, in the middle of which unfortunately I had to leave to go to our officers' dinner.

You will see that now we have got 2 halls going. Reserves from the trenches have been sent again to the village where our first hall is, which we did not close, and on

---

155 Rev. **Thomas Sydney Goudge** (b.1870 – d.1954). Regular army chaplain third class, promoted to first class in 1916 he would be the senior chaplain for Boulogne (Assistant Chaplain General), awarded a DSO in 1918.

156 "**Hark! The Herald Angels Sing**" is a Christmas carol that first appeared in 1739 in the collection *Hymns and Sacred Poems*, having been written by Charles Wesley. Music by Felix Mendelssohn from a cantata to commemorate Johann Gutenberg's invention of the printing press, adapted by the English musician William H. Cummings.

157 Private **William Widger** (b.1890 – d.1914), 2 Bn Devonshire Regiment, Son of George and Annie Widger, of Harberton, Totnes, Devon. Private **H. Ford** (b.1892 – d.1914) 2 Bn Northamptonshire Regiment. Son of Emma Ford, of 1, Burrells Court, West St., Stamford, Lincs, and the late John Ford. Private **William Hollings** (b.1891 – d.1914) 2 Bn Middlesex Regiment. Son of F. and Amelia Hollings, of 60, Bridport Place, Hoxton, London. All died 24th December 1914 and buried at Estaires Communal Cemetery.

158 "**If—**" is a poem by British Nobel laureate Rudyard Kipling, written in 1895 and first published in *Rewards and Fairies*, 1910. It is a tribute to Leander Starr Jameson,[1] and is written in the form of paternal advice to the poet's son. As poetry, "If–" is a literary example of Victorian-era stoicism. The well-known Indian historian and writer Khushwant Singh claims that Kipling's If is "the essence of the message of The Gita in English."

these cold wet days it gets much used. Tonight, as I passed by (and a wretched night it is, dreary and wet and sleety) the hall was quite full. The men's billets are farm sheds near there, rather smelly and demanding much philosophy to make them seem comfortable. The French farmers make their manure heap in the middle of their buildings, and these sheds are therefore a courtyard round an island or lake as the case may be, of dry or wet manure. In the straw stack inside the sheds the sleeping is passable enough, though there again in many cases, the fleas so much abound that some of the men have been quite ill. One, who came to me to ask for a hot bath, took off his clothes to show me, and his body was bitten as if he had chicken pox – he was a sight! Another poor fellow had to go to hospital for a similar cause. Now the men are organised by the brigades for baths in a disused and commandeered laundry. In this way, every man can get a hot bath about once every three weeks or a month. But there are difficulties – the men in the trenches and in the first reserve, do not as a rule take their boots off for 6 days at a time. It's only when they come into the 2nd reserves that it seems possible to allow them to do so. But how wonderfully cheerful they are and uncomplaining – they do not like the trenches and do not pretend to, but they like them, as a rule, better than their billets!

I must close. The Censor takes my word for not giving anything away, but if my letters are too long he will want to know whether it can be that one can say so much, without describing the movements of the troops.

Saturday, December 26th 1914, Estaires

A kind of curious truce on Christmas Day.[159] Conran walked today IN FRONT of our trenches, and saw about 70 Germans walking in front of theirs. At another point along our front we hear of the Germans playing a short game of football with our men, and yet, yesterday afternoon, one of our officers who was expecting a similar truce in front of his section, had no sooner put his head above the trench than he was shot dead[160]. They are strange doings. Not a sound of fighting tonight, though there was heavy firing as we came out of 8 o'clock service yesterday morning.

---

159 The **Christmas truce** was a series of widespread, unofficial ceasefires that took place along the Western Front around Christmas 1914, during World War I. Through the week leading up to Christmas, parties of German and British soldiers began to exchange seasonal greetings and songs between their trenches; on occasion, the tension was reduced to the point that individuals would walk across to talk to their opposite numbers bearing gifts. On Christmas Eve and Christmas Day, many soldiers from both sides, as well as, to a lesser degree, from French units, independently ventured into "no man's land", where they mingled, exchanging food and souvenirs. As well as joint burial ceremonies, several meetings ended in carol-singing. Troops from both sides were also friendly enough to play games of football with one another.

160 Capt. **Charles Harold Reynell Watts** (b.1882 – d.1914), 2 Bn Northamptonshire Regiment. Son of the late Charles Alexander Watts and Edith Alma Watts, of Lansdowne, Marlborough, New Zealand.

We wish you all a Happy Xmas and New Year success, Victory, and safe return.

Xmas . 1914 .

1915

from Lady. Rawlinson and The friends of the 4th Corps.

Sunday, December 27th 1914, Estaires

While I think of it, let it be known that scarves, waist belts and mittens are mostly over done now, but undergarments, pants and vests, are very acceptable.

I am very tired tonight. 7 and 8 a.m. Holy Communion, 10.30 Morning Prayer, 11.30 ditto and Holy Communion in a cold windy barn (very primitive). Bible reading with an ammunition convoy at 12.30, with a good long ride between each, and it was cold with a wet sleet. Evening Prayer in a barn loft close behind the firing line at 4 p.m. after another cold ride in cutting wet sleet, and a service of H.C. after that – how could I do otherwise when two officers had walked a mile in such weather for their Christmas Communion? It was a solemn and earnest service up there in the dim dark loft, the windows broken and windy, an old table in the middle lit by four tallow candles and a smoky lamp, the kneeling officers and two or three men, so quiet and reverent there in the gloom. It was an "Upper Room" and the Presence of the Loving Light of the World was with us – the guns rolling out very close, almost sharply near, now and again[161].

Two of their fellow Officers were killed on Christmas Day. It was the Mess from which I made my first visit down into the trenches. You remember the cottage in front of which we were machine-gunned? On each of the two succeeding days a man

---

161 The **Cenacle** (from Latin *cenaculum*), also known as the **"Upper Room"**, is a room in Jerusalem traditionally held to be the site of The Last Supper. The word is a derivative of the Latin word *cena*, which means *dinner*. In Christian tradition, based on Acts 1:13, the *"Upper Room"* was not only the site of the Last Supper (i.e. the *Cenacle*), but the usual place where the Apostles stayed in Jerusalem, and according to the Catholic Encyclopedia "the first Christian church".

was brought in hit in that place – it was a lucky escape and we have had a good many since. Fighting has almost stopped today. Then Evening Service at 6.30.

Day by day we discover how the Germans hereabouts frightened the lives out of women and children – literally that. Another young woman has been buried who was prostrated with shock by the shells and never recovered.

Wednesday, December 30th 1914, Estaires

This is a week 'off' from collecting the wounded, so we are living a more normal life, only receiving the sick who come in during the day, or an occasional casualty. I have also found a table to write by in my billet, and a little stove, both up in an attic. There is quite a difference in the billets and our present one is very pleasant. There is a chance of my coming home on leave – it is not quite clear … Fighting has been very quiet, and we think that the Germans may be retiring from our front, though there are rumours it may be a blind, and that they are massing quietly to try and break through just where we are now. If so the 'leave plan' will be stopped – we shall know more in a day or two.

Christmas meant a kind of truce near us. Germans came out of their trenches and conversed with our men! It is a comment on mutual trustworthiness that in no case that I have heard of, did our men leave their trenches first. In one instance two of our officers went across and had tea with some Germans in their trench. When they spoke of its being time to go, the Germans said "Yes. You will go back, but it will be via Berlin!" In another case, in one of my own very nice regiments, the officer who tried the rifle grenades my first night in the trenches, got out of the trench to move forward to greet the German and was shot dead. When a formal proposal of an Xmas truce was in the air, whether from our side or theirs I do not know, a rude message came from some Germans near us, calling our men 'mercenaries'.

Friday, January 1st 1915, Estaires

In a great hurry, all leave is off – such are the vicissitudes of a campaign. If I can, later I must come over as it will be simpler for the Fund and other things, and if I come, I must have 2 days clear I fear in London, on Chaplains' business. Do not write however until you hear again – we are in a tight place just here, but all goes well I think.

Later that same day

This is <u>final and definite – unless something happens in the next day or two!</u> Leave is being arranged for those longest mobilised, and I expect to be in London Tuesday night. Wednesday must be a busy day in town, seeing the Chaplain General, getting some fresh kit at the A and N Stores, calling at C.E.M.S. Church House (where I may hope to see Hubert Saumarez Smith)[162] and calling at Wippells about a campaign surplice, and probably at McGregors[163]. So I shall see you and the dear children again, but I think it will mean that I must stay in London Wednesday night as well. I must leave to return Sunday night, unless I spend Sunday in London to leave early Monday morning (entre nous, I am tempted to run down to West Farleigh for the good it might do – what do you think?)

Well, how wonderful it will be to see you all again, after the 'deaths' that have been died. The troopship voyage, the rail journey by a certain section, those nights that we were shelled, the nights in the trenches, the nights collecting the wounded and the freedom from disease – it will be nice and humanising to come back into the home circle again. This cannot go off before tomorrow (Saturday) afternoon, so I shall keep it open to see if your letter and the parcels arrive. I expect to arrive at Folkstone and will telegraph from there. If time permits, I shall call to see Deane Oliver about certain chaplain's supplies.

Fighting is very quiet today, except for much artillery which has not been replied to by the Germans. One report is that they are massing on the other side of their trenches, the other that they are retiring in an Easterly direction.

Saturday, January 2nd 1915, Estaires

This is <u>important</u> – the three parcels that you spoke of as having left before Christmas have NOT come. Were they sent via the Military Forwarding Office, Southampton? If they went by post, the Post Sergeant here says an enquiry ought to be begun at once. I note another parcel is spoken of as leaving the 29th December – I hope it will come before I leave. I think I shall certainly reach Folkstone Tuesday night, but all depends on getting to the coast and on the crossing.

---

162 RDG's brother-in-law.
163 J Whippel and Co, Clerical Outfitters.

Sunday, January 3rd 1915, Estaires

A curious 'knockabout' Sunday, but very encouraging. At 7.0am we had 4 communicants, 8.0am 10 communicants and at 10.30 a large congregation and we prayed hard. Then a service for some reserves for the trenches failed because notice had not reached them, and then a deeply earnest service with some men dressed for returning to the trenches immediately. I read part of the Archbishop's letter and we prayed hard again. The good cheer of the men is wonderful, but they do not pretend they like going back into these ditches. Mud everywhere.

I have been trying to get two of the officers and myself taken down to Boulogne for leave, but it is not easy! I hope to arrive somehow Tuesday or Wednesday – chicken for dinner! Aunt Mai's Jaeger blanket is a constant joy!

LEAVE

Monday, January 11th 1915

A fair journey so far. A slight contretemps crossing London as the taxi was in a crashing collision with one of Harrod's vans – the vans' fault but it might have been worse. It was a crash, broadside on, the van crossing the street without warning, but no one was hurt. A very refreshing stay – please thank your cousins again, and again! My love to the Chicks.

Tuesday, January 12th 1915, Estaires[164]

My darling, I am back in the old spot after a rather tedious journey. The motor bus this side broke down, and we had to ride outside the rest of our half journey in another bus in the convoy. I got to my billet about 1.30am and made myself a little Bovril and slept thoroughly. The system is now to be trained down to Boulogne, and most people are going on leave. The spartan Colonel Pickard I find has gone, partly sick, and one of the officers has had to give up sick, and one of the chaplains – Knapp RC. Also, Watson the Baptist minister they say could not abide to think the C of E was gone and he was left behind! And so has now gone on leave too – he chaffed the C of E man on tripping home!

A letter from the Chaplain General enclosing a cheque for the Church Army for £10 and another for £4. I hope not many more will be sent out here as it takes so much time answering, and there is much to do as Tyrwhitt went off last night. The Temporary Church they say, was crowded out last Sunday. Your letter was waiting, telling about the Belgium party, the lunch at Stonehurst etc. and also the parcel. Thank you very much, darling, for all the things especially the soap and the little flashlight. In my next letter I shall probably enclose one or two to be posted in England – it

---

164 He draws two faces, one smiling 'going on leave' and the other sad 'returning from leave'.

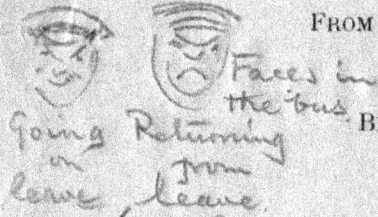

FROM REV. RICHARD GRIFFITHS C. F.
24th Field Ambulance
VIIIth. DIVISION
BRITISH EXPEDITIONARY FORCE.

Faces in the 'bus
Going in on leave   Returning from leave.

12/1/1915

My darling,

I am back in the old spot – after a rather new tedious journey. The motor bus this side, broke down! & we had to ride outside the rest of our half journey in another 'bus in the convoy. I got to my billet about 1.30 & made myself a little au Bovril & slept thoroughly. The system is now the train down to Boulogne: & most people are going on leave. The Spartan Colr Richards, 1, first, has gone: pretty sick. One of the officers has had to give up sick. And one of the Chaplains – Knapp (R.C.)

will save the censors. There is a lot to do, but things are quiet although the horrible casualties come in one by one. The deserted town has been more vigorously shelled, but the artillery generally is very quiet.

Conran is overjoyed because he can tap our Fund. He wants to start a club now for the billets near the deserted town and his General has been very keen about it, and he has found a set of men to work it. So now I have given him £50 and he will start operations tomorrow – he is very happy!

Tyrwhitt is a little in disgrace – to tell the whole facts, two men of the Middlesex Regt were found guilty of planning to desert, and were shot yesterday. They were of Tyrwhitt's Brigade and he requested that they should be left to him. But he was occupied with the last arrangements for his leave, and the men were executed with no chaplain present, and the Senior Chaplain is grieved about it[165].

Wednesday, January 13th 1915, Estaires
Such rain again, with floods everywhere and little artillery firing today. I have found where the 11th Bedfords are, in which is Dr. Brewin's son, about 4 miles from me, so I shall hope to go over and see him[166]. Another £5 for the Fund! The days lengthen and each day is one nearer the spring. What a mercy when that and the new armies come, and perhaps peace by June. It is obvious the Germans cannot conquer, and all the accounts say they realise it.

Thursday, January 14th 1915, Estaires
Thank you, the cold is better and everybody has had one. The surprise is, I think, no one has been worse. Well, in fact some have been worse and one doctor is sent home permanently sick, and an RC chaplain has gone down country with either pneumonia or typhoid.

I have been thinking about Eric's fees and I quite forget how much we pay, so I have written the enclosed and addressed an envelope all ready. I do not know quite how we stand at the bank – also Messrs Arnold, Baker and Day[167] generally send a statement of tithe at the end of the year – did they do so this time? Dear little boy – I fear he has a slight delicacy of the throat to contend with, and perhaps a little in the lungs. That will account for 'nervy' moments, but we must take him as God made him and help him to live his life with the material put upon him – he will grow into his responsibilities.

---

165 Private **F Sheffield**, Private **Joseph Ball**, both 2 Bn Middlesex Regiment, shot at dawn 12th January 1915, for desertion. Sheffield was 26, Ball, 20.
166 Private **Albert E Brewin**. The 11th was the Territorial Battalion of the The Bedfordshire Regiment (formerly the 16th Regiment of Foot), however this was only formed in 1917. It is possible that RDG is referring to the 1/1st Bedfordshire Yeomanry, who were in France at this time.
167 Arnold, Baker and Day, Solicitors, The Precincts, College Green, Rochester.

La Gorgue-Estaires, showing Le Pont de la Meuse

La Gorgue-Estaires

Friday, January 15th 1915, Estaires

I have been in it this afternoon! It was a clear day and a good opportunity for getting up to a point at the further end under the firing line to call on the officer who had such a narrow escape last month, and in whose regiment there is an old St Andrews boy (Lowry), on whom I thought it would be interesting to pay a call. All went well until I got within about a quarter of a mile of my goal. They had told me in a neighbouring hamlet they thought the '….s' had been shelled. When I turned the corner near a cottage that was all smashed about (there was the furniture in its place covered with dust and debris), there was an ugly scream – a sound one knows well enough now. Nothing was to be seen however, so I rode on. Then near another cottage there was again an ugly scream quite close, and the horse jumped and shied. Just the other side of the cottage up in the air I saw the big puff of black surrounded with white, only about 100 yards away – the shelling was true! Should I ride on? On the other side of the cottage about 30 men were sheltering under a kind of straw verandah, watching the shells coming in the field in front of them. I asked them if the farmhouse further along the road was my rendezvous and they said 'yes', so I decided to press on about 200 yards more. They seemed very long yards. Then there was another swish and a scream just along the little field on my right – another bang and a black puff – and I rode on. I passed a private hurrying back to the cottage, his eyes gleamed with a kind of hunted look as he went firmly on. At the farm doorway, a sergeant was standing holding the big door partly open. I asked if this was the billet and he said hurriedly "Yes, come in quick". Away in the field, not 50 yards off was another swish, a scream and a bang. They huddled my horse in, and myself, and you felt like coming in out of a heavy shower of rain. The sergeant had in his hand a piece of shell, an ugly jagged bit nearly as big as this sheet of paper, which had just been picked up near the farm wall on the left of the road that I had come along and I am keeping it as a souvenir of the closest bit of shelling I have encountered yet, each side of the road not 100 yards apart. Inside everyone was watchful but peaceful. The gallant captain was having his hair cut in the kitchen, tea would be ready in a quarter of an hour – so I stayed. A number of shells were still banging around us, making the windows rattle. Tea and toast and marmalade, … and a tablecloth, (the first I remember seeing out here) were all very nice. With the darkness the shelling stopped, but as you can imagine I did not discourage the homeward speed of the horse as we started off again.

About 12 men in church. The club gets uncomfortably full, and I understand that Conran's club is greatly enjoyed, as well it might be. It is right in that shelled area, but further on. I have just come up from the lighter ward and have left five Tommies all in a row on their blankets on the floor, hunting for fleas over their inner undergarments. It's a nightly practice, now called 'fighting fleas in Flanders'.

Saturday, January 16th 1915, Estaires

A letter from you again – which is very refreshing. I rode over to Brewin's regiment this afternoon only to find he had gone home on leave!

Monday, January 18th 1915, Estaires

Another great day – I think these days are great because they are milestones marking a journey to a great place, "what knitting severed friendships up, where partings are no more. Then eyes with joy shall sparkle, which brimmed with tears of late"[168].

I am afraid my letters will have to be less explicit than before – new and stringent orders have come out about many things. Censoring is difficult enough as it is, and hampers my Club work much – it is useless saying anything. I wonder what sort of a birthday you will be having – it will be a better one next year we will hope. It will be nice to see Mabel[169] and share it with her. I wrote to Miss Warde about the field. If they mean the field next to the tennis court, they are welcome to it, but I understood I let it to Weaver the butcher, however if he is not using it, by all means let them have it.

Such an interesting day yesterday. About 20 at Holy Communion at 8 am. I left the Cinema Church to Conran, who had a crowded service. About 120 men in a barn at 10.30 – the 2nd Reserves from the trenches, then a long, long ride to close to the firing line and about 120 men again 'stacked up' in a barn. They do sing at these services, but what a lot of quiet suffering there is – the cold and sore feet and unwashed bodies and clothes, scraggy chins (razors get lost or used up and the facilities for shaving are difficult to imagine). I am glad the socks are coming. The Club room is going with a great swing – it is so much enjoyed that it almost too good to be true. The men are almost afraid to enjoy it and Conran's, to his great delight, is going nobly also. It is a good work as well for the <u>body</u> as the soul.

I have heard from Col. Hughes and hope that soon you may be relieved of the greater burden of the Fund work. I am glad he sees about the contributions continuing, they will need 100s of pounds before they have finished.

Much love, my darling, and may we be together for your next birthday and for many years to come.

Tuesday, January 19th 1915, Estaires

Our Colonel has returned, bringing a cold turkey with him, and a tin of Devonshire cream. We have had a crowded sing song this evening, and I gave the men some

---

168 **Hymn:** *Ten Thousand Times Ten Thousand*, words Henry Aldord, music John B Dykes 1875 "O then what raptured greetings on Canaan's happy shore; What knitting severed friendships up, where partings are no more! Then eyes with joy shall sparkle, that brimmed with tears of late; Orphans no longer fatherless, nor widows desolate".

169 His sister-in-law.

cakes that were sent out in some parcels. Neuralgia is paining so many of them just now, and they like to come and sit by the stove and try to bake it out of their faces.

Wednesday, January 20th 1915, Estaires

We are having a fairly light hospital week, as it is our turn off from collecting the wounded. Most of the morning went in supervising Club arrangements. I have instituted a long tin bath in the wash house, bought some towels, and hired a table, some chairs and a strip or two of carpet, and the place looks very pleasant now. The cry all along our section now is 'baths'. The Generals have organised and the men are marched down to them, so that side of our effort becomes less urgent. Only, along our section there is much that tries the men, so that the private place is a comfort to the many who hear of it. For example, in the public baths about twenty men are swilled in the one tub of unchanged water. Also they have to hand in their underclothing and socks and many are dissatisfied with the garments they get in exchange, the system being that the clothes you hand over are washed and mended up, but you take instead of them those of someone else which were handed in on a previous occasion to be washed, and you never see yours again. The dodge the men have now is to wear down to the tubbing drill the rottenest old stuff they can get, rather than lose good material for inferior. It is very difficult to meet every situation, so I now give out some socks at the Club, members of the Committee having these and sundry other things to hand to any men who want them, and others we give through the Ambulance to men who go back to the trenches after being with us for short illnesses. A heavy cold or chilled feet which can be warmed up again in a week or so, and so one week is the period understood, with cases expected to take longer sent down country. I am only afraid in some cases the men go back a little too soon. I have just had an interesting chat with some of them. One asked did I believe the time would ever come when there would be no war. I said I did, and quoted Tennyson – 'When the war drums throbbed no longer, And the battle flags were furled' and a younger man said "yes, and don't you think it is interesting that just the verse but one before that, Tennyson spoke all those years ago about aeroplanes!" Then another man produced a pocket Tennyson and read the words, "aerial navies in the vaulted blue[170]"!

---

170 "**Locksley Hall**" is a poem written by Alfred Tennyson in 1835 and published in his 1842 volume of *Poems*. While narrating the emotions of a weary soldier come to his childhood home, the fictional Locksley Hall, the poem also presented the author's predictions about a future world government.
"Heard the heavens fill with shouting, and there rain'd a ghastly dew
From the nations' airy navies grappling in the central blue;
Far along the world-wide whisper of the south-wind rushing warm,
With the standards of the peoples plunging thro' the thunder-storm;
Till the war-drum throbb'd no longer, and the battle-flags were furl'd
In the Parliament of man, the Federation of the world".

It is a strange war. Fighting quiet tonight … snow and slush in the trenches. I saw an old Frenchman this morning being marched off as a suspected spy. He trembled so much that he could scarcely drag his feet along.

Friday, January 21st 1915, Estaires

Milder today – only shelling by our own guns. The enemy are very quiet here, a lull before the storm some say, as on the German Emperor's birthday (27th)[171] and the anniversary of the relief of Paris (28th) an effort will be made to strike hard at the allies. The hot baths are going strong and the men do really enjoy them.

Old Tyrwhitt is not made for Army Chaplaincy, and I hope they will soon find him a place at the Base! His ponderous pessimism in despairing about the men's not coming to early Communion and their difficulty to converse on the 'sacradotal' is so arrogant – and unconscious!

Friday, January 22nd 1915, Estaires

Our Scotch Major has found a violin in one of the billets and as he plays very well (and like Robert Falconer lives in his music[172]), he is regaling us at this very minute, after our mess dinner, with really very charming music. Illness is low and casualties are very few, fighting is very desultory and the doctors are having a quiet time. Our artillery have been brisk enough however as I found when visiting the further regiment this afternoon. To do that, you go in front of our guns, and as you do not know where they are, you get some surprises. An awful clap of thunder roars out from behind the hedge near you, the air over your head is filled with a scream that changes into a long wail out into the far off sky, now lowering with a rainy sunset, it ends with a whisper and you wait. Very faintly you can hear away over the German trenches a tiny, tiny bang. And you wonder what has happened – there? The horse has got quite used to it now and goes on unmoved, which is fortunate for the rider, as there are miles and miles of floods, and the roadway on either side is flanked with deep water ditches. Some of the road, in fact, is like a lake, and you have to splash on with the horse up to his knees in water … cold work!! It is a curious situation – the lurid flash of the great gun on your right, the gloomy flat unknown away on the left, and the hope, the strange hope that good destruction of human lives has been wrought. Only one shot came over our way today – it fell in the field just by the General's billet, and I saw it when I called. It reached the mud before it actually exploded so it was a mass of spread-out metal. What a stupid, wicked game it all is!

The Club is a constant joy but there is not room for everybody and many of the men have to stand about waiting to snap up a seat – and the baths go on, 'a stream

---

171 Kaiser **Wilhelm II** (27th January 1859 – 4th June 1941).
172 From the book by George MacDonald, *Robert Falconer* (1868), republished as *The Musician's Quest*.

of smiles'. There is no doubt about that effort answering. (Entre nous, it makes me a little popular – a dangerous experience. I wish it may mean the men are nearer to Him and I believe it does help.) Two men walked in two miles this evening to our Friday evening service at 6.30. They came out of the trenches last night, and so much liked a talk, and one man last week walked in over three miles along our front, just to have a talk!

Saturday January 23rd 1915, Estaires

There is a lot of serving at tables over the Club work, but it is worth it. I hear today that there is going to be a system of Clubs like this, a result, I hope, of the Chaplain General's visit. It would be a good thing if there were.

It is such a relief to have a better day, lakes of water everywhere. The rumble of artillery just across the fields, otherwise this little town proceeds quite placidly – the children splash into the gutters, little boys run up to hold your horse, busy women wash their doorsteps, but at evening they have all to be indoors by 8 p.m. Then you wait and listen, and the crackle of musketry begins getting livelier as the night advances. If the Germans get through our trenches, what a rush there would be to the next town!

Sunday January 24th 1915, Estaires

A very full but very moving and encouraging Sunday, 8 am – but only 3 communicants. 10.30 with 2nd Reserves in a barn – a crowded service with the men perched high on the straw up to the roof. 12 p.m. – the long ride further up by the firing line to another barn, full but a little more ceremonial, with 7 officers in a row on chairs which had been brought up from the farmhouse, a smoking coke fire in the middle (up in the loft), straw strewn around, and the men massed about behind the officers and behind me. How shall I describe these services? One's own feelings, the probable feelings of the officers and men – they are all back in the trenches tonight. There are gaps in the congregation since our last service and there have been wounds – will there be any more gaps the next time we can meet? Wounds there is every certainty of there being, but you do not say these things, or notice them in what passes at the service, but you never lose the undercurrent of them and so you try to speak 'all the words of this life[173]'; of 'the grace to help in time of need'[174]; of the Everlasting Love and the Everlasting Arms; the splendid manliness and the joy of right, justice and honour. Truly 'the Way of the Cross is the way of light'.

Then this evening the cinema has been 'filled' again and the numbers go on steadily improving, and soon we shall have every single seat occupied, I hope – all voluntary.

---

173 **Acts 5:20** 'Go, stand and speak in the temple to the people all the words of this life.'
174 **Hebrews 4:16** 'Let us therefore come boldly unto the throne of grace, that we may obtain mercy, and find grace to help in time of need.'

Tyrwitt says "O but my dear fellow, I had nearly 1000". "Yes, but not 'red hot' so to speak." Compulsory parade! But these are men who foregather of their own free will. O that the numbers more maybe drawn and that the next might gather them right into the Kingdom. The morning service was taken by Goudge – an army Chaplain Major rank, a good fellow.

Tuesday January 25th 1915, Estaires

Already some of the questions asked above are answered. I have just returned from burying one of the men of the Regiment that I visited on Friday, and at the door I met two men of the Regiment I first had the service with yesterday morning – both hit, one in the arm and one in the forehead, and in the same Regiment we hear, so far, of 25 casualties – one must be in certain and joyful earnest at these opportunities. In between one finds too much evidence that many men need help in realising that all the time they stand before God.

On my way back I popped into the farm kitchen of some interesting homely people. They are Protestants and they were pleased to have a visit from a Military "Pasteur", <sic>(I heard of their religion from Madame at my billet). They have been of this faith further back than the Grandmother can remember – she only knows that her Grandmother was so … and so on.

Our senior Major has just returned from 'leave', full of the atmosphere of England, and bringing the latest good news, the fight in the North Sea, the sinking of the Blucher, and the damage to two other cruisers. A helping forward to the end of this war[175]

More wounds, and a marvellous escape. Through the upper arm, in at the chest, out below the shoulder blade, no bone broken the lung not touched and the man quite cheerful. "Thank God for many mercies" I said to him. The next – horrible, the top of the skull smashed open, he must die soon[176]. The anguish of his friends, the pangs of pain he must have had. God did not mean this to be – his beautiful work mutilated by sin and wickedness. German shrapnel must be one of my deadliest fears henceforward.

---

175 The **Battle of Dogger Bank** was a naval battle fought near the Dogger Bank in the North Sea on 24th January 1915. Decoded radio intercepts had given the British advance knowledge that a German raiding squadron was heading for Dogger Bank, so they dispatched forces to intercept. Surprised, the smaller and slower German squadron fled for home. During a stern chase lasting several hours, the British slowly caught up with the Germans and engaged them with long-range gunfire. The British disabled *Blücher*, the rear German ship, but the Germans put the British flagship HMS *Lion* out of action. Due to a signalling mixup, the remaining British ships broke off pursuit in order to sink *Blücher*. The German squadron escaped and all the remaining German vessels returned safely to harbour, though some had heavy damage.

176 Lance Corporal **Henry Thompson**, (b.1892 – d.1915), 2 Bn Northamptonshire Regiment. Died of wounds, 25th January 1915, buried Estaires Communal Cemetery. Son of Walter and Elizabeth Thompson, of 16, Knightley Rd., Kingsthorpe Hollow, Northampton.

Another most interesting day, darling, but very full, and it is late, and nature fails! – tea in a scullery of a burnt-down farm, in the paddock and garden of which is a battery, which is going to celebrate the Kaiser's birthday tomorrow morning by sending them a heavy bombardment. Our talk was of Charterhouse, great Englishmen, Quakers, certain Generals, Macaulay, Tennyson and the naval victory yesterday. A lonely life it is in some of these batteries.

Thursday January 27th 1915, Estaires

I am tired tonight. Collecting wounded – it is a strange weird business. The creeping forms along the roads in the dim night light, the Ambulance car gliding along, feeling its way over the flat water-lined roads, the subdued tones at the dressing stations, usually a cottage or a farm house. The gradually nearing 'snap snap' of the rifle fire until you get to your nearest first-aid post and there you have the danger of long-range bullets, (three of our cars have been hit at one time or another). But tonight there were only two cases of wounds – one man hit over the head by a bullet sat crunched up in one corner of the car, dozing off and on, tired and sorry for himself[177]: opposite a bright lad, hit through the lungs just below the heart. In the kitchen he asked for a drink of water "just to quench my thirst before we start". A little later in the car he said, "oh, it is painful, I can't get my breath". The Major borrowed my flashlight and we turned him over on his side. He said that was easier, half a mile on the Major borrowed the flashlight again and said "he's dead"[178]. And so we rode on with our strange sacred burden – another life gone to pay the price. What a strange mad game it all is from one point of view. From another, it is God's quarrel for righteousness. How accustomed we get to things out here! A doctor has just been in with a big piece of sticking plaster on his cheek. He was called to the trenches yesterday afternoon, and he thinks a sniper saw him, at all events the bullet touched his nose and grazed his cheek and hit the cottage wall behind him. Another case last night of a doctor's orderly at the first aid Dressing Station stooping down for a bandage when a bullet came through the window of the cottage and grazed his eyebrow! And again, a man was observing through his binoculars – the bullet hit the edge and deflected to the left rather than to the right and grazed the side of his head, leaving a scrape in the auricular muscle[179]. As I write, my feet are very very cold – this is a cold feet country, and there just within hearing is the ceaseless crackle of musketry, men hurling death and destruction at each other along 100s of miles around Europe. God never, never meant this to be.

177 Private **John James Collington** (b.1886 – d.1914), "B" Coy. 1 Bn. Sherwood Foresters (Notts and Derby Regiment), died 28th January 1915, buried Estaires Communal Cemetery. Son of John and Rebecca Collington, of Wymeswold, Loughborough; husband of Julia Ann Collington, of 40, Mountsorrel Rd., Quorn, Loughborough.
178 Private **A. Fox**, 1 Bn. Sherwood Foresters (Notts and Derby Regiment), died 27th January 1915, buried Estaires Communal Cemetery.
179 War Diary, 24th Ambulance Division (WO95/1703/1) January 25th 'began collecting left half of lines (8.00 pm – 9.00 am). January 30th 'Finished collecting left half of lines'.

'One of our ambulances: a bullet hole, Jan 1915'

'One of our ambulances: another bullet hole (the slight smudge near the man's pointing hand) through the woodwork. Jan 1915. The man right in front my groom P. Waite with a bundle of socks!'

Friday January 28th 1915, Estaires

The lad who died with us in the car last night was to be buried and also the lad hit in the head the night before.

A most exciting afternoon today. As I got my horse out of the stable, one of the stable boys said excitedly "they are shelling the Church, have you heard them?" I had not, having to tell the truth been snoozing after lunch after a long ride this morning. But as I rode past the Church I found it was true as I heard the scream and the explosion of the shells falling on the other side. The cemetery is down a small side street and out into an open space and there the screaming became constant and I am afraid that not many men paid much attention to the service. It was impossible for them to avoid keeping turning their heads in the direction of each new scream, and now and again a shell fell unpleasantly near our neighbourhood. However – a miss is as good as a mile, and all passed well till, just as we were coming out of the cemetery again across the open space into the street, an ugly scream drew nearer and nearer so that you could not help cringing, it was so close, but it sailed on over us and just over the house on our right and fell in the field behind it – that was close enough! I rode round behind the house after – the shell had shot itself down into a long tunnel about 6 ft. into the frosty ground, and there performed such exploding as it was pleased to do. From 15 to 30 shells fell altogether and I wonder if we shall be moved off now as these buildings are next to the church. We wonder if some spy or other will tell them that they have got our range – and if that is so, we must go.

The Club is going on immensely. It is <u>packed</u> again this evening, uncomfortably, and we are going to open up the room above it.

A little good news today. The Government have decided to treat Chaplains as other officers and I received a paper today to fill up acknowledging recept of £30 for the provision of my kit. It is the rule to give this to officers but it was understood Chaplains were not included. A special order from the 17th now decides that they are! I shall get another Jaeger blanket and it is just in time for another pair of boots – the older pair has begun to get leaky in the soles.

Monday February 1st 1915, Estaires

Yesterday was a very full day and a very interesting one. I was too late and too tired to do anything last night but go to bed. 8 a.m. a nice service with about 12 men present: 10.30 a good assembly including a General and some officers and at 6.30 a very full evening service, followed by a most interesting service of enrolment of new members of the C.E.M.S.

IMPORTANT. Will you post, by the very next post possible to the Rev. Kirshbaum Knight[180], a copy of the Pastoral visit to the trenches as published in the West Farleigh

---

180 Rev. **Samuel (Kirshbaum) Knight** (b.1868 – d.1932) Trinity College, Dublin, ordained in 1892.

magazine (the long private account). A further thought – IMPORTANT – will you write to Mr.K.Knight and offer to let him see my journal? Though of course, unless the Censor allows it, the journal itself could not be published.

Tuesday February 2nd 1915, Estaires

A very full day – the baths are going like 'hot cakes'. The men book a place a day or two in advance, and some of the cunning ones now arrange to have two of them at the wash house at the same time to capture a turn! The Club is crowded out and Conran's club too is crowded out tonight. The Fund has indeed touched the spot. You will have seen what I said to Col. Hughes, and in view of further possibilities, especially if Mr Kirshbaum Knight takes up my point and gets the 'Times' behind a great Soldier's Club scheme, we shall need it all – would that we had more workers! And I ought to have a motor car – a small two-seater, as every hour is precious. A Chaplain of a Brigade is like being a Vicar of 5 or 6 small parishes – you need to visit each one. The men (C.E.M.S.) run the club very well, but of course one must be behind every detail to guide, suggest, inspire and control and other men could do the same at other points, if one could only get across to them what is needed at the time. Influenza symptoms are almost universal out here, though I am quite well now, going strong, albeit conscious that one must refuse to take on more than upto a limit.

They have got our range, and dropped another half dozen shells over us this afternoon again. No one hurt (one man hit I have just heard). I think the fight of a few days ago has rather called back their forces. But the men! They are splendid! They are such jovial sufferers. I censor a section of the patient's letters and you get the truth in them. Here is part of one:

"Dear Sister, you would have laught to of seen me going into the trenches. Besides my kit, I had my rifle and your parcel in one hand, and a bit of a plank to light our fire with in the other. Well, getting down the side I slipped and there I stuck. You should have seen me, neck and shoulders in the water until the Sergeant came and dragged me out. Laught! We all laught" *(this was on a frosty day, I know the date, sleet and snow morning and evening)* "but you cannot dry your clothes in the trenches. Feet wet, chest wet, and now I've got rheumatism and my left toe don't work … your Old Joker".

Last night a quaint Irishman, hit by a spattered bullet, came in. A nasty hole in the neck– a hole through the upper arm and the shoulder spattered with little holes. He

---

Curate at Wardleworth after which he was successively Priest-in-charge at St Paul's Barking and Vicar of St Mark's Notting Hill before being appointed a Lecturer at King's College London. A popular writer and publisher on Anglican issues. In 1919, he moved to the North East to become the Rural Dean for the Houghton-le-Spring area, then a Canon Residentiary at Durham Cathedral and finally in 1924 the Bishop of Jarrow.

was quite cheery and when he was stripped, his plump, smooth body was a wonderful sight – he was tattooed all over back and front. Across the waist in front, a lion-tamer putting his arm down the throat of a huge thick-maned lion. Flags, flowers, laurel wreathes and behind, really very well done, a sacred group, the Crucifixion! A scroll across 'The Light of the World'[181] Cherubim either side and the landscape of Calvary as a background! What touches of life!

Out 'collecting' again tonight. Foolishness! That is what these mad fellows have consented to hurl out upon the world, and in it let us hope they are now seeing that they have hurled wickedness.

Thursday February 4th 1915, Estaires
A glorious ride this morning, with green fields bursting out with thoughts of Spring and sheep grazing in the pastures.

I went to see a gunner Major, (one of whose men blew his right hand clean off last night by using an old German fuse to drive in a nail, we had taken the man in with us last night) to let him know how things were. Roaring artillery all the time. Tonight mutilations, blood, agony and death – one sees these things now and again massed in one's dreams. They come the last thing at night – I must not describe them. We have some splendid doctors here, no trouble, quick, keen, skilful, and most kind, it is a pleasure to see them. If we could only heal the heart wounds at home as they are able to do some of these body wounds out here, it would be a comfort. But that must be left to others, and the process in either case is generally slow and painful.

Friday February 5th 1915, Estaires
Another glorious ride this morning with the Colonel with a perfectly blue sky, soft air, rich green fields and the young corn blades showing up, but a very different ride this afternoon. I went with another officer to be company for him while he hunted for some souvenirs – some French shells said to be buried in a heap. I shall be careful in future to enquire beforehand all about his plans and localities, for his supposed treasure trove was near a small hamlet in which was a big-gun battery, and he blundered his way across a field right into the battery area. It was beginning an artillery duel with the Germans and before we knew where we were, we were on the fringe of it! Moreover I was riding another officer's horse, my own being tired with rather too much work these last three days, and unlike mine, this good creature could not stand gun fire, got wild and now and again almost out of hand. Eventually I told the officer that he must retire and he agreed. But the guns were so busy and my horse so alarmed that I jumped off and shut the poor creature up in a small farm nearby (occupied by three or four Indians – all to themselves) and made up my mind to wait. So I stood

---

181 **John 8:12** 'Then spake Jesus again unto them, saying, I am the light of the world: he that followeth me shall not walk in darkness, but shall have the light of life.'

outside the cottage watching the rain of shells. The battery was just across the road, as might be West Farleigh school from the vicarage, and it was a fascinating sight. The range was good, and the timing. The scream, the bang, the flash and the puff of shell after shell made a study in artillery action. The occupants of the cottage were a study too – a queer one. A little withered old man and a bent old woman: she was thickset with a square chin and a kindly expression. She told me they slept in a potato run – it is a kind of a hole in the ground covered over with a curved brick roof, and that being covered over with turf. It was dank and smelly and I shrank as I thought of any human-being sleeping there. The dear old soul took the screaming shells pretty unconcernedly, beating out her feelings upon the straw mattress she was dusting on the turf roof, until one of the shells came unpleasantly nearer than the others. Then she turned round and threatened it with her stick, crying out "Canaille!"[182] I asked her about her life and her family. She said she had three sons, the first – then her eyes filled with weeping and her voice choked – the first had been killed in the war. Then she was able to recover and tell me the other two sons were down country.

Behind me stood the row of Hindus, smiling when smiled at, but awestruck as the shells circled in front of us. But the afternoon wore on and fright or no fright, the horse had to be got away. So, though he danced a war-dance each time there was an explosion, I led him down the field and along the road to a burnt-down house, from the wall of which I mounted. Then I found that the shelling was taking a sweep right across us – across 100 yards from the one point to the other – and two more dropped now in the field to our right. The horse did not want any encouragement to put on speed. It was pleasanter to be further back at another battery where I had my tea with two nice gunners, one a clever artist and the other of special height, 6 ft 5" in fact! I helped at the sending off of four shells in reply to our friends over the way and just as I was leaving, there was a flare up to our left against the deepening evening sky. A German incendiary shell had found a house, long ago vacated and lately used as a headquarters for a regiment going in and out of the trenches, and evacuated by them just a few days ago. And so back along the dim winding road where we met silent cavalcades of men.

Such sorrow tonight again with the wounded brought in – a poor twisted frame from which the life breathed out just as it was being uncovered. The unusual presence of a train along this stretch of line led to a transport wagon being run into with one killed and two wounded – what a crushing it gave that poor body.

Saturday February 6th 1915, Estaires

Another nice letter from you today. Dear little Joyce, I am glad she is picking up and I hope she is in good spirits. Entre nous – I was afraid the quickness of the meals at Edge might interfere with nourishment. Let little children have plenty of time with their meals, Nature is a good guide and if there is a gastric tenderness, it is wrong to

---

182 Insult. The mass of people, the proletariat.

tell little people to hurry up as if they were wrong in taking Nature's intuition. That is a quarrel I have with Edge's quick meals and it is a plea I put in for our children everywhere – I know it makes a difference to me and if I can preserve better health by care in this way, it stands rather to reason on hereditary principles that those who are partly my children will benefit by it also[183].

A quiet day today, but salvoes of artillery from time to time – I am thrown rather much with death lately, so one has to guard against a morbid look at things.

Sunday February 7th 1915, Estaires
An encouraging day so far – a nice talk and a long walk with my General this morning.

The horse-shoe is for dear Joy. Much love my darling, Richie.

Wednesday February 10th 1915, Estaires
Shelling has been quieter here. We have not moved on – a good sign I think. I went to see Lowry this afternoon. He is at the farm which was being so closely shelled when I called about a month ago, but all was quiet today. Lowry is an old St Andrew's[184] boy and is evidently appreciated in his regiment.

This evening I have a full meeting of the C.E.M.S. men and have been trying to arrange bits of work for everybody possible. Men differ in capacity and intelligence, so one finds very simple tasks for some (e.g. hanging up a lantern and taking it down etc.) One of our best and most devout members was killed outright on Thursday by a shell – his life has been a sound blessing[185].

The snowdrops are beginning to peep, and little green ferns droop over the edge of newly made trenches. If only the gentle beauty of things like these were allowed to speak their message! Yet in a farm, I met a little 2 year old boy. To amuse the visitor the mother says to him "What did the Germans say?" "Piff! Poof! Homme!" is the answer, and it is explained that the little boy was in the kitchen and heard this sound piff-poof as the Germans shot a civilian in the yard outside. More head cases, how sad, and how awful some of the faces look – others so peaceful. I have just finished a sad task. I prayed with a little lad just before he went onto the operating table with a ghastly wound through his chest. The bullet passed through his pocket book and through a letter – such an affectionate one from a good son to his Mother. I have had to enclose the bullet-bored letter to the mother and send her what consolation and prayer that I could. A little Scotch lad, also shot through the chest, is today, after

---

183 In later years, RDG insisted on chewing every mouthful 24 times!
184 Prep school in Southborough, Kent. Eric attended St Andrew's.
185 Private **E C Oliver**, 2 Bn Royal Berkshire Regiment, died 4th February 1915. Buried Estaires Communal Cemetery.

2 days, making a wonderfully good pull for it, and is likely to heal. He is the only son of his mother and she is a widow.

Thank you, Darling, for the parcel. I am glad of it all. But I am also glad to say "do not bother till I bother again" about the soap and cocoa. The soap will last and the Army Service Corps is very good to us in the matter of cocoa!

Thursday February 11th 1915, Estaires
Conran's Club is going splendidly. I was over there this afternoon and it was very full, and the men looked very happy and restful. Our own Club overflows, and I observed two men sitting on one chair this evening. And the <u>baths!</u> It is something to have lived for to see how great pleasure and satisfaction a little arrangement like that can give, and it all draws the men round the Chaplain, and so within the atmosphere of better things.

Friday February 12th 1915, Estaires
There are so many letters to write, and as with the multitude, I have a throaty cold tonight. I write, when I can get the address, to the friends of men killed – it makes much to do. I hope friends at home will understand that I would like to write if there were more time and not the Censor!

The clubs are a delight and Conran is having the time of his life. His house is a fairly comfortable one – houses go cheap in a town emptied of everybody five weeks ago! But I said to him this morning "Have they been shelling much lately?" "Not for three days" he said, "but they did that!" and outside on the lawn under the afternoon tea tree not 20 yds from the window, he showed me the shell hole. It had burst and one bullet came through the window and knocked a slip off the marble top of the sideboard. Conran was not in the house at the time!

Saturday February 13th 1915, Estaires
The throatiness is still there. Wet – sleety – cold – it <u>is</u> a tiresome climate, and I suppose a phenomenally wet season. Some more shells over here today, and one burst right over the Cemetery – this time half an hour before one funeral, 7 altogether. Some mischief-making little gun away in some little village I suppose, and a wretched spy in this place who has let them know that they have got the range.

Did I say will you get 'The Times' daily to see in what form my notes appear? I hope they will put in about the small motors. It would be like the motor-boat on the Medway, only better, if we could have one for this work. The men are very much spread out and yet so easily manageable in their little scattered groups of billets. Sir F. Treves says rightly "this is a Motor War".[186]

---

186 **Sir Frederick Treves, 1st Baronet**, GCVO, CH, CB (b.1853 – d.1923) was a prominent British surgeon of the Victorian and Edwardian eras, now known for his friendship with Joseph Merrick,

By the bye, did you get an illuminated calendar from me for your birthday? I enclosed also a roll of films to be developed and am afraid they may both be lost. I will send, perhaps by this post, two interesting photographs. The one the group of trench-coated men taken on the day of the King's visit by the Marquis d'Albufera (one of General Joffe's staff), over which you may remember he and I had some fun at the time. He had just remarked to me that the taking of photographs <u>was forbidden</u> and said "send me any copies of yours that are good and I will send some of mine", when a special message came from the King asking if the Marquis would take a group of the goatskin men – the picture I send was the result and it will be historic[187].

Sunday February 14th 1915, Estaires

Such sleet, such weather – but some remarkable services. The one up nearest to the firing line, always deeply real and earnest, punctuated again today with roaring guns (our own, we have some huge ones up there), a very large service crowding out the rather chilly barn. One always feels at that Service, close to the edge of the other world, with the trenches nearby like the narrow valley of the Shadow of Death. <u>Always</u> the gap or two since the last time, and some very earnest officers, especially the Major. I hope he may be spared and that we shall meet again after the war – he is just a nice blunt unsentimental Christian, quite religious about reading his 'Happy Warrior' everyday and ticking the day off[188]. Men like that are fulfilling their mission now.

Good service this evening and a pretty full church, and Canon Tyrwhitt gave the address, the first I have heard from him. A loud voice hammering out some withering moralisings upon "God said – thou fool"[189] not very wise or reverent some of it, but a nice ending upon the three rules for keeping Lent, fasting, prayer and almsgiving. The first and the last are not easy on Active Service, but the middle one we can improve in this Lent. He is rather a hard man and in the benediction said "Unto God's gracious mercy and protection I commit you...."[190]

Monday February 16th 1915, Estaires

A glorious day for a change and a great relief for the combatants, for the constant cold and damp were getting very trying. A strange, quiet lull in the fighting also, except that two shells were dropped in the field behind the Club again this morning, and

---

"the Elephant Man".

187 See letter dated December 3rd, 1914.

188 *The Happy Warrior: Daily Thoughts [for 1915] for All who are Serving Their Country, Whether on Land, Or Sea, Or in Air, Etc.*, Edith Mary Gell, London, 1914. **"The Character of the Happy Warrior"** is a poem by the English Romantic poet William Wordsworth. Composed in 1806, after the death of Lord Nelson, hero of the Napoleonic Wars, and first published in 1807, the poem purports to describe the ideal "man in arms", and has, through ages since, been the source of much metaphor in political and military life.

189 **Luke 12:20** 'But God said unto him, *Thou* fool, this night thy soul shall be required of thee: then whose shall those things be, which thou hast provided?'

190 Text from the Book of Common Prayer's "Order for the Burial of the Dead".

Stretcher bearers

An ambulance with the Northampton regimental goat

Ambulances

'A picturesque and warlike group. My horse in the background.'

'The Northampton goat. Our late club behind.'

'A group of Sherwood Foresters.'

on Saturday afternoon two on the station of the deserted town, killing one of our men[191] and wounding three others.

I must not tell you of our doings or expectations, but if you want to get an extremely accurate and well-judged estimate of the whole position Hilaire Belloc's articles "The War on the Sand" in "Land and Water" (a weekly magazine[192]) will give it. I can say that the next three weeks or a month must see great and decisive developments but wherever influence can be exerted, the objective must be <u>more men</u>.

Thursday February 18th 1915, Estaires

What a trying winter it has been – sorrow everywhere, suffering and shadow. I think of the description of Minnehaha's dying in Hiawatha – a mind picture of bleak winter, sickness and love[193]. But with the spring, there comes a new song generally, and we will hope there may be a great one soon. Still quietude in front of us here – it is a mercy – only a head case now and then, and a foot case tonight, while at the same time we hear the Germans are being killed by hundreds and taken prisoner by the thousand. They must suffer until they see how wrong they are.

I have been playing off my 'heat' in a draughts tournament today – I lost after two drawn games. The baths! they are quite the thing – "like we get at home" one good fellow remarked today. I am trying to think of a new development – some of the men say they would like to come to the Holy Communion on Sunday, but if they do, they run the risk of losing their breakfast, or at least of having to take cold tea and bacon. It has occurred to one of the C.E.M.S. Committee men that we might get a joint breakfast served at the Club – I believe we could and I am going to try. An interesting talk a few minutes ago with a man (Watson) from Sydney! He lived at Paddington, knows Woollahra, Woollomolo, Randwick[194], etc. and came back to join his old regiment when the war began, and was present at the capture of the Emden[195]. He has been damaged in the eye by the splinters of the iron loop-hole

---

191 Private **Frederick Patterson** (b.1884 – d.1915), 1st Bn Worcestershire Regiment, died 13th February 1915. Buried Estaires Communal Cemetery.

192 **Land and Water** magazine was a British weekly journal published from 1914 to 1920. It was initiated by Jim Allison, then advertisement manager of The Times and devoted to the progress of the First World War and the events in its immediate aftermath. It was edited by the well-known Catholic writer Hilaire Belloc. Editing it was the only steady employment ever held by Belloc, who otherwise "lived by his pen". Belloc made numerous trips to the Western Front on behalf of the paper and collected information from well-placed friends in the ranks of the Army. The journal gained quick popularity and within a short time of being launched its circulation passed the hundred thousand mark.

193 *The Song of Hiawatha* is an 1855 epic poem, in trochaic tetrameter, by Henry Wadsworth Longfellow, featuring a Native American hero.

194 **Woollahra** and **Paddington** are suburbs in the East of Sydney, located 5 kilometres east of the Sydney central business district. **Woolloomooloo** is a harbourside, inner-city eastern suburb of Sydney, 1.5 kilometres east of the Sydney central business district.

195 **SMS Emden**, a *Dresden* class light cruiser built for the Imperial German Navy at the Danzig Imperial Dockyard in 1906. *Emden* spent the majority of her career overseas in the German

in the trenches, which cut him round the eye and partly entered it, but he will soon be better.

I have taken a picture today of the hole made in the Cemetery by yesterday's shell. Fortunately it just escaped the English graves and struck only the pathway but a little 'immediate' burying place just behind the trenches was not so fortunate. Five graves in a row have been upheaved, and the scattered bodies have had to be re-buried.

They are going to institute an envelope for private and personal use that need not be censored. We give our 'word of honour' and, so to speak, censor it ourselves. That will be a help. No channel steamer today we hear, and all leave is stopped – there is something on in the North Sea no doubt.

I hope the little boy will get on now – there is nothing I suppose except sentiment in being glad that it is the good honest English sort, and not German measles.

Friday February 19th 1915, Estaires
No letters, no papers today. They are probably guarding carefully the mail routes. "The Blockade!" We shall see what will come of it[196]. It is satisfactory to have something definite, and to hear that this isolation will last perhaps 4 or 5 days. It will not be so nice being without letters.

I hope the little boy is better. Today I was at the most trying operation I have known. A dear little French boy, 8 ½ years, wandering near the English billets picked

---

East Asia Squadron, based in Tsingtao, in the Kiautschou Bay concession in China. Under the command of Karl von Müller in 1913, *Emden* was detached for independent raiding in the Indian Ocean. The cruiser spent nearly two months operating in the region, and captured nearly two dozen ships. Müller then took *Emden* to raid the Australian territory of the Cocos Islands, where he landed a contingent of sailors to destroy British facilities. On 9th November 1914, *Emden* was attacked by the cruiser HMAS *Sydney*. The Australian ship inflicted serious damage and forced Müller to run his ship aground. Out of a crew of 376,133 were killed in the battle.

196   On February 4th, 1915, Kaiser Wilhelm announced Germany's intention to sink any and all ships sailing under the flags of Britain, Russia or France found within British waters. The Kaiser warned neutral countries that neither crews nor passengers were safe while travelling within the designated war zone around the British Isles. If neutral ships chose to enter British waters after February 18th, when the policy went into effect, they would be doing so at their own risk. German Declaration of Naval Blockade Against Shipping to Britain, 4th February 1915: "The waters round Great Britain and Ireland, including the English Channel, are hereby proclaimed a war region. On and after February 18th every enemy merchant vessel found in this region will be destroyed, without its always being possible to warn the crews or passengers of the dangers threatening. Neutral ships will also incur danger in the war region, where, in view of the misuse of neutral flags ordered by the British Government, and incidents inevitable in sea warfare, attacks intended for hostile ships may affect neutral ships also. The sea passage to the north of the Shetland Islands, and the eastern region of the North Sea in a zone of at least 30 miles along the Netherlands coast, are not menaced by any danger."
(Signed) Berlin, February 4th, VON POHL, Chief of Marine Staff.
After protests from the USA it was withdrawn after the Loss of the *Lucitania* in May 1915, then re-enstated in 1917, encouraging the US entry into WW1.

FROM REV. RICHARD GRIFFITHS C. F.
24th Field Ambulance
VIIIth. DIVISION
BRITISH EXPEDITIONARY FORCE.

19/7/1915

My Darling.

No letters, no papers
today. They are probably
guarding carefully the
mail routes. "The Blockade"
we shall see what will
come of it. It is satisfactory
to have something definite.
we hear this isolation
will last perhaps 4 or 5
days. It will not be so
nice being without letters, I
hope the little boy is better.
Today I was at the most
trying operation I have known.
A dear little French boy of
wandering near the English
billets picked up a fuse He
experimented with it to see

up a fuse. He experimented with it to see how it worked and it blew off the ends of his left-hand fingers and injured his right eye. It was decided that the later must be taken out. Our Colonel[197] is an eye expert, so he was asked to operate. Dear little lad, he wept aloud as he was laid on the blanket of the operating table, then the first whiff or two of chloroform reduced his cry to a sob or two, then to a quiet sleep. The shapely little form in the serge knickerbockers, with the mended black stockings and best Sunday shoes, lay breathing easily, the chin and neck like wax. Then the skilled master hand began to work. The lids were propped open with a little gold instrument. The white eye cover was carefully cut round and the ball of the eye was drawn forward like a chestnut out of a slit burr. The ligament attaching the 'vision' to the brain was severed, and there was the organ of vision in the hand. And the dear little lad lay there so white and still, just a twitch when the ligament was severed. And I thought of our children, their perfect forms, their beautiful eyes and wonderful being, a blessing to them, that this horrible war with all its' vicissitudes, might end and that this dispensation of pain and mystery might soon end. I did pray hard for that little lad, for the mother in the lobby outside, for the doctors that they might have wisdom and skill, for the kind, quick business-like orderlies that the event might be a blessing to them. I thought of this little lad and what the partial loss of sight might mean. I looked out of the window at the dull, leaden afternoon, the dismal garden merely a mass of mud, the broken-down fence, the old barge with one or two workmen in the distance, and the whole gloomy picture glowed with a new meaning. It was radiant – I could see it! I have eyes! And the dullest things can become beautiful. We examined the eyeball. There was a tiny filament of copper gleaming, about the size of the point end of a small needle, right in the centre. That was all! But had it stayed there, blindness would almost certainly have come on in both eyes. It was the strong hand wounding and even mutilating to save. I went out and comforted the mother. The little form was beginning to breathe life again, the wool pad and the bandage in their place. "il va bien" – how uplifted she was. "Trois ou quatre heures il restera ici, après M.de Medecin l'envoyerait chez vous dans une automobile. Vous resterez ici aussi?" [198] What an experience it has been and how much there is to be thankful for. Thank God for sight.

Watson, the Australian is very interesting. He has a clear way of seeing things and telling them. He was at Cairns in Queensland, when the English submarine was sunk[199]. His eye will get better it is hoped but his 'mate' who had come from Australia

---

197 After the war, Colonel Dr **Ransom Pickard** would be appointed Surgeon to the West of England Eye Infirmary (a post he held until his death in 1953), and was elected President of the Opthalmic Section of The Royal Society of Medicine.

198 "He will be well. He will stay here three or four hours, and after that the Doctor will take him back to your house in a car. You will stay here too?"

199 **HMAS *AE1*** (originally known as just *AE1*) was an *E*-class submarine of the Royal Australian Navy. Built in Barrow-in-Furness, and delivered in April 2014, she was the first submarine to serve in the RAN, and was lost at sea with all hands near East New Britain, Papua New Guinea,

with him was shot dead beside him. They saw the German who did it, he was a sniper in a cottage about 25 yds from our trench. Our artillery was warned, and they at last dropped a shell or two right on the cottage, which compelled the sniper to run. He was fired on by our men, and it was at last seen that he was hit, that he fell, and in all probability lay dead in his tracks.

Star shells again tonight – they are huge balls of white light which are fired in a curve over the space between the trenches, and for a few moments make things as clear almost as a searchlight. They give you a queer sensation when you are in the neighbourhood of the trenches – they glare at you like the eye of death, which indeed they sometimes are.[200]

I found young Brewin this afternoon – a nice boy – very pleased to be looked up. He had just received a present from Mrs. Trotter (widow of Canon Trotter of Gloster[201], who used to be Vicar of East Farleigh and whose niece married Cumming Bruce[202]). Just as I was getting off my horse, I heard "zing"!! and a loud bang and I said "that's a shell". I was quite right – it was about 190 yds along the road. I popped in to see it, in a small timber yard. It had sung through one baulk of timber and got down into another and then exploded. Two others fell thereabouts later they told me.

The little boy who lost the eye was cheerful enough this morning. I found him sitting up, dressed and smiling after a good night's rest and a good breakfast, which included an egg. I gave the mother, who is very poor, 5 francs out of 'the Fund' to buy nourishment. There are 6 other children, all small.

Sunday February 21st 1915, Estaires

A good Communion Service this morning with about 30 present – Tyrwhit took the Central Service, (entre nous – it is just as I said, he is pushing himself forward! A pity, for people remark things) Then a nice hearty service in my first barn, but at the second, my first real disappointment. The O.C., a Major just put in, had made no arrangements, hummed and hawed, and to be quite frank obviously thought slightingly of religion, finally rather shortly decided that I would agree that "as the

---

on 14th September 1914, after less than seven months in service. The wreck of the submarine has never been found, despite several searches.

200 A "star shell" was a form of artillery used as a means of illuminating the battlefield during the hours of darkness and as a means of passing signals. When fired, the star shell, which contained a fuse, would burst while at a given height igniting a magnesium flare. The shell, which also contained a parachute, would gradually fall to earth.

201 **Caroline Louisa Harvey** d.1923. Married 1879, Canon Rev. **Mowbray Trotter**, (b.1848 – d.1913).

202 **Grace Catherine Trotter** (b.1873 – d.1959). Married 1909 Rev. **Charles Edward Hovell-Thurlow-Cumming-Bruce**, 6th Baron Thurlow of Thorlow, (b.1869 – d.1952). Educated at Eton and then Trinity College, Cambridge, Thurlow was ordained in 1898 and undertook a number of overseas ministries before returning to the UK as Assistant Superindentant of the Mission to Seamen 1908–13, which is how RDG would have encountered him, ultimately as Rural Dean of Liverpool North.

men only came out of the trenches last night," we would have no service[203]. I did NOT agree, but he did not wait for that and 'voila', I was out manoevered. So I visited around and found some men who to my sorrow, had come over from other billets for the service, so I had a Bible reading with them. Then when I looked in at the farm house about someone else, I found the General and his A.D.C., in full church uniform who had also come over <u>for the service!</u> The Major O.C. smiled it blandly off, but I let him and the General see, I hope, that it was not my mind, and it was not the wish of many of the men I felt sure. They were doing nothing beyond lounging around in the sunshine and a half-hour service (we never have more) would have refreshed them more than anything. I felt grieved and depressed, so much so that I felt I must have a talk with the General about it and I looked in on him on my way back. He soon understood – the other regiment had arrived out of the trenches much later and their service was much earlier and in a dull cold mist, yet the men had rolled up in good numbers. And I do not think the Chaplain will have facilities for assembling the men so lightly dismissed again, with all due respect for the fullest discretion and authority of any O.C. Very kind in intention no doubt, but not in the most excellent way ("ye have need of patience where your treasure is")[204].

Monday 22nd February 1915, Estaires
It is trying about our little boy, the shadows this winter have been deep. The doctors here say that broncha-pneumonia is the one usual complication of measles – the common one, and his being, as I suspected, not strongest in that part of him makes it not surprising. We will hope it will strengthen him for the future and the illness will do good in that way. It will have shown where his constitution is less equal to a test and give us clear guidance as to care and adjustment.

My throat cold has greatly improved and yesterday was a beautiful day, but today is thick raw mist. Very few casualties, but two fatal ones last night. A loving sister had written (I see the letters of the deceased) "I pray for you every day that God will guard you and keep you from all danger. If at any time you are in difficulty just say 'Lord help me' and He will. When will this terrible War end? We are sure God is good and will do all for the best". Dear child, whoever she is, may all trust and peace be with her now that he has gone to the great beyond.

---

203 Given the harsh conditions, both psychological and physical, soldiers were regularly rotated in-and-out of the fire-line trenches (the first trench in a series of several defensive lines). British soldiers spent about 10 days a month in the trench system, and of those, rarely more than three days at the front line.

204 **Hebrews 10:36** 'For ye have need of patience, that, after ye have done the will of God, ye might receive the promise.'

A great General died today, shot near us – a distinct loss[205]. "Thou will keep him in perfect peace whose mind is stayed on Thee[206]". I should have Faith over if I were you, and be all together. Goodnight, my beloved darling.

P.S. Send the enclosed to the little boy, if he is well enough.

Wednesday Feburary 24th 1915, Estaires

Better news this afternoon I am thankful to say and you quote the telephone message 'distinctly better'. Dear little fellow, I expect it will be a longish convalescence and he will need much wise sympathy and patience. Dear Joy writes very cheerfully and her diagrams are <u>marvellous</u> quite marvellous.

O! But the weather here is quite disagreeable (there's restraint!) But the good lads are in the trenches still, and they are so unconscious of their heroism. Fighting is quieter, but death and suffering stalks in our midst night by night. One lad has been out up here only three days – we buried him yesterday. I hear measles has been rife among the soldiers and of the troops quartered round Bedford, hundreds of soldiers had it and about 30 died – there must be something in the air[207].

No shelling now for two clear days and I think things are going very well along our sector, and I hear all along this front. Each day seems to strengthen our position, but it is an awful, wicked business. Things are quieter here, but brave men are laying down their lives nobly, and the quiet courage of mostly everybody is a great experience.

---

205 Brigadier General **Sir John Edmond Gough** VC, KCB, CMG (b.1871 – d.1915). Awarded the VC for action in Somaliland, Gough went to France as a Brigadier-General with the British Expeditionary Force and Chief of Staff to Douglas Haig's I Corps. By February 1915 whilst working on planning for the forthcoming attack at Neuve Chapelle, Gough was chosen to command one of the New Army divisions. This appointment was due to commence sometime in March and would have meant his promotion to Major General. On 20th February 1915 Gough was visiting his old battalion, the 2nd Battalion, The Rifle Brigade, at Fauquissart, about 3 km north of Neuve Chapelle on the front line, about 2 km west of Aubers. His mortal wounding by a sniper there was very unlucky since the single shot that struck him in the abdomen was thought to have been a ricochet fired from approximately 1000 yards distance. He was moved to the 25th Field Ambulance at nearby Estaires, about 7 km behind the front line, where he eventually succumbed to his wound and died in the early morning of 22nd February. He was buried that afternoon in Estaires Communal Cemetery. Gough was quoted as making a famous remark in November 1914. 'As he watched the enemy swarming over a low ridge one of his staff said the fight was decided. Gough turned with his eyes ablaze and exclaimed: "God will never let those devils win."'

206 **Isaiah 26:3** 'Thou wilt keep *him* in perfect peace, *whose* mind *is* stayed *on thee*: because he trusteth in thee.'

207 1st/5th Bn Gordon Highlanders, during the first winter in Bedford [December 1914 to January 1915], several hundred cases of measles were diagnosed by the divisional Medical Officers. The number of deaths from measles appears to vary between sources – later authorities putting it as high as 58 while contemporary accounts place the death toll at 27. Men from the more remote regions of the Highlands and Islands suffered the greatest number of casualties.

The Dormouse sleeps the winter through,
As I myself would gladly do.
When springtime comes, once more he wakes,
And plentiful refreshment takes.

Nestlé's Milk makes bone and muscle.

BY APPOINTMENT

NESTLÉS POST CARD.

No. 8.

NESTLE'S SWISS MILK

Nestlé's Milk has often saved a baby's life.

(Communications may be written below.)

(Name and Address only.)

PASSED BY CENSOR

AFFIX HALFPENNY STAMP HERE

Much love from 'the Front'. D. 13/2/1915.

Thursday February 25th 1915, Estaires

I am so thankful to get the better news again today – may the improvement continue. Measles seems to have been rife in England with 50 fatal cases among the soldiers at Reading beside the 30 among the men at Bedford. I suppose it is something in the air, bred and fostered perhaps by the damp cold season, and thriving in the crowded atmosphere of the billets – "caught in the train ... or in the bus, or anywhere like that" the Colonel says. It will be a winter to be remembered by most of us – War and wickedness have a great deal to answer for.

Things are quiet here with no shells again. The Club quite hums. Two others have been opened now but only in a small way. I enclose a 'bath' sheet for fun.

I got in touch with Col.de Falbe's regiment[208] this afternoon – they are not many miles from here, and with luck I may get over to see them some day. Our billets are poor things. We have had another change in these latter, and rough as the fresh place is, it is preferable to the more elaborate one. The plainer place can be more simply kept clean. The weather is quite unpleasant – I hope for the Germans more so, but February is a hopeful month, each day is longer than its predecessor, and one day less of winter.

P.S. Entre nous – I have been thinking, he will probably feel the set back of this not for months only, but a year or so. Then I think he will get set, and in about 2 year D.V.[209] will begin to be really vigorous and athletic and so for about 3 or 4 years. At 16 or 17, he will want sympathy with his 'growing' age.

Friday February 26th 1915, Estaires

They are crowded days here and I do not know how much we ought to tell of what is happening and what is expected to happen. There is the grave, and the gay – the tragic and the sinful as well as the beautiful and noble. Seven men this morning all tied to a fence, their arms outstretched, their feet tied to the lower rail – 'field punishment' chiefly for getting drunk[210]! That is where a Club comes in. We ought

---

208 Brig.-Gen. **Vigant William de Falbe**, CMG, DSO, JP (b.1867 – d.1940). De Falbe was a family friend from Hastings, then serving as a Lt. Col. in The Prince of Wales (North Staffordshire) Regiment.

209 *Deus vult* (Latin for "God wills it") was the cry of the people at the declaration of the First Crusade by Pope Urban II in 1095.

210 **Field Punishment** was introduced into the British Army in 1881 following the abolition of flogging. A commanding officer could award field punishment for up to 28 days. Field Punishment Number One, often abbreviated to "F.P. No. 1" or even just "No. 1", consisted of the convicted man being placed in fetters and handcuffs or similar restraints and attached to a fixed object, such as a gun wheel or a fence post, for up to two hours per day. During the early part of World War I, the punishment was often applied with the arms stretched out and the legs tied together, giving rise to the nickname "crucifixion". This was applied for up to three days out of four, up to 21 days in total. It was usually applied in field punishment camps set up for this purpose a few miles behind the front line, but when the unit was on the move it would be carried out by the unit itself. It has been alleged that this punishment was sometimes applied

to have a dozen of them but I cannot, as things are, venture more than one. If only we could get a small car!

Two men condemned to death 'for attempted desertion while on active service' and the sentence was duly carried out[211].

Fighting is quiet and casualties are few. The hits are marvellous in the narrowness of the escape that they give – a man this evening struck from the bridge of the nose downwards through the palate, the nose split, and out under the chin – another, a hand, holding the rifle in front of the face, clean pierced through and so on: and our artillery goes pounding away, doing assuredly great execution. But I believe the situation is very promising – surely we may pray that reason may come, with a right understanding, to the German mind very soon.

Saturday Febuary 27th 1915 Estaires

I am glad again to get the better news, but your letter echoes mine – he will need great care. Indulgence about staying in bed of a morning until he is thoroughly rested, and tempted I think he will be to stay in bed for breakfast! The Spartan theory must go now for a long time to come. I do not think the spring is going to be a quick one and we must not anticipate it. What a trying time for Mr and Mrs Bull; things seem to have fallen round them like a house of cards[212].

Suffering all around this year. I do not think that Germany is very happy either. Mud everywhere now again, but happily no very heavy fighting, a lull perhaps, before the storm. We shall move I think in a few days, but I must not say where. For me, chiefly troop visiting, in strange dwelling places – little old thatched cottages, outhouses, even fowl houses, barns and the like. Four young officers in the dim back parlour of an old farm, their beds on the tiled floor laid out on straw with the room filled with smoke, yet everybody is quite cheerful though rather shrinking with the cold.

Sunday February 28th 1915, Estaires

I was glad to hear of further plans for the little son, air, dryness and light are very important. It is one of the complicated issues of what we are going through in all this 'sacrifice'. I trembled when I saw the little 'cell like' room the little boy had at Edge. It made me quite uneasy – the shape and position of it, the difficulty about getting enough light into it, and of having it fully aerated and dried. It was not a place I would have chosen to put a coldified young person into – rooms like that should

---

within range of enemy fire. During WW1 Field Punishment No.1 was issued by the British Army on 60 210 occasions.

211 Private **Joseph Byers**, 2nd Army, 1st Bn Royal Scots Fusiliers, tried for desertion. Executed 6th February 1915, aged 19. Private **Andrew Evans**, 2nd Army, 1st Bn Royal Scots Fusiliers, tried for desertion. Executed on 6th February 1915, aged 41. Both buried Locre churchyard, 4 miles N of Estaires.

212 Head and matron of Eric's prep school.

not be built. But who could say anything, or suggest even? The P.V Smiths would be horrified at the thought of its being deemed unsuitable for a small person! And be pained at the idea of its causing uneasiness. But nothing could be said or done of course and one only hoped for the best and plunged back out here. Let there be light, air and plenty of space and dryness, this must be a cardinal law for the care of health, and young people must have their chance. Their lives are before them and their early bodies have as much right to these various things as young plants and saplings, which are to be the larger growths. All this 'entre nous' of course.

I do not think there is anything very serious in the 'Blockade'. It is a policy that will recoil on the enemy very seriously, for it will mean the justification of all sea traffic being shut out from them altogether. The plot thickens day by day and I think we shall see something very decisive in the next three weeks.

A very enjoyable Sunday – about 22 communicants and I have started the breakfast plan, and it is going to answer. It is a great help to these men in their difficult lives. One difficulty is keeping clean – I wish I could manage more bath accommodation. A man came in sick yesterday, out of a smelly, dank, straw-spread billet. The Major said his shirt, when taken off, seemed to move before one, spread in one's hand like a live thing crawling with creatures – as there is much to be done in assisting the ordinary amenities of respectable living.

Two very hearty services in the barns of the Reserves from the trenches with an aeroplane circling again and being fired at – we have not had that for some Sundays, and our own huge gun pounding away, making the broken windows and the light woodwork rattle. One gets quite not to notice it now – just waiting for the roar, and repeating one's words perhaps and going on – in fact it would sound too peaceful now without it. Then an early evening service for a group of Transport mechanics, billeted in a skittle alley. Very hot, and with such a crowd of men, very stuffy but it was an earnest, reverent time. The Temporary Military Church crowded out full this evening – it was good. Tyrwhit gave the address and did it well on the unjust Steward[213], not as wordy as before and more humble – he confessed he was learning things day by day and he paid a tribute to the C.E.M.S. men and well he might, for they are doing things very well, this Temporary Military Church and services to wit. And so life creeps on. No great fighting, but one or two casualties and three fatal

---

213 The **Parable of the Unjust Steward** (also called the *Shrewd Manager*) is a parable of Jesus. According to Luke 16:1–13 a steward who is about to be fired curries favour with his master's debtors by forgiving some of their debts. "No servant can serve two masters: for either he will hate the one, and love the other; or else he will hold to the one, and despise the other. Ye cannot serve God and mammon".

ones[214]. One, an explosion of Luddite[215] made by a German shell, and this explosive does sad work, dyeing the victim all over a kind of yellow, like jaundice.

A beautiful day today. Long straight flat roads through a flat watery countryside, the lines of trees, the meagre patches of orchard, a clear blue sky and low lines of fleecy white clouds coursing along in level lines across the horizon, with a black puff here and there of the shells bursting round the aeroplanes far, far away. The quaint farmsteads, with here and there the quiet little thatched cottage – and little twinkling khaki-clad forms everywhere. We shall be more and more ready for the Germans when the hour comes.

I hope you are not overtired, darling. It is good to have plenty to do, and the doing helps us to keep going.

Monday March 1st 1915, Estaires

Things are very quiet here today, but hopeful. The tussle is not going to be an easy one, but I feel it being got in hand – and given Russia's ability to hold them in check that side, every day as it goes by is one day gained. Strength is accumulated by the Allies day by day. The war MUST work out right in time. England may be chastened, as no doubt it deserves to be, but no conscience can agree that it would be right for triumph to go with Germany, and God must uphold the right.

A wild day today, after a glorious warm sun rise, and a strange landscape tonight. The full moon, the blue star-lit sky, some star shells along the firing line, and a lurid flare against the horizon of some farm building burning (probably some billet set on fire by accident) and not a sound of big gun or rifle. But the air is full of movement and moment, and I must say no more.

Tuesday March 2nd 1915, Estaires

The plot thickens near us. I rode out this morning to search out a man, and then to see what was happening to Conran. The deserted town is being quite inhabited again by the residents and soldiers. Conran's Brigade has had to move, and his beautiful Club is in abeyance, but I saw a Quartermaster Officer who assured me that the General of that Brigade was keen on the Club idea and that the succeeding Chaplain would have every assistance in carrying on. My own Club still goes swinging on and the baths make one smile!

---

214   Private **R P Owen**, 2 Bn Middlesex Regiment: Rifleman **John Munster**, "C" Coy. 1st Bn Royal Irish Rifles, 34, Son of John Munster, of Drogheda; husband of R A Munster, of 44, Seaforde St., Belfast: Private **J W Weller**, 2 Bn Royal Berkshire Regiment. All died 28th Feburary 1915, and buried Estaires Communal Cemetery.

215   Lyddite explosive. Wet picric acid has been used as a skin dye or temporary branding agent. It reacts with proteins in the skin to give a dark brown color that may last as long as a month.

We have been given today some extracts from the diary of a German, whose body was recovered by us. It gives day by day the happenings of last month just in front of us. It is curious reading notes of what took place each night there, when we here felt so much in the dark. We returned the Germans unexploded bombs and our artillery made them very uncomfortable. They were preparing hand bombs, on a given day, which would give the English the same night 'God knows what'! Then they intended taking one of our trenches, but our firing was hot and they decided not. The British Artillery <u>shoot very well!</u> Then the diary ends by the writer himself being shot.

We have just found that we had with us a few days ago, a very interesting young Captain of the Black Watch, Wedderburn, stroke of the Oxford crew two years running and President of the Oxford Union – shot in the arm.[216] We very often do not know who is whom. A young private is in just now, who is the head of a firm of drapers and milliners and who is said to have an income of over £1000[217] a year!!

Wednesday March 3rd 1915, Estaires

Patient, cheerful confidence – that is the spirit that growing developments inspire in us here. It is delightful to feel that reinforcements are crowding up with us. We are feeling squashed a little – but we like it! And the kind of man we see coming along is very promising. Really there is an amazing amount of fine manhood in our favoured land and Empire, and the hard training has brought them to their best. We may be very thankful, and though we know little (when you are close up you cannot see the forest for the trees) the impression we have is that we have some wonderful guns with us now and plenty of them, and more to come. On the other hand, Germany is being set back on the Russian front, and internally it is getting a sinking feeling from shortening of food, and I think that Mr. Asquith's declaration in the House is masterful and entirely wise and well judged. I fear whether there will be any more leave now for long weeks to come. All leave is stopped from Monday last.

"Don't get up from your chair – you will lose it" one has to say to a man rising up to be respectful. From that you will guess how crowded the Club is, and now between this and the next Division there are 17 clubs in all. I must try and manage another now with all these troops crowding up, but it is a question of time and strength – oh, if only one were able to run a dozen!

---

216 Captain **Alexander Henry Melvill Wedderburn** (b.1892 – d.1968) was a barrister, justice of the peace and politician. Born in London, he was educated at Oxford, rowing in the Oxford XII in 1912 and 1913 and President of the Union in 1914. From 1919–36 he practised as a barrister. From 1931–34 he was a Municipal Reform Party member of the London County Council representing Kensington South. From 1946–61 he was chairman of the General Executive Committee of the Queen's Institute of District Nursing. He was awarded a CBE in 1956.

217 About £80 000 in 2017.

Thursday March 4th 1915, Estaires

My life has been given back to me again – at all events, it has been quite near enough to my being 'called away'! I had to go to the Headquarters of one of the battalions with whom we hope to have a service next Sunday, and got right in amongst the shelling, and one fell just as I was approaching the little farm. The officers I came to see were all engaged in a council of war, and I did not feel it could be interrupted. So I waited, chatting with two younger officers and some sergeants by the gatepost. Then came an ugly scream out of the sky, and another, and another and so on – seven in all, at intervals of about 3 minutes. The third one dropped right in the road over which I had just come, about 60 yds away. They make huge holes, scattering the earth and stones yards away, and those falling on harder ground fill the crater with a cloud of circling smoke. It does make you feel small when they come singing down on you like that – you feel rather like a cowering rabbit. They shriek up in the sky, and you know that they are coming straight in your direction, and you wonder, 'now where will this beast drop'? While you are wondering, the bang and whirl of earth has taken place before your eyes, and you see the mischief done, but it is amazing how the cottages escape. One shell dropped at this corner, splashing the sides and the roof, the other dropped in the little box-bordered garden behind, practically swallowing it up at one gulp. And yet, mercifully, when I mounted again, and resolved to make the dash over that infested patch of land which I must make to get on my return journey, there was a long lull, nor did I hear another one come before my home-trotting friend had got me well over the ground. Everybody looks a little serious at a time like that. One begins to know the danger signs – an unwonted stillness was over that part on one's approaching it, and one had one's suspicions. At home, sometimes, one remembers when a storm is brewing, and the sky gets black in the day time. People keep indoors and those outside walk on their errands intently and seriously, the birds are all silent and the whole air is still and the area where the shells are falling becomes like that. Only Tommy will laugh and whistle, and a strange thing – no sooner has the smoke in one or other of the shell craters subsided, than you are almost certain to see one or two khaki-clad forms, armed with a spade and so on, diving down out of sight, digging for souvenirs! Not merely for sentiments sake though, for an important thing to find is the fuse of the shell. This is valued by the experts (!) because the timing apparatus on it will, as a rule, tell how far the shell has come, a most important matter for replying batteries, and also it will give the age and quality of the ammunition. But that sky scream is always an ugly thing.

The plot thickens. It is inspiriting to be among these moving scenes. Every nook and cranny is packed with khaki. You ride down street after street of our little town, and every cottage door has its one or two soldiers. The French law is that the householder has one room for himself and the rest he must, if it is demanded, give over to the Army. How they manage I do not let myself try to think! Yet everyone is cheerful enough. Here is a good Tommy riding down with his ration of meat for his platoon – a great lump of red beef tied onto the carrier of his bicycle without paper (that is a rare commodity) and truth to tell it gets a little splashed with mud! Here is a stretcher party marching back for their time in the trenches. Perhaps the noblest and most heroic work of all is that done by stretcher bearers who carry the wounded out of the trenches. Now you pass a long threefold line of armed Khakis, swinging briskly along in the fresh morning air. Passing by them is a long fourfold line of French men, in their long grey or blue coats with the lapels fixed back, their red trousers a little soiled now-a-days, armed just now with long shovels, for they are mostly engaged in mending up the roads, digging reserve trenches and the like. The ride is an incessant greeting of saluting – we are very particular out here, it is an order and everyone salutes everybody and it keeps your arm warm! The low roofs, the cobbled roads, the narrow twisty pavements – you can imagine the scene.

We had another interesting boy through our ambulance station, Captain Dickens, grandson of the great C.D.[218]

Friday, March 5th 1916, Estaires

Yesterday's escape was accentuated today. One man was killed and four were wounded this afternoon at that place – how chastening it all is. Really these coarse-spoken, and I am afraid sin-stained, Khakis do come out in a noble light. You meet them of an evening, as you ride back from the firing line, marching silently by the hundred, along the narrow flat roads, over this wide flat country on into the night and that dark ditch of possible death, so calm and natural-looking. This lot with spades and tools for digging; this one to do duty with the big guns; this with the hand grenades; this with the rifles bristling up like a rigid thicket in the deepening twilight, and every man knows he <u>may</u> be the next turn for suffering or death. Who knows whether beneath his very feet that deadly German sap may not have become ripe to be the death-dealing mine?[219] Whether the shelling may not reach, this time, his platoon? He walks into a nightly gamble with death. Death may come on him from in front, maybe from above, maybe from below. He has to say, really "I die daily". Here is a man

---

218 Major **Cedric Charles Dickens** (b.1899 – d.1916) 13th Bn London Regt (Kensington) Battalion. Killed in action 9th September 1916. Educated at Eton and Trinity Hall, Cambridge, took a commission in his territorial battalion in 1909. Mobilised as a captain on 16th August 1914, he went to France in November and suffered a wound to his shoulder on March 4th 1915. Dickens gained his Majority in December 1915 and commanded a company at the Somme. As part of 56th Division, 13 Bn Londons were engaged at Bouleaux Wood when Dickens gallantly took a party north to cover a gap. Unknown to him their left flank was open due to the Irish Division having been held up at the Quadrilateral and it was heavy machine gun fire from that strongpoint which first wounded and then killed him. His men buried him in the shell hole where he fell.

219 The word "sapper" comes from the French *saper* (to undermine, to dig under a wall or building to cause its collapse). Any tunnel or trench designed to achieve this was called a sap. By extension in the British Army, a **sapper**, also called pioneer or combat engineer, came to mean any soldier who performed a variety of military engineering duties such as bridge-building, laying or clearing minefields, demolitions, field defences and general construction. They were also trained to serve as infantry personnel in defensive and offensive operations.

cleaning his teeth at the edge of that muddy pool out in the slush! How they seem to enjoy the morning wash at the canal side, even though the wind bites keenly. The other morning, one kneeling forward on a shallow patch, over-balanced himself and got his rolled-up shirt sleeves wet up to the shoulder. "Oh well" he said "while I am at it I may as well have it all" and he plunged in and had a good swim, clothes and all!

We had a very interesting visit today from Canon Scott, from Quebec[220], who is with the Canadian Contingent[221]. He hailed me from across the street as a brother Chaplain, and I brought him into lunch. His description of the departure of the Canadian Contingent from Canada bears repeating. 31 transports, painted grey, sailed off in lines of 3 abreast with escorts and without lights at night – a strange and beautiful sight at anchor in the bay, the night before they started[222]. Rudyard Kipling lunched with them (the headquarters people) the day before they set sail. One more transport from Newfoundland joined them outside. It must have been a sight, 32 great transports in column over that vast ocean. It is England's sea power! The Canadians are great fighters, almost too dashing as they want to be climbing out of the trenches and going for the men in front of them without waiting[223]! Good stuff that.

Saturday March 8th 1915, Estaires

There can be no doubt that the men are well looked after, and it is reassuring for the future. Good strength is well economised. Come down to the end of this little town street and there are a whole row of motor buses lined up! It is going to take the men up to the trenches and to bring others back. We <u>are</u> a pack! Actually too now

---

220 **Frederick George Scott** (b.1861 – d.1944) was a Canadian poet and author. He is associated with Canada's Confederation Poets, a group that included Charles G.D. Roberts, Bliss Carman, Archibald Lampman, and Duncan Campbell Scott. Scott published 13 books of Christian and patriotic poetry, and was a British imperialist who wrote many hymns to the British Empire – eulogising Canada's roles in the Boer Wars and WW1. Many of his poems use the natural world symbolically to convey deeper spiritual meaning.

221 The British Declaration of war automatically brought Canada into the war, because of Canada's legal status as a British dominion, which left foreign policy decisions in the hands of the UK parliament. However, the Canadian government had the freedom to determine the country's level of involvement in the war. On August 5th, 1914, the Governor General declared a war between Canada and Germany. The Militia was not mobilised and instead an independent Canadian Expeditionary Force was raised. For the first time in its history, Canadian forces fought as a distinct unit, first under a British commander and then under a Canadian-born commander. Canada's total casualties stood at the end of the war at 67 000 killed and 250 000 wounded, out of an expeditionary force of 620 000 people mobilised. Canadians of British descent – the majority – gave widespread support arguing that Canadians had a duty to fight on behalf of their Motherland. Sir Wilfrid Laurier, Canadian prime minister, although French-Canadian, spoke for the majority of Canadians when he proclaimed: "It is our duty to let Great Britain know and to let the friends and foes of Great Britain know that there is in Canada but one mind and one heart and that all Canadians are behind the Mother Country."

222 Thursday October 3rd 1914.

223 In the later stages of the European war, particularly after their success at Vimy Ridge and Passchendaele, the Canadian Corps was regarded by friend and foe alike as the most effective Allied military formation on the Western Front. The Germans went so far as to call them "storm troopers" for their great combat efficiency.

we have a little music. It is delightful to pause and let the brawny Scotchmen tramp by – wonderful food, porridge! Food for men in Scotland and horses in England, and where do you see such horses and such men[224]? The French people enjoy the Scotch uniform, and the bagpipes.

Alas today a near casualty. Just as we were sitting down to lunch, along the roadway across the garden and the canal, there passed a procession of five stretchers. It turned round over the bridge, and in a few minutes it was unloading in the long lower room. The shell had fallen upon a group of them cooking their dinner in the open. Two were horribly mutilated, still breathing but not conscious, and one of the three others got worse during the afternoon. The 4th is easier now that a big black bullet has been taken out of his fore-arm, where it had travelled from his shoulder. The 5th I hope will get some sleep when the shock of the gash in his arm has had time to subside. The General came in at teatime to enquire about them – he is our fourth General, whom I have not yet met.

The Club is a squash again. As I walked towards it from the site where the shell fell along the canal bank, a little black object, just visible in the deepening twilight, scuttled close by us on the water's edge. I asked an old Frenchman of 60 or so what it was. "A rat" he said "a black water rat, there are a great many of them about here and they make very good eating too!"

Tuesday March 9th 1915, Estaires

I am thankful that we had that dangerous service on Sunday morning, because the men who were there went to the trenches the same evening. This morning some of them are brought in. I have just seen a sergeant who I noticed on Sunday – the attentive way in which he joined in the prayers and his hearty singing. He is still, brave man that he is, trembling with the shock from last night when a shell burst in the trench. His legs are rather cut about but the man next to him "was blown up into pieces". He himself will recover but, as he said, it does make a man think.

Wednesday March 10th 1915, Estaires

A date to be remembered and one that perhaps will live on in history [225]– we have begun to take the offensive. At about 7.30 a.m. the huge salvo of our artillery began, miles of it and our Infantry sprang forward. The village of [...*censored*...][226] was

---

224 A play on Johnson's Dictionary (1755) definition of Oats: 'a grain, which in England is generally given to horses, but in Scotland supports the people.'

225 This was the **Battle of Neuve Chapelle** (10th –13th March, 1915). At 7:30 a.m. on 10th March, the British began a 35-minute artillery bombardment by 90 18-pdr field guns of the Indian Corps and the IV Corps, destroying the German wire within ten minutes. The bombardment was followed by an infantry assault at 8:05 a.m: German defences in the centre were quickly overrun on a 1600-yard front and the village of Neuve Chapelle was captured by 10:00 a.m.

226 Neuve Chapelle, captured 10.00 am March 10th. War Diary, 24th Ambulance Division (WO95/1703/1) March 10th 10.30 am 'first wounded cases from today's engagement arrived'.

soon taken and we hear that [*…censored…*] is taken, and it is expected that before tomorrow morning [*…censored…*] will have fallen. By the end of the week I should not be surprised [*…censored…*] will be in our hands. Large forces of the enemy are in steady retreat we hear. It is a curious calming and exhilarating sensation to be right on the forward line of so great a victory. This evening the report is that 3000 enemy prisoners have been taken, including a General. We shall know more tomorrow.

I got up this morning after a late night last night with the firing of the salvo, which we heard only in the faintest way. I splashed myself in my little rubber bath and outside there was a scream and a bang just like the day before yesterday. I heard afterwards that it was seen to burst rather nearer, on this side of the canal, in the air. After breakfast, as I was arranging plans for riding off to the firing line, there was a commotion in the little street outside. German prisoners! I ran across – there they were 56 of them, a grey-clad muddied and somewhat be-draggled crew, being marched into the Mairie buildings, the first Germans that I have seen. By this evening, I have seen hundreds more. We had broken through the trenches forthwith. Mounting some food and the thermos in my saddle holsters I rode off, along the now so well-known road. Khaki groups of reserves stood here and there and further on appeared a slowly marching group, grey and green fringed with khaki, more prisoners. In front of them in a torn cloak, was a dignified and gentlemanly figure, a tall young German officer. He was slightly wounded and his hands were carefully gloved in thick brown kid. On my approach he gravely saluted with all courtesy, and I returned the salute. There were about 20 or 30 with him. Then I came to our dressing station, and a crowd of bandaged men, mud-stained and blood-marked, some walking in, some helped by comrades, some carried in on stretchers and some debouched from horse and motor ambulances. Inside the little old school building, an unresting crowd of doctors, orderlies and men. "Well done" I said to each wounded man or similar words of appreciation and encouragement. How pleased they are to have the deed magnified "thank you, sir" some say and so on. All down the long road they come, some so weary and dazed – one with the blood streaming down his clothes, his sleeves hanging out loose, pulls himself up and says "I'm sorry I can't salute, sir" wounded in both arms. Our stretcher parties are detailed for further on, so thither I ride. All the way the same stream of wounded, walking, leaning, carried on stretchers, with now and again a group of prisoners. Outside the barn where we have held many services one little prisoner fellow sits cheerfully munching bread and cheese, surrounded by a sympathetic group of Tommies – his face is yellow with Lyddite. He has had a narrow escape and appreciates it. He is a Pole and I gather from the patched German I can use that he has no 'liebe' for the Kaiser or the Germans. He is very emphatic – 'none at all'.

On along the long road – greeting every single wounded man, encouraging the bearers in their dangerous work, for the shells are now flying busily either side of us

---

'Medical arrangements – besides large stocks of ordinary surgical material, much anaesthetic serum was obtained.'

and ten bearers have been hit today. The roar of the big guns is something terrific, behind us now. Where are they? That is a nice haystack – it is a gun and you can see the red flame shoot out of it! Further along there is the front row of straw manure heaps for manuring the field – it is a row of successive roars and tongues of flame in a minute or two! The German shells flash fire in the sky above us, along the skyline are puffs of circling clouds – down on the ground are little craters of white, black, and sometimes yellow, deep yellow, smoke. Everybody moves to and fro unconcernedly – it is curious you think nothing of possibilities yourself. In the general atmosphere you find that you cannot, for there is only one purpose – going forward.

I ride on to follow up the regiments of my Brigade, who I hear are pushing forward. Still the stream of wounded down the road, and the intermittent rattle of artillery. A pleasant young R.C. Chaplain has joined me, and together we go on. Not a man who can bear it, do I fail to address "Well done, dear lad, hope you'll get on alright" and so on, and the face lights up, tired sometimes and white with pain or strain. The man is glad – you can see he is thinking 'the day goes well'. We hear we have advanced. We come to our stockade, and I pass the mystic line past which is the <u>beyond</u>, before which we have spent these months and from which we have received the tales of suffering and death, and against which we have designed so much. I go beyond the trenches which I entered that first night with such intense feeling, past the barn on the left, the pathway of which has since been named 'Dead Cow Lane' and past the lines of troops till I enter the German trenches! They are poor, low uncomfortable places, the little dug-outs are like dog-kennels, and smell no better, rather worse, and everywhere lies dank yellow water, some of it knee-deep. Trophies lie here by the hundreds – and we can take what we choose. I find a Pickelhaube and a dirk, the belt buckle marked "Gott mit uns", a bundle of letters and a tassel[227]. We pass an officer dead in the mud – what are we to do? He has been awarded the Iron Cross[228] as you can see by his ribbon, and one can only offer a prayer for those who love him, and pass on, but not far.

---

227 The **Pickelhaube** (plural *Pickelhauben*; from the old German *Pickel* = "point" or "pickaxe", and *Haube* = "bonnet", a general word for headgear), also "Pickelhelm", was a spiked helmet worn in the 19th and 20th centuries by German military, firefighters, and police. The basic Pickelhaube was made of hardened (boiled) leather, given a glossy-black finish, and reinforced with metal trim (usually plated with gold or silver for officers) that included a metal spike at the crown. During the early months of WW1, it was soon discovered that these leather helmets offered virtually no protection against shell fragments and shrapnel and the conspicuous spike made its wearer a target. **Gott mit uns** (meaning *God with us*) is a phrase commonly used on armor in the German military from the German Empire to the end of the Third Reich.

228 The **Iron Cross** was established by King Friedrich Wilhelm III of Prussia and first awarded in 1813 during the Napoleonic Wars. The recommissioned Iron Cross was also awarded during the Franco-Prussian War. The Iron Cross was used as the symbol of the German Army from 1871 to April 1918, when it was replaced by the bar cross. Since the Iron Cross was issued over several different periods of German history, it was annotated with the year indicating the era in which it was issued.

Though our advance lines are some miles ahead, a group of sharp-shooters are somewhere on the edge of the village, and have this corner of the trench in their line of vision – we must go back, and it is as well we do, for shelling begins to be accurate round this corner. That and the sniping bullets over us make it warm, the backs of the trenches up to a point are low, and exposed to the rear. We breathe the better when we need crouch no longer, and back in our own trenches, which are now well out of range, we move at our ease. Groups of officers are glad to chat, and at last it is time to be getting to the real rear. In a farm as we pass by there is a group of German prisoners, about 35 of them. One can talk French – I ask him "When will the war end?" "Ne sais pas. Quand nous avons gagne" "You think you are going to win?" "Chacun a sont tour" "What do the people in Germany think?" "Oh, they will win" "They are getting short of bread and we hear they are short of potatoes?" (with a little laugh) "Oh, no sir. I have given my letters to the officer, or I could show you."

Another prisoner can speak English a little, and his most notable remark is that they are so surprised the English treat them so well. I ask what he expected and with a rather forced smile, he makes the sign of being bayoneted. They are all sorry about the war – the English artillery is 'terrible' and this group all agree the war must be over by June. A number of them have the typical round silver-rimmed German spectacles. One fellow is shivering with chattering teeth. I ask why and they show me his trousers wet through up to the waist and clotted with mud. I point him out to the officer, who agrees to his being allowed to walk about. I explain that I am a 'Pastor' and they are pleased.[229]

On back I go, and the stream of limping, leaning, mud stained, blood stained humans still passes on. Here at the hospital they lie everywhere, rows upon rows, Germans intermingled with the others, mostly all suffering so patiently, one or two head cases delirious with pain. They lie on the floors, blanket covered, but turning here and there in all direction trying to free themselves of that gnawing injury – all who can, smoke cigarettes. It is a long weary evening and night and the doctors, some of them, have had no lunch nor tea: I insist on dinner for everybody. At dinner the Colonel opens a letter from his wife in which there is a soft white piece of tissue, with a fresh pressed daffodil from Devonshire. The contrast of it with all the squalor and the suffering down below around us pulls one up short – dear, pure, beautiful thing, if only your spirit were in this world!

Thursday March 11th 1915, Estaires

After an official message from the General, all the Chaplains met this morning behind the village, to proceed to burying the bodies left out. It was impossible – the enemy have brought up bigger guns in the night, and have shelled us desperately, and they

---

229 War Diary, 24th Ambulance Division (WO95/1703/1). 'The East wing of the farm was set aside for German wounded.'

'One of rooms during Neuve Chapelle.
For 4 days and nights nobody properly went to rest.'

'Bomb throwers. After Neuve Chapelle First Day'

continue to do so. We pass along our own trenches, some lads lie there behind a parapet, behind a haystack, with the red blood streaming about them, waiting for the stretcher bearers. The officer in charge in a few words indicates how we all agree that the attempt at burying is out of the question, and we are advised to drop further back out of the direct line of fire. But two of us propose to wait in case of a lull in the firing later on. One came between 11 and 1, but the officer in charge is away 'changing' with his men, so another R.C. and I visit along the line of our trenches, which runs into the German evacuated one. The snipers have gone, and we visited one dug-out after another, like calling at little houses in a street – but such a dismal, twisty, filthy endless little street. And in the trenches we find spoils – but you cannot carry things with baggage limited to 36 lbs. However, I find a tube of pastilles, some belt buckles, and some picture postcards and so on. A scrap lunch behind the ruined farm we are waiting at, in the hope that the afternoon will be quieter.

Nay, directly after lunch, a perfect hurricane of the heavier shells finds our corner. One huge brute falls just across the road, spluttering shrapnel and mud everywhere – mud all down my back, and mercifully nothing whatever else, but a lad a yard from me cries out "Hit!" and the blood streams down his face from the top of his head. The transport officer, in bending, has fallen prone in the deep black mud, but comes up alright. This is too close, and in half a minute a whole cavalcade of ambulances, ammunition wagons and soldiers whose duties rest with them, are tearing down the road. Peter gets out our two horses – and then another huge shell drops just beside the road skirting the cavalcade. We wait for a third shell to drop, (they make enormous holes), and my groom and I plunge out into the road, nor do the horses need urging. Three quarters of a mile down the road is a Red Cross station and we will wait there. But half an hour later, the Jack Johnsons[230] find us. Shall I try to describe what it is like? They are like concentrated earthquakes – clouds of thick black smoke circle up into the air out of wide, deep craters. Everybody clears away, except the Hindu orderlies of some gunners in a battery close by, some signallers in a cottage, and Peter and myself. I have to wait to send a pre-arranged message about the burials. It is marvellous that these hurtling monsters do not find you. The cottage just vacated by the Red Cross is hit in the end, round here, and round there they drop. How noble the quiet courage of these gunners – it is grand. If the faces of some are pale, I expect my own is, it certainly feels like it, except for the flush of excitement. I go across to the signal cottage, my horses are in the cottage across the road from it. This screaming thunder goes on, but the message is sent and everything around is quiet and still, except for the sparrow's twitter. Then, smash, the little chapel by that cottage down there goes, the roadway strewn with brick-dust and debris. I wait on and on for a lull but none seem to come, so, at last, "well, if you're hit, you're hit".

---

230 A 'Jack Johnson' was the British nickname used to describe the impact of a heavy, black German 15 cm artillery shell. **John Arthur "Jack" Johnson** (b.1878 – d.1946), nicknamed the **Galveston Giant** was an American boxer, who – at the height of the Jim Crow era – became the first African American world heavy weight boxing champion (1908–1915).

How both horses do fly with these noises behind them – if they had wings they could scarcely do more and 300 yds down the road, I look back. A black, cruel, grinding cloud grips the whole road way. It will have gnawed a hole out of it large enough to put two motor cars in – these are the Jack Johnsons. Tonight how thankful one is for the quiet of this hospital, but out there those dear brave lads will be subject to this from daybreak tomorrow, hour after hour – it is no wonder that this war has meant so many mental cases.

Friday March 12th 1915, Estaires

Still the great battle rages[231]. People who write lines like, "and win the well-fought day," I just wonder if they have written them from the knowledge of the agony and peril which an awful battle means[232]. There is no describing the strain: how intense is the sense of the heart standing still when the conflict sways against us, how the spirit glows as it turns and progresses the other way. I have been up in our trenches today, and for a time at the General's Headquarters, shells came even near the latter. There are great black awful craters that have quarried themselves into the ground here, there and everywhere. My first attempt to get into the trenches failed, the shell ringing over them and this side of them was too intense. All communication with them was cut off, rations, ammunition, re-enforcements, the carrying away of the wounded, all stopped. While that went on, a counter attack came on and you could hear the rattle of the musketry get nearer and nearer. Then steadily our great guns kept searching for, and finding, their batteries – the counter attack was checked and our lines advanced. The stream of wounded and prisoners recommenced and they are so pleased to have the "Well done, good lad" and so on as one greets one after the other. Many have been at the Services, and the fruit of those prayerful times is being gathered now. A North country lad is still panting from the fight though he is now half an hour back from the fighting line. "Eh, I nearly killed mysen. A graat fella, must a' bin 7 ft , coom at me wi'is bayonet. I fired 10 rounds at 'im without stop. 'E didn't come on." We waited behind the corner of a farm while the shells flew opposite. The officer and I agreed that we must go back to another farm and have some lunch. We learnt afterwards that the officers' four men, who had been waiting with us, went inside the farm for some coffee and a shell flew in at the window without bursting! After luncheon, a hail of 'Jack Johnsons' fell round a battery near us, and the sight was quite awe-inspiring. Later we learnt that they had blown a field hospital to pieces and had fallen on the tail of a gang of German prisoners, 'hoisting them with their own petard'.

---

231 On 12th March, German forces commanded by Crown Prince Rupprecht, launched a counter-attack, which failed but forced the British to use most of their artillery ammunition. The British offensive was postponed on 13th March and abandoned two days later.

232 **Hymn**, *Soldiers of Christ, Arise* by Charles Wesley, 1707–1788 "From strength to strength go on, wrestle and fight and pray; tread all the powers of darkness down and win the well-fought day."

Then shelling subsided in the face of some of our biggest. I ventured on and though shells still fell, got onto our own trenches. What a scene! It is indescribable – bandages, blood, mud, mighty shell holes, with great ridges of earthworks. Tea is generously given by some officers squatting in the clay and after, I bury nine men in one grave, shrapnel bursting that way, a bullet or two spitting behind us in some trees, and our own guns roaring on our right. But as I turn to dash home, still past a ring of shells, the good news comes that we have practically 'won the well fought day' [...*censored*...] has been rushed by the [...*censored*...] and we shall certainly hope to retain it tonight. No more Jack Johnsons for tonight, in that case.

There was a grand attack this morning. I am burying the dead now in long trenches. A platoon was captured yesterday afternoon – taken by the Germans behind a barn and shot outright. Some of the Germans put up the white flag, yet fired behind it. 110 of them rushed out in another section and asked to be taken prisoner, our artillery they say, is terrible.

You will see by the London papers of the success that has been won – alas! – the cost writes itself into one's very soul. Those who gathered round us at the services, who have popped into the mess, how strange to think they are cold and still and will not wake from their sleep at all again in this world. The young officers are so 'game', so courteous, so fresh and pure in their gallantry. The men in the steadiness and the determination of their courage are so manly – they make one feel we are walking on firm ground. They are giving their lives truly and nobly for the honour of the Empire, but what a price to pay for righteousness!

Saturday March 13th 1915, Estaires

I went out to the trenches this morning, but at a certain point met my battalions coming out of them, relieved by their supports – it was a scene. They came literally out of the valley of the shadow of death. "We went in 120 of us" said one man "we came out only 17". "I am the only officer left of my company" said another. There was a wistful sense of relief about the way they sat down by the roadside and lit their cigarettes. They liked to tell their tales of things horrible and indescribable – of charges and maxims and huge shell destruction, of slain foes, of captured trenches and surrendering prisoners, and cheerfully they went up to the straw stacks nearby to prepare the first arranged bed they have had for three nights.

And as we talked huge 'coal box[233]' shells began, with loud crack and thunder, to fall down round the battery near us. These gunners, they are <u>magnificent</u> men, but the 'coal boxes' meant a counter attack was on. The orders had to go round that these men must prepare to go back into the trenches <u>at once</u>, (that is what the appeal for more men means). It is well to know that the enemy dread our artillery – they say

---

233 Any shell explosion causing a cloud of black smoke.

that the accuracy of its aiming is deadly. We hear today that we dropped two of our biggest shells on two of their trains of re-enforcements. Their artillery too, when it gets near, is an awful thing. You are ringed round with black craters of violent death. Truly the wrath of man cannot work the pure righteousness of God, who in His wrath thinks upon mercy.

Sunday March 14th 1915, Estaires

Today has been a strange and to me, an awful one, but intensely interesting at first. Holy Communion at 8 – only one man present, beside the three, which is not surprising, considering the enormous pressure. At Morning Prayer, only one man present besides the organist. Then I rode off to my four Battalions, all in reserve, thinking perhaps a service might be possible. It was soon clear enough that it was not – they were shaving, washing hands and feet, sorting out their bits of kit, rolling up the blankets that they had not used for three nights and gradually becoming a little more civilised. The chances came, however, in the talks around with groups of men in the different billets. You soon find a group of 10 or 15 men gathering round a sympathetic visitor, ready to talk and be listened to, and in each officers' 'mess' (the word is very literal just now) we had solemn times. "We are only 3 left out of 11". "Our Company went out 127 strong, we came back 51." "Oh Padre" said one officer, in a firm, strong, but gentle way, and that was all. He just handed me the list of the regimental casualties. It made me feel dazed. The regiment with whom I went out that first night into the trenches – the Colonel wounded – that noble gentleman the Major missing [234] – that nice adjutant killed – Capt [...*censored*...] killed, Capt [...*censored*...] killed and the list went on. In another regiment, the O.C. a thigh broken by a bullet. Capt [...*censored*...] one of the Chaplain's most earnest helpers, killed. And so on, and on. The men one has talked with, gone, and yet how cheerful and spirited the remainder generally are. "Thank you, only a black eye" says one showing his cap – the bullet had gone through the edge of it, after grazing the cheek bone. "They cry like little children," said another, "those Germans when you get to close quarters. I came on five of 'em in the trench, I shot two. Then one of the other three began to scream. 'Scream' I says to 'im 'I'll learn ye to scream', and I jumps down on his back. But the officer says 'don't shoot 'em, make 'em prisoners'". Another described how he had to lead back a young prisoner, who kept whining, "Coffee, wounded, me want coffee". "'Coffee' I says to 'im, 'I ain't had any coffee for three days and you want coffee!!'" Soon, towards lunchtime, the Prince of Wales passed by along the road, showing himself among the men, and strolling in the sunshine. As I rode on a little later, I encountered him, and we exchanged a little 'private and personal' salute. He is a pleasant looking lad, with a nice clear complexion, but not robustly made. I hear he went into lunch with the General who said "What are you doing here, young man! I order you back at once". His answer was, "That is the worst of you fellows,

---

234 See footnote 301.

you always make me feel so foolish". The General was right – the Prince had gone on about 50 yds before that, before he turned back. I went in to eat my lunch in a knocked about estaminet[235], another 50 yds further on which is used as a Red Cross dressing station. During my lunch about five shells fell harmlessly a little further on here and there, and behind us. About 20 yds on is another dishevelled estaminet in which part of a company of another of my battalions was billeted – I meant to visit them later on, as I had visited the others in the morning. Just as I was finishing my lunch, a scream and a crash sounding very near and, oh, such a scene! A group of men in front of the billet had been caught. I rushed out, to see a general stampede of them down the road, and what a scene just there. Dead men lying across and along the road, and others, some pleading, some caring for their mates, one thinking about his major's horse which had been cut, although he was wounded in the leg himself. "Cheer up, old chap", one had to say "we'll put you alright in a minute" and so on. I stopped to pray over seven of them huddled in a mass together, in all shapes. Willing hands came from different directions in spite of all the danger, with stretchers, an old shutter or two and so on. A doctor fortunately happened to be billeting in the next house, and we had our work cut out for the next hour and a half, an occasional shell whistling over meanwhile. 24 killed, 17 wounded by that single shell, and an 18th died on the way back. They are a wicked invention, those monstrous engines of destruction. How full the rest of the day has been, more visiting and arranging for the burial of those 24 men[236].

Evening Service – about 20 men present after all. I preached on "Let not your heart be troubled, neither let it be afraid"[237], and oh, how earnestly we all prayed for the day when right shall triumph. Many of these German prisoners think all must end not later than June. It must do so not much later than that – one nation is exterminating another – the life of the more 'highly civilised' cannot go on as the heathen races will outnumber them, unless wiser councils prevail[238].

---

235 **Estaminet:** a tavern, a synonym for coffee house, but generally serving beer and tobacco, located in Belgium, Nord-Pas-de-Calais and Picardie. These were the preferred places for soldiers to relax when rotated out of the trenches offering wine, song and the prospect of French girls. They were the rivals to RDG's clubs. In 1802, the French Academy defined it: "Assembly of drinkers and smokers," it is also stated that "This usage comes from the Netherlands has spread to Paris where we also say Tabagie to distinguish these kinds of meetings. According to the prevailing hypothesis, the word would be from the walloon and comes from "staminate", meaning a pillared hall. A Flemish origin is also attributed, from the word "Stamm", which means family, and the tavern would be a place for a family reunion. The Flemish landlord also invited customers to enter by calling out "Sta Menheer" (Stop off, Sir). Also: Spanish (the Flanders was a Spanish possession in the C17th) from *"Esta un minute"*, a place where you spend a quick drink.

236 The Commonwealth War Graves Commission lists 27 deaths and burials at Estaires Communal Cemetery on March 14th 1915.

237 **John 14:27** 'Peace I leave with you, my peace I give unto you: not as the world giveth, give I unto you. Let not your heart be troubled, neither let it be afraid.'

238 War Diary, 24th Field Ambulance (WO95/1703/1) March 16th 9.00 am 'Casualties March 10 – March 16th: Officers, 62; OR 1436; Indians, 47; Germans, Officers, 3, OR 142'. 40 000 Allied troops took part during the battle of Neuve Chapelle and suffered 7000 British and

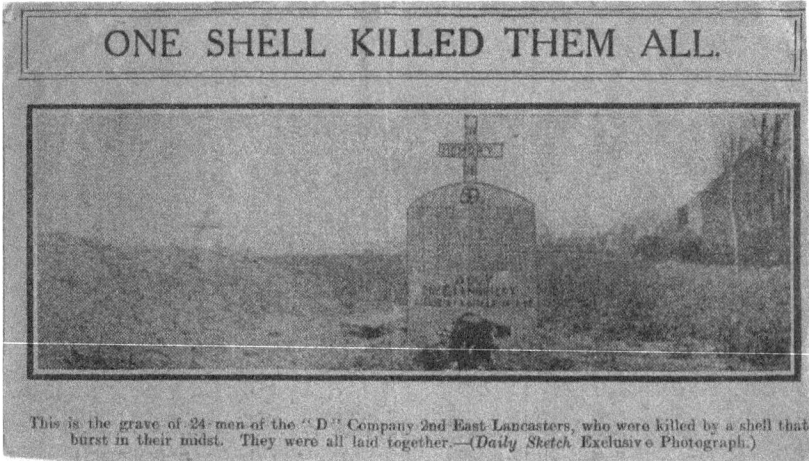

This is the grave of 24 men of the "D" Company 2nd East Lancasters, who were killed by a shell that burst in their midst. They were all laid together.—(*Daily Sketch* Exclusive Photograph.)

Monday March 15th 1915, Estaires

It would be a blessing and a mercy if one could efface and blot out many of the events and sights of the last few days. They come back to your ears and live before your closed eyes in spite of yourself. It is a gruesome and melancholy scene, a battlefield – smashed houses, damaged vehicles, cast-away clothing, bloodstains, fragments of bandages, bits of equipment – even valuables, and great yawning shell holes everywhere, and how some of us have lived through these things is incredible. I buried those 24 poor ghastly twisted forms this morning in two trenches. Two of them looked so placid, all the same. It was nervous work burying them in the field just behind the house with shells still whistling in the distance. Great 'coal boxes' were crashing half a mile away, feeling their way a few hundred yards at a time in our direction. However, nothing came near and the shelling finished soon after we did. They found three spies in an upper room of the farm, in the orchard where the battery is which was being shelled yesterday and five others in another farm – we do wonder why the authorities do not clear all these people away.

Tuesday March 16th 1915, Estaires

I have had two pieces of encouragement today. I stood beside a dead man of one of my regiments and a young soldier came up, wounded in the hand. He said "He was at that service in the barn on Sunday." "Ah", I said "those are the things we like to think of now". He agreed and said "I was there too, I liked it and have thought a good many times this week of what you said. One does think with a shell whistling over one, doesn't one?"

4200 Indian casualties. The 7th Division had 2791 casualties, the 8th Division 4814 losses, the Meerut Division 2353 casualties and the Lahore Division 1694 losses.

I have been censoring some patients' letters. One is from a man who has also been through all the fighting and he speaks of the preacher giving them "something to think about". The 'lecture' took their minds away from the fighting "and it was jolly good stuff too". How much these occasions may mean!

One of our Generals was so nice about things this morning – he is one of the common sense 'unstiff' sort. He spoke of the high price this battle had demanded, yet he added "it has been worth it". Out of ten of his younger officers put to a certain work, eight had been killed. He had had a quiet word with each one of them beforehand – there is a noble man! And he concluded with the consolation, "They died doing their duty". One is so thankful for Generals like that.

I have been able to spend this morning in the trenches. The strain is very great for everybody, and I know the mere fact of someone from outside coming along helps to relieve the tension, and the talks one can get are man to man in the Great Realities of life in the simple way that strengthens peace and makes duty happier.

Crossing over the ground lately held by the Germans is not pleasant. Some of their bodies are still lying about as it has been too dangerous to bury them. And how the men do love to talk over their fights! The hand-to-hand bayonet struggles must be the most dreadful of all, and a lad I talked with this morning had had one with a German lad of 17 years old. Somewhat of a lull has come, and the Club is crowded again to overflowing and the baths go with a 'roar', which after days in the trenches with scarcely a wash and without a change of clothes, can be guessed at. The sights, the smells, the devastation of a battlefield – how these things do hover close to one. It was a refreshment to be at the Holy Communion this morning, and to realise afresh the Glory world, the Angels and Archangels and all the Company of Heaven, and to thank Him for His great glory, who lives in the Land of Light, Righteousness and Love triumphing assuredly over darkness, sin and death.

Wednesday March 17th 1915, Estaires
I forgot to mention the name of the Baths caretaker is Douche!!

It seems likely our heavy fighting would have quieted the shell firing at this end, however I had not been in bed an hour last night when, after that first sweet sleep that you cannot easily get back, whizz, bang, three times, three had gone over our heads! It is very disturbing but all the same, what are you to do? It is best to go off to sleep again if you can, and one does generally sleep well these strenuous days. They tell me seven men died near us last night – it is some wretched gun tucked away cross country and I promised a Gunner Captain a V.C. this morning if only he would find it. There is still a lull, thank goodness and so it gives everybody time to smooth down their ruffled feathers a little – not that you can see much ruffling. There is a little gleam in the eye, just the least firm drawing-in of the breath, no stupid pretence of being unconscious of the seriousness of things, but a most strengthening quietness and cheerfulness through it all. No less splendid are the stretcher bearers, and it is agreed all round that the courageous fidelity of these men beats all praise, so let no one think that the Red Cross men do an inferior work to that of others.

Things are changing slightly in character and I think the long sitting down in trenches will not be the main feature of battle now for some time. I do earnestly hope that Lord Kitchener's appeal for no hindrance and delay in the output of ammunition will be responded to[239]. If only men knew how shells and guns stand between us and destruction and how in fact hours of delay mean so many lives lost of our brothers, and of course the postponement of the end of the war. Some means indeed ought not to be beyond the wit of man to discover the way of getting every ounce of the most urgent energy out of everybody at a time like this. Artillery is a grand force for protection and defence and the Germans have depended much upon it – I hope they may not be allowed to do so much longer. The tales of adventure and escape are endless, in fact, people cease to speak much about narrow escapes, as most have had such a number of them. But right must triumph in the end.

Thursday March 18th 1915, Estaires

We are gradually realising all that last week's sufferings stand for. So many one has chatted with, walked with, prayed with, are gone. It is difficult to think how their work can be carried on. In one Regiment <u>every</u> officer gone, in another, all but three – the price has been a high one, 12,000 they say. It is something that on the other side it has been greater – at least 17,000 killed and wounded besides the prisoners taken. A little girl of eight was brought in today with a shell wound in the hand and a young woman two days ago with a shell wound in the thigh. She had gone to hide in the straw in the barn and a piece of the shell crashed through the roof and the straw, carrying some of the latter into the wound.

The club is packed. It gives one a sinking feeling to see some having to walk out again, but you cannot merely stand in a crush to get recreation and I am afraid that I cannot undertake to organise a second one – there is so much to do.

The full tale of that one dreadful shell on Sunday was given me this afternoon: it was 24 killed (whom I buried) 33 wounded, 6 of whom subsequently died: 57 with one shell, and our side has been doing equally dreadful execution. I wonder if by now the Kaiser and his Chancellor are not beginning to think.

We have had an impressive parade this afternoon with a message from the General commanding the Corps and from the Chief Medical Officer, thanking and commending the men for their work – it was richly deserved. People sometimes think that Red Cross work is easy but I have seen it on the battlefield nobly and in

239 The Secretary of State for War made a speech on 17th March in the House of Lords concerning the issue of the shortage of artillery ammunition.

this Ambulance. Abbott of the 23rd Ambulance for instance, one of the coolest of men, who walked to and fro the whole of that first day caring for the wounded, reporting to the doctors and so on[240]: and Peel (from our own diocese) – he is a splendid fellow, a little sharp they tell me, in his sense of discipline, but devoted to a degree[241] and good old Conran has been indefatigable. Goudge with solemnly dangerous work, going in and out among the batteries with 'coal boxes' flying around, has had a searching time too. Two of our unit have been killed and 10 wounded (including De La Bere[242], the Oxford M.A., the curate and a private who got hit by shrapnel)[243]. Chaplains too have come out of it with injuries.

Today we have had snow again. The Germans do look after their men well, judging by those we have seen – knee boots, waterproof, clean well-tended feet, and two pairs of socks. I suppose they have plenty of men to change about with. Therefore, must we have more men.

Saturday March 20th 1915, Estaires

An aeroplane bombed the place today. It made a good shot, dropping a bomb on the furnace of the Gas Works. One man was killed outright, and the other, brought in to our Ambulance, lingers but tonight there is more chance for him (both civilians)[244]. There was another bomb also on a factory with 1 person killed and 12 injured – out of a clear blue sky, very high up. It is a mercy the thing did not drop on the Gas meter, as then there would have been an explosion. The works are not so far from us, and we heard a loud bang at breakfast time. Then came the aeroplane circling round over us on its way back, and then the (literally) dozens of puffs of smoke of the anti-aircraft guns, away far up in the sky. The rumour is that they were successful in their aim, but we have not heard. There is no gas in the town tonight, and I am so angry with the caretaker of the Club. The lazy, selfish old thing took it as an opportunity for an extra evening off, and, not troubling to get a few candles, closed up at twilight and shut off the baths as well.

This evening we had a concert in a factory. One or two of the men played and sang quite wonderfully well – there is real talent in them. The way one man picked out

---

240 Serjeant **John J Abbott**, 23rd Field Ambulance. He survived the war.
241 Rev. **Maurice Berkeley Peel**, Chaplain to the 1st Royal Welch Fusiliers. (b.1873 – d.1917). After leaving Oxford he worked for some years at Oxford House, Bethnal Green and was eventually ordained in 1899. From 1899 to 1906 he was attached to St Simon's Zelotes, Bethnal Green, becoming Rector of St Paul's, Beckenham, in 1909. Wounded in 1915, he was appointed Vicar of Tamworth; but returned to the front in 1917, winning an MC. Killed at Bullcourt on May 14th 1917.
242 Capt. **Charles Edward de la Bere**, (b.1890 – d.1918) 24th Wessex Field Ambulance, the Royal Army Medical Corps, thereafter Adjutant of the Royal Garrison Artillery, 66th "Y" Brigade, HQ. Died of influenza, 1918.
243 War Diary, 24th Field Ambulance (WO95/1703/1) March 19th. 'Statement of work of 24th Field Ambulance morning of March 10th to 9.00 pm March 14th. 24th Field Ambulance casualties: Officers nil, OR 1 killed 10 wounded, artillery fire 10, rifle fire 1'.
244 Sapper **Leopold Edward Davies** (b.1888 – d.1915), Royal Engineers, 15th Field Coy. Died 20th March 1915. Buried Estaires Communal Cemetery.

the air and wove in quite good accompaniments was very clever, and another had a fine, clear baritone voice and sang a nice song. Another song or two had the usual imperfection – it seems ingrained in the class to have the strain of thought that is poor in taste, bordering on worse. The men feel serious enough in all conscience, but the words are ready made, and they come upon their lips from the time when they first learned them.

A doctor, along our left front, was hit by a shell this afternoon, but he will come through alright. At present he sleeps peacefully under morphia – strange the happy peace that morphia gives. One man I noticed on the battlefield last week, badly hit on the head and quite unconscious, was beating time with his hand to imaginary music as he was carried on his stretcher. When the stretcher bearers stopped, the hand ceased and directly the motion began again, the hand was uplifted and the music was resumed – with a bullet wound through the brain! These doctors do noble work under fire, in and out of the trenches with shells flying round they go quietly on, and in the ambulance here they worked on a whole 24 hours at a stretch, the floors around them packed close with stretchers of wounded – a crowded, awful harvest of pain.

Sunday March 21st 1915, Estaires

In beautiful sunshine, beneath a clear blue sky with an occasional soft white fleecy cloud sailing across, with daffodils peeping out by a desolate hedgerow and the lark singing merrily in his exalted element, the War goes on. I have lost count of the days now, but it must be over five weeks since we have been shelled on <u>daily</u> in this place. Today neither bomb nor shell has come over us and it is a blessing to have had a more peaceful Sunday. The fighting continues heavily with the aggression on our side.

8 a.m. Holy Communion, about 40 present, including 2 Generals and 6 or 7 officers. It is good when the Generals attend and the temporary Military Church <u>has</u> been a success in that way. Goudge took the 10.30 service – I have not heard about the numbers but my service was in a suspended cotton-spinning factory. I felt the strain of it very much – out of 14 officers in one regiment only 4 left, out of 13 in another 5 left, and 160 men left out of an original 570. That infantry charge is surely worth ranking with Balaclava. Where is the Tennyson who will write of deeds like these?[245] The nerves of men and officers are letting them talk of it now, though even yet their shaking has not quite left them. The survivors! How we looked at each other this morning – the man in the surplice. I do not think I have ever been more conscious of an understanding that looked out upon one than that which I see from those rows of intent and serious faces. A piano among the cotton-spinning looms, and the men grouped in and out among the latter. The man who played the piano did very well

---

245 "**The Charge of the Light Brigade**" is an 1854 narrative poem by Alfred, Lord Tennyson about the Charge of the Light Brigade at the Battle of Balaclava during the Crimean War.

and you felt that the response really was, "O come, let us sing unto the Lord[246]." I hope there was strength and comfort in the message St.Matthew.VI. II [247] "Our Father, which art in Heaven" There were about 200 men present.

There was a misunderstanding about the place of the next service – our time and place being mixed up with some other troops, however eventually we foregathered in an orchard, the men sitting on ploughs, timber cart shafts, etc. and it was a glorious service with the blue sky, the soft sunny air, the rested men and the atmosphere of peace. Some of them were the comrades of the men who last Sunday, 57 of them, had been hit by that one shell. It was good to enter into the truth of Trench's lines:

"And we, and all men move
Under a canopy of love
As broad as the blue sky above.
That doubt and sorrow, fear and pain,
And anguish, all are shadows vain,
That death itself shall not remain,
And we, on various shores now cast
Shall meet, life's perilous voyage past
All in our Father's home at last[248]"

The afternoon was a busy one when I got back, getting lightning arrangements for the temporary Military church this evening. I have bought a number of cheap lanterns, which we can use in the Club as well. The hall looked rather picturesque with these hung at different points, assisted by some dozen or more candles stuck about in all sorts of available places, about 3 dozen points of light in all, relieving the darkness round them. The C.E.M.S. men worked nobly, and we all felt rewarded, for a very large congregation assembled, filling almost every single available seat. The singing resounded again and you could 'feel' the prayer as we thanked God who has done great things for us already, wherein we rejoice. I think God's Presence was very mercifully vouchsafed to us tonight.

Monday March 22nd 1915, Estaires

We shall move in a day or two and letters will be uncertain for that time. This morning I went up towards the line to accompany a party taking a head-board to the grave of a comrade killed there. We were stopped at the house I was in on Sunday week by the Medical Officer, who uses it as an Aid Station. They had just been shelled, one had dropped on the path outside, one had gone through the front wall, and

---

246 **Psalm 95:1** 'O come, let us sing unto the Lord: let us make a joyful noise to the rock of our salvation.'
247 The Lord's Prayer.
248 Hymn: *The Kingdom of God*. **Richard Chenevix Trench** (b.1807 – d.1886) was an Anglican archbishop of Dublin and poet.

another had pierced the side in a glancing way. Everybody was very excited, except the officer and his N.C.O., who had retired to a dug-out in the ploughed field behind.

Behold – a beautiful spring morning, the bright warm sunshine, the blue sky above, and a hovel dug down into the ground topped over with support boughs, straw and a thick covering of clods, the floor also lined with straw. Inside three Red Cross men, the medical officer, and the civilian occupants of the vacant house – a middle aged workman, his wife, a daughter of about 18 and Granny aged about 75 or 80, the latter all huddled in the shadows at the far end. I advised them to gather what effects they needed, and to move back into the town for a few days. They were reluctant, and a little frightened at moving out of the shelter, but with a little stiffening of everybody's courage all round, we sallied forth, my place of honour falling to giving a hand to Granny up out of the hole, and guiding her across the few yards to the house, although with a slow moving charge like that, I confess that I felt a little frightened. The German guns have found that corner to a nicety, and another shell might have come at any moment. We hurried our friends through their selection of their sundry necessities, all the time wondering when the next crash would come. At length, having seen their preparations nearly completed, I moved forward down the road with Granny. Poor old thing, I wondered if she was not too old and too feeble to feel frightened, yet her feet had a strong firm tread as of the peasant who is accustomed to sturdy walking, and her eyes had a gentle hunted look and her face was pale and flushed at the same time. We neither of us spoke much until we had got well along the road when I think I remarked only that it was fine weather and the sky was pretty. We breathed better when we had got out of the line of shelling, and I left her to journey on while I turned in to talk with some soldiers billeted nearby. I had not been there ten minutes when two more shells came whistling over us, both wide of the previous line, but fortunately dropping long – it is an ugly scream, the scream of a shell.

The Club will go on under another Chaplain, and we shall, I hope, run one where we go. I had a talk with the Chaplain who will take over, and he is delighted to know that the Fund will stand by him. We hope that the Bishop of London will come to the Cinema Church, though our Brigades I imagine, will have moved on.

A German prisoner brought in today shot in the leg with the bone broken, has been lying out eight days secreted in some ruins, hoping to be gathered in by his own people but our searchers found him, his smashed limb in a horrible state. Some of our men have been found after 3 or 4 days, but here is one out there for 8! He tells us he lived on bread and water and sausages got from the rations of the dead lying round him. They say that the German Emperor was at last week's fighting and is still in the vicinity. I wonder if he is mad – it seems sometimes as if it must be so.

Tuesday, March 23rd 1915, Estaires

A quieter day here, mainly concerned with trench holding. But the Church tower in the deserted town which we can see across the fields has been shelled about, and instead of being four-square to the winds, has become a mere pillar. The Churches all get foremost attention around here. We hear that the Kaiser has been to Lille and we wonder with what cogitations. There is more rain tonight and some ugly wounds from the trench fighting – I should like the Kaiser to see, massed before him, the mutilations these madnesses are causing. I cannot help holding him responsible for much that has come about, as people do vastly take their views from prominent persons, and in Germany the Kaiser has had a tremendous influence. Pity he could not have used it as did King Edward VII.

Wednesday, March 24th 1915, Estaires

We are moving on to a smaller place and letters may be slow. It is difficult amid movements and changes. I think shelling will be quieter for a time – they seem to have tracked down the gun that has been sending shells. We are thankful to see so many troops but more are needed and yet more, I am sure. It is depressing to read that Epsom and Ascot are to be held, if even in a modified form[249]. The 'morale' of the possibility of it is dissatisfying – are people taking the clear view of what is going on? Men are suffering and dying day by day to keep back a desperate enemy from our shores. That enemy and its people are straining every nerve and sinew with a grim seriousness to accomplish the mastery of us, and we can play with race horses, use up the strength and passion of numbers of <u>men</u> and squander the thought of a considerable populace on nothing of more importance than flashing first past a winning post, and the excitement of so many bets!! 'Punch' is sound on this, and he even has a cartoon on it.

Bye the bye, there is a 24th Field Ambulance joke in 'Punch' this week. One of our doctors quoted it from a Tommy's letter and I sent it. "Dear Sister, I send you these few lines hoping they find you as this leaves me at present I have a bullet wound in the hand."

We have marched today. A cold pouring morning, not so trying earlier, when all were warm and interested in a move, but it got unpleasant later and the wind was cutting. What a sight these country roads are with troops moving behind a firing line. You can see long winding columns in all directions across the flat landscape and every unit is timed to pass given cross roads at a given time. If one unit fails to keep time, miles of columns may be thrown out, which happened this morning – one unit stopped because a wagon got into a ditch. They should not have waited for it but they did and for too

---

249 A contentious issue in the newspapers in 1915, with a motion to cancel the races lead by Lord Curzon. The Jockey Club, it was reported, decided to hold both events, citing a cancellations effect on morale. In the end, Ascot was held without any of the attendant Royal trappings.

long and then had to leave, holding up hundreds of men and vehicles meanwhile. And one thinks of grey lines of crowding men doing the same winding moves on the other side of that long, tortuous, narrow gulf. The marching has done all ranks good. Spirits have well revived, and it is good to have a change of scene for people.[250]

Friday, March 26th 1915, Sailly sur-la-Lys

It is difficult to know what to do with the Bishop of London[251]on Monday. I have asked him to come over to our Brigade. He will come to this spot, but we are scattered along an extended line, and not in the vicinity of any central hall. The village church being a heap of ruins, the village hall is being used by the parish clergy for Mass, etc. and therefore is not available. I have been to look at a spinning factory further on – it may do.

Our Club opportunity here is a very small one, and we have no indoor place for making a church – the other Club goes on.

There are troops everywhere. Come out in the falling twilight, take half a dozen Ludgate Circuses, put them at intervals of a mile or a mile and a half apart – fill them with lines of Khaki-clad men – shadowing columns wreathing along in the deepening shade then put in the baggage wagons, and wraith-like camp cookers (wraith-like from the hovering steam and smoke that issues from them – solidly practical all the same), and here and there a farm, a knot of cottages, trees just budding, long, low stiff hedges, flat winding canals and narrow streams, and there you have a large section of a great army grouping itself for great actions.

I had an interesting talk with a soldier tonight. He had noticed my coming and going during the days of the battle of Neuve Chapelle, up at the trenches. He was near when the Jack Johnson crashed about us that heavy afternoon, and he happened to have gone by only 100 yds when that shell fell killing 24 and wounding 33. He said there was something in religion that made a chaplain walk about among men at a time like that, and he thought that he would begin to be religious. He didn't know whether he would come to church tomorrow, but he would someday soon. He has a drunken father, but a good mother to whom he allots a daily allowance.

---

250 War Diary, 24th Ambulance Division (WO95/1703/1) March 25th. 'Left ESTAIRES, came by road to SAILLY. Established hospital in buildings vacated by 3rd Canadian Field Ambulance at NE corner of crossroads'. Sailly sur-la-Lys is 3 miles NE of Estaires La Gorgue.

251 Bp. **Arthur Foley Winnington-Ingram** KCVO PC (b.1858 – d.1946) was Bishop of London from 1901 to 1939. During WW1 Winnington-Ingram threw himself into supporting the war effort. He saw the war as a 'great crusade to defend the weak against the strong' and accepted uncritically stories of German atrocities. For a clergyman, the language he used about the German people verged on xenophobia but Herbert Asquith, Prime Minister at the outbreak of the war, described his pitch as "jingoism of the shallowest kind." He spoke in aid of recruiting drives and later in the war urged his younger clergy to consider enlisting as combatants. Chaplain from 1901 to the London Rifle Brigade and London Royal Naval Volunteers, he visited the troops on both the Western Front and at Salonika and the Grand Fleet at Rosyth and Scapa Flow.

Wounds – notwithstanding the quietude, always wounds, and two deaths today, with a hostile aeroplane overhead today – merely squinting. Two of ours tackled it and drove it home again.

Sunday, March 28th 1915, Sailly sur-la-Lys

Today there is bright sunshine and a sharp frost, and a heavy bombardment very early from our side. After a superhuman effort, a place was obtained for a central service and a small room for Holy Communion with three present at the latter. As we came out there was a commotion along the little street. Two French soldiers pale with excitement – "A stretcher!" An aeroplane, now sailing away far up in the blue sky with little white puffs of anti-aircraft shells clustering round it, had dropped two bombs. One had dropped harmlessly in the field, the other had killed two soldiers and wounded another. It is evident the bomb had swung in its descent – it was meant for our village crossroads, 30 yds away. If it had dropped plumb, it would have been too near us. As it was, it went off 200 yds away. An escape I am sure – a message rather!

We had a nice service in the larger building at 9.30 and the bomb helped the earnestness of our prayers. Then a remarkably interesting service down near the fighting line at 10.30, with a sharp air, and the bright sun beating down upon us. The troops all round the square of the farm house, the poultry enjoying themselves on the straw manure heap in the centre, and when the singing grew in volume the hens settled themselves composedly to listen. Batteries nearby roared at intervals, and again how earnest everyone seemed to be. "Let this mind be in you"[252], we must be patient like Him, in bearing our trials now, in waiting God's will about the outcome: and we are promised to be partakers of His resurrection: we do not die, we are to live forever with God in the Great Land where sin is not and no more suffering or the fear of death. The next service was not to be. I had just got up to the area, on the edge of a village further along the line, and was chatting with the doctor in his little tumbled-down cottage (with the same regiment who had been shelled on Sunday week), when again that ugly scream, the bang and the shivering crash, and a red-tiled house across the triangular field in the village street belched up a cloud of pink, black and yellow smoke. There were some shouts, and men came streaming out in all directions. In two or three minutes another scream, the bang, the crash, the clouds of dust and smoke. Horses and carts came galloping along the road to us. Two or three minutes and another scream, bang, crash, and fumes. Four shells in all, each with the same deadly effect, up in the calm fresh morning sunshine. A few of the men remained in their cottages, going on with their washing and cooking and so on, and then stillness. We stood on the step, and thought of the dead, the wounded. They were in their billets, and the thought of that shell made its own picture. In the lull we had to think what was being done about the sufferers. At length the doctor agreed in deciding that we might venture forth, but it

---

252 **Phillipians** 2:5 'Let this mind be in you, which was also in Christ Jesus.'

must be with caution, for more shells with that deadly aim meant more destruction. But we went – one cannot bear to think of the men struggling there, uncared for. Very mercifully another shell did not come, though any minute, as we walked round the corner, we did not know when the next would come, or where. Every shell had hit a house, and yet we found only one killed and two wounded. Their mates had crept back to them and were attending to them. The man killed had a gash in the neck, but he died partly, I think, from shock. His face was so natural and composed – I prayed for those who loved him and whom he loved and we covered him with a blanket and a sack. The sergeant took in hand arrangements for getting him back for burial (he was one of Conran's men) and the rest of the time I was talking with the men for about half an hour as best I could, with 'words of life'. I confess I was a little relieved to have to get back for the rest of the day's work. A rest, and then preparation for the evening service. A large crowd in the disused grocer's store, our music a piano hauled in by the men from a house nearby, our lights – candles held here and there by the congregation with everybody standing. But we did sing, and read, and prayer – the thought of Christ's calmness through all this week of agitation, suffering, and death itself. I am sure that God's blessing was with us.

Monday, March 29th 1915, Sailly sur-la-Lys

A day of more peaceful interests today. Two great Lyddite[253] shells fell on the deserted town. An aeroplane fell with engine trouble just on the edge of this village, one of our own planes. I rode out in the car of the Captain of this section of aeroplanes. The machine had descended quite safely, though the engine had stopped suddenly – they are cool plucky men these aviators.

Rather a blow this morning – a message that the Bishop of London[254] could not come into our Division. So many dozens of people are keenly disappointed and all

---

253 In 1885, based on research by Hermann Sprengel, French chemist Eugène Turpin patented the use of pressed and cast picric acid in blasting charges and artillery shells. In 1887, the French government adopted a mixture of picric acid and guncotton under the name **Melinite**. In 1888, Britain started manufacturing a very similar mixture in Lydd, Kent, under the name **Lyddite**. Picric acid was used in the Battle of Omdurman, Second Boer War, the Russo-Japanese War, and WW1. Germany began filling artillery shells with TNT in 1902. Toluene was less readily available than phenol, and TNT is less powerful than picric acid, but improved safety of munitions manufacturing and storage caused replacement of picric acid by TNT for most military purposes between the World Wars.

254 At Easter 1915, the Bishop visited the front line at Ploegstreet, and celebrated Holy Communion for those members of the battalion not on duty in the front-line trenches and, on Easter Sunday, consecrated the battalion's graveyard there, but, *to his great regret was forbidden by the Commander-in-Chief to enter the wood* (the location of the front-line trench) and, *had to content himself with sending his chaplain, Rev G. Vernon Smith, who was also chaplain of the 2nd Battalion, in his place.* Apparently, there were a large number of other distinguished visitors to this trench as: *it was the only part of the British line that visitors could get into the front-line trench in daylight*; among these visitors were Gen. Allenby, Adm. Sir Lewis Bayley, Lieut.-Gen R. Baden Powell, Maj.-Gen. Sir R. Pole-Carew as well as Japanese and Russian officers. These visits might also explain the naming of the nearby "Tourist Line".

kinds of arrangements to be countermanded. However, he came into the next town and Conran and I rode over. They used my little Temporary Military Church to some effect and at 5.30 it was <u>packed out</u> with officers. I played the harmonium and the Bishop spoke so nicely. We, the 8th Division Chaplains, surrounded him before the meeting and got him to promise to come to the 8th Division! Then followed another meeting in the same place for the men – I played again and the place was fairly filled. At 6.30 he spoke from the steps of the Mairie in the Town Square, packed tight with Canadians and other soldiers – imagine it, 2000 to 3000 men! He could not be heard more than a few yards, but they cheered him again and again and sang "He's a jolly good fellow." In the distance round the corner, you can see the battered tower of the church in the deserted town and half an hour before you could have seen the fumes of the bursting shells rising up from it into a clear atmosphere. What scenes! I chatted with the Bishop a little about his brother, the Admiral Winnington Ingram[255], and with his Chaplain.

"I come" said the Bishop, "in the first place to bring you the love and the sympathy of all those at home who are thinking of you and praying for you – of all those thousands and hundreds of thousands whose homes you are saving by being out here. But I come also to claim the fruits of what I believe to be a 'Day of God' … The monstrous doctrine that 'might is right', that the Superman, that is the German State, shall rule the world by force has to be met and annulled[256]. It is given, I believe, to Britain as the Home of Freedom and the Mother of free countries, to do this. With this too we are fighting for the principle of National Honour. If treaties are only a 'scrap of paper' where is National Honour? The theory of the Superman is in direct contrast to the teaching of the Cross – the spirit of the Christ who came to serve, not to seek Self … this therefore is a Holy War. This being so, what manner of persons ought ye (the officers) to be in all holy life and godliness[257]? We must be men of prayer for peace, strength, guidance. If any of you lack wisdom, let him ask of God, who giveth liberally to all and upbraideth not"[258].

There was a quaint little scene this afternoon. Behind our billet is a strip of grass where the shop-keeper owner of the house has a small lawn-mower. 200 yds away,

---

255 Rear Admiral **Charles William Winnington-Ingram** (b.1850 – d.1923), grandson of Reverend Edward Winnington-Ingram, second son of the second Winnington Baronet, Sir Edward Winnington.

256 **superman**, German Übermensch, in philosophy, the superior man, who justifies the existence of the human race. "Superman" is a term significantly used by Friedrich Nietzsche, particularly in *Also sprach Zarathustra* (1883–85), although it had been employed by J.W. von Goethe and others. This superior man would not be a product of long evolution; rather, he would emerge when any man with superior potential completely masters himself and strikes off conventional Christian "herd morality" to create his own values, which are completely rooted in life on this earth.

257 **2 Peter 3:11** '*Seeing* then *that* all these things shall be dissolved, what manner *of persons* ought ye to be in *all* holy conversation and godliness.'

258 **James 1:5** 'If any of you lack wisdom, let him ask of God, that giveth to all *men* liberally, and upbraideth not; and it shall be given him.'

across two gardens is the big hole made by one of Sunday morning's bombs. This afternoon, an old refugee char-servant is amusing herself cutting the grass. High up in the blue sky one hears the buzz of an aeroplane – Madame hears it too. She looks up – pauses – goes on with the mowing. The aeroplane works nearer along the sky front – Madame pauses again, and you can see her thinking, "I think I'll do some potting in the potting shed". She strolls quickly into the potting shed in the corner, and shuts the door. By and by the aeroplane sails away – but Madame remains shut in, and there I leave her. It proves to be an English aeroplane – but a very wise precaution!

Tuesday, March 30th 1915, Sailly sur-la-Lys

A noisy night last night, as we are near the firing line here. Very few casualties on our side, but the machine guns and rifles kept up a tremendous fusillade. One looks out upon the flat landscape, under the clear moonlight just across the trees, and you think of the two lines of men facing each other, all bent on killing. The artillery shakes your windows, the machine guns rattle on the frosty air, and you go off to sleep.

I saw a sad scene this morning. As I rode down to the lines, there was a tremendous flare in the morning sunlight – evidently a farm burning. It had caught from one of the soldiers' fires and in an hour and a half it was a heap of ash dust. The distressing part was the grief of the poor farmwife who was young, and her husband a prisoner with the Germans, three small children, Henri a month old, a little girl of 3 and a half, and a boy of 4 and a half. She was inconsolable, and a group of neighbouring wives joined in her tears, and when her old mother came up from another farm, it all reached a climax. However, plenty of willing hands got out her cattle, a churn, some chairs and bedding and a few odds and ends. A farm cart was brought, drawn by some artillery horses, and soon she was settled in her brother-in-law's farm half a mile away – the baby boy slept on peacefully through it all. They are very poor, I fear, and were bewildered enough, so there was plenty to do in the way of putting the best face on it. It could have been worse, i.e. if it had been done by a German shell, which might have killed the children and herself as well, and she will get some compensation from the government, the accident being due to military occupation, and she has her brother-in-law's house to go to. But I felt deeply sorry for them and felt justified, after careful enquires, in giving her 20 francs for the emergency, out of the Emergency Fund. What strained and uncertain lives hundreds of these poor people are living in just now. Another poor soul, in a cottage close by, near which a shell burst on Sunday, was carrying on in the house somehow – I asked her how? She said on a Government allowance as her husband was at the war and she had not heard from him since September. "A prisoner?" "Nay" she did not know. "His comrades said that he was dead." She had not heard officially, so was hoping on. The Bishop of London, speaking of prayer for fortitude, said how we must see this thing through, we must 'stick it' and said how the women at home were sticking it too – and so do these patient souls also.

Wednesday, March 31st 1915, Sailly sur-la-Lys

It has been a busy day. A young officer to give breakfast to and then to help on his way and a long ride to the further lines, from which we could see a ridge held by the Germans, and the battered church, looking only a stone's throw away and daffodils and cornblades peeping. Big gun traction engines – a cutting wind – eggs, oranges, chocolate, butter, candles for sale in various cottage windows and crowds of men. I made preliminary plans for Good Friday and Easter Day, and had a visit from a keen young officer in charge of Bomb-throwers[259], asking for a service of Holy Communion among his men on Easter Day.

Conference with other Chaplains about co-operating where possible for H.C. services on Easter Day. Handed over £50 of the Fund to another Chaplain for his special purposes – Club and Churches – for which he was very grateful. I made a list of the burials during [...*censored*...] fight for recording on boards, including four Indians buried with Christian prayers.

Drink difficulty in England is evidently a most serious one, and the deputation of non-teetotallers asking for prohibition is most significant. Munitions are a most solemn need. We can see where the German guns lie from our billet windows and if they thought that we were likely to be short of shells, how soon they would hammer these houses down? Are they short of ammunition? Their guns have been silent today.

A beautiful sunset – an opal background with flakes of purple and brilliant crimson, and away in the East, one of our aeroplanes sailing away over the German lines, rings of smoke puffs following him in a long line as he wends on his brave way. Now and again you can see the flash of fire against the darkening sky, a little pin point of light of the bursting shell – splendid courage! He will come back later after a moonlight reconnaissance as the troops march mainly at night, and will probably bring back valuable information.

Friday, April 2nd 1915, Sailly sur-la-Lys

A very crowded day of services and arranging for Easter Day (I now have <u>six</u> battalions to shepherd) and fitting up a fresh Temporary Church. We now have a linen loft, long disused and rather dirty, but it will soon look better. It is rather out of the way and I confess that I am angry that, amid the many places there are about, the Authorities could not have afforded us a building and situation more worthy of the purpose. A beautiful day, with no bombs and only one shell which fell very wide.

---

259   The British bombing team usually consisted of nine men at a time: an NCO, two throwers, two carriers, two bayonet-men to defend the team and two 'spare' men for use when casualties were incurred. As an attack or raid reached an enemy trench the grenadiers would be responsible for racing down the trench and throwing grenades into each dugout they passed: this invariably succeeded in purging dugouts of their human occupants in an attempt at surrender (often not accepted as they were promptly shot or stabbed). This tactical group were termed 'bomb-throwers' at the direct request of the Grenadier Guards, who felt they already had a monopoly on the term 'grenadier'. See photo page 108.

Saturday, April 3rd 1915, Sailly sur-la-Lys

Another very full day – still arranging services and finishing fitting up the new temporary Military Church. I left the other to my successors, so this meant all here 'de novo'. But it is worth it – we have a much poorer building here, in fact a turnip-storing loft, but tonight with lanterns and a little simple draping it looks quite nice. The C.E.M.S. members work well. If only we had the late building! – one of the Chaplains has called it our Cathedral, and the other Chaplains have had lanterns services there. We wonder what the Germans are doing now. Only a shell or two today along our front, and no aeroplanes – but how badly they have behaved at sea, over the Falaba![260] Now that we have moved on I can say that the battle we were in was Neuve Chapelle. It <u>was</u> a fight – the crowds of dead and those horrible black shells, sights that we shall never forget and I shall never forget that one shell. The flowers are coming out, the buds are bursting – how wrong war seems. Some, who were at both, have described Neuve Chapelle as being as bad as Mons[261] – I think it must have been worse for the Germans than Mons was for us.

Sunday, April 4th Easter Day 1915, Sailly sur-la-Lys

Very tiring but a charming day. 7 a.m. Holy Communion in our tiny soldiers Club (two rooms in a cottage) 24 present including one of our latest V.C.[262]S. Neame[263] (who comes, by the bye, from Kent). At 8 a.m. about 110 in the fresh temporary Military Church, which really looked not so bad, though I think the rats and mice felt the commotion of so many humans! Three Generals present. An enormous service

---

260 The **Thrasher incident**, as it became known in U.S. media, nearly became the start of America's involvement in WW1. On March 28th, 1915, the British steamship RMS *Falaba* was torpedoed and sunk by German U-boat *U-28*. In the incident, 104 people were killed, including one American passenger – Leon Chester Thrasher, a 31-year-old mining engineer from Massachusetts.

261 The **Battle of Mons** was the first major action of the BEF, 23rd August 1914, a subsidiary action of the Battle of the Frontiers. At Mons, the British Army attempted to hold the line of the Mons-Condé Canal against the advancing German 1st Army. Although the British fought well and inflicted disproportionate casualties on the numerically superior Germans, they were eventually forced to retreat due both to the greater strength of the Germans and the sudden retreat of the French Fifth Army, which exposed the British right flank.

262 The **Victoria Cross (VC)** is the highest military decoration awarded for valour "in the face of the enemy" to members of the armed forces of Britain. It takes precedence over all other orders, decorations and medals. It may be awarded to a person of any rank in any service and to civilians under military command. The VC is usually presented to the recipient or to their next of kin by the British monarch at an investiture held at Buckingham Palace. The VC was introduced on 29th January 1856 by Queen Victoria to honour acts of valour during the Crimean War. Since then, the medal has been awarded 1357 times to 1354 individual recipients.

263 Lieutenant General **Sir Philip Neame** VC, KBE, CB, DSO, KStJ (b.1888 – d.1978). Neame was 26 years old, and a lieutenant in the 15th Field Company, Corps of Royal Engineers. On 19th December 1914 at Neuve Chapelle, Neame, in the face of very heavy fire, engaged the Germans in a single-handed bombing attack, killing and wounding a number of them. He was able to check the enemy advance for three-quarters of an hour and to rescue all the wounded whom it was possible to move. He was the member of the Neame family of Shepherd Neame, Faversham, Kent.

in a barn at 10.30 and another in yet another barn at 11.30, and a really beautiful one – beautiful in spirit (the regiment being a particularly nice one) in a factory at 12.15. All were nice, but the last one was so noticeably serious and attentive. I had ordered 1000 of the Bishop of London's Eastertide leaflet and gave away about 800 at the 11.30 and 12.15[264] After lunch the Bishop of London looked in on our mess but I was out and so missed him, but he saw the Colonel and two or three officers, and the Baptist Chaplain. The message announcing that he would be coming reached me an hour and a half after he had come! It was nice and sympathetic of him and he left a message which will do good, saying how sorry he was not to have been able to see more of the men in the Division. Everybody was pleased that the call was made. A very crowded service this evening – the Church was packed with men standing at the back and down the stairs, and a number had to go away. My heart was very full seeing officers and men from various regiments in whose ranks were so many gaps, as I spoke of Christ having abolished death, and brought life and immortality to light – those noble men, whom it has been such a pleasure to know. We shall meet them again.

No shells today, and no bombs. The Germans put out a scroll near the trenches, "A happy Easter, let us have peace today". Attached to one of the bombs that they dropped over [...*censored*...] on Thursday was a long streamer on which was written, "A happy Easter from those you have driven from the air."

Monday, April 5th 1915, Sailly sur-la-Lys

There has been pouring rain, almost incessantly all day today.

Holy Communion at 8 a.m. with only 1 present and another service at 10.30 in a barn with 46 present. Another at a further barn at 12 with 5 present with the arrangements made by a young officer who has received the D.S.O[265] just lately, and my horse held by a corporal who has had the D.C.M.[266]

---

264 *'Thoughts and Prayers for Soldiers at the Front by the **Bishop of London**'* Easter 1915 'O Lord, Who died for me to-day; forgive me all my sins, and forgive too my comrades their sins, and help us even while we fight them, not to hate our enemies'.

265 The **Distinguished Service Order (DSO)** is a military decoration of Britain awarded for meritorious or distinguished service by officers of the armed forces during wartime, typically in actual combat. Instituted on 6th September 1886 by Queen Victoria the first DSOs awarded were dated 25th November 1886. It is typically awarded to officers ranked Major (or its equivalent) or higher, but the honour has sometimes been awarded to especially valorous junior officers. 8981 DSOs were awarded during WW1.

266 The **Distinguished Conduct Medal (DCM)** was an extremely high-level award for bravery. It was a second level military decoration awarded to other ranks of the British Army. The medal was instituted in 1854, during the Crimean War, to recognise gallantry within the other ranks, for which it was equivalent of the Distinguished Service Order (DSO) awarded for bravery to commissioned officers.

Tuesday, April 6th 1915, Sailly sur-la-Lys

A long day and a very interesting one, ending with a ride that was pleasant only in the Mark Tapley[267] sense, with a cutting wind, prickly hail and a deep sympathy with the men of our brigade returning to the trenches after a week's respite, and passing into an area much shelled today.

Wednesday, April 7th 1915, Sailly sur-la-Lys

A long day, during which I saw some horse-jumping. It was strange sitting in a park with the band playing, and tea being served at one end of the stand, watching spirited and well-groomed horses being paraded and paced and put to hurdles and water jumps, while now and again our great guns boomed on the other side of the park walls, and outside many of the streets bore a dreary and deserted appearance. The lunatic asylum is not very far from the trenches on that side of town – so many things in this war are strange.

There is a marked change in the German tone, which I for one have found myself gauging. Now comes Hilaire Belloc's article in the last 'Land and Water' bearing out the same estimate. Their views are much more subdued and less arrogant now, and yet one misgiving came to me, as the loud conversation of some of the fast and horsey officers grouped there, betrayed lives so grievously unserious and immoral. Does not much in England need chastening? It must needs be that He will have 'brought us to our knees' – not in the German sense, but as a conquered people notwithstanding. Fine horses so many of them – how great is the goodness that provides us with servants like these to do our work and to afford us pleasure.

In the town I passed a Rue des Jesuites, and the Rue des 12 Apotres – I joked with our genial little Roman Catholic Chaplain, a cultured and very pleasant person who is a Jesuite, by explaining that to get safely home I had to turn away from the Jesuites and follow the way of the 12 Apostles.

Thursday, April 8th 1915, Sailly sur-la-Lys

My Brigade moved back towards the trenches, located on the outskirts of the village which was shelled last Sunday week. It has been shelled from time to time since – the day before yesterday about 30 came into it all in a direct line for the church, which was eventually reached and hammered. I went into the church, it was beautifully kept

---

267 A character in *The Life and Adventures of Martin Chuzzlewit* by Charles Dickens, (1843–44). Mark Tapley is always cheerful, which he decides does not reflect well on him because he is always in happy circumstances and it shows no strength of character to be happy when one has good fortune. He decides to test his cheerfulness by seeing if he can maintain it in the worst circumstances possible. To this end, he accompanies Martin to the United States. They attempt to start new lives in a swampy, disease-filled settlement named "Eden", but both nearly die of malaria. Mark finally finds himself in a situation in which it can be considered a virtue to remain in good spirits.

inside, but where the shell had struck it was battered and strewn. Some of the images were, of their kind, tastefully modelled and coloured, and a fine organ fills the small western gallery with aluminium pipes. The children's altar was rather nice, except for a doll-like figure of the Christ Child, dressed in a cope of gold over a crimson silk robe. The iron gateway was smashed by a shell, and some of it was melted by the heat. Fighting is suddenly very still with nothing from the German side, although our guns pound away occasionally. A terrific storm, hail, snow and a driving wind. A portable harmonium came today paid for out of the Fund and it will be a great gain.

Saturday April 10th 1915, Sailly sur-la-Lys

I took a ride round the newly shelled village and its outskirts this morning, arranging services. One lad was killed outright last night – he will be placed in the corner of a field near here, the Churchyard having been desolated, and the Church being practically a ruin[268]. Fighting is quiet near us, but I think things are brisk enough in some other directions.

Sunday April 11th 1915, Sailly sur-la-Lys

A beautiful day. Shelling during morning services and a funeral at 4 p.m., and Evening Service at 5.45. As on each Sunday we had an interesting discussion in the Mess on Socialism, Christian Socialism "Why does God allow wickedness and war to be?" – the differences between the churches, self-interestedness in politics and the possibility of a state of society in which there shall be no poor. The shells fell short and passed over our area, but none came any nearer than half a mile away during Service time. I noticed those big black puffs during one address. A large muster and a beautiful service in the warm spring sunshine, in a green field just at the edge of the shelled village, with another in a barn and a third in yet another barn, followed by Holy Communion, for which the portable harmonium is a great help. A number of aeroplanes this evening, our own and enemy ones – I hear that one of the latter was shot down in the clear rosy sunset of a still Sunday evening, while we in this temporary Military Church, and thousands of others everywhere, were singing Eastertide hymns of love and life – how wrong it all seems.

Monday April 12th 1915, Sailly sur-la-Lys

Better weather – more fighting in the night – they say that some shells fell short of us – but I heard nothing. They also say that a number of prisoners were taken each side of us. French came into the Division today – he passed by our Mess, also Douglas Haig, Rawlinson and Robertson – a galaxy of Generals. French spoke to

---

268 Sapper **Frederick John Couchman** (b.1891 – d.1915) Royal Engineers 1st (Home Counties) Field Coy. Son of William and Edith Louisa Couchman, of 55, Clarence Rd., Eastbourne. Born at Willingdon, Eastbourne.

one Brigade and I hear that he will do so to other of our Brigades during the week. Haig looks a fit and healthy specimen, Rawlinson looks keen and French seemed, in the clear sunshine, older looking than on the day of the King's visit. All the same, he is strong-looking and 'all there'.

Tuesday April 13th 1915, Sailly sur-la-Lys

We hear a Zeppelin went north of us and dropped 20 bombs last night[269] and also this afternoon an aeroplane dropped bombs over our late area.

I have bought a piano today from an evacuated Frenchman for £9, and a Commanding officer will find room on a baggage wagon behind the column when it moves on! Meanwhile, we are in for some nice concerts and many people are pleased. As things are, our Brigade will have a full week out of the trenches.

Weds April 14th 1915, Sailly sur-la-Lys

I have had a busy day arranging about the piano, etc. The Baptist has gone and I had to make a speech at his departure (as Mess President).

I got into the town we left and the Club still goes briskly – crowded and the baths! And they run the cinematograph pictures daily, making the place a properly 'chancelled' church at different times – it is all very nice. The Fund is doing <u>nobly</u> – I rather think that in another two or three months we shall have to ask for more. Four Chaplains are now using it and I see other developments. It is curious reading in the notes of 'Eyewitness at Headquarters' what I have written in these notes. His article in yesterday's Daily Telegraph e.g. gives what I wrote in my last two letters.

Thursday April 15th 1915, Sailly sur-la-Lys

Tonight, as every night, we hear the roar and rattle of the machine guns and the rifle fire, but – from the collecting point – not a single casualty. The men use their trenches well, and there are fewer instances of their getting careless and venturesome, peeping out over the parapet and so on, and by not disdaining to use the periscope, they can save themselves much. I have just had to let a mother know that it is certain that her son is killed, as one of his fellow officers' saw him hit, and fall.

Another Division near here today, and some boys from my first curacy I hear by name, are in it – I must try and look them up tomorrow. A Roman Catholic chaplain has come to this mess, who was at Shorncliffe at the same time as I was there – a nice man.

---

269 **Poperinghe**, 15 miles N of Sailly. During WW1, the town was one of only two in Belgium not under German occupation. As the railhead for the BEF, it was used to billet British troops and also provided a safe area for field hospitals.

In streams the Otter havoc makes,
So many fish from them he takes.
No wonder that the Anglers hate him,
And gladly would exterminate him.

Nestlé's Milk can always be relied on

NESTLÉ'S SWISS MILK
BY APPOINTMENT

NESTLÉ'S POST CARD.
No. 5.

Nestlé's Milk is far superior to ordinary town milk.

(Communications may be written below.)

(Name and Address only.)

AFFIX HALFPENNY STAMP HERE.

'The pictures I think are better than the poetry!
Much love from DADDY'

Wednesday, April 17th 1915, Sailly sur-la-Lys

One boy from the next parish to my first curacy was the son of one of my Sunday School teachers of those days!

Your Fund seems likely to expand its operations! The Chaplains of this new Division were casting about for opportunities, and had to check because of lack of means! Monies for the moment that they ought to have, and have not. I suggested to the Senior Chaplain (rank of Colonel) that they should apply to the Sailors' and Soldiers' C. of E. Institutes Association and meanwhile, if they will, they shall have £50 from us. It is just for when the troops are newly arrived, looking round for an environment, and impressionable, that our chance comes in to give them a place, or places at once. The Fund is literally an 'Emergency' one. The Col. Chaplain will come and talk with me on Monday about these things. I am busy talking with men nearly all the live-long day. The fighting is quiet with big guns roaring away in the long distance. French is in the village again this afternoon and he will inspect our Brigade, we think, on Wednesday.

God's providences some of them come home to us with extra benevolence. I learn tonight that Major Higginbotham had word of his wife's death only about a week before Neuve Chapelle. The separation was not long – such a nice man that[270].

Sunday April 18th 1915, Sailly sur-la-Lys

A full, but very interesting, Sunday – Holy Communion at 7 a.m. with 7 present, then Holy Communion at 9.30 a.m. with no one present, and a 10.15 Service in a field at the shelled village and at 11.15 another ditto and at 12 p.m. another ditto. All very hearty and serious, the first one not so large as people are nervous nearer the shelled area, and at 6 p.m. another large service with the bomb-throwers.

A beautiful day. Late hours. An eye case where the bullet grazed the rifle and something wood or bullet 'dusted' the eye. It is a boon for these men to have an expert like Colonel Pickard to know what to do in cases like these – he is clever with eyes, but it will have to come out. Poor lad, he had to be told this morning and he took it sadly, but quietly and simply, like a soldier. The good Colonel is a strong and kindly little man and very clever. Surely enough, when the eye was removed, it revealed a tiny fragment of lead about the size of a very small pin's head, close by the nerve channel.

---

270 Maj. **Charles Ernest Higginbotham**, Staff Officer, 2nd Bn, Northampton Regt (b.1866 – d.1915). Born in Glasgow. Higginbotham was appointed DAAG Standerton District, Transvaal on 2nd November 1903. On Staff at Devonport as Supt Gymnasia Western District (July 1899 to July 1902) during Boer War but served subsequently in South Africa October 1902 to May 1907. Made Major in June 1907. Went overseas with 2nd Bn in November 1914, killed whilst second in command at the Battle of Neuve Chapelle in March 1915. His Commanding Officer wrote from France "Had he alone survived I should be content for the future of the Regiment. He was everything to me, during the war, as a soldier." He was a notable cricketer for the Army team.

It will save the other eye. His father, strangely enough lost an eye also, in the Boer War. Good success last night – a house mined and blown up which is used by snipers. Five officers they say, taken and other prisoners.

Tuesday April 20th 1915, Sailly sur-la-Lys

The late Club is being carried on well and the place is <u>packed</u> with troops. One lives among streams of filing Khaki figures and the Club takes few enough, I think, for the great need. There must be no mistake about it – England must go into this fully supplied with every need, men, guns, bullets, and <u>shells</u>. How thankful we ought to be that the nation has men like Kitchener who know how to 'labour and to wait' – to get their forces in hand and not to strike before, but to strike then when ready.

Wednesday April 21st 1915, Sailly sur-la-Lys

Field Marshal French inspected our Brigade today. He is a fit looking man, short, thick-set, with a ruddy skin and neck and a very white moustache. He spoke to each Battalion in separate fields, and to us three Field Ambulances last. His words to our people were simple and good. "I have come as Commander-in-Chief to inspect these Field Ambulances. Your Divisional General has told me what splendid work you have done and I congratulate you on it. I think special praise is due to you as Territorials. You are engaged in professions and civil occupations differently to us, whose business it is, and I recognise the self-sacrifice and patriotism your coming out here has meant. I would like to say that I am proud to belong to a country in which such patriotism and self-sacrifice are possible. You have brought high abilities, willingly, to the service of your King and country. You have done your duty splendidly, and I know you will go on to do so as long as it lasts." Our Colonel of the <u>first</u> Territorial Field Ambulance was brought out to the front, and the senior Colonel of the Ambulances present then called for 'three cheers for Field Marshal Sir John French'. They were acknowledged with the military salute and the Field Marshal with the Generals, Sir Douglas Haig (1st Army), Sir Henry Rawlinson[271] (IV Army Corps), Major General Davies[272]

---

271 Sir **Henry Rawlinson** (b.1864 – d.1925) Served in the Myanmar expedition of 1886–87 under Lord Roberts, in the Sudan campaign (1898) with Lord Kitchener, and in the Second Boer War (1899–1901). In 1914 Rawlinson was given command of IV Corps sent to assist the Belgian Army against the Seige of Antwerp. In 1916 he was appointed Lieutenant General of Fourth Army, playing a primary role in the Battle of the Somme of July–November 1916, where his arguments for a limited infantry offensive contrasted markedly (and ultimately disastrously) with Sir Douglas Haig's breakthrough plans. In 1919, he was dispatched to Russia as commander of the allied forces sent to attempt to overthrow the Bolshevik government. In 1920, he was sent to command the British forces in India, a position he held until his death.

272 Major General Sir **Francis John Davies** GOC 8th Division.

(VIII Division), Brigadier Generals Lowry Cole (25th Brigade)[273], Pinny (23rd)[274], and Oxley [275](24th Brigade), with a big retinue of Staff Officers marched off, and we, after an hour's standing on a rather chilly afternoon were glad to warm ourselves by marching off also.

The piano is answering – there is a concert every night this week for the different battalions of my own Brigade, who are out this week from the trenches. The Battalion taking charge of it will have two nights and they are paying half the price – £4.10, so the Fund is less by that amount – we are getting on.

Thursday April 22nd 1915, Sailly sur-la-Lys
We have got out a badminton set! And have had some good games after tea today.

Friday April 23rd 1915, Sailly sur-la-Lys
Accumulating measures! It is a relief to read Asquith's re-assuring speech and Lloyd George's account of things in the House of Commons. The impression in the air was certainly that we are suffering at this moment from shortage of munitions. It appears the shortage is only a proportional one to the progress of time and increasing needs – a very different thing. One realises on the spot, in an acute way, how vital the question is. Shells on our side literally fall between us and death and they make us a 'salvation zone'. It is comforting to see the big guns coming along and we are obviously going to profit by the experience of Neuve Chapelle. The Artillery will

---

273 Brig General **Arthur Willougby George Lowry Cole**. 25th Infantry Brigade (b.1860 – d.1915). The son of Colonel Arthur Lowry Cole and Frances Elizabeth Hatton, married Mary Gertrude Browning, daughter of Thomas Browning. Fought in the Burma Campaign between 1885 and 1887, West African Campaign in 1900, Boer War in 1901. He was Commandant of the North Nigeria Regiment between 1904 and 1907. He fought in the West African Campaign in 1906. Died of wounds received May 3rd 1915. See footnote 295.

274 Major-General **Sir Reginald John Pinney**, KCB (b.1863 – d.1943). While commanding a division at the Battle of Arras in 1917, he was immortalised as the "cheery old card" of Siegfried Sassoon's poem "The General". Pinney served in South Africa during the Boer War with the Royal Fusiliers, and at the outbreak of the WW1 was given command of a brigade sent to reinforce the Western Front in November 1914. He led it in the early part of 1915, taking heavy losses at the Battle of Neuve Chapelle. That September he was given command of the 35th Division, a New Army division of "bantam" soldiers, which first saw action at the Battle of the Somme; after three months in action, he was exchanged with the commander of the 33rd Division. He commanded the 33rd at Arras in 1917, with mixed results, and through the Spring Offensive in 1918, where the division helped stabilise the defensive line after the Portuguese Expeditionary Corps was routed. After the war, he retired to rural Dorset.

275 Brig General **Reginald Stuart Oxley** (b.1863 – d.1951) CMC CB. Commissioned in the York and Lancaster Regiment in 1884, but transferred to the King's Royal Rifle Corps the following November. His only active service was in the Manipur Expedition (1891). Oxley served as Brigade Major, 12th Infantry Brigade, in South Africa (1899–1900). He was DAAG North-West District (1901–4), CO 1st Battalion King's Royal Rifle Corps (1907–11) and GSO1 Staff College (1912–14). He went to war as GSO1 II Corps (August–December 1914). After a period commanding GHQ Troops, he was made GOC 24th Brigade, 8th Division, on 17th March 1915, after its GOC, Brigadier-General F C Carter, had a nervous breakdown following the Battle of Neuve Chapelle (10–12 March) in which 8th Division had played a leading part.

'A part of the line waiting to be inspected by Sir John French
(the distinguished officer at the far off end is probably well known to you)'

adopt closer tactics, sweeping barbed-wire with greater thoroughness, and the Infantry will not be pushed forward too speedily, while we will hope that the Cavalry will be well up to time. It will certainly be a great battle and it appears clear that the enemy is massing reinforcements opposite. I have seen plans of some of the dispositions today. Our aeroplanes have done good work, and our maps can even note patches of barbed-wire.

Meanwhile, the country side just off the danger zone smiles with the opening of spring, in spite of a sharp east wind. Soldiers help the farmers with their ploughing, rolling and drilling: they make toys for the little children, give small boys (and girls) rides upon their horses: the little French people, boys and girls, kick away at the Tommies footballs and shout out "Goal!" "Off-side", "Well played" and sing "It's a long way to Tipperary" and "Hullo! Hullo". The swallows begin to twitter in the telegraph wires and the world is healthy and natural up to a line – but there potential death flies from time to time through the air by day, and nearly all through the night. Such a roar of guns at night, and the machine guns rattle just across the fields hour after hour.

Saturday April 24th 1915, Sailly sur-la-Lys
A man just in, shot through the arm while on listening patrol – good brave fellows, men like that. They creep along the ground between the English and the Germans, to see and hear what is doing, principally to listen for sounds of sapping from their

trench to ours. These saps are awful things – we have made some successful ones, you will have seen, under Hill 60[276]. How grieving it all is – men burrowing like savage animals to kill and overthrow.

Sunday April 25th 1915, Sailly sur-la-Lys

Sunday – a long day today. Early service at 7 a.m. – a nice full service in a barn and another crowded service in the turnip loft, the General (the chief one) present[277]. I am always glad when the Generals can be there. A very <u>large</u> number with men standing at the back and down the stairs again! It was a moving service and I spoke of God, the Good One, Al-mighty, who cannot let wrong triumph over Right, and Our Father, who loves each one of us perfectly – We are in His hands. We had a full service this afternoon, with convalescent soldiers going back to the firing lines soon (most of them). We did enjoy it, all of us I think, and a fairly full evening service but not so large as before. Goudge talked most helpfully on "Fear God – Honour the King."[278]

There was an intense discussion this evening as to whether we should retaliate on the Germans with asphyxiating gas[279]. We develop now, almost invariably, some intensely interesting and profitable discussions of a Sunday evening. Some of the hot spirits are for immediate and virulent retaliation after the German method. There happened to be a passage in the Daily Papers from the Archbishop of Canterbury on this very point, agreeing upon the provocation, but counselling restraint. Heavy firing all round tonight. The enemy are going to put forth their utmost strength now. I am sure that God prospers Right.

Monday April 26th 1915, Sailly sur-la-Lys

A lad from the Rifle Brigade has just been brought in wounded in the chin, while doing some brave patrol and barbed-wire work in front of the trenches. Another plucky fellow in the same patrol was killed, and four others wounded.

We have been in [...*censored*...] today actually to do some shopping and buy prizes! We have some sports tomorrow and I am one of the Committee – a jeweller's shop had quite a nice selection. There was an aeroplane alarm while we were there, (we motored in and out) and as we came out, one of our armoured trains was blazing away in the direction of [...*censored*...]. We stopped and watched for a little time.

---

276   **The Battle of Hill 60** (17th April – 7th May 1915) took place south of Ypres. Hill 60 was a spoil heap 250 yards (230 m) long and 150 feet (46 m) high, made from the diggings of a cutting for the Ypres-Comines railway. The hill formed a low rise on the crest of Ypres ridge, at the southern flank of the Ypres Salient and was named after the contour which marked its boundary. Both sides used gas warfare, as well as sappers tunneling under the hill to place demolishing mines. British mines were blown at 7.30 a.m. on April 17th.

277   Major General **Francis Davies**.

278   1 Peter 2:17 'Honour all *men*. Love the brotherhood. Fear God. Honour the king.'

279   First used on a large-scale by the Germans in 1915 at the Second Battle of Ypres. Chlorine Gas was a by-product of the German industrialised chemical and dying industries.

Very pleasant weather and it being Monday I had some badminton this evening. The Colonel is vigorous and athletic, but not nimble round a shuttlecock. We are all a little rusty, but we get great fun out of it all, and life is quite tolerable. However there has been much rifle fire today and a great clamour of heavy gun firing.

Tuesday April 27th 1915, Sailly sur-la-Lys

The sports have been historic and very successful, and the afternoon was brilliant. The Colonel tried my feelings a little by insisting on my giving out the prizes at the sports, even though he was present. He spoke nicely and all went well. No photographs, but it would have been good to take some. Artillery boomed all the time sounding quite close – it is always artillery just now. We are not far from Hill 60, and night and day the ammunition goes on being used up. Hill 60 seems to have been very costly, but as always, more costly to our friends over the way[280]. We are in for serious times, and the spirit of keenness of officers and men is most resolute and valorous, calm, anxious to achieve and subdue – in some cases to abolish and exterminate – they are good stuff.

We are part of the Ypres[281] fighting now apparently, though possibly making an attack soon on our own account – the conflict sways just at present along our front. The temper of the troops is splendid, the Kaiser will have found by now that the term 'contemptible' was long ago misplaced, before <u>he</u> was born.

Wednesday April 29th 1915, Sailly sur-la-Lys

There is no harm in your knowing that we are now to the left of Neuve Chapelle, and liable to move any day or hour. Shells now – shells and other munitions are what we want.

I have been today again into the reserve trenches – they were shelled yesterday afternoon after I had left and today the shelling was busy over the 'shelled' village to our left. It was a curious and fascinating experience to sit on one's horse chatting with an officer, in brilliant warm sunshine, beneath a clear blue sky in which a strong big British aeroplane circled above us. Rich green pastures before us, strewed with blazing daises and buttercups and ploughed fields around popping up long regular lines of corn blades, butterflies dancing here and there, and to look out across the fields at the pretty little village, its blue-tiled Church spire and its red-tiled houses and thatched cottages fringed with orchard buds and blossom – to hear the recurrent

---

280 In the attack on 7th April, the British lost only seven casualties. On 1st May the 1st Dorsets lost over 90 men to gas poisoning; 207 were brought to dressing stations where 46 men died immediately and another twelve men died later; the battalion had only 72 survivors. Of 2413 British casualties admitted to hospital, 227 men died. The 13th Brigade casualties from 17th–19th April were 1362 men and the 15th Brigade lost 1586 casualties from 1st–7th May, out of the 5th Division total of 3100 losses.

281 The **Second Battle of Ypres**; from 21st April – 25th May 1915 for control of the strategic Flemish town of Ypres.

'bang' and to see the thick clouds of red and brown dust circling up in the picture, as one shell after another reached its mark. Happily, the Germans still keep to the plan of going straight for the line of the church, and troops and people go on living in a circle of impunity in the houses and places round. Three enemy aeroplanes reconnoitered over us earlier in the morning, and the air was peppered with white cloudlets from our shells. I found one curiosity nearby – our anti-aircraft guns had been vigorously bombarding the aeroplanes and one often wonders why falling bits of shell have not dropped on someone's head. Well, this morning I saw the half of a shell that nearly did, as it fell into the little ditch of a hedge close to which one man was cutting another man's hair!

Thursday April 30th 1915, Sailly sur-la-Lys

The Ypres fighting is hot. We would like to be closer in it, but at the same time this month of quieter doings has been very restful. We are reaping the fruits of Neuve Chapelle. The other side have been increasingly cautious and their trenches are now more remote from ours, and it will take plenty of time for the respective lines to worm closer to each other.

There are now just one or two cases each night but I have been out collecting tonight – a weird and solemn proceeding, 300 yds from the fighting line, in the area of flying bullets. Everybody moves silently, no shouting, no loud conversation, no lights; dark figures greet each other in the star-lit gloom behind battered farm buildings and dishevelled hedgerows. All along the flank the incessant snap and sing of the bullets goes on. We pass through the shelled village this time straight down the line of the shelling. Three shells only today and they seldom come after twilight. Seeing lights in a cottage right under the line of fire, not 100 yds from the church, and four doors from a house that has been hit, I went in. It was occupied by a man, his wife and a son of 16 and they have been there all the time. It gave one a sense of astonishing trustfulness. I asked them had they not moved away at all – and they said not. Were they not afraid? "Yes. But where had they to go? One can only hope for the best". Poverty – Patience – Hope – Courage – Trust – Desperation – how much there is wrapped up in it.

Tea was fetched for us by the kindness of one of the young officers in the afternoon, in the farm billet of a small mess. One of them, Conybeare[282] received the Military Cross for Neuve Chapelle and his deed is recounted in yesterday's Daily Telegraph.

---

282 Lt. (Dr.) **John Josias Conybeare** MC (b.1888 – d.1967), Read classics before turning to medicine and was very nearly qualified when war broke out in 1914; active service in the Oxfordshire and Buckinghamshire Light Infantry in which he was already commissioned as a territorial. He served in France on the Somme.

Another £25 of the Fund to a Chaplain from a fresh Division, who was glad of tips and will do good work I think, his name is Pattinson and he was a trooper in the Jameson raid[283].

Friday May 1st 1915, Sailly sur-la-Lys

Tennyson wrote : "and by the meadow trenches blow the faint sweet cuckoo flowers[284]"

There were plenty of flowers to be found in the soft bright sunshine this morning, though no cuckoo ones. What we did find by <u>our</u> trenches was the glow of bursting shells. The day began at daybreak with a furious cannonade, first from their side and answered adequately, very adequately, by ours. I went down soon after 9, things being a little quieter. On the way to the 2nd Battalion which I was visiting, I was stopped by the ominous plunk, zing, plop. It was better being this side of the ring, so I stopped and watched 14 of them drop round about the cross pathway which was the route across the field. A plump country mother came running out of her house with her little son (about Eric's size) holding on to her hand. Her house was just the other side of the ring and four other peasants came out of their cottages too. I left them promenading disconsolately up and down the dusty roadway, waiting for the assault to abate – they will have returned by now, ready to take their chance of what may happen next.

Two hostile aeroplanes circled the town we had just left, and one took an ugly bee-line back over our heads here. They had no bombs, however, as far as we have heard. One of our shells, aimed at them we are told, dropped through the roof of the Mairie down into the unoccupied Council Chamber. It appears that the Germans wanted to carry us by attack, but found our position stronger than they had expected.

Not such good billets here – for some weeks past I have slept on the floor, over five weeks now, which is not so bad as my man Peter washes it every week or so, but the mice are a nuisance running about, and I have a suspicion, over oneself sometimes. This is the third lot of billets since my leave home, each lot a little worse than the last. But the real adventures will begin, no doubt, when we move on, whenever that may be.

Monday May 3rd 1915, Sailly sur-la-Lys

Over to the other place today, the Chaplain having gone in rather a hurry and the Club being rather, not at 'sixes and sevens', but at least at 'fives and sixes'.

---

283 The **Jameson Raid** (29th December 1895 – 2nd January 1896) was a botched raid on Paul Kruger's Transvaal Republic carried out by a British colonial statesman Leander Starr Jameson and Bechuanaland policemen over the New Year. It was intended to trigger an uprising by the primarily British expatriate workers (known as Uitlanders) in the Transvaal who were expected to recruit an army and prepare for an insurrection. No uprising took place, but the raid was an inciting factor in the 2nd Boer War and the Second Matabele War.

284 *The May Queen*, 1833 (in The Lady of Shalott and other poems).

A glorious morning, and I had a grand gallop along the river bank. I saw Mr. Stanley, who gives good account of Church Army plans for Red Cross cars, portable coffee stalls, etc. – excellent. Not much heavy gun firing, but musketry. The aeroplanes are a pretty sight (our own) in the twilight this evening, the flashes of bursting shells against the purple and mauve clouds.

Tuesday May 4th 1915, Sailly sur-la-Lys

I have had a full day – tea in the trenches and then visiting along in the dug-outs with plenty of excitement – flying bullets but no shells. As things have got more settled since the battle, the region of the trenches gets more workable and you can pay a visit with somewhat less risk, and this time I went at half past four. There had been some shelling at the cross roads earlier in the day, so I encouraged myself with the thought there probably would be none again till the evening. Beyond a point you come into very much desolation and loneliness – smashed cottages, the garden fence with a great hole in it, the flower beds wild and grassy, and the little pear and apple trees thick with white blossom stand out in contrast. Not a soul in sight now – a sparrow hops out of a low hedge and you hear now the sing of the long distance bullet, you are under fire! Like Agag, you walk delicately [285] when you hear the first snap or two – at least I do. Then you say "1 in 1000 that is only 2:997 yet". You come at length, at long length, to the barricade across the road – you creep low now, specially round a certain corner as the Germans are known to have trained rifles fixed onto certain corners, at which bullets fly at spasmodic intervals, and this corner is a marked one. You hurry sharp across to the wall of a smashed house and down into a ditch. This is the communication trench – the snapping is sustained, but the intervals are not very quick. You wriggle on, glad of each yard that brings you nearer to the front trench. The danger is greater at the longer distance on account of the bullet's trajectory, and so you come to the front tortuous line, the top protected with sand-bags, along which our men are doing the occasional 'ping-ping' which keeps telling the enemy to take care. I take tea in the dug-out with three of four officers, one a Military Cross, another wounded at Mons, another was at Mons also and the other at the Aisne[286]. After tea, I go visiting along from one dug-out to another and with a careful peep you can look out and see the German parapet, sand-bagged, across the field about 300 to 400 yards away. An occasional bullet snarls about you, hitting a tree or a bush. Too much must not be made of men of height for the army as less stature has its advantages. A corporal whom I

---

285 **1 Samuel 15:32** 'Then said Samuel, Bring ye hither to me Agag the king of the Amalekites. And Agag came unto him delicately. And Agag said, Surely the bitterness of death is past.'

286 The **First Battle of the Aisne** was the Allied follow-up offensive against the right wing of the German 1st and 2nd Armies as they retreated after the First Battle of the Marne earlier in September 1914. The offensive began on the evening of 13th September, after a hasty pursuit of the Germans and lasted until the 23rd.

saw in hospital this very morning, of this very regiment, got grazed on the top of the head by being nearly 6 ft tall.

Rain has fallen heavily – there has been a thunderstorm and the passageways are slippery and puddly, sometimes over your boots even on the boards. Visiting from one dug-out to another, at the last one I heard the men singing a hymn, and, happening to have a pocket Gospel with me (with half a dozen hymns with tunes at the back – a good idea), I found myself a welcome caller, and they were glad to have the book to keep, and as I left towards the red sunset it was nice to hear them singing "Sun of my Soul[287]".

The same dodgy wriggle back to the crossroads, then along a road parallel to the trenches for about a mile, here to meet the party collecting the wounded, then down towards the trenches at the further turning called 'Suicide Corner' because of the occasional bullets that have made hits there. Then down back to the First Aid Post to which cases are brought out of the firing line. With the deepening darkness the rifle fire has increased, and the machine guns make much noise. They hit the wall of the Aid Post farm and the mud walls further along with an incessant and ugly 'plug'. At the post, we find two men who have been hit, both by long-distance shots while sitting outside their dug-outs, both had lucky escapes – the one a clean flesh wound through the thigh, the other grazed across the chest bone and the knuckle of his thumb chipped off. The flesh wound man is cheerful – he is going back to England. I write a French postcard for him to his friends at his former reserve billet, to ask them to take care of his souvenirs (the usual helmet etc.) until he can claim them, and thanking them for kindness which has evidently been very real.

Wednesday May 5th 1915, Sailly sur-la-Lys
A busy day of odds and ends – getting together a concert – Club matters and such like. We are in for another fight in a few days and there are many things to think of.

Thursday May 6th 1915, Sailly sur-la-Lys
The concert has been a great success, rather a business, but worth it, with some of our bravest lads – the bomb-throwers. The piano under a tree not more than a mile from the trenches, lighted with shaded candles with the men grouped round. One thinks of what they will go through in the next few days – it made a nice break, and the songs were almost all in excellent taste, and some splendidly sung. They were all so pleased and a kind officer had managed to get the piano down on a lorry (it will remain in the farm now for the present).

Canon Tyrrhitt was shot, slightly, in the knee last night whilst burying some men. The telegram had come to me, asking me to take the funeral, but the men were of Tyrrhitt's

---

287 Hymn, *Sun of My Soul,* John Keble, 1820; first published in his The Christian Year, 1827.

Brigade, so I sent it on to him, or it might have been my fortune to come home and be nursed! These visits to the trenches and the concert and so on, all tell in helping the men. They know me, and look out on the road to exchange a greeting and so on.

Friday May 7th 1915, Sailly sur-la-Lys

We have been prepared today for what may well be the greatest battle of the war[288]. I have been round to the various battalions and everybody is full of expectancy and keenness. The spirit of the men is admirable, calm decision and purpose reigns, though there is the nervousness of taking chances – there is reasonable fear, but the cry is all for going at them, and getting the work done. The plans, as I have been allowed to see them, are most accurately arranged, with places for everybody and timed almost to the second. What strikes one is the wholesome readiness to take what may befall, officers and men and happily in so many cases, most in fact, to look to the Great Beyond. We have some heavy guns, one or two have been registering and they shake the very earth for a mile around. I hope we have plenty, I believe we have and, for the present, ammunition too. Our R.A.M.C. have been busy making 'smelly bags' against gas[289]. We have got a dreadful foe to deal with, surely now proving themselves neither of high principle nor ordinarily human, and these gases are an abominable contrivance.

Some sad cases in last night, but one I believe will pull round alright – they are extraordinarily tough, but it is a chest case about which you can never tell. A strange one happened at Neuve Chapelle where a young officer was so hit. One of the doctors thought him most likely gone, and got him to dictate a short letter to his mother but he lasted through the night, and next morning had to be carried on to the down country place. Three weeks after, the mother sent a warm letter thanking for what had been written, as just before the letter came to her, she had had an 'official' one notifying her boy 'killed in action'. He is, I believe, now doing very well and I see his name in the last awards as having received the Military Cross.

---

288 The **Battle of Aubers Ridge** was a British offensive on the Western Front on 9th May 1915. The battle was part of the British contribution to the Second Battle of Artois, an offensive intended to exploit the German diversion of troops to the Eastern Front. The French 10th Army was to attack the German 6th Army north of Arras and capture Vimy Ridge, then advance on Cambrai and Douai. The British 1st Army on the northern flank of the French was to attack on the same day and widen the gap made in German defences, preventing German troops from being moved south of La Bassée canal. This battle was an unmitigated disaster for the British army. No ground was won and no tactical advantage gained. It is doubted if it had the slightest positive effect on assisting the main French attack 15 miles to the south. The battle was renewed slightly to the south from 15th May and was then known as **the Battle of Festubert**. See footnote 291.

289 Immediately following the use of chlorine gas by the Germans, instructions were sent to British and French troops to hold wet handkerchiefs or cloths over their mouths. Simple pad respirators similar to those issued to German troops were soon proposed by Lieutenant-Colonel N.C. Ferguson, the A.D.M.S. of the 28th Division. These pads were intended to be used damp, preferably dipped into a solution of bicarbonate kept in buckets for that purpose, though other liquids were also used. Because such pads could not be expected to arrive at the front for several days, army divisions set about making them for themselves. Pad respirators were sent up with rations to British troops in the line as early as the evening of 24th April.

I have just been having tea with some of the officers getting ready for the fray. They have been through something already – one, at Mons, was twice buried by 'Jack Johnson' shells i.e. his dug-out was smothered, and the second time the dug-out was completely choked up and they had to dig themselves out. After the Mons battle, when at a certain place after a day and night of fighting they were getting back to a rest billet, they passed a farm near the firing line which had been badly shelled. Out from it came a comfortable housewife, who asked 'what about the Germans?' When told that they had gone back thereabouts, she placed her hands on the officer's shoulders and gave him a hearty kiss on either cheek and thanked him again and again. She then produced her husband and old father-in-law from the cellar, where all three had been during the fight.

The war is full of stories – what volumes mostly everybody will have to tell. Today comes one from a German aviator, shot down from one of our aeroplanes, describing the rifle duel in the air. First shot in the thigh, then his banking wire shot through, preventing his rising properly, then his petrol tank shot through and then his letter, written to his 'dear little mother' ends "let (his commanding officer) know – this may be worth an Iron Cross to me". A worthy lad, I should think.

We have our lighter moments. As I returned from the burying field just now, I passed a young Tommy who, I think, had been having something besides tea for tea. I overheard him, with heavy seriousness, impressing three small French boys with the greatness of impending events. "Demain – moi – mort" he said, repeating his words. The boys listen with round-eyed attention. Then one smiles, shakes his head and waves his hand "Non, Allemands mort". But Tommy will not have it, shaking his head "Non – moi – demain – mort", and he solemnly moves on, leaving the French boys wondering what they ought to think.

These gases <u>are</u> dreadful, but I am thankful to think that no retaliation in kind is proposed by us[290]. Hilaire Belloc was right – this sector is apparently the one selected for the main threat. We commit ourselves to Him who judgeth right.

May 8th 1915, Sailly sur-la-Lys

It is a fateful night and history will be made in these next three or four days, but at what cost, who can tell? Plans are being most carefully laid, we hear, and on a most extensive scale. Man hath proposed, now may God dispose for mercy and truth. The next few days must be crowded ones and I will write what is possible – you will know of the issues.

I have been encountering the groups as they move into their places for the different sections of attack. Many friends are now are among them and it is nice to exchange these greetings. There is splendid spirit – in the main the smile, the laugh, and the

---

290 The first use of gas by the British was at the Battle of Loos, 25th September 1915.

'getting at it' tone. Now and again there is the determined seriousness, the look of the man who knows about 'counting the cost' in a full degree. It is mostly the older man who looks like that, the man I have guessed, with a wife and children, and who has known that the claim is of home and country, and the wrong designed against all that must be resisted.

Beautiful weather – a red peaceful sunset and a cool fresh breeze. My Club will be given up for the wounded cases if needs be, every room and roof in the place is earmarked in case of need. Good news about the Chaplains work, in that I hear the Red Cross propose cars for Chaplains, and also that there are to be two Church of England Chaplains for each Brigade. These will be gains and I hope they will come off. I have had many sacred talks with individual men and officers these last few days. The real, true, tender, upright soul comes out at these times and people would not doubt the value of Chaplain's work if they knew.

Sunday May 9th 1915 Sailly sur-la-Lys[291]

Sunday morning 4.30 a.m. with a bright dawn and a favouring wind blowing away from us, and with only the occasional rumble of a larger gun. 5.am the rumbles have increased in frequency and volume so now it is like the waves of an awful sea upon a loud sea-shore, quicker than the waves the rolling comes. It is one incessant roar – think of a thousand machine guns, thousands of machine guns and these not the small mitrailleuses[292] but cannon – that is as it is. It must be awful on the other side. There surely never was a sweep of artillery like this in all history (it is to go on, I heard, for half an hour). It is being spread across miles of the front and surely not a soul can live for twenty miles along the front of this. This will turn the flank of Ypres, surely. Neuve Chapelle artillery was astounding – this outclasses it like a

---

291 The BEF renewed its attacks against the Aubers Ridge on 9th May, but the British artillery bombardment was too feeble to achieve a break-in. A series of unsupported and uncoordinated infantry frontal attacks, often made against uncut wire, collapsed in the face of German machine-gun fire. Brigadier-General **Reginald Oxley**, GOC 24th Brigade, ordered two companies of 1st Battalion Sherwood Foresters to re-inforce the failure of the initial attack by 2nd Battalion East Lancashire Regiment. When the GOC IV Corps, Sir **Henry Rawlinson**, enquired what had happened to the East Lancashires and the Sherwoods Oxley famously replied, 'They are lying out in No Man's Land, sir, and most of them will never stand again.' After the failure of the attempted breakthrough, tactics of a short hurricane bombardment and an infantry advance with unlimited objectives, were replaced by the new French practice of slow and deliberate artillery-fire intended to prepare the way for an infantry attack. A continuous three-day bombardment by the British heavy artillery was planned, to cut wire and demolish German machine-gun posts and infantry strong-points. The German defences were to be captured by a continuous attack, by one division from Rue du Bois to Chocolat Menier Corner and by a second division 600 yards north, which was to capture the German trenches to the left of **Festubert** village. The objectives were 1000 yards forward, rather than the 3000 yards depth of advance that had been intended at Aubers Ridge. The battle was the first British attempt at attrition, and the beginning of 'trench warfare'.

292 A **mitrailleuse** is a type of volley gun with multiple barrels of rifle calibre that can fire either multiple rounds at once, or several in rapid succession. In modern French, *mitrailleuse* is the word used for machine gun, including modern fully automatic weapons.

dream. I hear no reply from the other side. They must be all dead by now across there – it is impossible to think how they can live. There will be a counter-attack perhaps, during the day. Not a man will be alive in those trenches we peeped at last week. Not a man, or scarcely a man, along those ridges we have been peeping at day by day across the cherry trees and round those ruined church spires – what a long half hour it seems. I talked a day or so ago of the earth shaking with our big guns – it is shaking alright, to Force the appeal has been made.[293] You can see the smoke now circling faintly over the trees, below which are the trenches. Some shells are being fired at us, I can see them bursting – small ones – from a further distance than the enemy guns we knew of. They look faint and feeble little things against all this (there will be bigger ones later, no doubt). We hear too, that the French are joining in all this, along their south front. What name will be given to this battle? No local name, I think, will be able to fit it. John Bull is angry today and the spirit of the French is up. Kitchener, Joffre, French, Douglas Haig – (Winston Churchill – he was here yesterday afternoon) our national leaders all round are speaking for us faithfully today. An occasional big shell comes over, the Jack Johnson kind, but the range is not good. We have apparently changed the position of our batteries! Some shells have dropped five fields off, looking for a battery and not so far from it too!

6.30 a.m. the Niagara of bellowing destruction pauses, and our infantry are now moving forward. I am off to 7 a.m. Holy Communion. 7.30 a.m. no one present but like Moses we out here, like you at home, prayed. The procession of wounded begins[294] – I hear that we have taken three lines of trenches. Casualties arriving – not so many in proportion, I believe, as at Neuve Chapelle. But oh, the suffering! Two young officers whom I have got to know more specially, Lyon and Wynter.

Monday May 10th 1915 Sailly sur-la-Lys

Monday 2. am, a day of stress, valour and suffering. Our Brigade has suffered badly, but I believe much good has been done. There has been such carnage and I feel much sorrow in thinking over the list of the injured and the slain as I have heard of them, one after the other. 9 a.m. officers to look after. 10 a.m. To the temporary Military Church, expecting no one and expectation realised, but as the service had been given out and I was responsible, I was there, and I prayed. The guns roared outside, the roof trembled and the cuckoo (the first time I have heard him this year) sang. [memo – the German is a cuckoo, wanting nests without building them himself]

---

293 War Diary, 24th Ambulance (WO 95/1703/1). May 9th 5.0 am 'Artillery fire began' 6.30 am 'walking cases began to arrive at adv dressng stn'

294 War Diary, 24th Ambulance (WO 95/1703/1). '9.30 am 'a good many bad wounded to come in'. 4.00 pm 'work became very heavy, many lying cases'. Wounded were initially catagorised as walking, sitting or lying.

Down to the firing line – the procession of wounded as at Neuve Chapelle, though not so numerous. It is a hard fight and the enemy is a very strong opposition. After Neuve Chapelle they were not to be caught napping. They abode in their dug-outs during the heavy shelling, not that they escaped as there was the usual accounts of bodies by the half dozen and more being blown up in the air seen from our trenches. Trenches have been gained. A Brigadier-General has been hit, perhaps killed[295]. Down at the receiving point behind a cottage at the rear of the firing line – here the shells burst round us briskly and the nasty hiss of the bullets becomes a natural sound. My narrowest escape today was a bullet striking the tiled roof of the inside of the old farm next door and the falling pieces of tile make you hurry for the moment. Bit by bit you find out how things are gaining here, being held back there, who are wounded, who killed. Meanwhile you lend a hand with the maimed lads who come in. Some are now old friends [...*censored*...] wounded, you hear, and [...*censored*...] killed. One gets numbed to the personal feeling – it is all part of the day's work. Great tales of heroism, told unconsciously, or admiringly. Of the group of 8 or 9 officers at our Thursday night concert, only 2 have escaped unhurt. The nice young officer who played the harmonium – killed. Two others who were useful with the piano and good singers – killed, it is a carnival of death. Everybody is busy helping everybody – that is what is striking and people are wonderfully thoughtful and kind, especially those of an off-hand manner. The doctors have gone from gash to gash, from limb to limb, until it becomes almost mechanical to the onlooker. This case goes by ambulance train – that by improvised train – that to the Clearing Hospital for amputation or operation – that by barge (chest cases or any that cannot stand too much shaking), none are kept here now. Evacuate with all speed, and the men form up in queues with their wounds to be dressed and bandaged at one end of the receiving room, and they wait in queues at the other end for cars or other transport. Benches are placed by the roadside for the weaker ones and stretcher cases are laid in rows wherever space can be found for them inside, and in the quiet side roads outside. The spirit is, as usual, wonderful. Some of them even sing and whistle, stopping now and again with a spasm. Some, mainly those hit by high explosive shells, are white and strained. One man, a rare exception, has been crying like a child all the time – he is not hit, it is a nerve case and his capacity for weeping is colossal.

---

295 Brigadier General **Arthur Willougby George Lowry Cole**. 25th Infantry Brigade. The Rifle Brigade History of WW1 says the following of his death: "*The remaining troops of the 25th Brigade were herded together in the front line and assembly sap in an advanced state of disorganisation; and were so found by the Brigadier when he arrived at 6.20am – forty minutes after the attack began. In these circumstances, he ordered up his Brigade reserve (two companies of the 2nd Lincolnshire Regiment) and dispatched them in support of the 13th London Regiment with orders to bomb towards the 2nd Rifle Brigade (the only battalion to make any inroads) and join up with them. Almost immediately afterwards a further stroke of misfortune befell the attackers. In some mysterious manner, which has never been explained, an order to retire was circulated among the troops out in front (8th Division's account of the operation). It does not seem to have reached the 2nd RB, nor is there any record of it in their diaries, but from all directions men began retiring towards the original line. With conspicuous gallantry, General Lowry Cole sprang up on the parapet and succeeded in restoring order. The action cost him his life, for he was mortally wounded.*"

What a scene is this night collecting of the wounded. A shell has set light to a hay-rick – unfortunately it is between our road and the trench, and throws a clear light upon us as we dash by. It is a guide to the enemy rifle and shell fire, and both are getting this road rather well. 'Verey' lights[296] shoot up into the sky, making things look like daylight and along here and there, against the dark star-sprinkled sky you see bursting stars of flame and as you see, you hear. They are shrapnel shells. The burning hayrick, the stars, the Verey lights, the flashing shell pieces, smashed cottages, broken bare tree trunks, wild vegetation, vivid patches of red brick and green bush and Khaki-clad men dashing out of light into shadow, creeping along under cover of the grey square-topped Red Cross ambulances, dashing on amid so much crackle and bang, stillness and commotion – this is how it is. These regimental and aid post doctors are brave good men. They live in this kind of thing all day and all night, but we can go back out of it. Here is where the need for more men comes in, you can then change over your men and give them less hours of this continual strain.

The day's fortunes have been variable. I believe here we have not advanced. There is a strong line of guns against us. We want <u>more shells</u>. Elsewhere we hear of good success.

"But what of the field's fortune? That concerned their Leader,
Bold they struck their stroke not caring for doings left or right
Each his little bit".

Bright glorious weather. The procession diminishes and now comes the task of getting in those from the ditches, and between the trenches. We have not gained much here, but it seems that we have co-operated very substantially with the French in their successes along […*censored*…] and we were told that this was in the scheme. Worse cases are being collected now – those that have been out in the open. I met a young officer this morning at some cross roads – no hat, no collar, no equipment, no socks, boots, open neck, soaked through up to his chest – he did not know quite where he was. We were now well up from the firing line and he had been head of a bombing party of about 200 soldiers. They had exploded a mine and taken part of a trench, and then a re-attack had bombed them out of it. A short cut led him across some water into which he fell and the crowd behind him scampered over him. The water became deeper, and he found himself wading up to the armpits, and then barbed wire in the water impeded him. The day wore on, and night caught him, not in a place of safety, but where he could be quiet. And there he stayed, making his way out this morning. I put him on the track of his transport and have heard since that he had arrived. A queer figure he looked – he has been out here for only a month.

I have just been fetched to bury a Brigadier General and on the way there I meet Conran, whose Brigadier it was and so he went in my place. My horse fell this

---

296 **Edward Wilson Very** (b.1847 – d.1910) was an American naval officer who developed and popularised a single-shot breech-loading snub-nosed flare gun that fired flares that bear his name.

morning, slipping on the wet paved road whilst we were hurrying from a trench funeral. I had a lucky escape as he fell so suddenly that it was not possible to slip my foot out of the stirrup. Fortunately, though my leg was under him, the stirrup saved it from being crushed, so there was no more than a bruised feeling, and the arm also although the stirrup was curiously bent up! Such is the fortune of war.

The fighting continues, but with less intensity, with big shells falling in one area. We hear now that Italy wars on Turkey.

Tuesday May 11th 1915, Sailly sur-la-Lys[297]

It is 3.30 am and I have been out all night helping to bring in the wounded. It has been an exciting experience – we have been under fire for over three hours. In one open space a Maxim was trained over our line of retirement over a flat open landscape. There were about 90 stretcher-bearers in all and I had a hand in helping about 40 of them. What a scene! Dark, but starlight, and every few minutes the flares lit up everything about us like very clear moonlight. Now and again you pass over a dead body – we take none of these as they must be left to the burying parties who are busy doing their work. Our business is to save and carry back the living, but one cannot refrain from a second's prayer beside each man. As you kneel, and place a hand of benediction upon each mutilated form, "Dear lad, God bless him and comfort his friends". They lie in all sorts of places – here along a trench approach, huddled back just where the body fell. You place the body reverently where you can, but they are heavy and every minute is precious for the sake of the living. It is late.

The daylight opens up brightly. One or two of our big guns are at work and I can just see across the sky-line a blaze of some building, farm or hayrick that they have hit, and balls of flame shine out across the horizon of the dawn, where some of these shells burst. It is astonishing among the hundreds of bullets flying about how few of us get hit.

The account as I look over it, reads a little disjointedly. But it will give an idea of what this collecting work means[298]. We assembled at about 10.30, about a quarter of a mile behind the firing line. The trenches here are not more than 50 yds apart in places. You get 'under fire' at about 500 yds from the rendezvous. An uncomfortable smack of a bullet above us against the cottage wall beside us as we walk along to this or that rendezvous, reminds us of where we are. The assembly point is behind two small farm buildings with low roofs. It is very dark. You have to cross a ditch which is

297 War Diary, 24th Field Ambulance (WO 95/1703/1). May 12th noon 'This hour is taken as the end of this operation. Admissions of wounded: 9/5/15 Officers, 38, OR 794; 10/5 Officers, 6, OR 203; 11/5 Officers 1, OR 52. TOTAL 1103.' Classification of Wounds: Rifle, 561; Artillery, 495; Bayonet, 11; Grenade, 5; Accidental (Barbed Wire, etc.), 31; Deaths in hospital, 10. Lt. Col. R Pickard.
298 War Diary, 24th Field Ambulance (WO 95/1703/1). May 12th 'Collecting from rt. half No1 sector E & F lines'. Lt. Col. R Pickard.

in the line of fire between the two buildings. About 60 of the men are entirely new to the work (some fresh drafts) and full of excitement and extra precaution i.e. they creep low when they are now in the shelter of the protecting wall. It is, for the same reason, slow work getting the string of them along the long winding communication trenches, as they drop down at the openings which are really only windings of the trench. They make long waits, in groups, especially in the more shallow trenches, and it is difficult to keep them in touch and the journey up to the firing line, and along to the 'Sap' about which the wounded are grouped, takes fully over an hour. Then, because of the impossibility of carrying stretcher cases through the winding of the trenches, we skirt a road of stunted willows by a ditch, through three fields across the country to the two farm buildings. Here is where the main excitement comes in; we divide our party into three and I go forward with the first of about 40 men – 10 wounded that is, with 4 men to a stretcher. Every few yards, down comes the stretcher and everyone falls prone – a flare has gone up, lighting everything around. There are ditches, wires, shell holes, low parapet defences all to be passed, and until you have got about a third of your way back, you are in open ground, down which a machine gun has been trained. That was exciting. Fortunately, the firing line parapet makes the fire keep high as far as we can judge, but the bullets hit the trees round us and keep you low! Turning to the right you get only the stray shots, but you do not go far that way, for it is known that a sniper has a line there.

How patient the wounded are, being lifted up and put down again so often and so suddenly, being handled across ditches and hedges, inevitably shaken now and again however careful people are, and the men are wonderfully strong and careful in spite of the need for speed and continual dropping down for cover and twisted round corners in awkward ditch turnings.

As we retire, the excitement gets less, but the route is filled with sadness right to the end for the enemy shelling has reached this area with others, and you pass dead men who had been retiring from the fight wounded and were killed in their tracks, well up to the collecting point. These Red Cross men do wonderful, noble work, full of sympathy, courage and endurance and not less praiseworthy, as we feel our way back through rough by-ways all in the dark, is the devotion of the ambulance motor drivers, with their skill and courage and good temper.

Thursday May 13th 1915 Sailly sur-la-Lys

It is a strange Ascension Day, but what a blessing the message of it is in all this heavy mystery of conflict and death. Sunday's fight still goes on, although quieter on our immediate front, and my own Brigade is back out of the firing line in a deserted town, among the strange lonely streets and smashed houses. The gaps in the ranks! We do not talk of them – no one knows whose turn it might be next time.

7 am Holy Communion with just one person present, a Staff Colonel, and later on

in the morning another funeral. Booming artillery across the fields and visiting round the billets. Back, and back again in the afternoon – my battalion has moved lengthwise along the front. There have been great successes today but not being reaped at our end, but by the French.

The plan had been to have an evening service in the covered courtyard of a large house in a small smashed town where many of our battalions are billeted – a very convenient building. I got down in good time and had all ready, and looked out for the men, when suddenly there was a loud bang and then another. Some women came rushing down a street, with about 5 small girls all screaming – we were being shelled again after an interval here of four days. A man came with an armful of coverings, a quilt and so on, followed by his wife and two daughters. "I have a good cellar down here" he said and went a few doors off and disappeared. The service it seemed, must be off. It was trying, as these men have been through the fight of Sunday and in the trenches till this morning. About four more shells fell across the common ground behind us, then all was quiet. So, as about 8 men had come, I decided to go on. We had a very real and uplifting time, though once or twice the 'sing' and the 'plunk' of those unwelcome visitors made your thought and hearing stop. About 15 men came in all, and we rose in spirit with great thankfulness to our ascended Lord. After the service I had dinner with some officers in a side street with ration soup, kipper, ration mutton, potatoes, tinned peas, bread and butter pudding, dates, figs, ginger and cafe au lait – very nice thank you. But the gaps, and the new faces round that table, made it feel unreal.

Friday May 14th 1915 Sailly sur-la-Lys
How horrible the Lusitania[299] crime, and the report of the Commission of Enquiry about the Belgian atrocities[300] – we are up against an awful 'type' of person.

A full day visiting the scattered Brigade, resting thankfully in reserve billets, and hearing accounts of individual doings and escapes – they would fill a book. There has been wonderful courage again – one of the bomb-throwing group (with whom we had that concert) picked up German bombs before they had time to explode and threw them out of our trench – these explosions are a matter of seconds. A man shot by a spent bullet in the hand, finds the bullet at the bottom of his pocket! Two men crawled in this morning who have been lying out since Sunday – they did not know

299 **RMS** *Lusitania* was a British ocean liner, holder of the Blue Riband and briefly the world's biggest ship. Launched by the Cunard Line in 1907, in 1915 she was torpedoed and sunk by the U-20 commanded by Walter Schweiger, on May 7th 1915, causing the deaths of 1198 passengers and crew.
300 Britain sponsored the "Committee on Alleged German Outrages" known as the Bryce Report, produced by Vicount James Bryce, ambassador to the USA. Published on 12th May 1915, the Report provided elaborate details and first-hand accounts, including excerpts from diaries and letters found on captured German soldiers. The Report was a major factor in changing public opinion in neutral countries, especially the United States.

their whereabouts, and one crawled within a dozen yards of the German parapet. This man then 'entrenched' himself between the bodies of two dead comrades and lived on his own and their emergency rations.

In the smashed town, I came across a strange pair. A youngish lady shopkeeper in a small millinery place 200 yards from the demolished church and in the line of fire, has been living there with a maid-servant since January. The house has no glass in the windows, only boards. The roof has not been hit, but tiles have been loosened and the houses on either side are knocked about. When we remember that this church has been shelled sometimes for days together, at a rate of a dozen or more shells a day, it makes one think of hardihood. In Sunday morning's fight, a shell dropped on the edge of the pavement in front of their door and the great pit is there to tell the tale – they were in at the time, and remain there still. I called them "mechantes" and they laughed.

Wonderful sights at night time – from my billet I can see the ridge opposite, and the explosions, the flare lights, the searchlight, the rolling smoke and the reflections against the low night sky, with the tremendous booming of the guns, the snarl of the rifle fire and the crashing of the machine guns, all makes a wild spectacle. Comparatively very few of our people are hurt.

Saturday May 15th 1915, Sailly sur-la-Lys

Here is a special friend (please keep the picture – Capt and Adj. H. Powers) the warm hearted gallant officer who was my guide on the first night I went into the trenches. Of that first eerie dinner party, in the white cottage banged with bullets, at which we numbered four, one has been three times wounded and is still incapacitated, and two have been killed – I am the only survivor. A valorous and noble gentleman and no mistake, and a sacred and cherished memory[301].

Sunday May 16th 1915, Sailly sur-la-Lys

A joyful and refreshing day – beautiful weather and the fighting quieter at our end. We have news of great success on our right which might well have been after the terrific bombardment we gave them here as well as there at midnight, and at other times. It was a grandly, awful sight, under the deep night sky.

---

301   Capt. Adjt. **Herbert Power** (b.1886 – d.1915), Son of Lt. Col. Frederick Edward Power and Mrs Ellen Matilda Power. Sandhurst 1903, commissioned Second Lieutenant in the 2nd Battalion, Northamptonshire Regiment on 24th January 1906. Embarked to France on 4th November 1914, landing at Havre on 6th November 1914. Killed in action during the retirement from captured German trenches at Neuve Chapelle on 12th March 1915. A brother officer writes "Power was a terrific loss to the Regiment, an example of all that an officer and soldier should be."

Holy Communion at 8.am in the loft with 10 present, which included 8 officers. H.C. has been announced at 10 in the battered town. No one came, so I strolled round the magnificent garden and picked lilies of the valley, while one of our aeroplanes circled in the vaulted blue above, helping one of our bigger guns to do good practice. Four shell holes, two on the lawn, and two in the orchard, all over a month old. At 10.30 a good muster appeared – the concierge's wife had put two vases of lilac on the old oak table (we were in the covered courtyard), we had a very respectable piano and the service went with a great swing with about 60 present, and then I took another full service in a disused spinning factory – very hearty and serious. Across the plain behind the trenches, a German captive balloon ogled at us as we went to and fro. It seemed near, but they say it is some miles away – luckily for it! Nice evening service with the bomb-throwers.

Tuesday May 18th 1915, Sailly sur-la-Lys

A full day. The smashed town was shelled again this morning, along the street at the end of which is the Temporary Military Church. I arrived just in time to bring back to the Ambulance six men of one of my battalions, who had all been injured by a shell. One had a nasty wound in the neck, he will get on well however, the doctor thinks. I have been visiting this afternoon with no more shells, mercifully. Our Division has swung round and are co-operating very successfully with […*censored*…] and others.

960 prisoners are taken we hear tonight, and a battery taken by us and also trenches. I buried two men tonight, killed by a trench mortar while asleep, and five others wounded. A tremendous cannonading most of the day, mainly in our favour. I said last night after that captive balloon had ogled down on us that we should get something tomorrow. We did – but so did they! I do not think there will be any leave this summer. It is very unsettling, and I do not think that the effect would be advisable upon the officers and men in one's 'charge'. The only thing to call one home would be any possibility of usefulness in strengthening the output of munitions, or in recruiting as there is a special need it seems to be for more officers. All the same, things seem to be going the right way, if slowly, and at a stern cost. If Italy does come in at long last, it will help expedite matters. There is reason enough, in my opinion, for every civilised nation combining now to suppress a people that has proved itself at heart a cruel and unscrupulous one. I would not like to be the man who sank the Lusitania, even though acting under orders. The name of the German who did it will go down as a byword in history[302].

The fight begun on Sunday week still goes on as you will see in the papers, and though my associates have been injured severely, without any appreciable immediate gain to record for it, we know we have made a valuable contribution to the gains further next along our line.

---

302 Kplt. **Walther Schwieger** (b.1885 – d.1917), captain of U-20, did not survive the war.

Tonight we have some more good news, added to that of yesterday – they will never get through Ypres, and <u>we shall</u> advance our front steadily and continually I am convinced, from all the evidence available. The hot fighting has swung to the further end of my brigade, and though I did not mean to be in it today, I found myself so this afternoon. An officer, wounded and gone 'down country', asked me to go and preserve the site of a brother officer's grave (after Neuve Chapelle) and a letter from the mother came, wishing something could be done. I gathered that the heavier fighting had left the locality but on approaching it, I found that things were much too lively. The road down which we went was shelled in front of us, and further on I met two Generals (of a Division and Artillery) who both counselled a prudent retracing of the way. As the area in which the grave was supposed to be was thus still within range of the enemy guns, I did myself the honour of agreeing with the Generals! It was a picturesque sight from where we stood and I was with the group of the General and some of his staff. A typical battle scene – our own guns roaring behind us, occasionally men creeping across a field, along a path, and behind a ruined house, and the German shells bursting above our trenches and our own bursting over theirs. Puffs of white smoke – flashes against the sky – the roar and hiss behind, and everywhere battered buildings and wild vegetation.

Coming back, we picked up four men who had just been hit by a high explosive in the trench parallel to the road. What a mad business it all is!!! A man wounded on Sunday week who has been living between the trenches since then, crawled in this morning. Not a shot or sound tonight.

Wednesday May 19th 1915, Sailly sur-la-Lys

We are glad of books for the men, as when they are lying about in the dug-outs, they need some occupation besides cards, and stories take their minds off shells and other things. I believe that we are better off for men than for munitions. The Times man, however, I think is wrong in imputing a shortage on Sunday week[303]. It was my Brigade which was in the [...*censored*...] attack. The mistake seems to have been rather in using shrapnel instead of high explosives and not making the bombardment long enough, though to us looking on it appeared long and terrible enough in all conscience. I see in one case on the Eastern front, the Germans shelled for over four hours without intermission. Shrapnel is only second best against their strongly

---

303 After the failure of the Battle of Aubers Ridge (9th May 1915) *The Times* war correspondent, Colonel Charles à Court Repington sent a telegram to his newspaper blaming lack of High Explosive shells. French had, despite Repington's denial of his prior knowledge at the time, supplied him with information, and sent trusted officers (Brinsley Fitzgerald and Freddy Guest) to London to show the same documents to Lloyd George and senior Conservatives Bonar Law and Balfour. *The Times* headline (14th May 1915) was: "Need for shells: British attacks checked: Limited supply the cause: A Lesson from France". It commented "We had not sufficient high explosives to lower the enemy's parapets to the ground ... The want of an unlimited supply of high explosives was a fatal bar to our success". This clearly pointed the finger of blame at the government.

entrenched positions, but all the same, our guns did remarkable execution, as I happen to know. High explosives are very comfortable to be <u>behind</u>!

It remains to be seen whether Italy has come in, but their uncertainty has been useful to an extent, as it has made the Austrian frontier uncertain, and demanded the holding of some of the enemy forces in readiness – Italy has nothing to gain by keeping out of the conflict as they can only expect to be a vassal state of Germany. The Kaiser has an awful account to render.

Thursday May 20th 1915, Sailly sur-la-Lys

I have just been reading the Times of yesterday, and I do not think that the public can complain of being 'kept in the dark'. They have been told things to a detail that some of us think is almost dangerous for our success, and how foolish it is to clamour in the way some neurotic spirits are doing. They must know that the Germans read every word, and frame their plans accordingly. I do not like it.

So gas is to come – I feared it, yet my judgement tells me it is necessary[304]. The enemy must be met on his own ground, and since they have made the use of it a practice, it is true that our men are placed at too serious a disadvantage. However, 'smelly bags' can do a great deal to help.

A quiet day again today – visiting and planning for Sunday.

Friday May 21st 1915, Sailly sur-la-Lys

A quiet day today, but brisk firing tonight as I write. The [...*censored*...] they say, are doing very well on our right and they are making enough noise about it! Our sector is fairly quiet.

Saturday May 22nd 1915, Sailly sur-la-Lys

It is true about the [...*censored*...] on the right. They have gained the last German trench and held it and today there has been a German counter-attack, which has failed. These counter-attacks are good things from our point of view as they mean enemy losses, and a counter-attack that fails depresses and demoralises. Tonight things are quieter. We are all wondering about Italy – Austria at the last moment may have made impressive offers, with success. I am glad of the re-formation of the Cabinet[305] – it ought to make for strength.

---

304 While initially shocked by the German's use of poison gas, as early as 3rd May 1915 the British Secretary of State for War, Lord Kitchener, authorised the preparation of measures to retaliate. Experimental research work was carried out at Porton Down, and a laboratory established at Helfaut, near St Omer in France. The Kestner-Kellner Alkali Company, being the only firm in Britain capable of manufacturing Chlorine gases in quantity, supervised trials with the final large-scale one taking place at Runcorn on 4th June. Special Companies of technically skilled men, under Major C.H. Foulkes of the Royal Engineers, were formed with a Depot at Helfaut, to deal with the new weapon.

305 The visit of the Opposition Leaders to Asquith (17th May) was caused more by Fisher's

Things are apparently not yet ripe for a big move on. The Germans have great confidence in themselves still, and June was the month in which they expected to win the war (by the accounts of the prisoners). It will take a long time to wear them down. I feel I must stay on after the year is out as it would never do to leave the men in the lurch from the 'Chaplain' point of view.

The Daily Mail[306] deserves to be burnt on the Stock Exchange – I wonder what summer madness was in the brains of men who wrote like that at a time like this? We will hope it will only serve to make K[307] more popular than ever, but it helps the misgivings of the weak.

Sunday May 23rd 1915, Sailly sur-la-Lys

7 am Holy Communion with 18 present, including 2 officers. 8 am – to which I did not go, in the loft. 9.30 am a barn service which was very full. A soldier volunteered to play the harmonium which we had borrowed from the farm, but it would not work properly. However, we kept cheerful all round, and not a bad service resulted, though it was a little further interrupted by a stampede of horses!

10.30 am and a very pleasant service under the trees with a regiment who suffered much in the last fight – it was very nice in the soft sunshine. Some shells had been bursting across the fields earlier, but none came at this time, though we were on the trench side of the smashed-up town, with our own guns booming away. We had Holy Communion under an apple tree with soft white blossoms and ten men stayed. There are only two battalions out of the trenches, so the day was a lighter one. This evening's service in the loft was not such a crowded congregation as it sometimes is, though it was so I hear this morning. I spoke of the Ascension-tide glory promised us.

It has been a beautiful day with moderate fighting. A letter found on a prisoner at the other end of this sector, said of last week when we were having those night salvoes "Yesterday was Ascension Day. The British bombarded us furiously for a little while in the night with shrapnel. It was a sham attack and they are not going to frighten us

---

resignation (15th May) than by the Shells Scandal. As a result of the meeting Asquith wrote to his ministers demanding their resignations. Asquith formed a new coalition government and appointed Lloyd George as Minister of Munitions.

306   On May 15th, 1915, *The Times* published a telegram from its respected military correspondent, Lieutenant-Colonel Repington, highlighting the problem. After some critical editorials, on May 21st the *Mail* published an incendiary piece written by Lord Northcliffe himself and headlined '*The Tragedy of the Shells: Lord Kitchener's Grave Error*'. Northcliffe pinned the blame for the shells scandal directly on Kitchener: *Lord Kitchener has starved the army in France of high-explosive shells. The admitted fact is that Lord Kitchener ordered the wrong kind of shell … He persisted in sending shrapnel – a useless weapon in trench warfare … The kind of shell our poor soldiers have had has caused the death of thousands of them.* This direct public attack on such an esteemed figure at a time of national crisis was shocking and generated fury among many of Northcliffe's critics. Members of the London Stock Exchange burned copies of both *The Times* and the *Mail* and anxious advertisers cancelled contracts. Thousands of readers stopped buying the papers.

307   Lord Kitchener.

that way." Little did he know that it was part of the plan that won the very real success further along, and that part of the result would be his own distinguished capture!

Monday May 24th 1915, Sailly sur-la-Lys[308]

Thank you very much for the parcel. Eric's card was amusing about cooking a German sausage, and I have nailed it up in a part of the Ambulance where the men stay who are well enough to go back into the trenches soon – something cheerful for them to think about. I am glad of the chocolates, and I shall be popular in the mess for some days, having peppermints and three cakes to share round!

It has been a successful and enjoyable concert with the bomb-throwers, except that in the middle there was a terrific bombardment, and though the singers went on, they could scarcely be heard (it was part of a little attack by us on the right). You can imagine the scene, a flat field with the Fund piano under a tree and about 160 khaki-clad men. Also under a tree a good number of Scotchmen in kilts, lying in a circle around a dozen officers in chairs and a little platform made of ammunition boxes. The ragged tower of the ruined church and the jagged out-line of the buildings of the smashed town across the field in the pink sunset, with the pale moon creeping up and two of our aeroplanes being shelled against the skyline. And then as the darkness deepened, the terrific roar of our guns and the more distant boom of the enemy, and by and bye the flash of the enemy shells bursting over our front. Some came in the direction of our surroundings, but did not get near them and apart from the noise, it interfered nothing with the men's enjoyment. A remarkable birthday and Empire Day with the men singing until I <u>had</u> to close the programme – it is astonishing what a large number of songs and choruses are a common possession.

Tuesday May 25th 1915, Sailly sur-la-Lys

So Italy has come in. It will mean complications later no doubt, but it will appreciably shorten the fighting. The Teutonic mind must begin to feel itself woefully persecuted and misunderstood. It is distressing about the Daily Mail[309], but I suppose K is too big a man to be bothered too much by a matter mainly personal.

A full day, mostly Club managing, and after tea, Badminton! And then a terrific bombardment again at midnight – very fine to watch. As I went to 7 o'clock Holy

---

308 RDG's 48th birthday

309 See footnote 306. Lloyd George warned Northcliffe that the shells campaign was counterproductive and creating sympathy for Kitchener. Kitchener wanted to let the Shells Scandal drop. Van Donop, Master-General of the Ordnance, demanded an Inquiry to clear his name, but Kitchener persuaded him to withdraw the request as it would have led to French's dismissal. Although Lord Kitchener remained in office as Secretary of State for War, responsible for training and equipping the volunteer New Armies, he had lost control over munitions production and was increasingly sidelined from control of military strategy. Sir John French was also tarnished by his blatant meddling in politics, a factor which contributed to his enforced resignation in December 1915.

Communion in the loft I heard a shell drop in a field across the road. During the day, a number have fallen at that end of the village and one artillery man was killed. In the morning, the smashed town was reached just beyond the side where we were, but our people accomplished what they had set out to do – they have taken the position from the enemy and made it secure. The Red Barn, in which so many of our winter services were held, has been shelled in the Festubert fighting, but will still be available now that they are pushed back[310].

Wednesday May 26th 1915, Sailly sur-la-Lys

A terrific bombardment again last night, but no-one here seems to have been the worse for it. Near the roadside by three graves that are sideways to the rising and setting sun, on two or three evenings as I have passed I have seen two, and sometimes three, Hindus praying. They stand with their palms and hands turned upwards. Who do they pray to? And what do they ask?

Friday May 28th 1915, Sailly sur-la-Lys

The farm in which we held our Monday's concert was shelled last night: my bomb-thrower friends scattered post haste, and finished their sleep further down the village. The building in which I have been having my Sunday services in the smashed-up town was also hit – three shells came into the road outside and many of the windows were more smashed, and one piece of shell drove right through the brick wall.

I think I must close one of the Clubs as the Chaplain who took it over has moved on – in fact he has gone to England, but his Division has gone also, so his return will be to another locality. There are practically no troops in the place now, which in one way is a good sign. The baths also have not had the same run on them, as very many of the men take their dip in the river-canal. They find many things there, besides reeds and rushes, as it is a sluggish stream and French sanitation is not hyper-sensitive, and today two of the bathers encountered the dead body of a Sikh.

I propose to go on for another week with the Club as in the summer (as with sailors) there is not so much need for Club life.

This is a letter worth reading. To a nephew aged 23 from a not much older uncle at the front. The envelope was addressed "Master [...*censored*...]" "I notice that 75 percent of the men out here are married men. This proves beyond doubt that they realise the terrible results that would ensue if we were defeated by the Germans. I might say then, that when you say that several of the boys who went to the school where you went, have joined the Service, and then you say you are joining the [...

---

310 **The Battle of Festubert** (15th–25th May 1915) was an attack by the British army in the Artois region. The battle was the first British attempt at attrition, the beginning of the trench warfare stalemate.

censored…] Tennis Club, well, you ought to be ashamed to walk along the road. God help England if all young fellows were like you – I wonder what Grandfather would say if he were alive? He was a gentleman full of English blood, but it is hard for me to believe that you belong to the same family. I mix with all Regiments in the Division, both near the trenches and two miles further away, and I have seen men who have fought and been nearly blown to bits and still they smile. God alone knows how a man can play tennis while thousands of men are giving their lives for their country. The only advice I can offer you, and also to my aunt, is to be sure that you do not leave your winter clothes off, or you may catch cold. Also be careful when you play tennis because if you get a knock with the ball, it might hurt you and give you a shock".

Saturday May 29th 1915, Sailly sur-la-Lys

A day of running to and fro. The Division being widely scattered, services have to be arranged at various distant centres, and the planning for the two central 'Military Churches' now has to be done. Given fair weather there ought to be full and intent services on Sunday. There can be no evening service in the 'Cinema Church' as the town life is getting more settled since Neuve Chapelle, and the cinema man is coming back into his own. Sunday afternoon and evening he tells me, are his busiest time and I believe it. So we might migrate to the Town Hall for the Evening service. Conran is helping, and Pattinson (the Jameson raider), in addition to our respective Brigade services – so 'many hands make light etc.'

Sad news for our Division today – our Staff Colonel who left us lately to take up another Division, while riding near a bomb magazine, was killed by an accidental explosion[311].

The night bombardments have been very picturesque. There was no reply last night, but the night before some came unpleasantly close along our area. Tonight, everything is calm and strangely still. The great moon is like a metal disc in the cloudless sky and the trees are silhouetted up against it and not a leaf stirs. There is not a sound of a shot anywhere. They say large forces of the enemy have been withdrawn from our front to knock back the Italian advances at la Hindenberg, like a bull at a gate, which indeed gets its head through with much damage to the gate and we hope not a little to its head!

It's a good manifesto from the Bishops, "Every individual in the land must be a fighting force in some shape, and a praying force. There is no one, and there is nothing too dear or too sacred to be offered. What is at stake is not only the honour of our plighted word, but our safety and freedom, and the place entrusted to us among the nations of the earth. The spirit arrayed against us threatens the very foundations of civilised

---

311 Lt Colonel **Robie Fitzgerald Uniacke** (b.1869 – d.1915), General Staff, Asst. Adjt. & Quartermaster-General and Royal Inniskilling Fusiliers, died 28th May 1915. Son of the Rev. R. Fitzgerald Uniacke, late vicar of Tandridge, Surrey; husband of Jane Uniacke.

order in Christendom." I do not think that compulsory service would be amiss. Those ineligible for any reason would still remain at their posts. It is not policy to use up the worthy and valorous to preserve the shirker as the future 'body' of the nation.

We are alright now for prayer and hymn books for services. The Chaplain's Department has got well into line and these are now all issued, including tune books. I wish they would provide small cars as the distances are very great and large numbers of men are so widely scattered. It is a day of immense opportunity and need, and ought to be prospered with the very utmost efficiency.

Tonight again is strangely calm and still – you can almost feel that the Germans have run off to give Italy a hard knock, hoping thence to return and hammer at us harder than ever. One hears many views – I do not like the 'Times' and the 'Daily Mails' way of doing things. The personal onslaught upon Kitchener must surely have been as gratuitous as it is unprofitable. It was a disservice, in my opinion, to the national 'morale', and has certainly contributed to re-inspirit the enemy, always a thing to be avoided at all costs. It is a blessing there is a United Government – there must surely be a census of eligibles, and everyone must answer "Are you doing your part to the full? If not, why not?"

I have pretty well decided today to close the one Club. Things happen with no one to pop in unexpectedly and I am not sure that spirits are not being sold occasionally, and troops are now absent from that area for longer periods. It has done six month's excellent work and it is almost impossible to make it really go from this distance. I shall look round elsewhere.

Sunday May 30th 1915, Sailly sur-la-Lys

Twenty five years ago today I was ordained[312]. Little could one dream at a time like that what a quarter of a century will produce! A full anniversary – Trinity Sunday – 7 am Holy Communion only one person present and at 8 in the Temporary Military Church, three present including two officers. At 10 am a most uplifting open-air service with about 800 present and at 11 am another service in a factory building with about 250 present and at 12 o'clock a third service in a grazing field under a tree. At 6 p.m. yet another open-air service in the corner of an orchard in the nearer smashed town with about 50 present. All very sunny and peaceful and still, and then suddenly at about 7 o'clock the sound of shelling on the other side of the smashed town – a group from one of the Regiments I held service with in the morning had a shell dropped among them, wounding nine. Another shell got a trench to the right of us, wounding six. All this evening therefore has been spent at the dressing of the wounded – ugly wounds, some of them. A man's back all splattered with little bits, another's arm and shoulders, and another had the patella sprung upwards because

---

312 In Rippendon, Yorkshire 1891.

a piece of shell passed right through the knee, severing that particular sinew. Nasty head wounds and the dressing of them is painful, but the men are wonderfully stolid and silent – it is good stuff. A Lancashire lad however was very talkative, suffered a great deal obviously, but exclaimed about the dressing process in a cheerful, good-mannered way all the time. He was very nice-tempered about it all and said the breeziest things, making everybody laugh. I was struck that no bad expression came from him all through, including the setting of his broken leg. But there came the usual injection against lock-jaw and it was the last straw. "I've been inoculated twice" he said "You ain't going to do me again, mate. Nay, not that stoof a third time". They explained it was not anti-enteric. "Ah, but I know it is, by the needle, and it makes you bad after it" They explained the dangers of lock-jaw and that even only slight wounds necessitated this treatment, but he was unconvinced and, alas the swear words came. "Well,....................they go and shell me, and now they go and stick this into me". But when it was done, and didn't hurt, and we assured him that he would feel nothing more from it, he was content, and with his comical interludes, it was an entertaining episode.

Monday May 31st 1915, Sailly sur-la-Lys
An exciting morning. At about 5.30 am our anti-aircraft guns bombarded an enemy aeroplane buzzing round above, giving it about 90 shells. Some say there was a hit, but it got back to the German lines. About 7.30 am when you might have beheld me shaving, there was that ugly 'whizz' – well do we know it, and then the loud sharp crack, and then the black smoke. The anti-aircraft guns are just down the road, but it made one wonder, was the cracking and smoking going to travel on down our way? 28 times there came the same spiteful, insinuating sound – then silence. That meant 7 rounds from a 4 gun battery, and later it transpired it was good shooting, yet dozens of men were billeted around, and two only were killed and two wounded. I went down to look – not one shell was more than 60 yds from the mark, but after all only some machinery of the guns was damaged.

I am wondering about tomorrow – the aeroplanes will come with bombs perhaps, and will be delighted to find no anti-aircraft shells. Then we shall see and hear something and at least they will be able to report "Alright, Deutchland guns did well yesterday".

Tonight collecting the wounded – only one slight shrapnel cut, and a farm set on fire behind our trenches by an incendiary shell.

Tuesday June 1st 1915, Sailly sur-la-Lys
The aeroplane came at 7.30 a.m., but they had mounted the anti-aircraft guns elsewhere during the night, and two at least, instead of the usual three, were able to hammer away at him. Jolly snubs! There is heavy fighting on our right but here all has been beautiful and still, and except for an exciting ride across the corner of the

fighting zone, and passing over the ground of the last three shellings, I myself have had a peaceful day, and after tea, three sets of Badminton.

Wednesday June 2nd 1915, Sailly sur-la-Lys
A day of journeying, with a little shelling at our end this morning.

Thursday June 3rd 1915, Pont Logy
I received the shocking confidential information that one of the men has been condemned for repeated desertion and cowardice, and is to be shot.[313] The message came late last night and I have been with him most of the afternoon in a mud dug-out guardroom. I have spent most of the day interviewing staff and other officers on his behalf – my visiting had to be within the belt of shelling, and the bullets sung variously about, and I sat on the edge of the dug-out talking on and on, with him crouched on the straw. The bullets and shells did not matter, as this lad pleaded with me to do all I could for him, and I tried to bring him to truth, honour and God. The first, I fear, was the need, and so difficult to know about and yet forbearance and pity kept asserting themselves. "Tout savoir c'est tout pardonner". An only boy – let off after two offences out here. Many thoughts swayed up – Pro: His youth, not yet twenty, his circumstances – an only son and his mother a widow – his health – he repeatedly said that his head troubled him, and he did not know what he was doing. Con: The selfishness of a man wishing other people to face dangers for him, and unwilling to take his share. What right has any man to ask that? And then there is the falseness of some of his statements. The need of discipline – on two battlefields he had run away, after having been repeatedly warned. The assurance that every extenuation

---

313 Private **Oliver W. Hodgetts** (8662) 1 Bn Worcestershire Regiment. He was serving with the 1st Battalion when they arrived in Western Front on the 8th November 1914, fresh from Egypt. Some 5 days later the Battalion took up a defensive position in trenches facing Neuve Chapelle and came under heavy bombardment from the enemy during which 7 men were killed and 25 wounded. During the next 3 days (16th to 19th November 1914) a further 13 men were killed and 27 wounded. During this period, Private Hodgetts went missing but no action was taken against him. On the 19th November 1914, the men of the 1st Battalion climbed out of the trenches and made their way back to billets at La Gorgue, six miles away. They were exhausted, frozen and walking in heavy snowfall. One man in four suffered with frost-bitten hands or feet and in many cases feet or toes had to be amputated. On the 9th May 1915, just prior to the attack on Festubert, Hodgetts went missing again, just as the Battalion prepared to go into action. On the 12th May he reported to a nearby unit and claimed he had sprained his ankle, but when he was examined by the medical officer, no injury was discovered. On the 22nd May 1915, he was brought to trial for desertion and cowardice where he was undefended. Hodgetts' conduct sheet showed that he had been sentenced to 90 days field punishment on the 1st March 1915. His commanding officer Major **George W. St. G. Grogan** at the trial described Hodgetts as a worthless fighting soldier who was only intent on saving his own skin. At his court martial, Private Hodgetts was found guilty of cowardice. Field Marshal Sir **John French** confirmed the sentence and Private Hodgetts was shot by firing squad at HQ in Pont Logy in the morning of 4th June 1915. He was 20 years of age. He is buried at Royal Irish Rifles Graveyard, Laventie, Pas de Calais, France (Grave number IV.D.2). Pont Logy is 6 miles S of Sailly sur-la-Lys, 1 mile E of Neuve Chapelle, 24th Infantry Brigade HQ.

consideration must have been weighed by the Court Martial, the Brigadier, the General, the Corps Commander, the Army Commander and the Field-Marshal – and yet one's last lingering wonder is whether penal servitude would not have answered the offence? I cannot say. Those responsible have decided not. They have experience, and I suppose know where a milder penalty fails as a deterrent. Tomorrow morning at 4 am I am to be present at the execution. May God, who makes no mistakes, receive His erring son to Himself – death is after all, a smaller thing, dishonour is a worse, and here are both in the eyes of man. Yet, God knows, He is just and this life is not all.

We were on the edge of Neuve Chapelle, and on the edge also of the [...*censored*...] fighting. So I went past the Church and a little into the village. Amongst all the tangled waste of things, garden produce can be found – rhubarb a little wild, roses, carnations, peonies, cornflowers, poppies. Everybody seemed to have gathered there. In one corner is a sand-bag fort, in the centre of it a well, the water rather muddy. The younger men had collected old bottles, filled them with various bright-hued flowers and put them in a half ring round the well – their garden fountain!

Friday June 4th 1915 4.35 am, Pont Logy

It is all past – the hideous business.[314] The actual agony was over in three minutes the burial in another five, and the quick ambulance car kindly lent me by the Colonel has brought me back by this time. Everyone was assembled by 3.30 a.m. He was a man who had made many scenes, and it was thought well that I should not speak with him again, and I felt that it was right. The sand-bag bank and the hollow in front of it, with the stake. The long grass and oat stalks. The trench made for the purpose, along which were lined small detachments from other battalions. The firing party about 20 paces in front of about 12 men. The Provost Marshal, the Colonel, three or four officers, the doctor. I put on my black scarf only and stood at the side, almost too stunned to pray. Behind came the prisoner, scarcely able to walk, along a side path, pleading and groaning. Then as he turned the corner onto the grass, he suddenly dashed from his guard and ran wildly across the broken ground, stumbling, panting, straining, able in his despair to reach an astonishing speed, and for the time, to outdistance the men laden with their equipment. He was eventually caught, and as he came back facing us, he presented a pathetic figure of exhaustion and helpless appeal. He was tied to the stake. His eyes were

---

314 During WW1, there were 346 Military executions all by firing squad. Soldier executions served a dual purpose, to punish the deserters and to dispel similar ideas in their fellow soldiers. Offences under the British Army Act, which resulted in a court martial with a sentence to be shot at dawn, included alleged acts of cowardice, desertion, sleeping at post, casting away arms and disobedience. Those condemned to death usually had their sentences confirmed by the Field Marshal on the evening following their court-martial. On the evening before the execution a chaplain would be dispatched to spend the night in the cell with the condemned man. The next morning, at dawn, the execution would take place. Prior to the execution many of the condemned men drugged themselves with morphia or alcohol. The firing squad was usually composed of at least six soldiers. One of their rifles was customarily loaded with a blank round and no soldier could be sure he had fired a fatal shot.

bandaged. "Past 4 o'clock" said the Colonel to the Provost Marshal. A sudden quick crack and the huddled earthly form was separated from the soul gone to the beyond.

The larger party was quickly dismissed. The burial party carried the body behind the sand-bags to the grave already prepared. The O.C. and Adjutant came to the funeral, but I did not feel justified in taking the actual burial form. It seemed judging the judgement given, pre-judging the judgement to come. I took the opening sentences, the end part of the Lesson, the 'Lord have mercy', the Lord's Prayer, the Prayer for Compassion out of the Communion Service, and the Grace. God will make no mistakes. Desertion and cowardice are an awful crime. Leave it at all easy for men to desert to the enemy and how much information they may give away, and by it perhaps dozens, hundreds of other lives lost! It is a desperate offence that demands desperate measures. I felt deeply for the Colonel. He thanked me for coming and I could only answer one word "Duty". This man was an only child – it is less precious when there are other children. How terribly far-reaching is the reflection "No man liveth unto himself, or dieth unto himself[315]".

The strain of this morning's tragedy has been rather much. Other men have gone from us, so many now, good and gallant, sinful – known to be to be sinful, some of them, but redeeming so much by dying bravely at the call of duty. One likes to recall them at a time like this. How wrong any reluctance or misgivings of one's own have been, as one sees all there is behind the decision. Better inspiration than punishment, and I am sure that the Chaplains can help that way. I remember now the many times I myself have said to the men "There come tests at time like that that only the grace of God can carry one through".

That abject cry, "mainstay of the 'ome". "Can I have the bandage off, Sir? I want to see the sky" – cut short with the sharp crack, the quiet thud, the absolute silence, the motionless stillness. The quick order of "about turn" to the firing party. The swish of an enemy bullet in the long grass across the path – it was difficult to pray.

Saturday June 5th 1915, Sailly sur-la-Lys

Club work today, and arranging for Sunday. By dint of much urging we have succeeded in obtaining a kind of gig for the Chaplains, one or two of whom do not ride, and you cannot carry many hymn books on a bicycle – nor can you so easily carry many on a horse, and you find Communion vessels a real difficulty. But now there is the gig, for one or another of us. We can also borrow an ambulance car, but you are never sure of the availability. The next thing is to hope that we can get a horse for the cart. I am afraid that I have had to speak up in reference to this provision. As things are, there is no specified allowance of transport made for Chaplains. The establishment of a Field Ambulance allows for, say ten officers, and

---

315 **Romans 14:7** 'No man liveth unto himself, or dieth unto himself.'

baggage accommodation is provided for ten. The amount of cubic space and the weight per every individual, is calculated out to a cubic foot, to a lb. Now every chaplain has so many cubic feet and so many lbs, say 36lbs to add to this. Where is he to put it? It is true that we have managed so far and the Colonel and officers have been very kind, but the arrangement has always been 'on sufferance'. It has had to be said "Oh, the Chaplain, yes we must tuck his things in <u>somewhere</u>, and this, though amiable, is not right. We know that in war, everyone must put up with pressures, but on the whole question of providing Chaplains at all, it affects the principle. Again, they have sanctioned the issue of prayer books and hymn books, making no arrangement for the carrying of them, and four or five hymn hundred hymn books 'weigh up'! The tendency to regard Chaplains and their work as an annoying superfluity is found here and there, and has been openly expressed once or twice, though not in my hearing, by responsible persons in terms of bad language! If God's claims are in the right place, this cannot be. Moreover, I can think of no worse injury you can do to these men than to lessen the strength and consolation that comes to them through their religion.

The announcement is made today throughout the Division of yesterday's execution – and yet are there not men shirking round the corners of England at this present time who are too selfish and cowardly even to offer to serve? How difficult it is to see the way of clear justice. It is certain that if he deserved his fate, there are men battening at their ease in England to whom right and justice speak with equal sternness.

Sunday June 6th 1915, Sailly sur-la-Lys

It has been a nice day outwardly with glorious sunshine, but a little trying inwardly. Services were disarranged, inevitably, by late and unexpected changes of the battalion from the trenches. Holy Communion at 9.30 but no one present, though services taken for me at the Soldier's Club (here) at 7 and at the Temporary Military Church have had some attendants. Then there was Morning Prayer with the battalion to which my poor friend of Thursday and Friday belonged. I spoke on the day's Epistle "Let us love one another – perfect love casteth out fear[316]". The wrong in cowardice is its selfishness towards man, and that it is distrust towards God and His goodness. The next service failed on account of the battalion changing over so we meet again tomorrow instead. A not very large congregation in the Military Church this evening, but an earnest service and the banging of big guns the whole day, but no shells our way.

Monday June 7th 1915, Sailly sur-la-Lys

Guns all day. There is some heavy fighting along there. My own battalions are on the edge of it and fairly quiet, which is by arrangement no doubt, for they have been

---

316 1 John 4:18 'Let us love one another – perfect love casteth out fear.'

somewhat depleted and especially in the way of officers. It is sad meeting so many new faces – yet what a merciful thing it is that they are all forthcoming, and it is marvellous where all the men come from.

There is much sadness about. These officer friends who are no more – I find in the Illustrated papers news of three officers with whom I messed in former days. But it was a nice service this morning with about 300 present in an orchard – one of our very nice battalions. The officers spoke kindly afterwards – I think everybody feels things much now-a-days, so we sing, and pray and go on.

Tuesday June 8th 1915, Sailly sur-la-Lys
A little tired today and I have a touch of malaria – the extreme heat I expect. An aeroplane over about teatime, and as often, a burst of half a dozen nasty black shells down the road about an hour after – and no one hurt!

Wednesday June 9th 1915, Sailly sur-la-Lys
Your letter came this afternoon telling me that dear Dorothy had gone – I read it while waiting in the field for a funeral[317]. Then there came a telegram asking me to go down to a farm and bury three men burnt to death in another farm last night. These old buildings are so dry that, on a hot day like yesterday, they might almost be set ablaze with spontaneous combustion. At all events, these three men were caught at midnight and the place was burnt down in twenty minutes with 17 men injured. Poor charred remains! more rather three bundles put into the grave, tied up in blankets.

I felt bad this morning, and was almost going into hospital, but a sleep after lunch turned the corner and some pleasant cool rain this evening has helped. Nearly three days of dysentery is depressing.

Thursday June 10th 1915, Sailly sur-la-Lys
No news much today, except a few more shells down the road. Please ask my friends to excuse the delay in letters – last week's pressures and this week's indisposition have been overcoming.

Friday June 11th 1915, Sailly sur-la-Lys
Fighting is still very quiet near us, with just a shell or two down the road, and the rumble over the plain has ceased. We hope it is true that the Dardanelles are being forced more rapidly now, but every day brings with it its rumours. It is a blessing that President Wilson is taking a firm stand and it is obvious the German Mission to America, which pretended that the tales of barbarity in Belgium were fabrications of

---

317 RDG's sister-in-law Dorothy Saumarez-Smith, died June 7th 1915.

the Allies, leaves Germany now finally discredited by the Lusitania deed. The German mind is trained in a harsh school, and the overbearing spirit makes it incapable of reasoning with just tolerance and calmness, and there seems to be no limit to their capability for savagery. I wonder if America will be drawn in.

I am still keeping the two Clubs on, but apart from the baths, the first one is not so much used now. Yet there might be an influx of troops – one never knows – and that would make one glad to have the place fully going. So I am keeping it still.

Saturday June 12th 1915, Sailly sur-la-Lys

Better tonight, I think, but still a little off tone. It was wise to cry off tomorrow. There have been other cases, in fact rather a number – it has been the heat probably. So I have chiefly been doing the odd things – Club matters – visiting round the Ambulance rooms. There are some ugly wounds again, and the shock accompanying the shell wounds is sometimes very serious. Any shell has a vicious scream, and when it hits you as well, it must make you think.

We have a garden behind us, and among its wild contents are some nice carnations and roses – they make a pleasant sight to men wounded, and out of the trenches.

I had an interesting talk with an officer this morning. He has had to go off with a nervous breakdown, as he was in the fire three nights ago and helped gather the remains of the dead. One of the dead men was a special friend, and the officer has been thinking hard about God's ways. Things are a terrible strain to many just now, but the end is not yet. "What I do thou knowest not now, but thou shalt know hereafter[318]", and the very awfulness of things assures one's sense of goodness and right, that things will be adjusted.

I see that Germany is preparing the way for bombing Milan Cathedral and St. Mark's in Venice[319], by declaring that they have been used as observation towers and for anti-aircraft guns, which is strongly denied. What a hideous vandalism it is. It is like the time of, say, Julian the Apostate all over again[320].

I have been reading the official documents relating to the outbreak of the war. The German mind reveals itself there – in one juncture the contrast between the

---

318 **John 13:7**; What I do thou knowest not now, but thou shalt know hereafter'
319 October 24th, 1915 Austrian planes bombed Venice. The pilots aimed at the railway station and the iron bridge outside it, but instead they hit the 17th-century Church of Santa Maria de Nazaret, irreparably shattering its ceiling. February 14th 1916, Milan was bombed by eleven airplanes that took off in the region of Trentino. The bombers tried to hit the railway station but the greater part of the bombs fell in the Porta Volta area and near the cemetery. 15 people died in the attack.
320 **Julian**, Roman Emperor 361–63. Decendant of Constantine the first Christian emperor of the Roman Empire, Julian attempted to return the empire to the worship of the traditional Roman pantheon of Gods rather than Christanity. Killed fighting the Sassanid Persian Empire, his last words where, reportedly, "You have won, Galliean". He was the last pagan emperor of Rome.

courteous, earnest, solicitous tone of the Czar, and the dominating impatience of the German Emperor stands out unmistakably. This is the whole situation.

Fighting quiet – no shelling today, except at one of our aeroplanes, but there is plenty of rifle fire which is going hard as I write.

Sunday June 13th 1915, Sailly sur-la-Lys

Better today, thank you. Much cooler weather and this evening I was energised enough to go down to the convalescents, about 30 of them, and took a service under some trees. They were pleased, and I was pleased too.

There has been a recrudescence of fighting with heavy shelling and noisy rifle fire. It has kept to the trenches almost entirely, but there have been about three dozen casualties, almost all minor ones although one man was killed outright in a most distressing manner. It remains as striking as ever with what quiet patience the men take their injuries.

It is earnestly to be hoped the 'Shell' mission will progress increasingly. It is just the phrase – we may be thankful for advocacy like Lloyd George's "we must crash our way through"[321]. Writing by my candle at a road-side corner, where a hurricane of high explosives might drop at any moment, and where it <u>would</u> drop if the enemy chose to make this a point for an attempt at breaking through our lines, the sense of being able to get behind defences and to 'crash' at him until we silenced him, is one that pleads for every encouragement. Sandbags and shells are the sort of comforts for the troops that one likes to think of now!

Monday June 14th 1915, Sailly sur-la-Lys

Thankful to say, much better today and probably normal in another day or so, but it has been a warning to moderate off a little more!

A comparative lull today, but the 'pop-pop' goes on hour after hour and even more so through the night. What a stupid procedure it seems to be but rather fun tonight – a lot of 'bogus' noises being made by transport on various roads along here, through the night, to deceive the enemy.

Tuesday June 15th 1915, Sailly sur-la-Lys

It is a mercy to be feeling more natural, but it will take some days yet, no doubt, to be as fit as before. I have been working off various things, papers and letters, also reconnoitring in view of a possible change from here.

---

321 David Lloyd George, speech in Cardiff to munitions workers, June 11th 1915, "We want to turn out so much that once the hour arrives we shall just crash our way through to victory."

We are on a flank. There is much fighting and a thunder of attacking over away. Here we get bursts of shelling – not among my Brigade happily just now, except in the trenches and except this morning when some high explosives tried to find one battalion. One shell nearly got 15 men, but was stopped about twenty yards off by a tree – bursting there! Down the road there were about 80 shells, but not on our Brigade. Most of them fell harmlessly, but one fell among some transport, injuring 7 men, stampeding the horses injuring some and sending some other men out of their minds. Another set a farm alight this morning – it burnt furiously at the other end of the village. My beat lay at this end and I resisted the question of whether to go down there or not as duty presses along one's own route, and after all, one must just follow it. They are mostly all high explosives now, and though they are at the end of the village, the scream and crash sounds very near. They keep however, at a certain range which we hope is their limit, and we hope that they will not improve on it. Good progress on the whole seems general, East and West, but I do pray that the Eastern doings may be prospered. All the same, the resilient plan by the Russians seems effective – if they do not have to carry it too far.

Thursday June 17th 1915, Sailly sur-la-Lys

Two nice books, thank you. "Aunt Sarah and the War" is quaint and good[322]. I am making up my mind really to 'shut off' so much reading for every day, and now while things are quieter, turning in earlier at night. That is difficult, because the wounded cannot be brought in before dark, and the evenings are very long, and with the most serious injuries, one wants to be nearby. There was another head wound last night – no pain, I hope, after the first blow and no sign of consciousness – just breathing hard, and later – "God's finger touched him, and he slept[323]". A letter in his pocket from his mother showed how she loved and cared for him, a good lad, and how thankful she was that he was being preserved – and then, in three or four hours time, comes this. I have just been writing to her.

There has been shelling again today, across our trenches. So much of it tells on the men in time and a young fellow has had to come in all shaken by the constant night and day of it. All the pluck in the world cannot 'feed' the nerves that are anaemic for want of sleep and the opportunity of proper nourishment. I am glad that he, and the regimental doctor, have had the courage to be discreet. The dash and excitement of an occasional attack is quite a different thing. The man next to him, less seriously hit but also in the head, quite clean and glad of a word.

A fine big dog has been brought in from a farm that has been knocked about, and the inhabitants have all gone, no one knows where. The dog they said, during the remainder of the shelling, was by turns fierce and frightened. He would dash out

---

322 *Aunt Sarah & the War: A Tale of Transformations*, Wilfrid Meynell, 1915
323 Alfred, Lord Tennyson, *In Memoriam*

and bark at some of the shells as they burst, and others as they whistled down, caused him to rush for shelter anywhere he could. A horse and cart had to be left out on the road when the onset was hottest and about 40 shells in all fell around the cart without hitting it. The horse was undisturbed – he just turned his head in this or that direction of the explosion, but remained where he stood!

Friday June 18th 1915, Sailly sur-la-Lys[324]

We move tomorrow and much of today therefore has been taken up in preparation. Many pages could be written on the vicissitudes of billeting – it is late, and I must not stop to write. The rifles are popping away hard and the machine guns go pippering away.

An excitable little Yorkshire lad has just been brought in as a possible 'dementia' – he got up on the parapet and ran along it, flourishing his bayonet. I think really he is only a little venturesome, perhaps foolhardy – it would be interesting to follow him up and I shall try to get the Colonel to keep him here for observation.

Saturday June 19th 1915, Estaires

The Recording Angel must shed many a tear over the violent fabrications that are made by inhabitants grown weary of receiving military people, and wishing to be excused. Then, here and there, you meet with a devoted willingness to help and endure, which makes up for the others. A high, square, flat-faced house this, white-washed and white-shuttered, down the long street and out a little beyond a slummier area, overlooking a timber yard across the cobbled-paved road, with the river just visible round the corner of a roof in front. Over the cobbles the traffic rattles unmercifully. The house next but one, at a corner, is a many-eyed skeleton of a building shelled into that condition earlier in the war. We are just in the line of the shelling that pursued this place with five weeks of a daily visitation of that kind when last we were here. Why we are in this house is because it is the only one we could properly find rooms in, after a day's searching, as the town is rather full! Our welcome is cordial, which is a great thing. Whether this move is a swing round of the Division to another position is something we may not discuss – we wait and see.

Billeting!! Here is a house we think might be excellent for our mess – a sitting room, and then a long room with a chair or two and a grand piano and all unoccupied. But useless to us, as all the windows have been boarded up, except for a small one at the end, and they cannot be mended for want of glass. Madame, in another house, assures us with protestations, that there is only one bedroom and that is occupied. After much persuasion, she shows us three more, all huge apartments, but unfurnished except for an old mattress on the floor. Two bedrooms are locked, but after more persuasion,

---

324 War Diary, 24th Field Ambulance (WO 95/1703/1). June 19th 'Removed to PENSION de DEMOISELLES, ESTAIRES.'

she starts off to find the keys, but retraces her steps after a few yards, to asseverate that they are used by two relatives who are travelling, and have taken the keys with them!

At another house, we ring the bell and it is answered (the time is 6.15p.m.) by a round red-faced lady of some 50 summers in her night-dress, from a window looking on to the pavement just beside the doorway. She tells us solemnly that she is ill – true enough no doubt – and that her servant is out. We wait and the servant returns in five minutes to tell us that they do not have people billeted there although the red-faced lady's sister-in-law had told us not half-an-hour before that there had been billets there until five days ago. She did not tell us that the lady had long been 'invalidish' – we did not press for entrance there.

The welcome in this next house is very kind, and I have found billets for the two other chaplains next door. It is clean, and the elderly maiden lady is thankful to have Khaki here as a guarantee of security, but it is about a mile from the mess and it will use up too much time and energy merely in passing to and fro.

At the house I am going to now, the elderly widow began by objecting – then she wanted to know my rank, something of my habits, the nature of my officership, the character of my orderly, whether I would be sure to get the official 'billet de logement' and try to keep the passages clean. Being fully assured on all points, she ends by giving me a nice little bedroom over-looking the yard, and another, floor-clothed, next door for washing and dressing and a cupboard in which to hang up my clothes.

We marched in after breakfast, and a number of us used the motor ambulance, which saved much time and trouble. I shall be able to keep on the Club here and to the men's great satisfaction – delight in fact – the baths!

Sunday June 20th 1915, Estaires

Alas! let it be recorded with all tender forbearance that the good impulses of the elderly widow have collapsed! She watched for my passing by from her doorstep at mid-day today, and with a very concerned face, asked if I were accustomed to having a bath. I answered that, after the manner of my countrymen who liked being clean, I had a bath every day if I could, but I hastened to add that it was a very little one, "une petite affaire". I was so careful about "les taches" and my ordonnaire was also that I could safely "n'importerait du tout" or words to that effect. She was "desolee" but it was quite impossible to agree to that – if I would promise to give up my bath, I might come. I am afraid that I did a naughty thing – I asked her if she had thought at all what it would be like to spend a day or two in the trenches? She is really quite comfortably off with all this roomy house to herself and her stout serving woman. Her virtues have lain rather in other directions than home-making which, thinks an officer who himself failed on other scores to find an entrance there, is "why her husband chose to die so soon."

So I walk my mile to and fro to this house. She is an earnest good soul in her way, this one. When the shelling was about, she and her maid didn't come up-stairs at all. They lived in the kitchen at the back, and when the fights were on they sat up all night waiting for the three officers who were billeted here. They helped the orderlies wash the mud-stained clothes, made tea and coffee for them at any hour, and I believe behaved most hospitably.

The day has been a comparatively light one. Holy Communion at 7.30 am at which I did not officiate, a Chaplain of [...*censored*...] being due. 10 am a most hearty and earnest open air service with a very nice regiment, who always turn up in force voluntarily, four or five hundred of them. Then at 11.30 another very happy time with the regiment whose man was shot for desertion[325] and a number of whose officers I have had special friendships with, and of whom so many have been wounded or killed. In the next field nine men were hit by a shell on Sunday week. In the field next but one more shells fell yesterday afternoon, but we were fairly well away from the direction of fire. In connection with both services, some men lingered about for devotional words.

A full service in the Town Hall this evening at which I helped, the [...*censored*...] Chaplain preaching very helpfully on "Be strong in the Lord"[326].

The 'Daily Mail' Bird's Eye View of the British Front[327] will give you a good idea of our surroundings.

Monday June 21st 1915, Estaires
Things are fairly quiet and down here they are especially peaceful – one almost feels that there must be mischief brewing. A hostile aeroplane in the distance this morning dropped bombs wide of the next village.

Tuesday June 22nd 1915, Estaires
My time today has been very much taken up with work for the mess, trying to get a room and a kitchen, and literally serving at tables. Owing, in the first place, to my having some facility in the French tongue, I became Mess President, and was very glad at the time to do it till the end of November, but now I have tried once or twice to resign the honour to someone else, but no one is ready to take it on. Everybody is very glad to have a big mess with good supplies well served, and one or two have held themselves free to grumble when misadventures have occurred, or when supplies have been impossible, or when there have not been proper cooking facilities, but no one

---

325 1st Battalion, Worcestershire Regiment.
326 **Ephesians 6:10** 'Finally, my brethren, be strong in the Lord, and in the power of his might.'
327 *Daily Mail Bird's Eye Map of the British Front.* Published by the "Daily Mail" in London and printed by George Philip & Son, Ltd, the map features the Ypres area of Belgium and the Lille area of France. 6d, 1915.

will take up the management. I grudge the time very much when the men's lives call so much for every hour of ministry. I must seriously think whether someone will not do the right thing and take their due place. We have horrible cooking arrangements and French sanitation is primeval ignorance! But as we expect to be here for only a short time, I am making the best of it.

Apart from that, visiting behind the trenches, green fields, waving corn, reserve trenches, heaped up redoubts, battered buildings and farmhouses full of men – that is the scene.

Wednesday June 23rd 1915, Estaires

Most of today spent in the trenches and the firing line. No shells along our bit, but many further on, with plenty of bullets singing through the orchard trees, smacking and snarling against the parapets. The long road, running into wilder and more rank vegetation with cornfields and gardens sown before the battle now left desolate and unused. The corn and oats may be gathered, but the shelling has driven all the inhabitants away weeks ago. Here and there an Indian walking delicately close up to the road side, very picturesque – looking in the sun with a touch of yellow or brilliant red. Huge poppies are to be found now, and these Sikhs and Gurhkas love to decorate themselves, sticking them in bunches in their turbans and shoulder straps. Then the country gets very still and deserted as you draw near the firing line. Big houses can be occupied for the asking if you do not mind the gaping shell holes in the walls, and the prospect of more. Beds, bedding, an occasional chair or table, kitchen ranges and sometimes ornaments – they are all still there. People do not linger much as they go to and fro in those areas, and nobody cares to carry anything more than he need. Who wants a sewing machine, or a broken pair of kitchen scales at a time like this? Nearer the firing line it is safer than at a zone this side, and you always breathe more freely as you get closer to the dug-outs and the parapets.

Yesterday some huge shells got a house at the nearest turning to us and set fire to it, and today the remnants were still smouldering. One shell hole just on the edge of the road was fully deep enough and wide enough to put a motorcar into. My way lay right through the village of Neuve Chapelle – the church was shelled again yesterday. Here along the beaten path, or just beside it, is a stained patch of soil, buzzed over by bluebottles. It is the grave of a German, who is not buried deep enough and you see other patches like it as you move along. A covering-up process has been going on, but the weather has worn down the surface, necessarily left thin, the first necessity having been to make good the new trenches and defences. A shell hole has been used as a grave – it is filled across one side and above it is a rough cross "A British soldier lies buried here" – no name, no date, no identity disc – buried in all the rush and heat of the battle and probably at night. Here is a German officer's dug-out, in front of the little smashed up villa down the main street. They probably occupied the villa and dodged into the dug-out when shelling came on. One further wall of the dug-out has been tumbled in, a heap of earth and sand-bags. Over the door beam of it is painted in strong neat characters "Zur Schonen Hussenschift[328]". Here is a bottle-corking machine, and a kind of bottle stand like a hat stand, so this was obviously an 'estaminet'. A desk or two still stand among the debris of the village school and the Village Hall near the church is discernible by the beams and plastering. 'Smack' goes a bullet – well up fortunately. Across the next road, you drop down into the communication trench, rather muddy even in this dry weather. Just over there is a pump – an officer explained that after the fight, men tried different pumps for water but many were useless. One or two that did reach water, were found to have the bucket inside connected up with an electric wire, and the working of the pump was followed in each case by four or five shells from the German lines. It was joined up to an electric alarm!

Winding trenches, twisting every way and now and then you peep across at the German trenches, not more than 500 yds and at some points not more than 250 yds away. A German deserter came in last night, a bad character, who said he had been a prisoner for five months since the beginning of the war, and had deserted because they had been kept twenty days in the trenches. He says there are 15 machine guns along this line of the front.

I went to the graves of nine of our men killed two days ago and buried, (as is the rule in this Brigade,) the same night by the officers. Our Brigadier does not like Chaplains going to these burials, and indeed it becomes a complex and burdensome matter for many people. The Brigade Staff would have to be advised, the Chaplain would have to be warned, long awkward journeys at night would have to be made and guides provided – all an unsuitable tax on the personnel when fighting is going on. I said prayers over these graves and I then went to see the grave of the man who was executed. His comrades had provided a board "Pte [*…censored…*] Regt [*…censored…*] Died 4.6.1915". The grave of the 26 men, out of the 59 hit by one shell, has been nicely done up and is decorated with beautiful bunches of flowers, of which there are plenty everywhere, the houses at that crossway being now long ago deserted and some of them further smashed up.

Thursday June 24th 1915, Estaires

Last night one of the officers was particularly anxious to have company in 'collecting', so although I was very tired, I joined him. Collecting is late now – we do not start till 10 and tonight we got back by 11.30 as it happened, but it was late in the day for adventures[329]. The minor one was cutting a signal wire that sagged a little low across a road (it is all in the dark) and the major one was that the car-driver inadvertently

---

328 "Here are the Arts and Humanities"
329 War Diary, 24th Field Ambulance (WO 95/1703/1). June 21st '10.00 Collecting deferred from now to this hour' Lt.Col. R. Pickard.

over-shot the aid-post, and went sailing down the track to the trenches. We had gone a good 150 yds before our general observation discerned that things were not right, and pulled him up. The corner we passed is called 'Snipy Corner' and the roadway 'Snipy Lane'. While the officer and I stood in the road waiting for the car to turn round, we had an experience of 'snipiness' as two bullets sang over us with a very near and nasty noise. The senior officer of the Aid-post said, "If you had gone on much further you would have had a machine gun firing on to you". The one wounded man we collected there was one who had been hit on the other side of the house at about tea-time, by one of these snipers.

Another move! We are attached to another Corps. If this means a quasi-rest for the Division, I may get home. If, as is more probable, there is something up, then all leave will be off – the next week will show. I send you a little souvenir of Neuve Chapelle – a devotional book found in a vacated dug-out and a leaf of a prayer book found in a mined cottage.

Friday June 25th 1915, Estaires

Much to do today, preparing to move. Heavy rain. Visiting billets and I gave £25 for Club and other purposes to the Rev. E.K. Talbot[330] (a son of the Bishop of Winchester), who is very grateful.

Saturday June 26th 1915, Estaires

There is some prospect of leave, but not so late on as August as far as I can gather. We have not moved yet, but if we do and it is into quasi-rest, I might rush over in a hurry but we shall know more in four or five day's time.

The list of honours and awards has just come out and truth to tell, though in regard to the names given there has been some satisfaction, there have also been great heart searching and disapproval, and much enquiry. Where all have been so excellent, why particularise? With only rare exception every man and officer has done his level best – what can man do more? What more have those who have been honoured done than their fullest duty? It is difficult, but some are hurt and depressed – what a pity that questionings like these should have been raised at all.

---

330 **Edward Keble Talbot** MC (b.1877 – d.1949) The son of Edward Stuart Talbot. Talbot was educated at Winchester and Oxford, He was ordained in 1904 and was curate of St Mary's Church in Woolwich, south-east London. He joined the Community of the Resurrection in 1906. In 1914, he became a temporary Chaplain to the Forces, serving until 1919 and winning the Military Cross. He became Superior of the Community of the Resurrection in 1922, serving until 1940. He was also one of the Chaplains to King George VI between 1920 and 1945. His brother, Neville Talbot was the founder of Toc H (December 1915), a club for soldiers in Poperinghe, in memory of his younger brother Gilbert, killed at Hooge in 1915. Like RCG's clubs Toc H was "an alternative for the 'debauched' recreational life of the town".

Sunday June 27th 1915, Estaires

It is a question about leave and the difficulties do not diminish. July, they think, is going to be an important month and if it is, one's place is definitely here. We must see. We are again on the march, and have to be ready to move at 20 minutes notice!

7.30 a.m. Holy Communion in the Mairie of this now sheltered town, with 12 present.

9.30 and I am off to one of the smashed-up towns to propose a service later in the morning with the bomb-throwers. Everybody is on the move, and it has been impossible this week to arrange anything beforehand. Then on again to the area of the Reserve trenches. The billets near there were shelled yesterday afternoon, and the O.C. rightly would not sanction any bodies of men being gathered in groups, and I agreed with him. But on his own account, he had sent word round that any men wishing to might be marched up to the linen drying loft for a service about a mile and a half back, and indeed they were already assembled and starting off. So I rushed round by a cross country route, there to meet one of our Chaplains who had just heard that the Chaplain who was holding himself responsible for the day's service went on the march yesterday. So I proposed his taking the service and I would play the harmonium, the which we did. Others had arrived, including a General, and my men got in very late as the march was longer than they had expected, but they did eventually arrive at the hymn before the sermon. Then a rush back to the bomb-throwers, where we had a very nice service under a barn shed with about 80 present. I spoke among other things of the value of having Bible promises stored up in the mind, and about 40 men stayed behind wanting copies of Pocket Testaments – so my stock got mostly depleted.

The distances are very great and after a late lunch, I was glad of the usual Sunday afternoon pause. Then I had a rush around arranging for my little harmonium to be used at the Mairie evening service by the Chaplain who was taking it, and a journeying over to the linen loft again. Conran's people also are forbidden to assemble today, so we took the service as this morning – I played, and he spoke nicely on the unsatisfied spirit within ourselves, which God answers in Christ Jesus and by His life. As the last hymn was given out there was an ominous bang, then another and another. They sounded in a field nearby and some across the road. There was no mistaking them – for the first time for nearly three months they have started shelling these parts again. We found on finishing the service, that not only in our locality but also at the cross roads of the village, a dozen or so shells had fallen. It meant running the gauntlet again as there was no other road, and also Conran's billet is near these cross-roads. Surely enough, when we went along, we found that four of his ambulance men had been hit, one very seriously, perhaps dying, and also one or two horses and an ambulance car or so. I went in with him to the operating room, which is really the street parlour of the house that they have made into their hospital. The severely hit man was suffering greatly, and they were just going to give him an anaesthetic. Our house was next to this one, before we moved last week and a shell had dropped in the yard of it. Two more had hit the next house, and one had got into the yard of the next house where our men had had their cooking fire. All the Red Cross men were crowded under the lee of these houses on the pavement and I encouraged them to do this, as it was obviously the safer place. As I walked along among them – whizz – crash, there came another shell on the other side of this house and the majority of the men rushed away into a field across the road. I went into the house to go and view the needs at the back of the premises – bang – splash! there came another on the garden path, scattering mud everywhere. Two other Chaplains were already there and there was nothing more to be done. My own little Red Cross car, on loan by the Colonel's kindness was out in the road, so we wound it up and away we went. As we did so, another scream and a bang went down on the garden behind us and we were not sorry to be taking the direction pointing away from it.

I got in before the end of the service at the Mairie – it was quite a large one with over a 100 present and the Chaplain gave a nice earnest address. I met the Artillery Major who told me that those shells were going to get a heavy response from us in the next half hour.

After dinner I talked French with the worthy Proprietor of the house in which we have the Mess room, until rather tired. Apparently, during the German occupation, they had two non-commissioned officers billeted, who ate and drank all day long, especially drank – coffee, tea, beer, wine. They looted the town of wine, and in this house they took everything they wanted, paying for nothing.

Wednesday June 28th 1915, Estaires

We did not move today – it will probably be tomorrow, right out into some green fields, but where habitation is scarce. Tents are not provided – there are no tents in this campaign except those for the patients – so it means scattering, and for others, for example those who can get a ground sheet for a head covering, sleeping under the trees.

I have had an interesting talk today with a woman who was in Neuve Chapelle. When the Germans occupied the town she got separated from her children, and being a day too late in quitting her farm, found herself shut off on that side of the trenches and inside the German lines. This was in November and she got sent to Lille. In April, a general exodus of non-combatants was allowed to return to this side via Switzerland. The details she could give of life under the German occupation were enlightening. The view she got from the talk of the enemy soldiers was that it was now a fight for terms – a very different spirit from that held at the beginning, in which it was declared that Germany was going to dictate its wishes. The life of the farms, the workshops, the homes, the town shops goes on as usual, only always overshadowed by the domineering German chiefs. The soldiers rather cruelly taunted the people that although the Germans were not so completely master of the situation as they had expected to be – England having come in – France was <u>ruined</u>.

Thursday June 29th 1915[331]

We definitely move tomorrow, this time well out of shell range and I think out of the sound of firing, though they say it is nearer a 'certain place' where the sound of the guns travel over the plains very distinctly. Anyway, it is to a pleasant looking green spot, where the main part of the work is to be a convalescent place for lighter cases and if it is so, a number of us will put in for leave, and I shall hope to get across the water somehow[332].

I shall close this one Club here now – the baths are less used as men can swill and swim in the open and I think the expense is better reserved for the autumn and winter. Besides, our Division is moving right away from this area. I am keeping on the smaller Club in our own area i.e. still within the Division, our move being of the nature of a 'swing round'. Some of the Fund is going for the purchase of Illustrated Weeklies, which being used in the Hospital, are then passed on to the Club. I now think that it would be better to get two sets, one for the Club and another for the Hospital as there is a great run on them.

I shall be quite sorry to leave this billet – the distance is difficult but the kindness is remarkable. "With all my heart" said the kindly old lady today (a devout Roman Catholic) "you are welcome as if it were our Lord Himself" – a very real application of His wish "I was a stranger and ye took Me in[333]".

Wednesday June 30th 1915, Doulieu

I looked into the billets that we left last week over which the shells came on Sunday. One shell had dropped right on to where the cooks had had their fire out in the yard. Another hit the partition wall between two houses where some of the men are still billeted, but, as it happened, doing damage to neither interior, and a fragment of a third went high up through a window of a room in which I slept in, smashing a picture glass. It is a wicked game.

We are now right back in the country, well back from the firing line. A hostile aeroplane was visible this evening, surrounded by its' little black puffs, but we hear nothing of the rifle fire, nor any of the cannonading, if ought there be. The men are in a large field of the farm under waterproof sheets and I have managed to get into a cottage, as have five of the other senior officers. We are going to try and get canvas too – it would be pleasant sleeping in the open, but foolish on this mud without reasonable covering, especially as an order came this morning that billeting was to be sought for. I am close by the great church, which is now only a skeleton as the Germans, when in occupation of this village, saturated the building with petroleum

---

331 War Diary, 24th Field Ambulance (WO 95/1703/1). June 29th 'Moved from ESTAIRES to BRIELLE FARM near DOULIEU'.

332 La Brielle farm is about 4 miles N of La Gorgue.

333 **Matthew 25:35** 'I was a stranger and ye took Me in.'

and set fire to it, and incidentally used the opportunity to get rid of some of their own dead, placing them in a heap in the centre of the pile to be burnt with it[334]. The farm belongs to the Mayor of the Commune, a virile, thin-visaged keen old gentleman of about 70, who held me button-holed for about an hour this evening, recounting his experiences during the German occupation, and the return of the French, and the advent of the English in October last. It was a vivid account, full of exact detail, and it is clear that he behaved with great courage, gallantry and fidelity. He was eventually left alone in the place surrounded by over a thousand Germans, his body held as a hostage against any betrayal of them, and was made to stand the greater part of a night on a heap of potatoes, behind which German soldiers slept, and was kept for nearly 24 hours without food. Brought before the German General the next morning he was told by that dignitary "Mr Mayor, your Commune is now a German Commune, and you are a German mayor". Eight days after, he saw a French officer of cavalry at the corner by his farm, and he believed by then that the Germans had retreated, the bridge over the river in the next Commune having been blown up. He told this news to the French officer, who directed him to lead the way into the village. This he did, the officer's orderly walking with him, and the officer 20 paces behind. When they came to this corner by the church, they saw two German sentries on guard at the house to the right of the one that I am in. There was a sharp exchange of shots, revolver from the French officer, rifle from the sentries. Both sides missed, and the Frenchmen retired to behind a shrine half way between this and the farm. There was no pursuit, and two hours later another cautious inspection showed that the enemy had all disappeared.

There are two rumours – one that we are here only for a quick refit before pressing further along the line, and the other that it is a 'rest' occupation. If the later, I shall take some sort of leave and run over for a few days.

There are many signs of a prolonged British occupation in the town. Not least interesting are some of the window notices e.g. "Here washing of linen" - "Soldiers washing done here" – (Butter) "the very best ½ the pound" – "Here shoemaker" – "Cafee milk solhere". The last is pretty successful, it is in a cottage just outside the town and I remember that it replaced a sign which ran "Cafe aux lait". I conjecture both productions are due to the offices of some kind-hearted soldiers, who did their best.

Friday July 2nd 1915, Doulieu
This last week or two we have seen a good number of drunken Frenchmen, chiefly lads, excited at being called up for service. They parade the streets of the town, rolling and singing interminably the same doggerel which ends "après la guerre".

---

334 Doulieu, Church of the Assumption, burnt by the occupyimg Germans on 14th October 1914.

'Our three cooks and an aeroplane'

A quiet time, but tremendously busy preparing for Sunday – it does take time back in this country region.

Saturday July 3rd 1915, Doulieu
More preparing, and also Club business. I did much to wind up one Club today as it is quite unsatisfactory unless you can pop in often, and that is not possible in that quarter.

Sunday July 4th 1915, Doulieu
5th Sunday after Trinity and the eleventh month of the war completed. Why do mosquitoes choose to be most active at night? Because it is at night that their victims like best to rest – everybody is bite-y and lumpy all over but fortunately they are not the malarial kind, so their mischief is not too great.

I melted in church this morning – the linen drying loft must be very successful in peace time. Some of the men too were a livid red and streaming with perspiration. A London cook, I have read, put down for the Sunday dinner of the family 'Soup, Cold beef, Salad, Cold Sweats'. We have had the latter all day, but warmed up instead!

The early service was pleasant with three only present, all Staff Officers, but just as we were finishing there was the ominous "smash – smash" four times – the missives of a four-gun battery and then another quatrain – then another – and so on for over an hour. In the still morning air they sounded very near.

Breakfast at the Soldiers' Club and then the hot service at 10.30 again about 5 miles away with some 100 present, then back here, under the trees where we had a quiet nice time, with about 60 present and 3 officers. After tea, a 7 mile journey down into one of the smashed up towns behind the firing line and another nice service – about 30 present: I spoke about '<u>Sanctify</u> the Lord God in your hearts'[335] – the whole of today's epistle in fact. Coming back, our anti-aircraft gun was shelling a hostile aeroplane and one of its half-spent shells fell by the roadside just before we passed.

I am going to put in for leave as the Division is in quasi-rest. I wish the Government could issue the men with thinner summer clothes – they send them about everywhere with their usual kit and the thick winter Khaki – it is a dangerous economy as one man died suddenly today of apoplexy.

Monday July 5th 1915, Doulieu

I have sent in formal note for leave today – it is becoming general and I shall know in a day or two.

Fighting is quiet today. Much attention is being given now to anti-gas smelly bags. The order will be that we carry when issued, both a helmet and a smelling pad. Solution: 3 gals water 6lbs hydrosulphide of soda: 2lbs glycerine i.e. for the best known gas[336]. Another gas now being used does not affect the lungs, but burns the eyes, causing great lachrymation and temporary blindness[337]. Another farm was burnt down last

---

335 **1 Peter 3:15** 'But sanctify the Lord God in your hearts: and be ready always to give an answer to every man that asketh you a reason of the hope that is in you with meekness and fear.'

336 **Chlorine gas**. Chlorine is a powerful irritant that can inflict damage to the eyes, nose, throat and lungs, by reacting with bodily fluids to create hydrochloric acid. At high concentrations and prolonged exposure, it can cause death by asphyxiation. German chemical companies BASF, Hoechst and Bayer had been producing chlorine as a by-product of their dye manufacturing. In cooperation with Fritz Haber of the Kaiser Wilhelm Institute for Chemistry in Berlin, they began developing methods of discharging chlorine gas against enemy trenches, first used in January 1915. Caustic Soda (Sodium Hydroxide NaOH, soluable in glycerine), reacts with chlorine to produce a simple brine (sodium chloride solution).

337 **Tear gas**: Lacrimators, which exist most often in liquid or solid form, are usually dispersed into the air as gases by being exploded from grenades, bombs, or shells. (The liquid or solid lacrimators are vaporised by the heat of the explosion.) Liquid lacrimators, as well as solid

night, occupied by some Belgian refugees – they go very quickly these old buildings, once they get alight.

Tuesday July 6th 1915, Doulieu

I am assured today, on very good authority, that is was quite true that during the last heavy fight on the morning of the bombardment, a man was found with a telephone apparatus connected with an underground wire running past our trenches and to the German lines. The very fact, therefore, that the bombardment was postponed for 24 hours was apparently announced and all the rest of it.

It has been a beautiful day. I spent the morning visiting round a battalion who go back into the trenches tonight. They had heard that trench mortars were going rather busily just now, and also the cross roads behind their trench were being briskly shelled even while we talked, to the tune of about 40 shells.

One of the men who has been out here since Mons, and was going off next week for leave, was killed by a long-distance bullet as he walked up the road – a road one has often walked oneself[338]. So you never know your luck.

I have committed some poetry! We are intending to compile a little souvenir of the Ambulance under my own distinguished editorship. It remains to be seen if it comes to anything. One or two have made a beginning, and there will be photographs and possibly a sketch or two. The burden of the poem is that some of the Regulars were wont to speak lightly of the Territorials – they do not do so now. The Territorial Officer wears a badge 'T' with the other badges. The professional officer has regarded himself as something rather superior, but now the Territorial man is not at all inclined to apologise for himself and feels he is of use, and can be valued.

The Territorial 'T'
(R.A.M.C.)

The fragrant pipe, and the genial book
When the day's work's nearly done.
The greensward games, and the garden teas
Under the summer sun.
"But the day might come, we must be prepared"
Said the men who paused to see
And they spurned light joys and alert they took
The Teritorial T.

---

lacrimators dissolved in liquids, are sometimes sprayed into the air. The most widely used lacrimator is chloroacetophenone (CN); others include ochlorobenzalmalononitrile (CS) and chloropicrin (PS).

338 Private **C Shaw**, I Bn Highland Light Infantry, died 6th July 1915.

Oh cheery's the Camp on a glad warm day –
And cool is the evening shade.
But the mud sucks deep, and the rain wets much
And the work of a good brigade is stern and stiff.
And the careless stream
Smiled and said with quizzical glee.
"It's a game they play. An odd man's dream
This Territorial T."

It came. 'Twas war. And the land amazed
At a base foe's monstrous deed
Upraised its arm: around it gazed
For withal to strike with speed.
Every moment tells. Every man who can
A ransome's worth shall be.
And here stand these. Was it in vain they ran
The Territorial T?

And the R.A.M.C. to the general good
With courage and strength and skill
Forsaking home and livelihood
Did they not give with a will?
With a will they gave on Perram Down,
In the Hursley mud, by the sea
In the billet drear, in the shell-searched town,
Their Territorial T.

For the tale to be told, it will bear a thought.
Of the long night watch and toil,
Of the deft keen hand that so often caught
Back out of death's dread coil
The precious life. Of the dark, night ride
Of the tumble-down house and the tree
That were shelter bare when 'twas woe betide
The Territorial T.

And the trembling earth when the 'coal boa' drops
And the scream of the 'whizz-bang' shrill,
And the whistling bullets frequent 'flops',
Give you all that you want of thrills.
And indeed as the Book says "in deaths oft"
They walked full faithfully;
And some there are who have borne aloft
Their Territorial T.

Wednesday July 7th 1915, Doulieu

I wound up the one Club today. These long summer days the men are not indoors much, and troops have been moved from that side. The proprietress, who has not always acted with scrupulous Christian grace, was rather awry at losing her weekly francs. Douche, the bath man (a suitable name!) was quite sensible and nice about it, and we may resume again one day.

Visiting battalions. Arranging matters in the other Club, planning for Sunday and so on. Heavy firing on our right and we hear that some gas shells were sent over, so I looked out the smelly bags.

Leave seems rather remote again – if the way does not open soon, it will probably not come off, as something very decisive is not at all unlikely to take place, and I do not want to be away for that. What will the next month bring forth? The 12th month of the war?

Thursday July 8th 1915, Doulieu

I have piles of letters to write. We are moving out of the linen loft now into a cloth store near which two shells fell Sunday week, but it will make a nice little church.

At 10 a.m. I was present at the presentation by the General of some ribbons for valour to one of my battalions. One of the cases was a 'recognition' for the Lance-Corporal at the time those 59 men were hit, and the doctor on that occasion has been awarded the Military Cross, and this man the Distinguished Conduct Medal. It came out afterwards that 'recognitions' for Chaplains in this Division have gone by default, nobody quite knows how. Only one Chaplain in the Vlllth Division was mentioned in French's dispatches, and that one a R.C. in England two months ill and away at Neuve Chapelle and Fromelle. The Staff Captain remarked that the 24th Brigade had been specially unfortunate about these things, the Brigadier having broken down at the close of Neuve Chapelle and four Commanding Officers all having been wounded, and the Staff themselves have felt out of it a little. The Vllth Division, who was with us, had <u>six</u> Chaplains mentioned, moreover one was given a C.M.G.[339], one a D.S.O. and two Military Crosses.

The Club, and church arranging and planning services for Sunday. The Brigade Headquarters are now next but one to the field in which those 80 shells fell on Sunday morning without hurting anyone but an old apple tree. Two fell this morning while I was there, well wide of our surroundings.

---

339 Rev. **William Stevenson Jaffray**, DD, CMG, CBE, QSA (b.1867 – d.1941) South Africa, 1899–1900; British Expeditionary Force, 1914–1919 senior chaplain, 7th Division BEF; assistant principal chaplain, 5th Army; principal chaplain (Brigadier-General), British Salonica and Black Sea Forces.

Friday July 9th 1915, Doulieu

The leave form has just come and I shall probably get away from early Monday morning and arrive at Victoria Monday night or Tuesday morning at about 5. am – it will all be rather a rush and there will be a great deal to do in a very short time. Every hour will be wanted in England.

Saturday July 10th 1915, Doulieu

A full day, finishing up one Club and strengthening another. Talbot has a Club in a smashed town which they tell me is one of the best to be seen, a really thorough one, so that's alright!

I see waving cornfields, with two of our captive balloons looking out over the country, one being hauled down for relief and looking very near, another being shelled, and a German one in the far distance[340] and children playing round cottage doors – cackling hens and mother hens with chicks. Two little urchins fishing for frogs in the roadside dykes with a fishing rod, line and a little tiny piece of red tape for a bait! I am negotiating for another Club piano for which £4 is being asked and I have had a long talk with my new co-Chaplain, H.C. Hargreaves[341].

Sunday July 11th 1915

A full Sunday, on account of the distances to travel, with not much to show for it. Holy Communion in a barn at 8 am with seven present, and then a long ride to a factory which is the new Temporary Military Church, which was more than crowded in fact overfull, with about 250 present and seats for only a few with the rest sitting by the General's footstool. He was there and we had a nice service. There was no other service in the morning, the rule being now none nearer the trenches on account of very accurate shelling. So I went down to pick up Hargreaves, and we went together to the burying place behind the trenches, to deposit an artificial flower cross sent out to me for a much beloved Yorkshire lad. The car broke down coming back, and the

---

340   From the outset of warfare on the Western Front, the Germans had observation balloons, but they also had the advantage of being the occupying power and thus they usually ensured that they occupied the higher ground: even if this meant, initially, they had to cede some ground to the Allies. The German dominance of the Ypres Salient in Flanders, Belgium, being an example how they were able to control territory from the advantage of over-seeing, from the surrounding hills, the terrain below. The only way the British could even try to equalise the situation was to use captive observation balloons. The first British Kite Balloon Section arrived on the 8th May 1915 in the Aubers Ridge Sector. The kite balloons were usually located 3 miles behind the frontline trenches at a distance apart of 12 to 15 miles. At these bases, they would await suitable wind and weather conditions so the observation balloons could ascend bearing a tethering cable and a telephone line. The optimal operating altitude varied between 3000 and 4000 feet.

341   Rev. **Henry Cecil Hargreaves**, Pembroke College, Cambridge. Gained a B.A. in 1911 and a M.A. in 1914. In WW1, he served as a Chaplain to the Forces 4th Class and was mentioned in Despatches. After the war, he became Vicar of St. Mark's, Forest Gate, 1920–27, Chief Chaplain of Summerfield, Birmingham, 1927–37 and Harlow 1937–43, and then Vicar of Lower Amwell, St. Albans.

The family with Richard on leave.
From left to right, RDG, Agatha Faith, Eric, Joyce and Margaret

'Stepney' wheel also was found to be leaky, so we rumbled slowly onwards with the punctured tyre[342]. It was a bumpy process, and delaying for everybody.

An early evening service on another farm and the men very serious. It was all very peaceful in the quiet evening air, and the farm wife came out at the singing and I could see that she was touched, the tears coming into her eyes. The rest of the evening was spent preparing for travel on the morrow.

LEAVE

---

342 The Stepney Spare Wheel was invented by Thomas Morris Davies in 1904. Early motor cars were made without spare wheels, so a puncture was an event dreaded by all drivers. Davies's idea was to make a spokeless wheel rim fitted with an inflated tyre. Their 1909 catalogue claimed that Stepney Spare Wheels were fitted to all London taxis. However, the days of the patent spare wheel had drawn to a close, as car manufacturers began to provide spare wheels with all new cars, but the name lived on, long after the last spare wheel was made.

Tuesday July 20th 1915, Doulieu

Just a line to say that we have arrived alright – the passage was smooth and by 8.30 we were back within the old familiar boom of the guns. It was a crowded boat and all the lights were out. We were patrolled by a 'greyhound of the sea'[343]. The rail arrangements were rather confused and we were eventually muddled, six of us into one carriage and slept fitfully, waggling our heads and bodies about in various attitudes until nearly the end of the journey, when we separated. I came on alone to arrive at 8.30 am and four young Black Watch officers came on with me to breakfast, and now I have spent most of the day sleeping.

I found Hargreaves at 6.30 p.m. having a service of Holy Communion with some of my men and one of his own. His father, it appears, is one of the Council of St. Aidan's and he knew Robin Snowden-Smith at Ridley and he took on the class of lads which Robin used to hold[344].

Wednesday July 21st 1915, Doulieu

Everything goes on much as before. The same topics come up at the Mess – the numbers of the Germans, the next operations of our Division, the use of gas, the question of a winter campaign, tips as to kit, the value or otherwise of chlorinating the water, the outlook on the Russian front, tactics on the Dardanelles etc., etc. The same shells bursting with little spurts of flame, and balls of curling smoke round similar aeroplanes, and big captive balloons ogling down on us from the opposite lines and one of ours ogling at them.

The building next to our late temporary Military Church was shelled today while I was in the Club but thankfully no one was hurt. The General looked in at the Club today – the first time one has ever been into any of our places, and the caretaker said that he seemed pleased. The village street still trickles with the house fluids and refuse, and the farm ditches still have the same curious sour smell. So the work goes on.

Thursday July 22nd 1915, Doulieu

I travelled through a very smashed village – past a long Khaki-coloured canvas screen and at last to the communication trench. This is called Shaftesbury Avenue – you pass London Bridge, Charing Cross and a little gully called 'Jock's Joy'. Winding ways in all directions – here a toy aeroplane, there on the wall of a trench an eight day clock (taken from a farm) ticking away and telling the right time! And at the end of our windings, a little wooden hut behind a mud bank, and in there the object of my

---

343 Common nickname for the relatively new fast boats, 'Torpedo Boat Destroyer', or just, as is now, 'Destroyer'.
344 The twin of RDG's father-in-law, William Saumarez-Smith, both sons of Richard Snowden-Smith.

search, Mr. Piggott's gallant son[345]! There were three other officers as well. He is very well, tell his mother, and his Colonel spoke to me of him privately very appreciatedly, saying that he was a nice fellow and very promising. Last night he had been doing a plucky thing going out on patrol, and had done it well.

I am finishing this at a Soldiers Concert – a nicely conducted one with two of the Generals present. Some of the men have very good talent indeed. This afternoon there was a cricket match – our Division is, as you see, in quasi-rest, but there has been shelling. We have fired off our howitzers and they have retaliated, some flew over my head coming out of the trenches this morning[346].

Friday July 23rd 1915, Doulieu

A lot of time is spent, now that we are so far back, merely getting to and fro to where the men are, and Thursdays and Fridays are always rather taken up with planning for Sundays. There has also today been the matter of trying to buy a piano – the one bought previously is so much in demand and the Brigade is so scattered, that we feel we must try to afford a second one. There is one quoted at £4.

I overheard today from a patient in the barn "Orderlies are not to take the chalk from the patient's Billiard room" – "Orderlies are forbidden to pinch the coal from their mistress's Drawing room", so he is definitely getting better, seeing that the entire accommodation is one shed!

Saturday July 24th 1915, Doulieu

We bought the piano today for £4, and it is already asked for in two separate directions[347]. There has been an enemy aeroplane over this evening and a captive balloon ogling at us, but no shelling and very little rifle fire.

Sunday July 25th 1915, Doulieu

It <u>has</u> been a nice Sunday, after promising to be a flat and feeble day yesterday it has turned out to be full of good things owing to the disposition of my battalions, their position in a 'shelly' area and so on. I wondered if we could have a service at all – the ways however opened curiously. A group of Transport were found ready and willing to meet together and about 100 fell in at 9.30. Then the Brigadier found himself free and telegraphed Friday evening, with the result that about 300 in all met at his

---

345 **John Cecil Charles Piggott** (b.1897 – d.1973), 3 Bn, Duke of Cornwall's Light Infantry; promoted to Second Lieut. in August 1915. His mother was Ethel Mary Blackford Cox, father Charles Henry Piggott of Dursley, Glos, who was a chaplain on the Western Front also. In 1915, she would have been living in Hurstpierpoint, Sussex.
346 Short-barrelled artillery piece.
347 About £400 in 2017.

headquarters and we had a very nice quiet Communion Service afterwards. Then the O.C. of the regiment and I went visiting in the later part of the morning, himself proposed taking the risk of the shelling and invited me to come this evening, with the result of about 750 men and a very refreshing prayerful time, while he also proposed my coming for a Communion Service one evening this week when the men are most free just before returning into the trenches. So I am going on Wednesday and there is much to be thankful for, but the journeying and distances are a difficulty. Some sort of motor vehicle must be obtained somehow, even if I have to sell my watch – we want wings on days like these, 'gospel' wings.

We hear today of Bishop Gwynn's appointment as Bishop of us Chaplains' – and I am thankful.

Monday July 26th 1915, Doulieu

Days are much the same, yet each has its slightly varied happenings. I paid for the piano this morning and it is not so bad for £4 – one or two of the keys sit silent sometimes, as is the way with old pianos.

A telegram asking for a funeral in the afternoon, near the trenches, of a soldier shot in the head on a working party last night. The funeral was a little more exciting than usual with a German aeroplane circling over the village behind us, and two of our own reconnoitring backwards and forwards over the trenches, and being shelled vigorously by the anti-aircraft guns. The bursts sounded curiously close in the quiet evening air. Some of our artillery nearby were firing briskly guided by our aeroplanes. It was eventually a noisy scene and we had to be quick lest the enemy aeroplane should have drawn fire on us. The dear man was laid in the grave, just in his uniform as he had been picked up – there are some 40 graves now in that plot and some are marked still only by a bottle, with the name inside[348]. Later, the Burial Commission will place neat wooden crosses over them. The cross is a symbol of the Christian faith and we learn to think of its full meaning at a time like this. If we had not the Christian faith, what symbol should we be placing over these hundreds of noble men? Having it, what do we mean by it? God has spoken, through Jesus Christ His Son – He rules in righteousness and love and there is a better world and He has given us unto life everlasting in it. We are each individual persons, and dear to Him. We are to be with Him, and others dear to Him and us, in that better world. What symbol else is there? The Turkish Crescent,

---

348 Casualties were often buried where they fell in action, or in a burial ground on or near the battlefield. A simple cross or marker might be put up to mark the location and give brief details of the individuals who had died. In the early weeks of the war the British Army had no official register to whom these battlefield burials could be formally reported with a name and the location of the grave. Those individuals who reached a hospital in a safe area behind the fighting lines and who died of their wounds would usually be buried in a cemetery near to the hospital. Often it would be in an existing town or village cemetery or in a specially created annexed burial plot. These burials could be registered and their locations marked.

and the various ones of India, China, Japan, Central Africa and the others, and their message, how different to the Christian one! So all's well, <u>to the Christian</u>.

'Aunt Sarah and the War' is being read all round the Mess, and much liked.

Tuesday July 27th 1915, Doulieu

I have today signed and sent off the agreement for an extended period of service. There are many pros and cons, but I feel that there is a clear work to do, and that is the point.

Fighting, but everything very quiet here today. Living near here there is an old hand-loom weaver who I went to see this evening. He is very poor and over 85 years of age. His cottage is small and low-pitched – the loom is in a side room and the occupant sits in it with his back to the wall, hemmed round by the framework and with a tiny window at his side, in the winter for light, in the summer happily for a little air, for the room needs it. In the kitchen is a <u>hand</u> spindle for winding on the flax to the bobbin. The old man is virile enough, and likes to talk, but his patois is difficult to follow. He has seen four wars, Sebastopol, Italy, 1870 and this one[349]. In 1870, being married, he was past the age for fighting! He earns 30 francs for about 45 yards of canvas cloth[350].

Thursday July 29th 1915, Doulieu

The Evening Communion did not come off yesterday, through a mistake in the Battalion orders. I went down this evening, and two people turned up, a captain and a private, but it was a nice service notwithstanding. Two of our aeroplanes were being shelled vigorously on one side of the barn, and one of our batteries in a field on the other side commenced having its 'evening hate' right over our heads[351]. The noise of the guns like that, when you are right in front of them, is something tremendous, really tremendous and your flesh, like the farm rafters, shakes with the concussion. And there, kneeling in the straw, we did this in remembrance of Him[352].

There are great changes in the Division. So many of the officers have gone, wounded or into another world and now the General, who has had command, has gone off at half an hour's notice[353]. The village schoolmaster today told me an amusing thing – I

---

349 Crimean war (1853–56), Unification of Italy (from 1859), Franco-Prussian War (1870–71).

350 About £50 in 2017 value.

351 The artillery often opened fire in the first few hours of darkness when enemy soldiers would be going on patrol, or moving from the front line to the reserves. This became known as "the evening hate".

352 **Luke 22:19** 'And he took bread, and gave thanks, and brake *it*, and gave unto them, saying, This is my body which is given for you: this do in remembrance of me.'

353 After his breakdown, General **Sir Francis John Davies** was succeeded temporarily by Brigadier-General **Reginald Stewart Oxley** in command 8th Division on 27th July 1915, who was succeeded by Major-General **Havelock Hudson** on 1st August 1915. Major-General **William Heneker** took over on 10th December 1916.

am billeted in his house. When the Germans were here, a German captain had my room. We look out on the village square with the pump in the middle, a railing down the left side, then the road running crosswise. To the right there is the church and the Cure's house. Two German sentries were here and two outside the Cure's house, and the German flag was at the end of the railing, touching the road. One afternoon an English motor car flew by, the occupants pulled down the German flag and hauled up the English one, and before the amazed sentries had time to collect their senses enough to even think of firing, had dashed off again!

Friday July 30th 1915, Doulieu

The distances here do take up an immense amount of our time and I must really try to get the little car that I have longed for all this time – all the Chaplains feel it, but it is difficult to know what to do as so much depends upon the value that the authorities set upon religion. Visiting, taking one or two men down to arrange things at the Temporary Military Church, now more than 4 miles away, as indeed is all the work, and some of it 5 or 6 miles.

Saturday July 31st 1915, Doulieu

The last day of this month. Do you remember August 1st last year when we had all arranged in preparation for my going off to Shorncliffe, and the telegram "Camp struck last night, stand by?" What a full year since then!

I have been visiting some far down billets, arranging some details at the Club and making preparations for tomorrow. There was a German aeroplane circling over on our left at breakfast time, and dashing down country behind us, spying out the land no doubt. A very heavy cannonading on our left last night, we do not know whether it was ours or the enemy's.

A good speech by Lloyd George to the representatives of the miners – he is a gifted man and can speak to men of that kind in language that they can feel and understand. His analogies of the mottled sky, the 12ft. bridge and the 11ft plank, and the Australians at Gallipoli not going into hospital till the attack on the Turkish position was accomplished, are all good. Also the false idea of 'freedom which includes the right to shirk' is well put[354].

Sunday August 1st 1915, Doulieu

The last Sunday of the first year of the war. What have we been through during the year past – little did we dream it was before us – what has the coming year in store?

---

354 Miners in South Wales had striked in July 1915 over wages, wary of the 'war bonus' paid for higher productivity by the mine-owners. The Navy relied on South Wales coal, and they were back at work by the 20th July, and Munitions Minister David Lloyd George addressed them on July 30th.

These have been my thoughts in talking to the men. Almost invariably I take the message of the Sunday, and almost invariably it speaks to the hour and the need. "They drank of that spiritual Rock which followed them, and that Rock was Christ[355]". We, like the children of Israel, are passing through a wilderness of experience, with its hardships and dangers and its enemies to subdue. Our land of promise a rightful peace, the maintenance of right against wrong, the protection of the weak against brute force, the defence of honourable dealing as against violence and unscrupulousness. The way is already weary and difficult and the men are not so exuberant as they were. When the new drafts come out shouting "are we downhearted? No!" The men who have been out the longer time answer them "No, but you jolly well soon will be!" It is not a bad thing for us to be made to feel seriously – it brings us to a sense of need and to turn to where our strength lies.

There have been some very nice services – 8 am Holy Communion in the hospital barn with 11 present, 10.30 Morning Prayer in the Temporary Military Church but owing to local movement, only about 20 present. Then I took a large open-air service nearer the trenches at 11.30, with one of our aeroplanes being vigorously shelled away on our right, the scream of the bursting shells sounding curiously in the quiet morning air and some loud shelling and counter-shelling going on on our left. But we had the harmonium, and the partial shade of three small trees (by no means covering the people) but it was all very pleasant. We joined in intercession prayers in anticipation of Wednesday. Ten stayed behind for Holy Communion, which we held comfortably in a dug-out in which you could stand upright. Not much light, but the coolness was very acceptable, and it was nice and quiet. This evening a nice open-air service in a field, with rather loud artillery booming near and three of our own aeroplanes circling home to roost, low down. A heavy glow of gold-edged purple clouds, with the sun and strips of cloud across it like molten metal.

Monday August 2nd 1915, Doulieu

The town behind us has been hit this afternoon by a 12 inch shell from, they think, 12 or 15 miles away[356]. The clearing hospital was struck and four men were killed.

The Estaminets do not like our Clubs much and also the owners of them have been coming back, with the result that the chairs we had lent us by the Mairie are being asked for by the owners. It has been impossible to hire any, but I have been able to find some secondhand ones, and have bought them today. We must trust to turning them to account again 'apres la guerre'.

---

355 1 **Corinthians 10:4** 'They drank of that spiritual Rock which followed them, and that Rock was Christ.'

356 **Big Bertha** is the name of a type of super-heavy mortar developed by the armaments manufacturer Krupp in Germany on the eve of WWI. Its official designation was the L/12, *i.e.*, the barrel was 12 calibre in length, 42 cm (16.5 inch). 12 were used on the western front usually against fortifications.

The men are helping the farmers get in the harvest, much is done by hand, but one or two advanced farmers have patent reapers and binders, but heavy thunderstorms today, have rather interfered. It appears that the aeroplane which passed over us on Saturday morning went on to pay attentions to one of the greater towns behind us, and we see by yesterday's paper that they did some damage with their bombs.

Tuesday August 3rd 1915, Doulieu
Rain, rain, rain! And sloppy mud. Sir Douglas Haig came to see us today and shook hands all round[357]. We had a full C.E.M.S. meeting this evening. The 'knock about' has rather loosed people's efforts, but this evening quickened things up and the men are keen again – they ask for a club in this village and I think one could be managed, and so we have agreed to try again. If the authorities would give us a marquee it might be done. Then we are going to try for another concert and next week Major [...*censored*...] who is an Hon. Lay Reader in the Indian diocese where he lives, will give us a paper on Missions in India.

Wednesday August 4th 1915, Doulieu
A united service of intercession with the Ambulance this afternoon. Chairs obtained for the Club and another Club going well further on. New Chaplains arriving, fair weather and fighting quiet. The men were rather pleased at the united service and so were the other chaplains, and I think the Colonel likewise. They turned up in full numbers – that is, not one fell out from parade.

Thursday August 5th 1915, Doulieu
Chaplains meeting – arrangements for Sunday – visiting round patients.

Friday August 6th 1915, Doulieu
Ditto, ditto, ditto. Horse reared wildly today and I slipped from the saddle and twisted my ankle very slightly. Very busy visiting round.

Saturday August 7th 1915, Doulieu
The ankle is a little painful, but it is right enough when resting – rather the 'luck of the war'. The horse had a buzzing motor stop right in front of him, and two frightened French women fluttered just behind him and not knowing quite which way to turn, he stood finally on his hind legs with his nose in the air, and I slid off quicker than I thought. It will not happen again!

---

357 General commanding 1 Corps of the BEF in France.

One of the new Chaplains in the next Division, is a Missions to Seamen man – we are a pleasant family.

Sunday August 8th 1915, Doulieu

It has been an encouraging Sunday, but nothing like so full of the Spirit of prayer as one would have liked to see on the first Sunday of another year of war. 8 a.m. Holy Communion at the Temporary Military Church four miles off (I must leave my billet at 7 a.m.), with 5 officers, 2 privates and our new General present, then breakfast at the Soldiers Club[358]. 10:30 a.m. a big service in a barn on a road next but one to the trenches, with the men packed tightly in, in all about 130. I made it mainly a service of Thanksgiving for the unmerited mercies of the year past and a prayer for God's guidance, strength and blessings for the future. The Colonel and one officer present. 11.30 another full service in a barn further back and I followed the same plan there – Holy Communion following the service, one officer and six men stayed. I had then an early start immediately after tea and again the Military Church. The Battalions are changing over, so there were only 18 or 20 present, but we had an earnest time together. The ankle is much better but still swollen.

Monday August 9th 1915, Doulieu

It has been a very full day. Mess President work – Club work – Concert work – Guild work and letters. There was some heavy fighting near here last night and a tremendous cannonade for some hours off and on, and we hear that we have taken some trenches. But our own Brigade has been coming back into rest billets yesterday and today, and very glad they are and I am too, for them. The piano will be used every night this week for a concert and there will be extra services I hope, to make up for lost time.

A man brought into hospital this afternoon hand-cuffed with a self-inflicted wound in the hand or foot, we have not found which, and he is in custody for having threatened the N.C.O. when challenged about it. These self-inflicted wounds are a study – a man pretends that his rifle went off by accident, and makes a wound between two toes, or between thumb and finger. Sometimes it is more serious than he intended and it requires some courage to do it – why is it done? The monotony of the trenches gets

---

358 General **Sir Havelock 'huddie' Hudson** GCB KCIE (b.1862 – d.1944) General Officer Commanding 8th Division. Commissioned into the Northamptonshire Regiment in 1881. Transferred to the Indian Staff Corps in 1885 and became an officer of the 19th Lancers. He served on the staff on North West Frontier of India in 1897, took part in the Boxer Rebellion in 1900 and went on the second Miranzai expedition in 1901. Brigadier-General on the General Staff of the Indian Corps from 1914, General Officer Commanding 8th Division on the Western Front from 31st July 1915 until 8th December 1916 and was appointed Adjutant General, India from 5th February 1917 until 30th October 1920. Following the Amritsar massacre in 1919 he relieved Brigadier Reginald Dyer of his command. He went on to be General Officer Commanding-in-Chief, the Eastern Army in India in November 1920 before retiring in 1924.

too much? Or a man longs to get home and thinks to get through on a hospital ship? The penalty for a self-inflicted wound may be death[359].

Tuesday August 10th 1915, Doulieu

It is so very nice reading of all your home doings, but it makes me want to be back! But we look across Belgium and Russia and into those hard Russian faces, and we cannot think seriously of much else. Everyone must go on praying and working. I fear there are more serious sacrifices ahead for everybody and I begin to be concerned as to whether all England is taking it earnestly [seriously] enough.

Now three units have been supplied with a cheap work-a-day piano each – £4, £4.10 and £10, and it may be hoped that the price of them can be realised somewhat at the end of the War, and it will be cheaper than hiring them. The distances are very great. Very quiet doings now.

Wednesday August 11th 1915, Doulieu

Today, nothing much to chronicle – Club business matters, the Church and Mess and this afternoon a horse show. All the horses of the Ambulance were paraded, in harness and in saddles, and prizes given for the best kept. Afterwards there was some wrestling on horseback for prizes, and a horse race over hedges, the riders having to alight and pick up three potatoes and then drop them in buckets on the return race, jumping the hedges again. And a V.C. race – picking up a filled sack at the end of the outward run, and returning with it, jumping the same hedges on the return. It was all very good amusement. In the middle of it, two German aeroplanes skimmed away past us in the line of the trenches far away in the deep blue of the sky, glinting in the afternoon sun like tiny little silver fish, and our shells burst round them like little pinheads of cotton wool.

Friday August 13th 1915, Doulieu

A late evening after a concert, the arranging of which has meant plenty of work, though much of the detail has been gallantly born by three or four of our C.E.M.S. men. Many of the items were very good, in nice taste and providing good music, and our pianist is excellent, so we have much to be thankful for. Some items were incredibly vulgar, but on the whole they passed off shamefacedly enough.

A meeting of the C. of E. Chaplains this morning. The idea of a Central Military Church has now grown so that the new General has himself proposed the Divisional

---

359 The maximum penalty for a self-inflicted wound ("Wilfully maiming himself with intent to render himself unfit for service" as it was described) under Section 18 of the Army Act 1881 was imprisonment, rather than capital punishment. In the British Army, some 3894 men were found guilty, and were sent to prison for lengthy periods.

band coming for Sunday mornings. Some instruments have been got up country, and a Divisional band plays rather nicely, so we are progressing.

Last night at about 3 am there was a tremendous concussion and boom, which shook the houses for three miles or more, but no one knows what it was. A zeppelin passed over and some think it was something dropped from it, but others say it was a big shell from the German lines, but no one has seen any effects of it. Others say it was one of our own huge guns registering – we are not told, but the mystery will unravel. Visiting billets in farms all over the country, and arranging for Sunday.

Saturday August 14th 1915, Doulieu

The explosion mystery still remains, but some say it was a German ammunition store which blew up just across the trenches.

Today's chief occupation has been a horse show for the Division, and it was very good. There are some fine steeds among us and the jumping was good as the dry ground made it nice for the take off and also for the onlookers. There was a band and some bagpipes made glad the air after their manner. Sturdy men wrestled on stout horses with great vigour – the contestants were stripped to the waist and were not allowed boots and rode their horses without saddles, and the tugs when the men got to close grips were sometimes very exciting. Strange to think of a band, and horse parades, racing and jumping, and athletic sports all within four miles of the trenches. A 6" shell would easily have reached us and could have done awful damage if the Germans had only known of it. The Kaiser was there and the Crown Prince, riding about, clever caricatures by two soldiers and the Crown Prince had a huge cardboard Iron Cross on the shoulders of his cloak.

A strong and true cartoon in 'Punch' for Aug. 4th, the anniversary of the War.

Sunday August 15th 1915, Doulieu

The violent explosion is now said to have definitely been a bomb store on the German side of the trenches. One's first impulse is to hope that no one was hurt! There must be more prayer. Another day of prayer has gone by today and it has been fairly used as far as my own units are concerned. Twelve at Holy Communion at a quarter to 7 in the barn (2 of them patients) but at 8 at a farm three miles away, no one came. At 10 about 180 men packed tight into a barn about two miles further on and the rain fell in torrents. Then back to a farm, about two and a half miles away, for a service at 11 with again about 180 men. Both services were intensely quiet and earnest, the rain falling in torrents again and the thunder roared. One clap sounded just like a shell bursting nearby, and everybody stopped to hear. We have very short services, with much spoken in a little time, for example a prayer that we all say together – "Help us to think wisely, to speak rightly, to resolve bravely, to act kindly, to live purely. Bless us in body and soul, and make us a blessing to our comrades.

Strengthen us in life and comfort us in death[360]". I spoke on the 2nd Book of Kings XVIII.20 "Now on whom dost thou trust?[361]" It is a spiritual conflict in which we are engaged as Mr. Asquith said – the difference between the Turco-German spirit and that of the Allies. If the German spirit were to win, the world would be governed by brute force – again in Mr. Asquith's words "Is right or violence to rule the world?" The cartoon in England's greatest comic paper puts the position – on one side is the German Emperor scowling half defiantly, half shamefacedly, across the scene and on the other side is a roadside Crucifix and on it the Pattern Man, the Son of God. Under it is the inscription "The two Ideals". That is it. It is a contest between the Spirit of Christ and the spirit which is not of Him[362].

A bible reading in one of the barn hospital wards, then a peaceful evening service in an orchard under a pear tree, with about 20 present including 3 officers, and a very reverent quiet time.

Monday August 16th 1915, Doulieu

Today has been 'Monday-ish'. I cannot ride yet as the foot is untrustworthy for saddle work, and the doctor thinks that the bone just above the ankle was splintered and that being why it is slower at healing right up[363]. I had hoped to have got across to another Division, but could not have the use of a car, so I turned on to other things – Club, patients, parcels, haircut and correspondence. Heavy thunder storms, but no fighting today.

My battalion has gone further along the front, about 6 miles away. There is a Chaplain difficulty with these occasional far off separations. Last week one battalion was only a mile off. I think there will not be very much fighting here abouts for some time, though we hear rumbles of artillery fire in the distance.

Tuesday August 17th 1915, Doulieu

It has been a humdrum kind of a day here – patients, the Club, the Temporary Church and Mess business. I really think I must ask to be relieved of the Mess Presidency as it takes up very much time and thought. The catering, the finding of supplies and the paying for a mess of 13 people is rather much, especially as some of them have not any better sense than to grumble! As an old campaigner, one knows that a lot can be managed with knowledge and trouble, and how different things are 'a la laisser faire' without them! I have done it now since November, in addition to work outside, and

---

360 The Scout Prayer.

361 **Isiah 35:5** 'I say, sayest thou, (but they are but vain words) I have counsel and strength for war: now on whom dost thou trust, that thou rebellest against me'

362 Punch, August 4th 1915. Artist: Bernard Partridge: 'The Two Ideals'. RDG was a big fan of Punch, and his son Eric retained his complete bound volumes into the 1990's. This is presumably the cartoon also referred to in August 14th's entry.

363 Injury from August 6th.

now the battalions have gone 6 miles away. I am going to get hold of a two-seater car somehow.

Wednesday August 18th 1915, Doulieu

Somewhat cold, and the ankle is better but I cannot ride yet.

This evening I held an open-air sing-song for the convalescents. The piano is <u>most</u> valuable and a Scotchman, having volunteered one song went on and sang two others, the last one a French one. I gave out the title of one, partly owing to his Scotch accent, as "I'm wearing my hat away from you". It raised a laugh when I had to correct myself and announce it as "I'm wearing my <u>heart</u> away from you[364] ".

Thursday August 19th 1915, Doulieu

I had a nice visitor today from the 2nd West Yorks. In the winter he came in to us, one temple grazed by a bullet and the cap shot through above the other temple. A few days ago he was made Brevet Major[365]. I knew him at Necklace Kopje, near the Slangapies River in South Africa[366], where we had one of those violent storms when the hailstones were as big as hen's eggs and cut pieces out of the horses' backs. He says he saw the ammunition depot across the German trenches scattering with the explosion last week, so now we know that it was true, and what people thought was the rifle fire following, was the cartridges and small shells and bombs exploding for nearly half an hour afterwards.

They took a German prisoner last week in front of his trench. Two of our men had wandered exploring out of a sap-head (unarmed), and met two Germans also unarmed[367]. One German ran away and the other was cut off by one of our men and tried to fight his way past with his fists. He gave our man two black eyes, but was overpowered and brought in a prisoner and all this within 200 or 300 yards of his own trenches!

Friday August 20th 1915, Doulieu

A full busy day, and an important one – the Club plan is going to be strengthened. The Staff have got interested, and we are going to work on a plan by which each Brigade will have at least one Club permanently at its disposal. That is, instead of a

---

364 *I'm Wearing my Heart Away from You,* Charles K. Harris, 1902.

365 **A brevet** was a warrant authorising a commissioned officer to hold a higher rank temporarily, but usually without receiving the pay of that higher rank except when actually serving in that role.

366 About 100 miles SE of Johannesburg on the Eastern Cape.

367 A sap-head or listening post was a shallow, narrow, often disguised position used to monitor enemy activity and to gather intelligence information. Listening posts could sometimes be sited dangerously close to the enemy front line although they were typically some 30 yards ahead of the front line.

Club having to close by reason of the Chaplain's Brigade being sent to another area, he will keep it on wherever he is, and the respective Chaplains of the other Brigades will keep on theirs' also. Thus [...*censored*...] keeps his going in a smashed up town even though his Brigade has moved back. I keep mine on and [...*censored*...] will keep one going. This will be admirable – three main billeting centres being thus touched. We are going to be helped by having wounded soldiers deployed as caretakers, and when the darker, colder days come, there will be a regular allowance of coal and lights. We shall need funds, and more Funds, but they will go further and I hope the Club centres will be increased. It is all very refreshing, and the eternal 'estaminets' will possess the situation less. Games, books, stationery and cigarettes will be our main need. Provisions I think we will be able to get through the canteens, which are now coming into being, and if we can only get good tea and coffee and cocoa made, and lemonade and the like, I can see a happy and smiling future in front. The expense will come in chiefly with rent, the French caretaker (in certain cases), printing and incidental charges (utensils and the like), apart from games and literature. En avant!

Another enemy aeroplane this evening. It seems as if we hit him, the shells were very near – at all events, he turned round sharply and went back. Two shells in the smashed up town – no one hurt.

Some interesting insights came to me today into the life of Lille. They came from a Frenchman, through one of the indigent refugees who were allowed to come back via Switzerland. The town is under the control of a German governor[368] as the Prefect (of the Nord) has been long ago sent to Germany. The Mayor and some citizens are held as hostages[369]. High levies have to be paid and in addition, advances have to be made on requisitions signed by the Governor. The tramways are running and all Germans travel free. Some factories, not dismantled for the sake of the machinery, are kept running in order to keep the people employed. Trains run regularly to Brussels, made up of German coaches, and coaches for French and Belgian passengers are attached. There is a good service of trains. There are very strong fortifications and German workmen have been employed making these, and some 'Lillois' have also been commandeered, being paid from 2fr to 5fr a day. The 'morale' of the inhabitants is good, but they look forward eagerly and constantly to an early release. The health of the town is good and food, although not plentiful, is sufficient but going up in price. Fresh milk can be got from neighbouring villages, but it is dear and the supply is drying up. Nestles' milk (see postcard) is obtained in abundance from Switzerland and German brown bread was at first issued, but it was ill-liked and indigestible. Bread of a better kind can be bought marked 'K' bread at the rate of so many grammes

---

368 General of Artillery **Gustav Von Heinrich** (b.1854 – d.1942), 6th Army, Governor of Lille 1914–16, Governor of Bucharest 1916–18.
369 The Mayor **Charles Delesalle** (b.1850 – d.1929), came from a family of great spinners at La Madeleine.
Committee Chair Flax, he was mayor of Lille from 1904 to 1919 and General Counsel of the North (Township of East Lille) from 1907 to 1913.

a person[370]. The Banks are open and working, French business and French notes being negotiable, and payments in business are made in either money, French notes or German and German 'bons' have to be accepted[371]. Officers occupy untenanted houses as a rule, but in a number of cases they billet themselves with residents and sometimes demand food for which occasionally they pay with 'bons' and occasionally, one expects, for nothing. No goods are supposed to be had without 'bons', but often they are just simply taken. People are allowed passage in and out of the town by one route with a pass, free. There are three other routes, permission for which is obtained but only with difficulty, and for payments ranging from 2fr upwards according to the length of time covered by them, and the distance to be travelled. The railway station has been altered to allow only one entrance and exit for passengers, the other passenger exit having been enlarged to allow big motor cars to pass to and fro. German soldiers abound and the French barracks are full of them and the officers seem to have plenty of time to promenade the avenues. It is a large victualling centre and an immense quantity of motor transport is employed. English and French aeroplanes fly over sometimes high up, and drop journals which are eagerly seized on by any of the inhabitants into whose hands they fall.

Our cannonading is heard very distinctly, as is also the rifle and machine-gun fire. Some food supplies are known to be obtained from America and most of the inhabitants are confident of being relieved soon. About 1200 houses were destroyed by the German bombardment last year, and a larger number were burnt[372]. The Germans are not so universally confident as they were – it is now a fighting for 'terms'.

Saturday August 21st 1915, Doulieu
The air raids are disgusting – not more than three soldiers have been touched in the whole business, but it is civilians and a large proportion of women and children who are targeted[373]. As the Archbishop of Canterbury said, the further we go into this war

---

370 Lille diarist **Jeanne du Thoit** describes "K bread", the practically inedible wartime bread made from a mixture of potato, rye, and flour, which produced a bread, "with an exterior like a rock and a soft, slimy interior. It is impossible to eat it fresh and so we leave it three days in the basement … the doctors advise us to eat as little as possible and supplement it with potatoes."

371 Diechman-Bons; stamped German paper money for use in occupied territories. *Bon de Requistion*: Purchase Voucher.

372 German bombardments destroyed over 2200 buildings and homes. Lille was only 20 kilometers from the fighting, and it was common for troops to go through the city on their way to and from battle.

373 The German Navy resumed raids on Britain in August. On 9th–10th August, four Zeppelins were directed against London; none reached its target and one, L12, was damaged by ground fire near Dover and came down in the sea off Zeebrugge. The four-Zeppelin raid was repeated on 12th–13th August; again, only one airship, L10, made landfall, dropping its bombs on Harwich. A third four-Zeppelin raid tried to reach London on 17th–18th August; two turned back with mechanical problems, one bombed Ashford, Kent in the belief it was Woolwich, but L10 became the first Navy airship to reach London. L10 was also misnavigated, mistaking the reservoirs of the Lea Valley for the Thames, and consequently dropped its bombs on Walthamstow and Leytonstone. 10 people were killed, 48 injured and property damage was estimated at £30 750.

the plainer becomes the necessity for our having entered into it. Fighting is still quiet, with about 40 shells falling on the smashed town. As these all fall about in the same area, people go on living in the surrounding streets mostly unmoved.

Three Germans sniped opposite our lines by one of our men in a tree and a German officer in a white summer coat was seen with three men, pointing out a place for work, so the locality was shelled by us almost immediately, but with what effect we could not see – and so on – and so on. Today sports – very good fun. They were arranged by some of the provisioning units. The General was there who is a natural and pleasant-spoken man. Tilting the bucket was amusing and many got a ducking. The obstacle race was also good – up a rope, over a pole and down again, under a tarpaulin, under a very low bar, up over a very high one, over a hedge and into a made pool of water up to the waist and, as Pepys would say 'so home'. A half mile race and one of my nice C.E.M.S. men came in second.

Not very good news in the paper the last three or four days and some of the people are depressed, one poor officer in particular, who is the <u>only one left</u> of his battery at Mons and has been wounded twice since, which is enough to shake anybody.

I am busy arranging for tomorrow, with a very cold wetting driving rain and damping ride. I can manage the horse again now alright, but the doctor says it will be felt still for some weeks.

One of the Shorncliffe (embarkation camp) Chaplains passed through our line today, and I have just met him. He is a very nice fellow and very cordial.

Sunday August 22nd 1915, Doulieu

It has been a beautiful day, and one of many mercies. 6.45am Holy Communion in a hospital barn with seven present including one officer. 9.30 H.C. in the soldiers' Club in a smashed town with three present. 10.30 Morning Prayer in a barn nearer the firing line, with about 80 present and 4 officers – a nice devout service. 11.30 another Morning Prayer the other side of the smashed town in a barn with about 70 present and the same quiet earnestness seemed to prevail. The men are receptive now-a-days, and two stayed behind wanting to talk and one wants to be confirmed. Picked up two chaplains and then back on the long ride home to our local base. Later in the afternoon, after a visit from the Baptist minister, visiting round the hospital tents. 6.pm a hearty earnest service in the hospital barn with about 40 present and a number waited behind to talk, including a gunner who has been out here since August 17th last year, and wants to be confirmed.

Baptists sometimes show little sense of proportion[374]. They constitute about 4 per cent

---

Guns were fired at L10 and a few aircraft took off in pursuit, but the Zeppelin suffered no damage in the raid.

374 Identified in RDG's photographs as Rev E L **Loatson**.

of the Army, with other non-conformists making perhaps another 12% and the Church of England 70%. But the Baptist minister wanted to take all the Sundays evenings in this one Ambulance Brigade, fixing his own time and place. My conscience would not let me accede to that, so I proposed our coming to some working arrangement. The proposal was not taken up, and as I was really very busy, I fixed the time and place for C of E worship and announced them, taking care to avoid the time and place generally used by the non-conformists. That made the Baptist think and he came this afternoon to see if we could come to a working arrangement, the which I was very forward to do. These smaller un-national organisations are learning, I hope, from the good order, cohesion, and allegiance to a lawful centralised authority of Army life, where the danger lies in the dissidence of Dissent. Christendom suffers weakness from its being divided up into smaller sects, each with its little laws unto itself, and going on independently of others. You waste energy by overlapping spheres of effort and you lose in edification by over-emphasising some truths out of all proportion. You would save time and strength if you had not to think so much about methods for not getting into each others' way, and you would gain in appeal by being able to work upon a concerted plan of action.

Monday August 23rd 1915, Doulieu

An interesting visit today from [...*censored*...] who was Chaplain for a part of my time at Shorncliffe. He came out here three months ago, and has been under shell fire most of the time. He was confirmed by your father in Penrith Church. We talked over plans and methods, and he was very keen to pick up ideas. He took away some of my bills and forms and will go for a Club along our lines, and I agreed to letting him have help from the Fund. Our inference of last winter is being justified as he will make now the ninth Chaplain who has got a good footing by means of it. He wanted to see something fresh, so we got a refugee Belgian priest to take us inside the burnt out church here. It was a stately building, less flimsily adorned inside than are some of the churches, and the ruins still indicate its' fine proportions. Two stained glass oriel windows are still in almost complete preservation, and the stone reredos remains only chipped. A row of coloured figures of Prophets and Apostles very artistically portrayed, the bright colouring well-blended, remain uninjured. The rest of the place is a mess of rubbish. The priest was a nice earnest young man, well educated, a professor at a student's college and a parish priest as well. But his clothes are showing signs of long wear – he was driven back from near Dixmude in October[375].

Just incidents of trench fighting day by day. Yesterday afternoon one of our shells

---

[375] At the outset of the war German troops crossed the Belgian border near Arlon, then proceeded hurriedly towards the North Sea to secure the French ports of Calais and Dunkirk. The Belgians opened the flood gates holding back the Yser river and flooded the area. As a result, the river became a front line throughout WW1. Dixmude was first attacked on October 16th, 1914 and defended by Belgian and French troops. Colonel Alphonse Jacques de Dixmude led the troops that prevented the town from being taken.

was seen to hit a fortified house behind the enemy trenches. It took fire and was eventually consumed. Soon after the fire began, thick volumes of heavy green smoke clung round it, and they think it was possibly gas, and that some of the enemy was poisoned with their own poison. We brought down an aeroplane to our left and a machine gun found a working party, and saw that it had done its job by seeing one man at least falling, and the attack was received with loud yells.

Last night a German newspaper was found tied round a post about 80 yards in front of our trenches, probably put there the night before. An advance patrol of theirs was heard talking by a listening patrol of ours – and so on – and so on. I forgot to mention about the aeroplane which started to fly over the smashed town at Holy Communion time yesterday morning, 9.30, and which was then driven back by our rifle fire. Good news about German cruisers being sunk today.

Tuesday August 24th 1915, Doulieu
A Confirmation talk, writing, and a long morning in the smashed town. Better news in the papers.

(Letter to his 9 year-old son)[376]
My dear old Eric, "Comment allez vous?" and how are Cousin Margaret and Cousin William?[377] I am glad you have met a Hailybury boy and it was interesting his knowing cousin Stephen. Is Braughing a pretty place?[378] At all like Farleigh?

The place we are in is not very pretty, but it is interesting. The village is mainly a square of houses, near a bridge. In the centre of the square are two pumps over wells which are over 100 feet deep called Artesian wells. This is the part of the world from which that name comes, namely the province of Artois. The commune was very poor and the wells did not work nicely. The poor housewife pumped and pumped away 10 minutes at a time, but only spurts and trickles of water came, but our men have now mended the tubing. An Artisian well, as perhaps you know, is made by drilling a small bore on and on down into the earth with a long rod, and one section of rod is pinned into another section, until a sufficient depth is reached. The water is very pure, but owing to the chalk through which it soaks, is very hard. Besides mending these two wells, the men have made another in the field where our Hospital is, so the village will not be the losers by our stay!

The square is not used now for a market, because for one thing times are not prosperous enough, many of the inhabitants having gone back into the towns behind, and because also dozens of huge motor lorries occupy the space. These lorries fetch

---

376 RDG describes Doulieu (the smashed town) and the ambulance at De La Wastine farm.
377 **Margaret** and **William** John Saumarez-Smith, children of Hubert and Margaret Hanbury.
378 **Braughing** is a village and civil parish, between the rivers Quin and Rib, in the non-metropolitan district of East Hertfordshire.

food from the towns behind and pass it on to the wagons which carry it down to the trenches which, near here, are about 5 miles away. All the engines together make a busy buzzing noise in the early morning. The convoy of lorries which brings the food from the towns, is called the 'Supply Column'. Those that carry it on to the place where the horse waggons obtain it are called the 'Supply Train'. The place where the horse waggons meet is called the 'Refilling Point'. Hay and oats for horses, cheese, biscuits, tea, Bully Beef[379], bacon etc. for the men come up in large quantities.

At the end of the square is the large village Church. The walls and tower remain standing, but the inside was wilfully burnt out by the Germans. They spread petroleum about the wooden portion and set fire to it and the whole place was soon gutted. Along a very straight road, flanked by a row of trees on either side, and about half a mile away stands a large farm. It has five barns each about the size of our barn, and round the group of buildings is a moat. Behind them is a large field. The roadway entering the farm is marked during the day with a Union Jack, and the White Ensign, hung side by side, and at night by two lamps hung side by side. These indicate an Ambulance (or a Hospital as the case may be). Some of the patients are put in the barns, but in the field are two rows of bell-tents where the stronger patients are put. They have a long rough plank table longer than from the gateway to the barn (at our Vicarage), alongside which are planks on posts driven into the ground. At these tables the patients have their meals.

At this end of the field is a kind of kiln, made of old bricks and clay. This is called the incinerator, or destructor, and here every kind of rubbish, or scraps of refuse, or scrap of paper is brought to be burnt. Every day men are told off to pick up everything, even a tiny piece of bacon rind, or an old match-box, and a good camp is kept as clean as a new pin. The men who pick up scraps have long hand-baskets and a stick with a nail stuck in the end, thus they are able to pick up little things without stooping too often.

At the other end of the ground are long rows of little dwellings, made of rubber sheets, old sacks, pieces of canvas and tarpaulin. They are low, little coverings, sloping over a rough pole stretched upon two upright posts, and these are the men's bivouacs. Comfortable enough in dry weather but not so pleasant when it rains, and the ground is very muddy! It is like a little village – and the men like to give their dwellings 'fancy' names. Here are some 'Multurn in Parvo[380]', 'the Ginger Cat's home', 'The Rogues Rest'. The signallers' call theirs 'The Tappers Rest'. One is called 'Somewhere in Flanders' and another 'Wonford House', which is the name of a lunatic asylum in Devonshire[381]. Another is named 'Cryptoconchoidsyphonostomata'!![382]

---

379   **bully beef;** from the French *bouilli* ("boiled").
380   Latin: 'Much in Little'.
381   Now Wonford House hospital, and the HQ of the Devon Partnership NHS Trust, Exeter.
382   *Cryptoconchoidsyphonostomata, or While it's to be Had* was an 1875 one-act play styled a "successful romantic Extravaganza", written by R. H. Edgar and Charles Collette, an actor

'The incinerator for burning all our camp rubbish'

Give my love to Uncle Hubert, Aunt Muriel, Cousin Margaret and Cousin William and have a kiss from your loving Daddy.

Wednesday August 25th 1915, Doulieu

… and a long busy day today with Club work, and odds and ends, and a call to take a funeral behind the trenches. The corner had been shelled ¾ of an hour before I got there and there were plenty of bullets flying about, but chiefly against the parapet, with one now and again high among the trees. A wonderful dug-out is being made by the 'A' company of this regiment – a 'super dug-out' they call it with a tiled floor from a well-to-do house nearby (all the houses are smashed about) with some brighter hearth tiles to make a pattern in it, windows rescued from some houses, sloping sides plastered with lime and sand found on a farm and wild vegetation all round. Nearby is a smashed-up convent and a trench runs across its garden. The Germans opposite have put up a placard yesterday "What is going to happen to Russia now?" Our men shouted back "What about your Navy[383]?"

---

who also starred in the leading role of Plantagenet Smith and wrote the words and music of the play's hit song 'What An Afternoon'.

383 The **Battle of the Gulf of Riga**: naval operation of the German High Seas Fleet against the Russian Baltic Fleet in the Gulf of Riga in August 1915. The operation's objective was to destroy the Russian naval forces in the Gulf and facilitate the fall of Riga to the German army in the later stages of the Central Powers' offensive on the Eastern Front in 1915. The German fleet, however, failed to achieve its objective and was forced to return to its bases.

Thursday August 26th 1915, Doulieu

Chaplain's talk this morning and after that a confirmation talk in the smashed up town. The men were very attentive, but they live in such a different atmosphere – these matters, with the long distances to be covered, took up the whole morning. There were seven Chaplains present and we discussed Confirmation plans. A little circular note is going to be printed, nicely written by Talbot and paid for out of the Fund, by which it is hoped to reach some of the men who might otherwise not be reached, and at least that will give everyone a chance. On my suggestion also, we give information as to the date, and opportunities for talks which will go into Orders , and so help to get it better known[384].

The official intelligence paper sent round to us remarks, "allusions to the defeat of the German fleet by the Russians (across the trenches by our men) was followed by conversation which in turn evoked considerable machine gun and rifle fire!"

A German officer was seen in blue uniform with silver epaulettes and a peaked cap with a red band[385]. We smashed another large periscope – more newspapers have been put out between the trenches, but have been left alone lest they should be a trap. The papers obtained are copies of the *Gazette d'Argonnes* printed in French, but proving to be of German editorship and produced in Charleroi. It gives extravagant accounts of German successes, and the Allies want of it, and is scurrilous in its version of the English attitude towards the French and the Belgians, and of England's failures[386].

Friday August 27th 1915, Doulieu

Down to the trenches this morning to bury a Lance-Corporal, shot through the heart. He lay waxen white and still, with the deep red patch upon his clothes, and the warm summer sun shine glimmered round, so that it seemed quite natural to see him lying there. We have seen so many now, and we laid him to rest in his soldier's grave – a noble end, but one thinks of what it may mean elsewhere, if there is a wife or mother. I have not found out yet. A few bullets sang around, near enough as one knows by the sound, with one quite near. But it is astonishing how few people of the many present, get hit. We met one cheerful lad with his head all swathed in wrappings who had been grazed by a bullet. I do not think he realised what an escape he had

---

384 A copy of this circular is still in the possession of the family.
385 Probably, by the description, Prussian Landwehr (the Prussian equivalant of RDG's Territorials) cavalry uniform.
386 Information was strictly regulated in the occupied zones, and newspaper-printing facilities were suspended and requisitioned to begin printing German propaganda. The Germans produced a French language newspaper called the *Gazette des Ardennes*, and though the French civilians preferred to call it the "Gazette of Lies" in many cases it was the only source of information available. Jeanne du Thoit, a diarist from Lille, wrote in 1915, "The life we lead here is an automatic life, mind-numbing! [Not many choices of newspapers], except the *Good Public of Ghent*, censored by the Germans, and the *Gazette des Ardennes*, whose writing is all [done by] Germans."

had – a quarter of an inch makes such a difference to a head wound.

Wild vegetation, wild flowers and some trees laden with fruit. Club work, arrangements for Sunday, more effort about Confirmation and a very hot afternoon. I hear that the Dean of Sydney[387] has been wounded at the Dardanelles.

Saturday, August 28th 1915, Doulieu

I have been down into the smashed town with more arrangements for tomorrow. It appears that two shells fell on it yesterday afternoon soon after I had left, but no one was hurt. Into the next smashed town, more shells, with one killed and four wounded.

Wonderful weather, warm and sunny, is the outstanding feature of today. A dog was killed by an ambulance car and a little French urchin nearly killed also, little rascal, by the car that I was in. He was running along, trying to hold onto an adapted motor-bus, (one of those bringing men back from leave), and did not see us coming. Our driver slowed down, but we were going at a good pace and the young gentleman, barefooted, saw us just in time and bounded with his hands up against and away from our bonnet, and just saved himself. I think his hands must have been warmed by the hot bonnet casing and he ran away, looking rather relieved and naughty.

Back this evening in K's motorcar (K is the principal officer for the Ambulances) into the first town we entered last November[388]. It is astonishing how entirely it has recovered since then. We were there only a month after the Germans had left it, and houses were empty, the well-to-do had gone and only a few women and children were left. Now smartly dressed women walk about, the shop windows are alive, English notices are displayed "Beefsteaks, eggs, coffee, lemonade and other refreshments at moderate prices. Proprietress, Veuve Nidon" … and the like.

Sunday August 29th 1915, Doulieu

Who can reach so many men and at such distances? One starts out with great hopes but in a short day so little seems done. The men listened all round, with close attention when I talked about Confirmation, at 10.30 about 100, 11.30 about 250, 12.15 about 100. Holy Communion in a barn at 6.45, with the corn sheaves piled up to the roof on either side of us, and long rows of golden sheaves along the rafters making a ceiling above us. Three present with us to commune with the Bread of Life. An evening service in another barn, with the winnowing machine in the middle and

---

387 **Albert Edward Talbot** (b.1877– d.1936) Made Deacon in 1905, he was ordained priest by the Bishop of Manchester in 1906. He held liberal views and was rector of Stowell church, Salford (1909–12). In 1912, Talbot was appointed Dean and Archdeacon of Sydney. Having enlisted in the Australian Imperial Force as senior Anglican chaplain in October 1914, he embarked for Egypt with the 3rd Battalion. In Gallipoli, he developed a strong rapport with the troops and demonstrated his ecumenism. Wounded at Lone Pine in August 1915, he returned to Australia February 1916.

388 Estaires La Gorgue.

two long planks for seats, and one officer and 8 or 9 men. The cold rain beat upon things outside and some fell in through the great open doorway and the darkness fell on us suddenly with the lowering clouds, so we finished without a hymn only the National Anthem, as we were not able to see. The night has closed in gloomy and chill. Hundreds of Talbot's Confirmation letters have gone out today.

Monday August 30th 1915, Doulieu

It is pretty certain, I think, that we are out here for this winter, even if the back of things were broken before, as there must be an army of occupation for some time. The National leaders were wise in not withholding the prospect of suffering, and we must face it.

Today was meant to be a rest day, after the ride in to settle up the Club's weekly business, but it did not quite come off, an important medical officer having called at the Mess, needing to be talked to, and then some sports to be looked in on – the ankle too proved a little fractious.

Tuesday August 31st 1915

Another funeral just behind the trenches – so still and so restful the good lad looked. In these trench burials there is no wrapping in the blanket, the soldier is laid in his clean cut neat bed, in his uniform with his hands crossed and his feet placed together. Very simple and very appropriate, and now and then a bullet sings a kind of harmless farewell to the brave soul gone on. Bullets don't matter there. I went on into the trenches. They are greatly improved now-a-days to what they were those months ago. You have a good long communication trench, and can wind yourself along comparatively easily. Very tortuous are the entrance ways, like a Hampton Court maze, to prevent enfilading, and as a better protection against shelling. A shell comes, you drop flat in your narrow ditch and all is well. Some men go sick readily and others will not give in until they can really bear it no longer. At the back of the trench here sits a determined-looking good fellow, the back of his neck is being dressed by the doctor. It is wretchedly swollen and ablaze with soreness and the area is wide-spread. You would think that this man ought to be laid aside, but he will not have it, and yet another man will try to get into hospital almost with the scratch of a pin.

Peeps over the parapet are rather dull now, as the grass is so long and the vegetation so high that you can only see sandbags here and there, and no Germans. They send their bullets over you nevertheless. Now a snarl and a bang, now a high scream and a whistle – you never know where till after! People are all in very good spirits now-a-days in this cool dry weather and except for the confinement and the flying missiles, trench life is not so bad. They thought they caught sight of some mine earthworks, so proceeded to shell them vigorously, and this of course brought back shells in return. But today the returns had not begun till I was well up the road again and on my way back. Another good Confirmation talk. The two regular men are very earnest and attentive and nine more have sent their names in today. It remains to be seen what kind of material they are made of.

A specimen of spelling – (one of the patient's letters handed in to the Chaplain to be censored) – "dear sister i right you a few lynes hoping to fiend you all in the best heath for i have bean in the hopistl a weak and i am going on well worte to Jhon and got no answer yet so wen you right to Jhon tel him i wos asking after him and anny susey tommy so no mor at presend from your loving brother andrew."

Wednesday September 1st 1915, Doulieu

The weather is getting cold and wet, and the days are very full with these long distances to travel. Club work this morning and the ankle is almost right now, but stings a little when tired. My battalions come out of the trenches today or tonight, so will be more easily accessible, but it does take such a time for the Chaplain to get to and fro.

The suspicions were verified last night – the mound we shelled was stuff from a mine. Moreover, we had suspected a mine at that point, and so did not occupy the front trench thereabouts. Last night the Germans fired it, no one was within many yards of the place. Then they shelled the spot thinking we should be mustering there to pick up the wounded, and that there would be some confusion, "But Brer Fox he say nothing – He lay low[389]!". No one hurt in any way and so our men march on their merry way!!

Thursday September 2nd 1915, Doulieu

It is really rather cold here, but I think it has been warm enough on our left for somebody, a heavy shelling having continued most of this evening with the loud roaring of guns.

This morning we had a Chaplain's talk and billet visiting. This evening I tried a side road after billet visiting and found myself in the gathering darkness lost, over ploughed fields and potato and bean patches, which seemed endless. The rain fell heavily and the thick soil clung to the horse's feet. I was looking out over a gloomy fenland, with rolling clouds and a driving wind, across into an inky skyline that seemed to be far enough off to be nowhere, and over a wide space of soppy ground, then over another, all bounded by deep reed-lined ditches – there, if it be wanted, is an idea of the scene. The horse jumped the ditches well, and in about a quarter of an hour we struck a road that brought us at length under the shadow of the burnt out church. Welcome lights gleamed out of the little windows onto the dark wet roadway, and we eventually reached the farm really none the worse, thank you!

---

389 *The Wonderful Tar Baby Story,* trad. American.

Friday September 3rd 1915, Doulieu

Cold, wild and wet with deep mud and cutting chills round the corners. Church and Club matters in the morning and much serving at tables, with a Confirmation class this evening – 9 men as usual in a barn and all very earnest and attentive – they seem to mean business.

Saturday September 4th 1915, Doulieu

Sometimes things move rapidly in the Army. This evening I hear from the senior Chaplain of the VIIIth Division that the Deputy Chaplain General[390] has a change of station in view for me, and wished me to go to Head Quarters[391] and see him as soon as it is convenient. So my address will change and the entire scene of operations, with what different duties, I wonder? Some of my ideas have gone well – the Club, kept going continuously by hook or by crook, the known centre for meeting the Chaplain, the place where prayer is wont to be made, the regular service of Holy Communion at a given spot and a regular time, in the little or big Club, <u>always</u> with a place of devotion attached or working in connection with it – these have been the ideas I have tried to carry out, and they have been implemented in two large centres now. Other Chaplains have carried on the same ideas with the aid of 'the Fund' so I think that quite a good few centres have been set up and provided for. Other Chaplains have had their ideas and have worked them out too – one after this manner, another after that. Our plan must now apparently be pursued in another area. I shall try to leave this Club going on its healthy little way, crowded out each evening to its small utmost, and for the future, I await the events! The wild cold weather has given place to something balmier, but to noisier fighting.

Sunday September 5th 1915, Doulieu

With a big change impending, one's mind gets rather full, and I have had a busy day moreover. Holy Communion at 6.45 am with 2 present, then Morning Service at 9 in the mud of a farm with about 40 present, again at 10. am in a nice farm, with myself standing on the threshing floor, with about 200 present. At 11 a.m. in the stubble of another farm, a service with about 200 present and at 12 another bright service on dried mud, (the sun now being stronger) at yet another farm with about 200 present and after lunch, a rest, papers, candles and other arrangements to be made for the evening service. A run down to the little town where the Club is, to

---

390 Bp **Llewellyn Henry Gwynne**, CMG, CBE (b.1863 – d.1957) was the first Anglican Bishop of Egypt and Sudan (1920–1946). He began his overseas career in 1899 as a Christian missionary in east Africa. In 1905 Gwynne was appointed Archdeacon for the Sudan; and in 1908 he was consecrated Bishop of Khartoum.
   Recalled to Europe in World War I, Bishop Llewellyn joined the army as Chaplain. In July 1915, he was appointed Deputy Chaplain-General of the army in France, with the relative rank of Major-General.

391 St. Omer was the General Headquarters of the BEF from October 1914 to March 1916.

get some material, and at 6.30 a full service in the Hospital Barn, about 90 present and a service of Holy Communion following, at which 22 were present including 2 officers. For patients and some others, it is practically impossible to get to an early morning Communion under the regulations that they have to observe. It was very quiet and earnest in the solemn evening hour, the big barn lit by six or seven little specks of candle. How very quiet they were in listening to a talk on our entire dependence on the Holy Spirit.

Monday September 6th 1915, Doulieu

Busy getting things settled up after nearly a year with this Division. It is sad now, the going and the goodbyes and yet I think after losing so many friends, gallant and noble men, a change has its advantages.

A Confirmation talk at 11 to 13 men, all Scotch with a Black Watch Regiment and some very earnest men among them. Another, a settled class, to 11 candidates all bright and keen and about 14 'postulants' i.e. those who want to hear and know. I go down to General Headquarters[392] on Wednesday and shall then learn the next scene of my labours.

Tuesday September 7th 1915, Doulieu

A day of much interviewing and settling up. A Confirmation talk this evening and a meeting of C.E.M.S members. They spoke very nicely about my going.

I went with a young corporal back to his regiment this morning. He had a shrapnel bullet through his upper lip, down through his tongue and out through his lower palate under his chin! He said the pain was maddening, none but those who went through it could tell what it was like. After being sent out from the hospital in England his tongue still troubled him and he could not tell why, until two large pieces of tooth worked their way out from inside the tongue itself! What histories there are if only there were time to set them down.

Thursday September 9th 1915, St Omer

I was not able to write last night, being deprived of residence and materials, my baggage being afar off. I went to General Head Quarters, saw Bishop Gwynne, dined with him in fact, and had a talk. Tonight I am at a base camp, just having arrived very late. Here I am for I believe a slight season, and after that I do not know. It is a change – everything seems so peaceful, so civilised and so crowded with people. I

---

392 Organised during pre-war planning, this was the HQ of the British armies in France and Flanders on the Western Front. Up to December 1914, GHQ also acted as Army HQ; from there on, the army grew and proliferated several Armies and GHQ commanded vast numbers of troops. It was possibly the single most powerful 'management' Britain has ever formed. Originally located at St Omer, once the fighting had stabilised, Haig relocated it to Montreuil-sur-Mer.

cannot describe much now, not having seen much. The journey was slow, and French trainified! My orderly dropped my nice Thermos flask and it broke irretrievably!

Friday September 10th 1915, Étaples

Feelings are curious in this huge base camp. Hundreds of tents. We have here re-inforcements who go up to fill gaps in the firing line, and I am attached to one of the Divisions which have gone up to be instructed in French life by the VIIIth Division. You can combine therefore sympathy with the men in their new enterprise, and actual information about the trenches they will be going into and already it gives one a great introduction to the men. Another temporary Chaplain (besides myself) who's name is Warner, is working here among the thousands of men who are daily increasing. He has a parish near Gloucester and is a very nice earnest man[393]. We had a long talk on the sand bank, under the sunny shade of some trees this morning. He is <u>very</u> anxious to be sent up to the front –"Would give his eyes for it". He learned that I had been through Neuve Chapelle. "Ah" he said "I lost a nephew there". I asked the name and he said "Weigale". I said "I was talking with him the day before Neuve Chapelle" and I repeated the words we had exchanged. He was so glad to have that fact to pass on to the dear lad's mother. I feel sure she will like to hear of one who had spoken with her son in the flesh, the very day before he went away into that wonderful life[394].

In the train coming down there was a young officer travelling alone on duty, from the firing line to this Camp. I was glad to strike up an acquaintance with him because he was cheery and keen, and moreover going to the land that was strange to me. We went together to dinner at a little 'estaminet' by the railway side. I found that he came from Cardiff. I said that I knew Cardiff a little and that my godson nephew came from there, and was now an officer in the 7th E Yorks, his name, I added, was Thomas. He looked at me with round attentive eyes and said "George Vinson Thomas[395]?" I nodded and he then said "He is engaged to my sister[396]!"

Well, we parsons are persons, and our work has a very great deal to do with life's personal side, in addition to the conversion of souls. God is making conversions without human intervention. Many hundreds are born again, I do believe, by the passing through those waters that separate these two countries. Their military

---

393 Rev. **Wynyard Alexander Warner** (b.1875 – d.1926). 2nd Wiltshire Regt (21st Brigade, 7th Division) from August 1915 until he was gassed in December 1916. During this time, he was awarded the Military Cross for bravery during the Battle for Trones Wood (Somme, 8th–14th July 1916). Rector of St Andrew's (Sudely Castle), Toddington near Cheltenham. Rector of All Saints, Broseley, Shropshire, from 1922–1926.

394 Lt **Richard Edward Cromwell Weigall**, (b.1892 – d.1915), 1st Batt. Sherwood Foresters (Notts and Derby Regiment). Killed 11th March 1915. Son of Maj. and Mrs. Weigall, of 3, Christchurch Rd., Winchester.

395 2nd Lt **George Vinson Thomas** The East Yorkshire Regiment. He survived the war.

396 **Elizabeth Dora Lee**.

consecration, so self-sacrificing, so much a surrender of themselves to the service of Right against Wrong, is a death to sin in many forms – the sin of indifference about right, the sin of self-indulgence, of an undue self-cherishing, and a giving of themselves in a new birth unto the righteousness of a fight for right, a saving of others and a surrender in any way necessary, even to death itself, to the call of duty.

Saturday September 11th 1915, Étaples (20th Infantry Base Depot. A.P.O. S17 B.E.F.)[397]

A beautiful day with glorious sunshine. I went down into the rather smelly village[398], but it was nice breathing the salt sea air – very pure. There is a Church Army[399] hut, a Y.M.C.A. ditto, a Soldier's Christian Association ditto, and Preb. Pitt[400] helps the former to keep going.

Sunday September 12th 1915, Etaples

Another glorious day. Holy Communion at 7.30 am with 12 present. 10 o'clock a large Parade Service in the Soldier's Christian Association with about 350 to 400 present. Another service at 11, about which there must have been some mistake, as there were only about 40 men, although 300 were anticipated. However, there was more time for talking around. I went to lunch with Captain Skipwith[401], who has charge of this depot and is a very pleasant man. He has rooms in the village where an artist has a studio in the house, and Captain Skipwith has had a portrait painted. It is really very well done in flat tones, which makes a striking result.

397 **Etaples**, on the French coast opposite Le Touquet, 20 miles SW of St Omer, 30 miles west of Estaires La Gorgue, location of the Base Depot of the 20th Infantry Brigade, part of the 7th Division, consisting of: 2nd Bn, the Border Regt; 2nd Bn, the Gordon Highlanders; 1/6th Bn, the Gordon Highlanders; 8th Bn, the Devonshire Regt; 9th Bn, the Devonshire Regt. Étaples was the scene of much Allied activity during WW1 due to its safety from attack by enemy land forces and the existence of railway connections with both the northern and southern battlefields. The town was home to 16 hospitals and a convalescent depot, in addition to a number of reinforcement camps for Commonwealth soldiers and general barracks for the French Army. Site of the notorious Army mutiny in September 1917.

398 Lady Baden-Powell, volunteer YMCA worker "Etaples was a dirty, loathsome, smelly little town". Baden-Powell, Lady (1987). *Window on My Heart.*

399 The Church Army was founded in England in 1882 by the Revd. Wilson Carlile (afterwards prebendary of St. Paul's Cathedral), who banded together in an orderly army of soldiers, officers and a few working men and women, whom he and others trained to act as Church of England evangelists among the outcasts and criminals of the Westminster slums. During the First World War, the Church Army was very active among the troops in France, and ran around 2000 social clubs across France.

400 Rev. **Willam Baker Pitt**, Prebandary of Liddington, Wilts. (b.1856 – d.1936) was the founder of Swindon Town Football Club (1879) and also curate of Christ Church, Swindon until 1881 and rector of Liddington from then on.

401 Captain Sir **Grey Humberston d'Estoteville Skipwith**, 11th Baronet of Prestwould (b.1884 – d.1950). Captain TAR, 23rd Battalion City of London Regt, 2nd Lieutenant Warwicks Yeomanry. Obviously, he was interested in portraiture: his portrait in is in the National Portrait Gallery in London.

A good informal service in the Church Army hut this evening; the men were very attentive and I spoke about Confirmation, as the Bishop comes on Sunday. The Prince of Wales is also about here and he was on the beach this afternoon, one of our officers said.

Monday September 13th 1915, Etaples

Such a glorious day. Holy Communion at 6.30 am. There is beautiful water in this camp and a bath is joy! We get English papers the same day of issue, in the afternoon. I waited about for Carr Gregg[402], who was to have come for a talk, but he did not appear. I then went to see Warner and we had a talk under a pine tree, on a sandy slope. He was keen and eager to know everything about life and work to and from the trenches. There have been difficulties about the hut work here, which he wanted to talk about.

This evening I went and stood near a Salvation Army 'pitch'. They used our service books, but I am afraid that I was not impressed by the words of the speaker. There was the usual lurid confession of an ill-spent youth, a phrase or two intended to raise a laugh, and a rather amusing anecdote of his little boy, who was promised a bag of sweets if he kept good a whole day. He was found in bed in the afternoon with his clothes and boots on, giving as his reason that he was determined thus to keep good, and secure the bag of sweets – but then an earnest appeal to come to Christ.

Tuesday September 14th 1915, Etaples

I have talked today until my throat almost refuses to vibrate! After breakfast I had a walk and talk with Warner and we visited the Y.M.C.A. hut, and met a Mr. and Mrs. Dixon who run it. Then to see Day, the senior Chaplain for these base camps, who is a nice knowledgeable man[403]. Visiting the tents this afternoon and evening has been very interesting – I found the gardener of the vicar of Leeds, near Maidstone and lads from Maidstone, Boxley, Mereworth, Tonbridge, Tunbridge Wells, Strood, Chatham and a nice fellow from East Farleigh[404]. Of the last I asked, "What name?" "Pearson" "You are from Kent?"

"Yes, Sir."

"What part I wonder?"

"East Farleigh"

"Do you know Mr. Littlewood?"

"Yes, Sir."

---

402 Rev. **Ivo Francis Henry Carr-Gregg** (b.1876 – d.1958), amateur astronomer and vicar of Astley, Nuneaton 1917–1958

403 Rev. **Edward Rouviere Day**, CMG, CBE, MA (b.1867 – d.1948). Graduate Trinity College, Dublin, ordained 1891, served Boer War. 1914–15. Chaplain first class, Assistant Chaplain General, 3rd Army 1916–1918.

404 Leeds, 5 miles E of Maidstone; Boxley, 4 miles NE; Mereworth, 5 miles W; Tonbridge, 7 mile SW; Tunbridge Wells, 15 miles SW; Strood, 15 miles N; Chatham, 10 miles N.

"What is your Christian name?"

"George"

"Your grandfather lives in West Farleigh, up the hill towards Hunton?"

"Yes Sir, and my father lives with him."

"I know both well and your grandfather is an old friend. I gave your grandmother the Holy Communion two days before she died." – and so on. Tonight, at dinner an earnest discussion about Armageddon, the Millenium and the trustworthiness of Christ's words, the settled old senior officer being very interested to talk about these things, and then down to the Church Army hut for prayers. Many of these lads move off to the firing line tonight.

Wednesday September 15th 1915, Etaples

More visiting round the camps – it is endless. There is much help in being able to talk about life at the front actually, and the men are eager and impatient to get there. Most of them have been mobilised for over a year and have grown almost tired of waiting for the call.

Thursday September 16th 1915, Etaples

Some drafts went off last night and I was round among their tents beforehand, but missed seeing them off, as they were paraded a little sooner than was expected.

A meeting of Chaplains and workers this morning and Day, the Senior Chaplain of the Base, gave a nice address on the Cloud of witnesses[405] – he sounds a good man. Others present were Marsham, Preb. Pitt, some Chaplain out here on his own responsibility in connexion with the Duchess of Westminster's Hospital, and about six lay readers[406]. Much visiting round – it would take a book to tell you of all the talks, discussions and personal touches one encounters. Having been rather a 'rolling stone' about England and the world, I find it not a disadvantage – after all it is travel which has made the British Empire. At all events, it is a help to be able to say of one town or county, or even village, 'Oh yes, I have been there'.

Saturday September 18th 1915, Etaples

This work is not at all so 'advantageous' as closer up to the trenches, as the men are not so accessible, but the camp is nice and they are very comfortable although the

---

405 **Hebrews 12:1** 'Wherefore seeing we also are compassed about with so great a cloud of witnesses, let us lay aside every weight, and the sin which doth so easily beset *us*, and let us run with patience the race that is set before us.'

406 Lady **Constance Edwina Lewes**, CBE (formerly Grosvenor, née Cornwallis-West) (b.1876 – d.1970), also known as Shelagh, was an English socialite and peeress. The Duchess of Westminster's Hospital (No.1 B.R.C.S) was at Le Touquet from October, 1914, to July, 1918, and the British graves in the Communal Cemetery were made from that hospital. Le Touquet is across the estuary of the R. Canche from Etaples.

seriousness of their mission is rather far away from them. Also, as part of the personnel, there are people who have come down sick and physically unfit, the less sound in body and morale and they are not so inspiring. Still, there are a great number of the fresh, keen, eager ones and one dwells more with them, and their influence spreads.

No mails today – something happening. Two funerals in a tidy picturesque cemetery upon the sloping ground leading down to the sea shore with a number of men with whom one has been sharing fights[407].

Last Sunday I asked if there was anyone who would volunteer to play for the hymns at the 10 o'clock parade. A young man eventually stepped forward and played very nicely. At the end, I thanked him and hoped he would play again if he was free to do so. Tonight, he came to the Church Army hut volunteering for tomorrow again. Then he said that after looking closely at me last Sunday, he had made up his mind who I was – I had preached at his church (Shoreham in Kent) for the sailors ten years ago when he was then a choir boy, and his sister had played for the children's service in the afternoon. He remembered the sermons. The good sister had given him a 'Happy Warrior' and he is going to resume using it. The family now live at Sevenoaks, the father having retired from a small business and another sister is nursing at a hospital there. The Bishop's daughter is also nursing at the same hospital and is friendly with everybody and liked by all.

This evening we have been out on the hillock nearby [...*censored*...] with a hundred men drawn up under the pale moonlight on the sandy slope, dim khaki-clad forms, flitting flashlights moving in and out among them, and the thin grey sea line in the distance – all of them just off to the front. As they moved off, one of the reserves who stayed behind for a while longer, a sergeant, came up to me and said "Beg pardon, Sir, ain't you Mr Griffiths? I looked at you, and I says, it is – the other evening when you was going down our tents. Remember coming to see me aboard the 'Ventura'?"[408] Captain Smith, he's my uncle – he's got the Institute now, hasn't he? I went from Rochester to Lewes and I came to hear you that Sunday morning when you preached at St. Michael's", and so on.

More requests for Confirmation have come in from the Brigade that I have just left. I think that the men are more accessible up there than here. A young officer, a Jew

---

407 Of more than 11 500 soldiers interred in Étaples Military Cemetery, over 10 000 of these men were casualties of WW1 who died in Étaples or the surrounding area. Designed by Sir Edwin Lutyens, in 1920, Étaples Military Cemetery is the largest CWGC cemetery in France.

408 **SS Ventura**, Built by William Cramp, Philadelphia in 1900 for the Oceanic Steam Ship Co of San Francisco. She was a 6253 gross ton ship, two funnels, twin screw, 17 knots and with accommodation for 240 1st class together with 2nd and 3rd class passengers. She commenced sailings between San Francisco, Honolulu, Auckland and Sydney in 1901 and continued this service until 1907 when she was laid up in San Francisco, due to the company's financial problems. In 1912 she was reconditioned, converted from coal to oil fuel and rebuilt with only one funnel. Resumed the San Francisco – Honolulu – Pago Pago – Sydney service until 1917 when she was taken over for trooping duties in the Atlantic.

prepared in England, was hoping to be confirmed tomorrow, but he has gone off with a draft tonight.

An officer sat next to me in the Mess this evening. I asked him whether he had been out long. He said "Last evening". I asked if he had come from a nice camp like this one and he said "Not bad, just outside Rochester!"

A lady sends us some Times Broadsheets – I think they are an excellent idea as the men complain so much that there is nothing to do in these strange places, outside the soldiering.

Sunday September 19th 1915, Etaples

An 'occupied' day, yet not a very strenuous one. Holy Communion at 6.30 to which Loveland came with a friend he had helped and seven others, and the Bishop took the 7.30 service. I went home to breakfast, having 3 funerals at 9. You have to walk a mile and a quarter to the cemetery and when I got there just 'on time', I found the Wesleyan Chaplain in possession and I had to be back for a Parade service the other end of the camp by 10. It was a push, and each interment has to be made separately. Luckily, I got a lift on a Red Cross car returning which saved me five minutes, or I should have kept about 600 men waiting. As it was I felt rather steamy and puffy, but it was a nice service and Loveland played. One or two officers chatty afterwards, and that was all my official ministration for the day. The Bishop, Dr. Gwynne[409], took a large parade at 11.30 and gave an affectionate, fervent address and I am sure that the Holy Spirit used it to lead on and make more manly the listeners.

About 36 Confirmees at 3.30 including one nursing Sister. The Bishop had himself taken a Confirmation at Samaria, where we read of the earliest Confirmation service taking place. About 7 Chaplains present so you can guess it is a fairly large base! I had tea with Warner who knows and likes Dr Brewer and Bishop Frodsham[410]. The evening service in the Church Army hut was taken by a Church Army Chaplain and Preb. Pitt, the latter gave a kindly address on Temptation. Just before the service a soldier came up and said "Didn't you mention Sydney in your address last Sunday, Sir? And the Seamen's Institute? I know that place well – been there four or five times and had tea with Mr and Mrs Pain" etc.

Monday September 20th 1915, Etaples

A beautiful day and a very full one but more of that tomorrow.

---

409 The Deputy Chaplain General, rank of Brigadier.
410 **George Horsfall Frodsham** (b.1863 – d.1936). He was educated at Birkenhead School and University College, Durham and ordained in 1888. From 1896 he was Rector of St Thomas' Toowong, Queensland and then chaplain to the Bishop of Brisbane. From 1902 to 1913 he was the Bishop of North Queensland. On his return to England he was a canon residentiary at Gloucester Cathedral. In 1920 he became Vicar of Halifax.

Tuesday September 21st 1915, Etaples

The Bishop met the Chaplains yesterday morning for talk and afterwards had a personal talk with each. The address was a kind one, but not quite forceful. He asked for affection …

[*pages missing*] … to 'officer' the 300-to-500 'Temporary' Chaplains! To which, as so large a proportion of the permanent establishment are young, and very young men are not fitting on many counts. Not least in the precept of St Peter "Ye younger submit yourselves to the Elder: yea, all of you be subject one to another and be clothed in humility"[411]. However, it appears from the talk of the Deputy Chaplain General that I am sent here for a time of rest and change. Various young new Chaplains will work here before going up to the Front, and new drafts are quartered here for one, two, three or more days, some a month, before going up to join their regiments.

Wednesday September 22nd 1915, Etaples

Some more interesting talks today – having lived or stayed in many places during a lifetime, I am able to talk to men from various localities, and it makes friends to be able to speak of the road or village near the lad's own home.

Today I buried four brave men in the little Cemetery by the sea shore, facing over the blue waves out to where the golden sun leads on to the endless day. I passed a Princess Christian train[412] beautifully made and fitted up to perfection by all appearances. You could get just a glimpse of one or two of the patient men stretched out within – a train-load of suffering and self-sacrifice, marked outside with the Cross, speaking from inside of the Cross, also the Cross of pain and the Cross of help.

Friday September 24th 1915, Etaples

This evening a lad came up to me, all beaming smiles and very glad to meet someone he knew – a man from Teston.[413] Church Army hut and visiting round the lines, hundreds of men, thousands of men.

---

411 1 **Peter** 5:5 'Likewise, ye younger, submit yourselves unto the elder. Yea, all *of you* be subject one to another, and be clothed with humility: for God resisteth the proud, and giveth grace to the humble.'

412 A Red Cross hospital train. **Princess Helena** (Helena Augusta Victoria; **Princess Christian of Schleswig-Holstein** by marriage; b.1846 – d.1923) was the third daughter and fifth child of Queen Victoria and Prince Albert. Helena was the most active member of the royal family, carrying out an extensive programme of royal engagements at a time when royalty was not expected to appear often in public. She was also an active patron of charities, and was one of the founding members of the Red Cross. She was founding president of the Royal School of Needlework, and president of the Royal British Nurses' Association. As president of the latter, she was a strong supporter of nurse registration against the advice of Florence Nightingale.

413 **Teston** is a village in the Maidstone District. It is located on the A26 road out of Maidstone, four miles from the town centre.

Saturday September 25th 1915, Etaples

Yesterday was the Confirmation in the VIIIth Division and about 24 men were due to have been presented from my Brigade – I wonder what has been done.

Heavy rains here, but it is a beautifully dry and clean camp and the water soon soaks and shoots off. This evening a long walk over a winding hilly road, sandy and dry, between deep copses of pine trees, the damp earth and trees smelling delicious, all so cool and fresh, and a blazingly beautiful sunset behind, waves of crimson against an opal background – all most peaceful and refreshing. They are sending down all the Chaplains who have been up since the beginning, so I suppose one must not grumble, but I hope I shall not be here for very long.

Sunday September 26th 1915, Etaples

A beautiful day, and a crowded hearty and reverent service with about 500 or more present at 10 o'clock. Another parade service at 11.30 with about 600 people and a quiet service this evening – for the rest only visiting round.

A cold night, and we hear that the French have taken Souchez[414], are holding their ground, have advanced 3 to 4 kilometres along a front of 25 kilometres and have taken over 12000 prisoners. We may thank God and take courage, but how much we also need to humble ourselves before Him. Not least because some sections of the population, allowing themselves to be voiced by papers like "John Bull', resent the imputation that we deserve humbling. A nice service this evening and a good healthy address by Baggalay on prayer[415]. "Enoch walked with God"[416] That was prayer, but the meeting was kept a little long, but was otherwise very good.

When does Ursula go?[417] And has she quite decided against coming out here? There are many doing work, who I understand, have not done a complete training. A nice service this evening, and a good healthy address on prayer. There are very many Scripture Readers on the ground, and each is sensitive about his being given more or less attention and prominence.

Monday September 27th 1915, Etaples

Great news again today – prisoners by the French said to be above 20,000. Our own prisoners on this Front are said to be tonight about the same number and over 6000 prisoners taken by the Russians, and the wounded going back into Belgium,

---

414 **Souchez**, due to its location between the hills of Lorette and Vimy, suffered terribly during WW1. The Germans took possession of the hill from Lorette October 5th, 1914 and attempts to revive this strategic point (the hill overlooking the plain of Lens) by French troops failed until spring 1915.

415 Rev. **Frederick Wilson Baggalay** (b.1886 – d.1951) Pulborough, Sussex, educated Exeter College Oxford. BA 1909, MA 1912, Bp's Hotel Farnham 1910.

416 **Genesis 5:24** 'And Enoch walked with God: and he *was* not; for God took him.'

417 Ursula Saumarez-Smith (Sister in law)

an innumerable and pitiable procession. The enemy is beginning to feel our power. Now if we could only have plenty of munitions and could go hammering on!

Before coming down from the firing line, I had promised an officer to find the grave of a brother officer to assure the mother of its being cared for. I tried to get across, but was prevented by the shelling – then we were moved – then I came down here. Today in a strange way I met an officer who had seen the grave only five days ago, and who knew it had been cared for by another Regiment. So he will write to the mother – "there is a providence..............." [418]

You may remember some months ago I had to criticise one Regiment about its indifference to religious provision for the men. I have met here one of the officers of a previous generation. The present C.O. of this particular Regiment was then his Captain and these are one or two incidents that happened. When this officer joined as a young lieutenant, he was taken with one or two others, by the 'now' C.O. after mess, into the yard outside. There, in his full mess kit he was bidden to get into the dog kennel. On his knees, he was to put his head out of the kennel, bark like a dog for quite a long time, then to say "Subalterns is beasts". He did this and was passed! Another time in the summer, in India at 2 o'clock in the morning, this same now C.O. made him put on a dressing gown, outside his clothes, over that a fur-lined coat fastened round the waist with a belt, and on his head a knitted wool helmet. Under that covering he "steamed like a soup kitchen". He was then made, in this costume, to go down and perform his duty of <u>inspecting the guard</u>! It is not difficult to see from a little of the history of a Regiment, somewhat of an explanation of some of its tone!! Luckily there was one officer of godly earnestness who stood his ground, and greatly helped to a better way.

Well, goodnight my dear and special friend.

Tuesday, September 28th 1915, Etaples

If ever the writing is faint, whether by reason of the willing but fatigued hand that writes it, or by the poorness of the quality of the paper which receives it, or maybe on account of the haste with which it hath to be done, for what reason so ever it be, if that writing is faint, take water a cheap commodity even in these days of costliness. A little water, not a large quantity, so very little will be found to suffice, take it, I say, a thing not difficult to do either, for though many things are difficult to obtain not being in locality easy of access, being remote by cause of circumstance, the source or means of supply or otherwise – water we were saying, so easy to obtain for lives placed amid normal privileged even now-a-days, Yes! Take water, a little water, a rag, a little rag or cloth and just damp it and lo! Plainness strikes bold and unmistakeably well. There is water enough here at the moment.

---

418   **Hamlet Act V Scene 2** "There's a special providence in the fall of a sparrow. If it be now, 'tis not to come; if it be not to come, it will be now; if it be not now, yet it will come: the readiness is all. Since no man knows aught of what he leaves, what isn't to leave betimes? Let be.

It has been raining solidly for two hours. Everything outside is very wet and the tent is beginning to be 'musical' in that way one knows so well, the canvas answering like a drum to the least touch, the ropes taut and resonant like the thick strings on violincello, but the soil is sandy and on a slope, and it dries up very quickly. <u>No mud!</u> So a delightful camp in that way. It is well supplied also with a tin basin available for washing and there are floor boards. The O.C. has lent me his folding bedstead and if I stay here much longer I think I shall send for mine (no more sleeping on the floor for a time) and my faithful man Peter Waite has made a little bookshelf and dressing table out of some old biscuit boxes – the weather grows cold and fresh.

Visiting round today after Holy Communion in the Church Army hut at 7 am. These darker mornings we have put the time on a little. The men change almost every day, especially now this big fight is on – we seem to be doing well[419]. At the latter part of the morning, I went down into the smelly town and viewed the church[420]. It is very old, an old stone slab, and a description on it records that 'it was built originally by the <u>English</u> in 1004', sixty years before the Norman Conquest! It has been visited by Charles VIII and Henry VII 'rois d'Angleterre' and by the first Napoleon[421]. There is a miraculous statue of the Virgin – 'Notre Dame de Foy' and you behold it there above the Tabernacle, for all the world to see[422]. There are some very good figures carved in wood, notably St. Michael and there is a picturesque statue of Joan of Arc in shining armour and a quaint model under glass, made by a fisherman, of a local boat entering harbour (a curious thing this latter, to display in a church). A quaint wainscoting also displays twelve panels, each painted with its separate event in the narrative of 'the Miracle of the three Pilgrims'. Father, mother and son set out on a pilgrimage. At an inn at which they stayed, some hidden money was stolen and the son was accused and condemned for the theft. In the next panel you see him, in a white shirt and red knickerbockers, hanging upon the gallows, father and mother going disconsolately on their way. At the next inn, they watch the chickens in the chicken run when, lo and behold! The cock and hen begin to speak. The inference is that they say "Your son is not guilty, moreover he is not dead – return and fetch him" At the side is the red-liveried servant exhibiting much astonishment. In the next

---

419 The **Battle of Loos** (25th September –14th October) was the largest British offensive mounted in 1915. The first British use of poison gas occurred and the battle was the first mass engagement of New Army units. The British offensive was part of the attempt by the French to break through the German defences in Artois and Champagne. Despite improved methods, more ammunition and better equipment the Franco-British attacks were contained by the German armies, except for local losses of ground.

420 **St Michael's** church, Etaples. The old church decribed by RDG was completely destroyed in WW2 in an air raid by 12 B-24s on 15 June 1944, indended to disable the Etaples railway bridge.

421 Inscription in the side chapel dedicated to Notre Dame de St Foy. *Le Eglise Saint Michel, le seul restee de trios eglises d'Etaples, fur batie par les anglais en 1004. A travers la siècle elle a subi bein des modifications. Los de traite des paix en 1492 cet eglise fut visitee pas Charles VIII et Henri VII Roi de France et d'Angleterre.* Recorded by RS Bundy in the Saturday Review 18th August, 1906. The 'Camp de Boulogne' 1803–5. Marshal Ney's 6th Corps was encamped at Etaples sur Mer.

422 Notre Dame De Foy, (Our Lady of Faith) C12th.

picture you see father and mother, aided by the red-liveried servant, pulling down their smiling son from the gibbet. All three, father, mother and son are invited to a repast, to celebrate the release no doubt, with the magistrate, and their host provides for the meal a plump hen and cock. These are not to be eaten yet, however, for they are seen rising from the dishes on which they are served and again making a speech! What they say (again you infer) is to the effect that besides the son being not guilty, the real thief is the red-liveried servant. They would not have said this had not that miscreant selfishly to save his own skin, added to his other crimes this further one of planning the murder of those two innocent birds, who had born the witness that saved another from injustice and while they had forborne to deliver up the guilty, how that however he had not shown himself worthy of their clemency in that in order to save himself he had not stopped short of compassing their death, and so they punish him with full denunciation. From the rest of the panels, you perceive that the servant gets 'what for', the son becomes a 'religious' and father and mother walk off through the rocky hills away towards the sunset and the end of the story[423].

On a pillar near the door a boldly printed notice-bill warns young ladies about comeliness of costume, and forbids the priests to admit any to Confession or Communion who have open necks to their dresses. The holy water stoup is a very old and worn square of pumice stone which is said to have been picked up in the sea by a fishing vessel. A white marble memorial tablet records, in new gold letters, grateful recognition of a cure made by Notre Dame de Lourdes between 'March and August 1915' Indeed the Church is a little like a museum.

Wednesday September 29th 1915, Etaples
It has been a very cold wild day, with symptoms of winter, and tell Aunt Mai, if you will, the coat 'British warm' has been very comforting – it really is a possession. We begin to make winter preparations, though I dare say we shall see warm days yet.

Apart from a business talk with the Senior Chaplain of this huge base, (344 square miles of camps, hospitals and occupied villages) the work has been visiting round, writing letters, keeping warm, and taking service this evening at the Church Army

---

423 Miracle attributed to St.Dominic de la Calzada; In the 14th century, a German 18-year old named Hugonell, from Xanten, goes on pilgrimage to Santiago de Compostela with his parents. A Spanish girl at the hostel where they were staying makes sexual advances toward Hugonell; Hugonell rejects her advances. Angry at this, the girl hides a silver cup in the German's bag and then informs the authorities that the youth had taken it. Hugonell is sentenced to the gallows, in accordance with the laws of Alfonso X of Castile. The parents sadly decide to examine their son's body, still hanging on the gallows, but suddenly hear his voice – he tells them that Saint Dominic has saved his life. His parents quickly make their way to Santiago de Compostela to see the magistrate. The magistrate, who is at the time eating dinner, remarks: "Your son is as alive as this rooster and chicken that I was feasting on before you interrupted me." And in that moment, the two birds jump from the plate and begin to sing and crow happily. This is clearly the tale that RDG is relating, but how it was actually interpreted in St Michael's is unclear, and considering its destruction, unknown.

hut. Things are shaping up there rather, but they have been in a muddle! I am surprised at the Church Army doing things in that slipshod way. Very young evangelists who want to practice preaching on the soldiers, and who do it in a rather sentimental and patronising way. You cannot help thinking if they were more 'men' themselves they would rather be soldiering also instead of telling better men to be good (is that very cynical?). The social work is good, with reading and writing tables and the like. Your Fund is providing weekly Illustrateds, and they want now to borrow the portable harmonium provided by the same. Hurrah for the Fund!

Thursday September 30th 1915, Etaples

It is warmer, which is one comfort, and this afternoon in fact quite pleasant. At 10 o'clock there was a devotional meeting of all the Christian workers of the camp – in fact the whole Base. There were three other Chaplains and Preb. Pitt working the Church Army hut, also various lay workers and lay readers – about 25 in all. I was asked to give the address and spoke on our need of the Holy Spirit. The Churches need Him to show them how best to work among the soldiers – to choose the right men, to apply the right work to the right workers. How essential it is that the workers themselves shall be taught of the Holy Spirit. His promised gifts are wisdom and understanding, counsel and might, of knowledge and the fear of the Lord – love, joy, peace, long-suffering, gentleness, goodness, faith, meekness and self-control. It cannot but be noticed how these gifts stand in contrast to the confessed German spirit. Do we not feel their position wanting in wisdom, understanding, good sense and the fear of God? We do not easily associate a German with lovingness, his sombre manner with joy, his attitude with peace, long-suffering, gentleness (cf methods in Belgium), and goodness. Kind hearts are more than coronets and simple faith than Norman blood[424] – a man of good faith would not tear up a scrap of paper – meekness (cf the violence of the Hun), and self-control. The position is that, as Mr Asquith said in the House of Commons, the conflict we are engaged in is a spiritual conflict – the Spirit of Germany as against the spirit that animates us. If the German spirit wins, the world will be ruled by force and self-interest. Goodbye, indefinitely, to the good graces of life. Belgians can be trampled on, Lusitanias' can be submarined, and all that opposes that shall be poisoned with liquid fire and scorched from the face of the earth. It is the spirit of right against that spirit, and the mission of the Church, and of its workers, is to keep men's spirit right. How essential that the workers themselves shall be 'kept right' – that we should seek in our work wisdom and understanding to deal with individual men aright. The men of these <u>new</u> Armies need differently dealing with to the men of the <u>regular</u> Army – they have different traditions, they come from the quiet life of their parishes, and their settled 'home religion' many of them, the regular

---

424 *Lady Clara Vere de Vere* is an English poem written by Alfred Tennyson, part of his collected *Poems* published in 1842. The poem is about a lady in a family of aristocrats, and includes numerous references to nobles, such as to earls or coats of arms. One such line from the poem goes, "Kind hearts are more than coronets, and simple faith than Norman blood."

religions of the church of their denomination. We need the Holy Spirit to inspire us for the message for the man. Also to keep us right in spirit, besides being men of 'good sense' – how we need to be kept loving, cheerful, peaceful, long-suffering, gentle, good men of faith and true thro' and thro'– not easy in the Army atmosphere – and self-control and men of sweet reasonableness. "If ye, being evil, know how to give good gifts unto your children, how much more shall your Heavenly Father give the Holy Spirit to them that ask Him?"[425]

This evening I met Canon Barnett – he was Chaplain at Bordighera that fateful spring. He is superintending C.A. huts and I shall hope to get a fuller talk with him[426].

An unusual Communion Service this afternoon. A young Jew, an officer, had been prepared for Confirmation. He was to have been presented when the Deputy Chaplain General[427] was here a week or two ago, but was called away with a draft that same morning. Today he had sudden orders to go and join a regiment in the fighting and he asked for a Communion Service. There was a time to spare between 3 and 4, so we arranged for his coming into the Church Army Hut Chapel on his way to the station – so, an afternoon Communion Service with a Jew, and he unconfirmed! So in the 'presence of the Mediator of the New Covenant'[428] we draw near to the mercy seat 'to find grace to help in time of need'[429].

Friday October 1st 1915, Etaples
Most noble and particular Dame,
The first day of another month and over a year since I joined the 'colours' so to speak, viz. left West Farleigh clad in a uniform of khaki. Let us hope that this time next year the sword of men will have been "beaten into ploughshares and their spears into pruning hooks"[430], and would that the prayers may be fulfilled "neither shall they learn war any more".

It has been a very pastoral day here, visiting round among the tents, talking with the officers, trying the Word in season wherever it might seem to promise. With many of the men, the great need is the human touch – home, mother, those they love, and the

---

425 **Luke 11:13** 'If ye then, being evil, know how to give good gifts unto your children: how much more shall *your* heavenly Father give the Holy Spirit to them that ask him?'
426 Canon **Arthur Thomas Barnett** (b.1858) All Saints, Bordighera, Liguria, Italy from 1889–1911.
427 Bishop Gwynne.
428 **Hebrews 12:24** 'And to Jesus the mediator of the new covenant, and to the blood of sprinkling, that speaketh better things than *that of* Abel.'
429 **Hebrews 4:16** 'Let us therefore come boldly unto the throne of grace, that we may obtain mercy, and find grace to help in time of need.'
430 **Isiah 2:3-4** 'And many people shall go and say, Come ye, and let us go up to the mountain of the LORD, to the house of the God of Jacob; and He will teach us of His ways, and we will walk in His Paths: for out of Zion shall go forth the law, and the word of the LORD from Jerusalem. And He shall judge among the nations, and shall rebuke many people: and they shall beat their swords into plowshares, and their spears into pruning hooks: nation shall not lift up sword against nation, neither shall they learn war any more.'

bringing of this war to an end. How glad they are to talk, and really the patriotism and noble self-sacrifice are very gratifying and ennobling. So many of them – the entire majority of them – have come here from the truest and highest of motives. They have yielded to the grace of God, and are sublimely unconscious of any magnificent merit in it. A year's military training has been a severe trial to them, and they are thankful at least to be this side of the water. The next thing with them all is to make an end, and be back again.

A nice talk with Preb. Pitt, the vicar from near Swindon, who has come to give his help to the Church Army for a few weeks. Till just lately he has been serving behind the bar, coffee and cakes, but now the staff is better adjusted, and he can give proper time to ministering to the men's minds and souls.

Saturday October 2nd 1915, Etaples

This draft work keeps you at it, as strenuously as anyone can stand. The men are so eager to hear what you have to say, having come out of trench life, that mysterious underworld for which they have so long been preparing, and to which now after many weary months they are at last being sent. You talk till your throat can scarcely move any more. Lamps twinkle about in the dark, flashlights gleam into your face and pop out again and dim khaki figures move everywhere. Long khaki lines stand out in the gloom – you begin to talk and ten, twenty, thirty men swarm round you, and you get a word of commendation to God just in your closing phrase or two, or you touch on the love of home and those wondering, wishing and waiting here or there in the home parish. Officers flit up out of the darkness – you can often get in the few last words – Tonight a young officer, Dewar, very glad of a few words. "Were you related to Lt. Dewar who was killed last December?" "No, but I was at school with him. He was my football captain, and I did admire him". "I was with him when he died. He spoke five minutes before he passed away. I had a nice letter from his father". "Yes, I knew his people – they lived at Trinity, Edinburgh" "That was the address" and so on – it's a living work, isn't it?[431]

But what a commotion this week in the Church papers about the Chaplains Department! There is room for criticism, great criticism. But that is not the way of getting things forward, and I am sure the Chaplain General is a good man. The D.C.G also is a good man, but I wonder if he has the brains to grasp the full force of the situation that is arising. The Chaplains must be increased and they will become as much as two Dioceses in number, if not more; 'sweet reasonableness'[432] will get things right in time. I suppose that is why it has taken nearly a year for my 'official' commission to appear[433] unless these Commission parchments are a new instution. We had none in S Africa.

---

431 See letter December 23rd, 1914.
432 **Phillipians 4:5** 'Let your moderation (sweet reasonableness) be known unto all men. The Lord *is* at hand.'
433 RDG was 'gazetted' on 20th October 1914.

It is interesting to see that my commission starts from Hythe – not from the day I went down to Hursley Park (October), or … [*Pages missing*]

Sunday October 3rd 1915, Etaples

Thank you very much for the parcel. I am glad of the soap, just exactly right, and the sweets, and the cream is delicious. It has arrived in very good condition and I am very thankful for it. The experiment is worth trying again, if only we can get it fresh and it means, as you know, very much to my idiosyncratic taste! The Army order in these parts is that the purchasing of milk locally is forbidden, for fear of disease. Thank you also for the letter and the prophetic study for the Kaiser and his mark of the beast. It is very ingenious, if not very convincing – a little like the proof that the 46th Psalm was written by Shakespeare. Read from the beginning and the 46th word is <u>Shake</u>, read again from the end and you have <u>spear</u> – therefore the 46th Psalm was written by him!

It has been a beautiful day, the weather superb, most comfortable and refreshing. Holy Communion at 6.30 am with ten present including my friend Loveland from Sevenoaks who is still in the camp, and a hearty parade service in the Soldier's Christian Association Hut with about 600 present. Then another service at 11, with again about 600 present and a number having to stand outside. They are inspiring gatherings, albeit they do take somewhat out of you. The Epistle for the day speaks again "I thank God for the grace given you"[434] – the 'grace' that has brought these men boldly on the side of duty and self-sacrifice. I pray that ye may be (further) enriched by means of prayer, the Word and the Sacrament, that the manhood of the Empire may go back to their homes, this task over, a purified and an ennobling influence. After some words with different men, the morning ended. This afternoon some visiting round; and evening service in the Church Army Hut, walking round with the men, and now I must turn in my eyes being nearly closed.

I have just met a little fellow sent down to recover after a gas shell in the recent fighting – a 'lachrymatory' shell, which makes the eyes and the nostrils smart. He seemed pretty cheerful and will go back again in a few days.

Monday October 4th 1915, Etaples

This work is difficult. It is like living on a railway station, seeing people come in, striking up acquaintance with them, speaking with them a few days or a few hours, and off they go again. You are Chaplain to a kind of huge canvas hotel! I do not like the wafer-god ways of some of the celebrants. Rather beneath the dignity of their mission. He has ascended up far above all things, and in whom dwells the fullness of the Godhead bodily, "in whom all things consist", who dwelleth not in temples

---

434 **I Corinithians 1:4** 'I thank my God always on your behalf, for the grace of God which is given you by Jesus Christ.'

made with hands is not suitably placed in a wafer. Christ transcends our reason – He never goes contrary to it.

This evening I spoke at an open-air meeting, rather a 'faint' thing to begin with, wanting plan and arrangement I thought. Yet, it is one after this manner, another after that. Then later I gave an address at the Soldier's Christian Association Hut. The weak side of these occasions is – not feeling the definiteness of position that one gets in an ordered and consecutive church life. You appeal to a certain phase of emotion and excitement, you deal with a certain point, the point of a 'turning' to The Presence, but a soul needs educating: The Christian life is a life of ordered service and growth and the Church is the growing place, it is the business department "come and learn to pray, come and hear the word, come and use the great Sacrament". That appears to me is the Church's message and the Church's plan, and we learn to live in the Presence through it.

Good night, dear darling.

Tuesday October 5th 1915 Etaples

That was a grumble, rather, last night. Out of this War what will come to the Church of the Living God? It will see where it has failed? The nation, the nations, will see where they have been short-sighted in regard to it? Will the Church come out a simpler, more coherent organisation, with a more definte system, a more uniform front, and a clearer message? There are those who say Society is the Church. The temple of God is the lives of His people. The Body of Christ is the whole organism of human beings, interdependent, working from motive, to a purpose. Christ inspired, Christ guided, operating the Christ purposes in His universe. Even so, the Church then must be the central teaching, thinking, communicating, scene of human activity. There will still be function for a church – until He Himself appears – and the City shall need no temple, for He Himself shall be the temple, Who filleth all in all. What do you think?

Streams of officers and men into this sea of tents today. Out again in the morning – coming from everywhere, going to everywhere, you get almost giddy talking to so many. A blood-hound came into the camp today, on his way up to help in seeking out the wounded[435] – he has a long low musical bay, a strange sound in a camp where dogs and cats are not, nor any animals except an occasional horse.

A parcel today my dear friend. From you? Digestive biscuits, turkey and ham, chocolate biscuits, peppermints – all very nice and very acceptable. But the 'Otico' Thermos flask has not come. I only mention it because you mentioned it and I was wondering whether you would be wondering.

---

435 In total, the British and their allies were said to have used up to 20 000 dogs on the Western Front, many in roles which were extremely hazardous.

Goodnight – most gentle Margaret, kind, thoughtful, cool and calm,

Avaunt all sorrow and regret

Soothed by her genial balm.

Wednesday October 6th 1915, Etaples

Another letter from you – I am glad you got the better coat, it is as a rule cheaper in the long run. How interesting about getting through the Dardanelles – I had heard tales like that of a piece of string, or the like, signifying the 'fait accompi', I wonder if there is anything in it.

The Otico has come in quite good order and I am very glad of it; in these coming winter days it is sure to be of service, also thank you very much for the Horlicks Malted Milk tablets and the biscuits and potted meat that came last night, and made me feel at ease a little about nourishment at present. The good air here is certainly very pleasant and appetising. I remember a saying of John Wesley's that "the County of Cornwall was an uncommonly good one for creating an appetite, and an uncommonly poor one for satisfying it[436]".

Morning and evening walking round and talking with new arrived officers and men by the dozen. They will be off in a few hours, and are very eager to know first-hand accounts of the look of things, the equipment needed and 'tips' for the life in the trenches and in action.

The bloodhound is a nice person, forbidding-looking with his bloodshot eyes and heavy dewlaps, with his shoulders and back like a young lions', but he is really very friendly, and gentle as a pussy cat. I wonder how he will like shell-fire!

The French evening papers speak of the Greek Premier having resigned – that is an unpleasant development. I hope the people will insist on supporting him[437]. Do you remember that it was in his family, Venizelos, that Fraulein had lived before coming to us? and how they had escaped to the hills to prevent his being kidnapped?

---

436 *The Life of John Wesley*, John Tetford, 1898. Ch 14 "After one service Wesley stopped his horse to pick the blackberries, saying to his companion, 'Brother Nelson, we ought to be thankful that there are plenty of blackberries; for this is the best country I ever saw for getting a stomach, but the worst that ever I saw for getting food. Do the people think we can live by preaching?'"

437 **Eleftherios Venizelos** (b.1864 – d.1936) was a leader of the Greek national liberation movement and a charismatic statesman remembered for his promotion of liberal-democratic policies. Elected several times as Prime Minister of Greece, serving from 1910 to 1920 and from 1928 to 1932, Venizelos had such profound influence on the internal and external affairs of Greece that he is credited with being "the maker of modern Greece", and is still widely known as the "Ethnarch". His resignation (twice in 1915) was over Greek neutrality in the war; Venizelos wished to join the Entente, while King Constantine 1 favoured the Central powers.

Thursday October 7th 1915, Etaples

A good address this morning from the Y.M.C.A. hut leader on "Christ in you, in the hope of glory" just in danger of "saying beautiful things" about Him. He is too great for an offering of mere 'unction'. There was only the danger – which is, I fear, the common danger of Evangelicalism[438]. Hundreds and yet more hundreds of men to talk to and you can only take in some. This one is returning after frozen feet last winter – this one is rejoining after being gassed in the last fighting. These are quite new and very watchful to get facts and impressions. Two are Welshmen, proud of their nation and eager to prove their mettle. One comes from near the place of my birth, Pontypridd, and tells me the name means 'the Clay Bridge'[439]. You live among the tents here, and visit immediately you step out of your own – <u>most</u> interesting.

Friday October 8th 1915, Etaples

A beautiful day. In the morning, after H.C. at 7 I was rather occupied with piecing out Sunday's work. There are so many troops here now that it is a very considerable business getting to reach them all. Two new Chaplains arrived today, Robinson and Lee from the Southwell diocese, both nice men I should think, but very young. They will lighten the work a great deal, or rather take some of that which has had to be left undone.

This evening I had a look at half a dozen wounded German prisoners in a hospital hut. They appeared very comfortable and well-cared for and seemed very happy in their affliction. After the doctor had made his evening examination of them, they set to playing cards again with great zest – they trust our good-nature, evidently.

Since then, I have been taking Evening service in the C.A. hut (an idea of my own as they had been rather rough and tumble previously and afraid to set 'ordered' religion before the men) but it has been answering, with about 40 present. As I walked down, a young officer rushed up "Padre, is there a celebration anywhere tomorrow?" "Tomorrow morning at 7 am in the C A hut" "Oh, I am so glad, I am off to the trenches tomorrow, and I wanted to take it again before going. Almost all the officers of my battalion are wiped out – scarcely one is left. 7 o'clock tomorrow morning"

438 **Colossians 1:27** 'To whom God would make known what *is* the riches of the glory of this mystery among the Gentiles; which is Christ in you, the hope of glory.'
439 **Pontypridd** is the principal town of Rhondda Cynon Taf, Wales and is situated 12 miles north of Cardiff. The name means 'the bridge by the earthen house'. RDG was born here in 1867.

Saturday October 9th 1915, Etaples

How the weeks slip by: there comes the thought – which was literally applied, I think to war oppression – "the harvest is passed, the summer is ended and we are not saved[440]". Things look promising however in the West. In the near East we have somewhat of an enigma – the consolation all the time is that the Central Powers are an 'oozing' force and our own is an increasing one.

Rather a preparatory day today – papers and accounts this morning, besides getting my distinguished hair cut! It is a wonder yours and mine have not turned more grey ere this – from a worldly point of view mine would have been more worth to me if it had engaged itself more busily in that process. One of the new Chaplains, Robinson, came to tea with me this afternoon. He is <u>very</u> young and <u>very</u> high Church, but undoubtedly good and will 'do'. They perplex themselves about, to me, odd questions – "is there a <u>larger</u> wafer for the Priest out here?" Why should he have a larger one than his fellow Christians? A nice Communion service this morning – the officer, (Brulthee I think that is how he spells it) was there and is now gone I suppose. We are such an innumerable crowd – men and officers teeming along the sandy paths and lines and footways, that you can lose individuals. I learn that my stay here is to be 'for a time', not very satisfactory, and I gather a little depends upon the turn of events.

You will see from the enclosed what I have been doing this evening. Just imagine thinking of a son going to a public school, we shall have to 'wait and see' about the money. Taxes are going to be enormous, and prices high – they must make a difference.

Sunday October 10th 1915, Etaples

Changes! The Carr-Greggs went off a fortnight ago and Preb. Pitt goes in a day or two, so consequently he was content to be much used today, to our contentment too. He preached at my 11 o'clock 'Parade' and took this evening's service – so I have had only the 7.30 am with 20 men and the 9.30 am with about 600, and 100 or so turned back for want of room. As there were 4 other services of a like kind held in this camp alone, you can guess something of the work. But it is full of fascination, the situation presented. And God said "All souls are mine"[441]. Loveland goes off in a few hours, so I lose my organist and it means finding another. I have asked him to look out for Jack Page (it is the same battalion) and also Mr Ryan (it is the same Division).

I hear today that Gilbert Hannington, nephew of the late Bishop, has been accidentally killed when preparing to come out to the Front[442]. I am also grieved to see the picture of H.B. Stevens, son of our friends at Wateringbury has been killed. There can

---

440 **Jeremiah 8:20** 'The harvest is past, the summer is ended, and we are not saved.'

441 **Ezekiel 18:4** 'Behold, all souls are mine; as the soul of the father, so also the soul of the son is mine: the soul that sinneth, it shall die.'

442 Lieut. **Gilbert Joseph Hannington** (b.1884 – d.1915), Army Service Corps. Bishop James Hannington was an Anglican Bishop, missionary and martyr killed in Uganda in 1885.

be no mistake, I think, it is H.B. Stevens and the Royal West Kents – how grieving for them, and he was a very nice fellow. Poor Mrs. Stevens – but what an offering![443]

Men still moving to and fro – it is a great scene, but not to be described. You talk to an officer who has been a tea planter in Ceylon – another one has been horse-breeding in the Argentine, this one has put in so many terms at Oxford and this one has lived so many years in South India, but has also begun at Oxford, and the men from all parts present a multitude of mosaics in their varied localities and experience. This afternoon a trainload of Turcos goes by in their brilliant colours and swarthy skin, their gorgeous battle flag carried with them on the train[444]. Today some South Africans have joined the camp – and so they come from every land and every clime. It is a great tribute to the British Empire.

Monday October 11th 1915, Etaples
I do not like this kind of work at all so well – it lacks 'go' and enterprise. People are waiting about and they get stale. You have so little to catch on to, and the imagination is so little alive, then a 'movement' order comes and that particular group suddenly becomes alive and responsive – with the rest your effort is to evade 'vacuity', and that takes a great deal out of you. It is a mistake, I think, to call it a 'rest' sending people down here.

I had lunch this morning with Mr. Pyper, a very nice lunch! It was pleasant talking things over with him – he is a Chaplain and Casualty Clearing Station chaplain and has charge of an officers' hospital a few miles from here[445]. The Hospital is a superb one, everything is of the utmost best and it was a great pleasure going over it. I met one officer from my late Division who had been hit in the last fight by a smashing bullet and had had to lose his left arm. His matter of fact acceptance of the situation was very touching – he was thankful to be so well, and that it was the left arm and that was all. How splendid is the quiet resignation of so many of these people – so little conscious that they are heroes, if conscious at all. Indeed, we may surround them with every alleviation and comfort that can be conceived. They have suffered, they are suffering for us, and it is good to behold.

---

443 2nd Lieut. **Henry Francis Bingham Stevens** (b.1890 – d.1915) 6 Bn Queen's Own (Royal West Kent Regiment), killed 16th September 1915 at Armentières. Son of The Rev. Canon Bingham Stevens and Mrs. Bingham Stevens, of The Beck, Wateringbury, Kent.

444 The **Senegalese Tirailleurs** were a corps of colonial infantry in the French Army recruited from Senegal and French West Africa. The noun tirailleur, which translates as "skirmisher", was a designation given by the French Army to indigenous infantry recruited in the colonies. Despite recruitment not being limited to Senegal, these infantry units took on the adjective "sénégalais" since that was where the first black African Tirailleur regiment had been formed. The first *Senegalese Tirailleurs* were formed in 1857 and served France in a number of wars, in WW1 providing around 200 000 troops, more than 135 000 of whom fought in Europe and 30 000 of whom were killed. Other tirailleur regiments were raised in French North Africa from the Arab and Berber populations of Algeria, Tunisia and Morocco, collectively they were called *tirailleurs nord-africains* or *Turcos*.

445 *Rev* **Joseph Colling Pyper** (b.1858 – d.1932)

We have been depleted of men and officers today all keen to hear every word one could tell them of those trenches one has learnt to know so well – some you can see, apprehensive of the fate awaiting them. The subalterns openly excited, some of them, talking freely as boys would (they are not much more than that) of the things they anticipate, most of them expecting to be hit and hoping the wound would be a 'cushy' one, and occasionally quite decided they are going to get a 'knock out' altogether. So that is the kind of talk! Others, however, the majority perhaps, are quiet and philosophical about it. You meet some very sensible men, calm, strong characters – and to tell the truth, you meet some very weak ones too.

Tuesday October 12th 1915, Etaples

It is interesting hearing Dr Bury's point of view, and I think he is right about Rome[446]. It is a solemn warning to the Anglican Church to be united, strong and statesman-like. I note your comment on my observations – the quotation from S.D. Gordon I do not think a strong one. He is just of that type of rather emotional exclusionists that my attitude of mind was called out by – they are too eager to see men come to Christ after the manner of their own intensity[447]. If you are not intense to their degree in that particular form of Christwardness you are – they make no two questions about it – you are none of His. His parable said "Let both grow together until the Harvest" the tares will be separated by the unerring Hand later on[448]. Anyway, I find myself looking out over these seas of heroic men, stained as they undoubtedly are, with the widest charity. Preb. Pitt went today – an amiable man, anxious to do right, but his methods affected rather by the pettinesses that has to be reckoned with in a small county charge.

A little excitement among the Scripture Readers in the camp who have got themselves a little under disapproval by holding open-air meetings too closely in among the tents. The O.C. mentioned it, and talked of 'officially' requiring them to retire to a given corner, to save 'feelings'. I got him to agree to my having a word with them, privately. It will answer I hope, and it is an opportunity for evoking sympathy from the O.C. with their work, and also of preventing their being discouraged by directions which might have arrived at them in rather too blunt a form. It has fallen to me to mention it to them. It requires some careful management.

---

446 Dr. **Herbert** *Bury* (b.1854 – d.1933) Lived in Argentina, *Bishop* of Honduras, then the Anglican Church for *Northern and Central Europe. Prolific author:* "A Bishop among Bananas", 1911; "Here and There in the War Area", 1916; "My Visit to Ruhleben", 1917; and "Experiences of a Travelling Bishop", 1930.

447 **Samuel Dickey (S. D.) Gordon**, (b.1859 – d.1936). Born in Philadelphia, he was a leader and missionary in the YMCA. In the early 1900s, S.D. Gordon was a widely-travelled speaker in high demand. A prolific author, he wrote more than 25 devotional books, most with the phrase "Quiet Talks" in the title.

448 **Matthew 13:30** 'Let both grow together until the harvest: and in the time of harvest I will say to the reapers, Gather ye together first the tares, and bind them in bundles to burn them: but gather the wheat into my barn.'

Take care of yourself. Go to bed early. Have meals regularly. Guard against highly seasoned dishes. Read regularly. Do not think so much of reading many books as choosing thorough ones, and reading them thoroughly. As life goes on, one need not read all books, all through. Prefaces often may be skipped, as may introductions. Often from the beginning of a paragraph, one can see what the author wants to say, and so save time by passing on, and even if one should have happened to miss his meaning, it is often quicker to go back for that point than have to wade subserviently through every line. Life is short, and of making many books there is no end – but here I refrain from more moral maxims. A mere outburst of meditation aloud, so to speak, as life creeps on.

Wednesday October 13th 1915, Etaples

So many lines of dark forms on the sandy banks, up against the star-lit sky and various other forms flit before them, twinkling lanterns moving with them. An order came about 9.30 p.m. "So many men of the [...*censored*...] and the [...*censored*...] wanted for the front by 8 am," and these are the men paraded in response. The doctor has gone down the lines saying to each one, "Are you alright? Are you alright?" "Yes Sir, Yes Sir" and so on. But now and again, "Abscess on the gum, Sir" or "Swollen ankles," or here a man with neck and cheek bound up, obviously neuralgic and they cannot be passed. Nearby is a group standing to volunteer, so the gaps are quickly filled up. In the morning, they will receive ammunition, bandoliers, travelling and 'iron' rations, smelly bags and other equipment, and so will proceed on their way. I think we are a little like – was it the House Beautiful? "And in the morning Patience, Prudence and Charity helped Pilgrim on with his armour and furthered him on his journey with all God speed." [449]

Visiting round today and a very great amount of talking – how many thousands of men one seems to talk with. Glorious weather – what will Greece do? and Roumania? Bulgaria has undoubtedly been bought and has sold itself, like Judas, for gain. It will be disappointed of its lust[450]. Does England deserve to win? We need humbling – we are not at all as conscious of our shortcomings as we ought to be, and the lesson may be a costly one.

---

449 Pilgrims Progress, John Bunyan, 1678. One of RDG's favourite books. Atop the Hill of Difficulty, Christian makes his first stop for the night at the House of the Palace Beautiful, which is a place built by God for the refreshment of pilgrims and godly travellers. Christian spends three days here, and leaves clothed with the Armor of God (Eph. 6:11–18), which stands him in good stead in his battle against the demonic dragon-like Apollyon, (the lord and god of the City of Destruction) in the Valley of Humiliation.

450 Initially neutral, The Kingdom of Bulgaria participated in WW1 on the side of the Central Powers from 14th October 1915, when the country declared war on Serbia, until 30th September 1918, when the Armistice of Thessalonica was signed and came into effect. Free of the Ottoman Empire from 1908, the Bulgarians had hoped to gain territory from the Serbians.

Thursday October 14th 1915, Etaples

A momentous letter herewith (under a separate envelope). 100 guineas a year is enormous, can it be managed? Fixed incomes like those of the Clergy, are very seriously hit by the Income Tax, and the Insurance and Land Acts. Our only chance of getting the little man through is to drop the dilapidations next time, and chance to making them up afterwards[451].

Poor old Warner (really young Warner as he was ordained only in 1907) has broken down with nerves I am afraid. He is in danger of being overweighted with the importance of his position. He has been in the country only 3 months, but my being 'on the ground' here first, obtains a kind of leading role, and it is too much for him. He alternates from a curious subserviency to a strong-headed dictatorship – that will not do with a man nearly 20 years longer in Orders!! We agreed to take a 7 o/ clock Evening service alternately, with an address, in the Hut Chapel, following in Preb. Pitt's plan. Last night he announced that the Service would be only prayers, that the Coffee Bar would be closed, the Chapel doors thrown open, and the Service conducted for all in the Hut. Those who did not care to join might go on with their writing or reading. I do not think the experiment was justified – about 30 men in the Chapel, about 200 down in the hut. The Chapel doors were thrown open, but some of the men in the hut walked about, some were coming in and out of the doors at that end and there was a constant buzz of conversation. The Church Army Captain walked up and down keeping order, like a Beadle, but it was a little distracting at the very best. The point is that the notice he gave out commits me to carry on the same proceedings if I accord him the military submission his present mood expects! If I object – there will be trouble. If I acquiesce my conscience will be disturbed and my sense of reverence offended, and I submit to what hardly a Bishop would require! Also he gives out 'confession' and they have 'prayers for the dead' – that is an illustration of one of the difficulties the administration of the Chaplain's Dept. is suffering from. There is a need of adjusting man with man. All the staff of the hut have been changed during Warner's time and one or two 'fired' off. Having seen his fiery temper, I can understand it and I am sorry for those who have suffered. I should like to have a talk with Canon Barnett about it.

Friday October 15th 1915, Etaples

More Zeppelins over London and the damage I hear is more serious[452]. But they will come with less and less impunity as the days come on, and we get better gun equipment and aircraft. It ought to help with recruiting by making people so angry that they cannot sit still. England is not serious enough yet and my 'war' notes

---

451 Presumably public school fees for Eric Griffiths.
452 On the night of the 3rd October 1916, the Zeppelin commanders flew their heaviest bomb raid when five airships dropped a total of 189 bombs on London and its environs; seventy-one civilians died.

henceforward will be less local than ever. I am afraid that the journals will have to be less interesting because less informing, as the authorities are getting more and more perturbed about 'news' leaking out, and they are letting us know how emphatically necessary it is to refrain from comment, even of the most innocent kind – so you will understand. It cuts me off more, but I can see how serious the estimating of forces and positions is when filtering through to the enemy. The wonder is – and it is a constant wonder to some – that they have not bombed this place. They would do, in the way of military slaughter, a 1000 fold more work than in these East Coast raids. How perfectly disgusting the thought of those dear little children done to death in pain or agony. Another Herod slaughters the innocents.

Saturday October 16th 1915, Etaples

There are many problems in this Chaplain's work and they do not decrease as the number of Chaplains increase. The Church Times' has little room for complaint in our corner. The 'High Church' kind are overwhelming, and some of them, sad to say, are overbearing and glib-tongued. I remember one of Miller's sayings – "Yes – there are households that are called happy because there is one selfish will that dominates all the others wills, etc." That is their idea – "Let things be our way, and how nice it is to live like this, a happy family". However Warner, one of that kind, goes on Monday and a <u>very</u> young man has come in his place and it remains to be seen how he will do. I think some of them see me rather 'fossilised' and evangelical, and the Chaplain General is an 'anathema'! There is a good sentence of Prof. Gilbert Murrays', used at the recent conference of women workers, urging people to display good temper and common sense – "Don't" he says, "abuse anybody if you can possibly help it and do not let other people abuse them to you. There is far too much rather irresponsible ill spoken about people in authority, and in time of war such ill-speaking is not a trivial fault, but gravely disloyal"[453]

More drafts off in the moon-light, cheering throat-high to be going off.

Sunday October 17th 1915, Etaples

Another beautiful day, not a heavy day and a very encouraging one. 6.30 am Holy Communion with 10 present, 9 o'clock Morning Service with about 600, and at 10.15 about 450. After that, visiting round and making friendships – what a variety of experience and homes! You swim round, so to speak, in a sea of humanity. More visiting and the evening service taken by one of the younger Chaplains, they are keen to do things and it is good to listen and join in, but more Church accommodation is urgently needed. The other ends of the Camp are untouched, and the men may

---

453 **George Gilbert Aimé Murray**, OM (b.1866 – d.1957) was an Australian-born British classical scholar and public intellectual, with connections in many spheres. He was an outstanding scholar of the language and culture of Ancient Greece, perhaps the leading authority in the first half of the twentieth century.

not go outside their Division, being required to be ready, in many cases, at an hour's notice. Wonderfully nice clear, dry weather, and a good help on with the autumn.

Monday October 18th 1915 (St. Luke's Day), Etaples
Very busy and too tired tonight to write. Goodnight, sleep well.

Tuesday October 19th 1915, Etaples
Another beautiful day, but the night was very cold. Yesterday was taken up with trying to buy two pillow cases, the others being worn into holes, greeting the new extra Chaplain, writing, visiting round, and in the evening a most successful open air service in the moonlight. The Scripture Readers express themselves grateful for 'leadership'.

The open air came to nothing tonight! I left the beginning to the Readers and found that they had done nothing and some in fact had arrived late. The lines were unsettled, having been ordered to prepare for a move in the morning, so not a man joined in. One or two came shyly hovering around, but sheered off again. On to the Church Army Hut which was crowded out but the Chapel was not so full. Three men off to the front tomorrow asked for the Holy Communion, so I took it on there and then, and three other men joined in. The air is calmer since Warner went, he was a little hysterical I think, and boyish. He wants to go up to the Front, and then get back again "to have been through it!" Maddison, the new man, is from the Durham Diocese[454]. Good, in a blunt kind of way, and speaks with an Australian kind of accent, but keen and manly I should think and not so a fantastic a churchman as Warner. I have been writing a long letter to the Chaplain General. Consultation, co-operation and mutual counsel are better than criticism, and one naturally wants to throw all one's weight into getting things on. His attitude seems however, a little on the defensive, as one who was too eager to show how successful he was, taking up points in that light unnecessarily, and a little to one's surprise. I think it means that the administration has been rather assailed.

Zeppelins again – how deplorable and base beyond words, Germany is mad with wickedness. Yet their churches are being increasingly thronged with worshippers.

Wednesday October 20th 1915, Etaples
I am using one of the 'word of honour' envelopes, of which I am entitled to draw a number, having used none since the first issue – they will come in for an emergency. This is just to ask can you find the name of the head of Repton and of Marlborough. Repton was very good under Lionel Ford, I do not know who is there now, and Marlborough gives special consideration to Clergy sons. I am not sure the little son

---

454 Rev. **William Maddison,** educated Wadham College, Oxford BA 1905, MA 1908. Rector of Gosforth, Northumberland.

will be up to scholarship standard. It may be a matter of health and it is safer not to make point of the attainment in his case on that account – if he was of rugged physique it would be different. I wonder if you know of a small pocket concordance, or could find one through Treachers' when you are there. It is a push sometimes when one is in a hurry to find a given sentence, and it is rather pressured here just now.

Two Chaplains were killed last week – Hewitt, who was at one of the Brighton churches and Doudney, who was at College with me[455]. I see that Warwick Deeping is out here as a doctor in the R.A.M.C – you remember his book 'Sincerity'? I should like to meet him[456].

Visiting round today and then I went to the Y.M.C.A. to a concert given by Miss Lena Ashwell's Concert Party[457]. It was extremely good, the Farce 'Feed the Brute' in not at all bad taste and very clever. A working man's wife devoted to her cleaning and cooking, the surly, grumbly husband who comes in growling at everything and her perfectly imperturbable temper which sees nothing wrong in him, and turns his worst grumbles into amusing little loyalties, and the fury with which he takes these themselves into an admiration of his honest out-spokenness! Finally she comes to tears because he accuses her of being friendly with the butcher, thus showing that he really is jealous. Then it is remembered that it is the 12th anniversary of their wedding day and he recalls the sweet-hearting the first time he saw her, and how he stood her a sausage roll and a bottle of ginger-beer. They plan keeping up the day by an outing and it all ends happily. There was some very good singing by the first two ladies on the programme and violin-playing by the third. The place was crowded out – not a squinting little corner through the windows outside that was not occupied, and a good many officers. Really it is a very good idea, and excellently carried out and it must be acknowledged from what I know, that the Y.M.C.A. are out and away the

455 **Rev. Frederick Whitmore Hewitt**, (b.1880 – d.1915) Chaplain 4th Class, 20th Infantry Brigade. Killed on 27th September 1915, at Vermelles. Son of Stanley and Louisa Hughes Hewitt and the husband of Blanche E M Hewitt. A curate in Brighton, he was the Vicar of Brixton, Plymouth. **Rev. Charles Edmund Doudney** (b.1871 – d.1915) Chaplain 4th Class, 18 Brigade, 6th Division. He died from his wounds on 16th October 1915 at no. 10 Casualty Hospital, Abecle. Son of the late Rev David A, Rector of St Helen's, Hastings and Georgina Doudney and the husband of Joanna Clara Schroder. Curate at Penge, Rochester, then Australia, Vicar of South Lyncombe, Somerset, 1907–15. Both were at Corpus Christi College, Cambridge.

456 **George Warwick Deeping** (28th May 1877 – 20th April 1950) was a prolific English novelist and short story writer. Born in Southend-on-Sea, Essex, into a family of doctors, he was educated at Merchant Taylors' School. He proceeded to Trinity College, Cambridge, to study medicine and science, then went to Middlesex Hospital to finish his medical training. He served in the Royal Army Medical Corps. Deeping later gave up his job as a doctor to become a full-time writer. He married Phyllis Maude Merrill and lived for the rest of his life in Eastlands on Brooklands Road in Weybridge, Surrey. *Sincerity (The Strong Hand or The Challenge of Love)* 1912 – A strong-willed, young MD takes up his first position with an established MD in a small town. He discovers illnesses caused by poor sanitation but runs against town politics in trying to improve conditions.

457 **Lena Ashwell**, OBE (b.1872 – d.1957) was a British actress and acting manager, known as the first to organise large-scale entertainment for troops at the front, which she did during World War I. *Feed the Brute*, George Paston (1909).

superiors of everybody in their hut provision from the social side. On the 'spiritual' I am inclined to fear they are rather timid and not 'healthy-minded' or to be more exact, 'natural' enough. The men who enjoy this social amusement can as healthily enjoy the best things if they are not apologetically put before them. "Be natural in your spiritual life and spiritual in your natural life" that is my meaning. The Church Army is disappointing by comparison, their line having been among the very outcast and fallen I suppose affects their view. But here are thousands of young men, just healthy fellows away from ordinary social temptations, pulsing with life and good spirits and so ready to be taken at their best. The joy of the Lord must be our strength in working 'with Him' to lead them into his Presence 'where there is <u>fullness</u> of joy and pleasure for ever more'! I am certain that one of our first aims must be to push the 'Hut' scheme this coming winter.

Personally, I do not think now that we shall much change in the arrange dispositions of the Western Front this winter. Here is the 3rd week in October and another fortnight will see us in frost and slush, and another month will open up the weather that last winter crippled with rheumatisms and frozen feet. I hope, and believe, better safe-guards will be provided this season against the latter. By the bye I am going to ask for a small rubber hot water bottle. When one can get hot water and I think they will manage this more often under our better organised conditions, and it will be of use in the sleeping bag. Can you get a <u>small</u> one and post it and charge it to my account?

Thursday October 21st 1915, Etaples

Trafalgar Day! What will next Trafalgar Day see for our Great Empire? Do we talk too much of our great Empire and not enough of God's Great Empire?[458] "The lust of the flesh, the lust of the eyes and the Pride of life – will He wish to chasten us more for these? I fear we deserve it, as a nation. A nice address this morning by a Presbyterian "and the peace of God shall garrison your hearts"– a more helpful talk than that of some of our Church-y friends. I am disenchanted about the Church just now. The 'Church Times' need not complain: its clientale is getting its full share of Chaplain opportunities. By the bye, I notice in the paragraph sent to the West Farleigh Parish magazine, a name of a locality is mentioned, 'Artois' region – better to leave out all names of places, and even France itself!

A nice address this morning at our worker's devotional meeting by a Presbyterian "and the Peace of God shall garrison your hearts[459]". This afternoon and evening I have been in a sham fight, of all occupations! It was curiously real going down into

458 **Trafalgar Day** is the celebration of the victory won by the Royal Navy, commanded by Vice-Admiral Horatio Nelson, over the combined French and Spanish fleets at the Battle of Trafalgar on 21st October 1805. The formation of the Navy League in 1894 gave added impetus to the movement to recognise Nelson's legacy, and grand celebrations were held in Trafalgar Square on Trafalgar Day, 1896.

459 **Phillipians 4:7** 'And the peace of God, which passeth all understanding, shall keep your hearts and minds through Christ Jesus.'

the Communication trench, in the mud and the rain, and winding in and out of the deep passage ways and following your leader in the dark, and again the feeling came of what a mad, wild, wicked game it is – wriggling ditches like that now all over Europe, and it is calculated that over 700,000,000 cartridges a day are fired off over these vast areas. What a stupid waste of the time and work of the makers, of the carriers, of the users and of those who try to mend up the consequences!

A young officer whose brother I knew at Cambridge came in this evening, and another who knew Mr Karney very well at Buenos Aires[460].

Friday October 22nd 1915, Etaples

You remember at my first Shorncliffe Camp, our 'permanent' mess there consisted of six members – I have heard today that Captain Davidson has been killed. He makes the fourth of our number killed and the fifth was wounded – I am the only one left untouched. The same with the dinner party that first night when I went down into the trenches – the same with the motor bus load of officers the first time I came home on leave. <u>All</u>, the whole number, either wounded or killed – one cannot dare to think of all that it means to the many who are left behind.

I went over this afternoon to 'call on' Mr. Pyper, and found that he had left for England. It was peaceful looking out upon the calm sea in the clear evening moonlight, so unmoved it lay. The great ocean in its deep calmness contrasted itself with the welter of human passions stirring all along that dark line at one's back, and the restless caution, and the restless aggression, and the suffering. The huddled-up heaps of dead and mutilated bodies, the glazed eyes and the bloodless, set faces which recur so frequently on the retina of one's vision, set themselves in patches on the scene – God's handiwork contrasted with man's.

Entre nous – the man in Warner's place is a 'stick'. The service drawls and the hymns crawl and the men have dwindled. He has no cassock, and though a High Churchman, appears in a short surplice, which with the black chaplain scarf dangling over it, gives rather an odd effect as his long, gaitered legs go twinkling about underneath it. From which you will gather the Chaplain's Department is over-weighted just now – another man comes with cassock and a long surplice, and no scarf! C'est la

---

460 The Rt Revd **Arthur Baillie Lumsdaine Karney** (b.1874 – d.1963). He was ordained in the Church of England in 1897 and appointed assistant chaplain to the Missions to Seamen at Sunderland. In 1903, he was Rector of Woolpit in Suffolk. He had become fascinated in the work of seamen and was sent to work on the staff of the Seaman's Institute in San Francisco. The San Francisco Institute was destroyed by the earthquake in 1905. In 1906, he was Chaplain to the Missions to Seamen in Buenos Aires. In 1914, on the outbreak of the First World War he became a chaplain in the Royal Navy firstly on a hospital ship and then with pastoral care for a whole squadron. From 1918 to 1922 he was Oxford Diocesan Missioner. In 1922, he was awarded an honorary D.D. by the University of Cambridge. On 25th July 1922, he was consecrated first Bishop of Johannesburg. He became Bishop of Southampton from 1933 to 1943, Chaplain of Marlborough College until 1944 and Rector of Blendworth until 1949.

guerre! I am not allowed to say anything, Warner's heady highmindedness having been curiously passed on evidently in the talk they have had. One can only be loving, and patient, and watchful to be helped and to be helpful.

In the train was an officer just down from the Front, like ourselves, for a spell of change, he paid my train ticket just in a friendly way! He had just heard that the officer who had relieved him in that trench on Monday had had both legs blown off with an enemy rifle grenade, and he was hunting the hospitals round to find him. There is a wife, with five children, and no private means on either side. We learn later that the name is not on the Red Cross list of wounded, so it is concluded that it is another death – "and it might have been me" said the officer.

Saturday October 23rd 1915, Etaples

A beautiful day – busy getting ready for Sunday and doing various things. A nice letter from you with one from the little boy – he does not take so high a place in the new form as yet. I am glad that he is keen about the shooting. I hope that Sophie has not <u>sent off the bedstead?</u> I am not sure of being able to carry it with me – I told her that I would let her know. If it has started, well and good, but it stands the chance of being lost as in certain cases you are bound to leave them behind you. In any case the dispatch for parcels for this address is c/o the Military Forwarding Officer NEWHAVEN.

What a number of people one talks to in a day! One who knew Goodenough, my friend the naval chaplain at Sheerness. One who has been stationed at Sheerness and Minster looking out over the 'Nore'[461] and who described the damage done at Sittingbourne[462] Another has been describing his patrol work in the trenches and how he threw a bomb and hit a German on the chest, how with his revolver he shot a German officer who he meant only to wound and take prisoner, but the shot went too high, hitting the victim in the head. What a savage business it all is. And this execution of Miss Cavell is sickening – she was the daughter of a clergyman I see, and had done some nursing at Maidstone[463].

---

461 **Minster** is a small town on the north coast of the Isle of Sheppey and in the Swale district of Kent. The **Nore** is a sandbank at the mouth of the Thames Estuary, England. It marks the point where the River Thames meets the North Sea, roughly halfway between Havengore Creek in Essex and Warden Point in Kent.

462 **Sittingbourne, Kent**: Zeppelin raid, which occured on night of 4th June 1915. There were four HE bombs dropped on Sittingbourne in this raid but despite the damage caused to the buildings there were no serious casualties.

463 **Edith Louisa Cavell** (b.1865 – d.1915) was a British nurse. She is celebrated for saving the lives of soldiers from both sides without distinction and in helping some 200 Allied soldiers escape from German-occupied Belgium during WW1 for which she was arrested, court-martialled, found guilty of treason and sentenced to death. Despite international pressure for mercy, she was shot by a German firing squad, morning of October 12th. Her execution received worldwide condemnation and extensive press coverage. She is well known for her statement that "patriotism is not enough". She was quoted as saying, "I can't stop while there are lives to be saved." Her father was Rev **Frederick Cavell** of Swardeston, Norfolk. In the summer of 1897, an epidemic

The officer who had been hit in the legs has been traced, he died in [*…censored…*]
Hospital. A wife and 3 children left dependant only on his pension of about £120 a
year. How are we all going to live in the days to come? Captain Smith's nephew has
now gone off to the firing line. It is odd how natural his going is, just as if he started
from the banks of the Medway – he is a nicely behaved man, a sergeant, and worthy
of the 'Smith' connection.

Sunday October 24th 1915, Etaples

Heavy rain tonight, not pleasant for Camp dwellers and with the cold, serious enough
for those in the trenches, but a rather light day for me, owing to movement of troops.
At the 6.30 am service only two persons present. I went for a 9 o'clock but Day, the
Senior Chaplain came to this, by mistake, so I changed over, taking the 11.30 instead.
The service arranged for 10.15 came to nothing, many of the troops of the Division
concerned having moved off, but at the 11.30 there were a great number, 500 or
more, and a very nice service was held. Three ladies were present, one the lady who
had presented the hut, the widow of an officer who was in the Crimea and we had a
nice talk. She came to tears when talking of the loss of a nephew, and I was glad that
I had spoken in the address about God's power over the grave. The tears are the worst
part – you see them from time to time among the French women at the Station at the
foot of this hill, and they are the worst strain of any. What countless weepings there
must have been over this war, and how many minds must have gone! I remember I
used to visit an elderly lady at Nice, whose husband had been killed in the Indian
Mutiny[464]. She was not able to engage in conversation with you, but talked endlessly
about the 'white horse going up the hill' and 'the walls' and 'the shooting'. It is to be
feared the same kind of thing will be very general from this. That ended my 'duty'
for the day except that another draft went off and a number of officers, and it is busy
work trying to get word with as many as possible

Thank you for another letter – alas! I do not know of any dependable young man
of the desired stamp to consult about the billiard table left in Rochester. All of them
of that kind must have long ago gone to the War in some capacity. The simple thing
would be to refer to the makers, who are always reasonable and reliable, it being to
their interest to sustain the life of a table at a considerable cost. The name of the maker
is on the table – suggest to Mr Osborne that he write seeking for a price, and they
will send down a man (the journey is a short one) to report.

---

of typhoid fever broke out in Maidstone. Six London Hospital Nurses were seconded to
help, including Edith. Of 1700 who contracted the disease, only 132 died. Edith received the
Maidstone Medal for her work here – the only medal she was ever to receive from her country.

464 The **Indian Rebellion of 1857** began as a mutiny of sepoys of the East India Company's army
on 10th May 1857, in the cantonment of the town of Meerut, and soon escalated into other
mutinies and civilian rebellions largely in central India, with the major hostilities confined to
present-day Uttar Pradesh, Bihar, northern Madhya Pradesh, and the Delhi region. The rebellion
posed a considerable threat to East India Company power in that region, and was contained
only with the fall of Gwalior on 20th June 1858.

A rather flat service at the Church Army hut this evening, redeemed somewhat by a strenuous address by a new C.A. Captain. I think it looks as if one must settle down to things for the winter.

Monday, October 25th 1915, Etaples

Late, cold! Just had a young officer in for a talk – and to 'make his confession'!

Goodnight darling M

Tuesday, October 26th 1915, Etaples

The young officer who came to 'confession' last night is a son of the Vicar of Litherland, a parish with which I think your uncle had to do?[465] At all events I connected it in my mind. He is a young Oxford man, rather in with a High Church set. I am not happy in taking 'confessions', but I worked through with one of those manuals which I happened to have among the general lot of literature that comes in upon us. I do not like the practice as a 'practice', a straight talk is a different thing and I am making up my mind to steer that way in future whoever comes. But the Oxford teaching is so manifest and quite general enough so it has to be reckoned with, and one must take care not to offend the weak conscience. One can see how a good, healthy manliness will outlive the rather 'faddy' plan of examining too much into detail "The letter killeth, the Spirit giveth life"[466] An 'odds and ends' kind of day, talking to everyone possible: much frittering it seems – but it is still ministry.

Wednesday October 27th 1915, Etaples

A nice day. A talk with Day, the Senior Chaplain about the Sunday evening service, also about the keeping open of the Cinema on Sunday evenings, which personally I dislike, and I am glad to find that he does also, so probably something will be done to stop it.

I begin to feel tired enough for another 'leave', but there is an idea about here that it ought not to be asked for so soon as another quarter from the last. It seems pretty clear that we are in for another winter now.

Some typical talks. A neat-looking man washing up the dishes for the Sergeant's mess – speaks with quite a refined accent, and it turns out that he is a Civil Engineer, who has joined the Stockbroker's Battalion, and has worked under Sir John Jackson[467].

---

465 Vicar of St Philip's Litherland, Liverpool.

466 **2 Corinthians 3:6** 'Who also hath made us able ministers of the New Testament; not of the letter, but of the spirit: for the letter killeth, but the spirit giveth life.'

467 10th Battalion, Royal Fusilliers, raised in the City of London 1914. Sir **John Jackson** (b.1851 – d.1919), English engineer and contractor. He was educated at Edinburgh University and received his training as an engineer at Newcastle-on-Tyne. Amongst his more important constructions were the docks at Middlesbrough, Hartlepool and N. Sunderland, the commercial harbour at Dover and the extension there of the Admiralty pier, the last section of the Manchester Ship canal, the foundations of the Tower bridge, the new naval harbour at Simon's Town, Cape

Another man, a sergeant, comes from Ninfield and knows one or two of the Wakefield Diocese Clergy (whose photographs I have in my book at home). Since the Boer War, he has worked in a coal mine – another works ordinarily on the railway and lives in the parish of the Canon Smith who took West Farleigh Vicarage in August last year … and so on. A nice address this morning from the senior Chaplain at the Worker's meeting on God's gift to us as ministers and workers, and our gift to Him, fairly fluent but a little difficult to take in.

The Rev R.J. Campbell appeared in the Camp yesterday. He comes to missionise wherever he can be given a hearing and we expect to have his help in this camp three or four times.[468] I was very sorry to hear tonight that Mr E.J. Kennedy[469] is dead, after only two days illness. He was out here for a year and was thrown from his horse through a shell bursting near – he spoke at the Winchester Diocesan Conference only the week before last. So 'in such an hour as ye think not'.

Goodnight, my beloved darling.

Thursday October 28th 1915, Etaples
Heavy rains – they have been almost incessant since Sunday – the last 24 hours especially.

I am sorry to say I am feeling very unsettled. This Deputy Chaplain General has been going about rather restlessly. He seems to have a plan for turning chaplains over from one charge to another, giving everyone a short turn 'at the Front', and making a real 'general post'. He gossips, and says things about people that are not quite wise or just and, disloyal himself, thus makes it really hard for some of us to be loyal to him. He has upset my plans stupidly, writing with warm interest about certain things and promising his help in them and only a few days later, showing that he has quite forgotten what he has said and talking in an almost contrary sense, making you feel that he is a little 'distrait'. Things are too much for him I really believe, and the Department is overworked. The Chaplain General was reluctant to have a second Bishop at all – my judgement is that he should have a third. If it might be Bishop Frodsham I should not be sorry – more a man of education. After all, the attainments of Gwynne leave something to be desired in that way. A London College of Divinity man, a Missionary Suffrican Bishop without Order, or Archdeacons or Canons, who himself says he spent 7 months of the year itinerating in Egypt and Palestine, all

Colony, and the irrigation works in Mesopotamia.

468 Rev. Dr. **Reginald John Campbell** (b.1867 – d.1956), British Congregationalist and Anglican divine who became a popular preacher while the minister at the City Temple and a leading exponent of the socialist, liberal 'The New Theology' movement of 1907. In the summer of 1915, after a tour of the trenches, Campbell underwent a deep personal crisis, seeing a need for greater Christian unity, and for himself a return to the Church of England.

469 Rev. **Edmund John Kennedy** (b.1855 – d.1915). General Secretary YMCA, London, 1884–1894, vicar of St. James', Hatcham, 1896–1900, vicar of St. John's, Boscombe, 1901–1915, chaplain to H.M. forces, 1914–1915.

instructive for a Missioner, but not the best means towards a full understanding of the material of which these new armies are composed, Officers, Temporary (and other) Chaplains, and men alike. It is said there was a proposal to send out one of our strong English bishops – perhaps that may be possible yet, one who can administer with calm judgement.

<u>Private</u> It means in my case whether I can continue the whole of the second year. If the idea is to send men for short periods, first here, then there, to hold a few weeks of services among groups of men, and this rather indiscriminately as he himself did when an ordinary Chaplain, I shall find it difficult to agree. You want to feel you are called and sent for a <u>need</u>, and personally I am getting too old to learn too many new tricks!

Friday October 29th 1915, Etaples

It has been a better day – dry and warm. I called on the organist in the morning to find out more particulars about the Church, after that 7. am Holy Communion and a Chaplain's talk about Sunday and Campbell is to preach in the C.A. hut on Sunday evening – then visiting round. The Church here was built in the first place by some English who were refugees upon this coast from the invasion of the Danes in 983, although the church was actually built in 1004. The Virginia creeper was pretty – the French call it 'Vin Vierge'. At the Machine Gun I met a son[470] of the Rev. J. Lias! of Haywards Heath[471]. It was pleasant comparing notes. The father was up at Trinity with your father. When I went up to Cambridge in 1893, I had 3 letters of introduction: 1 to Mr. Burghley of Trinity, another to Dr. Perle of Christ's College and a third to Mr Lias!

More visiting and this afternoon I called to see a nice old Colonel, laid aside with bronchitis and heart weakness, perhaps he ought not to have come out as he is much over 60. He wanted to know all about one of the regiments I was with, which had been his when he was young – he was very pleased to see me. I see a Brigadier General Forbes Trefusis is killed – I hope not Lady Mary's husband[472].

A cinema has been started in the Camp, and has attracted large crowds, not unnaturally as the drab oneness of this life is a great drain on the troops, and also the dark evenings

---

470 Lieutenant, **Ronald John Mortlock Lias**. 9th Battalion, The Royal Sussex Regiment. 24th Division (b.1891 – d.1916). Killed in action at Hooge 23rd February. Educated at Marlborough College. His Father was Chancellor of Llandaff Cathedral. Buried Menin Road (South) Military Cemetery, Ypres, Belgium.

471 Rev & Mrs **John James Lias** (b.1834 – d.1923) of 'Broomfield', Oathall Road, Haywards Heath.

472 Brigadier General The Hon. **John Frederick Hepburn-Stuart-Forbes-Trefusis** (b.1878 – d.1915). Saw active service during the Second Boer War as a volunteer Trooper in the Imperial Yeomanry. He was commissioned as a 2nd Lieutenant into the Irish Guards in 1901 and promoted to Lieutenant a year later. In 1904, he became A.D.C. to General Lord Methuen, when the latter was appointed commander of IV Army Corps. Trefusis stayed with Methuen when the General moved to become Commander-in-Chief in South Africa (1908). He was promoted to Captain in 1909 and appointed Adjutant of the Irish Guards at Sandhurst. Led the battalion through the battles of Neuve Chapelle and Festubert, and during the trench and mine warfare

are long for this tent life. Poor men, they got so wet yesterday and these army coats do take such a long time to dry I wonder the authorities do not institute some drying places – it must be bad for the men.

A good many German prisoners sick and wounded in hospital.

Saturday October 30th 1915, Etaples

Thank you my darling, for another letter. What a truly distressing experience for the Piggotts – had they an idea, perhaps, that he might do some running away? Health, I daresay, and the strain of having to return to the rigours of school life, after a very comfortable home. Dear little Faith, please thank her for her letter, and dear Joyce, who seems to be happy enough. I am sorry her Mable (doll) has been ill. Tell her to let her have plenty of fresh air and to keep her feet dry. If her socks get the least bit damp, let them be changed. Even dolls are not made of brass.

Another day of visiting round – it would be tedious to tell of all the personalities met with. I met R.J. Campbell this morning, and had a short lift in his car when we went to the central office to arrange about tomorrow's services – he has nice eyes, a flock of white hair and a gentle smiling manner. He will take the address at my 11.30 Parade Service in the morning – strange things personalities! The King has not been to this Camp and now he has hurt himself. It was a lucky escape as it appears that his horse fell on his leg[473]. Kind Aunt Mai – I am so very glad about the Billiard table. The place seems to be greatly [?] this war time. I sometimes wish we might go back there – take a parish in the City – and have that in our interests as well!

I am tired tonight, I think the trials are – at the 'trench' end of the field 'nerves' and at this end 'boredom'. That is what so many of these good people are suffering from, and one feels it oneself. They have been drilled and drilled and drilled, some for over a year, until they are drilled 'stiff'. Goodnight sweetheart. 'O Lord, have mercy upon me for I am weak: heal me for my bones are vexed'![474]

---

around Ypres and Cuinchy. On 24th October 1915, Trefusis was arranging for his brigade to be relieved in the line by another brigade of the division. While taking the other Brigadier round the trenches, 'Jack Tre' was shot through the forehead by a sniper. He died of his wound almost immediately. He was not married. Lady **Mary Hepburn-Stuart-Forbes-Trefusis** (née Lygon) (b.1869 – d.1927), daughter of the 6th Earl of Beauchamp, was a composer and patron of the arts. She was the Brigadier General's sister-in-law, having married his brother, Lt-Col **Henry Walter Hepburn-Stuart-Forbes-Trefusis**.

473 King George V made several visits to the front: Nov 29th–Dec 5th 1914; Oct 21st–Nov 1st 1915; Aug 7th–Aug 15th 1916; July 3rd–July 14th 1917; March 28th–30th and Aug 5th–13th 1918. It was during his visit to the front in 1915 that, on Oct 28th, George met with a serious accident, through his horse rearing and falling backwards on him, being startled by the sudden cheering of a regiment whom he was inspecting. He fractured his pelvis, an injury that would cause him pain for the rest of his life.

474 **Psalm 6:2** 'Have mercy upon me, O LORD; for I *am* weak: O LORD, heal me; for my bones

Sunday October 31st 1915, Etaples

7.30 am Holy Communion with 13 present, including an amateur conjurer who is going about to the 'base' huts, (an excellent idea – one Herring by name). There is a cold, driving rain and high wind, very uncomfortable on this height. At 10.15 a very large parade service of about 550 and a peaceful and earnest time. 11.30 another parade of about 400 – I took the service part, to be exact, I led in the prayers and R J Campbell read the Lesson and gave the address "Rejoiceth not in iniquity, but rejoiceth in the truth[475]". It was high speaking and obviously 'above the heads' of a few of the men, and one or two were not 'arrested' but it was good – quick, quiet and full of right thoughts. The subtlety of rejoicing in another's wrong-doing, not trying to help them against it, since by their misfortune we can get some gain – the 'set-off' we give our own character when we see a flaw in another, and not being really sorry for that other because of the sense of relief we get in feeling so much better. The duty of keeping positive good and positive right as our aim, and which will keep us sympathetic and safe. He is a pleasant man, careful in his manner and dress, and quietly chatty. Appeared just in a 'mufti' suit, as he had brought no gown or bands, and of course does not yet wear a surplice. I talked with him about one of my favourite authors of his late church, Dr Dale, and quoted that writer's 'Sacramental' view as one being that might be held by a strong churchman. R.J.C. was struck and remarked "I think I must mention that to my Church Committee when I bid them farewell". I censored some letters for him – viz. taking his word for the contents and signing the envelopes. I noted one little thing, he had with him a little pocket comb with which he put right the back edges of his flowing white hair!

Talking with officers most of the rest of the day, Maddison took the evening service at the Church Hut. Day is not as successful as Deane Oliver in running clubs and huts so we have only one hut of a Church character for all this huge camp, and the circumstances are such that it is not easy to initiate another. There is a tradition in the Army that you do not move in advance of one senior in rank, albeit in <u>years</u> I happen to be the oldest Chaplain here. (The rank system is an inadvisable one in my opinion, and I think, with the 'Guardian', that it was unwise to give Chaplains military rank. It leads to many little unsatisfactory anomalies and there are instances of its leading to great ones.) Consequently, these dark evenings, one is condemned to a quiet time.

Aunt Mai's lamp came in to good purpose this evening as a Red Cross car had broken down in the darkness, and the 'Orilux' light was largely instrumental, after about half an hour, in bringing it right again[476].

Much talking with officers – the work here is not so thrilling as 'up the line' but it is very interesting and numberless links spring up. The verger from Newnham Church

---

are vexed.'
475 **I Corinithians 13:6** 'Rejoiceth not in iniquity, but rejoiceth in the truth.'
476 The Orilux Officers Trench Torch, 1915. This is still in the possession of our family.

near Cambridge turned out to be one man in a private's coat, and he <u>was</u> glad to be chatted with, Symonds the vicar being an old friend of mine from Cambridge days[477]. Another man is from the battalion of which Lady Mary Forbes Trefusis' husband is Colonel (Harrison)[478]. Maddison's talk was formal and proper, not likely to quicken the interest or devotion of the men and that evening service falls rather flat. My feeling about the whole Camp is that we do not find the officers much drawing round the Church and they will not much for such services as this Sunday Evening one. What do you think? I see that Chancellor P.V. Smith has been speaking strongly in favour of National Service – quite rightly[479]. Unfortunately, in our Army capacity we are not allowed to speak of these things!

Well my darlng, I must turn in. I shall think of the dear Archbishop tomorrow morning, as I often do in the prayers for the Church Militant. My best love to you, and darling Faith.

Monday November 1st 1915, Etaples

All Saints Day – I thought of many at the early service today, and since. "We feebly struggle, they in glory shine, yet all are one in Thee, for all are Thine[480]," though this horrible war makes Him seem far off sometimes. It is worse in a camp like this than in the strenuous valour of the Trench life. For instance, in visiting a sergeants' mess this evening I find one sergeant stupidly and garrulously drunk … it was a means of turning the conversation round for all the other dozen or so sergeants, who were ashamed for their comrade, and we got onto wholesome topics like Miss Weston's work[481], the pain of frozen feet (some had had them last winter), fighting incidents and Divine thought.

---

477 Rev **Septimus Symonds** (b.1865 – d.1950), St Mark's Newnham, St Catherines College, 1884. M. Mary Caroline Tindall.

478 Lt Col **Henry Walter Hepburn-Stuart-Forbes-Trefusis** (b.1864 – d.1948) 2nd Bat. Scots Guards. Educated at Eton, (Queen's) Medal for Transvaal, Cape Colony, and Wittebergen. Married Lady Mary (daughter of the 6th Earl Beauchamp) and Woman of the Bedchamber to Queen Mary. In later life, he became the High Sheriff of Cornwall, amongst other positions.

479 **Philip Vernon Smith** (b.1845 – d.1929), church layman, ecclesatical lawyer and church historian. He was appointed Chancellor of the dioceses of Manchester in 1894, Durham in 1903, Ripon in 1912, and Blackburn in 1927. A member of the Canterbury House of Laymen on its formation in 1887, he was vice-chairman from 1910 to 1920. He a vice-president of the Church Missionary Society, and visited a number of the Indian stations in 1908.

480 Hymn *For All The Saints Who From Their Labours Rest* Verse 7; "O blest communion, fellowship divine! we feebly struggle, they in glory shine; all are one in thee, for all are thine. Alleluia, Alleluia!" William Walsham How, 1864.

481 Dame **Elizabeth Agnes Weston** (b.1840 – d.1918) Founder of Sailors' Rests (later Royal Sailors' Rests) and temperance activist. Helped develop facilities for the 2nd Somerset Militia during their annual assembly in Bath, as alternative to congregation in public houses, and became committed to the Temperance cause; relocated to Plymouth in the 1870s and devoted rest of life to the development of naval welfare – fundraising nationally, launching correspondence mission circulated to every ship in the fleet along with her movement's magazine, *Ashore and Afloat*, addressing recruits on training ships on behalf of Royal Naval Temperance Society, and working to open large institutes with overnight accommodation close to the dockyards; also organised naval wives' groups and formed disaster funds to support seamen's dependants; published *My Life Among the Bluejackets* (1909).

RDG's Orilux Officer's Trench Torch

There are some sad things in a Base Camp – ne'er-do-well's come here, no less than those who have been broken physically by sickness, or hardship, or wounds.

Tuesday November 2nd 1915, Etaples

It has been a day of rain here, early and late, morning, noon, and night, blustery and cold withal. We had a nice quiet Holy Communion service in the Church Army Hut Chapel, and afterwards visiting around, after some more business and letters. A memorial service at the Cemetery had been proposed for 3 o'clock and I went to it, despite the pouring rain. About 40 people had assembled there, also a Presbyterian Chaplain and a Canadian Ch. of England, but no Day, who was to take the service. A lady in her car was among the number and she told me, with tears welling from her eyes, that she had lost all her three sons in the War. There were also a number of Sisters, who had brought beautiful flowers for the graves. After waiting about in the rain, some people got tired and drifted off, so eventually I telephoned to Day's office. He had not come because he had put in Orders 'weather permitting', though he had said to us in any case we might go into the Mortuary Chapel (the proviso did not appear in our orders). So the service fell to me and we went into the Mortuary Chapel. The lady seemed <u>very</u> glad that the service would be held. Fortunately, a surplice and a scarf of Day's were there and I had the S.P.C.K. Manual[482], and so we had a restful Memorial Service. The wild, dark weather outside, the dimly lighted Chapel inside, with two lighted candles and nice flowers and purple hangings all round within. I was thankful for it and I thought of the Archbishop[483] and many others and faces and names came to me in a long stream. "Part of the host have crossed the flood and part are crossing now". We had the 23rd Psalm, a part of 1 Cor XV and the Memorial Prayers in the S.P.C.K. book[484]. We are much with the other world now-a-days and how near it all is. More visiting – more drafts and movements which I am forbidden to describe.

Wednesday November 3rd 1915, Etaples

Just a hurried line to say I move on in a day or so, probably Friday, back behind the line again. I am very glad for many reasons – the address will be No. 12 Casualty Clearing Station. B.E.F.[485] I am glad to be going from this 'processional' work. The new work will be to 'see some off' to the Better Land I think, and what a blessing it is to know that we have that Land to go to.

Thursday November 4th 1915, Etaples

'Up the line' early in the morning, and I am sad at leaving the very nice officers and other people that I have met down here. A good meeting of workers this morning, and an address on God's presence with Moses.

---

482 Society for Promoting Christian Knowledge is the oldest Anglican mission organisation. It was founded in 1698 by Thomas Bray (an Anglican priest), and a small group of friends.

483 His father-in-law.

484 'Come Let Us Join Our Friends Above', Charles Wesley 1757. **Psalm 23** 'The Lord is My Shepherd, I Shall Not Want' **1 Corinthians 15** 'O death, where *is* thy sting? O grave, where *is* thy victory?'

485 No. 12 Casualty Clearing Station was based at Hazebrouck from June 1915 – May 1917. A Casualty Clearing Station (allocated at one per Division) was comprised of around 120 officers and men, commanded by a Lieutenant-Colonel with 3 Chaplains attached. A CCS would be situated out of enemy artillery range, and as close to the front line as possible with good communications both forward and back. Surgeons who had dealt with wounded from the First Battle of Ypres were convinced that facilities were required to enable surgery to take place nearer the front line and so prevent a potentially fatal delay in the treatment of infected wounds. Fortunately, the onset of trench warfare meant that the railheads and their associated units, which included the CCS's, became static. The CCS's now became virtual "hospitals" in which the bulk of the surgery on the Western Front was carried out. Most CCS's were of semi permanent construction and were able to treat casualties of all types including the most dangerous of injuries such as head and abdominal wounds. The CCS was the first place in the evacuation chain where successful surgery could realistically be carried out. The equipment scale for a CCS amounted to 22 1/3 Tons including 31 Marquees and 20 Bell Tents. To move one would require 17 General Service (horse drawn) wagons or 8 3-Ton lorries.

Friday November 5th 1915, St Omer[486]

On the anniversary of my leaving England, I am writing within the shadow of the buildings in which the Commander-in-Chief of this vast army out here conducts his unwearying and momentous councils. I go to my new charge tomorrow.

The country was very pretty with its autumn tinted woodlands and rich green pastures, and it was difficult to think that everywhere the awful game of killing was still going on, and how peaceful and comfortable the journey up compared to this time last year! Every mile of the journey was then fraught with discomfort and the sense of adventure – the uncertainty as to what might happen at any time. Only one line of troops between us and the Germans then, and only one between them and Calais!

I wonder if the Greeks will come in – the papers today speak of possibilities[487].

Saturday November 6th 1915, Hazebrouck[488]

I am at the Headquarters of an Army – I must not say which one of the first out here[489]. How impressive it all is and near where we arrived just a year ago tomorrow.

At a hospital in a huge College[490], where the casualties passed on by the Field Ambulances are received – they are the more serious ones. When operations are necessary, they are performed here, when they are of that class that cannot be postponed to a 'Base' hospital. Happily there are very few cases now. A rifle grenade exploded, killing 4 and wounding 19: toothache: rheumatism: jaundice: pneumonia, etc. The personnel are very interesting – the highest experts in their lines, it is a great organisation. Nearby is actually a factory for making mouth plates and fitting false teeth of all kinds. The town has three or four clearing stations, and my room is the dormitory of one of the Professors of this College. Part of the buildings are used by the students and you see them at dinner, eating vigorously and 'slopping' soup with pleasure, while a robed brother reads aloud. There is a beautiful Chapel used by them, and a large 'Salon' used by the Professors is turned into an officers' ward, which, when not much occupied, is used as a C of E Chapel. There is a theatre and lecture hall at the top of the building with stage and footlights and here tonight has

---

486 A commune and sub-prefecture of the Pas-de-Calais department 42 miles WNW of Lille on the railway to Calais. Field Marshal French officed out of 37 Rue St Bertin. GHQ was moved to Montreuil by Field Marshal Haig in March 1916.

487 Greece entered the war in support of the Triple entente in 1917.

488 **Hazebrouck** is a commune in the Nord department in northern France. Hazebrouck was a small market town before it became a railway junction in the 1860s. The development of the railways linked Hazebrouck to Lille to Calais and Dunkirk.

489 The **Second Army**, formed on 26th December 1914, when the British Expeditionary Force was split in two due to becoming too big to control its subordinate formations. The army controlled both III Corps and IV Corps. Second Army spent most of the war positioned around the Ypres salient. GOC Sir **Hubert Plumer**.

490 St Francis of Assisi College and Seminary, Hazebrouck, built 1854.

been given a concert by Kennerly Rumford[491] and some artistes that he has got together. They were late in arriving, so we filled up the time with items volunteered among the men. It fell to me eventually to announce some of the singers and others walked up voluntarily. The singing was moderately good – what it lacked in music it made up for in heartiness. Two other C of E chaplains were present, besides two non-conformists, and at a pause Chaplain Baldwin nobly stepped into the breech and sang 'Father O'Flynn' – he is vicar of Cinderford, a parish in the Forest of Dean where we lived when I was a tiny boy[492]! The Rumford party arrived eventually, and the concert was very well done, Sergeant Fry's Kipling recitations being excellent but it would take too long to comment on all the items. I had a chat with Kennerly Rumford and he remembered the visit to Sydney and remarked on my sister-in-law having written some very pretty songs[493], and for the fun of it, I got him to write his name on the programme. If you know of anyone who likes to collect autographs, this may give them pleasure!

Sunday November 7th 1915, Hazebrouck

Except for talking away with the men on and off through the day till my throat is tired, I have had an easy Sunday, having taken no services at all. We had Holy Communion at 8 am at the Maire[494] which was taken by Baldwin with 6 present, a 10 o'clock service taken by Jones with about 30 and a 6.30 taken by Baldwin with 35 present. Jones spoke nicely on "Render to Caesar – render to God[495]". There is so much enthusiasm about the former now-a-days that we are in danger of forgetting the other.

One good fellow very ill tonight – a fragment of a rifle grenade entered the wall of his stomach – he may not be talked with. It appears that the Earl of Crawford is one of our orderlies here, a Lance-Corporal, but I have not encountered him yet[496].

---

491 **Robert Henry Kennerley Rumford**, (b.1870 – d.1957) was an English baritone singer of the 20th century. He was first known for his performances of Oratorio, but following his marriage to the well-known contralto singer Clara Butt, he toured with her throughout the English-speaking world singing repertoire of a more popular type. He was twice mentioned in dispatches while serving in France during the First World War.

492 Rev. **Frederick William Baldwin**. Cinderford is a town forming part of the Forest of Dean, and including Ruspidge and Soudley, in the township of East Dean; it is in the Forest of Dean division of the county, 3 miles north-west from Newnham.

493 Mabel Saumrez-Smith, Margaret's sister, who toured with the composer Ivor Gurney in the 1920's.

494 The town hall, Hazebrouck. The Hotel De Ville was built in 1807 in an unusual classical style.

495 **Mark 12:17** 'And Jesus answering said unto them, Render to Caesar the things that are Caesar's, and to God the things that are God's. And they marvelled at him.'

496 **David Alexander Edward Lindsay, 27th Earl of Crawford and 10th Earl of Balcarres** KT, PC, DL, FRS, FSA (b.1871 – d.1940), styled **Lord Balniel** between 1880 and 1913, was a British Conservative politician and art connoisseur. He joined up as a private in the Royal Army Medical Corps. He volunteered for active service in 1915 aged 43, arriving in France just after the battle of Neuve Chapelle. His presence as a low-ranking medical orderly at Hazebrouck was a sensation, given his social status.

Lance-Corporal Earl

MANY tributes have been paid to the late Lord Crawford's many-sided and delightful personality. The Rev. Richard Griffiths, who was an Army chaplain in the last war, vividly recalls him as a corporal at the Hazebrouck casualty clearing station.

Some thought the matron enjoyed the humour of an opportunity of saying to the premier Earl of Scotland. "Corporal Crawford, that floor is not quite as clean as it ought to be," to receive the typical reply: "You see, Sister, so many people pass this way."

Mr. Griffiths tells me the story of the new chaplain who arrived at the stores office and asked the way to his quarters. These were at some little distance, and as he took up his kit a lance-corporal said, "I'll look after this, sir."

When the chaplain reached his room he found the N.C.O. just putting the burden down and slipped a shilling into his hand. He discovered afterwards that he had tipped Lord Crawford.

THE DAILY TELEGRAPH

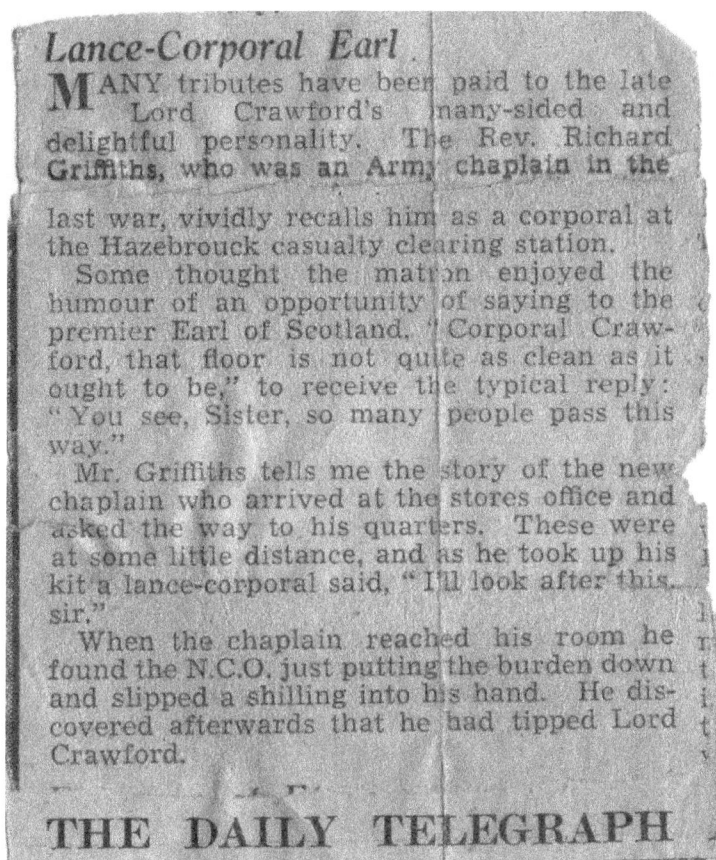

Obituary, Daily Telegraph, March, 1940

Monday November 8th 1915, Hazebrouck

I find that this can go off tonight, so I write just a word before passing it out. Yes, I am not sure about 'leave' this month, but I would like it and will try for it – I think I am owed it.

Another life has just been offered up on behalf of those of us left behind. I have just left a dear lad's body pale and cold in the stillness of death – the lips that this morning spoke patient and manly greetings of friendliness and acquiesced in a few words of prayer are set and motionless. He was handsome and I judged, healthy minded – we envy him the vision that he now looks upon[497].

---

497 Corporal **Frederick Ernest Clark**, (b.1882 – d.1915) The Buffs (East Kent Regiment) 1st Bn. Died 8th October 1915. Son of William and Louisa Clarke, of 24, Wilson St., Winchmore Hill, London, buried Hazebrouck Communal Cemetery.

Tuesday November 9th 1915, Hazebrouck

How like these French towns are the one to the other – the 'place' with the Maire on one side of it with the area of slippery 'pave' stones in front, the shops, the tailor's, the dressmaker's, the grocer's, the stationer's, the bootmaker's, the hairdresser's, all that goes to the sustenance, the clothing and the adornment of the person, (the bookseller is very rare!) range themselves along the other sides. On market days the place is full of stalls, laden with things for sustenance in abundance and all the best of quality and with clothing and adornment, but for those of humbler station. There is generally the 'chandellerie' where votive candles of rare ornateness are displayed side by side with various images and crucifixes – this town is just like all the rest.

We are roughly about 12 or 15 miles from the firing line and there are troops everywhere. The place is remarkably settled and civilised compared to what it was when we passed through just this day last year! So settled that you might wonder whether there is a war on at all. But this is brought home by the nature of the shop windows – everything that a soldier or officer can require is here – razors, English shaving soaps, 'Jaeger' sleeping blankets, 'khaki 'silk ties, underwear, sponges, canvas baths, rank badges, English war ribbons, Khaki caps, air pillows, etc. There is also a stationer's shop where they set out in the window 'Punch', 'The Times', 'The Illustrated London News', etc. In the very early morning, a small boy runs along the street crying "'Ere y'are, Delly Mell"! The side streets also are well alive to improving their opportunity with the Army. One notice informs you "Washing done here – ready in eight hours", another is not quite successful: "Tea, Coffee, Chocolate, Milks, Eggs".

We buried our nice Lance-Corporal this afternoon, in drizzling rain, the grave in a lonely corner of some spare ground at the end of the Cemetery. We hope that Kitchener's journey portends great things. He will be in his element in the Near East and I should not be surprised if the end came there rather than on this front – Germany is not in a radiantly happy condition![498] The Kaiser definitely promised there would be no winter campaign, and that the war would be over in October. That was his deliberate statement – let him prove it! We have very few cases in here at present. There is a club for soldiers in the town, but it is a dismal thing, a few chairs and tables in a large disused cinema and no fire – something ought to be done.

---

498 PM Asquith sent **Lord Kitchener** on a tour of inspection of Gallipoli and the Near East, in the hope that he could be persuaded to remain in the region as Commander-in-Chief. Asquith, who told Robertson that Kitchener was "an impossible colleague" and "his veracity left much to be desired", acted in charge of the War Office, but Kitchener took his seals of office with him so he could not be sacked in his absence. Kitchener visited Rome and Athens, but Murray warned that he would likely demand the diversion of British troops to fight the Turks in the Sinai.

'Market view'

Thursday November 11th 1915, Hazebrouck

Another lad killed by the rifle grenade explosion, buried today. A dreary, drizzling, dark November afternoon, rather suited to the putting to bed of a tired, fretful boy – he had not been a good patient[499].

I have been censoring over 300 letters, and I cannot do more than 100 an hour, so you can guess what that means. I think the Government ought to provide censoring officers. It is true an order has said "Censoring of letters is no part of a Chaplain's duties", but it is expected and in moderation – I like doing it as a means of knowing the minds and moods of the men, but there are limits.

Friday November 12th 1915, Hazebrouck

Cold tonight, with incessant rain, and a concert tonight. I am taking over a horse again, which will be a comfort for the work.

Saturday November 13th 1915, Hazebrouck

I have been busy today, thinking out a lecture on the Coronation[500]. It was to have been taken by the Wesleyan Chaplain, but he left. The Presbyterian Chaplain had

---

499 Lance Corporal **Joseph Frederick Hall** (b.1898 – d.1915), West Yorkshire Regiment (Prince of Wales's Own) 1st Bn. Died 11th November 1915, buried Hazebrouck Communal Cemetery. Son of Mrs. Sarah Dorothy Hall, of 3, Joblin's Yard, Bondgate, Darlington.

500 George V was crowned, By the Grace of God, of the United Kingdom of Great Britain and Ireland and of the British Dominions beyond the Seas, King, Defender of the Faith, Emperor of India on 6th May 1910.

then been asked, but demurred on the grounds of 'episcopacy', and I think a little 'slackness'. The slides were sent out by Tuckey[501] and the others rather urged my doing it. Anyway, it was a subject to draw out plenty of thought – and religion: the history of the Abbey, The Houses of Parliament, St. Paul's, the Beefeaters, Lord Roberts' example and life[502], the Indian Princes, the Colonial Troops, the South African representatives, and at the end, the hard work done by our King, our Queen, the Prince and others, and the way in which they share the lives of their people, and their nice <u>home</u> life which is a good example, Queen Mary having her children round her to sing hymns on Sunday evenings, and so on. The hospital is fairly empty, but about 40 men came to my lecture, and expressed themselves very warmly. The shirking Presbyterian took mock umbrage at my having said that Edward I brought the Coronation stone to England as a sign of his having <u>conquered</u> Scotland – Scotland, he said, had never been conquered! It has made topics for people to talk about, and in this dull passionless existence, any wholesome topic to occupy people's minds is a blessing. I think these talks must be continued.

The horse is a sound little person. There has been much 'red tape' to get over in order to obtain him, but I believe the point is now settled. The matter of transport and equipment for Chaplains' needs to be regulated firmly and decisively once and for all – at present there is <u>no</u> transport establishment for Chaplains whatsoever. I think I mentioned that Lord Grenfell and Lord Salisbury came out as a Commission for the Army Council to look into the questions affecting the better administration of the Chaplain's Department, and this is one of the matters they took up.

Sunday November 14th 1915, Hazebrouck

A rather light day – there is so little work for the non-conformist ministers to do that they need a 'hunting ground' and have therefore occupied the Clearing Station, the Presbyterian taking the 11 am and the Wesleyan the 6.30 p.m. I took the 8 am at the

---

501 Rev. **James Grove White Tuckey** (b.1864 – d.1947), educated at King's School, Canterbury and Trinity College, Oxford. A lecturer at Durham University from 1893 to 1895, he was ordained in the same period and appointed Chaplain of University College and of St. Margaret's, Durham. In 1895, however, he became a Chaplain to the Forces, serving first at Aldershot and then at York, embarking for South Africa in October 1899. Subsequently one of just five Chaplains present at Elandslaagte, Lombard's Kop and the defence of Ladysmith; and afterwards in the actions at Laing's Nek, Belfast and Lydenburg, he was advanced to Chaplain 3rd Class. From 1902–04 he did duty at Middleberg in the Transvaal, before coming home to an appointment at Caterham. Senior Chaplain at Woolwich Garrison in August 1914, he went out to France as Senior Chaplain, 4th Division, shortly thereafter transferring to III Corps and thence to the 2nd Army in 1915. Appointed Assistant Chaplain-General, Rouen Area in 1916. Later in the year he returned home to Southern Command, in which capacity he was still employed at the War's end. Having then been placed on the Retired List as a Chaplain 1st Class in 1923, Tuckey briefly served as Honorary Chaplain to the Bishop of Salisbury before being appointed Church of England Representative on the Interdenomination Advisory Committee at the War Office in 1935. He had, meanwhile, also been appointed Canon Residentiary of Ripon, in which capacity he remained employed until 1945.

502 Field Marshal Lord **Roberts**, Victorian military hero, had died in early November 1914.

Maire with only 2 present and attended the 10 am when Baldwin took prayers and gave the address on the soul – then I rode out in the direction of where I was due for the evening service, and to exercise the horse. I went to tea with the Matron – it is strange having womenfolk about the place, and the Colonel and Major appeared also. Then off in a motor car kindly lent by some officers, through the frosty moonlight away up country about seven miles and a very interesting service. A crowd of men packed into an improvised marquee. They are very hearty and it was a tight pack – the light extemporised acetylene, and I played a Dulcitone[503] for the hymns. The N.C.O.s had imported one for their concerts – have you seen them? You play with piano keys, in a kind of piano case, on tuning forks. The effect was thin, but not unmusical, and did well for leading the singing and then a long, keen and eventually earnest discussion here after dinner with four of the doctors.

Monday November 15th 1915, Hazebrouck

A busy night at the Club so not time for much now. The Fund is beginning to be most useful again – it has done good work. A football match this afternoon with both sides equal, No.12 C.C.S. v no.50 C.C.S.

Tuesday November 16th 1915, Hazebrouck

It is just as well perhaps that I did not attempt 'leave' this week as the communications have been very much disturbed, and indeed cut off from this corner, partly, I suppose, on account of the wild weather, but also I have no doubt for other reasons. I have been into the Club this evening, seeing what might be done about better lighting as it is rather dismal at present, and we must get warming arrangements of some kind – at present it is like a cellar. I think if I stay in this command long, and I must find that out soon, there must be some forward movement.

Among the officers in the Clearing Station is a brother-in-law of the Bishop of Barrow – the top of their dug-out fell in on him and some other brother officers, loosened and weighted by the late heavy rains, but he is not very seriously injured[504].

You would be amused at the short way the French have of counselling caution, about here there are notices "Taisez-vous! Mefrez-vous! Les enemies ont des oreilles!"[505]I see that Frederick Palmer, the American Correspondent, thinks the war will end next summer, with the Kaiser beaten[506]. The German tone is certainly different to what

---

503 A **dulcitone** is a keyboard instrument in which sound is produced by a range of tuning forks, which vibrate when struck by felt-covered hammers activated by the keyboard. The instrument was designed by Thomas Machell of Glasgow and manufactured by the firm of Thomas Machell & Sons during the late nineteenth and early twentieth centuries.
504 Bishop **Henry Ware** married to Mary Godwin, daughter of the Bishop of Carlisle.
505 "Be Quiet! Beware! Enemy ears are listening!"
506 **Frederick Palmer** (d.1873 – b.1958) was an American journalist and writer, covering the Boxer Rebellion, the Phillipine war, Balkan War, and WW1 for the New York Times among others.

it was this time last year, then it was "French's contemptible little army" – today they compare Kitchener to a second Wellington!

One begins now to know French provincial life pretty intimately. Here Flemish and French are generally interchangeable, just as in Wales you find people speaking Welsh generally and English as an additional tongue. The poorer homes are all on a common plan, with the room opening on to the street with a bed in it, highly mattressed and bolstered with curtains hung with little white balls, a big chest of drawers on one side, a stone floor well sanded and a stove like a big round flower pot on a pedestal standing out into the room. These stoves are very successful as they burn very little fuel, keep going hour after hour without much attention, and throw out a very satisfactory heat all round, even the stove pipe serving that purpose – too much heat sometimes! On the narrow mantelpiece behind there is generally a glass case under which is a wonderful confection of artificial grapes and orange flowers, with white ribbon bows, and a gold-edged scroll notifying the names and date of marriage of the husband and wife, and very often there is included in this also a rather doll-like image of the Virgin and Child. Upon the lime-washed walls in little black frames are pictures, always sacred, as a secular picture is almost an unknown thing. They represent most frequently the Crucifixion, the Burial and some local priest or bishop. The number of clergy whose portraits figure in the latter way, sometimes in resplendent Communion robes, sometimes in cape and cassock, is something enormous! The roadsides abound with crucifixes, or little wooden box shrines high up on a post or a tree. A farm builds its own little brick chapel at the corner of a road, or at the edge of a field and here votive candles are offered. But in this part of France they are not so common as in the more religious north. When a death occurs in a cottage, it is the practice to make a cross upon the ground of sheaves of straw placed by the gateway beside the road, and in the centre of the cross is placed a bunch of flowers.

The bombardment of a well-known town near us has been going on heavily all day today – the sound has a sort of fascination, you like to hear it in the sense that you are in a place where the 'cutting edge' is at work, but we are out of range here, except for the very long distance guns.

I have censored these last three days, over 400 probably 500, letters.

Wednesday November 17th 1915, Hazebrouck

The mails are very irregular just now in coming. It has been a hailing, changeable day, though pleasant in between. The horse got irritated by the weather, and was frightened at a train, so the morning journey was not dull! En route, I encountered a windmill working. The woman in the cottage below thought I was quite welcome to climb up into it to see how it was all done. The climb up a wide, long wooden stepladder, the wood of which was obviously very old, was quite exciting. The great sails of the mill plunged round, straining against the wind and creaking on the axle, and the whole thing kept trembling. A patient little old man inside fed the mill-stones with maize and corn, and the great wooden cog-wheels rumbled loudly on turning the corn into flour – nice wholemeal flour one kind was, and this again was winnowed into flour of the purest whiteness. It was a situation not without anxiety, for the wooden floor was very old and rickety-looking, and the great sails shook the whole place and it was not until you were in it, that you realised how high it was. The mill, the man informed me, was 150 years old, and it seemed to me that it was composed, in the main, of its original timbers[507] – I was not sorry to come down. But it was an odd experience to be up in a windmill in Flanders, in a hailstorm, with the great guns booming away in the gloomy distance, still going on with their ceaseless bombardment of the unlucky town, and here was Man, in primitive simplicity, using God's wind to grind the God-given corn to make bread for his wife and children. Below, the wife busied herself about the house and the children played by the door. A primitive wooden plough lay by the gate and in the distance was modernity and science, 'Kultur' dealing death.

We have had many dozens of frozen feet in today and it was strangely like this time last year. Poor men, they do look cold and 'starved' many of them. Otherwise visiting, visiting, and more visiting.

Thursday November 18th 1915, Hazebrouck
A bright frosty morning. At 9.30 a Chaplain's talk, where we went fully into the matter of improving the Club, the Fund being behind all plans, and a gift of £20 from Lady Crawford, some of which was spent on a lantern[508]. I think now that there will evolve a really nice attractive place – warmth and light, these two essentials at least will be improved. For the rest, it seems to have been rather a frittered kind of a day with many people talked to and not much said. Yet they do like someone outside to talk with, and a group of sick officers this evening said "thank you" for the visit. It is rather dull, I suppose being patients all the time.

Another deep discussion after dinner tonight, and one officer invited himself into my room for a further talk. Suffering, sacrifice, death and uncertainty are making men serious and real, and a discussion started upon a casual remark ends up upon the most earnest things.

Friday November 19th 1915, Hazebrouck
Yours posted yesterday morning arrived this evening! With it also came the one posted the day before, so I think the mails are working consistently again. Yes, it was sad about the Hospital ship – one gets a kind of numb 'insensibility' at length

---

507 That would be 1765.
508 Countess of Crawford, **Constance Lilian Carstairs Pelly**, (b.1879 – d.1947), daughter of Sir Henry Pelly, m. Lord Crawford 1900.

about all sorts of catastrophes, and one's sense of proportion goes.[509] Two men have been X rayed this afternoon. It is a wonderful discovery, and it is fascinating to look through the screen whereby (as the Psalmist says) "I may tell all my bones[510]". In fact the man with a piece of shrapnel in his heel was allowed to look through his own foot, and you could see the vicious little piece of metal lying embedded right within. The other man who received two pieces of bomb through the back is a more serious case. The one piece is embedded in the wall of the chest in front and the other piece was wandering about just behind. A photograph was taken, and was completed and exposed for examination in about 8 minutes, ribs, metal and everything else in detail. A young doctor has been in my 'cubicle' for a very long chat this evening. He has yachted among the Nore lightships, and has been through the Hohenzollern and Loos fights, and is not sorry to be a little further back[511].

Saturday November 20th 1915, Hazebrouck

One X ray man is rather bad but the 'heel' one is doing well – they all take time, with the many who have frozen feet also.

I rode out in the morning and saw some new troops recently arrived in a neighbouring village. The church is a very nice simple country one, dated 1630, with the art on the whole good. I saw the Cure's vestry book, which betokens deep and earnest piety, "prayers for our dear soldiers, prayers pour la patrie". On the chancel walls outside were the marks, evidently ancient, of the sharpening of arrow heads and I suppose other weapons.

There has been heavy and continuous bombardment over the hill, but a beautiful morning, a good road and a most enjoyable ride. Votive crosses stuck anywhere about at the roadside shrines. The brick–dog kennel is common here, as also are the dog wheels, but dog vehicles are not so common in this locality. Five weeks today to Christmas!

·

---

509 SS *Anglia* was a steam ship requisitioned for use as a hospital ship. On 17th November 1915 *Anglia* was returning from Calais to Dover, carrying 390 injured officers and soldiers. At around 12:30 pm, one mile east of Folkestone Gate, HMHS *Anglia* struck a mine laid by the German U-boat, *UC-5*. The nearby torpedo gunboat HMS *Hazard* helped evacuate the passengers and crew. Despite the assistance of the collier *Lusitania,* 134 people were killed in the sinking.

510 The use of X-rays for medical purposes (which developed into the field of radiation therapy) was pioneered by Major John Hall-Edwards in Birmingham General Hospital. The largest advancement of X-ray machines was Marie Curie's discovery of the radiological car. This automobile would help transport X-ray machines to the front line and help examine soldiers within a few hours of being injured. The electricity to run the X-ray machine was supplied by the oil directly from the engine of the automobile. **Psalm 22:17:** 'I may tell all my bones: they look *and* stare upon me'

511 The **Battle of the Hohenzollern Redoubt** took place during the Battle of Loos (25th September – 15th October 1915) near Auchy-les-Mines, 20 miles S of Hazebrouck. The British 9th Division captured the redoubt and then lost it to a German counter-attack. The final British assault on 13th October failed and resulted in 3643 casualties, mostly in the first few minutes.

Sunday November 21st 1915, Hazebrouck

'Stir up Sunday' – always a refreshing day[512]. It was <u>cold</u> in that car!! A cutting frosty wind, but clear moonlight. The same lot of men as last Sunday, a crammed full marquee and a very attentive congregation. The theme was that we must work as well as pray that 'Thy Kingdom may come'. Only two at the 8 am service in the Maire – the other Chaplain and myself, but a fair number at 10 at which I took the service and the address. I had meant to have a service for odd patients in the Clearing Station, but the room available for a Chapel was taken over to make additional accommodation for sick officers, and 'frozen feet 'cannot leave their wards.

Monday November 22nd 1915, Hazebrouck

I have been out of sorts today with a digestive cold I suppose, but this evening things have improved. The Club is depressing – two Chaplains together have tackled it, and it is difficult to say much. It <u>might</u> be so nice and could so easily be done. Meanwhile the winter nights are passing, and the place suffers from having a poor name!

Tuesday November 23rd 1915, Hazebrouck

I am moving tonight into a billet and I am going into a house where, for a while, Prince Arthur of Connaught was billeted[513]. The little old lady – <u>very</u> old – gives a kind welcome and, as long as the French temperament can keep it up, it will be pleasant enough. I think, too, it is not bad for one's work for a Chaplain to be able to come into the Hospital from the atmosphere of freshness outside. One of my lads, very seriously ill after an operation for appendicitis, comes from Birling[514] – it cheered him to be talked to about his home town, and he was so pleased.

The N.C.O. in charge of the lorry on which I popped my things in order to change my billet, was the Premier Peer of Scotland, the Right Honourable Lance-Corporal the Earl of Crawford! A full day of talking, talking and talking. Prince Maurice of Battenberg[515] was also in this billet – he was killed, I think, at Ypres. While he was wounded, his horse remained in the stable here and in acknowledgement of the

---

512 The traditional day on which to make Christmas puddings.

513 **Prince Arthur of Connaught and Strathearn** (b.1883 – d.1938) was a grandson of Queen Victoria. Educated at the Royal Military College Sandhurst and commissioned into the 7th (Queen's Own) Hussars. During the Second Boer War, he saw active duty with the 7th Hussars and spent several months stationed at Krugersdorp. In 1907, he was promoted to the rank of captain in the 2nd Dragoons (Royal Scots Greys). During WW1 Prince Arthur served as ADC to Generals Sir John French and Sir Douglas Haig. He was promoted to lieutenant colonel in 1919 and became a colonel in the reserves in 1922.

514 **Birling** is a village and civil parish in the Tonbridge and Malling district of Kent, England, about 7 miles W of Maidstone.

515 **Prince Maurice of Battenberg**, KCVO, (b.1891 – d.1914) was a member of the Hessian princely family and the youngest grandchild of Queen Victoria. His father, Prince Henry of Battenburg had married Princess Beatrice, fifth daughter and youngest child of the Queen. Killed on the Ypres salient, 27th October 1914.

various kindnesses shown by the good proprietress, Prince Henry of Battenberg sent a present of a clock, which is now an object of pride on the mantelpiece of the domestic sitting room.

Wednesday November 24th 1915, Hazebrouck

Damp mizzly weather but the billet is pretty good. There is a very old Monsieur, who has been reciting to me this evening, with great feeling, a poem entitled 'Maman', rather nice – the thoughts of a young soldier mortally wounded on the field of battle. He also likes to talk of the stay of Prince Maurice of Battenberg – the Prince went out shopping with Monsieur, who retains one remark vividly "I wish I could get some good butter!" Monsieur was allowed to ride the Prince's horse and he is inclined to wish to ride mine. As it is rather a fresh animal, and M'sieur is over 70, it is to be hoped that the wish will not be much urged!

A long discussion tonight about the 'messing', the usual three difficulties, the cook, the kitchen and the cost, and the Mess President wants to resign, as I sometimes did, and knowing that I have done the work, there is a movement for honouring me with the post – I am not drawn.

More talking endlessly, and it is difficult to concentrate one's mind sometimes as the men come from such infinitely varied experiences. They have lived so intensely these last few months and they are so glad to have someone who, by the very nature of his work, may be counted on to listen and be sympathetic.

A stove has been got going in the Club, but it fills the whole cavernous building with a damp smoke, so hopefully we may change in a few days to a better adapted place.

Postal arrangements are not at all good, and we have an indifferent management of them at the Clearing Station.

Thursday November 25th 1915, Hazebrouck

We had our Chaplain's talk this morning – the Deputy Chaplain General was here the day before yesterday, passing through to a Confirmation. (Winston Churchill was also here, by the bye[516]). The Chaplain General is expected here in a week or two, which will be interesting and I hope and expect helpful. The Club rather depresses us all. The 'Estaminets', light, warm, cheery, with an occasional gramophone, and one

---

516 Churchill had resigned as First Lord of the Admiralty after the Dardenelles campaign in 1915, accepting the post of Chancellor of the Duchy of Lancaster. He resigned from the government completely on 15th November 1915, and rejoined the British Army, attempting to obtain an appointment as brigade commander, but settling for command of a battalion. After spending some time as a Major with the 2 Bn Grenadier Guards, he was appointed Lieutenant-Colonel, commanding the 6 Bn, Royal Scots Fusiliers (part of the 9th (Scottish) Division), on 1st January 1916.

or two pretty French girls – how will a long, dark, cavernous hall, echoing with an occasional footstep and lit by a few widely separated handing lamps in a smoky fog and very cold – how can this compete with them?

Friday November 26th 1915, Hazebrouck

Snow today and I have been very busy. I rode out to see some of my old Division along the countryside. A hostile aeroplane shelled nearby, and a motor-bicycle in the middle of the dim, dark, deep long moonlit street, blazing up like a bonfire as I came back to my billet just now, accidentally set alight and so perished.

One of my VIIIth Division officers is sick and in the hospital this evening – a very nice man.

Saturday November 27th 1915, Hazebrouck

Very cold again, but dry and bracing. I must change my horse, or there will be another damaged ankle – he gets frantic in a street where there is any traffic, affording alternately amusement and terror for the onlookers, and mingled feelings for the rider! Some of these young horses are not fully broken and knowing that I wanted one with plenty of 'go' in it, the remount officer, I expect, turned in the direction of these, and perhaps took this one out of the lines a little too soon. What he would do close up to the guns it is difficult to guess – burst like a shell himself, perhaps, or go up in the air like one!

A ride this afternoon with Tuckey, who is interesting and I met Burgess, one of the nicest of my 24th Field circle[517]. It remains still where it was, separated from the Division – everybody in fact seems separated from everybody else and there is no Chaplain with the Ambulance. The Chaplains of the Division are changing all through – there is a kind of General Post and nobody knows anything!

Sunday November 28th 1915, Hazebrouck, Advent Sunday

These billeting people are really very nice for the present and it was wise to make the change – if for nothing else it is good to be out of the surroundings of sickness and suffering. We are very full at the Clearing Station, with more frozen feet and illnesses from exposure.

The homely old woman who possesses this large chateau lives in the kitchen and adjoining sitting-room, dressed as a peasant, and the one 'bonne' that they employ tells me that Madame does not know the 'fond de sa richesse', and I can quite believe it. She has property in Belgium, round Ypres, in this town, factories and the like. Wisely enough, she does not spend a penny more that she needs, and though she is extremely

---

517 Lt Burgess.

kind, I am strictly limited to 'la chandelle' prescribed by the billeting ticket. I have to supplement by buying others of course, if only for the preservation of eye-sight.

It has been COLD here. I had an 8 o'clock service with three present, all officers and one of them resplendent in red tabs, Captain Torr, who was in the VIIIth Division. He stayed behind and we exchanged a word or two, he is a remarkably nice man I think. At 9.30 am we had a short ward service, keenly appreciated by the men. The rest of the day I spent visiting as services are not very feasible at a Clearing Station, and the troops round happen to have Chaplains as far as I know. This evening a very hearty service in a large ward at the top of the building, with the singing led by two mouth organs, one of which was played by a breezy young Canadian.

Tuesday November 30th 1915 (St Andrew's Day), Hazebrouck
No English mail for two nights due to more floating mines or something like it, I suppose. They have been celebrating St. Andrew's night in the Mess in no very edifying manner, I am afraid[518].

We had an early service which I took, about a mile away. There were only three Chaplains there, Tuckey, Baldwin and Plate. It was a glorious morning and in the afternoon I had a long ride beside a picturesque canal, and through woodland copses and past a quaint and very old village church set on a little hill, in delightful weather. Some of my old Division were there and I met one of the R.C. Chaplains. The Division has been widely scattered and my old Brigade has gone in fact into another Division and it is in truth no longer a very efficient Brigade, being used up with so much fighting. Heavy bombardment over the hill most of yesterday and today – this afternoon it sounded very near and jarred on one's hearing a little, it is so incessant.

A Belgian motor car stopped at our door this evening. It had rushed down from a given town, and was going back again – Belgian officers and an interpreter, and the chauffeur, a Belgian, was still a little strained with the shelling he said they had gone through. This evening an Australian doctor came into the Mess, putting up for the night on his way through. He had lived for some years until 15 years ago in Randwick. He says that part, and all round by Coogee, is thickly built over now, and he knew Canon Hough and various other people[519]. His own name I have not got yet. Prof David is with a Red Cross hospital in Egypt.

Yesterday and today have been given up mainly to writing a report of 'experiences and work' since the beginning of the War for the Deputy Chaplain General. It makes a rather full volume, and I am suggesting that the main particulars of all of the Chaplains' reports should be selected and collated and published in a volume.

518 Patron Saint of Scotland.
519 **Randwick** is a suburb in the Eastern Suburbs of Sydney, in the state of New South Wales, with **Coogee** as the beach. Canon **Hough** (1843 – 1913) was the Rector of St Judes Anglican church, Randwick.

Wednesday December 1st 1915, Hazebrouck

A long and full day with a meeting of Chaplains, 50 or 60, addressed by the Chaplain General.

Thursday December 2nd 1915, Hazebrouck

It was a nice service and the prayers and hymns were of the old familiar words, but the address we felt was rather disappointing, too much epigram and not enough solid thought and reasoning. One thing was good – Christ for 18 years was content to lead a life of obscurity and drudgery. Tea afterward was good, it was provided by J.W Griffiths the Chaplain of that Clearing Station. He is at No.2[520] and the other Griffiths (R) is at No.12. He comes from Geelong, Australia and is an examining Chaplain to the Bishop of Ballarat[521]. We may be sure we did not meet in vain, and the Chaplain General was pleasantly sociable.

It is a blustery day today. Holy Communion at 8. am with a Chaplain's talk at 10.30 at which we discussed plans for the next week or two and for Christmas Day. Then arrangements for changing my horse and visiting, visiting, visiting!

The Earl of Crawford carrying a full clothes basket upstairs – and rolling artillery fire across the hills and flashes of gunfire light against the black night sky, are two outstanding impressions. An evening at the Club, closing with a short service, it is dismal but things are improving.

Saturday December 4th 1915, Hazebrouck

It was a blustery morning. After the King's accident, plus my own back in the summer, I decided that it was wiser to change the horse that I have had lately. It got so frantic in front of the traffic, in fact it could only be ridden along the country roads and then it was liable to tricks if motors of any kind passed by. A motor lorry made it wild, and the wildness generally took the form of prancing on the hind legs. As this was the way in which the King came to grief, I felt I would profit by his Majesty's object lesson. This last morning the little animal seemed to want to achieve a finale – it began by entirely refusing to pass under a railway bridge, and by doing so, lead another horse into the same evil spirit. So I had to jump off and take him through, a crowd of admiring peasants having gathered round to enjoy the circus, and then he refused to let me remount. I led him along a railway line and through a field, and then from a mud bank, got on his back by stealth. My success he greeted with some rebellious circuiting, but by making him stand quite still for three or four minutes

---

520 No2 CCS Bailleul: August 1914 – September 1917
521 Rev. **John W Griffiths**, Chaplain to **Julius Lewis**, Dean of Ballarat 1914 – 20. **Geelong** is the state of Victoria and the largest non-capital city. Located 47 miles SW of the state capital, Melbourne, the port city is situated around Corio Bay and the Barwon River. **Ballarat** is a city located on the Yarrowee River and lower western plains of the Great Dividing Range in the state of Victoria, approximately 65 miles WNW of Melbourne.

and to forget which way I wanted him to go, I eventually succeeded in making him believe that my way was the one he would like, and we got on nicely for about a mile. Then we met a motor lorry, and he dashed round and started off in an opposite direction to the top of his bent. It gets rather tiring holding a sturdy neck like that for any distance, but in a quarter of a mile he slowed down, and by repeating the former device, I got him again along the road to the Remount Depot – but that road still held the advancing lorry. So I had to again dismount and lead my wilful friend past his imaginary terrors. The next difficulty, after I had re-mounted by stealth from another mud bank, was a working windmill, the click, click of the sails, the great swing of the arms being a certain cause of alarm. He let himself be controlled past this however, and now we had only half a mile to the goal. He was settling into a respectable swing, when behind I heard the hoot, hoot of a big army motor car. It must be remembered that these Flemish roads are none of them wide, and many are narrow, and all of them are always flanked on either side by a continuous ditch at this time of year deep with water and slimy mud. You descend from the road to the ditch as from a long platform, and here was this car coming with an unconcerned fullness of speed behind us, and the horse knew it too! The only thing to do was to wave and slow down the car, and car, and occupants, and rider, had all to be subject to the will of a 7-year-old cob. Is man the 'Lord of Creation' always? The rest of the story would take too long, but eventually we found a mount that I think will do a respectable parson's work, and we came home with a decorum which after the last few days, and especially the last few hours, was something like bliss.

I have this afternoon been out to see some of my old Division – what changes! so few of the old officers left.

Sunday December 5th 1915, Hazebrouck

It has been a wonderfully mild and bright day – one day less of the winter and very pleasant for getting about. We have fewer cases in the hospital, and people's spirits everywhere are in better condition.

A rather nice Sunday, though not a heavy one. 8 am Holy Communion with 6 present and Baldwin took it, then at 9.30 a Ward service. We have arranged that the Presbyterian takes two wards, the Wesleyan two and the Anglican two, and we turn about Sunday by Sunday – it seems the best way. Last Sunday I started an evening service in the large room upstairs, and it was greatly appreciated. This evening I took the usual C of E Service in the Maire, the Presbyterian took the ward service and there were nearly 200 patients at it! That now is going to be a turn-about arrangement, and he is going to give up his Maire service which is held in the afternoon.

After the ward service this morning I had a journey on horseback to a neighbouring village, but no service was possible. This evening there was a very nice one in the Maire with some officers, two nurses and about 40 men present – there might be many more.

A dreadful wounded case this evening, very skilfully operated on – these doctors and nurses do work hard, and they do their work admirably, beyond all praise.

Monday December 6th 1915, Hazebrouck

I have today sent in the formal application for leave from December 28th to January 4th inclusive.

It has been rather a nice day here, a sunny morning, and a long talk of Chaplains – Joy! We are obtaining a NICE building for a Club. It is a lawyer's house, set back in its garden, rather near the station and on a main thoroughfare. A room for recreation, one for writing and a devotional room – it is almost too good to be realised, but they have promised to ear-mark it for us and so now we shall move on.

This afternoon we started for a ride out to look for troops, but the rain came on so heavily that we desisted. This evening I had a lantern meeting in the highest room – in school time it is a theatre and so does admirably for a gathering like this. About 150 men were there with about 50 stretchers. They listened very attentively to words on the pictures by Copping, illustrating the life of Christ Jesus[522], and they sang very reverently the three hymns, "O God our help in ages past", "Jesu, lover of my soul" and "Rock of Ages"[523]. I am purchasing a lantern for regular use now that we are fairly set in for the winter, and it will come in for the troops round also.

Tuesday December 7th 1915, Hazebrouck

Another sergeant, hit in a bomb accident, passed away today – he was a gallant man, well built, well nourished and fit. The turn came suddenly after the operation this morning. He fought for breath but gradually weakness overcame him and his mind wandered. An imaginary telephone worried him, it kept ringing him up and at last he asked that we would go and have it stopped as he could not cope with it, he said. He died about 20 minutes later, gradually sinking into silence – how grieving it all is[524]. A busy day, visiting and talking. The atmosphere of a full hospital is difficult to breathe in, physically, mentally and spiritually! There are so many of them, and each individual mind and body is different. It is best if you can catch the interest of a group and you then have an opportunity all round. I had a ride with Tuckey this afternoon, finishing in dark drizzling rain.

---

522 **Harold Copping** (b.1863 – d.1932) was a British artist best known as an illustrator of Biblical scenes. His 1910 book *The Copping Bible* illustrated by himself became a best-seller.

523 *Our God, Our Help in Ages Past* is a hymn by Isaac Watts and paraphrases Psalm 90, 1708. *Jesu, lover of my soul* words: Charles Wesley, 1740. Music: Joseph Parry, 1879. *Rock of Ages* is a popular Christian hymn by the Reverend Augustus Montague Toplady written in 1763.

524 Serjeant **Herbert Bonell**, 4th Bn Royal Fusiliers. Died 7th December 1915, buried Hazebrouck Communial Cemetery. A Civil Servant.

Wednesday December 8th 1915, Hazebrouck

We buried him this afternoon – a gallant and dutiful soldier, with a life full of promise of much usefulness and in the prime of health and strength. I have not found out yet who were his next of kin, but it is hard to think of their grief[525].

A full day of visiting. I burnt a hole in the back of my 18/- cap when drying it! I found a woman this morning, who has made quite a successful mend of it for 1 franc, so that after the fear that the cap had been made irretrievably disrespectable, this is rather a relief!

The new horse has developed its weak side which is to bolt at a terrific speed from anything coming behind it. It needs therefore 'holding in', always something! I have got a touch of blood poisoning in a finger, something people are liable to out here. By taking it in good time however, I think that any serious ill effect is prevented.

I went this morning to see a French Protestant soldier in the French Soldier hospital – it was interesting comparing the French methods with ours.

Thursday December 9th 1915, Hazebrouck

A long talk this morning between the Chaplains, and we got round to talk of the Club, and I must say the prospects look very pleasing. The Fund is there, and I think now with this new building, we are going to have a <u>very</u> nice place indeed. It is a comfort to think of – a nice large front room and two back rooms which can, on occasion, can be thrown into one. We entered it today – things are not in their places yet, but out of the black drizzling rain, and the flustering wind, it was a peaceful refuge. You, and all interested, would be glad to see it. We talked of Christmas plans – I hope my slides will have come by then.

Friday December 10th 1915, Hazebrouck

The finger was lanced this morning – a proceeding that made me, metaphorically, kick rather vigorously, but I think it is on the way to improvement. It is a nuisance only having one hand, but as I see some of the hands and feet here, I am thankful. I now wear a sling, and it makes great sympathy and amusement among the staff and patients to see me so much in the fashion.

Saturday December 11th 1915, Hazebrouck

It is question whether my leave date will be the 27th or the 29th as it is a matter of fitting in – one officer per day per unit is the system, I think. The Club goes admirably now, though not yet in proper working order, and it is a nice place. Two officers of

---

525 Commonwealth War Graves Commission: Serjeant Bonell was the son of Arthur Elias and Edith Bonell, of 14, Jedburgh St., Battersea, London

my old Division are in here today, both very cordial and cheerful. Today has been visiting as usual, and torrents of rain.

Sunday December 12th 1915, Hazebrouck

It is a tobacco-filled mess room upstairs – a round table, a French stove with the fire out, and the Colonel, Major and two Captain doctors are playing cards, and talking loudly about them. It is not a 'high-souled' scene and a little depressing. In the dormitories of the College lie about 300 men suffering from various ailments, bronchitis, rheumatism, earache, swollen faces, trench feet, abscesses and so on. The last named are common owing to the impure soil and water, and the hard living.

A nice day – I did not go to early service, nursing my finger (which is better) and being due for a ward service at 9.15. This was a hearty one, and I gave out some of Miss Blyth's books. At 10, a very large service in the Maire, very hearty and bright with nice lessons and I spoke on its being the business of our life to "Prepare the way of the Lord"[526]. It is a comfort to know that we can all be doing something, and must be doing our utmost. Then the dressing of the finger and visiting, visiting, visiting, with a pause for lunch. Then tea and a spinning ride away to a distant farm and a most earnest and cheerful service in a barn with three candles and about 50 men! It was uplifting and how quiet and intent they all were. I noticed one man harmonising in the hymns standing near me, and spoke to him. He answered in very correct English and said that "Yes", he was musical, and had taken his degree in Dublin although his rank is that of a private. It was a cold ride back in the moonlight.

Monday December 13th 1915, Hazebrouck

The finger is mercifully much better – I do not want another like it and it was a blessing being where it could be attended to, and it has helped one to understand and sympathise with the condition so many of our good fellows get into.

I made my official call today on the Abbe Lamire[527], the excommunicated priest who is the Mayor of a large commune, and a Member of Parliament. Prince Arthur of Connaught billeted with him and he is distinctly a personality. Some of his opponents have it against him that he once received a German Decoration and has not returned it. They think that he should, but others say that he is wise to keep it as a curiosity. However that may be, he has also received an important French Decoration during this war, and he works very hard in a tidy, kindly, keen and orderly manner, and is undoubtedly a blessing to this part of France, in spite of the Papal judgement on him.

A busy day and the Club is going well.

---

526 **Mark 1:3** 'The voice of one crying in the wilderness, Prepare ye the way of the Lord, make his paths straight'
527 Abbe **Jules Auguste Lemire,** Mayor of Hazebrouck.

Wednesday December 15th 1915, Hazebrouck

The 'billet' question makes rather a tale – one other officer is in this building, an elderly sub-lieutenant of the Flying Corps. He came into the sitting-room of Monsieur and Madame where I was making my goodnight as usual at about 9.30, and said that he understood that his Major was coming to take my room at 10 o'clock tomorrow (this) morning! This was rather sudden! We asked who had said so and he replied the French Interpreter attached to the Town Major[528]. Monseiur took up a role of most decided denial and disapproval. The officer was surprised that there had been no further preparation and very nicely steered back down from his announcement, and we agreed to go and see the Town Major together this morning. The interview revealed that the interpreter, and not without the cognisance of the Town Major, had got it into his head that the amenities due to a Chaplain, and of the rank of a Captain, were not quite of the same standard as those due to a Major of the Flying Corps Equipment. The Flying Corps Sub-Lieutenant, who in civilian life is a drawing master at Eton[529], was very understanding about it, and getting the Town Major alone, let him know his ideas about things. I said I wanted to help in the best way, but that there were a number of things to accommodate such as writing materials, Church things as well as kit, and there was another billet to find – I had a Chaplains talk at 10.30 and a funeral at 4 and so on. The Town Major was inclined to be high-handed and the interpreter was in danger of being flatly uncivil, but the Eton master was watchful, tactful and insistent and many points were discussed. The crowds of refugees swarming into the town, the fact that this house had been used as a Headquarters for Ordnance, the selfishness of Monsieur and Madame in wishing to have their house free of these people. (I sympathise with them, after they have had the place full of officers and orderlies for 9 months and been turned out of their own kitchen for cooking, having to cook their own meals in their sitting room and being kept up till 1 and 2 in the morning – my quieter ways I can see, made me more acceptable to them, as both M'sieur and M'dm are nearly 70), the fact that they would easily find me another billet, (I trembled as I heard them mentioning one or two localities!) and so on. The end of it is that at midday I was told that I would not be disturbed. It gives an idea of another of the difficulties of campaigning and also

---

528 Staff officer (not necessarily a major) responsible for billeting arrangements in a town or village behind the lines.

529 Lieut. **Eric Walter Powell** RFC RAMC (b.1886 – d.1933) at London. Certificate taken on Maurice Farman Biplane / At: British Flying School, Le Crotoy, France, 29th May 1915. Obituary 21st August 1933 (he died in a climbing accident), Dr Alington, headmaster of Eton *"Eric Powell was a man of genius which showed itself in many fields. The world perhaps knew him best as an oarsman, the winner of the Diamond Sculls, but there are others who think of his distinction in the Flying Corps, and yet more to whom his wonderful talent as an artist made a stronger appeal. To watch the marvellous speed with which he transferred to paper the beauty which he saw with an unerring eye was a pleasure of which one never tired, and in later years he was developing an accuracy of detail and a variety of technique which seemed to hold the highest promise. Of what he did for drawing at Eton it is impossible to speak too highly; and his success as one of the most popular and best beloved of house masters was so remarkable that it might have been grudge to anyone but him … His was indeed a rare combination of courage, strength, and tenderness, and it is given to few to leave behind so fair a memory"*.

of the difficulties of a Town Major, and also of the ways of some of the interpreters. I think that on reflection, the Town Major saw he had behaved, let us say, 'carelessly'.

Thursday December 16th 1915, Hazebrouck

The arrangements for leave all go through the Headquarters of the Army to which you belong, and each army arranges for so many officers to have a place on the leave boat each day. If an officer due for leave is wounded or falls sick, that alters arrangements, and nobody knows about that from day to day. For example, an officer came into us sick yesterday morning and he was due to start on leave that morning, and to be married on Friday! It is wonderful how the leave system works as well as it does and one must be thankful. I am trying to get a week for my faithful man Peter Waite, who has had no leave since our coming into the country over 13 months ago. He is a good and faithful lad and I am very pleased with him. All the time that I have had him he has needed a rebuke only once, and we stood and rode, surrounded by death together during the battle of Neuve Chapelle in a way that neither of us will ever forget.

A Chaplains' talk for a long time this morning, preparing for Christmas. We are going to have a social evening at the Club and I am showing some of our sailor slides, and Dickens' Christmas Carol, and we shall have coffee and cakes, we hope. Much of this afternoon has gone in arrangements like that, and in hunting for a piano. One man told me he had found 18 pianos for different regiments in the country round for use at Christmas-tide! My quest so far has been unsuccessful.

Friday December 17th 1915, Hazebrouck

I have learned today that I am booked for the 27th (and my faithful 'man Friday' also). I hope to arrive at Victoria the same afternoon at 4.30.

Saturday December 18th 1915, Hazebrouck

We are very busy here getting ready for the Season, and it is a blessing being able to give everyone plenty to think about. It has been a full day, arranging things for the Clearing Station Christmas, and others for the Club. The latter is certainly getting to be a very pleasant place, and by Christmas Day I hope we shall have something excellent. Our quest today has still been for a piano, (I believe that with this evening, success is in sight) and chairs. These last are a great difficulty as the early occupation by troops in this year have used much furniture, and it is one of those things which trade does not quickly replace as so many of the men of France are, of course, under arms.

Sunday December 19th 1915, Hazebrouck

A rather tiring day – Holy Communion at 8 am with 3 present and at 9.15 a large 'ward' service and another at 11, then visiting and after lunch arrangements and then letter censoring. This sometimes takes up as much as an hour and a half. At 6.30 another service in the Town Hall with about 60 there. There is heavy firing round us today and some circling aeroplanes which they say went out to scout some of the enemy who have been dropping bombs on a neighbouring town. Turkey and plum pudding tonight provided for us through one of the officers!

Tuesday December 21st 1915, Hazebrouck

It is now uncertain if we can get across for our leave. I hear that communications are in abeyance for an indefinite time. Will a sense of chivalry and reasonableness gradually come into the German head? One wakes up from time to time and realises that there is a big, stupid, wicked war going on – houses are battered, men are mutilated, men are killed, women and little children are driven from their homes. A lot of them passed through here today – a dishevelled pale-faced, ill-fed and listless crowd they looked, and deeply pitiable. I hear that gas was experienced within four or five miles of us, right back behind the trenches, but the effect on our soldiers has been small. All the time, happily, I think the enemy are being used up, and their exuberance is subdued. It is a good farewell order from Sir John French, and the firm tone of confidence is very healthy.

We heard tonight that the leave boats were not running – I hope the cessation is only very temporary and that on Monday the faithful Peter and I can set our feet once more on Albion's shore. There is still a tremendous amount to do, and one of the severest tasks here is the censoring – it takes hours.

Last night when we were censoring in the Wesleyan Chaplain's room, an N.C.O. came in with some official letters and a parcel to get them censored. I asked the Chaplain if he had noticed how particularly respectful the Lance Corporal had been. He had noticed it, but was not prepared for my information that it was the Earl of Crawford! Then he remembered that last week when he had arrived, he had some baggage which had been taken to the officers' end of the Hospital by mistake. He was questioning what to do with it, when this same Lance Corporal offered to get it over to the proper place. The Chaplain afterwards, in thanking the Lance Corporal, gave him a franc for his trouble – it was the premier Earl of Scotland!

Wednesday December 22nd 1915, Hazebrouck

What a full day it has been again. I am turning a blacksmith's forge into a Chapel, and it is beginning to look very nice, and at least it will begin well on Christmas Day. At present it is difficult to see how one can get everything in – getting ready for leave, finishing the Chapel, helping to fit out the Club better (it is improving), arranging a concert, giving a lantern talk on Christmas night, helping with the decorations in the Clearing Station, in the Club, in one's own Chapel as well as the Maire Chapel, arranging for refreshments at the Club Xmas night, finding a piano and chairs, editing the Christmas dinner menu, and having in view two, perhaps three, services on Christmas Day and three on Sunday, with also about 300 letters to censor – leave will be acceptable!

Thursday December 23rd 1915, Hazebrouck

It <u>has</u> been a full and long day! And just as I was making my way gratefully to my billet, I encountered a brother Chaplain stranded on his way to another Army, and went from one point to another first to try and find him the means of travel (unsuccessfully), and now happily to get him a bed – not at all an easy task. He is one Leigh, a minor Canon of Southwell, and they have changed his station for him this evening, the day but one before Christmas! He had all his plans made for his people at the base (where we had met) so all these had to go, and as far as he knows, no one takes his plans up![530]

The censoring work becomes something tremendous at the Christmas season – I have been wanting to write to the children and to the Parish for Christmas, but it has been quite impossible.

Friday December 24th 1915, Hazebrouck

A crowded day – fitting up the little Chapel, giving notice of the services, arranging the concert and lantern pictures, I shall be very glad of a rest.

Sunday December 26th 1915, Hazebrouck

A train journeying down country with five other officers in the compartment, and a dismal little acetylene flame does its best to show us the darkness outside

Yesterday was a strenuous day. I was up at 6.30 with Holy Communion at 7.15 in the Blacksmith's forge – 4 nurses and 8 men present, and the place looked not too unpresentable with red and blue bunting covering up the machinery, the anvils and the forge. Some old Army blankets from the Quartermaster for kneelers, and the Blacksmith's bench transformed into the Holy Table. At 9 am a very large ward service, full of happiness and reality and about 250 present. Then a rush off to the Maire for Morning Prayer at 10 and another peaceful and joyful service with about 100 present – how we feel the strength of the Christmas spirit at a time like this! Then a rush back to the Clearing Station for another service of H.C. to which no one came. Back to my billet to change then a hasty lunch with all the patients eating, and about 50 had to be left over till the rest had gone, all on my hands with only

---

530 Rev. **Thomas Arnold Lee** (b.1889 – d.1972). Durham graduate who had taught in schools in Cambridge, Singapore and Leeds; he had also served as a curate in Southwark Cathedral and at Leeds, a chaplain to HM Forces in WW1. In 1948, rector of Gedling with Stoke Bardolph (1948 – 57), and was made a full canon of Southwell in 1955. He then retired to Buckinghamshire, where he was vicar of Grendon Underwood and Edgcott 1957 – 61.

three or four orderlies to help. Back to my billet to lie on my back for half an hour reading over Dickens' Christmas Carol for the evening show, and writing a note to round up the banjoist for my Club concert (his banjo did not come, so no more could he!). Back to the Clearing Station to peep in at a smoking concert, and at the Soldiers' Club two performers failed to appear. However, Brockington[531] (the new Chaplain) turned out to be an accompanist and reciter, so we had an enjoyable 'home' concert. Two large cakes and a box of sweets sent by a kind sympathiser proved a valuable addition to the simple provision made by a French pastry cook. The place eventually got crowded up, and people warmed together cheerily. My sea pictures proved to be of great interest, illustrating what our maritime strength means, while pictures of Ceylon, Hongkong, Sydney etc. brought before us our imperial outlook. Back again to the Clearing Station for another concert and then the Staff dinner, with a wonderful production by the Quartermaster considering that it is wartime (on the menu everyone of the Staff was brought in under some facetious form or another), and at 10.30 I left the party to themselves – still cheerful.

This morning an 8 a.m service at the Maire (1 present!), 9.15 another ward service with 100 present, very hearty and real. 11 o'clock service at the officers' hospital across the town, also in my charge, and a time of real grace, I think.

EIGHT DAYS LEAVE

---

531   Rev. **Alfred Allen Brockington**, (b.1872 – d.1938) poet and collaborator with Cecil Sharp in the collection of folk-songs. Chaplain attached to the 15th Casualty Clearing Station RAMC, June 1916, and with the 23rd Brigade RFA (3rd Division), June – September 1916. His son was killed in September 1916, he was apparently transferred to the UK by January 1917, there is brief mention of work at the Avonmouth and 2nd Southern General Hospitals. As the time of his son's death, he was resident in Taunton.

Tuesday January 4th 1916 (on the way back from leave)

Here I am in a French Hotel, not a first class one and <u>not</u> very clean. It is full – the leave boat arrived so late that the up country 'leave' train had long gone and a chalked-up order on the quay requested all officers 2nd Army to report to R.T.O. <u>tomorrow</u> evening at 6.30p.m. A whole day again to wander round in – we are all officers. It was rather a wild crossing, the night fell dark and thick with a foggy rain which was difficult to see through, and the black smoke from the steamer fell around us like a pall. When we drew clear of Folkestone Pier the ship began to plunge and roll diligently. Green lights, red lights, search lights shone at intervals through the haze, but not a light showed on our ship. We slowed down now and again, as the ship seemed to be dodging, and in the end I submitted to illness once, one of a goodly company. The boat was crowded to its utmost capacity.

I write in the assembly hall of the hotel; one or two young officers have arrived to find no accommodation left, and my thermos flask has broken, and flooded some of my clothing with tea!

Wednesday January 5th 1916, Hazebrouck

Instead of waiting for the 'leave' train, I found an ordinary one departing at 10.45 and just caught it after walking round the docks making enquires, and I now write en route at Calais. The little boys as the train slows up call out to the English "Souvenir, Sir" and to the French "Bouteillies vide". They get about 12 empty bottles from this train, and I suppose that they will get about 2 sous a dozen for them. Each journey impresses one more with the resettled condition of travel – passengers come to and fro much in the ordinary way, and the railway terminus is much as it is in peacetime. I had just written so far when bang, bang, rattle, as our train begins to move out of the station. It is a hostile aeroplane circling over the town and harbour. The anti-aircraft have given it all their attention and it has come near the station and now moves north-west. Some of the shots were very close and the air is full of little black and grey smoke balls – it is just as well to be moving on.

As one journeys on, one notices how less well-kept the streets and houses are and I expect that England must begin to show similar signs ere long. I am glad that those 651,160 unattested bachelors are to be 'fetched', or must give the reason why not[532].

---

532 **The Derby Scheme** was a voluntary Army recruitment policy in Britain created in 1915 by Edward Stanley, 17th Earl of Derby. Men who voluntarily registered their name would be enlisted only when necessary. Married men had an added incentive in that they were advised they would be called up only once the supply of single men was exhausted. The scheme was also referred to as the "Group System" as men were classified in groups according to their year of birth and marital status and were to be called up with their group when it was required. The scheme was abandoned in December 1915 and was superseded by the Military Service Act 1916 which introduced conscription for the first time. 215 000 men enlisted under the Derby Scheme and another 2 185 000 attested for later enlistment. However, 38 per cent of single men and 54 per cent of married men who were not in 'starred' occupations failed to come forward: that 38% numbered 651 160.

All the railway crossings are managed by women, and there is still an advertisement well preserved of the 'Exposition Universelle – Bruxelles – 1910'. I noticed at lunch just now how much a Frenchman makes of his mid-day meal. He entrenches himself behind a large dinner napkin and, surrounded by little dishes – haricots, sardines, tomatoes, salads and the rest, goes forwards to his task like a man.

Long, flat roads, many of them paved, flanked forever with regular dotted poplar trees, long stretches of canal and many windmills, that is the landscape. 5.30p.m. arrived quite comfortably to a warm welcome in the billet.

It has been a busy return and it is astonishing how many people greet you after an absence. It does good to go away! A number of papers, parcels, and letters were waiting, and a very nice parcel from West Farleigh, doing me the real kindness of remembering me with the others who are serving. A pipe and tobacco, a box of peppermints, a tin looking-glass, writing materials, chocolate, Carbolic soap (most useful) and a pipe lighter, all done up in a cleaning cloth.

Thursday January 6th 1916, Hazebrouck
The rush and the swing again – there are indeed many to speak with, and so many of them sad and dreary, and therefore open to my sympathy. 7.30 a.m. Holy Communion and at 10 o'clock a long talk of the Chaplains, the Club, services in the town and for the troops round. Arranging for more seating in the Club, a lantern meeting, taking round literature and of course, censoring.

Friday January 7th 1916, Hazebrouck
Most people here are overworked – three doctors sick and one on leave, and the work to be done by just two others and the nurses, with nearly 500 patients requiring treatment. I am sure that something ought to be done. There are one or two gas cases and the rest are accidents, trench fevers, rheumatisms and colds. The weather is still wild and very trying for those going and coming 'on leave', with some of the passages having taken 4 or 5 hours – poor things!

I write this in the Soldiers' Club in which three tables are occupied by men all writing, and three by others reading and playing games

Saturday January 8th 1916, Hazebrouck
It has been a day of preparations and doings. In the morning it was a great pleasure to meet three of my old Brigade officers, who were most warm and cordial. They were rather 'in a pickle' as they had expected the 'leave' train from Victoria would go at the later hour but it changed that morning to the earlier hour! That meant their coming round by another route, and arriving up here a day and a half late – all three of them, and one or two officers waiting to go on leave in their place. I did what I

could to help them get a vehicle to take them some 15 miles or so to their Battalion, but we had to separate before I knew if they were successful. One of them was the officer who had taken me through the front trenches at Neuve Chapelle on one of my visits, and another had been a keen friend at a bombing school. In the afternoon I had a long and pleasant ride with the regular Chaplain, Tuckey, surveying the country round for troops. He goes on leave in a few days and is arranging for my being Acting Senior Chaplain of the 2nd Army

Sunday January 9th 1916, Hazebrouck

It has been a bright Sunday outwardly, but regarding the people, I do not know how it is, but there does not seem to be the grip and the response one saw up in the trenches and with the Field Ambulance. There is perhaps a little reaction from Christmas and the New Year. 8 a.m. service at the Mairie – a beautiful morning. At 10 o'clock a full congregation and a very hearty service, then a long ride out into the country in a sumptuous motor car to a very nice service in a Soldiers' Club there which has been subsidised from the Fund, and is managed by an officer who is really very attractive looking. Also it is very largely used indeed, so that is refreshing and it was a very good service. Besides taking Tuckey's work in part (he is going a round of his station), I am also taking an oversight of another Clearing Station while that Chaplain is on leave, so there is plenty to do.

Loud and continuous bombarding all today, and a number of aeroplanes, but no hostile ones near us.

Monday January 10th 1916, Hazebrouck

Very fine weather, and after a very good nights' rest following a tiring Sunday, it was pleasant moving along in the sunshine and made one thankful not to be some of the patients. The worst was a Yorkshire lad where a shrapnel bullet had entered near the knee and travelled downwards, opening out a hideous patch above the foot where it came out. The whole frame of the lad shook with wincing caused by the washing, and cutting away. But he smiled wanly when talked to. Then I met a little hunchbacked Frenchwoman, about 50 years old, pale and drawn and very thin, and not more that 4ft. high. She was stepping along quite firmly all the same, and smiled 'Good morning' with a little gleam of pleasure. Later I passed a little old cripple with no hands and no legs – he seems all spindles as he swings along. He stopped at a door and knocked, but could make no one hear. Quickly he turned to the bell and put the stump of his arm into the ring on the chain and pulled it down – how thankful one felt not to be maimed or crippled.

At about 12.30 I went into the railway station to try and get an English newspaper – as it happens with success. Just as I came out of the door on to the street, there were signs of alarm, heads popping out everywhere, people at their doors and on the pavements, and without a moment's warning – crack – smash – a dreadful rumbling and a cloud of thick black smoke at the end of the station platform. Up in the sky, like two little transparent brown flies, were two German aeroplanes. Presently another crash and a boom, and you stood there wondering if you were near enough to be in the way of an other one that might come. People ran away in all directions. The next thing to do was to step out on the road and to watch those creatures spinning their way on through the white clouds into the deep blue, little flecks alternately of gold and silver and pale brown, far, far up – so beautiful and yet so false! The one bomb had dropped harmlessly by the railway side further back, the next at the end of the station platform, had fallen INTO the tender of a engine. By wonderful good fortune neither the driver nor the stoker were on the engine at that moment, though it was under steam. The coal served as an excellent deadener, though it was scattered yards in all directions. Nearly every pane of glass in the train standing on the next rail was shivered. A train with all its windows broken – a curious sight! An Ambulance train lying on the next rails was untouched! The station soon became deserted, but soldiers and railway employee's gathered round the engine, the stoker of which, pale and shaking a little, was philosophically stirring up the fire and getting the tools sorted out to see if the engine would move alright. You can imagine I walked back to lunch meditating thankfully.

Taking a funeral in the afternoon, I learnt that a third bomb had been dropped near the Cemetery, again a harmless one, in the garden of a house about 50 yds away. Tonight we are told, they went on to the next town and dropped nine bombs, killing a woman, cutting off a dear little boy's legs and killing him, and wounding three people. Do the enemy expect to make friends this way?

Tuesday January 11th 1916, Hazebrouck

A busy day. The other Clearing Station in the morning, and preparations for a lantern talk then a ride out with Tuckey, and meeting again with some of my old Division. The men entered into the spirit of the lantern pictures heartily and the Carols gave them much pleasure – it is drab life that they lead, many of them. Our poor staff here get very tired, as well they might, with so many dozens of sore throats to look at, so many sore fingers, so many tired feet.

There was an interesting incident this morning when one soldier said he knew Chatham. "Did you ever see the Mission steamer on the Medway?" "Yes" he said, "I used to work on the water a bit, and there was a Mission place near Rochester station, where I used to like to go and play billiards". "I had the interest," I said "of seeing that place built".

Wednesday January 12th 1916, Hazebrouck

That poor lad's foot is in an awful state, but the treatment, the frequent washing with disinfectant, the life in the open air, the feeding up, are doing marvels and the corruption is gradually receding. The lad, when brought in, was thought to be dying.

He does shout when he is being done, and they let him as it is an outlet. He is very frail and young-looking, not more than 18 years old. He dreads each turn, but chats away freely when it is all over. The Sister is a noble woman as the task each day with all the dead matter is most unpleasant, and the two orderlies who help are noble fellows too. I mention these details because I think that sometimes the lay mind gets the idea that nursing, and the work of the R.A.M.C. is chiefly romantic and picturesque. Neither for the stretcher bearers, nor for the people here, is it that – they bear their cross truly.

Letters, business and details, and visiting for the rest of the day.

Thursday January 13th 1916, Hazebrouck
A very full day with Holy Communion at 7.30 a.m., and at 10 o/clock the Chaplain's talk. It is nicely guided by Tuckey – it began devotionally and I hope that we shall work it up to finishing that way too. Letters, visiting, lunch, more visiting, censoring of letters, and the Club which quietly, though slowly, improves and a service there. How glad the men are to talk, and their desire for friendship is very touching.

Friday January 14th 1916, Hazebrouck
Visiting today, chiefly. This evening I met a young officer from Manley, Sydney, and another is in civil life a marine engineer who knows the Mission to Seamen in Liverpool and elsewhere.

At dinner tonight we had Dr Simms, the Irish Presbyterian Chaplain, who before Bishop Gwynne came, was the Senior Chaplain out here. He is a pleasantly spoken man with a short white beard, looking rather tired, but warming up after dinner[533]. He was chiefly interested in the King's accident – it appears an order had been given that a horse was to be provided that was safe and quiet, irrespective of appearance. Two horses of this description were sent by the Cavalry, but a certain General did not like their appearance and said that his own horse was quite reliable, and gave it for the King to ride. The King congratulated the Colonel on the turn out of the men, and rode up to shake hands with him. The Colonel, perhaps a little excited with the greeting, as the King turned round to get into position to receive the cheers of the men, called out there and then "Three cheers for the King". The clamour of all their shouting immediately behind it frightened the horse out of its wits. It reared up and

---

533 Major-General Rt. Rev. **John Morrow Simms**, DD, CB, CMG, (b.1854 – d.1934). Born in Newtownards, Simms studied at the Old Academy, Belfast, the Coleraine Academical Institution, and Queens University. In 1882, he was ordained as a Church of Ireland clergyman, becoming a Regular Army Chaplain in 1887, serving in the Sudan, Somaliland and South Africa. From 1914 to 1920, he was Principal Chaplain to the Forces, and held the rank of Major-General, though he was outranked, much to his displeasure by the appointment of Bishop Gwynne as DCG in July 1916. He subsequently became Honorary Chaplain to King George V. He was elected for the Ulster Unionist Party at the North Down by-election, July 1922, and when the seat was abolished later in the year, won a seat in Down, serving until 1931.

fell backwards onto the King. Both rider and horse lay there for a few moments motionless, and until they ran forward to lift him, the onlookers did not know whether the King was alive or dead. His thighs might have been broken and he still has to be very careful and it will be sometime yet before he can do anything active[534].

Saturday, January 15th 1916, Hazebrouck

I had my coat loosely over my shoulder this evening when going to visit the Officers' Hospital. An orderly ran up after me into the Ward with attentions who I did not at first recognise, and he also was set back because, as he was proceeding to divest me of my coat he said, "oh! I thought you were an officer coming to us with a broken arm". It was once again Lance-Corporal the Earl of Crawford! He has just returned from leave, from seeing his seventh new baby, a daughter, who was born just before Christmas[535].

Sunday January 16th 1916, Hazebrouck

No one came to an early service in the Forge, nor to another at 11 o'clock. It takes time to get known, and in a Clearing Station the men are always changing. However, there was a large and devout service at the Mairie this morning.

Monday January 17th 1916, Hazebrouck

It has been a busy day again here. Visiting serious cases – a motor-cyclist unconscious from an accident, a corporal with an internal complaint, and the little lad with the leg, just getting on, no more than that. Then a long talk with Tuckey as to arrangements to be made during his absence, and after lunch a ride out with him and a nice talk. A drizzling rain soon cleared up – heavy bombarding over the hills. A hostile aeroplane came over the again this morning, but dropped nothing.

Wednesday January 19th 1916, Hazebrouck

I had a nice ride this afternoon with the Remount Colonel, by name Palmer. We rode across country, and instead of getting a nice canter for the horses, found the pasture land flooded up to the horses' knees. However, it was a beautiful afternoon and the ride was a refreshing one. The Colonel paraded about a dozen chargers, choosing one for a General and two others for his staff, and they were some fine mounts.

Thursday January 20th 1916, Hazebrouck

The little dog in this billet is called 'Quatre-roues' because when he was a fat little puppy he used to paddle along on his four round little paws as if they were four

---

534 October 27th 1915. The horse from which the King fell was General Haig's.
535 Seventh child and fifth daughter of Lord Crawford, Lady Barbara Lindsay was born on 31st December 1915. She died on 20 July 2001 at age 85.

wheels! The day has been a beautiful one and a good help on with the winter. Not much to chronicle besides the usual visiting – an ugly septic hand and a man shot through the eye. Early service at 7.30, arranging Club matters and censoring.

Friday January 21st 1916, Hazebrouck

An interesting link with the Missions to Seamen this evening – one of our doctors, a nice one, was on the 'Port Jackson' training vessel which went round the world via Sydney, and the Chaplain of which came down to Rochester to see whether he should take over the Nore Assistant Chaplaincy – they were 11 months without touching land![536]

A long morning taking over details from Tuckey, who goes on leave on Sunday night, and also a busy evening setting going the arrangements for a concert for the patients on Wednesday. We have found a Sergeant who has a Pathescope Cinema big enough to show quite large pictures – that will be a great diversion as their lives are really very dreary sometimes.

Saturday January 22nd 1916, Hazebrouck

At the club there was a soldier from the Division that relieved my Division. They have moved suddenly and he is stranded here for the night. He has been one of the caretakers of a Club that followed on one of mine 'up the line'. They do remember after all these months "I remember you, Sir, wasn't it you that said your wife's grandfather was in the Rifle Brigade?"

It is a clear moonlight, almost like day. The guns have been booming over the hill – perhaps that is why that Division moved so quickly – but now all is quite still, except for a large number of cockerels who are crowing away lustily, perhaps they think it is early morning.

Sunday January 23rd 1916, Hazebrouck

A beautiful day, sharp and cold. A very nice ward service and then H.C. in the Blacksmiths' forge with only 3 present. The town is busy with troops – how splendidly these good fellows bear themselves on the way up into – one does not know what. This evening we had a very nice and hearty ward service.

---

536 The **Port Jackson**: Designed by Alexander Duthie. Under 1st commander Capt. Crombie some fast passages – notably 39 days Sydney-San Francisco; best run in 24 hrs. 345 miles; 77 days Channel-Sydney 1882. 1907 bought by Devitt and Moore as a cadet training ship, under a partnership with Thomas Brassey, 1st Earl Brassey GCB, TD, JP, DL, (1836 – 1918) a British Liberal Party politician, Governor of Victoria and founder of *The Naval Annual*. During WW1 reverted to cargo carrying. On April 28th 1917 (under ownership of Swift S.S. Co.) was torpedoed and sunk by German submarine 180 miles west by north of Fasnet. Captain and 13 of crew killed.

Booming guns all day – a friendly aeroplane circled above us in the mid-day sunshine scouting and it gives you a sense of assurance. A Chaplain, standing outside his billet in a neighbouring village, had an aeroplane bomb dropped near him, and was so badly injured in the leg that it is feared an amputation may be necessary.

Monday January 24th 1916, Hazebrouck

I don't think I like office work much! A good deal of this morning was taken up by it, interesting enough but not inspiring, so not much time for visiting today. The little lad with the putrifying foot had to have the leg cut off today and it is a question now if he will live. Dear lad, it might be better if he went, he has suffered intensely.

I played this evening at a billet on a harmonium that has been rescued from a shelled house in […*censored*…] I played the chant of intercession that was sung in the Church of the Madeleine in Paris during the war of 1870.

A kind parcel from someone today containing two mufflers, and a book of Raemakers' Cartoons[537]. They are dreadfully realistic and too terribly true. They make one feel what a revolting horror one is dealing with in subduing Germanism. They will live an abiding indictment against the Kaiser.

Tuesday January 25th 1916, Hazebrouck

There is nothing much to chronicle today outside the many talks and interviews. I had the Communion Service all to myself this morning of the commemoration of the Conversion of St. Paul – what an event in history that conversion has proved.

I see the seaplanes have been busy in the east of Kent, and I wonder if it was down Sheerness way – as so often, it is the women and children who have suffered.

I am rather extra busy arranging for a concert for the patients tomorrow night. An N.C.O. (who is in the 'professional' line) has an amateur Cinematography machine and will show some films tomorrow, army and navy pictures, and one or two of the renowned Charlie Chaplin.

---

537 **Louis Raemaekers** (b.1869– d.1956) was a Dutch painter and cartoonist for the Amsterdam Telegraaf during WW1, noted for his anti-German stance. He was born in Roermond in 1869, the son of an ethnically German newspaper editor. His graphic cartoons depicted the rule of the German military in Belgium, portrayed the Germans as barbarians and Kaiser Wilhelm II as an ally of Satan. The German government forced the Dutch government to place Raemaekers on trial for 'endangering Dutch neutrality', but he was acquitted. He later left for England because of the bounty on his head. There, his work was published in *The Times* and he released a collection, *Raemaekers Cartoon History of the War*, in 1919.

Wednesday January 26th 1916, Hazebrouck

We had quite a successful concert tonight, the items clean and safe all through. Everybody was very pleased, so it was worth all the trouble and the Wesleyan Chaplain has been a 'brick' over it, not minding what he did.

A full morning with the office work and visiting the the serious illnesses. Then in the afternoon I had the Senior Chaplain's car to run over to [*…censored…*] a town up there, to see Griffiths, my namesake, who used to be Vicar of Warnambool, and Principal of St. Aidan's College in the diocese of Ballarat, and Chaplain to the Bishop of Ballarat, etc.[538] He was ill in bed with bronchitis and overwork, so we chatted, and then partook of a sick officer's afternoon tea which was rather nice, thank you, including buttered toast and cake! Then on to a neighbouring town, to a service in the Recreation Room, there with 15 present and a very earnest time of prayer and praise. I spoke of St. Paul's conversion and the difference it makes to live when, as it were, the scales fall away from the eyes, and we see GOD in His perfect and Everlasting Love. Then back to the concert, which was really good fun, with some nice sincere songs in between – give the men good things and they will rise to them. The Colonel insisted on my proposing the vote of thanks at the end.

Thursday January 27th 1916, Hazebrouck

There is much to do and time passes very quickly. This morning we had an early service at 7.30, and the Chaplain's talk at 10, which proved to be a long and earnest one, then office work and visiting, preparations for another concert, more visiting, and business with various people about the club and hospital.

Friday January 28th 1916, Hazebrouck

"Schlaf goot" my genial host has just said – he generally gets it that way, sometimes "Schleep goot" and now and again he remembers and says "Schleep well", but the times he succeeds come barely above those when he doesn't. Madam laughs and we all laugh all round, and he says "Schaf well", and so it ends! He has been busy all day in getting together a string orchestra to give our men some music next Wednesday evening.

I have just come from a long friendly chat with an officer, who was very glad of a talk as he is in an isolation ward and time hangs dully upon their hands – I make it a practice to go in each evening.

A very full day, arranging for Sunday, taking the Club, following up the concert and the like. I rode out in the middle of the afternoon for a breath of air and it was very

---

538 **Warrnambool** is a regional centre and former port city on the south-western coast of Victoria. Situated on the Princes Highway, Warrnambool marks the western end of the Great Ocean Road and the southern end of the Hopkins Highway. **Ballarat** is a city located on the Yarrowee River and lower western plains of the Great Dividing Range in Victoria, approximately 65 miles west-north-west of the state capital, Melbourne.

pleasant. The snowdrops are peeping, a fat red hare started up and flew across a green field and the sky was far off pale blue, behind faint grey and pink clouds. An aeroplane – our own – buzzed dreamily aloft and there were no guns to be heard. It was a rest to get away from the stuffiness and strain of the Clearing Station.

Saturday January 29th 1916, Hazebrouck

Things are really very busy here just now. A corporal in difficulties about a piano took up a slice of the afternoon, which I could not help grudging, but we succeeded in our quest and they were intensely relieved, so it was all to the good.

Sunday January 30th 1916, Hazebrouck

This evening crowds went off to a concert, which made no pretence of being 'sacred' but it has been a nice day although cold, foggy and clammy. Two others present at 7.15 for a service in the blacksmith's forge, and at 10 a very hearty service with about 60 motor and supply men, involving a long motor-car drive. Then at 11 there was an interesting and well attended service in an old concert hall, with the General[539] and a good many of the Headquarters' Staff of the 2nd Army present. These, with the long motor ride, took up the whole morning till late lunch and then afterwards a pause, and then preparation for the evening service, and the usual slice of censoring immediately after tea. The service was not largely attended, which was just as well for the lantern worked poorly and would not rise to a full light. The pictures were however beautiful and I hope conveyed the message, helping to bring home the wondrous fact that God came into the world in the likeness of human flesh, and spoke our own language, and lived our life and told us who we are, and whence we came and whither we are wending – and so another day has passed.

Monday January 31st 1916, Hazebrouck

I am 'on duty' in Tuckey's office, awaiting telephone messages, or passers through needing consultation. Today again a day of odds and ends, and pulling together details of our concert for Wednesday. I believe that Kennerley Rumford is coming again, about Saturday week and I find that he was at the King's School, Canterbury.

Tuesday February 1st 1916, Hazebrouck

The Concert seems to be going ahead well and I think we shall have a good programme, but it does mean a lot of work! It cheers people on however.

---

539 General **Hubert Plumer**.

Wednesday February 2nd 1916, Hazebrouck

It has been a very successful concert, but none but the promoter knows how tiring! Especially when 3 of the performers in the early part of the programme did not arrive, and there had to be a pause and an explanation for a short minute or so (which really felt like a quarter of an hour!). However, we did patch it up, and no hitch was perceptible except to the perspiring promoter. So many people behind the scenes also all fly to the Master of the Ceremonies with enquires. The comic man "where can I paint my face?" "Can you get a walking stick from one of the audience?" The clarinet soloist has forgotten his music! "Will you put his piece at the end of the first half and let the violin and 'cello come next to the comic man instead of before?" "The piccolo man can play a nice solo – would you like him to come in the second half instead of the piano?" and so on! The pianist was a <u>great</u> success, making the instrument really swirl with life and the men liked him greatly. The French orchestra also, gave us really good music. We have in the unit a professional clown, who really was very droll, for example, he started to play 'Tipperary' on his mandolin when a (pretence) blue-bottle came in with a buzz. He chased it all round the platform and eventually knocked it off the end of his own nose, but knocked himself head-over-heels with the blow! We had the 4 national anthems at the end which were all very well played.

Some sad cases of illness in the hospital and two German prisoners very glad to be caught, both only slightly wounded.

Thursday February 4th 1916, Hazebrouck

It has been a beautiful day, toning people up after the damp fog of Sunday and Monday. At 7.30 a.m we had the Chaplains' Holy Communion and at 10.am our weekly talk, with plans and thoughts for better work. The denominational question is a complicating one in a Clearing Station where you have two non-conformists whose imagination does not travel much outside the building in which they live, though they are supposed to be here for the non-conformist needs of the whole town. The concert, however, was greatly appreciated. I have managed to get the piano that I left in the Field Ambulance (now I understand seldom, if ever, used) and it has been installed this evening in the Club, already with cheering results. The Club is improving steadily and at times is quite over-crowded – a great advance! Much of the day seems to be 'small talk', but it is 'diffused Christianity' in various ways we hope.

Friday February 5th 1916, Hazebrouck

We have had an exciting day here with more hostile aeroplanes 'circling in the vaulted blue', and they came very near this end of our town. Our anti-aircraft firing was a little wide, but I think it warned them off, and after giving us an interesting hour or so of sky-gazing, they sailed on, pursued by our aircraft. At the next town, they dropped four bombs, wounding and killing some and also at another town above us I hear they dropped some – it was obliging of them to leave us alone. They flew a little lower today, which suggests their being more on reconnaissance work.

I had a chat with the wounded German prisoner. He was quite friendly and glad to talk, and agreed that we were all friends at heart! He said "Why should I shoot you, or why should you shoot me?" He is a fresh-looking well built young man, in excellent condition. He says the Kaiser is well and as busy as ever and they expect to be in Paris in three months' time – will they? A hostile aeroplane came over again yesterday – merely peeping.

A beautiful day and a most refreshing ride with Tuckey. I went to change the horse, the other one being too big, and the new one now seems suitable in every way. I was sorry to let the other one go, but it was really very awkward when visiting around getting on and off and in that way was rather like the wooden Horse of Troy.

Saturday February 6th 1916, Hazebrouck

Five present at the early service in the blacksmith's forge and a short service at the Mairie after. I found a long one in vogue when I came here and have aimed at shortening it, and though one shrinks from people grudging time to God when it is patently obvious that a number give him so little or none at all – but people cannot keep fresh for a long time together. At 11.30 a very real time with some sick officers, with 16 in the ward. I met an old friend from the very nice battalion with which I spent my first night in the trenches, and it is wonderful how the sterling worth of two or three good senior officers has pervaded the whole regiment – what a thing to be thankful for. Then a long spell of censoring letters, and a well attended service this evening in the large ward. I was rather amused, when trying to illustrate asking for 'right things' in our prayers (speaking of the 2nd lesson for this morning "All things, whatsoever ye shall ask in prayer, believing, ye shall receive[540]"), I said, having described how God came to Solomon after his evening service at Gibeon, "Supposing before you go to bed tonight, after this evenings' service, that offer was made to you – Ask what I shall give thee[541] – what would you say?" "Blighty, Sir" cried one of the men. There was no doubt about having held his attention! 'Blighty', as perhaps you know, is the word they have for being invalided home to England. It is derived, I believe, from a Hindi word 'Belati' (I cannot give the spelling) as Indian soldiers speak about going to England as going to Belati, and Tommy has adopted the term, with his own way of rendering it! [542] Another man quite as spontaneously answered 'Peace' and both replies got to the point I had in mind, that if we want the war to end, we must pray

---

540 **Matthew 21:22** 'And all things, whatsoever ye shall ask in prayer, believing, ye shall receive.'
541 **2 Chronicles 1:7** 'In that night did God appear unto Solomon, and said unto him, Ask what I shall give thee?'
542 OED "Blighty" derives from "bilayati", a regional variant of the Urdu word "vilayati", meaning "foreign", "British", "English" or "European". In India, *vilayati* came to be known as an adjective meaning European, and specifically English or British.

for it – "Ye have not because ye ask not[543]". In the absence of our prayers, can we be surprised if the war does not end?" and if God seems to be afar off from it all? Also, it is possible that God may be saying "I cannot let you have victory yet because I do not know how you will use it" – is our wish for 'blighty' and 'peace' only in order that we may go back to having a roaring good time leaving God out of it all just as much as before? One man stayed behind and talking very earnestly and nicely.

The orderly who looked after the German prisoner said the prisoner had said in the opinion of many of his comrades, the war would be over in four or five months, Germany being allowed to retain possession of the lands she had occupied (with little change) and England retaining command of the sea.

Sunday February 7th 1916, Hazebrouck

I am afraid it is true that that beautiful cruel thing circling above us in the blue on Saturday morning among the little white puffs, did go on and killed three people in the next town, even while we were looking at it – and the daily tale goes on. I wonder what America will do as the sinking of the 'Lusitania' must be acknowledged to be illegal. That seems to be President Wilson's firm demand and it will be a hard task for Germany to 'come to', and if she cannot, what then?

I have lived most of today among slides, sorting out and getting ready for one of two talks, all this apart from visiting and talking with the soldiers. One man has been sent here after three days with a wound in the head by shrapnel, and had not been made a 'lying down' case until he was examined here, and they found that the skull has been broken and a little piece driven in – he must have a hard head. A delightful ride with Tuckey this afternoon and the new horse is the right one at last I think!

Monday February 8th 1916, Hazebrouck

The lecture passed off very well – I called it "How we won the last War" and showed the South African slides. The men spoke very warmly and I think that they enjoyed it and in fact they said so, so it was worth the trouble. The next thing is the Kennerly Rumford concert, the arrangements for which are out of my hands, and so the winter is creeping on.

Tuesday February 9th 1916, Hazebrouck

Another Taube this morning but no bombs here[544]. An inhabitant remarked yesterday

---

543 James 4:3 'Ye ask, and receive not, because ye ask amiss, that ye may consume *it* upon your lusts.'
544 The **Etrich** *Taube* (Dove) also known by the names of the various later manufacturers who build versions of the type, such as the **Rumpler** *Taube*, was a pre-World War I monoplane aircraft. It was the first military aeroplane to be mass-produced in Germany. As Imperial Germany's first practical military aircraft, the *Taube* ("dove") was used for virtually all military aircraft applications, as a fighter, bomber, surveillance aircraft and trainer from 1910 until the start of WW1. It was so common that even after it had been withdrawn from service Taube became a generic term for German aircraft.

"In [...*censored*...] if it isn't raining the wind is blowing, and if the wind is not blowing, they are dropping bombs!"

A ride over to [...*censored*...] in the car with Tuckey, and there we inspected an Institute and a new Church Army hut which is altogether in the rough[545]. The former was crowded and the latter is nice and roomy, and ought to prove a very serviceable place. A hostile aeroplane circled over the outskirts of the place, and was vigorously bombarded – the one this morning circled round above us like an annoying gnat, but attempted no harm.

We had a nice evening service in the Soldiers' Recreation Room at that place, with the attendance being very large. The service and the address fell to me, and it was quite a real time I thought. We then visited the Headquarters Signalling Room of the Army, a wonderful place with an amazing network of wires and instruments of all kinds and descriptions.[546] We hope that the Signallers' minstrel troupe will come and give an entertainment to our patients, as it would do a lot of good I think.

Wednesday February 10th 1916, Hazebrouck

We went to plan some services and we found that for some Sundays lately, the services had been held by a Lance Corporal from a neighbouring Field Ambulance, a Mr Stainsby from near Durham. He has been in Holy Orders four years or so, and is a B.A. of Leeds and had his theological training at Mirfield[547].

We passed under a flight of our aeroplanes, six in all, returning home like rooks to roost. They flew in pairs, and looked very picturesque against the pale pink clouds – we must have an immense number of aircraft by now. It appears one of the enemy aircraft that we saw yesterday morning did drop two bombs at neighbouring village but they fell harmlessly in fields near the railway crossing, one bomb exploded and the other did not.

The German exchange still goes down and it appears clear that they have made liberal overtures to Belgium – "Nearly the whole country has come to the conclusion that its enemies, especially Great Britain, cannot be crushed" so says Dr Koht, the Norwegian Professor of Political History, after a long stay in Germany[548].

---

545 From March 1916, General Haig's GHQ was located in Montreuil-sur-Mer, 50 miles SW of Hazebrouck. The move from the original site at St Omer took place in the early months of 1916.

546 The C16th **Citadelle** (citadel) at Montreuil held the communications hub for GHQ and the BEF, in the subterranean C19th casements. A Scottish Churches Hut stood at the entrance, where services were held on Sundays and soldiers could relax at other times when off duty. This was, presumably, where RDG held his service.

547 **George William Stainsby** (b.1887 – d.1951), from Linthorpe, Middlesborough. Theological student at the College of the Resurrection, Mirfield, Dewsbury, Yorks. George enlisted at Jarrow, Co. Durham in April 1915 in the RAMC. His occupation was clerk in Holy Orders. George belonged to the 65th, Field Ambulance and acted as a stretcher bearer. He joined the British Expeditionary Force from September 1915 to March 1916. On the 14th March 1916, he was appointed to a commission as Chaplain to the Forces.

548 **Halvdan Koht** (b.1873 – d.1965) was a Norwegian historian and politician representing the

Thursday February 11th 1916, Hazebrouck

When I was going home on leave at a certain station between here and the base at about midnight, a French soldier, very much the worse for drink, got up into the carriage and wanted to find a seat among the 1st class passengers. It fell to me with my knowledge of his language, to guide his wanderings into a more appropriate and less agitated location! This evening, in the long row of beds of sick officers, was an officer who had been in the carriage that night. I did not recognise him, but he did me – so you can never tell!

It has been a sleety day here with the downpour almost incessant, so a relief from aeroplanes therefore, and a day for indoor work. I have been handing on the contents of the Stonehouse parcel and others – the games and puzzles especially have been most acceptable. Also, the cartoon in 'Punch' showing the German mark as a patient sick in bed with the German Chancellor the doctor and the Kaiser looking on depressed and miserable, with the temperature chart behind going steadily down and the title 'Sinking'. A good cartoon, and one rather congruous to hospital patients, who displayed a strange levity over a decline so serious[549].

Friday February 12th 1916, Hazebrouck

More aeroplanes! I rode out in the afternoon for a constitutional and to see some soldiers from Cambridgeshire, in beautiful sunlight. As I passed a cottage by the roadside – bang! bang! I thought some of our big guns were rather near. The woman of the cottage came rushing to the door holding a little one-year-old. She said "Bombs! Allemands!" I said "No, I thought it was English cannon". "No", she said, then listened and looked up. Two ploughmen also stopped and looked up. A group of people came to the farm door and looked up. Far, far away on the edge of white cloud, that little brown waspish thing buzzed and fussed on – it circled round our heads and it was unmistakeably a German, and I held my horse at a standstill on the road, wondering what might happen next. Then it shot on its course in a straight line back over the town. I rode on about half a mile to the edge of the hill and there saw great excitement. Half a dozen farm labourers, and some women and children were gathered round a large new hole in the cart track across the field. Fresh turned sods of earth lay scattered around and there was also the Wesleyan Chaplain, who had been only 150 yds off when the thing fell, but there was no harm to anyone and the nearest cottage was 100 yds

---

Labour Party.
He represented that party in the Bærum municipal council for parts of the interwar period. He was never elected a member of Parliament, but served nonetheless as Norwegian Minister of Foreign Affairs from 1935 to 1941. As an academic he was a professor of history at the Royal Frederick University from 1910 to 1935, having become a research fellow in 1900 and docent in 1908. He was a prolific writer, and touched on numerous subjects during his long academic career. He became known for syntheses on Norwegian history, and emphasised the roles of peasants and wage laborers as historical agents who found their place in an expanding notion of the Norwegian nation.

549 Punch, 2nd February, 1916. *Sinking* by cartoonist **Leonard Raven-Hill** (b.1867 – d.1942).

away. We wonder if the object aimed at was the farm, or whether it was a long shot at the town, making too much allowance for the swing – a haphazard business at best, with a good chance of getting some poor innocent peasant woman, or one or two of her children. I picked up one or two fragments of the missile for a souvenir, though they do not appeal to me much. What I think is a nice souvenir is a root of snowdrops that an officer told me he had got from a smashed-up town last week, which he had posted home. If it lives, it will be interesting in days to come.

The Kennerly Rumford concert this evening was almost an exact repetition of the previous one and he left early as it is Saturday night.

Sunday February 13th 1916, Hazebrouck

Two very encouraging Ward services as the men have now got into the way of taking part heartily and readily, and they find the aim is to help. Three at H.C. in the blacksmiths' forge at 11.30 and this evening a fairly large service in the Maire, where everything went with a good swing. I quoted Admiral Beatty's letter, putting it all very forcibly – "Until there is a religious revival at home, just so long will the war continue. When England looks out to the future with a humbler eye and a prayer upon its lips, then we may begin to count the days towards the end[550]".

Monday February 14th 1916, Hazebrouck

Monday is always an odds and ends day, and also there has been the business of fixing up another concert for the patients, for which we shall get some amateur cinema pictures I hope, and an amateur minstrel troupe.

Tuesday February 15th 1916, Hazebrouck

At the mess this evening, we got round to the topic of eugenics[551] and the population of Great Britain after the War – will it mean that America will become the most virile people? And if so, what mission will America carry on into the future? In the absence of a coherent religious system (America's religion is a collection of ideas without any unifying organisation) will its mission be mainly that of the 'Almighty dollar', this worldliness?

Wednesday February 16th 1916, Hazebrouck

A wild windy day and I have just been talking to another wounded German prisoner who has just been brought in, and who is very homesick and <u>very</u> appreciative of

---

550 Admiral Sir **David Richard Beatty** (b.1871 – d.1936), letter to The Society for the Promotion of Christian Knowledge, January 28th, 1916.

551 Sir **Francis Galton**, term coined in 1883, *Inquiries into Human Faculty and Its Development*, a book in which he meant "to touch on various topics more or less connected with that of the cultivation of race, or, as we might call it, with 'eugenic' questions."

the kindness he has received in hospital. I fear though, from his tone now and then, that he is one of the 'hating' sort, a product of the national mind for which a few no doubt, and not least the Kaiser, are responsible.

Thursday February 17th 1916, Hazebrouck

The German prisoner is interesting to talk with. He is in a bank and had been at the University of Gottingen and speaks English pretty well. The October after war broke out he was to have gone to a bank in London and thence to one in Manchester. He has attained to the rank of Sergeant Major during the War and has earned the Iron Cross. His capture came about through his having been out on patrol where the party was heard and a hand grenade was thrown at them. He was injured and his companions left him and got away. Dazed by the blow, he wandered into what he thought were the German trenches, but which proved to be those of the English. He is not a strong looking man, and if his hair were not shorn so inordinately close, might look refined. He has been on this front the whole of the war, not having gone twenty miles one way or another from the point at which he was taken. He has a father and mother living in Hanover, his father being what the man called a 'statesman'. I suggested 'Member of Parliament' and he said "Yes". He has one brother who is 19 and has been many months on the Russian front. He would not enter into the question of how or when the War would end, but he will be very glad when it does. The old jocular spirit of assurance that we saw in some of the prisoners after Neuve Chapelle is wanting in these men. No milk, I see, in Germany except for children under 6 and the use of cream is forbidden.

One of our doctors finishes his years' engagement next month, and goes back to Australia – Adelaide The concert has gone off very well indeed and everyone was pleased so it has been worth all the trouble. It is late and there have been many people to talk to, so more tomorrow............

Friday February 18th 1916, Hazebrouck

........to continue yesterday. The morning was busy with arrangements for the concert, after the H.C. at 7.30 with 5 present, and visiting the serious cases. Then the Chaplains' meeting at 10 and a talk with the German prisoner. After lunch Canon Adderley[552] called (from the Cathedral, Limerick) and remained all the afternoon and eventually the evening. Two other officers also came and kept us occupied – one was in the attack upon our trenches that the papers have told you about and my nephew George is in the same regiment. They had a very trying time of it with a bombardment against them lasting over four and a half hours. Then the band of the Coldstream Guards appeared in the market place – they do play very nicely. I captured the Director of the band and got our Clearing Station before his attention

---

552 Rev. **Joseph Adderley,** canon of St Mary's Cathedral, Limerick.

for a visit. The concert proved a great success and the nigger troupe were amusing and some of the items were tastefully given. The conductor of the minstrel troupe found that Canon Adderley had christened his daughter the month before war broke out!

I had been in between my blankets about half an hour when, half asleep, I thought "someone is banging that front door rather much – it must be something urgent" – it was not. Only a bomb in the next garden to this and fortunately this is a long garden – then came another bang, then another –and then the unmistakeable hiss and crash. It was a matter to be looked into – clear moon-light and very still. Then, as I looked out of the window, there was another hiss and crash and a flare over the houses in front. The anti-aircraft gun began popping and then I knew it was either aeroplanes or zeppelins. I went down into the street, where mine host was also in an overcoat and dishabille, and many heads popped out of windows with various partly dressed people at doors and on the pavement. There were no more bangs but a slight air humming in the distance – aeroplanes! I find this morning that 8 or perhaps 9 men have been hit, 2 seriously, as a bomb dropped on their billet. No one else injured and no civilians hurt. One bomb dropped on the edge of the pavement near the church, smashing dozens of window panes. It is like being under shell-fire closer up to the trenches, and the number of bombs that fell is variously stated as from 6 to 14.

The Coldstream Guards band came into our Clearing Station tonight and gave us a great treat. Captain J.M. Rogan Mus.Doc. M.V.O.[553], the Director is a great enthusiast, and very agreeable company. This is his 50th year in the Army and he will be 65 next year – the music was really very good. The performers number 35 and there were some humorous pieces which delighted the men, one a play upon 'Tipperary' with the bassoon taking odd variations in a way that tickled everybody. There was also a descriptive piece giving a motor ride – the whistling birds of early morning, the clock striking 7, the start, the happy ride, a collision – bang! the mending of the tyre, and moving on again. Then a grand potpourri arranged by the Director "You'll remember me" catches and refrains of a great number of airs all very well grouped – e.g. when it came to the Grandfather's clock which "stopped short, never to go again", the music did stop short – and went off elsewhere! A good programme and nicely thought out.

A ride out with Tuckey, shortened by drenching rain, and another call from Canon Adderely.

---

553 Lieut-Colonel **John MacKenzie-Rogan** (b.1885 – d.1932), Coldstream Guards. 'Britain's Greatest Bandmaster.' For 20 years he was the senior director of music of the Brigade of Guards, responsible for the massed bands of the Brigade at the funeral of Queen Victoria, the coronation and funeral of King Edward VII and the coronation of King George V. Under his direction, the Band achieved several notable "firsts". In 1896, a Coldstream officer heard Tschaikovsky's 1812 Overture in St Petersburg, and brought back a copy of the score. Mackenzie Rogan played it at concerts throughout the country and brought it to the attention of Henry Wood. The Band was the first British Army band to visit one of the Dominions, touring Canada in 1896, and in 1907 they were the first Guards Band to visit France at the invitation of the French Government. He retired in 1920.

Saturday February 19th 1916, Hazebrouck

Thursday night's bombing is gradually accounting for itself – twelve bombs in all can be traced, two were incendiary, but did not come off. I went to look at the next door garden which belongs to a market gardener who has been a prisoner for 14 months. His wife had only left about 10 minutes ago from renewing the fire in the glasshouse, and it is marvellous how little damage there was considering.

You will like to know that my bed is in a recess in the bedroom – an old-fashioned arrangement – and above it is a little square turret chamber, all to the good when things are falling from the skies. It is a clear, still, moonlight night again tonight. It has been a busy day, getting ready for Sunday, and there are many little things to think of.

Sunday February 20th 1916, Hazebrouck

There were two bombs last night, rather wide fortunately. We have been warned about giving too much information about air raids, so you will understand if the references are limited. One appeared in the distance this afternoon but it was well scouted and I think we shall not have much more trouble with them tonight.

I think today has been encouraging – we had a service in the Blacksmith's Forge at 7.15 with 3 men present, then two very nice Ward services at 9.30 and 9.50, then a Communion Service in the Officers' hospital at 11.30 with 8 present. The Coldstreams' played in the Market place at 12 and at 4 o'clock. We had a nice Ward service at 6 and a large number stayed behind for Gospels afterwards.

Monday February 21st 1916, Hazebrouck

Rather nice weather and too nice for the aeroplanes! 4 bombs in the night. I had been asleep about an hour when there was the ominous boom and concussion. This time they fell in the suburbs, mercifully without damage to humans, and then this afternoon as we finished our frugal lunch, we were conscious of a commotion outside to find four fine aeroplanes circling busily right over our heads. Our anti-aircraft soon got among them for they flew very low, but I think did nothing to them. They dropped three bombs and one, if you please, within 120 yds of my billet, and the other about 100 yds! The one in the next door garden the other night I find measured only about 60 yds away, so that has a touch of excitement about it! I have just been to see where the 120 yd one fell, and it had dropped into a kitchen where four of our men and the French Dame were having their mid-day meal – it didn't explode! It was flaming, and one of the men dashed some water over it before it had time to do anything else. Why it did not drop on the dinner table instead of just behind the door, the Great Heart of Love and Wisdom to which every life is perfectly present in minutest detail, knows. Another dropped on the railway line 300 yds away and it too did not explode. Later some French soldiers set it off, and it made a terrific concussion, which made many think that there was something further afield! By all of this you will gather the enemy aircraft are fairly busy just now. We have one officer in today who has been stuck by a fragment in the street. Steadily, all the same, the enemy is being worn down – Erzrurm[554], the Blockade, their exchange, supplies and their heavy losses of men, are telling.

Tuesday February 22nd 1916, Hazebrouck
A clouded night with no bombs and the morning broke with a snowstorm and at 9.30 the snow, after intervals, is falling again. It must be trying work in the trenches, only happily things must be better provided for than they were last year.

I went for a spin on the horse this morning, really to show to the Remount Colonel a trick that it has. Curiously the trick did not happen, though the horse slipped on the sleety turf and came down with the Colonel – 'plop'. I rode his horse, an Australian, which has plenty of 'go' in it, but rather tired my arm by so much pulling – it is not easy to get a good mount now-a-days.

Wednesday February 23rd 1916, Hazebrouck
More bombs fell last night, all harmless but noisy and that in spite of a clouded moon. Everybody here talks 'bombs' now-a-days, but for my part, I try to forget them. The moon was hazy, but it got clearer by 11.30p.m. then came one boom and another and the anti-aircraft cannon made plenty of noise. Four in all are said to have fallen, but that number has not been verified.

The concert went off very well I thought and the applause showed much appreciation. It passed an evening away, and helped some to forget they were sick, and others to forget many things. One of the men recited the 'Green-eyed God' rather well[555] and there was a good duet between a cornet and a trombone.

Thursday February 24th 1916, Hazebrouck
St. Matthias' Day.
Holy Communion at 7.30 at which three other Chaplains, a nurse and a soldier were present. The Chaplains' meeting was briefer than usual, yet good business was done. Then visiting and talking with various people, but it has been bitingly cold. A nice evening at the Club – one of the men could play very well and we used Mabel's song books and had a very successful 'sing-song'. One man sang 'Until we meet again' and 'The Trumpeter', another 'We'll keep the home fires burning', another 'The Old Folks

---

554 The **Erzurum Offensive** (10th January 1916 – 16th February 1916) was a major winter offensive by the Imperial Russian Army on the Caucasus Campaign that led to the capture of the strategic city of Erzurum, Armenia. Turkish Ottoman forces, in winter quarters, suffered a series of unexpected reverses that led to a decisive Russian victory.
555 *The Green Eye of the Little Yellow God* is a 1911 poem by J. Milton Hayes that is a famous example of the genre of "dramatic monologue", which was a music hall staple in the early twentieth century.

at Home' and I sang 'Every morn I bring thee Violets' and 'Drink to me only with thine eyes' and also 'Will ye no come back again?[556]' At the end we had our Evening Prayers and I hope the men were glad of them – I think they were. No bombs last night, so we had a clear night's rest – a great thing.

It was great the French getting L77 – it is said that means the 24th zeppelin lost – a costly business compared to the execution done[557]. I wonder if the German navy is really 'bottled up', or if they are preparing some wonderful floating craft with which to make a great and determined sea effort. They are daily becoming weaker, commercially, financially and morally.

Friday, February 25th 1916, Hazebrouck

Snow is falling fast and it will be bad for the men in the trenches, but how content everyone is here with plenty of snow, no aeroplanes and no bombs! All leave is stopped, on account of rough channel crossing passages perhaps. After visiting and visiting and preparing for the evening lantern talk, I went out for a long walk with Tuckey. The snow blew in our faces across a flat ice-bound Flanders landscape, a ruined windmill peeping at us through a long line of trees and we felt (a little) what it must have been like going to look for the South Pole.

The Peace talk in the House of Commons was interesting and I am glad that Mr Asquith spoke firmly and definitely, as there must be no doubt about Germany having to recognise the conscience of civilisation, but I fear that England must also feels its' chastening also through and through.

Saturday, February 26th 1916, Hazebrouck

This afternoon we buried the lad who died yesterday from the effect of one of the bombs which fell the other night – a victim near to us[558]. But how many cases like it have been multiplied in this mad game of 'blood and iron'![559] However, the enemy have paid an awful price for their policy – over a million Germans killed!

The men liked the sea pictures very much last night – on their own account they started rounds of applause at the end, which is not their way usually, and now we are hoping to have out some pictures of Serbia, Roumania and Gallipoli.

---

556 RDG's sister-in-law, Mabel Saumarez-Smith was a musician and composer. *God be with you till we meet again*, Jeremiah Eames Rankin, 1916. *The Trumpeter*, Music J Arlie Dix, words John Barron, 1904. *Keep the Home-Fires Burning ('Till the Boys Come Home)* Ivor Novello with words by Lena Gilbert Ford, 1914. *Old Folks at Home* (also known as "Swanee River", "Swanee Ribber" or "Suwannee River"), Stephen Foster, 1851. *Drink to Me Only with Thine Eyes*: Ben Jonson 1616. *Will ye no come back again*: **Lady Carolina Nairne.**

557 Zeppelin L77, shot down with an incendiary shell near Brabant-le-Roi, 21st February 1916.

558 Pvte **J W Nicolson**, Middlesex Regiment attd. 182nd Tunnelling Coy. Royal Engineers, died 21st February 1916.

559 ***Blood and Iron*** *(Blut und Eisen)* is the title of a speech by German Chancellor Otto von Bismarck given in 1862 about the unification of the German territories.

Sunday, February 27th 1916, Hazebrouck

The snow has melted a little, and everywhere there is slush. We had a good ward service at 9.15 am and a crowded Parade service at 10 with a great many of the comrades of the man who was killed by the bomb there – and felt it all I am sure. We had a nice time in the Officers Hospital at 3, and one patient slept through it all (I had no hymns), so you will see it was not a violently loud devotion!

Monday, February 28th 1916, Hazebrouck

A dark, rainy day, and yet peaceful in the sense that it is not the weather for hostile aircraft. Heavy fighting is afoot, but one must not repeat either knowledge or rumours – we can know many things after the event[560].

Tuesday, February 29th 1916, Hazebrouck

It has been a very full day and my eyelids are feeling rather a 'close fit' and it would seem wisdom to humour them, the night being dark and stormy and 'unaircrafty'. Clearer nights are not so good for sleeping, wherefore the moral is "sleep while you can".

Each day how many dozens of people does one talk to, and how difficult to record! If one begins one must explain so many details, or not attempt at all. Regarding the fighting – if you ask me things look well and promising. Great guns are booming near us, day and night and I do trust and believe we are accumulating strength with the accumulating days.

Rain this afternoon so no hostile aircraft although one appeared this morning, but it was both scouted and fired at by one of ours, so did not come near.

Wednesday, March 1st 1916, Hazebrouck[561]

A great and memorable day, dear lady, when the earth shone with new colours and the stars took on a more brilliant light! And there is more to come. Thank you for another letter, posted on Sunday. I read of Major Campion's death and the funeral is described in Tuesday's Daily Telegraph[562]. How many gallant lives have been offered up in this mad form of arbitrament?

Yes, Waller's way of scolding about the Holy Communion spoils the blessing of it. In time you begin to feel it is the man's pettishness at not being able to count more noses of attendance than anything deeper. You actually hear young 'purists' comparing

---

560   The German assault on Verdun began on 21st February 1916.
561   RDG's and Margaret's 13th wedding anniversary.
562   Major and Temp. Lieut-Col **Edward Campion** (b.1873 – d.1915), 2nd Bn. (78th Foot) Seaforth Highlanders (Ross-shire Buffs, The Duke of Albany's), youngest son of Col. William Henry Campion, of Danny, Hassocks, Sussex. Eton; gazetted 2nd Lieut. Seaforth Highlanders, served in Crete in 1897; A.D.C to the Major-General, Infantry Brigade, Aldershot, 1900–1901; served in the Nile Expedition 1898; Battles of the Atbara and Khartoum also in the South African War

records – "I always got about 10 more communicants a Sunday when I had charge of the Mission Church than when he had. It used to make him so angry. I laughed." Alas!

Whenever the 'leave' is I am sure this time it will be wisest to get quietude, but I want to see as much of the children as possible. The time becomes due about the end of this month.

No more bombs last night and our aircraft are on the alert scouting. One of ours came over this afternoon and made a wonderful dive and turn as it changed its course going back over the town. My belief is the enemy wants to do hurt by every means and on every spot that they can, and we are easily accessible from their lines.

Thursday March 2nd 1916, Hazebrouck

7.30 am Holy Communion this morning, which I took with just three of the Chaplains there and a matron, and then at 10 the Chaplains' talk. A Taube flew over and was shelled, but attempted no damage.

I changed my horse as the other (my third) proved nervy and vicious – it is not easy to get workable mounts away from the Division now-a-days, which is rather as it should be. I studied up a talk for tomorrow on Turkey, Bulgaria and Serbia, a fairly good set of slides having arrived. Then I watched over the progress of a very good concert got up by a Lieut Pimian. It was really very good indeed, with high class music and good healthy nonsense and one of the very best we have had. It helped some of us to forget our illnesses, some to forget their work, and passed away for all a dull, drizzly winter's evening.

Rather good news today we hear – we have retaken some trenches near here and captured about 200 prisoners.

Friday March 3rd 1916, Hazebrouck

The lantern talk has taken up quite a long time, sorting the slides and thinking out thoughts, but it has been worth it as a dull sleety dark winters' evening went by profitably I hope, in thinking how we shall win the present War, and in studying more particularly the Near East, the characteristics of the lands and people of Turkey, Bulgaria and Serbia. Everything is on so immense a scale. I think the upshot of our studies was "Thank God and take courage and be patient[563]" – but how much there is to think about and pray about and wish about!

(1901–2), chiefly in the Lydenberg district of the Transvaal. Gassed, near Ypres, in May, 1915; he had a relapse during convalescence in England, and died from the effects of the gas poison in London, 25th Feb. 1916. Buried at Hurstpierpoint, Sussex.

563 **Psalm 27:14** 'Wait on the LORD: be of good courage, and he shall strengthen thine heart: wait, I say, on the LORD'.

Saturday March 4th 1916, Hazebrouck

The talk at the evening meal glided into a most wholesome channel – Shakespeare, Scott, Kipling, 'Lorna Doone'[564], Rolf Bolderwood[565], education, mind vacuity, and the danger on active service of mental rot setting in, which was all very salutary. Sleet and rain and dark clouds have been the weather to enjoy with its freedom from aeroplanes, though on the other hand one thinks of the enemy being able to move troops unobserved.

The three accidental cases are all very serious – at a motor machine gun lecture rounds were fired, some of which were not <u>blank</u> cartridge – someone's carelessness! And how maddening to think it need not have been!

A good talk this evening with the Quaker Lieutenant and the Wesleyan Chaplain with the question raised by the former, "Do we deserve to win this War?" When one marks the lack of earnestness for 'right' in many directions, one does feel that it is of God's mercy only if we are allowed to come out on the winning side.

Sunday March 5th 1916, Hazebrouck

Quinquagesima Sunday – always a refreshing day[566]. It makes one think of how much loving kindness and forbearance there must be round about us among the 'blessed company of all faithful people'[567] and one gets courage to go on trying again. Some nice services with 6 present at Holy Communion at 8 am and very hearty Ward services at 9.20, 9.40, and at 11.30 a very prayerful and devotional service in the Officers hospital. A long sitting at censoring, but we have a plan now by which each officer takes a proper share and this much reduces the Chaplains' part. The ward evening service was spoilt by a rush of new patients, brought in by the continued cold and snowy weather, but I took two smaller services in wards where the medical officers were able reasonably to adapt themselves, and the seed was sown. A Ward service takes a lot out of you as all your arrangements have to be made impromptu, and your assembly formed by your own invitation.

---

564 *Lorna Doone: A Romance of Exmoor* is a novel by English author Richard Doddridge Blackmore, published in 1869. It is a romance based on a group of historical characters and set in the late 17th century in Devon and Somerset, particularly around the East Lyn Valley area of Exmoor.

565 **Thomas Alexander Browne** (1826 – 1915) was an Australian author, who sometimes published under the pseudonym **Rolf Boldrewood**. He is best known for his novel *Robbery Under Arms*.

566 The Sunday before Ash Wednesday, 50 days before Easter.

567 Church of England Holy Eucharist, Rite one, concluding prayer – Almighty and everliving God, we most heartily thank thee for that thou dost feed us, in these holy mysteries, with the spiritual food of the most precious Body and Blood of thy Son our Saviour Jesus Christ; and dost assure us thereby of thy favour and goodness towards us; and that we are very members incorporate in the mystical body of thy Son, the blessed company of all faithful people; and are also heirs, through hope, of thy everlasting kingdom. And we humbly beseech thee, O heavenly Father, so to assist us with thy grace, that we may continue in that holy fellowship, and do all such good works as thou hast prepared for us to walk in; through Jesus Christ our Lord, to whom with thee and the Holy Ghost, be all honor and glory, world without end. *Amen.*

Monday March 6th 1916, Hazebrouck

Cold, sleet and snow with warm sunshine in between, so we are very full up with 'weather' patients. A hostile aeroplane at mid-day, but no bombs. Dr. Grenfell, of the Labrador Coast[568], popped into the Clearing Station this afternoon – I did not see him, but the visit did good.

Tuesday March 7th 1916 (Shrove Tuesday), Hazebrouck

A long, ceaseless fall of quiet snow that melts almost before it reaches the ground, and does not do more than tint it a thin white. It is cold to the feet and wetting, but the air on the whole is mild and not unpleasant – and in the midst of it all is being waged one of the most eventful battles in history. I hope that God's praying people are hard at it now. The French about here are taking things seriously and I rather like the Pope's appeal to womankind and those that are left behind to do their utmost in prayer.

Wednesday March 8th 1916 (Ash Wednesday), Hazebrouck

It is very difficult to keep in touch, and to address thoughts, with <u>everybody</u>. One's very nerve force will not pulsate to it. Every man of the 100s' that one looks at and greets, day by day, looks for an intelligent exchange of sympathy, and directly one comes into contact with him, he opens out a whole life of needs and interests and will have you go with him into them. That is one advantage of these collective occasions; one can speak to the many as to each, and they receive the words as to each and reply upon them in subsequent individual conversations. A young man from Cambridge this evening (we have a number of them here just now) from St Barnabus's parish – how pleased he was to talk of the Vicar I knew, and the Curate, and the church in which he had worshipped and I had preached.

I am glad that the Admiral thinks that the allies are doing well in the way of munitions as I think the French will need a great quantity where the pressure is now[569]. What will Turkey do? They will try to dodge onto the safe side once again?[570]

I held a lantern service this evening in the larger ward and it was well attended. I let it be frankly Evangelistic and felt that the response was real and appreciative. One of the soldiers said "Sure to be a blessing?" I feel there must be courage now more and

---

568 Sir **Wilfred Thomason Grenfell**, KCMG (b.1865 – d.1940) was a medical missionary to Newfoundland and Labrador. The Royal National Mission to Deep Sea Fishermen sent Grenfell to Newfoundland in 1892 to improve the plight of coastal inhabitants and fishermen. Although originally founded to serve the local area, the mission developed to include the aboriginal peoples and settlers along the coasts of Labrador.

569 The German attack on the French fort of Verdun about 100 miles SE of Hazebrouck began in early March 1916.

570 The Russian offensive in northeastern Turkey started with a victory at Battle of Koprukoy and culminated with the capture of Erzurum in February and Trabzon in April 1916. By the Battle of Erzincan the Third Army was no longer capable of launching an offensive nor could it stop the advance of the Russian Army in Anatolia.

more for nothing but the truest realities – consecration to God, prayer, the building up of His Kingdom, peace in Him, and work for Him.

Thursday March 9th 1916, Hazebrouck

These concerts are very tiring, although they do much good. Much trouble has to be taken by many people, much good nature is given out, and the dull monotony of the lives of the patients is thus dispelled for a time, in forgetting various unpleasant things. Otherwise one does begrudge the labour and the time and if only one or other of the officers in the staff would only catch on to the idea, they could do so much good by making this work their 'offering', but they do not really see into it. (Entre nous the elder of them – now the Major has gone – is an extraordinarily self-centred person, and his influence goes down to the others. I will describe him to you one day – privately). As it is, this evenings' concert was a great success. Beard, the Wesleyan Chaplain, had to do with bringing it in on this date. Captain Gibson's Motor Ambulance Convoy supplied the talent, Lieutenant Summers – a nice man – arranged the programme of music, songs, violin, cornet and piano, Private Briggs, out of his pocket money, had bought a portable cinema lantern and provided the films and worked them, good Sergeant Richards supervised all the arrangements and laboured unsparingly at the piano, and two or three privates carried on with songs grave and gay. That extraordinary character Charlie Chaplin figured in the films (one gets rather tired of him) – there was a silly story about a man being fastened up in an empty cider barrel and rolled down a hill and a clever story of a man going to see a conjuror, and then trying to perform some of the tricks at his Grandmother's birthday party with disastrous results, and a touching, strong, rather exciting story of Yellow Flame, the old Red Indian, and his devotion to the Sheriff who had saved him from drowning[571].

In the middle of the Chaplains' meeting this morning there was an awful bang, then another and another. A bomb had dropped about half a mile away, and the rest was anti-aircraft – five hostile planes. Then came along 7 of ours scouting them like a flight of wild ducks, up in the sky, glinting against the sunshine, and that one which had dropped the bomb looking like a vicious little pale brown dragonfly. But no harm was done, just a hole in a garden.

In the afternoon, I met Lord Salisbury[572] with Tuckey. Salisbury is out here for

---

571 *Yellow Flame* (1914). Dr. Charles Giblyn. Film short with Earnest French and Charles K Swallow.
572 **James Edward Hubert Gascoyne-Cecil**, 4th Marquess of Salisbury, KG, GCVO, CB, PC (b.1861 – d.1947), known as **Viscount Cranborne** from 1868 to 1903, was a British statesman. Lord Salisbury sat as Conservative Member of Parliament for Darwen from 1885 to 1892 and for Rochester from 1893 to 1903, when he succeeded his father and entered the House of Lords. His father was **Robert Arthur Talbot Gascoyne-Cecil, 3rd Marquess of Salisbury**, KG, GCVO, PC (1830 –1903), styled **Lord Robert Cecil** before 1865 and **Viscount Cranborne** from June 1865 until April 1868. He was a British Conservative statesman and thrice Prime Minister, serving for a total of over 13 years. The first British Prime Minister of the 20th century, he was the last Prime Minister to head his full administration from the House of Lords.

the Advisory Committee of the Army Council in the interests of the Chaplains' Department. He talked away keenly and I told him that I was glad to see him here as I felt sure that he was 'up for some good'. He seemed surprised that we were able to do so much in the way of ministry among the patients of a Clearing Station. He seemed also to feel the difficulty about the non-conformists, and was interested in the means I had taken to try and make the least of the difficulties organising ward services throughout, and giving the non-conformists their turn in them all circulating round the wards impartially, and keeping my denominational services for the Blacksmiths' Forge opposite. The partisan spirit was so obvious when I came to the place – it was hateful to think of letting it come into play. At the end, I told him I had known his father at Nice 23 years ago, when I was assistant Chaplain there[573] and also that I had lived in Rochester (he was MP for Rochester), and he was surprised that I had been 'in harness' for so long. He strikes me as a clear-headed good-minded 'natural' man, out here with a prayerful sense of his responsibilities. They have immense undertaking laid upon them to organise the Chaplain's work for a nation in arms.

Thank you for another letter, enclosing one from Eric. The little boy is getting on – it was a good letter, but a 'touch of cold' is significant. If he is not in quite good form, it may be expected to show in his place in the class – he will make up later on. Yes, I agree about the Fawn's style of living, and he must recognize that a) it is a small charge and b) one does not pay a Locum Tenens much more than a curate. I think we must go back to the house in the autumn – I am much above the military age, 49 in May! So that honestly one will have done one's bit and the Department is all for the younger man – except for the old experienced militarist – to take the commanding position. P.S. I am glad of the better account of Mother – Katie and Sophie will be a better help than Lizzie!

Friday March 10th 1916, Hazebrouck

It has been a full day, cold and murky, all the better against aeroplanes! The bomb that fell yesterday morning proved to be only about 500 yds away from the hospital. There is a big hole in the corner of the field, a good shot for the railway, and I hear that five others were dropped further along the line. But compare that with the 124 bombs dropped a few days ago by the Allies on Metz station[574] – but also alas! for the deadly naughtiness of it all!

I have tonight done a serious thing – I have let myself be elected Mess President. It is an undertaking and I speak sincerely when I say it is very serious. Men do grumble so, some of them, over their feeding, and it is those who do least for the general good who are readiest to complain. Only a sense of wanting to help the right temper of things

---

573 Lord Salisbury had a house in Nice, France: La Bastide, built in 1889. La Bastide is set in five hectares of parkland between the city of Nice and Monaco.

574 French air raid, 10th March. 16 aeroplanes attacked Metz railway station.

made me yield, and I did it very reluctantly and strictly for the time of one month. It is the old principle – if any man will compel you to go one mile, go with him twain![575]

Good night, my sweet lady.

Saturday March 11th 1916, Hazebrouck

I have been thinking what a mint of trouble you would have been saved if you had not married me! No sense of a loss of a home, no worries about the children and my absence from them, quiet and untrammelled work in some way to further the success of the war, and not much to be anxious about – a strange complexity in life!

The lecture on Victoria and Tasmania which was to have been given by Dr. Beale[576] did not come off because the lecturer had to take to his bed sick, so I turned on a set of Punch pictures. I had carefully selected a bundle of these, putting on one side those that are not likely to be amusing to soldiers but in the hurry of a crowded evening, I took these to the lecture instead of the selected ones and it was too far to repair the error when I discovered it! However, the men really did enjoy them, so it was not quite so disappointing.

I rode off with Tuckey to look for some of the Cambridge soldiers, but a cold clammy drizzle came on, and as I had two meetings to follow and did not want the bother of changing, I hurried back.

Sunday March 12th 1916, Hazebrouck

Today is the anniversary of Neuve Chapelle – that fateful Sunday when the shell fell and killed 29 and wounded 25, and at this moment the Germans are falling by the thousand, a costly failure[577] today's report calls it. The first psalm for the day is full of "in God is my strength and trust" – "trust in Him at all times: pour out your heart before Him, for God is our hope" "Power belongeth unto God: and … thou Lord art merciful". Power and mercy – how we need them both. And England needs them – of the first it is conscious, how soon will it learn the other equally vital one?

I am tired tonight and this morning felt like collapsing, bother it, really faint and sickified, but I simply shut myself in during the afternoon and slept, waking refreshed. At 11.30 we had a small but very attentive Ward service in the Officers' Hospital and this evening a nice quiet service held at Headquarters with about 20 present.

I got in touch with Captain Wright[578], though I did not manage to see him, who

---

575 **Matthew 5:21** 'And whosoever shall compel thee to go a mile, go with him twain'
576 *Capt. Stanley* James Annear Beale R.A.M.C.
577 See entry for March 14th, 1915 at Estaires La Gorgue.
578 2nd Lieut **Charles Seymour Wright** (b.1887 – d?), in Toronto, Canada and educated at Upper Canada College. Was an undergraduate at Gonville and Caius College, Cambridge and did research at the Cavendish Laboratory between 1908 and 1910. Member of the first Terra Nova expedition 1910–13. WW1 2 Lt Royal Engineers, Military Cross and OBE. Director of the

was one of Captain Scott's party in the South Polar Expedition. He has a number of his slides with him and I have good hopes he will come and give them to our patients. Voila!

Monday March 13th 1916, Hazebrouck

A very refreshing day with bright sunshine and a hostile aeroplane in the distance. I have had a touch of malaria but am a little better tonight.

Tuesday March 14th 1916, Hazebrouck

Another beautiful day and a great help on from the winter. Two hostile aeroplanes took advantage of the sunshine this morning to visit us, but both were chased away without doing any damage. It has been a busy day, re-arranging the date of the weeks' concert, the Sergeant Major having chosen to arrange a concert party of his own and wants to give it to all and sundry at one of the billets on a different night to the one he had told me – it meant a number of people being put about. Then we had a lantern talk by a young doctor (Dakin-Smith) on Greece and the Balkan States[579]. He did it very well, giving a good clear sketch of their history and political characteristics, their recent wars and their position today and I worked the lantern.

Wednesday March 15th 1916, Hazebrouck

Another nice day and I have been busy with many oddments which comprise too much I am afraid, and so keep one from the true mission of one's office and it is difficult to know where to draw the line. I am just off to a concert given by this unit in the town.

The concert threw our dinner very late. Some of the items were good and a man with a nice voice sang "The Diver" and "It is my wedding morn[580]" musically and forcefully.

Thursday March 16th 1916, Hazebrouck

A very successful concert tonight – my host in this billet, rallied up his 'Symphonic Francaise' and they gave us an admirable evening. The most popular item was "Tipperary[581]" which was sung by an English flying man, and played by the orchestra

---

Admiralty Research Laboratory and Director of Scientific Research at the Admiralty.

579 Lieut. Dr **William Henry Dakin-Smith**, R.A.M.C.
580 *The Diver*, 1880; *The Yeoman's Wedding Song*, 1899
581 "It's a Long Way to Tipperary" is a British music hall song co-written by Jack Judge and Henry James "Harry" Williams. *Daily Mail* correspondent George Curnock saw the Irish regiment the Connaught Rangers singing this song as they marched through Boulogne on 13th August 1914 and reported it on 18th August 1914. The song was quickly picked up by other units of the British Army. In November 1914, it was recorded by the well-known tenor John McCormack, which helped its worldwide popularity.

with immense enthusiasm. The other items were a march, a mazurka, a classical flute solo, a cornet solo (very well given) violin and cello – the big bass fiddle parted in two just as a concerted piece finished to the wild amusement of everyone, audience and performers alike, and the body of it fell on to the floor with a loud bump!

During the Chaplains' meeting this morning, five hostile aeroplanes passed over the edge of the town, and were shelled.

Friday March 17th 1916, Hazebrouck

The aeroplane lecture gave great pleasure. The lecturer was a little prosy, he is curious in that way, Mr. Thomas Atkins. Some of the men had bad coughs which they have no idea of suppressing and a pneumonia patient talked loudly now and then in delirium, but there was an undercurrent of deep and rapt interest all the time that was unmistakable.

We went up in the air and looked down upon our own town! Upon Ypres, and upon certain towns in the German lines where we saw in one case a field of German transport – a great target for one of <u>our</u> bombers. We had a photograph from an aeroplane, between some clouds, of a gas attack going on down below (the first time the English used gas), and we saw, fore and aft, the F.E.8 our aeroplane[582] which goes one better than the German Fokker, and we saw zeppelins, sea-planes, hydroplanes and airships in plenty – and so our war-weary men passed one more pleasant evening. All leave is off for the present.

Saturday March 18th 1916, Hazebrouck

Nice weather, with a beautiful moonlit night which is rather a temptation to aircraft. Two appeared this morning early and were vigorously shelled at about 7.30 and then at 10.30 another appeared and was scouted off by three of ours. The rest of the day has been full of the usual visiting and preparations for Sunday, and also censoring letters. Also thinking out a message for tomorrow – it is not easy as many topics present themselves. The subject for the day is 'humility' and a divine discontent doubting our own strength, yet confident in the Perfect Strength, seeing that we have no power of ourselves to help ourselves "keep us both outwardly in our bodies, and ontwardly in our souls, that we may be defended from all adversities which may happen to the body and all evil thoughts that may assault and hurt the soul."[583] The only thing is a complete surrender of ourselves 'to be kept'. No one can be safe until he is able to say "the Lord is my keeper". That means a complete surrender to God's standard –

---

582 The **Royal Aircraft Factory F.E.8** was a British single-seat fighter of the First World War designed at the Royal Aircraft Factory. The F.E.8 was one of the first so-called "scout" aircraft designed from the outset as a single-seat fighter. In the absence of a synchronisation gear to provide a forward firing machine gun for a tractor scout such as the S.E.2, it was given a pusher layout.

583 Book of Common Prayer, Prayer for the Third Sunday in Lent.

"be ye perfect even as your Father which is in heaven is perfect[584]". Safety lies in the highest standards: anything lower counts as weakness. If you want to hit the church, aim at the steeple – he will not hit a tree that will not aim at a mountain. "Keep well outside of temptation, and it's clean all the way" – a phrase your father once used. "If you keep in touch with the highest, you'll keep away from the lowest" as a sailor once said. I am only just learning how to be a Christian.

Lord Thurlow, I see, is dead: and Cumming Bruce succeeds to the title – and considerable estates[585].

Sunday March 19th 1916, Hazebrouck

I was glad to get your letter this evening at the end of a long and tiring Sunday. Dear little Faith's letter was very nicely written. Please thank her for it, and say how glad I am that she is such a useful little girl – I wish I could come and pick primroses with her down the lane. I understand about the shortage of man and woman labour – it will not be a bad thing to return to the 'simple life'. After the war I think that 'woman' labour will become plentiful enough, but – the scale all round will have to be simpler.

A beautiful day – 7.15a.m. H.C in the Blacksmith Forge with one soldier present, and a good ward service at 9.15 then a large service at the Maire at 10, followed by H.C. with 5 present. This evening a good large ward service where most of those present seemed to mean business. We must mean business – hundreds of these men are ready to have their part in the National Mission of Repentance and Hope[586]. At present I feel my own need to be that of zeal and persistency – the 'one thing I do'. People are looking for distractions out here, they are very tired of the War and too listless to take an interest in anything much, and yet glad to catch at anything that diverts their attention. They – we – want the one thing needful, an all-satisfying object in life – "Thou hast made us for Thyself and we do not find our satisfaction until we find it in Thee"[587], and to work for the bringing about of the perfect Kingdom – how definite in object, what a task and what an occupation! "Thy Kingdom Come".

---

584 **Matthew 5:48** 'Be ye therefore perfect, even as your Father which is in heaven is perfect.'

585 **Thomas John Hovell-Thurlow-Cumming-Bruce, 5th Baron Thurlow**, PC, FRS (b.1838 – d.1916), was a Liberal politician who served as Paymaster-General in 1886 for Gladstone. He served as High Commissioner to the General Assembly of the Church of Scotland in 1886. He was succeeded by his son **Charles Edward Hovell-Thurlow-Cumming-Bruce, 6th Baron Thurlow** (b.1869– d.1952). See footnote 202.

586 A national initiative lead by the Archbishop of Canterbury, **Randall Davidson**, intended to be a 'collective act of self-examination and fundamental reorientation' by the Church of England in October and November 1916. It was not judged a success in that it coincided with the close of the Battle of the Somme and was unclear in its aims. While RDG, as usual, was supportive, he also seems to have been lukewarm to the National Mission. The Archbishop's visit to the front (16th – 24th May 1916) was intended to gather information and generate interest in the National Mission with the Army Chaplaincy.

587 St Augustine of Hippo, Confessions book 1.

We hear the aeroplane that came over yesterday morning was brought down by one of the planes that we saw pursuing it, and I hear that two of the enemy aeroplanes which were fussing round us yesterday were also brought down, one by the new fast fighter the F.E.8 which I remember noticing being very fast and the other by one of our anti-aircraft guns. We think that this will make them chary of visits to these quarters[588].

Monday March 20th 1916, Hazebrouck

I have got quit of the Mess Presidency, and it is a relief. One or two of the younger lazier spirits were a little surprised, but I pointed out that the conception of a Mess President as they viewed it, was different to what it is in England, and under peaceful conditions. In England, you 'preside' and the Mess sergeant does the catering, whereas here they rather expect you to preside, cater, and take all the grumbling! In a Field Ambulance, and when there is much movement and much fighting, it is a different thing. Here some of the young 'fast' spirits are all for having all kinds of things in the way of 'good living' to be thought out and provided by – the Mess President! They are very young. We were wakened at 6.15 am by 'Archibald[589]' (the anti-aircraft gun) firing away at four hostile aeroplanes, successfully keeping them at a respectful distance.

Goodnight my beloved.

Tuesday March 21st 1916, Hazebrouck

A nice dull day with a perfect freedom from aircraft. But the price you pay is some amount of raw chilliness – there is always something "C'est la guerre!" All the same, they dropped one bomb pretty near – I heard the hiss. This afternoon I saw the garden across the railway where it fell, very near a humble little cottage, and not far from the daffodils – a German idyll!

I have been rather disappointed this afternoon as I heard that George Thomas's regiment was about 4 miles away and so rode over to find his battalion and another, and I found that they had moved off this morning! They were chosen to move forward in advance and I am wondering now if it will be possible to get to them, as they march on again at 6 o'clock tomorrow morning[590].

---

588 The **Royal Aircraft Factory F.E.8** was a single-seat fighter of a 'pusher' (engine mounted in the rear) configuration. Although a clean and well designed aeroplane for a pusher, it could not escape the drag penalty imposed by its complex tail structure and was no match for the German Albatros fighters that appeared in late 1916.

589 Nickname given to anti-aircraft fire, said to derive from a British pilot who reacted to enemy anti-aircraft fire by shouting the line from a music hall song 'Archibald certainly not'. Often shortened to Archie.

590 The East Yorkshire Regiment.

You may have noticed my name in the London Gazette this morning – it was merely to recognise those days at the beginning of the war when we were 'marking time' and doing nothing at Ladbroke Grove. About a dozen Chaplains seem to have been in a similar position, including Bishop Gwynne. Our commissions are all dated back to the 6th of August 1914 – mine to the 4th, but it all adds up. What it means I think, is that I get £5 pay which was then due to me, a neat little windfall. I shall be aware of it when I get it! You never can tell. I sent you Edith's letter, because I want you to know – the future of my parents causes me some anxiety.

Wednesday March 22nd 1916, Hazebrouck

It has been a most remarkable day today, darling. I have been through a wild, battered and devastated region and then finally through Ypres itself, wandering through the Cathedral[591] ruins, the ruins of the Cloth Hall[592], while our artillery roared around us (the Germans fortunately making NO reply whatever, which was a mercy!) and it feels like having been through a chapter in a tale of fiction. The Belgian frontier is of course strictly guarded, and we could only get through by Tuckey's pass. You go through one village or small town after another, mostly damaged, and the nearer you get to the line the worse the conditions, and the further you go the more battered the Church always is, until you come into regions where a strange stillness and desolation broods over everthing. You pass the zone of civilians – no longer children playing, or clothes hanging out to dry, and then you come to where the cottages become even less habitable, and huge dug-outs are common, and finally to where no buildings at all are inhabited above ground i.e. the skirts of Ypres – and then you are in the town itself. So pathetic are the remainders of its simple and trustful picturesqueness, its ornamental architecture, its carved wood and stonework. Now a beautiful old oak doorway with figures carved in full or in relief, now some facade with its sculptured statues and, bravely asserting its witness of beauty amid its crippled fellows, is the jagged outline of the Cathedral side by side with its no less brave neighbour, the Clothworker's Hall. We wandered, not too leisurely, along the floor of each – at the corner of the Cathedral vestry is a heap of ruins, and a board states that under it lie the bodies of 19 men of the 6th Battalion of the Duke of Cornwall's Light Infantry, (Jack Piggott's regt[593]) buried there by one 15 inch shell, and so we left[594].

---

591 St Martin's, Ypres. Completely destroyed 1914–18, rebuilt 1922–30.

592 The **Cloth Hall**, Ypres, was one of the largest commercial buildings of the Middle Ages, when it served as the main market and warehouse for the Flemish city's prosperous cloth industry. Destroyed 1914–18, rebuilt 1930–67.

593 2 Lt **John Cecil Charles Piggott**, 3 Bn Duke of Cornwall's Light Infantry.

594 6th (Service) Bn, Duke of Cornwall's Light Infantry was raised in August 1914 as part of Kitchener's First New Army and joined 43rd Brigade, 14th (Light) Division. They landed at Boulogne on the 22nd of May 1915. They fought in the The Action of Hooge, being the first division to be attacked by flamethrowers. The 19 are: Lieutenant **R C Blagrove**, Major **Carew Barnett** (b.1867 – d.1915); Lance Corporals: **Albert Henry Armer** (b.1888 – d.1915), **Burnard Jeffery** (b.1896 – d.1915), **R Lee**, **H E May** and **Howard Taylor** (b.1890 – d.1915); Privates: **Frederick Arthur Andrews**, (b.1896 – d.1915), **T C Arthur**, **J Chadwick**, **Thomas Collins**

At the entry of the vestry are the yet visible bloodstains on floor and walls of the two sentries who were killed also by a shell, mercifully outright. On the Clothworkers' Hall one figure stands out, smiling and natural, as if in cheerful defiance of having lost both its feet. On one of the churches just outside the town, the one figure of the Living Christ stands its hands raised in benediction, with a suggestion of wondering pity as it seemed to me about it. The graves in the Cathedral yard around have been upheaved pell-mell and human bones lie scattered in all directions. In the midst, near one side, lies a large shell which I suppose fell unexploded, a 'dud' as the expression is. There is no time to attend to these things apparently, and probably there is no opportunity as shelling is continual.

The main street is like the page of a book – some things yet remain in the shops, sewing machines seem common as no-one carries away a sewing machine as a souvenir! A chemist's shop has broken jars and bottles strewn about a shell-splintered floor, and the sulphur drawer has strewn its contents across in the corner and has spread itself in pieces to riot over it, and nearby a drawer of some kind of cobalt-looking stuff, perhaps washing blue, has done the same.

Here is a beautiful old cloth-weavers' house, old and of strong design. On the centre frame of the double doorway is carved, in full relief, the figure of what looks like a bishop and upstairs through the smashed front of the house, you can still see the weaver's hand loom. Over the door is carved the date 1633. I send you a little souvenir from this house, there were probably children in it and I hope that they all escaped. Among the fragments of a broken sewing-machine and scraps of dress material I see the picture of a 'Daisy'[595]. It is one of a collection of flowers which are intended for sticking into a scrapbook. Would you like to stick them into some book, darling, perhaps in the shape of the name YPRES, in token of my having remembered you in the midst of that beautiful, old ruined home, and of being thankful that it was not ours? (there is one short of the 29, except the two odd scraps be used – token also of a broken name!)

The most tenable building is the prison, the solidity of its walls serves some purpose now-a-days, as a part of it is used as a dressing station for the R.A.M.C. and a part as the living-place for the Town Guard. In a vaulted cellar the Church Army are running a little recreation room for the soldiers – it is one of the strangest Soldiers' Clubs that I have ever seen and it is certainly one of the finest bits of war work the

(b.1895 – d.1915), **Henry James Eades** (b.1898 – d.1915), **D John, W Jones, W Kay, Alfred Albert Lever** (b.1883 – d.1915), **G J Murray, D Rowe** (b.1887 – d.1915), **William John Smith** (b.1894 – d.1915). They were killed on 12th August 1915, and are all buried at Ypres Reservoir Cemetery, Plot V, Row AA. C and D Companies 6 Bn were billeted in the vaults of St Martin's, the crypt was collapsed at about 6.30 am on 12th August, through shelling from a 17" gun, nicknamed the "Ypres Express" firing from Houthulst Forest, about 10 miles away. The survivors were rescued by the 11th King's Liverpool's, not before Major Barnett and Lt Blagrove had also perished trying rescue the trapped men.
595 Margaret's nickname.

The paper flowers from Ypres

Church Army have done. The Town Major remarked "A jolly good thing this" and from such a quarter that is high praise. He is the eleventh Town Major the place has had since its investment as it is not an office men crave to hold onto for long, the record being three months in office. Two shells dropped on the far end of the building last week – the upper part is of course, unoccupied.

In the afternoon at a Soldiers' Club in the town nearby I had an interesting encounter, I met the first two missioners of the Navy Mission, who have just got out here – they arrived the night before last. They seem to be good, bright capable men, and likely to make full use of the immense and splendid opportunities that they will find in that quarter. No where, I think, is work more responsive than close up to the firing line.

Thursday March 23rd 1916, Hazebrouck
Tuckey is leaving and going to an important base – it is possible that I may be moved also[596].

Friday March 24th 1916, Hazebrouck
Things have developed a little here today. Tuckey goes to a new district and the plan seems to be that I am to follow him. The change, if it takes place, will come about at the end of next month, and Tuckey proposes that I should take a leave then and as it will be between two spheres of work ask for a fortnight, the more so as the possibility of another leave is rather remote. He takes his leave next week and does not return here except for a day or so to finish up. I carry on as Senior Chaplain 2nd Army until his successor comes.

---

596 They would meet again in Rouen later in 1916.

Saturday March 25th 1916, Hazebrouck

Cold squalls but warm sunshine in between. We are surrounded by Australians and they are a splendid-looking lot of men. The tired look that one sees on so many Tommies is absent with them – they will do good work. It has been a day rather crowded up of Australians – and of Tuckey! It is difficult for him under the Army system I suppose, to be otherwise – but he is rather full up of himself and is departing with more fuss than I am sure Field Marshall French made when he quitted the Army Command. A good Senior Chaplain is reputed to have said once "Alas! With so many of us it means that when we enter the Department we are 'missioners' and when we leave it, we are 'Chaplains'" Much of Tuckey's has been about keeping up his position in the new station "living up to style, etc." "I am going to be so and so". "So and so will succeed me", etc. – Oh! To be nothing! Yet I suppose we are all relatively something. One thing is very clear – it is conspicuous all round – the men of the permanent Department are out to get for themselves the very utmost advancement possible, and they will climb on any back for the purpose. The temporary men – all and sundry – are a grand 'stalking horse' in the process. I am sorry. I am bored today I think and it has not helped preparation for tomorrow.

A young Corporal in one of the wards announces himself to me as a candidate for Holy Orders, he is the son of Canon Hornabrook of South Adelaide[597]. He is a bright, healthy-minded man, exercising a good influence.

As I rode on my horse three or four afternoons ago to see a group of men outside the town, a good wife in the road greeted me, with quite a clear accent, with "Good afternoon, Sir". I stopped and chatted and she told me that her father came from Manchester and her mother from Leeds. They had settled in Lille, and their children brought up French. This 'child' of now over 60 summers is a refugee from [… *censored*…]. She keeps a tea room in a street rather used by the troops at one corner of the town so yesterday I went and had tea there. Her married son, a Territorial soldier, lives with her and is able to do his service in this part and they preserved, I saw, a very nice tone of home life. Then eventually it transpires that they are very earnest Protestants. I mentioned that I had made the acquaintance of another French Protestant family near Neuve Chapelle, and quoted the name, and they were rejoiced to find they were their old friends of years gone by.

A young Canadian officer late last night asked if there would be Holy Communion on Sunday, and it was very nice to be able to say that I could arrange it in his ward.

Sad things happen – and a warning about teeth! An officer has been in now for over 10 days and is unable to open his mouth through the hardening of the jaw tissue by septacemia. They gave him gas to try and cut in behind, but were unable to do so in the time. This morning he is to have ether as something must be done – he can

---

597 Sapper **Harold Newton Hornabrook**, b.1892. (Reserve Engineering Field Companies), son of Canon C.S. Hornabrook. He survived the war.

only take food by suction. What mysteries of suffering there are. The Club is now a greatly improved place – a piano, a fire, bright lights, tables, papers and a gramophone, and now what I wanted most, a devotional room downstairs. The next thing is prayer and zeal that this may be used.

A young Australian officer came in this evening – he lives in the parish of St. John's, Balmain[598]. In one bed there is the nice young Canadian officer, in the other this young Australian, both talking hard across the Chaplain from England – it is indeed stretching hands across the sea.

Sunday March 26th 1916, Hazebrouck

The seed has been sown again – in how much weakness God knows. One wishes sometimes we were like the Society of Friends, and that the good thoughts and feelings in the seats could share themselves aloud with the thoughts of the speaker. It would guide him, and strengthen him. The silence, and the appearance of impassivity are difficult to combat sometimes. It is a great responsibility to have to be voicing the meditation of a large gathering of people minute after minute, knowing how many and various are the temperaments, the degrees of attainment, the moods, the 'states of grace'. Nothing but the command "Go, speak all the words of this life", and the promise that "the word … shall accomplish that where most it is sent" could make the position tenable. Yet, in a wonderful way, the words do get used – and so the Kingdom comes. After all, "the work that is done upon earth, He doeth it Himself" and what people think about the speaker, or the worker does not much matter. "Thou art the Organ whose full breath is thunder" – "we are the keys beneath Thy fingers pressed"[599]

The Presbytarian Doctor Major has been replaced by an Anglican Dr. Major – a nicely spoken and gentlemanly man (rather a contrast to the one gone) – and he was at the H.C. this morning (Maj. Nightingale), so that is a crumb of comfort. The Ward services, also, went better than usual as the staff are getting used to them and that makes a great difference. It was a help at the service in the Officers' Hospital having a Chaplain among the invalids. He is here from a throat trouble and is on his way to Nice, by name Jaffary Nicholson, and has been Chaplain in the XVIII Division and of the Brigade in which George Thomas is: I remarked that G.T. was my nephew and the first baby that I had christened: the Chaplain's comment was "Well, he does you

---

598 **Balmain** is a suburb in the Inner West of Sydney, located 6 km west of the Sydney central business district, in the local government area of the Municipality of Leichhardt.

599 **Acts 5:20** 'Go, stand and speak in the temple to the people all the words of this life.'
 Isiah 55:11 'So shall my word be that goeth forth out of my mouth: it shall not return unto me void, but it shall accomplish that which I please, and it shall prosper *in the thing* whereto I sent it.' **John 5:17** 'But Jesus answered them, My Father worketh hitherto, and I work.' From Alexander MacLaren (b.1826 – d.1910) "Thou art the Organ whose full breath is thunder, I am the keys beneath Thy fingers pressed" *Expositions of Holy Scripture: Ezekiel, Daniel and the Minor Prophets; and Matthew Chaps. I to VIII* .

credit" – so far so good![600] This evening we had a very nice service in the Mairie, followed by Holy Communion for which 13 stayed including an officer. One of the Chaplains is opposed to this Evening Communion, but never since he has been in this place has he seen more than 7 or 8 at an earlier service – sometimes no one. Who is to say, with an unurged attendance like that, that the Evening C is unadvisable – still less wrong! We lose the end by worrying over the means.

Thank you my darling, for another letter, and one from Faith (I wrote three childrens' letters – one to Joyce, another to [?] and that one to Miss Primrose). The home touches about no.4 are very interesting – the very day and hour during which you were busy fitting in wardrobes and washstands, flowerpots and linoleums, and seeing to a cheerful fire – I was standing in the desolated clothweaver's home at Ypres, looking round upon chests of drawers smashed to matchwood, curtains draggled in heaps of brick dust and mud, walls and windows a shapeless mass and for all I know, stained with blood as well. How much we have to be thankful for to God and to the brave men who, with their lives in their hands, (and from some the offered sacrifice has been accepted) have stood between the same sort of thing, and us!

Monday March 27th 1916, Hazebrouck

How can one go preaching on "Walk in love, as Christ also loved us"[601] and yet feel so unforbearing as I do tonight? Some of these young officers are very "heady, highminded" and I think, unreasoning, and they are eager to have elaborate dinners, entertaining, jovialities. The question of expense comes in and also of the time it takes up – also the strength. They are not conscious of the 500 patients who also have to be thought about – neither have we the accommodation in our cramped mess-sitting room and nor have we the staff of mess men that you have in a peacetime mess. Nor, if you do muster together a scratch crew, have you anyone who can properly give the time, on active service, to training them and the result is a 'botch'. An affectation of a ceremonious dinner on rations and expensive accessories – not very well corked frequently – and no one is satisfied. A little less ambition, and plain and well-done and well-served meals could be much more comfortable for everybody if they only knew it. I have dropped out of the Committee – my ideas are too 'war economy' to suit those more ardent tastes, and I should feel happier too if I did not know that some of them really cannot afford the cost. One or two, especially, ought to be saving for they have careers to make, and I know they will be sorry for it, by and bye.

I have been carrying on for Tuckey today and this evening presided at a concert, going out half way in order to take Evening prayers at the Club for the Presbyterian, who keeps up a bad throat by late hours and drinking much alcohol – and does not

---

600 Rev **Jaffray Brisbane Nicolson** 2nd Lt (b.1869 – d.1928).
601 **Ephesians 5:2** 'And walk in love, as Christ also hath loved us, and hath given himself for us an offering and a sacrifice to God for a sweetsmelling savour.'

realise it. Platt, the C of E Chaplain of another Clearing Station came to voice the difficulties of some of his Presbyterian staff, including an officer and a Sister, who complain of no Presbyterian services being held – we dare say nothing! What a complaining chapter this seems!

Tuesday March 28th 1916, Hazebrouck

Having some of Tuckey's things to look at, as well as the Clearing Station, and the turns at the Club, all keeps me pretty busy. A pleasant young Australian Chaplain came into the office this morning to report to the Senior Chaplain 2nd Army. He belonged to the Bush Brotherhood, and was very glad to talk about Australia[602]. He had been in N. Queensland and went out on the same boat with the Rector of Windsor, who was accompanied by his wife and mother. This you will recognize, was no other than the Rev. W. H. W. Stevenson whose mother you know and I believe his wife also! He had been in Gallipoli and Egypt and was very glad of various hints I could give him about his new sphere of operations. A sad case tonight – shot through the head.

The Germans are filling up the cup of their enormities, and yet the Kaiser repeats his avowals 'in the name of God'. It is a new chapter of the primitive Old Testament history – as David did with the sons of Saul, he 'hung them up unto the Lord!'[603]

Thank you darling, for another letter – it is a good sign mother being able to write so fully and so firmly, but I suspect it will take her time to be really active again. My bank balance is not an enormous one! Rates and taxes are a business and I wonder how we are going to manage 'apres la guerre'? But – the morrow must, in the ultimate resort, take care for the things of itself.

Wednesday March 29th 1916, Hazebrouck

Besides my own individual change, that is pre-shadowed by the rumours for change for the whole unit – it may come speedily or with more deliberation so do not be surprised if all at once letters have an interval, for these rumours come off sometimes very suddenly at the last minute. I shall be very sorry indeed for many reasons, but whether it is further forward or away from the lines remains to be seen. Either way has its attractions!

I am not in quite good fortune lately – I had the Chaplain's car today and got as far as a certain town, then on account of a certain Colonel, had to return in this direction. My plan had been to go and see the Senior Chaplain of George Thomas's Division and while seeing him, to find out George's battalion. Ten minutes after the time arranged for our starting, a message came that the car had broken down, and the

---

602 A loose affiliation of missonising Anglican clergy who would travel the outback in Australia. Begun in 1880s and continues to this day.

603 2 Samuel 21:6 'Let seven men of his sons be delivered unto us, and we will hang them up unto the LORD in Gibeah of Saul, *whom* the LORD did choose. And the king said, I will give *them*.'

repairs needed necessitated its being towed away to the workshops. The distance is too far to be accomplished any other way, and the battalion moves off today or tomorrow, and after that one does not know what will be its movements. In the town I saw a sight which made me say 'thank you' once again. Yesterday afternoon a Brigadier's car was passing along a given strip of road where we were this day week outside a famous town, when A SHELL FELL RIGHT IN FRONT OF IT. The front of the bonnet was knocked off, the stock of the steering wheel was gashed, the glasses were all smashed through, and as from a fierce pepperbox, the back of the car on one side was riddled through from the front. The Brigadier happened to be sitting on the left-hand of the seat instead of on the right. The driver was quick enough to be aware of the arrival of the shell and ducked down into the well of the steering place, and neither Brigadier nor driver were touched, nor was the car overset!

You and dear Joyce have been at the concert today, I hope, and have seen the dear son – I have been thinking of you and of what a nice day it will have been. It is a blessing that the educationists are able to go on with some due regularity. It is a trying time for some children and speaks of anxiety for the future.

Goodnight, my beloved.

Friday March 31st 1916, Hazebrouck

A glorious day here, but you seem to have been having rough weather in England. We had only the edge of the blizzard the papers have been speaking about[604]. I do hope Miss Primrose is better. I expect what she had was a chill on the liver, or on the stomach: Alas! That we should have such organs!

There is much to do when 'carrying on' for another Chaplain as well, especially as Tuckey's successor is moving in while Tuckey is away. He will not live in this town, but in a village outside – I think on account of the bombs! And things that might be done in Tuckey's name, cannot be done in the others' name, because he has not said so yet!

We had an admirable lantern lecture this evening which was kindly taken by my friend Dr. Beale – he is a good fellow. We followed Amundsen to the South Pole and Beale knew his subject very well and kept about 200 men attentive in the silence of mice for over an hour. It does them a world of good to forget the war, their sickness and their wounds, the trenches and the rest of it all. Your Fund bought us this lantern, and it is proving the greatest boon. I have had two or three lantern services as well and hope to have another one on Sunday. (The Presbyterian sleeps, giggles, or ambles on – one of the most successfully lazy men 2 or 3 of our Base have ever known. That is a trial.)

I am glad to have the poem 'In Flanders' in print! I do not know when it appeared first – it seems in the Spectator. If you could manage 100 they would be most acceptable[605].

---

604 1916 was an exceptionally snowy year with blizzards and snow up to 14" reported.
605 Lucy Foster Whitmell's poem 'Christ in Flanders' appeared in The Spectator, September 11th,

Saturday April 1st 1916, Hazebrouck

A very full day again. The Deputy Chaplain General comes tomorrow and we received word of it only this morning, and this meant much telephoning and planning about various details. There are 3 candidates for Confirmation, prepared by Brockington, and the Bishop will preach also at the evening service in the Mairie. I am wondering if it would be possible to get a word with him tomorrow, as that might open out what may be coming in the nearer future. At present I am planning to take 'leave' on say, Easter Monday, but for the moment I cannot get clear in my mind what ought to be done with the time in England. Two things are clear – to be with the children as much as possible, and to get the teeth 'tinkered' up enough to carry on to the end of this year. I really do not think, as things are in the Chaplains Department here as well also as regards the parish, that my staying on after this year is indicated. I think it is the occasion for younger men.

The man with the head wound may recover! But a case of cerebro-spinal meningitis came in – dreadfully sad.

Sunday April 2nd 1916, Hazebrouck

Thank you vey much darling M, for another letter. It was disappointing about Southbro' and the weather. I think under the circumstances I should have taken the strong line and gone: open air and travel do not as a rule induce colds, and it meant a great deal for the young people. But – the day is past and the milk spilt. We have it on record that as the years come on, "fears shall be in the way"[606]. By the time you get this perhaps, the little boy will be home, so it will all be in the past.

It has been a nice day – there were 4 present at H.C. at 8 am and a good big ward service with a hearty spirit, followed by a very good officers' service. This afternoon the D.C.G. took a confirmation, and spoke very well. After tea with him at that Clearing Station, I went for a half hours' walk with the Bishop, out among the green fields. It gave me a little fuller insight into the working of the Chaplains' Department. The military authorities keep a firm hand, (not to say a firm foot!) on it, and the Deputy, as well as the Chaplain General, finds their powers are very much limited as the Army is afraid to be frankly religious and indeed it is difficult to see how they can be. For if it is to be, how can you co-ordinate the diverse sectarian elements? It is rather depressing. The plan is that, in all probability, I shall change from here for a big Base, after my leave at Easter, probably Rouen, but there is nothing certain or definite. There might be a switch, sending me off into quite a different direction.

1915. It was reprinted several times over the course of the war (50 000 copies) and was hugely popular. RDG appears to be ordering reprint copies via his wife. Whitmell died in May 1917, and was the daughter of Sir William Foster and wife of the astronomer and poet Charles Thomas Whitmell.

606 **Eccelesiastes 12:5** 'Also *when* they shall be afraid of *that which is* high, and fears *shall be* in the way, and the almond tree shall flourish, and the grasshopper shall be a burden, and desire shall fail: because man goeth to his long home, and the mourners go about the streets.'

The move is not to the superficially more attractive or more interesting work, and I dislike the idea of a 'base' more than words can say, but we are not out to choose 'places in the limelight!'

I got some knowledge of the Presbytarian's previous history. He was largely responsible for the agitation about the rank of the Principle Chaplain! He also claimed to hold services for C of E troops, when chaplains were wanting, which was kind of him, but proposed that chaplains need not be sent as he was ready to take the services, and would read the absolution, or do anything else you liked if it were desired! Which was a way of covering over the fewness of his own following, that does not commend itself to many men whose Church views were more definite!

A very nice lantern service this evening and I believe much blessing was vouchsafed.

I am delighted to hear that we have brought down another Zeppelin – that will help chasten their zeal, and also that we are building zeppelins – the meshes are closing in[607].

Monday April 3rd 1916, Hazebrouck
My darling – quite a fat-looking letter from you tonight – posted apparently on Friday, and arriving this evening (Monday) – fairly good travelling from a country district. Money is tight now-a-days all round. Mr Bull's letter seems to acknowledge that – as his previous one did not, which was probably not unintentional. Except that it would be such a blessing after the strenuous and perilous life out here, and after your comparative homelessness, to sit down amid the peaceful pleasantness of the west Farleigh countryside. It would be desireable to get, if we could, a sphere of operations nearer some educational centre – I wonder if it could be? But it would be a blessing to haste home again some time!

A glorious day and a busy one, but I broke off and had a ride in the country among the green hedges, and was then much refreshed. Fighting is rather quiet and our patients are few.

Tuesday April 4th 1916, Hazebrouck
Great flashes of light across the sky tonight, like repeated lightening and loud rumblings of artillery – there is a little something on which I divine, but may not say. It is cooler, with threatening of rain. Thank you for the parcel, all good, and not least acceptable, if not very romantic the Carbolic Soap, as dirt and septecimia are one of our worst enemies. The good man with the head wound died after all. Strange to say he was able to talk intelligently to within an hour and a half of his death. It is just as well as he must inevitably have been paralysed on that left side to the end of his days

607 Zeppelin L 15. Commanded by Kapitänleutnant Joachim Breithaupt, Damaged by ground fire from Dartford AA battery during a raid on London on April 1st, 1916, it was stranded at Knock Deep in the Thames estuary and 17 members of the crew were captured, one having died.

and always a drag on someone[608]. How many of them there will be in England after this – and in Germany! It was good work bringing down that Zepplin, and there are rumours of a second. And as we are building them too, I think the days of that kind of menace are going to be shortened.

I start early in the morning to run down to Boulogne, Tuckey wished it, I assume, for a talk about his future plans as he leaves two days later for the new sphere. I take Beale with me, the nice Doctor who is off on leave, and intends then to rejoin for another year. A hitch at the last moment has been an uncertainty about the car! A Colonel, not wishing to be without his for the day, (although Wednesday is the day for the Chaplain's first call on it), and the substitute car which has been obtained having promised a seat to a Major also going on leave! Life has complications manifold.

Wednesday April 5th 1916, Hazebrouck
It has been a full and interesting day with a cold ride at first in the car, but improving with the rising sun. The woods near Boulogne are beautiful with a blaze of wild flowers, aconites, primroses, violets and cowslips. The rise and fall of the land resembles the Downs as you get nearer to the sea. How settled and peaceful the life of the town looked after these parts. The 'Sussex' was in dock – a pitiable sight with her bows knocked away, and the spirit of all those innocent victims seemed to speak like a crowd of appellants from her wreckage-strewn deck[609]. Outside the harbour too, about a mile north, you can see the masts and funnel of another wreck standing out of the water – the ship was torpedoed near Lemareux about a month ago. The Germans have a great deal to answer for[610].

I duly deposited my doctor on the 'leave' boat, and also a Major who goes on leave with his hand in plaster of Paris, the muscles clogged through a gun accident. The Officers Club, which has been opened by some generous lady, is an excellent institution. There I picked up Tuckey, we had lunch and I have just got back after a call at the D.C.G.'s office.

---

608 Pte **A. Wilkinson**, 8th Bn East Yorkshire Regiment, died 4th April 1916. Buried Hazebrouck Communal Cemetery.

609 *Sussex* was a cross-English Channel passenger ferry, built in 1896 for the London, Brighton and South Coast Railway (LBSCR). On 24th March 1916, *Sussex* was on a voyage from Folkestone to Dieppe when she was torpedoed by SM *UB-29*. The ship was severely damaged, with the entire bow forward of the bridge blown off. Some lifeboats were launched, but at least two of them capsized and many passengers were drowned. Of the 53 crew and 325 passengers, at least 50 were killed, although a figure of between 80 and 100 is also suggested. *Sussex* remained afloat and was eventually towed stern-first into Boulogne harbour.

610 8th March 1916. SS *Harmatris*. The cargo ship was torpedoed and sunk in the English Channel off Boulogne, Pas-de-Calais by SM *UB-18* with the loss of four of her crew.

Thursday April 6th 1916, Hazebrouck

The plan for my moving is in abeyance. There is the question, as he puts it, as to whether under the new arrangements which are being made for the working of this Army, my work ought not to lie here, and this town and district be a Senior Chaplaincy, separate from the Senior Chaplaincy of the Army – and "There arose amongst them who should be the greatest? And whoso will be great among you, let him be your minister........."[611] There is a tremendous lot of 'seeking for place' among even the Chaplains on Active Service – it makes me tired. The right and the great things are lost, and yet one is afraid to be humble with some people: they seek the 'position' without giving 'full proof' of it. The Presbyterian for instance decidedly does drink too much, cackles over obscene jokes endlessly, but he is a great fellow for asserting his status as a long-established 'regular' Chaplain (I MUST keep off him!)

This evening we had a really good concert by some men of the Flying Corps. There are voices of high quality among them and they sang songs in good taste and as far as I could judge, with ability and discernment, while the comic turns were clever and clean. One man described the difference between how things are according to the newspaper description, the novelette and the opera, as compared with real life e.g. in the last, the bride in being taken out to the yacht, falls into the sea. In real life she would be rescued in a few minutes by a boat-hook, or someone jumping in after her. In Grand Opera, they take an hour and rather more to do it and all the while the hero sings –

"My bri – i – ide is in the sea,
In the sea, in the sea, in the sea,
Yes, in the sea, my bri – i- ide is in the sea,

While the chorus of sailors, fishermen and on-lookers sing –
"Yes, his bride is in the sea"
and so on.

The hero sings – "I will save her,
I will save her, with my own life she shall be saved "
The chorus sings – "Yes, he will save her, by jumping in and save her
Yes he will save her
He will save her
Yes – he will save her by jumping in
Even at the risk of his own life for the great love in which he loves her
He will jump in and (notes swelling up to the roof- full chorus)
He will save HER

Meanwhile the bride sings –

---

611 **Matthew 20:26** 'But it shall not be so among you: but whosoever will be great among you, let him be your minister'

Oh Rupert, into the sea I fall
The water covers me over all
The sea, the sea, the wet, wet sea
Oh Rupert – From the wet, wet sea
Behold me as I cry to thee
Oh save me from the wet, wet sea", etc.

and the soldiers whistled again and again for an encore! It is nice when you can pull off a good and bright evening like that.

More about 'leave.' I think I shall definitely try and get away on Easter Monday. If any move does not take place it may not be so easy to get the extended leave – but I shall try. The delapidations ought to be finished up – and the <u>teeth</u>, and there ought to be a few days of clean 'leave' besides.

Friday April 7th 1916, Hazebrouck
A lot of this morning was taken up with Tuckey, talking of much that did not signify – I can understand the complaint of the people who say that he bores them. Well! How much do we, perhaps, bore other people? I think if I can that I shall stay on in this charge – if only other people will 'do their work' and let you do yours!

It was interesting to have a shrapnel-wounded man run up this evening, who was <u>very</u> glad of a talk, and saying to me, "Weren't you our Chaplain at [*…censored…*] well, I am glad to see you again".

I wonder what the young people will find to do with themselves? I think a regular bit of work of some kind daily keeps the mind from becoming vagrant and dissipated.

Saturday April 8th 1916, Hazebrouck
A pretty full day of odds and ends, as Saturday generally is and more work to do, the nice Wesleyan Chaplain, Beard, having gone to a Division, our Chaplain Brockington having gone on leave and Tuckey having left – three Chaplains less in one week (and as you know, the Presbyterian is not a tower of strength!). However, you have to cut your coat accordingly.

Heavy booming all day and this evening, and flashes across the sky. There were two loud explosions about an hour ago, which some think are aeroplane bombs again – peut etre que oui, peut etre que non! My move from here is now all uncertain – if this does not take place, there will possibly be difficulty about an extended leave.

Sunday April 9th 1916, Hazebrouck
I am glad that you and the children had tea at a creamery. It sounds like a little treat and the very word cream! – only the very rich houses in Germany have fat in their

foods and cream I take it, is practically unknown. There is fresh milk for children under 6 years of age and only a quarter of a pound of butter per person per week, and the mark is still going down.

The old Presbyterian is out-reaching himself. I have begun a Sunday evening service – the second Sunday I was unable to be there, so invited him to take it. He was immensely pleased to have a large assembly to deal with – and without consultation with me, proceeded to take the following Sunday evening as well. The next Sunday I had to be away again and so it fell to him without question. The Sunday following, I proposed to resume it, putting it that I was free and that it came to be my turn. He was a little startled, but agreed as well he might, and so we have gone on since. Each Sunday evening that I was free, I took my turn and each time his attitude was rather that of letting me take the service – the service that I had inaugurated. This Sunday it was his turn, and I stated it so, and he agreed, but note, he had the service announced in the Town Orders as one for Presbyterians and non-conformists! They have strange ideas, some of these men but things gradually work out 'and by their fruits ye shall know them'[612]. Now further, he has taken his usual quarterly 'leave' (which for those going to Scotland is 11 days) in spite of having had over a month for going to, and returning from and staying at Nice all at the Government's expense. He truly does, as he himself says "know how to work it". He goes tomorrow, and we are reduced from 7 Chaplains to 3 for all these Clearing Stations, and the troops in and about the town – Platt and myself Anglicans and the Roman Catholic. I offered myself for the Non-Conformist service in the Y.M.C.A. tent this evening and the offer was cordially welcomed. There were about 18 present and we had an enjoyable and devout time and a taste of the old Trinity Cambridge days in the Trinity Place Mission room – our assembly was of all and sundry, including a Salvation Army 'envoy' and a Baptist local preacher.

Monday April 10th 1916, Hazebrouck

It has been a day of full pressure, as the Presbyterian has gone on leave and left me his serious cases to visit, and to bury in some cases, and there are also some serious cases of our own. We feel the effect of the recent fighting that you will have read about, but plenty of work is good for health of body, mind and spirit.

Tuesday April 11th 1916, Hazebrouck

I was up late last night with an Australian from Manly, in with acute appendicitis[613]. He is a strong man but he was nervous and anxious about the operation and very thankful for a talk about it and for my assurance of how skilfully it is managed now-a-days. It

---

612 **Matthew 7:16;** 'Ye shall know them by their fruits. Do men gather grapes of thorns, or figs of thistles?'

613 Manly is a beach-side suburb of northern Sydney.

was something to be able to tell him of how Griff[614]got through his – and what good it did. Today he is critically ill after the operation, but his constitution is good and the doctors think he will possibly pull right. Those travels in Sydney Diocese, to Melbourne and Ballarat and so on are proving of great service in all this pastoral work among the Australian men. "What part do you come from?" "Near Randwick, by the zoo". "That used to be Dr. Manning's parish" "Yes, Dr Manning married me"[615] – you can guess how the talk leads on, how I know Randwick, how he knew by sight Archbishop Saumarez-Smith, the way he puts it as "I knew him well". It is a great institution, the Pastoral System of the Church of England, and I think of a saying of Dr. Moule's "The Church in the abstract is Christ in the concrete"[616]. All this is a furthering of his arms round His brethren "the blessed company of all faithful people"[617] and we have many Australians with us now. The sudden change from the climate of Gallipoli, then Egypt and directly into snow as it has happened when they came into these parts, has set up pneumonia and other chest troubles, and the Australian constitution is not built for violent cold.

This evening has been taken up by two German prisoners, and one of our English doctor officers, who brought them in. The former are well kept, and say that the food is good nearer the trenches, and not so good further back, and not worth speaking of much in their country. I have not heard what they think about the issue of the war yet. The doctor is interesting because he was himself a prisoner in Germany. He was in a group surrounded near Neuve Chapelle in October last year, just before our Division got up to hold that line of trenches. When he was marched a prisoner through Neuve Chapelle, the village was in flames. As they went through the French villages, the people used to come out and cheer them up and the Germans were very angry and drove them away. He thinks that the behaviour of the Germans to their prisoners is consistently unkind and coarse. As he was being taken from one train to another in a German station, two men with fixed bayonets escorted him to the carriage, one in front and one behind, but as he was getting up into the carriage, a civilian in a compartment nearby saw him and, running forward, called him a violent ugly name of some sort and gave him a most terrific kick from behind. A British officer asked a German Red Cross woman for a drink of water – she brought it to him but as she was handing it to him, she spat into it. They had practically to live upon the parcels sent to them from home, and the Russians, who cannot at all quickly get their parcels since they have to travel via Norway or the like, scarcely get enough to keep them going. It rather bears out what the Court of Enquiry have just issued as they report on the statement of Maj. Priestley, Capt. Vidal and Capt Lander – all RAMC. We are fighting against no imaginary evil[618].

---

614 RDG's brother
615 Rev. Dr. **J N Manning**, Rector, St Jude's, Randwick
616 **Handley Carr Glyn Moule** (b.1841 – d.1920) was an evangelical Anglican theologian, writer, poet, and Bishop of Durham from 1901–1920.
617 Book of Common Prayer, Holy Eucharist, Rite 1.
618 Wittenberg, officially Lutherstadt Wittenberg, is a city in Germany in the Bundesland Saxony-Anhalt, on the river Elbe. German Camp for POWs. Government Committee of Inquiry,

Wednesday April 12th 1916, Hazebrouck

Cold rain. A very busy and full day, the odds and ends of 3 chaplains as well as my own, but it does make the time go by! I gave my S. African slides again this evening, but the lantern did not work very well – the first time it has failed, but I feel sure that the men were interested. What a serious business the Wittenberg Camp seems to have been: perhaps still is!

Thursday April 13th 1916, Hazebrouck

Rather a set-back today as all leave is stopped after the 18th, so that even if one went tomorrow or the day after, everybody is expected to have returned by the 18th, which would mean about one day in England. I do not know if there is a likelihood of getting a special leave – it is possible, but you have to give very weighty reasons to get it. (PRIVATE – Rumour has it that this means very heavy fighting – if it does, one must pray and trust.) Never was there more need for the power of prayer than there will be this time. Whichever side attacks, and the rumour is that it will be the enemy, it will mean an unprecedented effort, and it may be the turning point of the war – let us hope it will be. There is a possibility of a 4th Chaplain here, as there should be, and we shall be a 'command' to ourselves, with I myself as what they call the 'bishop'.

I am watching the passing away of a number of souls just now. Strange – that sleep and unresponsiveness of the body, the wandering mind, the dullness, the mechanical twitching. Yet, the Word that cannot fail says "because I live, ye shall live also[619]". He "shall change our vile body that it may be like unto His glorious body[620]". "I am come that they might have life, and might have it more abundantly[621]." "Yet in my flesh shall I see God[622]".

A wretched guest night dinner – much wine and whiskey drunk and a great deal of chattering nonsense. A new doctor (called Tannahill) has come, a quiet, literary man and a teetotaller and congenial company, and sits next to me[623].

Sleep well, my darling.

---

presided over by Mr Justice Younger. The report is based on the statements from repatriated prisoners of war, and especially from Major Priestley, Captain Vidal and Captain Lauder R.A.M.C. the only survivors of six British doctors sent from another camp to take the place of duty abandoned by the German medical staff when the typhus manifested itself (winter 1914–15). The camp was grossly overcrowded. While typhus was raging 15 000 prisoners (700 British) were contained to its ten and half acres. Prisoners were also severely mistreated.

619 **John 14:19** 'Yet a little while, and the world seeth me no more; but ye see me: because I live, ye shall live also.'

620 **Phillipians 3:21** 'Who shall change our vile body, that it may be fashioned like unto his glorious body, according to the working whereby he is able even to subdue all things unto himself.'

621 **John 10:10** 'The thief cometh not, but for to steal, and to kill, and to destroy: I am come that they might have life, and that they might have *it* more abundantly.'

622 **Job 19:26** 'And *though* after my skin *worms* destroy this *body*, yet in my flesh shall I see God.'

623 Lieut **William Bow Tannahill**, RAMC (b.1881 – d.1941)

Friday April 14th 1916, Hazebrouck

I shall be thankful when our strength of Chaplains is restored nearer its normal. There is much to do with our own Clearing Station, Brockington's[624], the Office, the Officers' Hospital, the Presbyterians' odds and ends, the Wesleyans' also and the Club.

The weather has been trying today with hail, cold rain, sleet, snow, wind and thunder. There were three burials, which at the last minute, Pratt took over at the burying ground gate, and I was thankful. It is a question when 'leave' will re-open again – they hold out no prospect for some time. I must find out for certain next week. I may find time to write to one or two of the children, but it is high pressure here just now.

Sunday April 15th 1916, Hazebrouck

Much booming across in the direction of [...*censored*...][625] and so the game of killing goes on, and there it is, all along that black sinuous line across Europe, out into Asia and up to the Baltic Sea, while anywhere at any moment out upon the ocean, lurking perils may burst into destruction for numbers of innocent lives. What a nightmare the Kaiser must be laying up for himself – the Kaiser and his military advisers – unless "their conscience is seared with a hot iron, speaking lies in hypocrisy"[626] a kind of hypocrisy that comes of hardened self-deceit. Their reply over the 'Sussex' reads like a derision. Since America has taken up the matter at all, I cannot understand their long-drawn patience – perhaps they are waiting until they are strong enough to be able to speak peremptorily?

Sunday is very full of odds and ends – the Australian, operated on for appendicitis, is getting on well, but it will be a pull for him. A shell wound in the spine has gone down to the Base and the shell wound in the head is gradually sinking day by day. Able to speak 'yes' and 'no','drink' but breathing on evenly and steadily, like a little child, out into another life.

We have succeeded in gaining a notable concession from the Abbe Lemire who is the acting Mayor of the town. All our Holy Week, Good Friday and Easter Day services are to be put up at the Town Hall – Tuckey failed to get permission at Christmas-tide! Was it my excellent French, my gentle and persuasive manner (which you know so well, old rascal!), or that, as I urged Eastertide was so very special an occasion? The last, no doubt.

There is a new rumour now – leave may re-open after the 28th, then I shall come that day or the next, if it be so. Please let me come to the Red House[627] for a few days – I

---

624 Rev **Alfred Allan Brockington** (b.1872 – d.1938) chaplain attached to the 15th Casualty Clearing Station RAMC, June 1916, and with the 23rd Brigade RFA (3rd Division), June – September 1916. His son was killed in September 1916, he was apparently transferred to the UK by January 1917.

625 Probably Verdun to the south, then entering into its third phase, with the German bombardment of Avocourt Wood.

626 I Timothy 4:2 'Speaking lies in hypocrisy; having their conscience seared with a hot iron.'

627 The Red House, Hurstpierpoint, Sussex. Built by the church commissioners as the rectory for the Rev. Richard Bevan (Trinity, Cambs) in 1900. When the Reverend Bevan moved away to

want to go somewhere and be quiet and 'human' again. How much prayer one needs in the midst of so much ceaselessness and foolishness that is existing here. The strain becomes very great sometimes and some of the younger men seem possessed with a kind of madness of folly. They read fast French magazines, they drink too much wine, they get through their work as speedily and indifferently as possible and then complain that they have nothing to do with their time. Yet, you cannot live people's lives for them. I am sorry the little son has to lose a tooth. I hope it is not a difficult one and, as I expect, will be so kind as to come out readily. The chief thing is keeping the mouth well rinsed with a pure mouth-wash afterwards.

Monday April 16th 1916, Hazebrouck

A beautiful day, and a nice ending with a letter from you. I was unable to have any ward service, having promised to ride out to an ambulance in a neighbouring village, viz. the one attached to George Thomas's Division. The ride was delightful, with beautiful birds, tom-tits, yellow-hammers, magpies, thrushes, windmills, one or two busy though on a Sunday morning, masses of flowers, daisies, violets, cowslips and some primroses, and a nice open-air service in the glad morning sunshine. Then a nice lunch and a long talk with an officer whose work, early on in the war, had included buying up for the Government some of the Tunbridge Wells motor buses, and some of those running to Maidstone and Chatham, etc., then a long ride back to censoring, and this evening a very largely attended service, hearty and real and receptive in the Mairie.

It was nice to find your letter this evening – that is a time when one feels emptied out and rather worthless.

Tuesday April 17th 1916, Hazebrouck

It is a beautiful moonlit night which is a temptation to aircraft of an obnoxious kind, but at present there have been no signs of them. It is true that they dropped four bombs in the vicinity of the town on Saturday night – the military spirit in Germany has much to answer for, and we can only pray "for we wrestle not with flesh and blood but against principalities, against powers, against the rulers of the darkness of this world, against spiritual wickedness in high places"[628], and there prayer is a power which is ultimately the deciding power. Germany needs a new mind and a different inspiration, but England <u>does</u> need cleansing also.

---

become Rector of Binfield, Berkshire in 1909, the Church Commissioners sold it. Now called Furlong House, it was the residence of Mary De Bryune and Henry de Bruyne until 1976. Ownership of the Red House between 1909 and the early 1930's is not known, but Mary Campbell Smith Foster ('Aunt Mai', the sister of Archbishop William Saumarez-Smith – RDG's wife's aunt, and wife of Ebenzer Bird Foster), died there on 25 July 1927, so presumably it was owned by some faction of the Foster Campbells. It is possible that Aunt Mai moved to the Red House from Anstey Hall in Trumpington, after the death of her husband, in 1908.

628 **Ephesians 6:12** 'For we wrestle not against flesh and blood, but against principalities, against powers, against the rulers of the darkness of this world, against spiritual wickedness in high *places*.'

In the little chapel at the Soldiers Club this evening we had a short service of prayer and meditation – one quiet New Zealander only, besides Platt and myself.

Leave may re-open on the 28th, but I can learn nothing definite as at present all is dumb silence about any possibilities, as far as any authority is concerned.

Wednesday April 18th 1916, Hazebrouck

I have been thinking aloud at our evening meeting in the Soldiers Club on Christ's words "Today shalt thou <u>be with</u> Me in Paradise[629]" They are a wonderful promise – 'those we have loved long since and lost awhile' have seen the fulfilment of that promise[630]. There were only 2 soldiers and Pratt in the devotional room, but we shall get on now by degrees, I think.

Brockington returned from 'leave' today, very depressed at coming away, so I offered him plenty of work – it is a great absorbent of the virus of vain regrets! Our hands are very full just now – the Recreation Room gets crowded and there are many patients also in this unpleasant weather, many of them New Zealanders and Australians. The Australian appendicitis is doing very well indeed now. I find that the Senior Chaplain's work for a large town demands very much time and energy, and many details come up that would scarcely be thought of from outside.

Thursday April 20th 1916, Hazebrouck

Some people have an idea that clergymen have not much to do except killing time – let them come and try it! I find that being the Senior Chaplain of a large town is a fairly arduous occupation, though it is very interesting.

Today, Platt having a New Zealander to look up in a neighbouring village, I went out with him in the hope of being able to find the Dean of Sydney, who I heard was quartered in the same village[631]. It took much longer that I thought, or wanted, as it appears that Platt is a very nervous rider and does not like his horse to go beyond a walk, except now and again as a fearful venture along quiet bits of road! The wind was keen and cutting too, and it would have been nice to get warm with a good spin! By dint of pressure gently applied we got a good many brave little spurts, but it was slow work and Platt is not very apologetic about wanting to keep the pace mainly at a walking rate – Voila! A good Lenten discipline. We passed a charming copse with the buds bursting gladly and as the sun was out and the ground ablaze with wild flowers, it was very pleasant. Platt did not actually find his man but traced him, but we could find nothing of the movements of the Very Rev. Dean, so I suppose that he has moved

---

629 **Luke 23:43** 'And Jesus said unto him, Verily I say unto thee, Today shalt thou be with me in paradise.'

630 Hymn: *Lead, Kindly Light* is a hymn with words written in 1833 by John Henry Newman as a poem titled "the Pillar of Cloud".

631 Rev. **Albert Edward Talbot**, Dean of St Andrew's Sydney, 1912–1936

on. Then visiting about, censoring and preparing for tomorrow and Sunday, and this evening we had a nice Passiontide service in the little Chapel.

The N.Z.s and Australians are making full use of the Club, and the numbers at the little service were quite good, the room being nearly full, while about the middle in came a N. Z. Major and a Captain. The former proved to be a chaplain – Archdeacon Hawkins from Auckland[632]. Pratt gave a nice address on the words of desolation "My God, my God, why hast thou forsaken me?" (a little hard perhaps, but how easily one's feelings can critisise!) He was sympathetic about how many of us know the meaning of separation in this War.

Friday April 21st 1916 (Good Friday), Hazebrouck

Heavy rain – odds and ends – and much visiting – "And what part of the world do you come from?" "Paddock Wood[633], Sir" "Do you know West Farleigh?" "I do a bit, Sir" "That is my part of the country!"– and the man's face lights up and he begins to talk of all kinds of people and places round about, and I am the first person he says that he has met from his part of the country for over a year. Our Australian friend is not going on so well – his name is Vickers.

At the last moment, I hear that leave will be re-opened shortly but the chances of an extended leave are only very remote. In view of so much uncertainty, may I ask to come to Aunt Mai – a kind of stranger who took me in. At this distance and with these uncertainties I feel rather feeble about making arrangements, but if it be true about this re-opening, I shall try and come <u>at the end of next week</u>.

In censoring the letters this evening, the Presbyterian noticed that one letter was addressed by a patient to a name similar to that of one of the sick officers (who signed his own envelope). He had the curiosity to follow it up and then it transpired that they were brothers, the one an officer in an English regiment brought to this Officers' Hospital by chance, the other a private in a New Zealand regiment brought into the men's hospital also by chance. Neither was aware of the other's vicinity, and they have not met for four years since the younger brother went out to New Zealand[634]. Their surprise and delight has been interesting, and we hope that they may meet in a day or two, and furthermore, their name is Cranswick, so I asked them if they knew Canon Cranswick of Sydney, and they are cousins![635]

---

632 Rev. **Hector Alfred Hawkins** (b.1871 – b.1948) of Remuera, Auckland, New Zealand. Missionary to the Maori, 1900–12.

633 Paddock Wood is a small town and civil parish in the Borough of Tunbridge Wells and county of Kent in England, about 8 miles southwest of Maidstone.

634 Pvte **Thomas Bertram Cranswick** (b.1888 – d.1917) 1st Bn, Wellington Regiment, N.Z.E.F. Son of John and Charlotte Cranswick, of The Red House, Scalby, Scarborough. Killed 7th June 1917.

635 Rev **Edward Glensville Cranswick** (d.1934), canon of St Andrew's Cathedral, Sydney (1911– 1934). Born in Stalybridge, E Yorkshire.

A nice service in the Club Chapel this evening with six present and I spoke on the words "I thirst: It is finished", we can rest on that[636]. The services on the whole have been good – at the Maire a good attendance this morning, and a fair one this evening. Our nice Major (Nightingale) went today – constant changes.

Saturday April 22nd 1916, Hazebrouck

The little son 12 years old today! Old enough to enter the Navy, had that been his calling!

A nice talk this evening at the Club by Brockington, he thinks good things so it is curious that with such good thoughts he should be so uncourageous in dealing with the men. It is a matter of nerves very much. In the club, among the men, a smiling face kept looking towards me which at first I did not recognise, then it came home to me the remembrance of young (Tom?) Hayward from Teston whom I met that one evening at the Base 7 months ago. He has been through his 'baptism of fire' and is now batman to an officer who has come into our hospital sick.

Sunday April 23rd 1916, Hazebrouck. Easter Day

This is the time of day, darling, when I ask much mercy, and only hope that there are still some praying friends who really mean their prayers. It has been a long day with varying experiences – light and shade – the light, the joy and grace of God and the goodness of many people, and the beautiful weather: the shade, the absentees, the indifferent ones and the humanness of one's own feeling. One shadier side was a little unecessary – the Town Major, in some ways an odd man, had offered to decorate the Temporary Military Church for the day, and as in private life he is an Estate Agent (though also a retired officer), he succeeded well in that way, and I must say, made the chancel look exceedingly nice with roses, white flowers and plants. But, he has mixed ecclesiastical views – likes to go to listen to the Mass in the R.C. Church and comes to us for Evening Communion. It appears he thought how nice the altar would look in the vesper lights, so without asking anyone he propped up two lots of three lights behind the flowers, never dreaming they might not be acceptable to some. At the 7.0am service I found them there and did not quite know what to do. At length, I decided to remove them. Then when I had them on the harmonium, I wondered whether I would not return them. Then I thought I would place them in a side place, and while I was debating, one of the candles toppled off, and I find that they are fixed on small nails. So that decided me, and I put them on one side. This evening they are restored by someone – so I let them be! Alas I did so want the day to be a day of 'souls' rest for everyone.

---

636 **John 19:28** 'After this, Jesus knowing that all things were now accomplished, that the scripture might be fulfilled, saith, I thirst.'

The services seem to have been very well attended, and the spirit of devotion seemed full and glad in the service. At 7 am there were 16, at 8 and 10 I do not know, and this evening the Hall was quite full, and 10 stayed for Holy Communion. We had a nice service at the Officers' Hospital and also one at the Clearing Station at which a staff officer stayed behind and chatted. We both had the feeling of a previous meeting and recognised each other almost simultaneously. He was Captain Rasch[637], who was adjutant of the Grenadier Guards that Sunday when we had a service with the Prince of Wales present – it was a pleasant meeting, so many of the officers present then are gone! And in this weeks Illustrated News I see the last officer but one from that nice regiment I spent that first night in the trenches with, has gone. Major Haldane 2nd Northamptonshire[638] – how much Easter means!

Monday April 24th 1916, Hazebrouck

A very full day with a lecture this evening by Anderson with Ponting's Cinema pictures, the same as we saw at Maidstone with a few good additional ones – a most successful evening[639].

A new clerk has come to superintend the mails (in an old Pawn shop here by the bye!). We looked at each other, sure that there had been a previous acquaintance. Yes, he had come out with the VIIIth Division, and we had had friendly words there. Then it came out that he had been in Tunbridge Wells, and in two choirs, Holy Trinity and St. Johns' (Mr Parsons, who was at St Aidans the same time as myself.) I mentioned having a son at school at Southborough, and he asked, "Mr. Bulls'?" and said that he had seen the boys going down to Tunbridge Wells etc.

I am asking for leave at the end of this week!

Tuesday April 25th 1916, Hazebrouck

I have just heard that a warrant is available for Saturday night – rather a rush of things in prospect of leave again. I have written to Mr Fawns proposing to go down for the day on Monday and stay the night of that day with Sophie, and if it is really quite convenient come to the Red House for Tuesday.

---

637 Capt. **Guy Elland Carne Rasch** (b.1885 – d.1955), DSO, Grenadier Guards. He was the younger son of Carne Rasch, Conservative Member of Parliament for South East Essex and Chelmsford. The **Rasch Baronetcy**, of Woodhill in Danbury in the County of Essex, is a title in the Baronetage of the United Kingdom. It was created on 29th August 1903.

638 Maj. **Laurence Aylmer Haldane** DSO (b.1884 – d.1916) 2nd Northamptonshire

639 **Herbert George Ponting**, FRGS (b.1870 – d.1935) was a professional photographer. He is best known as the expedition photographer and cinematographer for Robert Falcon Scott's Terra Nova Expedition to the Ross Sea and South Pole (1910–1913). 'Mr Herbert G Ponting's Cinema Lecture, With Captain Scott in the Antarctic', and leaflets promoting the lecture, paper, published; T Whittingham & Co Ltd, England, 1914.

Bombs in the next town yesterday with some motor ambulances destroyed, but no one hit! There were 24 bombs in all, and 15 in another neighbouring town this morning with some victims – our turn again no doubt in a day or two, if this weather continues.

Wednesday April 26th 1916, Hazebrouck

A beautiful day – at about 10 am a hostile aeroplane buzzed loudly above us, he went reconnoitring out to the suburbs of the town, and there half an hour afterward, we heard that he had been shot down. That is the third enemy plane brought down in this locality in these last two days. Another dying face today – one gets so sad and weary of them.

I quite expect to leave here Saturday and so get to London Saturday evening. If not, it will be Sunday afternoon and I do not like travelling on the Sunday even in War time.

Thursday April 27th 1916, Hazebrouck

I am wondering if anything might happen at the last minute to make the journey impossible! A busy day preparing things in advance and handing over details to my Locum Tenens here, and a good concert tonight.

Friday April 28th 1916, Hazebrouck

I hope we shall meet very soon, my dear lady and please thank Aunt Mai most warmly for letting me come. I do leave here tomorrow, Saturday, and if I get the boat, I shall be in London tomorrow night, at Sophie's. I have proposed going down to West Farleigh on Monday – there will be some business to do in London on Tuesday morning. I should like to be able to come down to Hurstpierpoint (*the Red House*) Tuesday evening – I daresay there is some afternoon train (we have no timetables here). If this nice weather continues, what a help it will be. It is unfortunate about the cow. I think after this, we must get rid of her, and when we set up again, get ordinary shorthorns. I am posting this tonight – it will cross the Channel probably about the same time as I do!

I went across the hill this morning to the spot where the enemy aeroplane was brought down the day before yesterday. It fell into a ditch by the roadside, a drop of 12000ft, and the pilot was killed by a machine gun from one of our aeroplanes, and the observer died from the fall. Written instructions were found on one of them to reconnoitre this place and two others, and to drop bombs on a third. Enemy aeroplanes over early this morning – they are fairly active just now.

Saturday April 29th 1916 In the train – Folkstone to Victoria 10.30pm

After various minor adventures, I write once again on English soil. I left my billet at 5.55 am this morning and reached Boulogne at 11, and the boat did not leave till

8.15 p.m.! A peremptory notice on the quay says "The Leave Boat departs this day at 8.15 p.m. There is <u>absolutely no other</u> boat <u>before 8.15 p.m.</u>" Boulogne is getting more and more inhabited by the British, as the shops, hotels and even the banks, show. Lady Dudley has set up a free Club for British Officers, and it is an immense boon[640]. Thither I fared, for a wash and brush-up, and then I went off to the Bank as I find myself short of money and tomorrow is Sunday. In the window of a hatters' shop are displayed fragments of anti-aircraft shells which had fallen at different times about the town. They are out there as an incitement to the inhabitants to obey the military instructions that everyone must <u>keep indoors</u> when enemy aircraft visit the place. On the quay, I met Baldwin, Chaplain of one of our Clearing Stations – he has been on 6 weeks sick leave. Nearby I met one of the young doctors who was with the 24th Field Ambulance and in the street over the bridge appeared Lieut. Weekes, brother of George Thomas' fiancée and we had tea together later. On the ship was a Canadian Officer, who remembered my visiting the Officers' Hospital – and so on!

A beautiful sunset, and a successful passage with the aid of due patrols and, the first time it has happened on my own journeying, an order came round the ship that we were all to get a life belt and wear it. A whole crowded boat-load of Khaki-clad passengers look rather odd in the half light of the stars and dim deck lights, all wearing cork straightjackets! Three of my fellow passengers as I write, are annoyed to find that as the arrival here is so late (10.05) at Folkstone, they miss the midnight train for the north and it being Sunday, they cannot get another one till the evening – a second day to fritter through!

TWO WEEKS LEAVE

Thursday May 11th 1916, Hazebrouck

I am in the whirl of the life of the Army again, my darling.

I met the Deputy Chaplain General (on the ship), Crick, one of the former VIII Division Chaplains and Lycett, who we called to see once at Snodland, do you remember? He remembered Eric and how he clung to a little blind bunny![641] and Buxton, now a vicar in Southport, who is just joining as a Chaplain[642].

Goodnight, Darling.

---

640 **Georgina Elisabeth Ward, Countess of Dudley** RRC DStJ (b.1846 – d.1929) was the wife of William Ward, 1st Earl of Dudley (d.1885) and a noted beauty of the Victorian era. She was a daughter of Sir Thomas Moncreiffe of that Ilk, 7th Baronet, and Lady Louisa Hay-Drummond. During the Boer War and WW1, Lady Dudley served with the British Red Cross Society.

641 **Snodland** is a small town in the county of Kent, England, located on the River Medway between Rochester and Maidstone.

642 Rev. **Arthur Buxton** (b.1882 – d.1958). He was the son of John Henry Buxton and Emma Maria Pelly. He married Esme Caroline Pixley, daughter of Colonel Francis William Pixley, on 14th January 1908. Educated at Harrow, graduated from Trinity College, Cambridge in 1908. He was the Rector between 1920 – 1936 at All Souls, Langham Place. He was the Rector at All Saints, Southport, Lancashire.

Friday May 12th 1916, Hazebrouck

It is all deeply interesting, though there is the reaction of coming back here, and away from you all. I travelled up with Buxton, who made a very acceptable companion. At a certain station we were joined by a Chaplain from New Zealand, who had been one of Canon Burrough's curates, knew Dr Flynn very well and was very glad to get tips about work out here. He occupies the house next to the one that I slept in last year, and the place has been shelled again as it was this time last year!

There has been a plague of work but it is very pleasant to see the smiles of recognition and greeting among the men. And now, most interestingly, I have just had a long chat with Prof. David of Sydney, who is here 2nd in Command in the same Australian Troops. He wears the Antarctic medal ribbon, which is pure white[643]. He was interested to know that I had spoken with Sir Lewis Beaumont the day before yesterday. Then a chat with Capt. Anderson, son of the Bishop of Riverina[644] – he was so glad to talk with someone who knows his father. You would not remember how we used to chat with Bp. Anderson while he smoked on the veranda at Bishopthorpe. These Australians are fascinating, and how they 'light up' when we talk of Coogee Bay, Bondi beach, Illawarra and so on. One weather-worn Australian warrior, from Brisbane, drifting from one link at that end to the fact that I came from a parish near Orpington, Kent, got into a long confidential explanation about the merits of blending White Wyandotter with Buff Orpingtons[645], (being that he is in the poultry

---

643 Prof. Sir **Tannatt William Edgeworth David**, KBE, CMG, DSO, FRS, (b.1858 – d.1934), was a Welsh Australian geologist and Antarctic explorer. David's most significant achievements were discovering the major Hunter Valley coalfield in New South Wales and leading the first expedition to reach the South Magnetic Pole. In 1891, David was appointed Professor of Geology at the University of Sydney, a position he held until 1924. In August 1915, after reading reports about mining operations and tunelling during the Gallipoli Campaign, David wrote a proposal suggesting that the government raise a military force to undertake mining and tunnelling. He set up the Australian Mining Corps, and on 25th October 1915 he was appointed as a major, at the age of 57. The first contingent of the corps consisted of 1300 officers and men, arriving on the Western Front in May 1916. Given the title 'Geological Adviser to the Controllers of Mines in the First, Second and Third Armies', David became relatively independent and spent his time in geological investigations, using his expertise to advise on the construction of dugouts, trenches, and tunnels, the siting of wells for provision of pure drinking water from underground supplies, giving lectures, and producing maps. On 7th June 1917, his wartime contribution culminated in the mining of German positions in the Battle of Messines.

644 Capt. **Ralph Anderson** (b.1992 – d.1917) 52 Bn Australian Infantry, A.I.F. Died of wounds 8th June 1917.
Bp **Ernest Augustus Anderson** (b.1859 – d.1945). Queens' College, Cambridge. North Queensland as a mission preacher in 1882, was made deacon, and in 1883 ordained priest. Married Amelia Constance Isabel Ross (d.1917). Rector of St Thomas's, Hughenden, in 1886–91. In 1891, appointed to St Paul's, West Maitland, where he became known as a vigorous Low Church preacher. In 1894 Bishop of the Riverina.

645 The **Orpington** is a breed of chicken named after Orpington, England, which was made famous in part by this breed. Belonging to the English class of chickens, it was bred to be an excellent layer with good meat quality. Their large size and soft appearance together with their rich colour and gentle contours make them very attractive, and as such its popularity has grown as a show bird. The **Wyandotte** is a breed of chicken originating in the United States. The first examples of the breed appeared in the 1870s. Wyandottes are a docile, dual-purpose breed kept for their

farming line himself) and grew wistful as at last he remarked how he would like to see that famous poultry neighbourhood himself, now that he is so near!!

I do hope that you are not overtired with our journeying. It is rather annoying to think that it was not essential to leave until 2.55 from Charing Cross, though I believe coming by that train means paying one's own fare, the 'leave' voucher not being available. It is just as well, perhaps, that they do not make the 'leave' journeying too simple – it is a great thing being able to get it at all. How interesting, wasn't it, to find Prof. David and Capt. Anderson in this place. The former took down Sir Lewis Beaumont's address – asked for it: I hope I was right in giving it as St Georges' Hurstpierpoint. I am trusting to see something of him again. They were glad to hear of our C of E services, as by the Australian plan only one Chaplian is appointed to a Brigade, and the one they have is a Wesleyan. I find on my return that the Fund has been enriched by further voluntary offerings £7.13.6 in all with £5.13.6. transmitted from Singapore, and two gifts of £1 each sent direct. All of which, as I find that the Club has been crowded out again, is so much to the good – the Club is a great boon.

It is well to have plenty to do as there is than less room for feelings, and we are in an atmosphere electric with activity.

Saturday May 13th 1916, Hazebrouck
A notice received today tells us that the Archbishop of Canterbury[646] is coming into our neighbourhood on Wednesday next, into a town that has been considerably bombed and somewhat shelled. I hope it may be possible for me to go over.

It has been a full day and it is a great consolation to be full up with work. One soldier after another! "Where do you come from?" "Hobart" – and you get the home touch very soon[647]. Another man has written a long letter to his mother, near Sydney, and is very anxious to know how soon it may go off. We ring up the Army Post Office, and they tell us it may go off on Wednesday, and that is one of the uses of the telephone! Three men in to prayers in the little side chapel today.

---

brown eggs and for meat. They appear in a wide variety of colour patterns, and are popular show birds. The Wyandotte lays pale brown or tan eggs and usually has a white ring of feathers around its neck.

646 Archbishop **Randall Thomas Davidson**, GCVO, PC (b.1848 – d.1930) was an Anglican bishop of Scottish origin who served as Archbishop of Canterbury from 1903 to 1928. He was the longest holder of the office since the English Reformation. He was also the first Archbishop of Canterbury to retire, all his predecessors having died in office. Roger Lloyd, Church of England historian, thought that Davidson was one of the two or three greatest Archbishops of Canterbury. Davidson reacted to the papal bull *Apostolicae Curae* by stressing "the strength and depth of the Protestantism of England" and regarded other differences with Rome as much more important than its views on Anglican orders.

647 **Hobart** is the capital and most populous city of the Australian island state of Tasmania. Founded in 1804 as a penal colony, Hobart is Australia's second oldest capital city after Sydney.

It was nice to get your letter this evening and to know that you had got back safely after a fairly successful day, but alas! I cannot comply with the little son's request to come and see him 'soon'! Now it is late and tomorrow is Sunday.

Sunday May 14th 1916, Hazebrouck

It is cold, and dull, and damp and I daresay it is the same with you, and the tent in which we take our food, is dank and draughty! Were it not that one knows the open air life is good, it would be less easy to bear. As it is – we are on Active Service!

8.0am H.C. with 7 present, and then a service in the Officer's Hospital, in the middle of which a new young starling popped out from under a bed, and hopped around cheerfully visiting one chair after another to pay his greetings. One officer played with him a little, to their mutual satisfaction. I went up to the Y.M.C.A. tent to take the Evening Service, but found that during my 'leave', the man in charge had changed, and the newcomer, being very full of his ability to do more and yet more, I left him to it! He was a bit like the lady who would play the harmonium at Wentworth Falls "I don't wish to offend you …" [648] I have today sent in Claims for £72 back allowances – I am wondering what will be said about it, and hoping for the best!

I met the Australian Wesleyian and put him in the way of having the Maire for an afternoon service, for which he was very pleased. His men came in large numbers at 3.0 o'clock and I found subsequently, made full use of the accommodation, including the placing of chairs all round inside the Chancel rails. Mr. Wilson (the Chaplain) asked me to make it a united service with him, but as I understood that a C of E Chaplain was expected to join the Battalion soon, it seemed desirable not to anticipate any line of action he might have to re-consider.

Monday May 15th 1916, Hazebrouck

It is very splendid – the quiet bravery with which they go into the operating room. I have just been with another, an Australian whose name is Newley. And I have just left him at the operating room for an operation for appendicitis, a little apprehensive but consoled with a talk. The appendicitis man from Auckland is getting on well and a patient from Christchurch N.Z. a disciple of Bishop Julius[649], was looking after him for a while. One talks with these Anzac men over various parts of their continent, Illawarra, the Blue Mountains, Koowa, Cairns, and so on. Today "I come from Coogee myself!" from a straight young soldier. "I know Coogee a little" I said "I once lived at Bishopscourt. Do you know it?" "Do I, well I should think I do – many a hunt I've

---

648 **Wentworth Falls** is a town in the Blue Mountains region of New South Wales, situated approximately 60 miles west of Sydney.

649 Archbishop **Churchill Julius** (b.1847 – d.1938) was an Anglican cleric in England, then in Australia and New Zealand, from 1890 Bishop of Christchurch, and from 1922 becoming the first Archbishop of New Zealand.

had in that gully". "And many a hunt Tom Tunnicliffe had for you, my dear rascal"[650] I thought though I did not say it. "Do you know the Rector there, Mr Greenwwod?" – but his knowledge there was at fault, which told its own tale. It appears that this place was visited by aeroplanes once during my 'leave' and bombs were dropped just outside – their visits are getting rarer, touch wood![651]

Wednesday May 17th 1916, Hazebrouck

We have had a car lent to us, by dint of gentle courtesy, so Pratt and I got to the town of our rendezvous[652] without mishap, but not without adventure, for the village near this side had been visited by aeroplanes an hour and a half before we passed through, and had dropped bombs. One bomb had fallen on the pavement and the debris was everywhere as we passed on – one man had been killed and 7 wounded. The town itself had no visitation today, though it had had yesterday and the day before, with bombs and shells.

The meetings have been successful and valuable. We had a short 'conference' in the open in the garden behind the Soldiers' Club[653], Talbot House to be exact. That was useful, except that one or two who had not much to say, kept talking. We had tea and then a service in an upper room, which the Archbishop described truly, as a <u>very</u> Upper Room as it was above the third floor[654]. He helped our views admirably – "our position was an enviable one, to be the direct agents called of God to deal with the flower of England's manhood at a period of unique opportunity in all history." He said they were strong words but, he repeated, he believed there had never been an equal opportunity in the history of the Christian Church. There were about 100 or more chaplains present, and I suppose the Archbishop will go to the six other administrative Centres during the week, thus meeting perhaps 600 or 700 chaplains from Canada, Australia, New Zealand, Africa, Wales, Scotland, Ireland and so on.

Saturday May 20th 1916, Hazebrouck

It has been a full day and a lot of time has been taken up in arranging a visit of etiquette from the Archbishop of Canterbury to the Abbe Lemire[655]. The Abbe was

---

650 **Coogee**, a seaside suburb 8 miles SE of Sydney. Bishopscourt, the residence, since 1911 of the Archbishops of Sydney, built 1841.
651 **Etaples** was a major target of German bombing raids.
652 **Poperinghe**. A market-town and railhead for the BEF; gateway to the Ypres Salient, 10 miles NE of Hazebrouck, over the Belgium border.
653 Talbot House, Poperinghe. "Then we went to Talbot House where, in the garden there was a large gathering of Church of England Chaplains, some 60 in number. We had a fairly lively discussion on the question of the relation of Army work at present to the National Mission; on a possible supply of new ordinands after the war; and on other kindred topics." Diary, Archbp Davidson May 17th, 1916.
654 "Then we went to an exceedingly 'upper room', a long garret that has been cleverly transformed into a Chapel at the top of Talbot House. There in an overflowing meeting we had prayers and a full address from m upon the uniqueness of our present responsibilities and the splendour of our opportunity'. Diary, Archbp Davidson May 17th, 1916.
655 Abbe **Jules Auguste Lemire** (b.1853 – d.1928), French priest and social reformer, was born

pleased to have the proposal and said that nowadays, "there must be no Presbyterians, Wesleyans, Greek Orthodox, Latin Papists or Anglicans, but we must meet all on the platform of our common humanity." We understood one another in the 'essentials', and to that we agreed, and he approved of my observation that for that "we need not be very conversant with one another's language – we understood one another in a few words". The visit is to take place (D.V) on Tuesday. The Abbe proposes a dejeuner, to which I doubt the Archbishop agreeing!

Now poor Brockington has been in a little distress, both in mind and body. In mind because he hoped that his son would be coming out of the firing line where he has been many months, but the regiment has gone back into the trenches yesterday[656]. In body – because the heat has brought out the toothache, and the tooth has had to follow suit. So he begs off a little of the work, and I am glad to be able to carry on for him.

How gloriously warm it has been – it keeps down the number of patients, which is good for them and not so good for some of the younger doctors, who get into mischief. Newley, the Australian who knows W Stevenson[657], is getting on well and likes to talk of Brisbane. They all like to talk of places they come from naturally, and it is wonderful how useful a comparativly wandering life comes in! I have just noticed another successful attempt at an English notice – "TEA, COFFEE, CHOCOLATE, FOR SOLD HERE", meant apparently for "FOR SOLDIERS" Another one runs "TEA, COFFEE, AND WASHING FORD SOLDIERS". I take the FORD as being the phonetic spelling of the French way of saying "For the", the "th" being difficult and run into "For de"! Another runs without stops "TEA COFFEE WITHIN EGGS AND MILK" Yet another starting so well deserves a better fate "SEPERATE ROOM FOR MEALS FOR ORFFICES. Enquire within". So, it will be seen that some of the inhabitants are not losing by the British occupation, and also that there is a courageous entente in the direction of the language. Many of the children cry out "Hulloa" and "Good Morning".

Heavy bombing over a town near here we are told, with over 100 bombs dropped, however, we are getting nearer to them in the Air Service I think.

The Presbytarian is talking (I am writing at the Mess table) "Well, I've never found Brussell sprouts disagree with me. Yes, I'm fond of Brussell sprouts. I like pork in

---

at Vieux-Berquin (Nord). He was educated at the College of St Francis of Assisi, Hazebrouck, where he subsequently taught philosophy and rhetoric. In 1897, he was elected deputy for Hazebrouck and was returned unopposed at the elections of 1898, 1902 and 1906. He organised a society called *La Ligue française du coin de terre et du foyer*, the object of which was to secure, at the expense of the state, a piece of land for every French family desirous of possessing one. The Abbé Lemire sat in the chamber of deputies as a conservative republican and Christian Socialist.

656   Lieut. **Conrad Clive Brockington**, 2 Bn The Welch Regiment, the son of the Reverend **A A Brockington**, was killed in action on 8th September 1916 during the attack on High Wood on the Somme.

657   William Stevenson married Dorothy Saumarez-Smith, one of RDG's sisters-in-law.

December. I like it always, but give me pork in December. Come on A, have a liqueur – B, have a liqueur, C come on" "Padre", says a young man, "I am surprised at your encouraging the young men to drink like this." The remark is greeted with a gurgle and a guffaw.

A beautiful day with nice services, and then much censoring. A number of men are in wounded and one man from South Wales very full of what he had done. I said "Well, I dare say you gave them as much as they gave you". "Oh yes, Sir" he said "We retaliated back!"

Monday May 22nd 1916, Hazebrouck

Monday has been a quiet day. I found that yesterday had been more tiring than I thought and under the influence of the heat as well, found it expedient to go softly. I called on the Abbe Lemire to arrange the final points about the visit of the Archbishop tomorrow, and visited some of the officers in the hospital. Then I had a few words with one of the Sisters who proved enthusiastic, and had been down near Paddock Wood for hop-picking, and saw my friend Newey again, who is getting on well and will go down to a Base tomorrow. I talked with a number of patients – topography plays a large part in this work! Now I must be off to attend on His Grace of Canterbury, to see in case anything might be wanted, and to represent the Church that is in […*censored*…]. I wondered if he would need an interpreter but in case he did, one can be got and not from down the street!

Tuesday May 23rd 1916, Hazebrouck

It is beautiful weather and has been a most interesting day. The Archbishop came over at 11.30, accompanied by Bishop Gwynne and a Chaplain[658]. The Abbe received us in his study and Bishop Gwynne drew me in with the party, so I had the interest of listening to one of the most impressive interviews I have ever witnessed. The Abbe, in his chair, genial, quick, remarkably quick of thought and topic, the Archbishop facing him with Bishop Gwynne in a chair nearby, the Chaplain (whose name I do not know) next and myself modestly in the background. Through the open French window some trelliswork, some greenery and two or three young pink roses, touched by the sunlight. (I do not think that this part had better go outside our circle) – the Abbe and the Archbishop talked busily on one topic after another for over three quarters of an hour.

"Was the Archbishop the head of the English Church?" asked the Abbe. "The first Bishop," he announced "There were other Archbishops of York etc, but he ranked

---

658 'At 11 am after a stroll in St Omer, we three drove off to Hazebrouck to see Abbe Lemire' Diary, Archbp Davidson May 23rd, 1916. The Chaplain was **John Victor Macmillan** (Mac) (b.1877 – d.1956), one of the Archbishop's domestic Chaplains (1904 – 15) before joining the Army. He was Military Chaplain at Treport, Bologne. He would become bishop of Guildford.

as first of all the Anglican Archbishops and Bishops throughout the world" (The word 'rank' was prompted by the Abbe – 'rang' being the word he used) "Did the Archbishop think the war was going to end soon?" The question was answered by another "What did the Abbe think?" "Perhaps soon." The Archbishop thought "perhaps so, perhaps not" "A year more?" said the Abbe. "Perhaps" said the Archbishop sadly. "The English will go through to the end?" "Oh yes" said the Archbishop with a smile "how otherwise? Would not the French?" "The French would, yes" then a little dubiously "the English are more patient than the French, and the South are not feeling it as much as the North, nor would they feel the effect so much later, and they are by temperament less steady "la tete chaude!" [659] "Was the Archbishop encouraged by the religious life of the troops: were the Chaplains meeting good success?" The Archbishop replied in the affirmative "especially as regards some directions. Did the Abbe think the war was helping religion in France?" "Yes, decidedly yes. Especially in the North which was naturally more religious" "Even among the men?" said the Archbishop.

"Yes, the men were becoming more religious and the priests were understanding them better, and were more considerate. Before, the priests had asked too much of the men – too many devotions, too many ceremonies, too many masses, too much in the way of discipline. The men were less improved by the war than the women and children, but they were better than before (moins mais mieux). The Roman Church was learning its lessons (incidentally, he remarked, celibacy wherein we differed, was a question of discipline and one it might be able to reconsider. There was great good in the home and family life of the Clergy of England). They were, for the reason of over-discipline, meeting the difficulties they had in the schools. The public schools admitted much freedom in religion, the promotion of Church schools was running the risk of repelling freer spirits by harshness, and Parish clergy refuse the Sacrament to parents sending their children to other schools i.e. the priests ask too much. Sisters are not allowed to teach in the schools, but they do so none the less by permission of their Bishops and by putting aside their official dress in order to do so. The objection to the Church Schools was not so much that they taught religion as that their cause was adopted by 'conservatives' as against 'republicans' of a more radical sort."

The personal particulars were interesting – the Archbishop asked the Abbe point blank how he came to be not 'en regle' with his Bishop. Put shortly, the answer was that the bishop objected to the Abbe's growing social success and wished to check his activities in the direction of social service[660]. He objected also, to some of the

---

659 'We then passed onto the condition of France in other respects and he was not inclined to be very buoyant. He himself is quite clear and determined about the war, but he says that in many parts of France the people are losing patience – You English have more patience than we have. You know our temperament, especially in the South' Diary, Archbp Davidson May 23rd, 1916.

660 In 1916, the Bishop of Lille had Lemire suspended from the priesthood for his political activism. In 1893, Abbé Lemire had protested against the action of the Dupuy cabinet in closing the Bourses du Travail, characterising it as the expression of a policy of disdain of the workers. In

freer views as above illustrated. A law was passed by the Vatican that no 'nouveau candidat' should offer himself for a Town Council appointment, or for Parliament, without the consent of the Bishop. Lemire has been a member of Parliament for 18 years, but the Bishop signified that, before the next elections, consent should be asked from him. Lemire made the point, however, that the law said 'a new candidate', and that he was not that. He added, he knew at the same time that if he did ask consent, he would not get it – hence the rupture. He is not allowed to officiate, he attends Mass, but is never 'communicated' unless in a strange place. He holds that 'Christianitie' is deeper than these things, and in that spirit, was honoured by the Archbishop's visit. The war is, at base, a struggle for Christianism 'contre la barbarie, la force etc.' Incidentally, in reply to an enquiry from the Archbishop, he confirmed the account of German misbehavior, and some of his own relations had suffered, but they misbehaved far worse on Belgian soil than on French, seeming to run wanton more readily among the weaker people. He explained how his newspaper was being used for communicating between friends on this side of the line and those in Lille, on the other side. A list is printed of all those having friends in Lille, who want to say that they are well. There must be only the name and address. The paper is taken in large numbers by our aeroplanes and dropped in the town. At first the Germans objected, but now they have even allowed it to be posted up on walls. The paper is the 'Cri de Flanders'. I must get a copy – the Archbishop took one with him[661].

Very impressive was the last moment, when the Abbe asked for the Archbishop's blessing, and received it kneeling, in Latin ending in "in nomine Partri, Filii et Spiritu Sancti" – I could not hear all the rest. In the next room, the Abbe had waiting his married sister who had lost two sons in the war, and he asked for her the Archbishop's consolation. It was a devout moment and you get a glimpse of what a living thing sincere and pious episcopacy – which is sometime obscured by 'state' and 'social' superficialities – can be[662].

2 German officers to be buried tomorrow.

Wednesday May 24th 1916, Hazebrouck (his 49th birthday)
Thank you, my darling for your letter and the loving birthday wish, which is very precious to me.

December 1893, he was seriously injured by a bomb thrown by the anarchist Auguste Vaillant from the gallery of the chamber; against whose death sentence he campaigned.

661 'The Abbe edits a newspaper which has now a peculiar character. It is called Le Cri de Flandres … he gave me a copy of it'. Diary, Archbp Davidson May 23rd, 1916.

662 'Before I left he knelt down and asked for my blessing. What his Bishop would have said I do not know. I gave him the full benediction from our Communion Office in Latin as we use in Convocation. He was pleased with this and asked afterwards to have the words said again that he might know them.' Diary, Archbishop Davidson, May 23rd, 1916.

Friday May 26th 1916, Hazebrouck

You are back in (what is left of) the bosom of your family, and very glad to be, I daresay. Your visit to Birkenhead was very interesting – how I would have liked to be there too. Little did we think, in the year 1888 or 1889 as we wrought in body, soul and spirit our respective aims beneath that same roof, that one day our body, soul and spirit would be united in joint service! Now 28 years ago, and neither of us had reached that age then. I think I must go and see it for myself again, someday, if we are spared. It will reinforce various ideals, and establish much in the way of comfort. I work in despair, sometimes, and then find unexpected successes – which perhaps means that when we think we are doing least, we are doing best. I expect the Snowdons were very glad to have you and it is nice that they are able to do war work.

I heard that my claims for allowances went through, so that my bank balance is about £50 better than when I found it! I think nothing might have happened if I had not gone to see, so much is done by routine in the Army.

The usual round today, talking on numberless subjects to a world, literally a world, of different experiences. At one minute in Somerset, at another in Geelong, at another in Hackney, at another in Sydney, and at another in Hunton! "I was born in Hunton originally" was the phrase. "Do you know West Farleigh?" "Don't I! And East Farleigh, and Coxheath, and Collier Street and Marden!" Happily, we often manage to find deeper things to talk about[663]. I talked to a nice lad this afternoon with a C of E Men's Society badge on a watch chain above his head. I am sorry about the split between Archdeacon Lloyd and the C.C.C.S. It seems a pity that compromise was not somehow possible. I talked with a man this morning who came from Saskatoon and had heard Archdeacon Lloyd speak once or twice – and so the Church goes on 'weaving its' meshes.

Saturday May 27th 1916, Hazebrouck

Cooler today, which was just as well as there has been much travelling to and fro, and we have another concert tonight in the open.

I was very glad to hear that poem by Bishop Pakenham Walsh "1916 Darkness and Light"[664] It happened to fit in with what I have in mind to say tomorrow, leading up to "a City which hath foundations whose Builder and Maker is God[665]" and we do

---

663 **Hunton** is a village near the town of Maidstone in Kent. **Collier Street** and **Coxheath** are villages and civil parishes within the Borough of Maidstone, Kent; approximately 2.5 miles S of Maidstone. **Marden** is 8 miles S of Maidstone.

664 Rt. Rev. **Herbert Pakenham-Walsh** (b.1871 – d.1959) was an Anglican bishop, educator, scholar and lyricist. He received a doctorate in divinity from Trinity College, Dublin. In 1916, he married Clara Hayes. He was a missionary at Bangalore, India from 1907 to 1908. He was warden of Bishop Cotton Boys' School in Bangalore, Karnataka, India from 1907–1913. In 1915, he became the first Bishop of Assam when the diocese of Assam was created out of part of the territory of the diocese of Calcutta.

665 **Hebrews 11:10** 'For he looked for a city which hath foundations, whose builder and maker

know that is to look forward to, when a condition of society will exist wherein there shall be no fear, or uncertainty, much less mutual destruction and upheaval – but there shall be mutual trust and strength upon the sure foundation of God's righteousness. That righteousness which, as it says on Mr George Foster's tombstone "is like the great mountains[666]". Chattering voices shall be silenced then and mischief-dealing hands shall be impotent.

Five of our aeroplanes over today – do you know how long it takes to get from here to Aldershot in an aeroplane? One hour twenty minutes! I do not hear that they propose issuing aeroplanes to Chaplains – as yet!

Sunday May 28th 1916, Hazebrouck

Two letters from you today, ma cherie, owing to a turn-about of the mails. The parcel came alright and thank you many times for it my sweetheart – it is nice to be loved! The prayer book is just the very thing as we get into lights sometimes, when even with glasses it is not easy to see, and it is nice to be able to read without my glasses. I am so glad to have the Browning also as one craves the 'good thoughts' in the midst of so much that tends to deteriorate, and the socks are just the very thing! Please thank your Aunt Chattie for the first class super cake! It is really very kind and cakes of that kind are almost impossible to get in these parts.

A beautiful day, but not very successful from the ministerial point of view, as owing to my Presbyterian friend, it has not been possible to re-inaugurate a Sunday morning service for the Clearing Station. He is one of the laziest men I know!! We had an early service at 7.15 to which no one came and as I was finishing my toilet at 8.15 a message came from Brockington to ask if I could take the 8.0 am HC at the Mairie as, I could not quite gather, there was something about some Dragoons! I have not yet discovered quite what happened as B is getting really a little unnerved, and on Thursday he was a little hysterical! His anxiety about his son who is in the trenches and the hot weather are, I think, too much for him.

At 10.0 we had a nice service in the Mairie which was fairly well attended, then at 11.30 we had a ward service at the Officers' Hospital which I felt was devotional all through – "I did like it" said one officer to me afterwards. Visiting, visiting and visiting afterwards, and making arrangements for the evening service to be held in the Soldiers Club, the Mairie being needed by the French people.

---

is God.'

666 **Psalm 36:6** 'Thy righteousness *is* like the great mountains; thy judgments *are* a great deep: O LORD, thou preservest man and beast.' George Ebenezer Foster, (b.1811 – d.1870). Father of Ebenzer Bird Foster, the husband of Mary Smith Foster (Aunt Mai). Principal of Foster & Sons bank, Cambridge. He is buried at St Mary & St Michael's, Trumpington, Cambs.

Monday May 29th 1916, Hazebrouck

A 'Mondayish' sort of a day – good Mr Platt has come back – he is more of a 'sound mind' than our other friend and helps to keep things steady. An interesting paper from the Bishop of Kensington about how to bring the advantages of the Mission of Repentance and Hope to the men – a most important question which has occupied my mind most of the day, except for the visiting and other necessary matters in between.

Can we think more about the summer holidays? There is a rumour that all 'leave' stops next month[667].

Ainsi le journal d'aujourd'hui s'appellant "Le Matin[668]"

"L'Archeveque de Canterbury, primat d'Angleterre, accompagne de l'eveque de Khartoum, a rendu visite, a Hazebrouck a l'abbe Lemire qui a recu les deux prelats a la mairie. Le primat d'Angleterre a vivement remercie l'abbe Lemire des dispositions qu'il a prises, en sa qualite de maire d'Hazebrouck, pour faciliter aux soldat anglais l'exercise de leur culte." [669]

Et vous avez recu in conte particulier, et tout a fait complet! I think probably the publication was due to to the Abbe Lemire himself.

"In the course of your Ministry in the Army, what have you found to be the chief difficulties and deficiencies in the religion and religious life of the men?" 1). Unsympathy upon the part of those in authority where religion is 'patronised' or 'tolerated'. It has lacked energetic support and that enthusiasm which was its due. The religious keenness, or want of it of the officers, has a most marked effect upon the men. Many thoughts supervere upon that reflection and produce others, which it is too late to set down here, even in the most condensed form.

To add a side reflection – our hot-headed young Mess caterer made a little dissertation yesterday explaining why the Mess could not afford porridge and milk for breakfast (he does not like breakfast himself). This evening he produced tinned salmon and cucumber before the soup, and ice cream after the pudding! I think I shall have to leave that Mess!

Goodnight, my darling – "there is a deal of human nature in most of us, especially in some!"

---

667   Preparation for the Somme offensive on 1st July 1916.
668   *"and here is today's paper, called The Morning"*. **Le Matin** was a French daily newspaper first published in 1884 and discontinued in 1944.
669   *"The Archbishop of Canterbury, Primate of England, accompanied by the bishop of Khartoum* (Bishop Gwynne)*, has visited Hazebrouck as the Abbe Lemire which received two prelates was mayor. The Primate of England is very grateful to the Abbe Lemire of the steps taken, in his capacity as mayor of Hazebrouck to facilitate the English soldier exercise of their religion."* RDG: *And you have received this particular tale quite fully!*

Tuesday May 30th 1916, Hazebrouck

There is a tremendous bombardment going on, flaming the night sky and making things to tremble even at this distance. It has been going on for two hours now and the slight jar of the 'thud, thud' gets a little monotonous. (Please excuse the two spots of grease on this letter – the candle grew suddenly erratic.)

You remarked receiving a copy of the Certificate of the W.F. Delapidations – will you please sent it to me, and as it is rather important, register the envelope? I am sorry for the bother, but it becomes a security of some value. The little boy has sent me a flash light and refills, but I happen to have two flashlights already – a large one and a small one. Do not tell him so – I will keep my present ones in reserve.

The nice Chaplain, Platt, has received orders today and moves tomorrow – I am sorry. His successor came today, a tired looking man, quite young, who has been doing duty at No. 4 London General Hospital, so this more knock-about life may help him although he does not look very fit at first sight. I am not sure of his name yet – I think it is Byrne.

Wednesday May 31st 1916, Hazebrouck

A successful day and a busy morning. Farewell to Platt, who moved off this afternoon and then a long car ride across country and at last I have succeeded in meeting my godson/nephew, George Thomas, christened at my hands in 1890. He will be 26 next month. He is a good keen fellow and seemed liked by his brother officers. His Division is 'in rest' now in a charming part of the country, far back in the quiet, under the slope of a wood-covered hill, not unlike Woolstonbury[670]. I had over two hours with him and we were able to talk of many things, past, present and to come. His mother, my sister Mary, was very unwell when he was on leave. I think she feels the strain of his being out here very much. His uncle, my brother Griff, is somewhere in France and George has had some hard fighting and some thrilling times. The ride took me over much new country, which I may not describe.

I had the car, which was the Chaplain's for this place. Now that the Senior Chaplaincy has been re-moved, a car has been allotted thereto exclusively, this car being shared by a Veterinary Colonel for 5 days of a week, and the Chaplain for the Jews, 2 days. This day was the Jew Chaplain's day and as he was doing some of his work by train, he very kindly, in fact in a most Christian way, gave it me for the rest of the day. I met him – he is a young, pleasantly spoken man, with a fair moustache, very like a British Officer and an M.A of London I think, wears a uniform like ours, but with collar badges composed of entwined triangles instead of the Cross of Jesus of Nazareth, his Messiah. I hope he does not despise the Nazarine ignorantly, in unbelief. He is, he told me, the one Jewish Chaplain for the whole of the 2nd Army[671].

---

670 **Wolstonbury Hill** is a chalk prominence in the South Downs National Park, approximately 2.5 miles N of Brighton and 1 mile W of Clayton, in the parish of Pyecombe, West Sussex

671 Rev. **Vivian George Simmons** (b.1886 – d.1968) of the West London Synagogue (1913–1942).

collar badges composed of
entwined triangles,
instead of the Cross
of Jesus of Nazareth, his
Messiah. I hope he does
not despise the Nazarene
ignorantly, in unbelief. He is,
he told me, the one Jewish
Chaplain for the whole of the
IInd. Army.
A nice letter from
Aunt Loo waiting
my return. I left "an
Outpost in Papua" in the
Car. I hope it may turn up
again.
Goodnight - my own darling.
-1/6/16. A very 'flat' Ascension Day -
darling from the point of view of fellow
worshippers. God knows.
Both much love.
Your loving Ritchie.

Sunday June 4th 1916, Hazebrouck

So the rumours were not unfounded – there was a big naval fight and the losses have been severe[672]. Anxiously we wait to hear how the enemy fared. If they have had a real success it will impose the utmost strain upon us and our Allies. The bantering tone, which I have never quite liked, will be deservedly chastened. I wonder if Winston Churchill was so ill-placed at the Admiralty – Mr Tritton remarked that there might be worse things than his being back there. That our 'balance' has been upset is, of course, not possible, as our reserve of craft is considerable – I hope very large, and there is more on the way. But we have been gashed in our strongest part, and it behoves us to "walk humbly before our God"[673].

In the same newspaper that announced these happenings appear also the lists of honours and awards. Tonight much strong drink will be flowing. It has been flowing freely in the shape of champagne and whiskey in our own Mess – I have come away quickly. One thinks of that loss of life which is described as 'grievous', the absence of particulars as 'ominous', and those hundreds of bodies swaying in their watery resting places – the hundreds of bereaved homes and aching hearts and the tear-stung eyes. There must be more prayer – that the Divine Comfort may come down and that the end may come soon.

I find myself very thankful for the witness of the Church of Rome, and the Ascensiontide Season has shown them up favourably. At least the numbers have rejoiced in the recollection of the Event – the message has been heeded and the fact has been 'observed'. It is all so much idle indifference for Protestantism, for Nonconformists, and shallow Anglicans, to pretend they have the larger, healthier life, the life that is superior to observing 'days and months and times of year', the freer life. It is an excuse for laziness, and they lose the blessing of the facts thereby. The non-observation of Ascensiontide has been very depressing, except among those who belong to the Church of Rome: with them the message has been heeded, the fact observed, and how much it means to us at a time like this. They claim 'liberty' from forms, and ceremonies and an official ministry, and what do they adopt instead – political forms and social gratification. "Oh Liberty, how many a crime is committed in thy name!"[674]

Son of a jewish minister, Simmons was only the second Jewish Chaplain to be appointed after Dr Michael Adler, who had brought the issue of worship for Jewish soldiers to the attention of the authorities at the BEF from 1914. Simmons was appointed on the advice of Albert Jessel KC. The collar badges were to Adler's own design. In summer 1916, Adler and Simmons (aged 30) were the only Jewish Chaplains for the entire front. Simmons would lead various progressive synagogues after the war, as well as teach Jewish pupils at Stowe and Rugby.

672 The **Battle of Jutland** was a naval battle fought by the Royal Navy's Grand Fleet (which also included ships and individual personnel from the Royal Australian Navy and Royal Canadian Navy) against the Imperial German Navy's High Seas Fleet during the First World War. The battle was fought on 31st May and 1st June 1916 in the North Sea near Jutland, Denmark. It was the largest naval battle and the only full-scale clash of battleships in the war.

673 **Micah 6:8** 'He hath shewed thee, O man, what *is* good; and what doth the LORD require of thee, but to do justly, and to love mercy, and to walk humbly with thy God?'

674 Saying attributed to **Marie-Jeanne Phlippon Roland**, better known simply as **Madame**

An early Service was impossible in the Clearing Station but we managed a very hearty Ward Service at 11.0. The place is very busy though, and a large number of the men filed off to go to a base immediately we had finished, and then a very large number came in from the recent fighting – a proportion suffering from the blowing up of a German mine. Horrible business!! A young Australian officer died yesterday morning, he was shot accidentally[675].

Our Colonel has received a D.S.O. – perhaps just deservedly – I am not quite sure of him, and the Presbyterian is sore because he has received no recognition. That shows only too well the nature of people in some cases – that that type can expect to receive one. However, his skin is very tight, and oozy with the Colonel's champagne tonight, so he is not without making some advantage out of it – there's a critical sentiment! But really, it makes one rather sore and sad that the one nonconformist Chaplain in the town, and 3 Anglicans and some R.C.s being pretty fully occupied, he has not said one word of public prayer or done as far as we know, one act of ministry beyond handing in two dozen boxes of cigarettes to the Wards, this whole Sunday. In which sweet frame of mind, after I have prayed for mercy and forgiveness and new zeal and simpler faith, I shall say 'Goodnight', my dear darling!

Monday June 5th 1916, Hazebrouck

The news about the naval fight gets more balanced as more information comes through. There is a persistent rumour now that a portion of the German fleet is shut up in neutral waters, and it would be good if that were true – but what a distressing loss of precious life!

Many conversations of much interest today and the news tonight tends to place the balance of the Naval fight yet more favourably for the Allies. If the Germans have lost in any degree proportionately, it must hasten the end of the war, they cannot go on. We hear tonight of adverse doings in the salient, a Canadian Divisional General a prisoner in the hands of the enemy – we can only go on praying, it is slow work.

I met a lad from Stonehouse this afternoon – it is very remarkable this blending of the Empire in all its doings, and the ambulatory Chaplain has much to do in the way of carrying on the treads to their entwinement here and there.

Roland (1754 – 8th November 1793). She was, together with her husband Jean-Marie Roland de la Platière, a supporter of the French Revolution and influential member of the Girondist faction. She fell out of favour during the Reign of Terror and died on the guillotine. These were her supposed last words.

675 Lt **John Charles Davidson**, (b.1895 – d.1916) 1 Bn Australian Infantry, A.I.F., died 3rd June 1916, 'of accidental injuries'. Son of James and Ellen Davidson, of "Kalang", Bellingen, New South Wales. Native of Bathurst.

Tuesday June 6th 1916 Hazebrouck

I have been busy today, chiefly with the Club and scattered units about the town. Six men came to the little chapel this evening – two stayed behind for a talk and were very warm about the prayers. They are passers through and have been for weeks at a time without the opportunity of a service. I fear a strenuous time is before us for a week or two – for those who want this War to end soon and those who long for England to be a better place after the War.

Wednesday June 7th 1916, Hazebrouck

Alas! What a stunning blow this is about Lord Kitchener[676]. We can only fall back in fuller trust upon the great Commander Himself. The little souls who wished Kitchener's removal will have cause to think now. One's first impressions are of treachery (not from that quarter of course), but one awaits details. It is a day of immense and awful events. Men and officers alike are visibly stricken with grief, and some of the French people have shed tears. The Dean at the Parish church, the town Interpreter, and a woman in one of the shops and others all say, "Une parte universelle". Now we must go on.

Friday June 9th 1916, Hazebrouck

It has been a tense week altogether, with the Naval battle and waiting for accounts of it. I could not for myself take the first particulars as final, and now Mr Balfour's excellent speech explains it all[677]. Then Lord Kitchener's departure – mercifully after the foundations of his work had been laid, and his unique organising abilities having practically accomplished their contribution – and the heavy German pressure both on this side and on the Verdun side. And now tonight the Town Mayor comes and takes our Soldiers' Club Room at 24 hours notice and we are in the middle of turning everything topsy-turvy – if he could be as zealous helping work of this kind as he is in running soldiers in when they get drunk and foolish, one would not feel so annoyed. However, I have rung up 2nd Army Headquarters and if it cannot be stopped this time it will not let us hope, come again.

An interesting message this afternoon asking me to go and hold a service for a New Zealand unit, one of the officers was with us, I think sick but got interested.

---

676 Lord **Kitchener** sailed from Scapa Flow on 5th June 1916 aboard HMS *Oak* before transferring to HMS *Hampshire* for a diplomatic mission to Russia. Shortly before 1930 hrs the same day, while en route to the Russian port of Arkhangelsk during a Force 9 gale, *Hampshire* struck a mine laid by U-boat *U-75* and sank west of the Orkney Islands. Kitchener, his staff, and 643 of a crew of 655 were drowned or died of exposure. His body was never found. The survivors who caught sight of him in those last moments testified to his outward calm and resolution.

677 A speech by **Arthur James Balfour, 1st Earl of Balfour**, then First Lord of the Admiralty, on 8th June to The British Imperial Council of Commerce, covering both the battle of Jutland and Kitchener's death.

Saturday June 10th 1916, Hazebrouck

I must try to get home for some time in August – it is a month tomorrow since my return from 'leave'. However, for the next few days I am too busy to be able to think clearly about it. A suggestion has come from the D.C.G. that we hold a memorial service for Lord Kitchener. I am very glad, especially as I think the idea originated with our new Chaplain, Mr Byrne.

We have got ourselves into the new temporary Club building, but it is a poor place and rather a return to the old dismal conditions of last winter, and as far as lays in my own utmost strenuous power, I will not have it. Voila!

Sunday June 11th 1916, Whitsunday, Hazebrouck

A quiet service of the Holy Communion at 8.0 with 5 present and then a ride out into the country, and a most hearty, bright service with the New Zealanders. They liked my being able to speak about having had a glimpse of their beautiful country, and at all events I do believe very many of us were all together "in the spirit on this Lord's day[678]". A nice service at the Officers' Hospital where, just now, Canadians predominate! They were very nice about matters afterwards which, at least, is a great comfort and the rest must be left in faith. Those were all the services I managed. I tried the Reinforcements, but as it happens, they were vacated last night – tomorrow there may be 500 again! So I followed up about the arrangements for the Tuesday Memorial Service and just got in for the end of the Maire's Evening service. Brockington preached nicely on "These died, in faith"[679], but he spoiled himself by sudden lapses into slanging phases like 'pals' and 'taking it lying down', all rather brought in for effect and losing in dignity. Those central services are bringing in the men by degrees, but my evening service has been supplanted in favour of nothing at all, i.e. it is not possible to hold one for the present, by the idle intervention of the Presbyterian, about whom I can hardly bring myself to speak with patience. I wish he would go!

Monday June 12th 1916, Hazebrouck

It has been a crowded day with the morning rather full with preparing for the Memorial Service tomorrow, and a long time was taken up, quite unnecessarily with having to explain to the Town Major about why I was negotiating things. It appears that the Presbyterian thought that he ought to have been asked to arrange it – a C of E service! He did not grasp it as that, but as it was to be more or less of a 'public' memorial, and as he is the "only reg'lar Chaplain in the town" and "a Major" in rank,

---

678 **Revelation 1:10** 'I was in the Spirit on the Lord's day, and heard behind me a great voice, as of a trumpet.'

679 **Hebrews 11:13** 'These all died in faith, not having received the promises, but having seen them afar off, and were persuaded of *them*, and embraced *them*, and confessed that they were strangers and pilgrims on the earth.'

he held it as a grievance not to be the head of the proceedings. It gives you a weary, weakening kind of feeling – very difficult to conquer. I had to assure the Town Major that the Presbyterian had nothing whatever to do with us much less, (fortunately though I did not add the adverb) any authority, as we had had our instructions directly from the D.C.G. in the form of a suggestion and the Presbyterian had been asked to read the lesson, also according to the D.C.G.'s suggestion – but it shows what is in the air!

At the end of the day has been the opening of a Y.M.C.A. amateur cinema, which is going to remain here, in a large barn. It promises to be quite useful, and personally I am glad of it. The Secretary came to borrow all the chairs from our Temporary Church at the Maire, on the strict promise of returning them for tomorrow's 8.0am service. As I lent the portable harmonium to a young man last week, who was hurt because I emphasised the importance of its being returned in time for our service, showing his pain by saying reproachfully 'on the word of an officer and a gentleman' – and yet, who did <u>not</u> return the instrument after all! – one has qualms. It all goes in with the day but good news again 107,000 prisoners, things are moving.

Tuesday June 13th 1916, Hazebrouck

The Memorial Service went very well and it was packed out. It was nice to see the honour done to a great man, and to feel how much of God was behind the same man's character and life. The Town Major was agreeably surprised at the response, and it really was very touching. The rank and file came in large numbers to pay their tribute to the memory of a respected servant of God and of his people. A number of Officers and Sisters came also in the same spirit – the Abbe Lemire came and one General. One or two came with a mixed sense of a regard for Kitchener and of their own importance and an opportunity of improving it, but we were in the presence, thanking God for a great man, realising the wonderful wider world where he is now, asking for the Divine Power, feeling the solemnity and joy of death and looking forward to the ever brightening future, both in this immediate cause and in the Great Beyond. The organist played the old big harmonium nobly, the hymns rang out through one's soul. Byrne sang the prayers, two buglers sounded the Last Post in a rugged, soldierly way, slightly out of practice, and the National Anthem must have come from the hearts of most of us.

There seems no chance of getting a fourth chaplain here, they have made up their minds that no one ought to be at a Hospital more than so many months and I quite agree. I don't think I could healthily stay on at the Hospital work and carry on the outside work as well – and the system demands that no hospital shall be without a Chaplain. So it is left for me to choose – I do not think I ought to stay on at the Hospital – so it is the outside work must go, but where next for myself remains to be seen.

Wednesday June 14th 1916, Hazebrouck

Our Club has had to give way to a General and his staff, and we are so to speak, on the streets – it might have been avoided, or ought to have be. I happened to meet the General and quite unexpectedly he observed the same, remarking "it was a pity for so short a time".

Good news from our front tonight – trenches re-taken and some hundreds of prisoners. I have not seen any of the latter, but an officer has told us how cheerful they were, and glad to be safe out of it and on this side.

Tonight the French clocks and our own Army time here 'advance themselves' one hour, so off to bed early goes the distinguished writer of these brilliant pages.

Thursday June 15th 1916, Hazebrouck

The Colonel is leaving for another command, so much champagne has flowed this evening. With a pile of work to be done it is not easy to sit at table for 2 hours, so I have withdrawn myself. With the French Interpreter (who represents the French Government in these things), I looked at a corner house which is practically unoccupied, the windows all broken by the last bombing raid. There is a great chance we can get it for Soldiers' Rooms. If only we may – we shall know tomorrow.

Friday June 16th 1916, Hazebrouck

The Interpreter by his own confession, drank too much champagne last night and was in bed till late in the day, consequently the Club plans have been held up for this day. Luckily they use the temporary place a little – but the place is full of troops and we have not the 'out-stretched' hand for them, and I am determined to do something.

What an eloquent cartoon in 'Punch' this week to the memory of Lord Kitchener[680], and what a clever lampoon of Germany's actions after the Naval victory! We had the unit photographed this afternoon – special permission has to be given by the Town Mayor and the photographer had to be escorted by a soldier. The picture was taken as a farewell for the Colonel.

It is curious going to bed by daylight, but the arrangement is a good one – it saves candles.

Sunday June 18th 1916, Hazebrouck

26 years ago today I was admitted to the Deaconate, and I have lived another lifetime since then. The Bishop was Walsham How[681] – writer of the hymn 'For all the Saints'

---

680 Punch cartoon, June 14th 1916: THE LOST CHIEF In Memory of Field-Marshal Earl Kitchener, Maker of Armies.

681 Rev. **William Walsham How** (b.1823 – d.1897) was an Anglican bishop. Educated at Shrewsbury, Oxford and Durham. Ordained in 1846, after a curacy at Kidderminster, he began

etc and the Vicar of the Cathedral Church (of Wakefield) was Archdeacon Straton, since Bishop of the Isle of Man and later, of Newcastle[682] and there was present Canon Ellerton[683], writer of the hymn 'the day Thou gavest Lord is ended' and the preacher was C J Ridgeway now Bp of Chichester[684]. I have worked (hard enough sometimes) a lot since then, and have suffered, and learnt and unlearnt much. You get less in love with yourself with the increasing years, yet – one has to be careful – an abject self-distrust becomes oddness and feebleness. It requires much faith to despise oneself, and I have to learn whether one is expected to invite others to despise one. "Uriah 'Eap was so very 'umble"[685]. Forgetting those things that are behind, we press toward the mark … "on stepping stones of their dead selves to higher things[686]".

Two services here and then a rush off to the Clearing Station for a Ward Service – also well attended. The comic man (of the Clearing Station Concert party, in private a pierrot singer on Margate sands!) offered to play the harmonium – he had High Church notions about intoning the responses, which I had to nip in the bud – and he played the tunes with just a suggestion of the vamp with which he accompanies his stage songs, (in fact I had to suppress the sense of his bursting into something jiggy and frivolous, it is so much at his finger ends,) but he did well, he helped the service and I think the service helped him – it did me.

Other than that it has been censoring and visiting, and this evening a most interesting open-air service with the New Zealanders. A Divinity student from Dunedin played the violin, and then one 'led' the opening prayers and a bandsman came up and volunteered his mandolin, which blended in admirably and a Salvation Army man

---

more than thirty years actively engaged in parish work in Shropshire, as curate at the Abbey Church in Shrewsbury in 1848. In 1879 he became a suffragan bishop in London, under the title of bishop of Bedford, his province being the East End. There he became the inspiring influence of a revival of church work, especially among the poor. He took a stand against what he regarded as immoral literature. In 1888, he was made the first bishop of Wakefield, which is when RDG would have known him.

682 Rev. **Norman Dumenil John Straton** (b.1840 – d.1918) was an Anglican bishop. Stratton was educated at Cambridge, and ordained in 1865. His first post was as a curate at Market Drayton from where he became vicar of Kirkby Wharfe then from 1875 vicar and rural dean of Wakefield. From 1888 to 1892 he was Archdeacon of Huddersfield. In 1892 he became the Bishop of Sodor and Man and 15 years later was translated to Newcastle, serving until his retirement in 1915.

683 The Rev. **John Ellerton** (b.1826 – d.1893) was a hymn writer and hymnologist. He was born in Clerkenwell, Middlesex, England, to George Ellerton, the head of an Evangelical family. He was educated at King William's College on the Isle of Man, and Trinity College, Cambridge, (BA 1849; MA 1854), where he came under the influence of Frederick D. Maurice.

684 **Charles John Ridgeway** DD (b.1841 – d.1927) was the Bishop of Chichester from 1908 to 1919.
Trinity College, Cambridge. Curacy at Christ Church, Tunbridge Wells before becoming Vicar of North Malvern, Rector of Buckhurst Hill, Vicar of Christchurch Lancaster Gate and Rural Dean of Paddington.
After two years as Dean of Carlisle he was raised to the Episcopate as Bishop of Chichester in 1908.

685 **Uriah Heep** character in Dickens' *David Copperfield*, notable for his cloying humility, obsequiousness, and insincerity, making frequent references to his own "humbleness".

686 Alfred, Lord Tennyson, *In Memoriam AHH*, Poem 1: Grief

volunteered his concertina, with not so much success as the pitch was about half a note out, and decidedly forbade itself continuing. How wonderful!! From far New Zealand, from Canada, and myself from the Homeland under the deep blue, cloud-ridden sky, the warm bright sunlight behind us, the green trees round us, tents and canvas huts across the field and the heavy boom of big guns coming down on the evening breeze. The mystery of the Holy Trinity and the tragedy of sin, finding its solution for our perplexed and burdened human spirits in His own simple message "God is Love". It will be alright soon! Well, well – it is a strange yet interesting dwelling place this world of ours. Goodnight, dear old fellow pilgrim.

Monday June 19th 1916, Hazebrouck

I have just been gently hustling the Town Major by telephone. We had found a piece of ground, <u>admirably</u> suited for our purposes. Anderson came over from Headquarters, sniffed at all the difficulties at first, then found himself talked into an enthusiastic support of my plan. The Town Major approved promptly and heartily. The Interpreter proposed freely, and almost effusively, to write to the owner of the land, who he felt sure would agree to let us have it "immediately". He would write "this very day", and let me see the letter before he sent it. I went to see him this evening. How the French temperament changes! He was full of excuses – there were other things much pressing on him just now – the Soldiers' Rooms was a luxury. Our first business was to win this war (undoubtedly, but if so, why not shut three quarters of the estaminets and beerhouses, and keep the men rigidly to campaigning life? If you give those places so much freedom, at least give other kinds of places a chance!). He hoped he would be able to write the letter tomorrow! In fact, he did not know the address. I have been at him again this evening, and telephoned the needed address, after a tramp along to get it.

Tuesday June 20th 1916, Hazebrouck

Tuesday – movements are on, which I may not describe[687]. Last night there were two heavy explosions, which woke me up. I assumed it was more bombing. Another explanation was the explosion of two mines near Hill [...*censored*...]. If it was, there must have been a terrific quantity of explosives to sound so near from that distance[688].

It has been a busy day again – and Hospital visiting is a long business at best. The Australians and New Zealanders are full of interest – they are quaint sometimes. One time-worn warrior tells of having so many children and two of them out here fighting. "Yes" I said, "evidently you can say with the Psalmist, I shall not be afraid when I speak with my enemies in the gate". "Ah", was the reply "the gate – I think old Peter'll let me through".

Tomorrow is the longest day – and <u>frost</u> last week in Yorkshire!

---

687 Preparation for the Somme offensive, 1st July 1916.
688 Most likely Hill 321 at Verdun

Envelope of letter post marked 'Field Post Office, 19th Ju 16

Wednesday June 21st 1916, Hazebrouck

The longest day has seemed rather short, being so clouded. George Thomas' birthday – I am delighted to find that he has been mentioned in dispatches. It has seemed an odds and ends kind of day – writing a letter for the West Farleigh Magazine – a ride out to one of our villages with Byrne. We found various mutual acquaintances in our talk, including Mr Waugh, the Vicar of Stonehouse[689]. Just before dinner there was an aeroplane battle, away across over the plain outside the town. Three of ours and we could not see how many Germans – no result that we could see, and ours drew off again back to their park, leaving the battle scene mottled with little black puffs for half an hour afterwards.

Sir Douglas Haig is in town tonight, and a new unit just out from England, has with it I hear, an old acquaintance, Dr Roper. He used to be a member of our congregation at Holy Trinity Cambridge.

Thursday June 22nd 1916, Hazebrouck

A public holiday today – Corpus Christi. La premiere Communion – little girls all in white, with long veils and long gowns, trip about the streets – little boys in their finest clothes, with a rich silk bow upon the arm, walk about showing much pride

---

689 Rev **Robert Waugh** was Vicar of St Cyr's, Stonehouse, Glos. 1911 – 1920.

in their grown-up importance. There is much outward show about it – and one fears how much devoutness may be in it.

A busy afternoon. I had to take tea in a refreshment room near the station. There came in a Major in an Australian uniform – he was disposed to talk. He was on his way up country it appeared. I remarked that I knew Australia a little, having been Chaplain to the Archbishop of Sydney – he asked which one and I replied, "Saumarez-Smith" – his quick rejoinder was, "A good man that!" he had noticed our list of services near the Mairie, and said how refreshing it was to see an established set like that in this part of the country. His name is Sweet and we talked of many things – of his travels in Queensland, and in the Holy Land and we parted quite friends.

Friday June 24th 1916, Hazebrouck
A beautiful day here. The Australian Wesleyan Chaplain has gone sick and has been sent down to a base. The Town Major has been thrown from his horse – the horse rolled on him in a ditch, and we went to look for yet another place for the Club, without success.

A ride out along some pretty roads to a cavalry unit about a service tomorrow, and a 'Christian' has arrived, with a nice appreciation of Sir Douglas Haig – which I was very glad to see.

Saturday June 25th 1916, Hazebrouck
A confused but encouraging day – the New Zealanders have moved off, and their successors made some mistake about the time, and so did not send a car. I borrowed one, and found on arrival what had happened, so made another journey for the service postponed to 2.30. A nice service in the Officers' Hospital, which was happily not disturbed by the big ceremonial procession through the town in honour of Corpus Christi. Our organist had got permission to go a day sooner for his 'leave', and so left us 'in the lurch'. Eventually at 6.10 – the service was at 6.30 – I ran to ground our professional Pierrot among the orderlies, and he very willingly came and played very nicely.

Sunday June 26th 1916, Hazebrouck
An impromptu concert for the Officers' Hospital took up all my morning. It was intended to give an 'occasion' for Lt. Whitehead, who has a very good baritone voice, whistles very well, plays very well and is, in fact, of the Drawing Room Entertainer kind. I think after the War if it does not last too long, that will be his line. He 'got up' the concert – but I did most of the work, hunting up the other performers, etc. It gave him much pleasure and happily also gave the sick officers a pleasant change.

(Entre nous – how much of our best work is done without praise and how many of our noblest self-sacrifices are those that have been entirely unrecognised – e.g yours for me, my darling, forgive me when I haven't even known how nice you've been – but the angels know!)

Still delays about the Club – the proprietor of the land, a Major Doctor in the French Army, replies by telegram that he cannot settle the matter by writing, and wants that 'leave' shall be asked for him so that he may come to the town to see about it! Then, supposing 'leave' was got for him, and he refused after all? An alternative is to requisition the ground by the Army – and let his 'leave' come in the ordinary course!

They say the procession of yesterday is to be repeated next Sunday and I am sorry as thinking it was over, it jars even more than before. A dozen little children dressed as cherubs, with flimsy gold wings, walk along with their hands folded for prayer. The Angel Gabriel, a big girl with great blue and gold wings, walks along with her hand (rather painfully as it seemed) held upward with the index finger pointing skyward for all the length of the march. A rather big girl, with a dark complexion (most jarring of all) dressed in a flowing red robe, with a crown of thorns upon her tousled head, bears a large wooden cross – she does not stand out much in the procession but is just one of the many. There is wanting the "I, if I be lifted up, will draw all men unto Me"[690]. The aesthetic, the spectacular and the egotistic "I acted a part in the show also" are the principal impressions born in upon me. The inwardness of it all is not easy to my untrained mind, though I have no doubt it is very real to some of these people. They feared trouble because it was said that the Papal Flag would be borne in the procession, so the civil authorities, voiced through the Abbe Lemire, had forbidden it as threatening political issues, and the Churchmen at the last moment derided against aggression.

I am glad that you like the War Supply work – the need for Hospital supplies is certainly something appalling, and cleanliness is so vital. I can understand all the insistence upon a scepticism and in this place alone I suppose we must have used tons of dressings. It is a comfort to see the wretched wounds and weeping sores cleanly wrapped away into healing seclusion.

Monday June 27th 1916, Hazebrouck

I see Geo. Harland Bowden 'has decided to retire' from N.E. Derbyshire. It is a dreadfully sad failure. His was a life capable of very great usefulness, moving steadily along the road of prosperity and success, and then betrayed by its own folly, its self-conceit, and moral and physical self-indulgence. Other lives fail, worse no doubt, but one feels it the most when it touches one through one's own blood. It made me ill last year but this year, time has eased the shock and prepared one for the inevitable[691]. He had his chance and I warned him specially in so many terms about 'carrying his

---

690 **John 12:32** 'And I, if I be lifted up from the earth, will draw all *men* unto me.'
691 Lieutenant-Colonel **George Robert Harland Bowden** (b.1873 – d.1927) In North East

full cup with a steady hand'. And thou mourn at the last and say 'how have I hated instruction, and my heart despised reproof'[692].

Some heavy fighting, and a number of wounded – things are moving a little. We had one German brought in wounded, a surly young lad from Hanover, surprised at the kindness shown him and acknowledging it gratefully in a rough way. I gave him a text or two as usual – "All things work together for good" "rejoicing in hope, patient in tribulation" and he responded earnestly with "Yah! Yah!"

The dear little boy is improving in tidiness you say – I <u>think</u> it must be Tonbridge, and the school for Joy sounds just the thing, but I wish she could be nearer W.F. too, later on. Remember, we shall be getting older, and W.F is a quiet place – we must think. A telephone message today speaks of my moving, possibly soon. The Club business is still tediously held up by the Major Doctor, fussing to be brought up.

Tuesday June 28th 1916, Hazebrouck

The Club business has moved a step forward. The Town Major is in a good humour, because Town Majors have now been made Staff officers – and it is just possible they may wear red tabs – so he put a little pressure on about getting the ground for the club.

I had a chat with the German prisoner, who is rather grumpy. He is a Roman Catholic, as also are his mother, five sisters and a brother, but his father is Lutheran – he is rather bored by the fighting.

Wednesday June 29th 1916, Hazebrouck

I go on to the new work next week. The Deputy Chaplain General was going to write a letter, I understand, which has not come. But my 'relief' has come, in the person of a very nice fellow Mr Plowden Wardlaw, vicar of St Edward's Cambridge, formerly a barrister-at-law, who lived for a time in Henry Somers Cocks' parish at Edenbridge, and is rather friendly with him[693].

England in 1896 as manager of D Selby Bigge and Company, an engineering company based in Newcastle. In 1902, he founded his own company, G Harland Bowden and Company. In 1907 Bowden was granted a Volunteer Force commission in the Royal Garrison Artillery. Bowden was active in Conservative Party politics, and in April 1912 was adopted as the party's prospective candidate for the constituency of North East Derbyshire. In April 1914 the sitting Labour Party MP for North East Derbyshire died, causing a by-election and Bowden was elected to the Commons, gaining the seat for the Conservatives with a majority of 314 votes. He continued to hold his parliamentary seat during the war, but found himself estranged from the Conservative Party, going so far as to issue libel proceedings against a party official. He stepped down and ran as a Unionist.

692 **Proverbs 5:12** 'And say, How have I hated instruction, and my heart despised reproof'

693 The Revd **James Tait Plowden-Wardlaw** KC, MA (b.1873 – d.1971) was Vicar of St Clement's Cambridge and a barrister (Lincoln's Inn), an Old Malvernian and graduate of King's College, Cambridge, who served as an advocate in the Supreme Court of the Cape Colony, South Africa. He had been a curate at St George's, Beckenham. Revd. **Henry L Somers Cocks**, Church of St Peter and St Paul, Edenbridge. **Edenbridge** is a town and civil parish in the Sevenoaks district

Thursday June 30th 1916, Hazebrouck

I move off on Monday, and as it is one of the places one is allowed to mention, I can say that it is in the first place, to Rouen. On the whole, it will be a relief to get away from a continual round of sick and suffering men. A busy day passing things on to the succeeding senior man for this area, Mr Tichborne, and getting ready to move – letters may be fragmentary now for a few days and all leave is stopped after today. It is interesting being among the Australians and I met a very nice Chaplain this evening, who jumped off his bicycle eagerly to greet an English Chaplain, and was very interested to find that there was so much of the Australian in him!

Friday July 1st 1916, Hazebrouck

Do not be surprised if there is a break for some days in my letters as movements and letter writing may be stopped.

Going from point to point today, helping <u>four</u> chaplains with tips and local information. I went with Tichborne to see the Town Major and then had a very interesting talk with Abbe Lemire. Then arrangements about getting Peter Waite and my horse taken with me – good luck! Then to see a corporal of Engine drivers to play tomorrow morning – then a Chaplain's talk – then taking P. Wardlaw through the Clearing Station, and pointing out plans for Sunday, also adjusting a difficulty about a bicycle for him. There are three bicycles, and they wanted to give him the most broken whereas the best one was the one my man Peter had been taking care of up to the last minute!

Government papers about travel – arrangements about my packages, magic lantern, etc., another chaplain's talk, a concert by the French students which was very good. A professor who was the curate I met that second night of our travelling up country November last year and with whom I was billeted, sang nicely in English 'Sergeant Daddy V.C'[694] and our English Clown made many funny jokes in French. An English officer sang the Marselllaise – and the Abbe professor sang 'God save the King'!

Very heavy booming tonight, and flashes across the sky, but very good news today – quite a good success[695].

Saturday July 2nd 1916, Hazebrouck

Rather a sad evening – the last page of another little chapter of toil and hope, suffering and joy. I am a little sad at leaving this place after all.

---

of Kent. It is located on the Kent/Surrey border on the upper floodplain of the River Medway and gives its name to the latter's tributary, the River Eden.

694 *Sergeant Daddy, V.C.* written and composed by J. P. Long, A. J. Mills and Bennett Scott.

695 The first day of the Battle of the Somme, July 1st – November 27th. British casualties, 57 470.

Sunday July 3rd 1916, Hazebrouck

Great haste – travelling tonight. The horse and Peter Waite have gone on ahead – I am very glad to be able to take them both. One or two of the senior officers have been most kind. There is always some sorrow in parting, but on the whole I am glad to change.

An uneventful journey, and a <u>very</u> cordial good-bye from the Mess. The country is much more settled, and passengers go about more freely.

Monday July 4th 1916, Rouen

A night in the train, and the usual sleeping at intervals, but fortunately a carriage all to myself.

For the first time I am in the French lines. Instead of nothing but khaki everywhere, there is nothing but grey-blue everywhere, and always the steel helmet[696]. They look very picturesque, those long columns of mounted men winding in and out of the little forests and up the green-clad hills. Shut your eyes a little, and you see a cavalcade of knights of old, followed by their men at arms. It is very pretty country, the churches and houses slate-roofed, and many of them affecting turreted and pinnacle decoration. I have just stood outside a waiting station and seen a brigade of artillery go by. There is no doubt about the French guns – their number and their quality. Many of them have pet names marked in chalk – 'Joyeuse' – 'Chant Clair' with a cockerel all alive! 'La p'tite folle' and so on – that shows the spirit of the French troops.

An English Officer, rather older, is travelling down by the same train, going to see his young son who was wounded on Saturday, not knowing whether he will find him dead or alive – he was at the Kings School, Rochester. Two French officers returning from leave, have many questions to ask of us – they are surprised that the pay of the English Officers, though it is not much, is better than theirs.

Evening. I have arrived alright – and alas! I am temporarily at a Hospital again. I do hope to change in a few days – the place swarms with sick and suffering[697].
I went into the Cathedral this morning. As a boy I painted, from a copy, the interior of this Cathedral – it seemed strangely familiar to stand at the identical point of view, and see how nicely I had painted it! Tuckey is here – and very busy.

---

696 The French Adrian Helmet was issued at the beginning of 1915. The BEF only began issuing the steel Brodie Helmet in April 1916.

697 Rouen – alongside Boulogne, Etaples and Trouville – acted as one of the primary Hospital Centres for the BEF, with some 20 000 beds by March 1918. The British scheme of evacuation was based chiefly on Rouen, to which casualties were conveyed mostly by train, ambulance or improvised, but also by barges down the Somme and by *char-à-bancs*. About 15 hospitals were based in the town. Hospitals July 1916: No 1 Stationary; No 2 British Red Cross; No 3 General; No 3 Stationary; No 5 General; No 6 General; No 8 General; No 9 General; No 10 General; No 11 Stationary; No 12 General; No 25 Stationary; No 58 General; No 59 General; No 2 Australian General.

Tuesday July 5th 1916, Rouen

Piles of torn and blood-stained clothing; torn and weary men, some groaning, some gently moaning, rows and rows of them patiently silent, but looking so tired. Busy Sisters and tired Doctors, everybody hard, hard at work – the place is overflowing with sufferers and tenderers.[698]

To Tuckey's office at 10 – after a walk around with Lowndes (the Chaplain who is leaving), then I took the horse up to the re-mount camp. No Chaplains down here have horses for use and mine cannot be authorised, but I can get it for use by asking for it! Peter Waite is rather tired with his two nights in the train. In the car with Tuckey to an R.E. Office, waiting for a funeral – here a funeral is published in the local paper, and some civilians attend.

Wednesday July 6th 1916, Rouen

Three funerals this morning, three tomorrow and a German. The crush of patients is subsiding, but it is by these places that you know what is going on – these, and the Reinforcement Camps – the gaps in the ranks to be filled by willing and brave men, who go smiling and singing, eager to smite their blow. The ships also came in loaded up, it is a wonder of organization and yet the life of the city goes on in full liveliness – delicacies of food, dainty garments and costly – and some places of entertainment doing brisk business.

It is now settled that I go to a Camp on the hills, reinforcements etc., and I shall be thankful. We are in a rush here … things are going well. For the present please address as before c/o A.C.G. A.P.O. 2 B.E.F. It has been a very full day – suffering, dying and dead – and the recovering. I have just given Holy Communion to a very cheery, friendly little fellow, shot in the chest with little chance of recovery[699]. How good some of these Doctors are, and how gentle and untiring are the Sisters. There is surely something divine in the tender self-forgetfulness of a good and faithful woman.

I have lost only my walking stick over this change which is something to be thankful for. Good Peter Waite knows his work well by now, and does it steadily.

Friday July 8th 1916, Rouen

A beautiful day, not too hot and unlike yesterday, no rain, but a very full one. Three hours taken over a funeral – going and returning! The Cemetery is beautifully situated, and the graves of the English Officers and soldiers are well looked after. The French tombs are, some of them, very interesting. In the little chapels over them there are very nice stained glass windows and in one of them I noticed the portraits of a

---

698 5th Day of the Battle of The Somme.
699 Pte **Edwin Charles Ireland**, A Company, 7th Battalion, East Kent Regiment ('The Buffs', RDG's old regiment) (b.1894 – died 12th July 1916).

husband and wife – very modern-looking. But how some of these men suffer, and how glad one is of one's own health and faculties.

Saturday July 9th 1916 Rouen

A beautiful day. H.C. at 6.30 with ten present. The Sisters had arranged flowers in the Chapel very nicely indeed. An upset rather because the place (really the long attic under the roof) had been laid out with beds on the floor for an overflow, which happily did not take place. For the first time since I have been out here we had a collection. At 11.15 we had a service but no patients or soldiers came, only 5 Sisters and a nice Indian Medical Officer. In the evening, nobody came, except a Sister to play. So off to a central Church in the town, which is held in the chapel of the Archbishop's Palace, and a service also in the infectious tent.

Sunday July 10th 1916, Rouen

I went down to the Hospital this evening and saw the Sister who nursed George Thomas, she says they operated and removed the bullet. To be mentioned in Dispatches and to be wounded both are distinctions many would envy him. I also met the father who came down in the same train to see his son, who was critically wounded, in the same Hospital. Mercifully, his boy has taken the right turn and is going on well. The father had noticed George Thomas's bright face in the bed nearby, and had chatted with him – so life pieces itself together.

"Won't you sit down and talk to me, Sir?" Who can resist that? And the weary pain-stained man is so thankful for the relief of being chatted with. Eventually we glided into prayer – he was weary of his sin, and he did want to get back to his young wife near Lincoln. He remembered seeing me going about near Neuve Chappelle and in the Fromelles fight. He was in the next Brigade to mine and was thankful for the prayer. And we have a little each time I can spare to get to him. "Will you ask the Chaplain if he will come and read to me?" and the Sister laughed at the simple coolness of the request in the busy visiting of many dozens of serious cases. But I went across, and he wanted – a little of Rudyard Kipling! He had just come out of the Operating Room so I read him a paragraph of or two of "Mr Puffles", and he soon dozed off. As I was going away, he murmured "Will you come and read a bit out of the Bible later on?" The cheery little lad I took Holy Communion to is sinking – at one moment he is managing a transport, at another he is getting his rifle up to the loop-hole. At another he can see a shell coming in his direction and scattering dirt all round. Yet he knows you – always with a happy smile – in the intervals. His mother has been sent for – he comes from a parish near Canterbury[700]. Another, who had to have his arm cut off, is reconciled – he smiled when reminded that he still has his right

---

700 Pte Ireland was the son of Thomas Rainer Ireland and **Louisa Ireland** of Church Corner, St. Nicholas at Wade, Isle of Thanet, Kent.

arm left, and quite chuckled when told that he would soon have his Father, Mother and sisters all clustered round when he gets to England. I remember reading at the beginning of the War, of a French Officer saying that the first two things a wounded Tommy asks for are a barber and a chaplain – he was pretty right!

Monday July 11th 1916, Rouen

"Sweet-natured large hearted Sisters" – thus the Daily Mail – and it is quite right. They are <u>very</u> admirable, invariably so patient and tactful, and they must be strong to keep the hours that they do. Ireland is sinking; he has been nicely brought up I should think. He loses his temper in the delirium, but his words are always restrained. "Dear Mother, do bring the candle please, I want to see who I am talking to". It is strange this separation of mind, body and soul. I do not want to linger when I die! It would be wearying to anyone who cared. The man with the head wound is in happier mood now the anaesthetic has gone off. Another had half an inch of copper taken out of his back this morning and is as pleased as a hen who has laid an egg – a nasty jagged piece.

I have been busy with the business papers, odds and ends and visiting around. This evening I climbed the hill, from whence you get a full panorama of the City and it certainly is very picturesque. The green clad, winding hills around, the slate-covered houses, the picturesque churches and the Cathedral, and St. Maclou and St. Ouen churches on a slight eminence in the midst of the mass of buildings with the gleaming Seine in the distance and the fading lines away to the hills beyond[701]. It is difficult to imagine it an immense 'base', or that there is a war going on at all. Only the faint haze of some huge camp on the far-off hills writes that upon the eye. The outside of the Cathedral and the churches is delicate, varied and attractive, tho' I fear my ignorance of architectural styles forbids my describing.

Goodnight my beloved – I send you a little wild mint gathered on the hilltop[702].

1.40 am Another 'convoy' in – George Thomas' regiment has suffered badly with two of the officers killed and almost all wounded, and very many of the men knocked out. The shell-shock cases are very sad – some stonily dazed, one twitching, cringing, the hands trembling (a characteristic symptom), seeing shells coming every few seconds. Rather tiring that.

---

701 The Church of **Saint-Maclou** is Roman Catholic, considered one of the best examples of the Flamboyant style of Gothic architecture in France (1435). The Church of **St. Ouen** is a large Gothic Roman Catholic, famous for both its architecture and its large, unaltered Cavaillé-Coll organ, which Charles-Marie Widor described as "a Michelangelo of an organ". Built on a similar scale to nearby Rouen Cathedral, it is, along with the church of Saint Maclou, one of the principal Gothic monuments of Rouen.

702 This pressed flower is still in the family's possession.

'wild mint gathered on the hilltop'

Tuesday July 12th 1916, Rouen

Still the stream comes on. They are in good spirits having gained trenches and villages.

Ireland's mother came this morning, to find that her son had died during the night. By some very sad carelessness she was not passed on here yesterday afternoon – she was in the town only a mile away by 4 o'clock, but some unsophisticated person persuaded her that the place was too far away for her to try coming over then. How unnecessary it seemed.

Another batch in today – all full of good spirits at the successes gained. But how some of them suffer, and they are thankful for prayers which some of them ask for. The Scotchman in the small hours of the morning was amusing, arm, neck, and thigh all badly gashed and his head bound. At first he began explaining his case to me as a doctor but I hastened to say that I was a Chaplain. "Oh well," he said "thank you, Sir. You do as much good as the doctors!" I left him asking the doctor if he could please give him an 'antidote to send him off to sleep'! Another little fellow, talking really quite intelligently and pleasantly, apologises "if he isn't talking sense, he is that distracted with pain", and one of the shell shocks is coming round. Another, who would not speak to the Doctors, suddenly spoke when I adopted Our Lord's plan with the Gadarene lunatics, asking "What is your name?"[703] I read once that that is a scientific method of trying to use whatever reason is there. Two new doctors have come. One a fresh-looking Territorial happened to find a seat at table next to me. Eventually he asked me where was my parish? I said 'in Kent'. He said "I come from Kent, my practice is in Maidstone" I said "my Parish is four miles outside Maidstone!" His name is Johnstone – I do not know him but he has attended the Misses Warde and has visited the Wardes at 'Gallants'[704] and has also attended the Sinclairs – and so on! He thinks that Dr Hoare ought to retire and give the younger men a chance. Dr Falwasser is serving with the troops, as is Dr Gibb, the Trittons' doctor[705]. I see that Lance Corporal the Earl of Crawford has been made a cabinet minister in succession to Lord Selborne!

Wednesday, July 13th 1916, Rouen

It is a mercy that the weather remains cool, or it would be so much the worse for these suffering men. How these Sisters and Doctors do work! Another convoy came in this morning – such hideous damages in so many cases and legs and arms have had to be cut off, bits of metal and bullets extracted and gashes cleaned and sewn up. Of course, the Chaplain visits the worst cases, and in the hot and crowded, necessarily crowded atmosphere, the smell of the suppurating injuries is very intense and very disagreeable at times. I wonder more people do not get blood-poisoning! It says wonders for the care taken to keep all things aseptic and in working order. A lad of 17 comes in with his right arm gone from the shoulder – another man has to lose one leg at the knee, the other just above. Two other arms have been cut off above the elbow, and a man has a huge slice of flesh taken away by a fragment of shell, exposing a rib and the chest wall. A sergeant, a cheery man, who remembers me in the 8th Division, has a bullet through the chest, but is going on well. What a list might be made, you talk almost mechanically towards the end of the day.

We buried Ireland this morning. His mother, a good type of a quiet healthy-minded and healthy-bodied English peasant woman, who must have been handsome when she was young, small in build but with wonderfully thick and rich chestnut hair now shot with grey, followed everything in a wondering and interested kind of way, her eyes now and then filled with tears when we talked of him. She stood up bravely and firmly when the Last Post was sounded, and there were no tears. It was a look of motherly pride, I suppose, to think that she had given her son for her country – at all

---

703   The Gaderene Swine. **Mark 5:9** 'And he asked him, What *is* thy name? And he answered, saying, My name *is* Legion: for we are many.'
704   Gallants Manor Farm House, East Farleigh, Kent.
705   Lieut. Col. Dr. **Arthur Thomas** *Falwasser (b.1874 – d.1943)*, MRCS, LRCP, DSO, Lond., Chairman *Maidstone* Division, BMA, West Malling, Kent.

events, she had given her son to do as other brave lads had done. I think these were the kind of thoughts I read. She was pleased to see how the graves are cared for.[706] There were five other English relatives of different soldiers there. One had arrived too late to see his brother, he was from Carlisle, but was grateful for a talk – and hurt my hand as he said goodbye! He remarked that trying to get about out here, not knowing any French, was 'like trying to cut hair with blunt scissors'! The Y.M.C.A. has done good work in sending out these relatives and Mrs. Ireland returns this evening at 5 o'clock.

The worst shell shock has slept, and is improving. To tell of all the different talks, the varied cases and experiences, the groups that like to gather round and describe the fights, the trenches, the symptoms and all the rest would take pages. There are plenty of souvenirs again! Pickelhaubers, rings, watches, mark notes – and the rest!

Thursday July 14th 1916, Rouen

It has been a long and very full day with many dangerous cases, and more deaths. The amputations are sad and worrying, some with good constitutions pull through and others do not, but the Sisters are <u>marvellous</u> and the quality of doctors that we have in this place is really superior – I am thankful. The O.C. is a thoughtful man who has written a book on surgery in wartime[707]. It does make a difference – and NO Presbyterian, at least the Presbyterian who visits is an earnest man so there is much to be thankful for.

Friday, July 15th 1916, Rouen

Streams of wounded again – a good many bringing German helmets as trophies, which is a good sign and all are in very good spirits. You talk until your throat becomes stiff. One man full of interest is from Cambridge – Chesterton – and used to attend Holy Trinity. He remarked, when I said I knew Trumpington, how sad was the death of Canon Pemberton's only son[708]. Another comer from Lydney, Gloucestershire – Primrose Hill, a hill I walked up not seldom as a boy and further chat revealed the fact that his mother was in service with Mr. Pope, the little County Town tailor, who made some of your distinguished husband's clothes just about 30 years ago[709]. With that same tailor lodged a clever Civil Engineer who helped with the making of the Severn Bridge, by name Count

---

706 **Louisa Ireland**. Her son is buried at St Sever Cemetery, Rouen, Seine-Maritime, France.

707 **Sir Henry McIlree Wiliamson Gray** (b.1870 – d.1938), base surgeon consultant at Rouen 1915–16. *Treatment of Gunshot wounds by Excision and Primary Suture*, Journal of the Royal Army Medical Corps, June 1915, the first publication of this technique for treating gunshot/shrapnel wounds.

708 Capt. **Francis Percy Campbell Pemberton**, (b.1885 – d.1914). 2nd Life Guards. Killed in action, 19th October 1914. Only son of Canon and Mrs Pemberton of Trumpington Hall, Cambridge; husband of Winifred Mary Colegate (formerly Pemberton), of 16, Prince's Gardens, London.

709 **Alfred Pope**, (b.1830) tailor, Newerne, Lydney, Glos.

Reichenbach[710] – a German.

More deaths. At 12.0 I was called in to see a dangerous case, a nice quiet unselfish man. He dictated this postcard: "My dear Sister, I hope this postcard finds you well. You will be surprised to hear I have been wounded. I hope to be on the way home soon. Will write when I get there. Your affectionate brother, Frank." At one o'clock I was called in again, and a few minutes later he died[711]. "On the way Home," we hope, though that was not in his thoughts – if only some might be allowed to write to us when they get there! "It's like going through fire and death," remarked one man of the crowd tonight, "there's many hundreds have prayed who haven't done so for a long time before."

Saturday, July 16th 1916, Rouen
Goodnight, dear lady, very late and very tired.

Sunday, July 17th 1916, Rouen
Very busy again today, in Cavalry camp – 3 funerals. I have just been, for an hour and a half, trying to persuade Townsend from jumping out of bed in delirium after having had his legs amputated[712]. Everybody is overwhelmed with work, so patients have to look after themselves in many cases. They are lying in all kinds of corners, and some under the awning in the open, as well as upon the floors. More news later.

Monday, July 18th 1916, Rouen
I hope it is not shirking, but I am thankful to be away from gangrenous wounds and jagged limb stumps, the delirium and moans of pain and the smell of crowded-out wards. General Plummer[713] is right – 3 months at a time is enough for a Chaplain at a hospital these days. It is fresh, open and alive up here at the Cavalry depot – an immense camp with a very nice Colonel (of Viscount Wolseley's regiment – the

---

710 George William Keeling and Count **Oscar Reichenbach**, engineers. The Severn Railway bridge was built by the Severn Bridge Railway company in the 1870s to transport coal from the Forest of Dean on the Severn and Wye Railway. The span across the Gloucester and Sharpness Canal operated as a swing bridge.

711 Private **Frank Corke** (b.1894 – d.1916), 10th Bn. Cheshire Regiment, died 15th June 1916. Son of William and Sarah Corke, of 37, Stafford St., Market Drayton, Salop.

712 Second Corporal **Herbert Francis Townsend** (b.1888 – d.1916), 203rd Field Company, Royal Engineers. Wounded 12th July, died of wounds 25th July 1916. Born and enlisted at Cambridge, the husband of Francis Daisy Townsend.

713 Field Marshal **Herbert Charles Onslow Plumer**, 1st Viscount Plumer, GCB, GCMG, GCVO, GBE (b.1857 – d.1932). After commanding V Corps at the Second Battle of Ypres in April 1915, he took command of the Second Army, HQ Hazebrouck, in May 1915. Victory over the German Army at the Battle of Messines in June 1917. Served as Commander-in-Chief of the British Army of the Rhine and then Governor of Malta before becoming High Commissioner of the British Mandate for Palestine in 1925 and retiring in 1928. 'Daddy' Plumer was the model for Colonel Blimp; a devout high churchman and favourite with the troops.

Cameronians[714]) in charge and all kinds of 'live' work going on round[715]. I am in an entirely new kind of dwelling place, one of those portable canvas cabins on the plan of a small log hut! Two 'friends' in the Mess – Capt Lord Caledon[716], whom I used to meet on the front, and Lt Pelly of the Life Guards[717] – a welcome change from the raw and rather vulgar Irish Dentist and the Presbyterian!

Tuesday, July 19th 1916, Rouen

Please note the change of address! No.5 GENERAL BASE DEPOT APO 2[718].

It is very pleasant here for the present. The C.O. is a kindly, courteous gentleman, and there is a genial Adjutant who took me all round his camp this afternoon very keen about everything, such as the accommodation for the men's showers and a number of nice officers, to say nothing of the tone of the men[719]. We have 1st Life Guards, 2nd Life Guards, 5th Dragoon Guards, etc. etc. all fit, fresh and keen to go off up the line – over 800 marched off after lunch, to where I may not tell you! I shall be content to stay here awhile. A full, a very full day – the war goes well.

Wednesday, July 20th 1916, Rouen

A full day of much work, and mingled feelings (the latter of which I hope I may be able to recount to you, my darling, in private!) A meeting of the Chaplains of this group presided over by Colbeck[720], a regular army Chaplain with the rank of

---

714 The **Cameronians (Scottish Rifles)** was an infantry regiment of the British Army, the only regiment of rifles amongst the Scottish regiments of infantry. It was formed in 1881 under the Childers Reforms by the amalgamation of two other regiments: 26th Cameronian Regiment, 90th Perthshire Light Infantry. Field Marshal **Garnet Joseph Wolseley**, 1st Viscount Wolseley, KP, GCB, OM, GCMG, VD, PC (b.1833 – d.1913) served in Burma, the Crimean War, the Indian Mutiny, China, Canada, and widely throughout Africa – including his Ashanti campaign (1873–1874) and the Nile Expedition against Mahdist Sudan in 1884–85. He served as Commander-in-Chief of the Forces from 1895 to 1900. His reputation for efficiency led to the late 19th-century English phrase "everything's all Sir Garnet", meaning "all is in order".
715 Colonel **Thomas Townley Macan** (b.1862 – d?1940) 1st Bn Cameronians (Scottish Rifles). Irish cavalry officer who had also fought in the Boer war. He survived the war, retired to Devon, where he was a keen polo player.
716 Major **Eric James Desmond Alexander, 5th Earl of Caledon** (b.1885 – d.1968), The Life Guards, eldest son of James Alexander, 4th Earl of Caledon and Lady Elizabeth Graham-Toler. Succeeded to the title of **Earl of Caledon** on the death of his father in 1898. Eton, Trinity College, Cambridge. He fought and was wounded in 1915, served in the Baltic from 1919 to 1921.
717 Lt. **Phillip Vincent Pelly** (b.1898 – d.1991). Household Battalion (1st, 2nd Life Guards and Royal Horse Guards from September 1916) and Grenadier Guards. He was the 4th son of Sir Harold Pelly, 4th Bt. and Anna Maria Poore. He married Pamela Mary Des Voeux. He was educated at Wellington College.
718 Base Depot, established at Rouen, Normandy in 1914. Supplies, reinforcements and remounts, ordnance, mechanical transport, sick and wounded (hospitals); No 4 General Base Depot for Royal Engineers; No 5 General Base Depot for Cavalry and RAMC (RDG's attachment); Territorial Force Base Depot; Indian Advanced Base Depot; Army Ordnance Corps Base Depot.
719 No 5 General Base Depot for Cavalry and RAMC. C.O. Col. Thomas T. Macan.
720 Rev. **George Henry Colbeck** (b.1860 – d.?) Ordained a Deacon in 1887 and a Priest in 1888

Lt Colonel, who was in the V11th Division (and took £25 of the fund for his work there), a fussy, fiery little man who likes to be "je suis en haut vous etre en bras." Then on to my old place to see Phillips the new Chaplain and two patients, Townsend from Cambridge and Pollard from Yorkshire, the latter doing rather well, the former in an uncertain condition as his second leg is getting a little septic – I wonder if he will be spared[721].

It was nice lunching in the Mess again and chatting with Jimmy Stewart's brother and then to buy some summer socks (they do wear out!) and light vests. Then to rescue the little harmonium I had left in the town and a Macintosh cloak I had left in the robing room of the Cemetery only to find that someone had appropriated it – another Chaplain? let us hope not! Goodbye dear Macintosh[722]. Popping the harmonium into the temporary Church of this town, I came into my hut to find a message saying that Tuckey was coming and would like to borrow the harmonium! Tuckey came, and Colbeck, and I found to my honest distress that a part of their purpose was to tackle me about the Evening Communion that my predecessor has had. I did not go into the matter a word more than I could help, suffice it to say they seemed trying, in their Senior Chaplain capacity, to be suggesting more than a Bishop would do! It was a relief to go and sit quietly looking on at a pretty good game of cricket our unit was playing. Let us play cricket! Let us play the game!

Thursday July 21st 1916, Rouen

There seems to be a little conspiracy between Tuckey and Colbeck to 'squash' the Evening Communion to which I hear 20 or 30 men have been accustomed to attend – communicants are too precious, I think, to shut down opportunities if they are needed. Alas! It is a new little trial in its way, for Colbeck is a hot peremptory little person, very ready to use his military authority. As I remarked, some of these smaller men will do or try to do, what a bigger man like a Bishop or even an Archdeacon would not think of doing! At the Church tent, the following dialogue occurred Tuckey (after a firm enquiry came at the announcement of H.C. each Sunday in the Y.M.C.A. Quiet Room at 8p.m.) "I say, Mr. Griffiths, if I were you I would alter that" G. "I'll see" T. "If it were a good, big popular service it would be different. But the Holy Communion is so special I should alter that and put it once a month". G.

---

in Rangoon, Burma. He was Chaplain of the Society of the Propagation of the Gospels Mission at Mandalay and Principal of the Religious School, Burma, 1887–90, Acting Chaplain to the Burma Field Force 1887–90. During the Boer War, he was a Chaplain to the Forces, 4th Class, 1900–01. He was then Chaplain at Woolwich, 1901–03; Warley, 1903–04; Standerton, South Africa, 1904–05; Potchefstroom, 1905–09; Dublin, 1909–12, and Portsmouth, 1912–14.). After the war, he was Curate of St. Cross, Winchester, 1921–22; Chaplain to Enham Village Centre, 1922–24; Curate of St. Peter, Eaton Square, Westminster, 1925–27; and Curate of St. George, Hanover Square, 1927–31. He was appointed Vicar of Stanford-on-Avon with Swinford in 1931.

721 **Townsend** had had his other leg amputated July 17th, and died on July 25th of septicemia.

722 **Charles Macintosh** FRS (b.1766 – d.1843) was a Scottish chemist and inventor of waterproof fabrics. The Mackintosh raincoat (the variant spelling is now standard) is named for him.

"They tell me that the service is much appreciated. I must see". Colbeck. "They want a big, popular service more". G. "I imagine they must have had that, by the Y.M.C.A. people. I'll see" as indeed they do. So the men adjourn from the usually crowded 'popular' service, to the Holy Communion time in the Quiet Room behind. The arrangement shall continue for the present. The new administrative posts are rather much for some of our Chaplain brethren, so If I come home to England at the end of this mission, dear lady, a little depressed, blame that for it, partly. One gets almost a sense of outrage to think that a military uniform should be used in such a direction.

I mentioned meeting Jimmy Stewart's brother – I think he is a good fellow. Did he not once go to Anstey in the year 1904?

In this mess are one or two rather especially nice persons. Major Tuson, of the same regiment to which the nice Capt. Sloane Stanley[723] belonged, do you remember, and who was A.D.C to Lord Hampden?[724] Also Lord Caledon who came in sick to no.12 Casualty Clearing station and Lt. Pelly who I met last May – you seem to be not among strangers anywhere. Much good goes on here – there is a nice YMCA hut and a son of Canon Aitkin helps, also Prof. Thomas (Prof of Greek?) at Bala College[725], and others – so we can go on trying.

There is no 'leave', I fear, for months! Pressure everywhere.

Thursday July 28th 1916, Rouen

I am at a concert, where there is a large crowd of around 200 on seats – it is in the open air. Speaking roundly, there are probably a dozen concerts going on at the moment in various parts of this huge camp, some within 50 yards of each other. A string band is playing rather well (the same that plays for our Church Service) and a trooper has recited 'The Bells' with great power and effect, and the man with the 'cello is plunging away at this second – grandly! The cool sun-dried air is perfect and everyone is happy and contented, but many will go off <u>up there</u> day by day – it is a pleasant interlude. It is good for these different performers to have the hobby of learning their instruments – cornets, violins, piano, 'cello, flute and so on. The night is cool and I had a long walk with a young officer who is hoping to have a letter tomorrow telling him he is engaged – Lt Latreille of the GB Cavalry![726] Such is the kind of work in a Chaplain's life.

---

723 Major **George Edward Tuson**, (b.1885 – d.1935), 12th (Prince of Wales) Royal Lancers, 16th Cavvalry Brigade South Africa. Father, Edward Bailey Tuson, Surgeon General. Capt **Cecil Vivian Sloane-Stanley**, 12th (Prince of Wales) Royal Lancers, ADC Governor New South Wales, 12th Cavalry Brigade S Africa.

724 **Henry Robert Brand**, 2nd Viscount Hampden, GCMG (b.1841 – d.1906) was Governor of New South Wales from 1895 to 1899.

725 **Bala-Bangor** was a theological seminary belonging to the Welsh Independents, an association of Welsh congregationalists. It was founded in 1841 at Llanuwchllyn, then moved to a permanent location at Bala, Gwynedd in 1842 under the principalship of Michael Jones (b.1787 – d.1853).

726 2nd Lt **Leonard Latreille**, King Edward's Horse (b.1892).

A message from Tuckey by telephone asking for a call on him in the morning – why am I apprehensive? What a pity! Why cannot they go on with their work and get religion spread as a health-giving influence? I may be wrong – I hope I am. But one loses spirit in time (just as Peel did – the 'regular' Chaplains would not leave him alone). However, this is the thought, "Ye serve the Lord Christ[727]".

Friday, July 29th 1916, Rouen

It was as I feared, darling. The interview will remain with me as a painful and melancholy memory. Tuckey said he had had complaints that the men coming from this camp said they were not going to go to morning Communion when they could have it comfortably in the evening – that we were setting a bad example – that we were going to send men back to England after the war with a bad tradition – that if men were more 'real' they would take the trouble to turn out early in the morning. And then "speaking as my <u>superior Officer</u>", he requested that the practice should cease and that an ordinary Evening Service should be instituted instead. And alas! He took on a dreadful tone, the minatory one, and said if I did not conform he should ask the Deputy Chaplain General to have me removed to another district. I said I was very, very sorry if any interruption were to come into my own, Tuckey's and Colbeck's friendship. Also, I said I was deeply sorry for what seemed to me the harsh view that was being taken of the whole thing, the needs of the men and their difficulties as Communicants were precious, and I could not lightly think of turning any aside. I said that I did not favour the Evening Communion in preference to the morning, but the men really had difficulties e.g their Adjutant had said to me immediately, when I named the earlier service, "it was not a bit of good putting it in orders as the men could not get away". And the service, I was told, had been used by large numbers compared to the few who came to the early. That a service of Evening Prayer was desirable I quite agreed (and the plan for one was there and then adopted – I think I should have come to it independently – I have only been here <u>one</u> Sunday!) but a re-mount, and a reinforcement Camp were exceptional places, and an occasional Evening Communion would not meet the case of men only here for a short stay who might be glad, and many of them were glad, as at Etaples, to receive the Sacrament before going off to the Front. Also that this matter had never been raised with me by my own Bishop, or any Patrons – that it seemed to me Our Lord would wish this Service made as easily available as possible, and at this time especially, and I could not help thinking we were in danger of the warning against 'binding burdens heavy and grievous to be borne[728]', of making it harder for men to enter the Kingdom of Heaven – and that I wanted to be here to help the men as much as possible. That in any case any semblance of trying to put

---

727 **Colossians 3:4** 'Knowing that of the Lord ye shall receive the reward of the inheritance: for ye serve the Lord Christ'.
728 **Matthew 23:4** 'For they bind heavy burdens and grievous to be borne, and lay them on men's shoulders; but they themselves will not move them with one of their fingers.'

upon me a 'force majeure', in a matter that was one not of military exigency but of religious principle, and a principle upon which a large section of the Church had very strong feelings, must call for very great care on both sides. The practice had been long in use at this camp, and I repeated the peculiar difficulty men attending on horses have about the early hour of the day, and I could not, at short notice, take the responsibility of hindering a custom which so many of the men, sometimes as many as 30 or 40 I had been told, were glad of. It ended by Tuckey saying I had better see him again next Thursday at 10.30, and to think it all over in the meanwhile. A strenuous effort might be made to get them to a very early Morning Service – 5.30 or so ("Cri bono vous?" my heart says). But in any case, that was the import – the regular fixture ought to be, <u>must be</u> I think was the tone – given up. What to do now?? Be removed? What a hateful experience – how painful the discussion of it! I have learnt from the workers this evening that the <u>very early</u> plan <u>was</u> tried some months ago, but after much effort, failed – I wonder how this unhappy business will work out[729].

Saturday, July 30th 1916, Rouen
A very full day of officers and troops and it is very hot. Just off to a parade. One of the men of the 24th Field ambulance appeared this afternoon, the third that I have met lately – Bailey, one of my special friends among them, has been killed[730].

Sunday, July 31st 1916, Rouen
COPY OF THE LETTER TO BISHOP HARMER[731] "My Lord Bishop,
I am in a difficulty about which I cannot do anything else than ask to consult you. I found in existence here, when taking on this Cavalry Base Depot, a regular service of the Holy Communion in the evening. It was instituted, I have ascertained, by arrangement with the S.C.F. of this Base, particularly at the request of the men of the Remount Depot in the month of November last, and has been continued since.

---

729 RDG talks of many of his fellow Chaplains as opportunist and careerist; though at this point he was a Captain, equivalent to Tuckey's full Colonel. The issue of late versus early communion was a current one within Anglicanism, with traditionalists taking the view that communion should be proceeded by a fast, and therefore could only be taken in the morning. RDG seems typically both slightly diffident (simply following what was already practice at the Cavalry Base Depot) and concerned for the welfare of the men by making communion something that all could partake.

730 Pvte **Frederick Henry Bailey**, (b.1895 – 1 July 1916) RAMC 24th Field Ambulance. Son of RH and Annie Bailey, Exeter.

731 Rev. **John Reginald Harmer** (b.1857 – d.1944), Bishop of Rochester, thus RDG's civilian clerical superior. Harmer was born into a clerical family (his father the Rev. George Harmer), educated Eton and King's College, Cambridge. Ordained priest in 1884, a curate at Monkwearmouth before becoming Vice-Principal of the Clergy Training School in Cambridge. From 1892, he was Dean of Corpus Christi before his election as Bishop of Adelaide in March 1895. In 1905, he was translated back to England when he was elected Bishop of Rochester, serving for a quarter of a century before his retirement in 1930.

The matter was referred to me by both Mr Colbeck and Mr Tuckey (at the time of my joining last Tuesday week), who were of the opinion that the practice of holding the service each Sunday should cease, and that a Service once a month should be substituted. I had been informed that it was a Service very much used – as many as 30 or 40 men being present at it, and I asked for time to know more about things, and see and judge for myself.

The circumstances of these Cavalry and Remount men are exceptional by reason of their duties with their horses – stables at 6.0am, feeding, cleaning, breakfasts and horses all saddled ready for Squadron Exercise Rides daily at 8.45am.

The *alternative* arrangement for a very early service of the Holy Communion at 5.0am has been tried, I understand, without a good result.

These facts I was ascertaining in the meanwhile – but on Saturday morning, Mr Tuckey summoned me by telephone to his office, and as it seemed to me obviously without sufficient knowledge of the local particulars, informed me that unless I conformed in this matter, my removal from the district would be asked for.

I said I was very sorry that there should be any disunity of spirit about a matter so sacred, that there should be any attempt at a 'force majeure' about any plan to help the religious lives of the men, that communicants were precious and I could not lightly think of turning any aside, that my sympathies were very much with the men in their difficulties, that our Lord's words about the "smoking flax[732]" and "burdens heavy and grievous to be born[733]" weighed with me greatly in anything that had to do with making this Service, His own Ordinance and the Principal Service of the church, as accessible as possible, especially at a time like this when men go off any day to danger and death, and that at a notice so short the step proposed regarding myself seemed rather a harsh and drastic one.

I may say that in a matter of this kind the line taken by Mr Tuckey did not commend itself to my judgement. He spoke as "ordering" me in this as my "superior officer" – using those terms.

I suggested our giving ourselves time to know more of the circumstances; whether we should be wise in suddenly arresting arrangements valued by both officers and men (for I find that both have used these services); whether as at Etaples, where the Communion Service is offered to men in notices at the Parade Services in the Reinforcement Camps, whose migratory conditions make all the difference "at any hour of the day or night", a wider latitude is not demanded of us.

---

732 **Matthew 12:20** 'A bruised reed shall he not break, and smoking flax shall he not quench, till he send forth judgment unto victory.'
733 **Matthew 23:4** 'For they bind heavy burdens and grievous to be borne, and lay them on men's shoulders; but they themselves will not move them with one of their fingers.'

And I said my difficulty was that I could not submit my judgement, and the judgement of fellow communicants, on a matter on which my own Bishop and my patrons had left me free, a matter of wide-reaching doctrinal significance about which strong opinions are held in the Church at large, and one which has no really military significance, to a local and military direction. But the answer given me is that I am to see Mr Tuckey again on Thursday morning next at 10.30, and give him my reply.

My difficulty is to know just what reply to give.

What would you advise?

I am, my Lord Bishop,
Very faithfully yours

Tuesday August 1st 1916, Rouen

Marvellously hot! A long beautiful ride this morning to see some of the 'horse people' making hay! And then I rode through a cool pine forest to some sandpits and all the afternoon I have been taking burials – 13 in all. This evening I did not feel worth much – the afternoon sun was so fiercely hot in the cemetery. We now have a proper firing party who fire salutes over the graves. Poor heart-broken young wives, two of them there brought over by the Y.M.C.A., and a young mother sitting in a stony kind of grief with tears streaming down her cheeks – it is a grievous business.

Thursday August 3rd 1916, Rouen

There was a Chaplain's meeting at 10, and by ill-fortune Colbeck and I missed a tram and got into the meeting late. Tuckey made a long speech about punctuality which hit one after the other, about 6 Chaplains! Then a talk by Burroughs[734], his

---

734 Rev. **Edward Arthur Burroughs**, (b.1882 – d.1934), bishop of Ripon. Active in evangelical circles in Oxford, supporting the Oxford Inter-Collegiate Christian Union and the Oxford Pastorate, an evangelistic agency working with undergraduates. Burroughs came to public attention with a series of letters to The Times in the early months of 1915. Moved by the loss of friends and former pupils in the first year of the war, he challenged the nation to recover the spiritual ideals with which it had entered the conflict in August 1914. His letters were collected and published as *The Eternal Goal* (1915) and the theme of spiritual renewal was developed more fully in *The Valley of Decision* (1916). He criticised the lazy pragmatism of contemporary British society, comparing it unfavourably with the deep (though misguided) intellectual seriousness of Germany. He castigated self-centredness and moral decline, particularly targeting gambling, immorality, the craze for leisure, and the political influence of the drink trade, and called for repentance and faith. This message caught the national mood and chimed with the Church of England's plan for a National Mission of Repentance and Hope in 1916. Declared unfit for military service, Burroughs busied himself with the **League of the Spiritual War** (1915–20), an organisation seeking to stimulate the spiritual lives of men on active service through publications, personal correspondence, and a regular 'Letter from HQ'. He made visits to France, assisted forces chaplains, and was in much demand as a preacher and public speaker. 'Bursting into fame' (Methodist Recorder, 4th Feb 1937) with the publication of The Eternal Goal, he was hailed as a prophet for the times, and he received preferment, being appointed a chaplain to the king and canon of Peterborough Cathedral in 1917.

keenness very refreshing, about the League of the Spiritual War, and then a service in the Chapel which belongs to the Archbishop's Palace[735]. I had a nice little talk with Mr Shallard en route whom I hope to see more of later[736]. Mr Tuckey asked what I had arranged about the Evening Communion, and I said that I had found the matter so difficult that I had written to consult the Deputy Chaplain General[737].

Friday August 4th 1916, Rouen

I rode out in the fresh air after the morning's work (no one came to the Early Service) to prepare addresses and sermons. It was glorious – a cool fresh breeze, the sunlight danced between the innumerable trees over the fresh green and graceful ferns. An old black crow now and then glided across a little space, lazily as it seemed, all in keeping with the easy-going atmosphere, and suddenly a gleaming young red deer lept up from among the ferns, and sprang and skipped speedily out of harm's way – that being me or my horse! The horse is a fine person, well set up with arching neck, and is what is called a 'flea-bitten grey', partly white and with graceful action and very good manners. So you can imagine, it was not all sorrow this morning.

After lunch, Mr Shallard and his two daughters called, and we had a long and very full chat – I am going to lunch there on Wednesday. Then a long 'confab' with Mr Burroughs and a chaplain called Page about a programme for the former on Monday.

Tuesday August 8th 1916, Rouen

A beautiful day. I had business in Rouen, and spent a quarter of an hour in the Cathedral – it is a picturesque and interesting building. There is a beautiful marble altar to Joan of Arc which is much in danger of breaking the first commandment and decidedly the second! But beautifully proportioned. An altar nearby was profusely adorned with the relics of saints – bits of their bones, their rings, etc. There was a stone figure of the thorn-crowned Christ, the feet of which had been kissed by thousands of lips, but it seemed to be a little outshone by the monument of Joan of Arc nearby.

Wednesday August 9th 1916, Rouen

A long interesting day, but tiring. The Seamans' Institute – Mr Shallards' Church – a talk with Tuckey (he is stuck-up, alas!). Then lunch at the Shallards and a call at the Officers Hospital where I met Col Lewin (who married Lord Roberts' daughter[738]).

---

735 The chapel where Joan of Arc was tried in 1431.

736 Rev **G M Shallard**, All Saints church, Ile Lacroix, 38 Rue Centrale. Wesley Church, 20 Rue Lafosse, Rouen. Daughters Gertrude and Constance.

737 Bishop Harmer

738   Ada Edwina Stewart Roberts, (b.1875 – d.1955). She was the daughter of Earl Roberts, V.C. and Nora Henrietta Bews. She married **Brig.-Gen. Henry Frederick Elliott Lewin**, on 26th February 1913.

The Shallards know Sister Kewley (one of the sisters in No 1 Casualty Clearing Station) and Kingsley Ault, son of the clergyman we all sat under, as a family in 1887!

Thursday August 10th 1916, Rouen

It was remarkable hearing about Kingsley Ault – his father was our clergyman at Sharpness. Kingsley Ault entered a bank, and he came out here as a sergeant, but I hear now that he is in a Staff Office at General Headquarters[739]. It was also remarkable meeting Col Lewin[740]. A Miss Cooke, who had tea at the Shallards, went to a hospital to see a patient (an officer). I went also to see one of the doctors whom I knew up the line, and Mr Shallard also visits this hospital. I spoke to a wounded officer and remarked to Miss Cooke of having done so, and spoke his name. She said "I wonder if it is my cousin whom I have not seen for 10 years". It was, Colonel Lewin! The Shallards seem to have a nice natural and simple home life – une femme de menage and everyone else helping – rather tiring. Today a <u>most</u> unedifying Chaplains' meeting, which ruffles me rather – a chorus of Chaplains resenting Y.M.C.A. workers visiting in the Hospitals "he followeth not with me, and I forbade him!"[741] A nice ride in the forest to open up my lungs (I have something rather like an obnoxious hay-fever), then reading, writing and this evening visiting the tents. The particular men there have pet rabbits, a jay, 5 puppy terriers and a queer-faced monkey who likes to bite the phosphorescent ends of matches and eat them! But – the number of people one talks to – the life histories and the like! I <u>am</u> tired.

Friday August 11th 1916, Rouen

I think I may have had a touch of malaria but three doses of quinine have made things seem pretty normal again tonight, thank you. At the same time I have had to take things quietly, which perhaps is not all to the bad!

Letters[742] and a cool ride in the forest then visiting one or two people that matter for the Sunday services (the bandmaster, the Y.M.C.A. staff and so on). A rest, chatting round among the men at cricket, some visiting round, dinner and, as Mr Pepys would say, "so to bed". I am reading 'Ordeal by Battle[743]' which appears to be a soundly reasoned book.

---

739 Serj. **Herbert Kingsley Ault**, (b. 1884), son of **Rev. Herbert Ault** of Sharpness, Gloucestershire and Katherine Elizabeth Jane Ault (Bachelor).

740 Brig.-Gen. **Henry Frederick Elliott Lewin** was the son of Commander William Herbert Lewin. (d.1946). He gained the rank of Brigadier-General in the service of the Royal Artillery. He was invested as a Companion, Order of the Bath (CB). He was invested as a Companion, Order of St. Michael and St. George (CMG).

741 **Mark 9:38** 'And John answered him, saying, Master, we saw one casting out devils in thy name, and he followeth not us: and we forbad him, because he followeth not us.'

742 One of RDG's tasks was to write to the families of those killed.

743 *Ordeal By Battle* (1915) **Frederick Scott Oliver**, or F.S. Oliver (1864–1934), was a prominent British political writer and businessman who advocated tariff reform and imperial union for the British Empire. He played an important role in the Round Table movement, collaborated in the downfall of Prime Minister H.H. Asquith's wartime government and its replacement

I have, at last, been able to get a letter off to Kitty – one nearly 18 months late, and I must try and find time to write to my dear children, but just now it is not at all easy, and the posts too are very irregular.

Saturday August 12th 1916, Rouen

Furiously hot today, and our Mess has been depleted a great deal by officers going up the line. All on the right side. I had a long talk with one of the Colonels this morning – he is a 'low churchman', with strong views against the Bishop of London (the traitor!) and in favour of Evening Communion, so it is not easy to steer aright for everybody.

Sunday August 13th 1916, Rouen

5.0am Holy Communion with nobody present so rather a dismal proceeding, but at 8 a.m. there were 14. At 11.15 a good hearty Parade service and 2 men stayed behind for 'confidences' which is always a good sign. At 12.15 an enormous Parade, going with a great swing, the instrumental band giving great spirit to things, and they always seem to 'rise' specially to this second service. Many, many men have been strengthened and comforted, and some fresh ones captured. Entre nous – a letter from Deane Oliver holding out the prospect of Army Ministry in England. We must keep this in view, dependent upon the Fawns' movements. I would like to see the end of the War among the soldiers, and I do not feel my message is spent, but that it accumulates with the added months of experience.

I was tired in the afternoon – the Depot played cricket and at 7p.m., 12 were present for Evening Service. There are about 100 services of various kinds going on within the 4 square miles at about that time.

I wonder if the members of my diligent young family would like to send me each a drawing of one or other of the interesting objects or scenes in and around about their holiday home? This is a picture of my small Church tent – the object to the right is a gong, which is really a part of an aeroplane engine.

Monday August 14th 1916, Rouen

The tone of this Mess is a decidedly good one. There has been refreshing rain and I rode across the end of the forest and came into a little village, where I met a large company of German prisoners being marched back from some work. They did not look at all kindly or buoyant![744] A great many were strong and healthy-looking

---

by David Lloyd George in 1916, and pressed for "home rule all round" to resolve the political conflict between Britain and Irish nationalists.

744 By 1916, most non-officer prisoners of war, were put to work, some returning to the POW camp at night, others lodged under guard near to their place of work. For those housed outside the camp conditions could vary considerably. While POW camps were inspected during the

– a contrast to the impression one gets of our own prisoners at Ruhleben and elsewhere[745]. We had a long discussion after dinner tonight on Socialism – there are some keen and thoughtful officers here.

Tuesday August 15th 1916, Rouen

Torrents of refreshing rain and my touch of malaria is over. It is fortunate being able to pop in and drink your dose of quinine 'whenever you feel so disposed', the Medical hut being a few yards off.

A refreshing ride through the forest, often ridden I feel sure, by my old friend William the Conqueror, of whom you have heard me speak! A quick lunch and then funerals, preceded by drenching rain. We have here the firing parties and the Last Post, all very suitable and the men do their part well.

Parish visiting among the tents, and I popped into a Y.M.C.A. hut, packed like a wash-house on washing day with steaming khaki, where a self-confident young lady sang rather silly songs which she need not have done.

Wednesday August 16th 1916, Rouen

The rain cools the air and that is a mercy, for these canvas huts get very oven-like. The morning was taken up with looking up one of two people and arranging with the band-master about the services, then a glorious ride through the forest to get some things in the village of St Etienne[746]. The scent of the pines was brought out strongly by the rain I suppose and I felt perceptibly better of the malaria. Your letter came – we suppose the mails have been delayed through the King's visit but it is enterprising of him to have come.

I am glad that Mr Fawns has rested – it was a great occasion to have had <u>two</u> Bishops for a little parish like that! It will have written a chapter in history: its Vicar two years way at the war, its Locum Tenens a rector from Australia, its faithful and devout Churchwarden a Life Vice-President of the Navy League, his wife a sister of a General

---

war by the International Red Cross, working units outside the camp were rarely inspected. The worst camps, however, were those run by armies near the front line. By 1916, the British, French, German, Austro-Hungarian and Russian armies were all keeping permanent units of prisoners as forced labourers for the army at or near the front. These men had to work under shellfire and live in desolate, unhygienic conditions.

745 Ruhleben internment camp was a civilian detention camp, located 6 miles to the west of Berlin. The camp detainees included male citizens of the Allied Powers living, studying, working or on holiday in Germany at the outbreak of WW1. They also included the crews of several civilian ships stranded in German harbours or captured at sea. There were also quite a number of fishermen captured from trawlers, which were sunk in the North Sea in the first days of the war – these were mainly men from Hull, Grimsby and Boston. The camp contained between 4000 and 5500 prisoners, most of them British

746 **Saint-Étienne-du-Rouvray** is a commune in the Seine-Maritime department in the Haute-Normandie. A large suburban town of light industry and forestry situated by the banks of the Seine, some 4 miles (6.4 km) south of the centre of Rouen on the D18 and the D18e roads.

in the War Office, the service taken on consecutive Sundays by Bishops, to say nothing of the Vicar's wife being the eldest daughter of the Primate of Australia! – kind Sir Lewis Beaumont writes characteristically[747].

After lunch reading, and then I had arranged a short ride with an officer, who could not come, so after a short turn round, I went 'parish' visiting. There were none at the 7.30 service – the three huts take the crowds of men and the new Church tent is not easily known by these passers by. So I talked round amongst the men, and we shall do better perhaps when we get the Central Church for these Camps built.

Thursday August 17th 1916, Rouen

Another very uninspiring Chaplains meeting this morning – it has to be confessed that some of these 'regular' Army Chaplains are a flat and mechanical sample. I am not surprised at all at the men in this area wanting to get away.

This afternoon – a 16 mile ride with the Colonel along the banks of the Seine, through the forest and back along another bank. Superb weather, cool, fresh, clear, sunny and perfect scenery. Great grey stones bluffs, standing out from grass-covered hills, wooded over and between with varied green woodlands, a chateau here and there, clear blue skies beyond with fleecy banks of cloud, and the clear pale green waters of the Seine rolling placidly along. Tramp steamers with their bright colouring, lying here and there at clean-looking jetties, now and again a stately sailing ship, and now a big tug-steamer with a string of bright-coloured barges. We passed the making of a little temporary railway on which was working a big gang of German prisoners. They looked clean, well and cared for, but their expression towards us was one of a gloomy and hard curiosity with not a smile among them. At one bend, on the opposite bank, was a church built into the cliff – I must try and see it sometime[748]. That side of the forest was like the scenery in Benson's Midsummers' Night Dream[749]. It was (too long to describe fully) really a most refreshing ride.

---

747 Admiral Sir **Lewis Anthony Beaumont** KCB KCMG (b.1847 – d.1922) Beaumont joined the Royal Navy as a boy and was engaged in operations in Malaya by 1875. Command of HMS *Excellent* in 1893, Director of Naval Intelligence in 1895. He went on to be Commander-in-Chief, Pacific Station in 1899 and Commander-in-Chief, Australia Station in 1900. He was appointed Commander-in-Chief, Plymouth in 1902 and First and Principal Naval Aide-de-Camp to the King in 1911. He retired in 1912 to St. George's, Hurstpierpoint, Sussex, which is where RDG would have met him.

748 See November 3rd 1916.

749 **Sir Francis Robert Benson** (b.1858 – d.1939), commonly known as **Frank Benson** or **F. R. Benson**, was a British actor-manager. He founded his own company in 1883, and produced a number of productions of A Midsummer Night's Dream.

This evening we had a strongly rendered performance of 'The Bells[750]' by some of the troopers – very good and some of the acting quite powerful. A little hindered by the two ladies having to be acted by men, and you could not help laughing at their gruff voices.

Friday August 18th 1916, Rouen

Mercifully another cool morning, but not torrentially rainy. It is wonderful how time goes in a camp – you talk to many people, and you question whether you have achieved much. Dr Dale has a warning to people about measuring the amount of work they do by the amount of conscious effort put forth. A precarious doctrine, but founded on a deep truth. "The first business of life is to be". I am in a puzzle to know quite what to do for the future. There is the message of these years of campaigning, and what it may be of use for among the men, and there is also doing one's full bit in the War to the end, but there is also health, home and going on.

We passed under a remarkable bridge I must mention yesterday – a great iron viaduct over the Seine, which the Germans nearly blew up at the beginning of the War. When the English base retreated from Havre to St Nazare, two enemy armoured cars made a dash for this bridge. If they had blown it up there would have been a most serious hampering of both French and English – they did not succeed[751]. Another of the mercies of those fateful early days.

Saturday August 19th 1916, Rouen

It is cool and pleasant and I had a spin in the forest on my horse, who was rather fresh after being in a whole day, following on an inoculation, and then a long journey to pay a proper call on the Shallards. The tram system was held up for nearly an hour through a dear little baby traction engine having broken down in the middle, between the two sets of tramway lines. That shows how one awkward little person, without perhaps knowing it, can upset half a city! Mrs Shallard was at home, and their two daughters and the little son, who wants to be a Naval Engineer.

Sunday August 20th 1916, Rouen

Only one officer at 6.0am HC, and at 8.am one officer and 8 others. Parade service at 11.15 with about 600 present, closely packed and very stuffy, but a nice service.

---

750 *The Bells* is a play in three acts by Leopold Davis Lewis which was one of the greatest successes of the British actor Henry Irving. The play opened on 25th November 1871 at the Lyceum Theatre in London and initially ran for 151 performances. It is a translation of the 1867 play *Le Juif Polonais (The Polish Jew)* by Erckmann-Chatrian. The Erckmann-Chatrian play was also adapted into an opera of the same name in three acts by Camille Erlanger, composed to a libretto by Henri Cain.

751 The German sweep across France in August 1914 caused the British concern with regard to Le Havre. The British supply Base Depot was temporarily moved to St-Nazaire by Sir John French but by October was once again moved back to Le Havre.

At 12.15 our Cavalry Parade, about 500 present, always nicely conducted and the quietness of the men is very remarkable, so it is much easier to take than some of the other Parades for that reason. I am sure it is in marked measure due to Col Macan's influence, he is so persistent in his attendance and young officers come too.

Only 4 people came to our evening Service, but great numbers crowd to the Y.M.C.A. and S.C.A. huts. Only those would come to us who want a quiet and devotional time in the Anglican way and those who did come, said how much they liked it. A long and earnest discussion after dinner with the three senior officers of the Depot on life's disappointments, the interference of unscrupulous or self-interested persons etc.

Tuesday August 22nd 1916, Rouen
There is not time to tell of the very long concert of yesterday, but it was good, and one was glad to see so many men occupied with wholesome things – good music, good fun, and in some cases, some very nice thoughts. Another concert tonight (Miss Lena Ashwell's party) which was very good.

Busy with letters this morning, and a very nice short ride, where a dear old red squirrel ran along the ground, then behind a fallen tree trunk, then up a high, slim smooth fir-tree, with just the nimbleness of a squirrel, then he lay snugly along a high branch out of sight.

Wednesday August 23rd 1916, Rouen

It was rather nice to find this soldier's note laid on the prayer desk this morning, left by some grateful passer-by:

'Dear Sir & Brother,
Just a line to say how pleased we were to be able to join in the Holy Communion on
Sunday last. God Bless you in your work for Him.
Yours Truly B. Cone R.A.M.C.'

COPY OF THE LETTER FROM REV RICHARD GRIFFITHS TO THE BISHOP, DATED 23/8/1916

"My Lord Bishop,

The time has come for my having to trouble you about my plans for the future.

The War may end soon – it may not, but my second year ends in November. It would have been a satisfaction to have 'seen it out' with the Expeditionary Force. But, all things considered, I have come to the opinion that I might not be able to go through a third winter, roughing it anywhere and so on, successfully. I rather gather too, that the policy of the Department is to give the field to younger men.

Whether to propose continuing with soldiers in England I am not quite clear. The way is open to me to going to work somewhere in the Eastern Command, but there is the question of the Parish.

I cannot help being conscious that the accumulated experience and knowledge of campaigning carries its weight with the men, and could be turned to great account. One still has a message – one can see that by the way they listen and respond – and the message grows with use.

And it is a great privilege to be in the swing with all this glad, fresh life: to be on the crest of the wave that, with all the sparkle and dash of English manhood at its best, is steadily rolling on to a great victory!

But the wave may be slow in breaking, and time is going on. And one does not get much in the way of holiday at times like these.

What I am venturing to propose is that I should go to work among soldiers at home for six months, and this would give Mr. Fawns time to look around. And by then, even if the War is not ended, I feel I should have had about as much of that endless press that War work means as I could do with. It is a break that one wants.

At the same time, if Mr. Fawns found other work to his liking earlier, I should be content to return to the parish earlier – and I know my wife would. The home side and Mrs Griffiths' work must have their weight.

I have written to Mr. Fawns somewhat to the same effect as this, but have no idea what may be in his mind. He will probably write soon now, but I thought that I had better write to you as time goes on and plans must be shaped. Albeit – West Farleigh will be rather quiet after all these stirring doings. Ten months in and out of the trenches and two battles, ten months among the sick, and suffering, and dying, and four months of the mingled strenuousness, dullness and keen preoccupation of Camp life. It will be necessary to burst out in some direction "why should a man whose blood is warm within sit……[752]!

---

752 W. Shakespeare, *The Merchant of Venice*, Act 1 Sc 1.

I am glad to hear that you have been enjoying a good holiday at Church Stretton, in charming country.

If I can help in any way, please say.
I am, my Lord Bishop
Very faithfully yours
Richard Griffiths."

Friday August 25th 1916, Rouen

I have been down into the town this evening spending money. There are no lights in our Church tent and the Government will not supply them. So – they have to be purchased, mercifully by 'the Fund'. They have opened a Club for the officers, near the river, Lady Dudley has been the moving spirit and it is an excellent idea. All officers and one thinks particularly of the young ones, have been at the mercy of the cafes, and one or two rather expensively run hotels, so this place will be a set off against them.

Saturday August 26th 1916, Rouen

How depressed one gets sometimes, and all the prescriptions of the doctors of medicine, and the great Christian Confessors only mock you at such times. As helpful as anything is the Cockney meditation: "Wot's the good of anyfink? Nuffink!" Peoples' little ambitions bore you. Their little fussings about their rank bore you. The unnatural views – wildly unnatural views – you have to listen to alarm you. Peoples' severities hurt you. Their gruntleness seems tedious weakness. Their superficiality wearies you, and your own incompleteness discourages you – we all want saving.

A long talk this morning with the low-church Colonel of one of the camps of this charge. He is flatly defiant of the Deputy Chaplain General and his advice! Which, with my own feeling in the matter, does not make it easy for me to be dutiful and loyal! Between the Ultra–Montanist[753] and say the Baptists or the Society of Friends, what is the central position, say, regarding the Holy Communion? And we talk of this War bringing everyone together! In many ways the National Mission is in danger of intensifying peoples' differences.

A French aeroplane came down near here yesterday and I walked across to see it. They are improving the patterns rapidly. This was the kind that has the propeller behind the observer, and the floor under his feet is made of plate glass – it all looked very secure and inviting.

Visiting round this morning and a cricket match this afternoon. This evening the General dined in this Mess and some of us had to go to a second performance of 'The Bells'. It was still rather amateurish and I have felt too busy to remain after the first scene.

---

753 **Ultramontanism** is a religious belief within the Catholic Church that places strong emphasis on the prerogatives and powers of the Pope.

---- THE BELLS ----

PRODUCED BY

Tpr. F. VALLENTINE 1st E.E.H.

STAGE MANAGER

Sgt. DAN DERRY Innis. Fusl.

SCENERY BY

Drmr. E.A. KEEFE Roy. Fusl.

PIANIST

Cpl. A.S. HEATH Gord. Highls.

--- --- --- ---

All arrangements under the
Direction of

R.S.M. A.F. DEAN Roy. Scots Greys.

PROGRAMME.

OF A
THREE ACT DRAMA
ENTITLED

"T H E   B E L L S."

BY
Leopold Lewis
as played by
The late Sir Henry Irving.

Given in the Library
of
No 2 Convalescent Depot Rouen.
on
Saturday 26th August 1916.

Followed by
A Variety Programme and
One Act Comedy Entitled

"C O L L A B O R A T O R S."

Given By Ladies of
MISS. LENA ASHELL'S CONCERT PARTY

By Kind Permission of LIEUT.COL.
H.L.W. NORRINGTON, D.S.O., R.A.M.C.
Commanding No. 2 Convalescent Depot.

C. A S T E .

Mathais (The Burgomaster)	Tpr. Vallentine.
Walter	L/Cpl. Dunscombe.
Hans	Pte. Newsam.
Christian (Quartermaster of Gendarmes)	Pte. Broughton.
Mesmerist	Sgt. Derry.
Doctor Zimmer	Drmr. Keefe.
Notary	Tpr. Green.
Tony	L/Cpl. Barker.
Fritz	Pte. Hill.
Judge of the Court	Cpl. Maule.
Clerk to the Court	Pte. Morgan.
Sozel	Sgt. Gillon.
Annette	Corpl. Jones.
Catherine	Corpl. Maule.

Acts 1 & 11 .... Interior of Village Inn in Alsace.
Act 111
　　Scene 1 .... Corridor in the Burgomaster's House.
　　Scene 11 .... Interior of Court. (Dream Scene).
　　Scene 111 .... Corridor in the Burgomaster's House.
　　　　Period December 24th. and 26th. 1833.

VARIETY PROGRAMME.

1. Song . . . . . Miss Katharine Vincent
2. Chello Solo Miss Marguerite Godfrey
3. Song   Miss Mollie Eadie
4. Songs   Miss Marguerite Godfrey
　At the Piano

"COLLABORATORS"
A one act Comedy

Mary ------ Miss Katharine Vincent
Reginald--- Tpr. P. Vallentine.
Time - The present.

G O D   S A V E   T H E   K I N G.

Sunday August 27th 1916, Rouen

(Let us learn as we go on – an aeroplane which has the driving blades behind the operator is called a 'pusher' and that which has them in front is called a 'tractor'.) The depression passed somewhat thank you, and the day has been, on the whole, an encouraging one. Two men have enquired about confirmation.

6.0am H.C. no one present and at 8.am only one communicant (rainy). A very large service at 11.15 with the hall crowded out and at 12.15 also a very large service – you felt at both that 'good' was being granted. This afternoon torrents of rain so I was glad to be quiet as these Parade services are pretty heavy work!

The aeroplanes sailed off in the midst of thunder and pouring rain. At 7p.m. Evening Service only four persons present – the Chaplain, the harmoniumnist and two others but at the Y.M.C.A. hut 250 yds away were 400 or 500 men at a popular Service, the conductor this evening being Minor Canon Perkins of Westminster Abbey[754]. The situation is a difficult one. With all these crowded inter-denominational services being held within a quarter of a mile of each other, it is only the well-instructed Churchman who can be expected to come aside to the quieter place. One must be content to see what best can be done under the circumstances.

Monday August 28th 1916, Rouen

Great rumours today – they say that Romania has come in. If only Greece would make up its mind and join also, the end might be near[755]. I had a talk with a remarkably interesting Irishman Sergeant Stark, who had to shoot down some of his own neighbours in the Sein Fein Rebellion – it has preyed on his mind[756].

---

754 Revd. **Jocelyn Perkins**. (b.1870 – d.1962) Ordained 1894 and was organist and assistant master at St Edward's School, Oxford and minor canon of Ely cathedral 1895–1900. He was appointed to Westminster in December 1899 and installed in 1901. He did much to introduce new vestments and plate to enhance worship at the Abbey and wrote a three-volume work on its Worship and Ornaments. He took part in four coronations and was also on Westminster City Council 1919–45. Another Anglican celebrity.

755 On 27th August 1916, Romania joined the Allies, declaring war on Austria-Hungary. For this action, under the terms of the secret military convention, Romania was promised support for its goal of national unity of all the territories populated with Romanians. The Romanian military campaign began disastrously as the Central Powers occupied 2/3 of the country within months; the invading forces were finally blocked in 1917. Total losses from 1916 to 1918, military and civilian, within contemporary borders, were estimated at 748 000.

The struggle between King Constantine I and charismatic Prime Minister Eleftherios Venizelos of Greece over the country's foreign policy on the eve of WW1 dominated the country's political scene, and divided the country into two opposing groups. During parts of the War, Greece had two governments; a royalist pro-German government in Athens and a Venizelist pro-Britain one in Thessaloniki. The two governments were united in 1917, when Greece officially entered the war on the side of the Allies.

756 The **Easter Rising** (Irish: *Éirí Amach na Cásca*), an armed insurrection staged in Ireland during Easter Week, 24th April, 1916. The Rising was mounted by Irish republicans with the aims of ending British rule in Ireland, seceding from the United Kingdom of Great Britain and Ireland, and establishing an independent Irish Republic at a time when the United Kingdom was heavily engaged in WW1.

Tuesday August 29th 1916, Rouen

(This 'camp' ink is maddening!). The two Confirmation candidates prove manly, responsive fellows – both from Kent. One from Deal, the other from St Lukes' Tunbridge Wells, and they seem much in earnest. Having finished the first talk with them, I went off and lunched with – Miss Lena Ashwell!! I had written a note to her about the possibility of one or two of her parties going up to towns nearer the line, and she asked for a talk. As a matter of fact of course, that is her stage name. What her proper name is I do not know, but she is wedded to an Edinburgh doctor[757]. She struck me as capable and business-like and very kind hearted, and keen about getting her parties further up. She manages a fresh party each month, and she has sent one lately to Egypt and another round the Fleet. She does a good work in providing wholesome amusement for these men and her programmes are, as far as I know, unexceptionable, and she selects performers of the highest quality. She said that at some of her 'audition' days she had heard as many as 50 candidates in a day. I hope that she may be able to get up to that town where I was.

A tremendous thunderstorm this afternoon and the train system in this direction was delayed nearly an hour through one train being slightly struck. The city has had a great washing down today.

This evening I took my prayer meeting at the Soldiers' Christian Association Hut – I always like that atmosphere, and the nice sergeant (Stark) was there. He was wounded in the retreat from Mons, through the chest, the bullet coming out by the shoulder-blade. The doctor said "had he any messages for anybody?" Stark said "that doesn't look very promising does it doctor?" The doctor said "it isn't the wound I am so much afraid of, though that is bad, but whether I'll be able to get you out of this. There are Germans all round" – the doctor himself was killed half an hour after. When convalescent in Dublin, Stark was called on to help suppress the rebellion. The sights he saw there, he said, were driving him mad. He sat in his house, and he felt his reason was going and his wife could see too – "she had to look on and see me going mad". Then he said "I prayed – I said "O Lord, have mercy on me and save my reason". When he prayed this, he saw the clear form of an angel standing in front of him in the cottage room – a strong, shining angel, who smiled. And from that day he has been at peace.

Great news about Romania! It brings the end appreciably nearer. What will Greece now do? There are rumours of another sea fight[758].

---

757 Born **Lena Margaret Pocock**. Lena Ashwell (b.1872 – d.1957). British actress and acting manager, known as the first person to organise large-scale entertainment for troops at the front. In 1915, she began to organise companies of actors, singers and entertainers to travel to France and perform – by the end of the war there were 25 of them, travelling in small groups found France. She also organised all-male concert parties to perform shows near to the front line. In her writings about this experience, she emphasised that ordinary soldiers had been enthusiastic about high culture, in particular Shakespeare plays. She married the royal obstetrician Henry Simpson in 1908.

758 The **Action of 19th August 1916** was one of two attempts made by the German High Seas

August 30th 1916, Rouen

Thank you for another letter – I wonder what Mr Fawns will do. There is a hint from Deane Oliver that I should help him at the Church House, Westminster, but it does not draw me much. An open-air life seems likely to be more manageable in my particular case. I have heard nothing from Mr Fawns or the Bishop – possibly they are both enquiring elsewhere and of each other and letters take time, and also the Bishop is on holiday.

How dreadfully sad it is about Colonel Longridge – poor woman, it must nearly break her heart[759]. A broken heart!! Think what that means and there will be a good many after this War. It will need great grace and strength from one and another. A broken heart gets querulous, or morbidly depressed, or may try to seek relief in unworthy directions. Many lives will be scarcely quite normal again, or will gain their naturalness only with tremendous effort. The company of faithful people will have their work to do – how shall we be equal to it all? "Our conversation is in Heaven."

August 30th 1916, Rouen (Letter to his eldest daughter)

"My darling daughter,

I am sorry you fell and grazed your arm. It reminds me of the old joke, 'it happened notwithstanding'! But seriously, I hope it is not very serious.

Farms are nice places for holidays, as I expect you will find; dear boys and girls ought to be very thankful to have nice places like that and nice holidays. And in your letter you said CREAM!!!! And here there has come out an order that even if you can get fresh milk you must not use it! They are afraid of some kind of infection, I understand. That does seem rather hard, doesn't it? But such is life in the Army.

We have been cheered by learning that Romania has now come into the War on our side. It will help quicken the end very appreciably we hope. There are now 10 nations on our side, against 4 on the other, Russia, France, Belgium, Serbia, Montenegro, Portugal, Japan, Italy, Romania, and the British Empire, and on the other Germany, Austria, Turkey and Bulgaria. It is a comfort to know how many are firmly on the side of right – it makes me think of the Apostles in Jerusalem who, when they were

---

Fleet in 1916 to engage elements of the British Royal Navy. Four Zeppelins were deployed to scout the North Sea between Scotland and Norway for signs of British ships and four more scouted immediately ahead of German ships. Twenty-four German submarines participated off the English coast. The result was inconclusive, with minor losses on bioth sides.

759 Lt Col **James Atkinson Longridge** (b.1875 – d.1916) 43rd Erinpura Regt. India in 1897, involved in the Boxer and Somalia Campaigns. In 1912, he was selected to assist Sir Beauchamp Duff at the India Office, becoming the Assistant Secretary to the Committee of Imperial Defence. In September 1914, the Army in France as General Staff Officer (3rd Grade) of the Indian Contingent. Eventually, in June 1916, he became Major & Brevet Lt-Colonel – CMG of the Indian Army and first General Staff Officer (1st Division British Expeditionary Force). Killed 12th August 1916; shot by a sniper while visiting the front line. Mrs **Alice Lillian Longridge** lived at Bow Cot, Headley, Hampshire.

beaten for speaking "in the name of Jesus" rejoiced that they were counted worthy to suffer shame for His Name. So, with all England's faults, it makes me glad to know that the nation has enough sense of right to be ready to suffer for it. Now we must go on praying and working that the nation may be right all through. And pray for the Germans and others "that they may unlearn their misunderstandings, lay aside their bitterness, see where they have done wrong and be ready to make amends.

I have been reading again about Joan of Arc. You know that it was at Rouen that she was imprisoned. She was only 16 when she led the French Army to victory against the English and Rouen has many statues and memorials of her. It appears that she was even braver than the French king – the Dauphin as he was called. But, at the age of 19 they accused her of being a witch, and had her burnt, then twenty-five years afterwards they called her a saint! At all events the English were so affected by her courage that when she was taken a prisoner by the Duke of Bedford, the English King was ready to pay as much as 10,000 gold pieces to have her handed over to be imprisoned by him! On the whole, I am sure she was a good woman.
I must go. Write soon."

Friday September 1st 1916, Rouen

A cool sunny and fresh day, and very full it has seemed. In the morning, papers and plans and a ride out of camp with a squadron going off to the front, just to see them on their way: then a ride on back home round a turn through the forest. More papers and writing then reading up about Romania – they are a promising ally. After lunch, a pause, then talking and visiting round until one's throat gets sore with chatting. Grumpy men – a few, you meet all sorts, they are a little tiring but all like to talk. This one is from Worcester – his son is 2 days older than Lord Beauchamp's son and he was taken by the mother up to Madresfield Court to celebrate the christenings![760] This man comes from Tiverton, this one from Luton, next Chatham, and this one from Barming, but has not been home for 10 years, having been on Foreign Service, but he has been 'hopping' in West Farleigh. This man is verger at St. Nicholas's Gloster and is able to tell of Mr. Luce the vicar, and of his son who died, and of Miss Luce, who was C.M.S. missionary in India, and is now in Canada and very ill and likely to be reported dead of consumption any day[761].

---

760 **Madresfield Court** is a Grade I country house in England, in the village of Madresfield near Malvern in Worcestershire. **William Lygon, 7th Earl Beauchamp** KG, KCMG, PC (b.1872 – d.1938), styled **Viscount Elmley** until 1891, was a British Liberal politician. He was Governor of New South Wales between 1899 and 1901, a member of the Liberal administrations of Sir Henry Campbell-Bannerman and H. H. Asquith between 1905 and 1915 and leader of the Liberal Party in the House of Lords between 1924 and 1931. When political enemies threatened to make public his homosexuality he resigned from office to go into exile in the US. Lord Beauchamp is generally supposed to have been the model for Lord Marchmain in Evelyn Waugh's novel, *Brideshead Revisited.*

761 Rev **John James Luce**, Vicar of St Nicholas' Gloucester, daughter Miss **E A Luce**.

A part of the time I went to see the Indians playing football – they go at it with full British vigour, all of course with their shirts flying loosely about them, some with hob-nailed Tommy boots on, and some running about in their grey socks <u>without</u> boots on. One great fellow, surely six feet and a half high, broad and bulky in proportion, with a long flowing Khaki shirt and baggy, light-coloured trousers tucked into his socks, hovering round the group of players and pouncing down upon the ball from outside from time to time, with a broad determined grin on his face like some giant genius out of the Arabian Nights. Then a packed meeting in the Y.M.C.A. and a short speech to back up the Superintendent in presenting the willing bandmaster with a farewell present – a leather dispatch case for mss music.

Saturday September 2nd 1916, Rouen

The chief event today – a cricket match in which our side got just beaten, but it was a good game, and some of the players were from S. Africa. When one visits round these men, one feels one must stay among them longer. My talk this afternoon with one of the men took us to the farm where he has settled, in the Veldt, a part well known to me. While we were talking, a little tame springbok came and put his cold nose into my hand – a fascinating creature. By and bye a dog came up, and was chased away by it with contumely.

There is a new confirmation candidate this morning – a remarkable man. At 17 he ran away and went to sea because his father, a stern man, wanted to 'insist' on his being confirmed. A typical sailor story, about large accumulation of wages, people of the wrong sort waiting for him, his getting into a decent lodging house in Hartlepool and, having plenty of money, insisting on paying more for board and bed than was asked, turning up at the same port again a year after and getting married to the landlord's daughter. His father is an N.C.O. in the Artillery, his 3 brothers are all fighting, he was 'the worst of the lot' (a good fellow really), his sister is a nurse in a hospital in England, and a prayerful person, rather nice-looking (he showed me her photograph). A chaplain doctor had proposed to her, but she said "no, she must keep to her place". My friend has been sent down here with shell wounds and is now convalescent. When I asked him when he had decided on confirmation, he turned up his New Testament and came to the 14th verse of the 21st chapter of St. Matthew – that was the date: the 14th of August and he read a verse a day![762]

Sunday September 3rd 1916, Rouen

Tonight is rather cool – it has been a long and tiring day, but very happy in responses. I have just been talking with a young officer, Lt. Penrose, from British Columbia, who was at Mr. Freeman's school, Park House, Southborough, and afterwards at Haileybury. He was glad to talk of his boyhood days.

---

762 **Matthew 21:14** 'And the blind and the lame came to him in the temple; and he healed them.'

6 a.m Holy Communion with no one present – I am not going on with that service, it is too artificial. At 8.a.m there were 27 present, including a Colonel. Two nice parade services, with very large attendance, between 400 and 500, and men waited behind to talk which is a good sign. The Colonel asked for a mid-day Communion Service and I was glad as we now can put the Parade a little earlier. Previously a Colonel had objected to this on account of the times for his stables, but now he has gone. We had a pretty full Evening Service, but the wind blew our tent about much, and made the lights very flickering and one light was blown out – such are the difficulties. We had Evening Communion this evening with 31 present.

I am interested to see letters in the 'Challenge' advocating Evening Communion, both on the grounds of the convenience of some servants, mothers and, we might add, working fathers, and also on grounds of fellowship and I am impressed by these considerations. A pretty strenuous day, with all the people to talk to in between – but not dull!

I took the horse for exercise for half an hour after tea. He was very pleased, remarking "it's good for me, and good for you, Sir. Thank you very much!" You saw the occupations of the men: here two good fellows behind a thick oak helping one another in Bible study: here an officer lying flat face-downwards buried in what looked like some study volume: here a solidly-built 'Geordie' in running shorts, with his pacemaker, getting in trim for some sports next month. These are the sort – healthy-minded – to whom you can say with some effect when you get the chance "So run, that ye may obtain[763]" – you understand the metaphor better when you have some part in it.

Monday September 4th 1916, Rouen

A sad record tonight, my darling. Tuckey and Colbeck have turned spiteful over the Evening Communion and I am being moved. I must think what to do. There was general outcry in the Mess when mention was made of it, and the Colonel proposed my riding down with him to see Tuckey. We found him <u>dreadfully</u> under strain, and what was worse, we found at the end of the talk that he had just heard his son was killed[764] – a young officer, who only got his commission in June, and came out a fortnight ago. "He had already passed over the heads of 4 or 5 of his fellow cadets" said this poor, pathetic man. He spoke wildly about my having referred to the Bishop about it "May God forgive you that letter" he repeated[765]. "Be Thou our advocate with God for grace, that in all our sufferings and trials we may follow Thy example and be supported in all difficulties and discouragements with which

---

763 **1 Corinthians 9:24** 'Know ye not that they which run in a race run all, but one receiveth the prize? So run, that ye may obtain.'
764 2nd Lt. **John Caufield Tuckey** (b.1895 – d.1916) killed in action on the Somme, 13th Bn, Middlesex Regiment on 31st August 1916, aged 19.
765 See 23rd August 1916, Letter To Robert Harmer, Bishop of Rochester.

God shall see fit to exercise the patience and fidelity of us, His servants, for Thine honour and glory".[766]

Both the Colonel and I urged that for the short time that I am to remain out here, it seemed a pity to move now: that I was just getting into the swing of this charge, there were the confirmation candidates and I was getting to know the men of the depot, and the work was growing under my hand. The Colonel urged also his dislike of changes like these and in this case so abruptly and without a word of reference to him or to me, Tuckey answered like a hysterical baby as I have quoted above, and I am not quite sure whether his mind is quite well. Now, I shall be thankful to be home. I do not know whether it will be possible to remain with the soldiers. Tuckey took an ugly line, speaking extravagantly and vindictively and of course, his position gives him power[767]. How much better if only the whole aim and energy were thrown into seeing how it would be possible to make the best of those committed to his 'direction', as he loves to call it, and to help things on. The Colonel almost laughed at his melodramatic "God forgive you for that letter"! and there is obviously a time-serving policy behind his actions.

Tuesday September 5th 1916, Rouen

I am more thankful than I can say – the crisis is over and I do <u>not</u> move! And the work goes on. What revealing of inner workings it has meant – what patience and restraint, I hope not abjectness, but something rather like it. When you have a haughty and high-minded character to deal with, very full of the powers of its office, piqued at a slight, unmistakeably vindictive, craving for worldly distinction, the D.S.O. or the C.M.G., using any person in the more advantageous way, setting down if that may seem to promise an end, or lauding and pushing forward if that is going to help, then you are handling dangerous material. Yet, poor man, he has lost his son! It has softened him. He was to have gone over to England today, but the steamers are all stopped.

The Mess was very cordial in testifying its satisfaction at my remaining on – that is something, and it came out quite spontaneously and unexpectedly. We had a large meeting at the S.C.A. this evening with every seat occupied, and the men standing. It helped me much as we thought together of God's peace realised in the midst of tribulation.

I went to see the bakeries today, the wonderful bakeries of a large *military* base, and Eric will be interested to know that I went across the Seine twice, in the transporter. Two horses and carts went also, a pram and many men, women and children. It is worked by electric, which sends the transporter along overhead rails, and it does not, as I had supposed, touch the water[768].

---

766 *Prayer in Times of Anxiety*, Thomas Wilson, Bishop of Sodor and Man, 1663
767 Tuckey was then Assistant Chaplain-General, Rouen Area. His rank would have been a full Colonel. Colbeck's rank was Major, RDG was Captain.
768 Rouen Transporter Bridge, 1898, by Ferdinand Arnodin, destroyed June 1940. The postcard sent

Goodnight, my darling (I think what made the change was that I told him that if this change was made I should refer it to the Bishop.)

Thursday September 7th 1916 Rouen

It has been a day of some reaction really after the somewhat violent unsettlement of the day before. 7.45 am H.C. – no one present. After breakfast, I have been arranging with the band for Church Services – the Y.M.C.A. are very good in providing the men with any instruments they need. Then a Confirmation talk, the candidate a very keen and responsive fellow, quick to take up points, and remarking now and again his understanding and approval of some line of reasoning. He will be a useful man I hope. Then a ride out to meet some troops returning – on these squadron rides you get to chat with men and officers under very pleasant conditions!

Then after lunch and a pause, down to watch the cricket. This depot has come out equal in the League matches for the season with another depot, and this was to decide the winner. This depot made 167, and the other side was 6 out for 16 runs when it was time to draw stumps owing to the light – a most surprising set back as in the last match they were the winners! One curious thing happened – a man hit a ball high and far and they were tempted to make a 3 of it, but the fielder made a remarkably good throw in and the ball flew off the wicket-keeper's pads against the wicket, running the man out. He was walking off disconsolately to the scoring group when somebody remarked "was not that a boundary hit?" It proved it was so, in which case the man was entitled to 4 runs and the throw-in could not be recognised! So he returned and continued batting – however he was caught out about 5 overs later, after 3 or 4 more runs. But it was an interesting peep into sportsmanship, him being put in again!

I went off to the city to send a telegram to 2nd Lieut. George Vinson Thomas on the occasion of his marriage this day. It is a business getting a telegram through and I hope that it may arrive in time. He will have had an eventful 1916 – heavy fighting, mentioned in dispatches, wounded and married! At dinner there were some important guests. Col. Grove (Base Commandant), and Col. Buchanan, a rather nice Scotchman, who got the Humane Society's Medal for jumping into the Liffey to save a woman from drowning. He had one or two nice stories – going out to India, he had on the ship a sergeant whose wife and little girl were there also. The little girl sadly died and at the very moment she died, the ship's watch cried out "All's Well". That led us on to discussing the dying of children unbaptised. The Colonel's father did not believe in the 'condemned unbaptised' theory, and he used to say he did "not believe the Almighty would be so unChristian". The base Commandant, also, had some nice thoughts about 'peace' amidst tribulation, and he is anxious for the well-being of womenkind after the war as their numbers will be so preponderant. When he was an Adjutant in India, he was able to inspect some of the regimental records and among them was a formal complaint in the Mess suggestion

---

to Eric is posession of the family. See postcard dated 10/10/1916.

book (or to be safely exact, a book of such a kind) of the charge made by the native punkah-wallahs for swinging the wine cooler – the wine bottles were placed in water in canvas baskets and swung in the air and were thus very successfully cooler. The complaint was made over the signature of 'Wellesley' (the Duke of Wellington!).

Today has been very much a 'parish' day – all amongst the men. One I met came from Gillingham, another from Gravesend and a third worked for the grocer, Mr Hedgeoak on St Margaret's Bank. Then a nice confirmation talk with my Irish Sergeant friend, but yet he may go up the line before the Bishop comes – he is a good brave man. The Medical Board had offered to mark him still 'temporary base', but he would not have it, "by God's grace" he "pulled himself together" and got marked for up the line. He is good stuff, that man. He showed me his young wife's photograph – she is handsome-looking and has a nice face, and is I gather, a good woman. What a hideous war.

Friday September 8th 1916, Rouen

A letter from you at last, again finished on Sunday so nearly a week in transit. You have had the Bishop's pastoral read at you. My frank opinion about the present Bishop of Chichester is that (like Tuckey is in a minor way) they have wished for, and sought, and liked *the* position which they have worked themselves into, rather than lived and loved themselves into, and their idea is now to work for a certain respectability of show in the way of results, and if these do not come by any other means, to force them into existence. There is a nice sharp piece of cynicism after reading 1 Cor. X111 last Sunday[769].

Not a word yet from the Bishop, or Mr. Fawns. I do not quite agree with all Mr Talbot's impressions that a large majority of men are everywhere willing to be won – the rest is much a matter of individual capacity and the number of Chaplains to capture the possibilities. It has been a broken, busy day with an interesting finish as I dined with Colonel Bulman who is a strong low Churchman, well off, and has run lads and girls Clubs and is maintaining one or two still[770]. The League match was finished this afternoon and the other side were out for 37 runs, leaving our Cavalry Depot victors by 120 runs, and head of the League! This evening a typical Tommy Concert, programme enclosed. Sapper Rees has a voice of remarkable strength and quality, very true and clear.

Saturday September 9th 1916 Rouen

9/9/1916 – what a lot of 9s! A long and tiring day today. Colbeck has gone on 'leave' and left his work for tomorrow unprovided for, and the combined plans for the

---

769   1 Corinthians 13:1-3 'If I speak in the tongues of men or of angels, but do not have love, I am only a resounding gong or a clanging cymbal. If I have the gift of prophecy and can fathom all mysteries and all knowledge, and if I have a faith that can move mountains, but do not have love, I am nothing. If I give all I possess to the poor and give over my body to hardship that I may boast, but do not have love, I gain nothing.'

770   Colonel **Philip Bulman**, (b.1857 – d.?) 2nd Kings Shropshire Light Infantry, Staff Officer.

various Chaplains (regarding funerals, marriages, etc.) unarranged and that has meant much thought. More tomorrow, or Monday, goodnight darling. I have a touch of fever again and a wasp pursued my poor horse this morning till he was almost distracted.

Sunday September 10th 1916 Rouen

It <u>has</u> to be more tomorrow! Very tired. Holy Communion at 6 am, no one present – I am going to give up that effort. 8.0 am H.C. with 10 present and then two good parades, going with a swing, and 32 francs given at the first, 31 at the second all for the Church Army. Then from 2 to 3.30, in a blazing sun, burying the bodies of brave and faithful men who have suffered and died in the cause, one an officer. 5.30 a large Evening Service in another camp with an earnest seeming and reverent company and at 7.p.m. another service in my own camp with only 5 present, but one a new confirmation candidate and this evening confidential chats with two officers. Goodnight my darling. Another letter from you today, thank you, they are very precious to me.

Monday September 11th 1916, Rouen

My darling,

This letter will give you pleasure. Mr Fawns is definite in wishing to give up in November and I do not think he could well do otherwise, all things considered. I do not think I can take up the weary business of finding another 'locum' to take on, and I feel I could benefit by a long rest, and though the taking up again of the Parish must mean an extra strain, it will be possible to have things enough in hand to let the home life be a sufficient rest with the month of December. What would be best would be an entire absence of anything for a whole 3 weeks or a month, but this cannot be just yet. So – I propose getting the benefit of the 10 days 'leave' that will be due to me at that time, leaving here about the 27th of October, and prepare to go and live again in <u>West Farleigh Vicarage</u> say on the 6th or 7th of November. Perhaps you would be inclined to come too at about that time?[771]. I expect Mr. Fawns will not be sorry to escape another winter in West Farleigh, and will be glad to be free, for a while, from the constant claims which the charge of a parish means. The loss of Mr Fawns, too, from his household and from helping in the Parish, must make a great difference. At all events, it looks as if we were going to have Christmas all together again in our own home! Agatha Faith will be glad to have Daddy "put off his soldier clothes and put on his Daddy clothes" and so shall I, and you will be glad to be back with your own household. I must cancel any plans that Deane Oliver may have got in view. The War does not seem likely now to be over by that date, but it is well 'over the ridge', and it may be possible to arrange later to be with the soldiers again for a time, and to be 'in at the death' (in England). The thought of being home again makes my mind run on ideas of going to bed somewhere and sleeping for a month! To have a properly made bed! To sit at a 'home' table and have home food! And

---

771 RDG's wife Margaret was was staying in Hurstpierpoint with relatives at this time.

what a repose of spirit for you to be back, I hope, though I am afraid the home does not mean less work. At all events, the plan that presents itself to me now is that we return to WF vicarage some time in the week beginning the 5th of November.

P.S. We may as well let the family committee now know! I am sorry not to have seen the War out, but it will have been nearly 2 1/4 years and 2 years actually at the front!

Tuesday, September 12th 1916

Curiously, the idea of remaining on with the soldiers until the end of the War still persists:

1. Added knowledge and experience does not lessen one's interest in them, and I am sure increased familiarity with them helps aptitude in dealing with them.
2. All the travel of previous years helps getting into touch with men brought together from all quarters of the globe.
3. While one still has 'go' it is a great thing to speak with the men, numbers of whom are not easily reached by Clergy at all in ordinary times.

Perhaps the thing will be to go back to West Farleigh in November, get you settled in there, have parish things in hand again, and then have another short period with the soldiers before, or up to, the end of the War. In England, you are not required to 'take on' by the year, so that would be simpler. We could thus look around, as it would not be possible to do here, for another Locum Tenens for the short period? Compris?

I had an interesting encounter this morning in the train – an officer from Buenos Aires, a Mr. Clarke, who knows Canon Arthur Karney very well – you do meet people in an extraordinary way. Yesterday I met a young officer who came into our Field Ambulance just before Neuve Chapelle, and with whom I had tea in the trenches the week before Fromelles[772], and whom I met coming out of the trenches the first day of Fromelles, wounded in the neck and for whom I wrote a postcard that morning to his mother. He has recovered and been out to Gallipoli since then, and has been wounded a third time! He is Lt. Wynter[773] of the Worcesters (the same regiment to which Lt. Robinson V.C. the Flying Officer, belongs[774]). He was very cordial and has 3 strips of gold braid on his arm.

I have written this evening to the Foreign Office to see if there is any chance of recovering your Hungarian Stock. It will be interesting to see if they hold out any hope – keep the paper in case they refer to you for particulars. It would be satisfactory

---

772 The **Battle of Fromelles** (19th – 20th July, 1916), was a British military operation on the Western Front during World War I, subsidiary to the Battle of the Somme. The attack took place 9.9 miles from Lille between the Fauquissart–Trivelet road and Cordonnerie Farm, an area overlooked from Aubers Ridge to the south. The Battle of Fromelles had inflicted some losses on the German defenders but gained no ground nor deflected many German troops bound for the Somme.

773 Lt. **Robert Charles Wynter**, 4th Battalion, The Worcestershire Regiment.

774 **William Leefe Robinson** VC (b.1895 – d.1918) was the first British pilot to shoot down a

if this was settled up, and with all the Austrian and German property there is in our hands, it ought not to be difficult to get all back with interest!

Wednesday, September 13th 1916

A rather eventful day. The letter from Mr. Rhys saying the dilapidations business[775] was finally closed up – thank goodness. A letter from Tuckey saying his tenure here was closing – thank goodness. He has learnt his lessons and I have helped him to learn some, but it has cost me much, the 'regular' Army Chaplain has lived in a little world of his own for too long. And a most kind letter from the Bishop approving of our return to West Farleigh as soon as may be. I must say that with the prospect of rest and comfort once again is mingled a very acute reluctance to move away from the scene of England's men at their best, and even yet there is a feeling with me that a different door may open – we must see. The Bishop spoke very considerately, "I could not help feeling that the exceptional claims which your military service has made would have justified the War Office in giving you a high position among the permanent staff of Military Chaplains". (He went to the War Office) "I find, however, that the rules which govern Chaplains do not permit of this to one of your age". The Bishop does not know, as one in the midst of things has to, of how much of 'looking askance' at another, of rivalry, and of open place-seeking there is. But it was kind of him, and I am content. It is a great thing to have had strength for so much, and to have been allowed to try and help men at such a time and in such places, and to have seen such glorious doings.

Thursday, September 14th 1916, Rouen

I do not think that Mr. Fawns will really regret leaving West Farleigh. When he wrote asking for a fee in addition to the other remuneration, he spoke as "pluming his wings for flight", if an arrangement did not come about, and without Mrs. Fawns it would be very difficult for him to carry on – you will see what I have said in my letter to him. It will be a business getting in again – fixing up servants and so on. That, and the idea of Mr. Fawns 'rounding up' his work for the National Mission, incline me to putting off our entry until the end of November, what do you think? Say we go in the first week of December?

Great haste, my darling, let me know, bit by bit how you think!

German airship over Britain. For this he was awarded the Victoria Cross, the first person to be awarded the VC for action in the UK. He died of influenza in December 1918.

775 At West Farleigh Church

Friday, September 15th 1916, Rouen

A most interesting lecture tonight by Prof. Holland Rose (Prof. of Modern History, Cambridge) to Officers, on the Balkan tangle. It is <u>very</u> cold[776].

"And whether a man goes right or wrong, It's a woman that holds the reins" – so a sergeant in a very stentorian recitation just across the compound. In this huge camp there are entertainments literally by the dozen every night. Five or six cinemas, ten or twelve Y.M.C.A. places, camp library huts, camp entertainment huts, and the Church Army and Soldier's Christian Association also afford their share. The amount of talent among the men is amazing, especially in the piano line.

Hospital visiting this evening – we are short of Chaplains, so I am lending a hand for a day or two as there are 6 hospitals here. A refreshing spin through the forest, which is green and pure-aired – two little rabbits frisked round some blackberry bushes and did not seem to mind a visitor.

Saturday, September 16th 1916, Rouen

A pale moon, a misty landscape. Thousands of tents with candles gleaming through the openings, hundreds of huts' lights twinkling through the windows. Streams of wounded have come in, special trains bringing them up in addition to the usual ambulances. The men are all very cheerful, but it is odd to see a wounded man standing at the front of a train, wearing a German helmet. A cool 'twang' in the air, and in the Mess hut we have started a stove. My little canvas cabin strikes 'fresh' as I sit in it. Nearby the piano sergeant is pounding away at "I want my home in Dixie[777]" and a loud chorus is joining in with the music. I 'blew in' earlier to a Y.M.C.A. hut, where Prof. Rose was lecturing and just saying "the Germans complain that one of the causes of our seeking war with them was that we wanted to steal away their trade. We answer that they were free to trade anywhere they wished, including not least in <u>our own colonies</u> without let or hindrance, indeed to the extent of an unwise freedom – e.g. in our colony of Singapore there were more German traders than English. I then 'blew in' to another Y.M.C.A. hut, where one of the South African contingent was singing a comic song in Dutch!

As I walked across the end of the stable lines I met a staid old soldier taking his pet monkey for a walk in the forest, led upon a long cord.

Music to arrange for tomorrow, details of services, chats with officers leaving for the front, a theological discussion as to the origins of evil, and another as to how the

---

776   **John Holland Rose** (b.1855 – d.1942) was an influential English historian who wrote a famous biography of French emperor Napoleon Bonaparte and also wrote a history of Europe, entitled *The Development of the European Nations*. Rose was the basis for C. P. Snow's fictional character M. H. L. Gay (see "Years of Hope: Cambridge, Colonial Administrator in the South Seas, and Cricket" by Philip Snow.)

777   *I want to be in Dixie,* Irving Berlin, 1912.

majority of the men will settle down after the War. Some will be too restless to go back into the old ways and will make for the colonies, others will be only too thankful to be at home again – both opinions were challenged, but in the main agreed to, I think, and so goes another day.

Good news from most fronts, especially our own. Goodnight, my darling.

Sunday, September 17th 1916, Rouen

A cold, dark foggy morning. Turning out at 6.am I put my foot, squash, upon a green caterpillar reposing in my slipper, a warning against dressing in the dark in a canvas hut. Four or five minutes later, 'squash' again, putting my foot into my gumboot! They swarm everywhere these little reptiles and you have to get rid of their remains after an accident like that, and at this end of the day time is precious. The early service at a Camp hospital about half a mile off, 5 nurses and an orderly present, a windy tent, but electric light! 8 a.m. (a very cold morning) H.C. in our Church tent with 3 present. 11a.m. a very large parade, they seemed attentive, but they were a rougher kind of man.

Confirmation letters were offered them at the door, I hope they may be read. It is very hard to explain in a 'popular' way what 'confirmation' means in a ten-minute address. But some listen very attentively – you can see by the way their eyes are on you. A large parade also at 12.0 and one man stayed to the midday communion and then talks around later in the afternoon. It is very pathetic how some of the earnest ones like to unburden themselves and they tell you some remarkable confidences, very frequently about the 'girl' who helped them to stick to the church regularly, or the one who wasn't much good, and carried on with the other fellows. This man is going to be confirmed, and then going to let his people know as a pleasant surprise "they will be pleased". Here are two men who are downright in earnest, waiting behind in the Chapel for a long private prayer. One wonders which of them is the strong one who has helped the other. We want more Chaplains for individual dealings among these crowds who are constantly passing through – moving up or coming down.

They have been asking for volunteers, among the officers, for Egypt – would it bother you if I went there?

Monday September 18th 1916, Rouen

Rain, rain, rain. Rather busy with the wounded. How tired one gets of the waning bodies, the mutilations, and the reeking wounds! It is a brutal business, is war. A busy evening, after a visit to the Indian Hospital, and a cold clammy night. I wonder if the way points to my going to Egypt – things seem to speak!

Tuesday September 19th 1916, Rouen

19/9/1916 – observe the 9's dear lady!

Torrents of rain, and a keenly interested Confirmation sitting. A dull and comfortless day outside, which made one all the more glad to get your letter. You have had the letter proposing our return to West Farleigh in November? Now there is the call, very insistent, to go on living the life of one's fellow men in the larger world outside. How – if we return to the confines of that little place? Ought all the knowledge of men, and the appeal that varied experience makes to them, to be shut up amongst those few? Is it, such as it is, a talent going to be buried in a napkin if there is energy, health, and strength enough for wider activities? Home must not be the first claim.

I hear today that Tuckey has gone East! Whether to Egypt, I wonder? That would be a reason for <u>not</u> going!

The nights are getting cold. I had thought of the little son as returning next week – however I have written to him today and I hope the letter will reach him on Friday, which will be the day of his return. I wonder what career he will choose – it is to be feared the engineering idea is a 'boyish' one, it is very common among boys and they little realise the tremendous drudgery it means.[778] I called on the Shallards this evening, both the girls have met with success, Gertrude having passed the Intermediate for the London B.A. and gone to Bedford College and Constance has passed the Senior Local (Oxford) with distinction in French – happy people!

A crowded meeting at the S.C.A. hut this evening and a manifest response, the men listened most intently, as it seemed to every syllable, over 400 of them – with the tempest swirling outside I read and spoke on the XXIXth Psalm[779] and God added voice through Christ Jesus: He is King, but he is also our <u>Father</u>. How much that means. Our Father saying "I have loved thee with an everlasting Love".[780]

A talk with Maj. Tuson after dinner – he has property near Nairobi, farms there and has had great times hunting lions and other wild animals. He has been in Australia too and knows the Blue Mountains.

Wednesday September 20th 1916, Rouen

A full day, rather tiring and a touch of neuralgia tonight.

7.45am H.C. with one man present and then a morning of business details. In the afternoon, a rest and then looking up Confirmees and a 7.30 Evening Service – some

---

778 **Eric**, RDG's son, went on to Cambridge where he achieved a double first in Electrical Engineering.

779 **Psalm 29:3** 'The voice of the Lord is over the waters; the God of glory thunders, the Lord thunders over the mighty waters.'

780 **Jeremiah 31:3** 'The LORD hath appeared of old unto me, *saying*, Yea, I have loved thee with an everlasting love: therefore with lovingkindness have I drawn thee.'

came for a communion service as we gave out at Parade men so wishing can have it arranged but there were only 3 present. This evening there was a guest night, which tired me much. A rather nice Major Kirby, who was at Queens College, Oxford, and though worldly-minded enough in a common 'officer' kind of way, is a good-hearted person, who sang to help in the College choir, and has been down to the poorer parts of London to lecture on S. Africa and so on[781].

Thursday September 21st 1916, Rouen

It began with (incidentally a twinge of neuralgia) H.C. at 7.45am to which no one came, followed by a Chaplain's meeting – a little more edifying than sometimes, but alas! The visit of Canon Cunningham[782] is cancelled and the confirmation is put off. This latter is specially trying because the men set great store by a given date, and the officers arrange a long while before that they shall have extra talks and so on. However, it is War. One of the Chaplains is giving up after a few months and going home on sick leave. He has had a very trying time, I must say, having been for some months at an infectious hospital. These are heroisms that show as 'little' in the public eye, but how much they mean. After visiting round, and following up a man, I had a spin on the old grey horse, (paying a visit incidentally) – he is a nice old person and enters into the proceeding quite as one who enjoys it.

Another letter from you and the home-coming idea is shaping itself. What will happen will depend now, apparently, on what Mr Fawns wishes. The difficulty about a Locum Tenens will interfere with more soldier-work later, I am afraid. In any case, it will be better not to give up the house again? Perhaps another Locum might like to take the Skelton's house – or even Mr. Fawns? The war does not seem likely to finally end now before next autumn.

In the afternoon I had to go down into Rouen to see a 'proof' and then the Evening service to which two sturdy Devon Lads came, putting their whole hearts into the responses and the 'Amen' and following the lesson in their own books – so quality was there if not quantity!

The lecture by Prof. Rose was very clear and full, showing what a bid Germany had made for power in the East, the Palestine and Baghdad railways: the Kaiser's promise to be the friend of 300,000,000 Mahommedans: the possible strategy of certain

---

781 Lt.-Col. **William Lewis Clark Kirby** (b.1879 – d.1962) 12th Royal Lancers, DSO, OBE, Queens College, Fellow of Royal Geographical Society (F.R.G.S.), JP.

782 Canon **Bertram K Cunningham**, (b.1871 – d.1944) rector of the Bishop's Hotel in Farnham (Surrey), a theological training college for Anglican Clergy (1899 – 1915), founded by the Bishop of Winchester. Graduates were known as "The Farnham Brotherhood". As such, he was an Anglican celebrity. From 1917, Cunningham was invited to set up a training facility at GCHQ in St. Omer to train C of E Chaplains for the British Army. His visit to the front in August and September was intended to prepare Chaplains for the forthcoming National Mission of Repentance and Hope. After the war, he became principal of Wescott House theological college in Cambridge.

moves by Romania on the one hand and General Sarrail on the other[783]. A Colonel present asked about a curious point e.g. whether it was true that the Baltic side of the Kiel canal had been blocked by our submarines at the time of the Jutland fight, thereby defeating the German plan to let out a number of their merchant craft to attack Russia also on that side by the sea, and thus leaving Russia more free to make good her land attack all that side.

Friday September 22nd 1916, Rouen

Colonel Macan has just come back from leave which he has spent with his wife and two roistering little boys. He had a good time and is thankful for past mercies. They were at a seaside place called Charmouth near Bridport in Dorset[784], but he thought his small boys made rather free with their officer father.

After sending your letter this morning (our post goes out at 2.0) I wrote to Deane Oliver speaking about soldier-work in England. I wonder what will evolve. In the alternative, I can see our two lives growing, with the years, as the accompanying illustration.[785] Let us at least hope mental caterpillars will not consume what simple usefulness which may, by change, be in us.

This evening, we had a concert, just 'so – so' and dinner after with Col. Bulman who is a bachelor and a little crusty, but willing to be friendly and a fairly considerable reader. He has kept some Clubs going in London, and is a little 'down' on the Clergy of the parishes in which they are, because the Clubs have gone off during the war. Mr. Shallard called this afternoon – I am glad that I was in for he is a kind man, but very gently dull and 'talky'. He was brought up on the edge of the Forest of Dean – and I was for a time brought up in it!

Saturday September 23rd 1916, Rouen

A profitable evening and very enjoyable – a recital by the Rev. J.E. Smith, a Baptist who is helping at our Cavalry Y.M.C.A. hut, of Ben Hur. He has a very retentive memory, and recounted the various passages with very telling effect, especially the Chariot race, and the release of the mother and sister from the Roman prison, their leprosy and consequent banishment and their eventual cure by Our Lord, and restoration to the son and brother (Ben Hur).[786]

---

783 **Maurice-Paul-Emmanuel Sarrail** (b.1856 – d.1929) was a French general. Sarrail's openly socialist views made him a rarity amongst the Catholics, conservatives and monarchists who dominated the French Army. Appointed to command at Salonika, Greece, after Verdun in 1915.

784 **Charmouth** is a village and civil parish at the mouth of the River Char in West Dorset.

785 Drawing of two cabbages side by side.

786 *Ben-Hur: A Tale of the Christ* is a Novel by Lew Wallace published on November 12th, 1880 by Harper & Brothers. Considered "the most influential Christian book of the nineteenth century", it was the best-selling American Novel from the time of its publication, superseding Harriet Beecher Stowe's *Uncle Tom's Cabin* (1852)

A confirmation talk this morning, arrangements for tomorrow and a talk with a young man who wants a commission and then a refreshing spin on the old grey horse.

Sunday September 24th 1916, Rouen

I was to have taken Evening Service for another Chaplain (W.E. Harper) who is returning to England at his own request, and was just putting on my surplice in his Chapel tent when he appeared! A message sent to intercept me did not come in time – it rests on the table as I write. But as it would have been a rush from there to my Evening Service, I was relieved to get away.

An interesting and encouraging Sunday so far with H.C. at 6.45 to which none came and at 8 a.m. there were 7. Then two very crowded parades at 11.0 and 12.0 with hearty singing and quiet reverent prayers – that quiet during prayers always encourages me, and very attentive listening. A parade service is a time of great opportunity, and though some of the men find occasion to grumble (I do not know that any of ours do) I believe it is a good institution. The band is a great help and 8 stayed to Holy Communion after, including 3 officers, and one knows that people get helped by the way they talk afterwards. Our little Church Tent is not well placed as it is down in a corner, and people have to pass 2 sentries to get to it. The Y.M.C.A. C. of E. service is about 150 yards off on a main road – an officer was making for our service and got into that one, and was mystified not to see myself officiating! However, as that service is apparently well run, it does not matter very much. Two men only came to my evening service – but they were very intent. One was one of the two I mentioned before and the other was new, but he was very earnest, and you could see how really he meant the thanks he stopped to give as he passed out.

Some nice talks with officers during the evening – a residing Chaplain does get immense opportunities as people talk freely and the real message of our faith comes out naturally. Some doubted, but when one, for example, sees the greatness of the Gospel Revelation placing itself right in the way for the acceptance of his own life, it is good to hear him say "Yes, I can see that. That's good." So is the bread cast on the waters.

Monday September 25th 1916, Rouen

A glorious morning, not too hot and not too cold, and a restful one after a tiring Sunday. Good news about the 2 more Zepplins brought down, perhaps 3! They will not feel so exuberant in that enterprise any more than they do in that of the submarines – England is a powerful country. A number of 'farewells' as many of the officers who have been with us for some time have moved off to the front (entre nous – some of those who come out to fill their places, newly made from the ranks, are excellent men, but the 'style' and 'manners' are not quite that of, say the Blues!) After a refreshing spin on the old grey horse, I had a nice chat with one of my <u>very</u> gallant friends, Lt. Francis, who has been twice wounded, once on this front, the other time at Gallipoli where he lost an eye. A bright, natural person, not in the least self-conscious, and talks of his glass eye as he would of a pencil, or his walking stick! The first did not work very well and he has just had another one out by post and was laughing this afternoon because it is not <u>quite</u> of the right shade of grey! Also, it fits no better than the other – these are some of the heroisms of this wonderful time.

A nice young officer of the South Irish Horse[787] also has just come in. Tonight he has had to turn in early as he is rather over-taxed. He was in the Sinn Fein rebellion and under fire the whole length of one of the streets of Dublin, with no chance of taking cover.

Tuesday September 26th 1916, Rouen
Another day full of work and crammed with interest – no time to describe it all.

18 burials – 2 officers. The father of one of the young officers buried was there. He was a proud, grieving man who held up firmly, but you could see it was an effort. I confess I found it hard to hold up also.

Mr Colbeck came round to talk over 2 difficulties; 1) We need dreadfully a Church Army or similar Quiet Hut for the Infectious Hospital – the Church Army cannot take it up and the Y.M.C.A. cannot provide the kind of thing needed. The Colonel is an earnest, Christian man and is keen to have something put there. <u>Our</u> Fund cannot go beyond £150 or so to help. We have been talking over what to do for the other £250. It is trying and tempting, making a great wish in me to stay on here (now T has gone!). A Lena Ashwell party, with <u>excellent</u> music, especially a violinist full of power, but I had to leave in the middle to go to a crowded meeting in the Soldiers Church. How can one leave all these living interests and 'pastoral' as well as 'preaching' opportunities?

Wednesday September 27th 1916, Rouen
Good news in the paper today – Thiepval taken, an important strategic point – and Combles, and many prisoners taken. Events are taking place in support[788]. A long and weary guest night, with no guests to speak of! Dinner not over till 10.5, no dinner to speak of! 8.0am H.C. – no one present, but a very interesting evening service with

---

787 The **South Irish Horse** was a Special Reserve cavalry regiment of the British Army. Formed on 2nd January 1902 as the **South of Ireland Imperial Yeomanry**. It was renamed as the South Irish Horse from 7th July 1908 and transferred to the Special Reserve (Cavalry).

788 The **Battle of Thiepval Ridge** was the first large offensive mounted by the Reserve Army of Lieutenant General Hubert Gough, during the Battle of the Somme and was intended to benefit from the Fourth Army attack at Morval, by starting 24 hours afterwards. The battle was fought on a front from Courcelette in the east, near the Albert–Bapaume road to Thiepval and the *Schwaben* Redoubt in the west. Thiepval Ridge was well fortified and the German defenders fought with great determination, while the British coordination of infantry and artillery declined after the first day, due to the confused nature of the fighting in the mazes of trenches, dug-outs and shell-craters.

the church tent full. There were some R.A.M.C. men and one waited behind to ask if I would take his confession and I said I would tomorrow, and another who was there they told me, was a curate and a third who spoke to me is a B.A. of Manchester and preparing for Holy Orders.

We had a farewell Concert at the Y.M.C.A. to Miss Pullar who returns to Scotland this week – of Pullar's Dye works. She has been a devoted, and wise and useful worker, lending her own car for work. Very good news from up the line today.

Thursday September 28th 1916, Rouen
A crowded day – after a <u>not</u> very profitable Chaplain's meeting – I give you the peep from the hut door which diverting my feelings while the Senior Chaplain was peskily laying down the law about letting a Salvation Army patient share in the Holy Communion. Then a spin on the old horse, and the taking of a good fellow's confession (a rather mechanical business this latter proved to be. I tried following the line of Walsham How Self Examination at the beginning of his book, but my friend wanted the 'Catholic' form and a Catholic absolution).

At 6.45 we had a huge Evangelistic meeting in the Cavalry Hut Y.M.C.A., with the band. There must be a large number of earnest men among them, they listened so quietly and joined in so intently. We had to finish a little abruptly taking 2 hymns instead of one, because heavy rain came down on the roof, making it impossible to be heard. A man stayed behind to talk, in difficulties because his wife has been unfaithful and he does not know what to do.

After dinner, another lecture by Prof. Rose on 'France and Germany', but not quite up to the normal dignified level, with some slides of the German Commemoration medals tempting the lecturer to make some rather cheap allusions to German mentality, which, I was very interested to find our Colonel depreciated also – he volunteered the opinion.

Friday, September 29th 1916, Rouen
A wet and rather soaky day. H.C. at 8.0am with 4 present and the looking up of Confirmees and a Confirmation talk with one sensible man – they are very thoughtful and understanding some of these good men. A friend of this particular man I found had been in the VIIIth Division and had been confirmed while in it, under Goudge's instruction.

Then in the pouring rain, an extra interesting encounter. A bright-looking soldier ran up and said "Excuse me, Sir! Did you ever live at Rochester?" I said "Yes" "You're Mr Griffiths?" I acknowledged the self-impeachment. "Do you remember Mr F.F. Smith who lived in Watt's Avenue?" "Yes" "I'm his son!" Do you remember? My recollection of him was thus. Today he was as thus! One has to realise it is

who lived in Watts Avenue?" Yes.
"live his son'." Do you remember?
my recollection of him
was there. Today
he was as there!

One has to realise it is
about 8 years since we
[...] used to see them first by
going to S. Margaret's Ch. (He was at
our Court School - Tunstall - also -
when I used to [...] preach for the
Seamen's Mission). He has
since been to Rutley School,
& then to Christ Church
Oxford, where he took his degree.
He was some [...] on in
his course at Cuddesdon when
war came on, & he joined up
as a private in the R.A.M.C.
Today he is a sergeant! His
name is C. L. Smith. We
talked of much. [...]
[...] Smith - who is still happy

about 8 years since we used to see this good boy going to St. Margaret's Church and he has since been to Radley School and then to Christ Church Oxford, where he took his degree, and he was some distance on in his course at Cuddesdon when war came on, and he joined up as a private in the R.A.M.C. – today he is a Sergeant! His name is C.L. Smith. We talked of much – Miss Hilda Snowden-Smith, who is still happy teaching and inspiring younger boys in Rochester: the Dartnells: the Bishop: Mrs Wharton and various Rochester personalities. You felt it was almost uncanny chatting with this gallant young Sergeant, in the mud and the pouring rain, who you remembered as the smart boy in the Eton jacket in that peaceful and decorous and superior quarter of the city of Rochester all those years ago![789] So life creeps on.

More visiting and then a camp concert given by the Cavalry men. There is good talent among them and their concerts are always of a high order, and the fun is healthy. One man came on dressed up as a cricketer and sang a song all about a cricket match and what happened to him and his side. The other people beat them by about an innings and 1000 runs. The song consisted of at least 12 verses and was sung at a tremendous speed, without a single pause for breaths, ie non-stop between the verses. It was a wonderful effort of breath, and of memory.

Saturday September 30th 1916
Tomorrow the 'National Mission' opens. It does not seem to have caught the sympathy of the many as one could have wished it would, and I am disappointed and sorry that the 'Church Times' has been luke-warm towards it. "When two of you shall agree together".[790]

Today has been occupied in preparing for tomorrow, <u>and</u> no order had come out about the <u>Army</u> taking up the alteration of the Clock time. One Camp Commandant said he should make the alteration himself – another said he could not do it except orders came from headquarters – which would have meant 2 lots of men coming for a Parade Service where there would only be room for the one lot. Happily at 7 o'clock this evening came round an <u>after order</u> – there will be some confusion nevertheless[791].

Another Lena Ashwell concert this evening – the talent was of a high order and all in excellent taste (except for the comic man, who just succeeded in being vulgar!). I was sorry for the ladies of the party, though of course they had to make the best of

---

789 Sergeant **Cyril Lawrence Smith** (b.1894 – d.?), RAMC, Son of Frederick Francis Smith, Rochester.
790 **Matthew 18:19** 'Again I say unto you, That if two of you shall agree on earth as touching any thing that they shall ask, it shall be done for them of my Father which is in heaven.'
791 British Summer Time was first established by the Summer Time Act 1916, after a campaign by builder William Willett. His original proposal was to move the clocks forward by 80 minutes, in 20-minute weekly steps on Sundays in April and by the reverse procedure in September. In 1916 BST began on 21st May and ended on 1st October.

it. One lady (I think a Miss Clark) played the violin marvellously and what was so nice, the men recalled her twice. It shows how if you trust the better taste, it is there, but if you play down to the lower taste, of course the men will take that too, alas!

Thank you for another letter, dearest. Yes, it must be home for a little, but while I have any spring left in me, and with all these blazing opportunities open there, with all the life and interest, and with so much knowledge of the world, of the ways and needs of men, of war, sea, and travel, I do not think I can sit down in a little corner like West Farleigh yet. Nous verrons.

This morning I met another VIII Division ally. It is interesting comparing notes over those strenuous early days – "the Dead Yesterday" as someone has called that time, 'dead' I suppose, as to the memory of the tremendous strain and anxiety that it was. There's strain and anxiety enough yet to come, but the outlook is very different now to what it was then as the German Chancellor's speech shows! How different his tone is now, no more the contemptible army, and the hacking the way to victory, but "fighting for life and liberty!"[792]

Sunday October 1st 1916, Rouen

There was a curious reposefulness about the camp early this morning. Everyone was taking the extra hour in with much contentment and so did I, but the habit of waking earlier kept me just wakeful and resting. Holy Communion at 6.45am with only one present, viz. Cyril Smith of Watts Avenue, Rochester, now Sergeant Smith! I think he was a little sad at moving off. At 8am 19 communicants and at 11.0 am a very crowded parade, and at 12am not quite so large. The Colonel, nursing a bad cold, was not able to be present, but some very attentive men were. At 5pm I went for a pine wood walk with a nice Major Staveson of Glasgow. Then at 6.0 pm we had a large service at a General Hospital and at 7pm a full service in my Church Tent, very quiet and intent. After it the Rev. S. Evans, a Red Cross private, made himself known to me, and I asked him to help at the Evening Communion. It was the first he had ever been to in his life, and he liked it – the work is full of interest. On the whole, it was an auspicious opening for our share of the National Mission, especially the large Parade service, the General Hospital and the Evening tent service. But – there are many, many Gallio's even among quite nice men and officers, and one Chaplain feels small and of little avail, but with rightly divined words, great things can be done[793].

---

792 Theobald Theodor Friedrich Alfred von Bethmann-Hollweg (b.1856 – d.1921) was a German politician and statesman who served as Chancellor of the German Empire from 1909 to 1917. At the opening of the Reichstag September 28th, 1916, Germany was fighting 'for nothing but defence of her right to life and liberty'.

793 **Lucius Junius Gallio Annaeanus** or **Gallio** was a Roman senator and brother of famous writer Seneca. According to the Book of Acts he dismissed the charge brought by the Jews against the Apostle Paul. (Acts 18:12-17). The key phrase for RDG is v.17: 'but Gallio cared for none of these things'.

What a nice letter Mr Asquith's nephew wrote to his mother in case he died – which he did[794]. Goodnight, my queen.

Monday October 2nd 1916, Rouen

No English mail today. Good news – another Zeppelin down and the French aeroplanes have bombed Essen[795]. I do not think the enemy's management in the air is any greater than that which they receive under the sea! Much rain, but a pleasant ride in the afternoon with Capt Younghusband,[796] (whose father was once vicar of Henfield) a man who is living a nice-minded life among some whose views are not right ones. On these hills the sandy soil soon dries up, and the autumn fragrance of the pines and bracken brought out by the dampness of the pure rain was very refreshing. I was to have ridden with Major Staveson, but his horse was unexpectedly sent off to be shod.

When I went into the Church tent this evening in the dark, I found a soldier kneeling there saying his prayers. To get a quiet place like that in a Camp like this I perceive, is a great boon. So I am going to have two of the lamps lit each evening at 6.0, and our next difficulty will be the warming – hence, again, the Fund! I had a long talk this evening with the 2nd Lt who was in the VIII Division. He is interested in the church, but a little against his vicar who has lately become an Army Chaplain "and a good one he will make too" which was an admission. The officer's young brother has lately been ordained, and wants to become an Army Chaplain. A talk with a foolish young trooper of yeomanry who states at first jocundly, and then seeing that I was not amused, sheepishly, how he had come out with the VIII Division as a full corporal but was disrated to a private "for doing what was right" – the 'right' he meant, I found, was being drunk while in charge of a practice firing party, maintenant – coucher! How will it be possible, dear lady, to settle down to the local and simple limitations of that pretty little countryside after all these living and wide-reaching interests?

Tuesday October 3rd 1916, Rouen

No mail again today – rumour has it that some mines have got loose, and have to be swept up before regular traffic can be resumed. The weather is beautiful and warm – good fighting weather, and we may hope for encouraging reports. A central meeting of Chaplains in Rouen, which was preceded by a 'Choral' celebration of the Holy Communion – I am sorry to say that it oppressed me. It was taken by Colbeck, who at times was very indistinct (he drops his h's) and parts were sung to Gregorian

---

794 Lieutenant The Hon **Charles Alfred Lister**, (b.1888 – d.1915) Royal Marines Hood Bn RN Div. Killed 28th August 1915. Son of Thomas 4th Lord Ribblesdale, and Charlotte, his wife, of Gisburne Park, near Clitheroe, Lancs. Secretary in H.M. Diplomatic Service. A noted socialist, his letters were published in 1917 by his father.
795 French air raid September 24th. Zeppelin raid on London 23/24th September.
796 Capt. *E. W. Younghusband*, 6th (Inniskilling). Dragoons, Special Reserve.

plainsong! And the Agnus Dei was sung and the celebrant read the wrong Collect, Epistle and Gospel for the 14th Sunday after Trinity. A redeeming feature was an address by Preb. Swayne[797], on "All ye are brethren"[798]. It was a little 'scolding' in parts, "the Church is hopelessly divided" and "we are disastrously unbrotherly" and "ought to be ashamed of ourselves", and his mannerism is just that which is rightly caricatured on the stage – the mouthing and the intonation up into a falsetto just not avoided, and once or twice it almost made me laugh (of that I am ashamed). But the reasoning was sound, and there was a manliness of Christian faith about the outlook which made one feel better. The Chaplain's talk was not of a high level, most people smoked, and they got down to talking to one another across the meeting. Colbeck wisely brought things up to the business again, but he is not a strong leader.

Tuckey's successor is Barnes, who arrives at midnight tonight, and Canon Cunningham comes early in November for a quiet day with the Chaplains. The Bishop is definitely booked for Sunday week, and on Monday has a talk with the Chaplains.

After tea a spin through the pine forest on the nice old horse, and at 6.0 a talk to a confirmation candidate, a nice manly man, who said he had been drawn out by what I had said in an address about "a soldier being brave enough to do what is right".

Wednesday October 4th 1916, Rouen

Regarding the accompanying papers which have just come out, Mr Foster[799] has usually been so very kind in all your money matters so perhaps the Bank would do it? Anyway, there will be comfort in the fact that you are <u>commanded</u> to make this claim by the <u>King</u>, and that you are to get the back interest as well. You may be able to give yourself a nice little well-earned holiday with that, a little to recover what you have given out as 'your bit' in the worst war in history.

It is a beautiful night, calm, mild and dry with a pale moon sinking away into the horizon. A sea of tents and huts everywhere and away on the fringe, a belt of fir trees which is the edge of the forest. In the other direction, just visible over the edge of long grass fields, some of the roofs and spires of the city, bathed in a soft, blue-grey transparency, rather pretty to look at. I have come out of a chatting Mess company – myself, the Colonel, the doctor and a nice visiting doctor have been talking over the sound sanitary laws of Leviticus[800], and the possibility of conquering cancer. The last post has sounded from one camp after another, no two seem to keep to exactly the same moment of time, and the far off ones have sounded faintly in the distance like

---

797 Prebendary Rev. **Robert George Swayne**, Chancellor and Canon Residentiary, Salisbury Cathedral.
798 **Matthew 23:8** 'But be not ye called Rabbi: for one is your Master, *even* Christ; and all ye are brethren.'
799 Charles Finch Foster (b.1842 – d.1922), third son of George Ebenezer Foster, and brother-in-law to Mary Smith Foster, 'Aunt Mai'. Principal of Foster & Sons bank, Cambridge.
800 **Leviticus 13**, concerning the treatment and transmission of bacterial leprosy.

the effect called for in a stage scene or written of in a book. It is the end of another day – one day less of the war. My impression is that there is much more for the Nation to endure: in the Divine Providence the 'much more' that the Nation will have to endure is because it needs it.

It has been a busy day with early Service in the pouring rain to which no one came. A chat with Colonel Bulman – he is a nice (though blunt) man and has much cared for patches of grass and flower borders in his camp, the salvias making a special show. He always talks of good things e.g. the future of England, whether the soldiers are getting more harm than good out of France, and so on. Some letters and the newspaper, and a ride on the old grey horse. I got some chestnuts (following Lloyd George's example)[801] and fir cones from the forest, proposing to plant them in West Farleigh garden to see if they will grow as souvenirs.

Thursday October 5th 1916, Rouen
Such is camp life – a sudden order this morning means that half our ground goes over to another area! The Colonel was most kind and he himself suggested another site for our little Church tent, and by this afternoon it is up again in another spot! (rather more convenient as it happens!). The Chaplains' talk – <u>not</u> very practical, then a nice ride right through the forest with Major Salmon to the bridge the Germans nearly blew up at the beginning of the War, and a coffee in a little estaminet house in drenching rain. A <u>most</u> interesting lecture (the last of the series) By Prof. Holland Rose on the culminating causes of this war.

As far as I can see I shall not be able to get away before the end of this month – I mean there does not seem much, if any, prospect of a 'leave' before the end of my time.

Friday October 7th 1916, Rouen
I took fourteen burials this afternoon, under a gloomy sky and with a cold, fitful wind blowing occasionally and sprinklings of rain over everything. The Cemetery arrangements leave much to be desired, and it is to be hoped more attention may be given to them by Tuckey's successor.

I met an old comrade earlier in the afternoon from the Base Depot I was at in the

---

801 Cordite had been used by the British military since 1889, replacing black powder. It consisted chiefly of the high-explosives nitroglycerine and nitrocellulose (gun-cotton), with acetone as solvent in the manufacturing process. Prior to WW1, the acetone used in British munitions was made almost entirely from the dry distillation (pyrolysis) of wood, imported from the United States. At outbreak of war, the stocks for military use were just 3200 tonnes, and it was soon obvious that an alternative domestic supply would be needed. One of the first initiatives of The Ministry of Munitions, run by David Lloyd George, was to ask the chemist Chaim Weizmann of Manchester University to develop an alternative way of making acetone in large quantities; and one of proposed solutions was from conkers and fir cones, both of which the public were exhorted to collect in large numbers.

autumn – Rifleman Bennett. He is rather happy in having done his turn in the trenches, and being now on his way home to England, for munitions work.

Capt Boyd also passing through, he comes from Mr Schreiber's parish (Shipbourne)[802] and knows and likes him well. I had two very earnest Confirmation candidates this evening. "I wouldn't like" said one "to go back on all I learnt in the Church Lad's Brigade. I want to go forward." (A remarkable ugly fellow, but remarkably nice and with an obviously 'healthy' mind.) The other is of the more educated kind, with a mind for history – a grocer, in a small way I should think.

Sunday October 8th 1916, Rouen

The Communion Service is the Principal Service of the Church, it is the Ordinance of Christ Himself. The Roman Catholic Church, the Greek Orthodox, and the Lutheran do rightly in giving it priority of position. What is the Anglican Church doing? The Evangelical section have made much of Morning Prayer, or Evening Prayer according to local conditions, always with exalted attention to the momentous mission of Preaching: the idea being public family worship, with plenty of exhortation and instruction. The 'Catholic' section have given great prominence to the Sacrament and less to preaching and instruction. They have been right in placing the Sacrament thus to the fore, and wrong in not affording their disciples the opportunity for being fed with "knowledge and understanding."

Does a remedy lie – a better adjustment – in forsaking the rigid insistence on the early morning for that Service and putting more in the place of Morning Prayer, making it the Service for family worship and giving the sermon and instruction full scope in the appointed place: and letting Morning Prayer be a service by itself, without a sermon? In the Army, a condensed Morning Prayer – the Parade service – grows to be the one recognised service and the whole routine of the Regiment or Garrison as the case may be, centres upon that. I wonder whether it could not be as simply centred upon the Holy Communion, it would give the import to the Communicant life which I believe our faith demands. It would guide men in putting first things first, and the Communion Ordinance being what it is, would bring men nearer to Christ, for where are we more one with His mind than in His own Personal Service? There would be less the idea then, that the Parade Service as such is more important than a Communion Service, and that the Communion Service is an occasion of very significancant import – which as the practice proves is the view under the existing custom.

Two services of Christ's Holy Communion today – and no one present at them (at the second, it is true, was present the Rev. S. Evans, a private in the R.A.M.C., but that was because he had offered to help, and I accepted his offer). I wonder if the National Mission can help in this way. Otherwise, it seems to me, the Church is in

---

802 Rev **Francis Longe Schreiber** (b.? – d.1938), St Giles' Shipbourne, situated between the towns of Sevenoaks and Tonbridge, in the borough of Tonbridge and Malling.

danger of sliding away to Congregationalism. Of course, if Congregationalism is the right conception of the Church – there is something to be said for that[803].

But even so ought it not to be a Congregationalism centered round the Divinely Personal Service – the Ordinance that in its nature draws the disciples to congregate round the Personal Presence and in drawing out the communion of various spririts, brings them into more real and full communion one with another? There's a meditation!

This evening we had an overflowing Evening service at a S.C.A. hut, followed by a quiet and closely united Evening Service also in the Church tent – a further Confirmation candidate came to this Service, a fine upstanding young Guardsman, who spoke firmly and naturally as if meaning business.

Monday October 9th 1916, Rouen

How the days slip by! Tomorrow we are in 2 figures for this month. I have addressed your letter today to the Red House so I hope it will not arrive before you. Your letters sometimes take 3 or 4 days to come, but perhaps mine go hence quicker. I wonder what day you will go over to W. Farleigh, and what all the arrangements to be made will be. Did I glean that the Fawns had had special blinds put to the windows for darkening purposes, or did we pay for them? Then there is the anthracite stove in the hall. I am sorry, but I am afraid I do not take to it – perhaps you do? If so, I dare say we could come to an arrangement. Are servants going to be more of a difficulty under War conditions? They will be less so directly the Armies begin to return.

Today, after feeling a little 'Mondayish', I went out on the old grey to the drill ground, and witnessed some very good squadron manoeuvring (let us write 'manoeuvres' to be safe, otherwise would it be manoeuvring or manoeuvreing?) It is really an aviation ground – sandy soil over a very wide plateau, with fringes of pine forest all round, very fresh and pure-aired. The old horse was very amusing in wanting to take part in the drill, he had evidently been there before!

Visiting a confirmation candidate – a pause – then three separate confirmation talks with two guardsmen and an ex-Congregationalist, all of them in downright earnest and listening with a remarkable tenseness of quiet reception – not moving a finger, not a cough or a turn of the head for a full half hour on the stretch – the remembering of the passages given previously to be read and pondered, by chapter and verse, is very striking. One feels with the men of England, that they would be more fully 'Church' if the Church had had more opportunity for reaching them and instructing

803 **Congregationalism**, is a system of church governance in which every local church congregation is independent, ecclesiastically sovereign, or "autonomous". Among those major Protestant Christian traditions that employ congregationalism are those Congregational Churches known by the "Congregationalist" name that descended from the Anglo-American Puritan movement of the 17th century, the Baptist churches, and most of the groups brought about by the Anabaptist movement in Germany that immigrated to the U.S. in the late 18th century.

them individually. That is if the men, also, had been able to be more detached from the duties of their calling, the necessity of earning their living, anxiety about getting their place and keeping it, and would then be more free to receive of the things of God. It is a time they can never forget "it can never not have been".

Goodnight – dear Miss-eldest-daughter-of-the-Principal-of-St. Aidans-and-of-the-Primate-of-Australia – formerly!!

Tuesday October 10th 1916, Rouen

A party of R.A.M.C. men from Yorkshire are singing glees, unaccompanied, in the Sergeants Mess. They have voices of rare quality, and are singing with great taste and accuracy[804]. Some of the pieces are beautiful, and at this moment a soldier is singing a song very greatly in favour just now "A perfect day"[805]. It is rather appropriate, for today has been a very encouraging one – the weather has been delightful, there have been some nice talks with the men, two of the confirmation candidates have shown a remarkably 'healthy' spirit, and we have had a crowded and very responsive meeting in the S.C.A. hut. This evening is calm, mild and bathed in soft moonlight. The gentler, wholesome side of man is with us, and the promise of hope stands out.

I mentioned, without names of course, about Mrs Mills this evening, to illustrate Christian unselfishness, which takes pleasure in other people's pleasure "I don't begrudge anybody anything. If I walk along and see a nice garden, I say 'what a nice garden. Thank God they've got a nice garden, or I see somebody who's got a pig. I can't afford to keep a pig myself, but I say 'thank God, they can keep a pig!' Rejoice with them that do rejoice!"[806]

One of the confirmation candidates was troubled about the Commandment "Thou shalt not kill". I quoted Romans 13 "He beareth not the sword in vain .... he is the minister of God"[807], and we read the 37th Article, and decided that for the present distress, it was a necessary evil – the men are thinking[808].

---

804 A **glee** is an English type of part song spanning the late baroque, classical and early romantic periods. It is usually scored for at least three voices, and generally intended to be sung unaccompanied. Glees often consist of a number of short, musically contrasted movements and their texts can be convivial, fraternal, idyllic, tender, philosophical or dramatic.

805 **"A Perfect Day"** (first line: "When you come to the end of a perfect day") is a parlour song written by Carrie Jacobs-Bond (b.1862 – d.1946) in 1909. "A Perfect Day" was phenomenally successful when first published in 1910. 8 million copies of the sheet music and 5 million recordings sold within a year; 25 million copies of the sheet music sold during Jacobs-Bond's lifetime, and many millions of recordings circulated as various artists performed the song on the fast-growing means of audio duplication. It was her most-requested number when Jacobs-Bond entertained the soldiers at U.S. Army camps in Europe during WW1.

806 **Romans 12:15** 'Rejoice with them that do rejoice, and weep with them that weep.'

807 **Romans 13:4** 'For he is the minister of God to thee for good. But if thou do that which is evil, be afraid; for he beareth not the sword in vain: for he is the minister of God, a revenger to *execute* wrath upon him that doeth evil.'

808 Romans 8:37-39 'Nay, in all these things we are more than conquerors through him that loved us. For I am persuaded, that neither death, nor life, nor angels, nor principalities, nor powers,

A remarkable sight last night was to see the Y.M.C.A. hut crowded up, while a sergeant talked to them on "the inner meaning of the War". He was going deeply into things and they were listening most intently. I could not stay for more than a sentence or two, but it was solid thought.

Thank you for another letter and your plan for West Farleigh. Once more, I cannot think that all this full world experience must go to be secluded in West Farleigh, and yet I suppose it must be if my body cannot go the pace necessary. Bodies are a nuisance – all your knowledge of the life of a Theological College, of the Bible, of travels across the world, of missionaries, of mission doings, of the workings of a Diocese, must they be shut up in West Farleigh too? Yet – how many thousands will have come out into a vastly widened world experience over this war, those going to India, Egypt, Turkey, Greece and the African Colonies as well as out here to France, and who will have to drop back into some limited little sphere! What is to come of it all? And then those kind hearts, all which will have lived in sympathy with all these travelling, toiling and suffering lives, to what now must that far-thrown interest be turned?

Friday October 13th 1916, Rouen

It <u>has</u> been a strenuous day, with all the usual arrangements for Sunday being changed by the opening of the New Camp Church on Sunday, and a visit from one of the successors of the Apostles[809], and we, Mr Colbeck and I, walked and talked incessantly most of the morning: then a pause, and walking and talking again, and then a spin on the nice old grey horse (whose affection is very touching!). Separate interviews with Confirmation candidates and a further talk with Colbeck about the opening of the Church – he has had £25 out of the Fund for the equipment of the Church and the Hall. It is the largest building of its kind in the whole Expeditionary Force, the main difficulty will be the heating of it I think, with the coming winter. It has been a most valuable Fund, and how much blessing will have come by it no one can measure.

Then, a kind of last straw, we had the weekly concert of the Territorial Base Depot (which is part of my parish)! It was pretty good – the Colonel's presence commands its tone. It is astonishing where all their jokes come from. Then to dinner with Col Bulman, who is well-read and well-travelled and always interesting to talk with, and he has good firm ideals also. He had been noticing the pictures in 'Country Life' of Christ's Church Cambridge's Master's Lodge, and the Sanctuary windows looking down into the Chapel from the study[810]. I told him of how Eric, then a little boy

---

nor things present, nor things to come, nor height, nor depth, nor any other creature, shall be able to separate us from the love of God, which is in Christ Jesus our Lord.'

809   A Bishop, presumably.

810   A. E. Shipley, 'The Master's Lodgings, Christ's College, Cambridge', *Country Life* (1916), vol 40, 406-12.

Postcard to Eric 'Very busy getting ready for a confirmation and the opening of a new church. Thank you for your post card. Very glad of good reports. Lovely weather here: with you too I hope. Much love From Father'

of 3 or 4, asked the Master's blind wife who was standing by "Does she have this because she is blind?"[811]

He is going to be severe on Germany after the war. Germany is to have no Colonies – I wonder if that will be wise? As a country, must they not have an outlet, though strictly under treaty control?

Then finally, a chat with 2 or 3 fresh officers passing through our own Depot. One has just returned after a week of the fighting and one, they told me, who had passed up three weeks ago, was killed his first day up. The conversation got onto dog stories, and one officer told of a big wheel dog he knew up country, who was always left to himself by the farm people, and the wheel gate was left open. This dog used to slow down the wheel when he was getting a little tired, jump out, and go for a little stroll, then come back and resume the wheeling vigorously as before!

---

811 **Annette Peile (Kitchener)** (b.1835 – d.1920), wife of **John Peile** (b.1838 – d.1910) was an English philologist. Peile was educated at Repton, St. Bees School and Christ's College, Cambridge. After a distinguished career (Craven Scholar, Senior Classic and First Chancellor's Medallist), he became Fellow and Tutor of his college, Reader of Comparative Philology in the university (1884–1891), and in 1887 was elected Master of Christ's. He took a great interest in the higher education of women and became president of Newnham College. He was the first to introduce the great philological works of Georg Curtius and Wilhelm Corssen to the English student in his *Introduction to Greek and Latin Etymology* (1869).

Saturday October 14th 1916, Rouen

It is a dull day, but not unpleasant. After much pressure the Church is in a state of readiness for the opening – it is bare and simple enough, but looks welcoming. The band lost heart at the last moment, but will come up to scratch we hope, in the morning.

A glorious ride with the Colonel, through filmy beech copses, green and golden autumn tints, long fairy-like avenues of about 12 or 15 miles. My old horse got a little tired but will be able to rest tomorrow.

A piano friend in the Mess has the loud pedal down and is thumping out airs with varying degrees of accuracy – he will go on into the night, but mercifully the Mess closes at 11.30 so no one need be kept awake after that!

Peter had orders to be moving today – but at the last minute they were cancelled to admit of his being here over the dedication of the new Church.

Sunday October 15th 1916, Rouen

A busy but very interesting day and an encouraging day for everyone, I think.

H.C. at 8.0 with three men present, and at 10.0 a very nice parade Service with my Territorial Base Depot. They had it in their Hut, and liked being there I know – esprit de corps inclines them to prayer being within their own borders, and they will not like coming over to the central Church! At 11.15 they rolled up in their hundreds. The senior Colonel of the Camps, who belongs to this end really not at all, made a mischievous muddle in parading some hundreds of troops not in this area. Some of them got in early and some hundreds had to be turned away, among them, alas, some of my own Cavalry! That was a pity. A very good brass band stood near the entrance and played in everybody to spirited martial airs. The string band pulled itself together and it did very creditably indeed. The place holds over 1000 people and it was packed. It was a touching sight, the sea of faces with some hundreds of fresh arrivals on their way up to the line – what awaits them there? Some hundreds of returned and broken warriors, content to be in the shade doing service in quiet ways, glad to be able to move about, if not always at quick march. Baines[812], Tuckey's successor, was there and one other Chaplain, Baird, Colbeck and myself. I was private Chaplain to the Bishop, and preceded the successor to the Apostles to his seat, and sat beside him, then to the pulpit, and back again – as of old! It is an eloquent service, and one felt the meaning of sentence after sentence in the building which made all the difference between a Divine Meeting place and a mere wilderness of tents and huts. We, who have been born into Churches ready-made, learn like this to be thankful for them when we see them brought down to us where formerly they have not been. The Bishop's sermon was admirable, stout, simple, tender, and sincere – no preaching but

---

812 Rev **C F Baines**, Chaplain 1st Class.

a godly word "They shall go from strength to strength"[813]. This Church might be a wayside place of refreshing to these many pilgrims out of England, perhaps homesick, full of the seriousness of the sacrifice, the sense of what might be to come, thoughts of wives and children left behind – it would be to them hereabouts a vale of misery. Might they come here and find life-giving strains of new grace, new trust and new self-surrender. Afterwards we lunched at Colbeck's Mess – 7 Colonels!

The confirmation service was also very devout and real, two of the Bishop's anecdotes were good – one of two men sitting on a London bus. One said that he was sorry as much as anybody about this war for Sir Edward Grey[814] who had worked so hard for peace. The other said that he felt sorry for the Kaiser, for he was going 'to get it in the neck'! The third man was a bit of a philosopher – he said that he was sorry most of all for the Almighty God who had laboured so hard to bring the world to blessing, and Who so suffered with the afflictions of His people. The other story was how Sir Douglas Haig came into the ante-room at the officers' mess at Headquarters, where some Generals were also present, and said to the Bishop how he wanted him to know how he appreciated the work of the Chaplains which he regarded as 'invaluable' "and," he added "you know I am one who believes in prayer". There were about 60 Confirmation candidates, all came forward of their own free will as the Bishop said "no pressing", and it was nice to think of the earnest coming-forward of the 9 men of my own lot who were there, and about a dozen others have had partial preparation, but have been drafted on meanwhile.

Monday October 16th 1916, Rouen

A conference with the Bishop at 10.00 with all the Chaplains and a totally different tune to the usual Tuckey kind! We discuss the provision of Clergy after the war, the keeping open of an eye for ordinands, the discussion varied between the lesser open door, or the wider open door. A useful point was made about making it easy for Non-Conformists to come over to this Communion – easy that is, from a business point of view as they are seeing in the Army chaplains what an advantage the C of E organisation has, which theirs has not.

After the conference, I had a private talk with the Bishop and he approved of the idea of my resuming work among the soldiers after Parish matters had been arranged. They are short of Chaplains suitable for the work, 35 short even with the present establishment out here. Personally, I think Egypt or the Balkans, but that must be seen. I wonder if Mr Fawns may not like to take the Skelton's house and then you could

---

813 **Psalm 84:7** 'They go from strength to strength, *every one of them* in Zion appeareth before God.'
814 **Edward Grey, 1st Viscount Grey of Fallodon**, Bt KG PC FZL DL (b.1862 – d.1933), better known as **Sir Edward Grey, 3rd Baronet**, was a British Liberal statesman. He served as Foreign Secretary from 1905 to 1916. He is probably best remembered for his remark at the outbreak of WW1 "The lamps are going out all over Europe. We shall not see them lit again in our life-time."

remain at the Vicarage and do the 'lady' work that offers? It would hardly be for more than 6 months I should think before the end, and there would be the satisfaction of having gone through the Campaign. Anyway, we shall all have Christmas together D.V. I do not expect to leave here now, before the week preceding November 5th on the Thursday or the Friday I suppose, to arrive in Southampton, (or Folkstone no one knows) on the Saturday. They will hardly wish to fix my landing on the Sunday! Would it be well, I wonder, to go straight off to Stonehouse then, and take a pause of rest after that – I ought to hear from Deane Oliver in a few days. If nothing comes, it may be assumed the plan for a short period during November will not come off, wherefore I must go idling round somewhere and I cannot abide a purposeless holiday nowadays. Things will shape themselves I do not doubt.

I hope the fruit from West Farleigh has been plentiful – the prices are said to range high. It is evident we ought to sell the cow but it is a great boon being sure of your milk and having it pure, and as things go now-a-days with our land at our own disposal, it would be an economy, except perhaps that feed may be costly therefore we might be well advised to buy two sturdy shorthorns.

Alas! I rushed off, directly I got Mr Dickinson's letter, to the hospital about five miles away only to find his brother had died before the letter was sent off[815]. It was a sorrowful mauling – an eye had to be removed and an arm amputated, and he died following the operation. They that "suffer with Him" will surely share His reigning[816].

Tuesday October 17th 1916, Rouen
The letters are coming through more quickly just now – one posted on the 12th got here on the 16th, they have sometimes taken a week.

I have written to Mr Fawns, sounding him out about future possibilities – I wonder what will come of it? One feels one must follow up these men with the accumulated knowledge of their ways, circumstances and needs, and as long as one has movement in one, that it seems to be the way it could best be used, we must see how things shape. Wesley said "the world is my parish!"[817] I think it must be the wider world yet for both of us, if the body will keep up steam.

Goodbye for the present, dear Margaret – we pay the price of Empire.

---

815 2nd Lieut **Humphrey Neville Dickinson** (b.1882 – d.1916) 3rd Bn. attd. 6th Bn Queen's Own (Royal West Kent Regiment). Died of wounds 13th October 1916, St Sever Cemetery, Rouen. Son of Henry and Ellen Marion Dickinson, of "Martins", Burnham, Bucks. Student, Balliol College, Oxford. Barrister at Law, Inner Temple.

816 **2 Timothy 2:12** 'If we suffer, we shall also reign with *him*: if we deny *him*, he also will deny us.'

817 "I look on all the world as my parish; thus far I mean, that, in whatever part of it I am, I judge it meet, right, and my bounden duty, to declare unto all that are willing to hear, the glad tidings of salvation". Charles Wesley, Journal (11th June 1739).

Wednesday October 18th 1916, Rouen

A clammy day with squalls of rain. Busy with plans for Sunday and 'parish visiting' – what lives one unravels in the latter! He went to sea at 13 and travelled the world, and the influence of a good home along round him: he has been 5 years in the Royal Corps of Mounted Police of Canada and is here as a trooper and wants to resume communion after "getting out of the way of it". This one comes from Trinidad, was brought up in a good home and was prepared for confirmation at school and confirmed just before leaving, but has never received the Communion and would like to do so, and so on!

The arrangements for the Parade are going to be a little complicated. Each Depot wants a parade to itself, and they can't all be fitted in, so it means squeezing up the morning time rather closely. The Colonels are nice about it but each is keen for the esprit de corps of his Depot. It will mean in one case, the development of a second band, which will not be a bad thing. There will be plenty of work for my successor – the same is to be G.E.P. Cave-Moyle who is Rector of Abbey Dore, Hereford[818].

A spin on the old horse after tea, not spoilt by the rain for the soil here is sandy and dries quickly.

With the men of England out here like this, presenting such response and such opportunities, I confess that I look towards the quiet and limited prospects of West Farleigh with reluctance. This evening a passing officer comes from Wales, knows the place of my birth very well and is brother of a nice man who was up at CC in my time – A H Swan, now vicar of Christ Church, Fulham[819]. Life's meetings!

Thursday October 19th 1916, Rouen

Alas! My gentle partner, I wonder what you will say – I have written to the Bishop the prospect to my returning to the soldiers early next year. While the men of England are out here, one feels one must be out with them, as long as one has legs to stand on[820].

Friday October 20th 1916, Rouen

Cold!! but seasonable. The old warriors are beginning to scent winter and avenues that present a possibility of getting back to England, such as Munitions or Garrison work,

---

818 Rev. **George Edward Phillip Cave-Moyle** (b.1876 – d.1971) Gonville-Caius College, Cambs. Ordained Chester 1899, St John's Cheltenham 1902–4, St Paul's Cheltenham 1904–10, Abbey Dore 1911– ? Holder of Patent 946,674. Patented Jan. 18,1910 "Be it known that we, William Ricahard Hughes, motor-engineer, and Phillip Cave-Moyle, clerk in holy orders, subjects of the King of Great Britain, residing, respectively, at Airedale, Victoria Terrace, and Belmont, both of Cheltenham, in the county of Gloucester, England, have invented new and useful Improved Means for Securing a Spare Rim to the Wheel of a Vehicle."

819 Rev. **Arthur Henry Swann** (b.1868 – d.1930).

820 See letter dated August 23rd, where RDG writes the exact opposite.

are making their attraction felt. Two have come to see what a kind-hearted Chaplain might be able to do to help them! One needs care, lest one should be discouraging a man from doing his full bit. In a case where he has not been up the line, he does not deserve sympathy, except under very unusual conditions – age or definite infirmity.

My gallant servant, Baker, has had a severe time in Mesopotamia so I do not mind him remaining at a base. The malaria is a little better today, but the cold is searching.

A morning of looking up bandsmen and making arrangements, and then this evening a concert at my Territorial Depot which was quite good. The tone of the party manifestly tends higher when they know, I think, that the Colonel sees and that the Chaplain backs that up too. As the Colonel said "it is such a pity that such good voices should be wasted in paltry words."

Saturday October 21st 1916, Rouen

Trafalgar Day – of great memories, and we are making events nowadays for what future? When Eric, Joyce and Faith are men and women, if they are spared, for what in England will they be living and how serving? Like "as the arrows in the hand of a giant, even as well the young children[821]". To what directed? With what driving force? With what power to affect? Direction, strength, keenness and efficiency?

It has been cold and last night tried most people. So many found the same thing – they could not get their feet warm. That, on through the night, in a tent or a canvas hut, suggests meditation – we shall hear more of trench feet again, I suppose, though no doubt this winter we shall be much better prepared against difficulties of that sort. England, and the Allies, <u>must</u> win this war.

The weather was nice at midday, and after a busy morning, I enjoyed a spin on the old grey horse. The cold weather makes him snort and he enjoys his exercise.

The new Church is not ready for proper occupation. There are no heating arrangements and the electric light men declare that they must (*will*) finish before the early service tomorrow, and could not before! Colbeck is a fuzzy muddler in some ways, and short and 'tempery' with people – he is not so with me, though he would be if he did not know that it would not be accepted – militarism or no militarism! Baines came up with him this afternoon – an amiable man, but like many of these 'Regular' Army Chaplains a little conscious of his importance, and not first and foremost the 'fellows' clergyman. That the war should be a short one is desirable for the good of the Chaplain's Department, unless much grace shall abound. He has no idea what day my movement to England may come off – a previous Chaplain was kept over his time nearly a month and then only went away by notifying that he did not propose to conduct any more services after a given Sunday! Whether

---

821 **Psalm 127 3-5** 'As the arrows in the hand of a giant, even as well the young children.'

I get back for the 5th or after that day remains to be seen! Baker, the new orderly, is a promising fellow. He has been wounded three times, once at the Dardanelles, once in the Ypres salient and once near Albert. He has a twin brother, a baker, in the Army (Baker by name as well!). He wrote to him saying that he was in France and a week or so later the brother turned up at his tent door, and now he is in the bakeries at this base.

This cold weather drives the men into their huts, and much work may be done talking around. The poor Indians! We have a number near us and the way they 'hug' any scrap of fire is pathetic.

I think I might go to Stonehouse as soon as possible after getting to England. Busyness often out of the midst of quiet – wherever one goes, one longs for quiet and privacy. Here every moment almost is in public, very nice and brotherly, and a <u>man's</u> life, but one needs to retire from it for a time. It is nevertheless great in the way of inspiring companionship, and there are some splendid men in the English race spite of much pettiness and wrong.

Sunday October 22nd 1916, Rouen
Cold, a little ruffled through fussy Mr Colbeck making arrangements without knowing what he was doing!

Tuesday October 24th 1916, Rouen
They cannot tell me what day I go from here – it makes it less easy to make arrangements.

Torrents of rain today.

Wednesday October 25th 1916, Rouen
Again, a late evening – the Colonel has taken to keeping it up rather long at dinner, and none moves, of course, till he does. But he is a nice good man, and you certainly improve acquaintances by talking on, Major Tuscon is especially interesting with his descriptions of land-cultivation in Nairobi[822] – it is a wide and interesting world and we <u>cannot</u> remain closed in at West Farleigh. Shall we go to some overseas Mission Charge think you?

I was fortunate today – the funerals I was due for were taken by a Chaplain on the spot, which released me for a ride on the old, kind grey, who grows increasingly tearful with the nearing of our separation.

---

822 **Major C E Tucson**'s family farmed the Sabatia Estate in the Eldina Ravine district of the Rift Valley, Kenya.

Thursday October 26th 1916, Rouen

Things have moved – the least fraction. I understand now the custom is to return a Chaplain that he may report at the War Office the day his term expires. I ought to be in London therefore to report <u>on</u> Sunday the 5th of November. There is a certain vagueness, however, one soi-disant authority speaking one thing, the other another. Colbeck airily remarked I would go back for the Sunday "if my help was not required here!" Little he understands – the War Office does not pay a day beyond the specified agreement. Therefore, I ought to be near enough my domicile the day of my ceasing to act *in order* not to necessitate my occupying additional days in returning thereto!

A peculiarly unfortunate Chaplains' meeting again this morning – C gets garrulous, and occupied the major part of our time denouncing two Colonels as delinquents in respective particulars. Alas! And alas!! It makes one very depressed. The keen, uplifting subject of the National Mission received its' brief and formal attention, and then duly as a subject was dropped. However, this day week, I anticipate, I shall be en route.

My new servant, Baker, (who looks very respectable with his 3 wound bars on his arm) had a telegram "Come at once, wife very ill, a son" from his sister-in-law. The rule is to send a telegram to the police of the area "Is husband's presence necessary?" Then if the illness is extremely serious, special leave of absence is granted. The reply came "Husband's presence is unnecessary". So, though there is the disappointment of the non-return, there is the relief of the better condition, and sometimes these telegrams are a sentimental 'try on'.

I have begun to 'square things up' for moving off. They seem uncertain now about 'posting' the man here who was decided on. I hope they will succeed in keeping their word, but one of two 'hoity-toity' young new-comers are taking much on themselves in the Base Chaplain's Office, and I found it hard not to be depressed as I witnessed their tone this afternoon. The War is putting some of these younger Clergy through a serious test and one fears, and wishes it may not last long for that reason. If it lasts long some must suffer – either their hearts or the men whose work they are exploiting.

The dear old horse, with again two or three tears, went very well this morning, and the pine forest in the glinting sunshine, with the deepening bracken and the soft, fresh air, was soothing.

Shall we ever settle down in West Farleigh – we must burst out somewhere thence.

Friday October 27th 1916, Rouen

The 'void' has spoken once again – thank you very much for your letter, written under various difficulties. West Farleigh, Gravesend, Hurst, comes this morning, posted on the <u>19th</u>! Rather slow! I wonder when you will get this? Your letter does not say anything about Mr Fawns having received my proposal to resume later – I hope he will come after Christmas. As long as the men of England are 'in the swing' of all this

National effort, I want to be 'in the swing' with them – "better wear out than rust[823]".

I have written to two other possible substitutes on the off-chance. It has been a long time for the Fawns with 2 years in another person's house. If he is prudent he will remain in the Rochester diocese with another year say at West Farleigh and two more years elsewhere and he will then qualify for a preferment of some kind, which is his due. He might do much worse, apart from the interest of his work, than take up the Skelton's house.

How damp everything gets in a canvas hut, even to the writing paper. This evening we had a very good concert at the Territorial Depot with some really nice songs, well sung. One, "A giant I am" (a windmill) sung with great effect by Sergt. Hopkins and Corporal Harrison R.E. also has a well trained voice of unusual quality. Colonel Bulman is admirable in the way he lets it be known that the things that we wanted are those of good taste and quality. I have been hard at work writing notes for my successor and tearing up odds and ends of paper. I dined with Col Bulman again this evening, and though he has a bluff snappy goodness – it is goodness, and I like him. I hope we shall meet again, though I should rather pity the man who was vicar to him!

Yes, I think we would do well to get rid of the Jersey, and get two rough and ready Shorthorns. I feel sure – measuring up all values – it is domestic economy in our case that is economy.

My poor servant is disappointed that the telegram did not say "Husband's presence is necessary" so it is difficult for us all to be pleased. He would rather have his wife seriously ill enough to demand his being in England!

At the moment of writing this page, my return for Sunday week is uncertain. A Chaplain has gone off ill (to England) and the place of another has not been filled, while further up the line Chaplains have been dropping out wounded, or sick, in the Somme fighting. So we are not a supererogation! But I expect to leave about Friday next week, November 3rd, and will send a telegram from the port of arrival as speedily as possible – I wonder if this will arrive before that day!

I like this, quoted in one of E.A. Burrough's addresses:

"I would not to Thy bosom fly
To shirk off till the storms go by.
Flog me, and spur me, set me straight
At some vile job I fear and hate"[824].

---

823 It is better to remain active than to succumb to idleness: used particularly with reference to elderly people. Frequently attributed in its current form to Bishop Richard Cumberland (d.1718). Better it is to shine with labour, then to rouste for idlenes; [1598 Shakespeare *Henry IV, Pt. 2* i. ii. 206]

824 *A Faith for the Firing Line*, E A Burrough, 1915. The poem is anonymous, popular in patriotic

Saturday October 28th 1916, Rouen

<u>Two</u> letters from you today, one dispatched on the 22nd and the other on the 23rd, enclosing more particulars about West Farleigh. Mr Fawns does not seem inclined to carry on at West Farleigh, so I hope that the correspondence with other possible men may lead to something – M Fletcher seemed interested and interesting and Mr Tritton is keen. W. Farleigh will seem very tiny after life among men by thousands, across part of a continent, over battlefields and all the rest of it. I still think Mr Fawns might be well-guided to adopt the arrangements proposed – suitable charges to men of his qualifications are not simply found, and there is a great deal to be said for knowing your surroundings. I think my time at West Farleigh will be a fairly quiescent one, the activities will be chiefly feminine as also very much elsewhere, outside military circles.

Today the weather has been fair and I took my last chance of seeing one of the views of this ancient city. Climbing a height overlooking the town (climbing by train that is), I stood by a fine statue of Joan of Arc, and saw what is probably one of the most striking views in Europe[825]. The statue and its surroundings are gracefully and strongly conceived and it is flanked on either side by statues of her two patron saints – St Marguerite and St Catherine. In front are four recumbent figures of sheep, recollecting, I suppose, her occupation[826]. Nearby is a modern Church, the Notre Dame Chapel[827], which is greatly affected by pilgrims. It was a blaze of candles – the white silk cloak of the statue of the Virgin with its gold braiding, looked rather stiff and tawdry, dollish in fact. I looked into the Cathedral and found 'Salut' in process and so I stayed. Much, much repetition and the priest, conducting up in a high prayer pulpit in the nave, looked distrait and formal. He scratched his head and yawned, but went on grinding out the reiterated sentences of some kind of Litany. Yet, there was an atmosphere of prayer over all, which you felt and joined in, and I am sure our Church has much to gain in preserving stateliness and beauty of outward things in worship. The dignity of great arches and pillars and the fitness of beautiful fittings – the best human artifice can contrive to appeal to me. I thought of you, darling – and

---

literature in WW1, known as 'The Soldier's Poem'.

825 **Bonsecours:** A southern residential suburb of Rouen situated at the junction of the D6014, D6105 and the D95 roads.

826 **The Memorial of Joan of Arc** (Louis-Ernest Barrias b.1841 – d.1905), Bonsecours, is executed in an early Renaissance style and stands in front of the Basilica de Bonsecours on granite terrace overlooking the Seine valley. The central shrine is made of pillars supporting a cupola and a bell tower of lead and gilt copper (made by Ferdinand Marrou). The dome is topped by a lantern with St. Michael slaying the Dragon in gilded bronze, made by Thomas. Under the dome, are the coats of arms of the major cities and regions that have marked the life of Joan of Arc: Lorraine, Normandie, Domrémy, Orléans, Reims and Rouen. On the six pillars are putti with coat of arms. In the center of the shrine is the statue of Joan of Arc by Barrias. The two side pavilions house the the statues of Saint Margaret (by Édouard Pépin – south) and Saint Catherine (by Robert Verlet – north). The balustrade of the terrace accommodates four sheep (sculpted by Georges Gardet).

827 **Basilica de Bonsecours:** 1840–1844. The basilica was designed by architect Jacques Barthélemy in Eugene. neogothic style – this is also the first example of this style in France. It has a nave flanked by aisles, without transept and a tower topped by a spire above the western portal.

of how our two lives have come out of Eternity to walk this pilgrimage together on into Eternity. This grand old old Cathedral[828] (whose interior I painted a study of as a boy) stands there as one of the strong, peaceful, strengthening houses of rest along the journey. I could easily be a 'High' churchman, except that they soon lose themselves in a maze of fidgetting details and minor personalities, but it a comfort to think of how many are at the 'feet of God' – some after this manner and some after that.

Goodnight, my darling – we must have W. Farleigh Church and the services beautiful and dignified somehow, small as the place is.

Sunday October 29th 1916, Rouen

Catholic ritual with Evangelical tradition – is that the position the Church of England will come to? Both are so appealing, but I tremble as I remember some shambling 'familiar' Communions I have been present at – the assertion of the individual who prays cleverly, and who likes to pray because he could pray 'nicely' and other Evangelical enormities, while also one trembles as one remembers some irritated formalist, some hard and particular observer of, say, the Sarum use[829] who barely avoided demonstrating to you that "Knowledge that puffeth up[830]". To tell you the truth, I longed a little for that outward uniformity of Rome that presents to the world at least a united front. How are we all going to come together into 'a perfect man' into the measure of the stature of the fullness of Christ? The High Churchman thinks I am unbrotherly because I insist on having an Evening Communion, he is shocked and hurt. I am tempted to think him unbrotherly because he makes the law of God of no effect by his tradition, and as he observes times and seasons, days and years, he omits the weightier matters of judgement and mercy, of kindness and brotherly love. "Our little systems have their day, they have their day and cease to be, we are but broken lights..........[831]" But A B C or D claims overmuch to be the Light in its fullness.

Rain, cold and blustery, made an unpropitious beginning to the day – 9 people came to the 8.0am Holy Communion, 3 of them of the newly confirmed. There was an enormous parade at 11.0 with over 900 men, some standing up at the back. They were very quiet, and I do trust that a blessing reached them – we know it must. The

---

828 In 1892, RDG was an Assistant Chaplain at Holy Trinity, Nice, an Anglican church in Nice from 1862, under the diocese of the Bishop of London.

829 The **Sarum Rite** (more properly called the **Use of Salisbury**) was a variant ("use") of the Roman Rite widely used for the ordering of Christian public worship, including the Mass and the Divine Office. It was established by Saint Osmund, Bishop of Salisbury, England in the 11th century and was originally the local form used in the Cathedral and Diocese of Salisbury. Many of the ornaments and ceremonial practices associated with the Sarum Rite – though not the full liturgy itself – were revived in the Anglican Communion in the late 19th and early 20th centuries, as part of the Anglo-Catholic Oxford Movement in the Church of England.

830 **1 Corinthians 8:1** 'Now as touching things offered unto idols, we know that we all have knowledge. Knowledge puffeth up, but charity edifieth.'

831 Tennyson, *In Memoriam AHH*, completed 1849. Prologue, Stanza 5.

new band, helped by your Fund, did very well indeed – they have bought a cornet (second-hand) for 60 francs and the player fully let himself go, so with 3 violins and a very capable organist, the cornet in full strength and the men well kept in hand, the result was reassuring. The second parade was cancelled, but about 100 turned up voluntarily and we had a nice 'homely' service – we do not get a hundred men to hear the Gospel in W. Farleigh at one moment! A large crowd went to the 6.30 Service in the central Church, not 400 yards away from my camp, but none came to my 7.0 pm Evening prayer. 31 however came at 8 o'clock and I do believe it was a communion to many of them and there was a sense of fellowship. Will W. Farleigh be like letting our lives run away into the sands – a stream drying up nowhere?

Monday October 30th 1916, Rouen

I gave myself an afternoon off again today, and really enjoyed it by going over the Cathedral[832]. It is very realistic seeing the actual tomb where reposes the body of Matilda, wife of William the Conqueror. The guide book says she was buried at Caen, but the Swiss Guardsman showed me the tomb in the Cathedral. Certainly there reposes the body of Henry II, with his recumbent effigy of a plump, comfortable-looking gentleman with a very round chin and his sceptre of kingship clasped under his left arm[833]. There is the tomb of the Duke of Bedford, now represented by some noble descent, but of unenviable repute *owing* to the volaries of Joan of Arc. He bought that gallant girl for the King of England from the Duke of Burgundy for 10,000 pieces, and afterwards in collusion with the Cardinal of Winchester handed her over to the French Church representatives for trial[834].

There also you see the tomb and recumbent effigy of Richard Coeur de Lion, Richard 1st of England, (little did he know how a distinguished lady would wed a distinguished warrior-priest of his own name though of the more honourable and ancient nationality than his own – the original Britisher![835]) whose brain and bodily

---

832 **Rouen Cathedral** is a Roman Catholic Gothic cathedral, it is the seat of the Archbishop of Rouen and Normandy. RDG's guide was mistaken; Matilda is buried at The **Abbey of Sainte-Trinité** (the Holy Trinity), also known as **Abbaye aux Dames**, is a former monastery of women in Caen.

833 **Henry**, known as **the Young King** (b.1155 – d.1183), was the second of five sons of Henry II of England and Eleanor of Aquitaine but the first to survive infancy. Beginning in 1170, he officially reigned alongside his father as King of England, Duke of Normandy, Count of Anjou and Maine. Because he predeceased his father, he is not counted in the numerical succession of kings of England. His remains are in Rouen Cathedral, where his tomb is on the opposite side of the altar from the tomb of his younger brother, Richard, with whom he was perpetually quarrelling. The tomb of the Archbishop of Rouen, who had married him and Margaret, lies nearby in the ambulatory. His brothers Richard and John both later became kings of England.

834 **John Plantagenet, 1st Duke of Bedford**, KG (b.1389 – d.1435) was the third surviving son of King Henry IV of England by Mary de Bohun, and acted as regent of France for his nephew, King Henry VI. Jean (Joan) D'Arc was ransomed from John of Luxemburg by the Duke, handed over to the French Inquisition and burnt as a witch on 30th May 1431 in Rouen.

835 RDG was born in Wales, his wife Margaret, was born in Jersey. The Welsh are, of course, the original Britons.

machinery he bequeathed to Poitiers, whose body's framework lies at Fontevrault, and whose heart he sent to repose here "on account of the great love he bore to the Normans" – he shared himself liberally[836]. His admirers must have meant to ascribe to himself an impressive bearing, for the effigy is seven feet in length.

Here also repose the bodies of 5 cardinals, their red hats suspended high up in the vaulted roof above them, as we used to suspend the banners and casquets of knights, still red enough, but suffering one would think a little, from the dust of ages. The relics of certain saints, bits of bone and cloth, I am afraid did not impress me. There is some remarkably fine carving on some of the tombs – one, that of the Cardinale d'Amboise, (two of them, uncle and nephew – curious that a nephew happened to succeed his uncle as Cardinal!) in alabaster is a remarkable display of ingenuity and patience. There are dozens of figures, and the whole work took seven years to carry through. The first Cardinal was named Georges and for that reason there is in the centre of the tomb a rather fine and detailed study of St George and the Dragon. There are also 6 figures representing the chief virtues, charity, purity, etc, and each figure is flanked by two tiny little monks, one of whom sleeps with his book closed upon his knee, the other wakes watching and praying, showing how there should be service and rest, turn and turn about[837].

Goodnight for the present – it is raining in torrents, as it has been most of the day.

Tuesday October 31st 1916, Rouen

A wild night with tents blown down, although I am thankful to say that I slept through it all. The Hospital tent was blown over bodily so the 11 patients took refuge in our Church tent (making rather a mess of things!) – "for once" the infidel doctor remarked "the Church has done something useful. The first time I've ever known it to – I'm one of these practical men myself, etc., etc."! Again no mail and persons journeying hither and thither do not progress. I wonder if my journeying hence will be prevented also. It has been a beautiful day – the storm will have beaten itself out let us hope, before the most important passenger in the world to myself i.e. myself, has to cross. So we expect the universe to radiate round minute centres.

It is most likely now that Cave-Moyle takes over this work, and we meet for a talk over things tomorrow morning. The men who occupied the Church Tent last night in the midst of the storm showed little consciousness of the nature of its' use, employing

---

836   Richard 1's heart was buried at Rouen, his entrails in Châlus (where he died), and the rest of his body at the feet of his father at Fontevraud Abbey in Anjou.

837   Started in 1515, and completed in 1525, this tomb is an early example of French Renaissance art by Rouen cathedral's master mason, Roullant Le Roux. The monument is a memorial to the French Cardinal George D'Amboise (d.1510) archbishop of Rouen, and his nephew George d'Amboise (d.1550) who, on the death of his uncle, took the post of archbishop of Rouen, and who also became a cardinal in later life. The two priant figures are kneeling with their hands raised in prayer and are beadsmen.

the Church candles for their own needs and generally disposing themselves in genuine 'sanctuary'. The carpet before the holy table was appreciated as a bed, and I could not begrudge it, though one could have wished for evidence of some definite reverence. It is one of those 'let-downs' of which Army life has many. Men are what they are told to be, or what is suggested to them to be at the time – reverent when they are required to be, but not on their own initiative. On his <u>own</u> initiative the strong things the soldier indicates are comradeship, enterprise, and sentimentality, especially towards the opposite sex.

I went down into the city to get some money for 'journeying' purposes, and hope to have enough, but in doing so, I just missed Mr Shallard, but had a few words with him between two trams! Otherwise visiting, and a football match – the good old Rugby game between an Australian team and some Cavalry details. The Cavalry won easily though a good game was put up at the start. It was a game I rather succeeded in, long years ago, and it stirred one's pulses to see the dash and vigour both sides showed. Rugby is a spirited game to watch, having more in it, I think, than Association[838].

The dear old horse was pleased to have a short run and was diligent in calling attention to the various autumn beauties of the forest. The tints were certainly radiant and rich, and if the horse does not enter into them, he talks as if he does in horse language, which you know as well as I do.

A crowded meeting in the S.C.A. hut and we all entered into the communion of Saints on the eve of tomorrow. Most of these men are more 'saints' than they know in their loyalty to the call of duty, their standards of manliness and courage, their unselfishness, their surrender of themselves to labour, suffering, and fight for right against wrong. Take every man at his best, and God's image is there.

Goodnight, dear, gentle sweetheart. Reading today an account of the retreat from Mons, I am thankful, myself not to have known anything of a retreat[839]. What wonderful mercies were shown to us all as a people, those first 3 months of the War!

Wednesday November 1st 1916, Rouen All Saints' Day
For all the Saints – who made the world a better world for man's brief earthly dwelling. A good many names crowd up – your father, Major Higginbotham – some names I find stand forward regularly in the Prayer for the Church Militant.

Cave-Moyle came, according to his telephone message. While we were talking, Colbeck came into the tent on a matter of the Central Church. He was furious to find that Cave-Moyle had come without reference to him. He took him off

---

838 'Rugger', rather than 'Soccer'.
839 Imperial German Armies at the Battle of Charleroi (21st August) and the Battle of Mons (23rd August).

to "show him the Church" but really to let him have a piece of his mind, and in addition to insist that Evening Communion be dropped altogether, or Cave-Moyle does not come here. Cave-Moyle is an old Ridley Hall[840] man, and quite decided on the Service continuing if there is a call for it! But wisely enough I think, decided to avoid that question being made a test of his coming. But how dreadfully sad it all is. So now – we agreed it would not be well to take him round introducing him to the Colonels. Colbeck does not know them, but to magnify his office 'requests that it be left to him' – he does not know how it lets him down before those same Colonels, and incidentally the work of the Chaplains' Dept. Bother it!! Really, from these human bickerings one has no place to flee unto, except you conform to their whims and wishes to a fraction, and Colbeck is of an age that it is not easy for anyone to tell him things. Bother it!!!

No mail – no word about movement, but I hear movements are being made. A small Evening Service and this after a ride on the old grey friends' comfortable back.

Major Tucson has been regaling us with his lion-hunting stories since dinner. He is a plucky man and they are like tales in a book, and then Colonel Bulman came round to say 'Goodbye' – he is a good man. On Sunday morning early he had to be at the execution of a man for insubordination and it has whetted his keenness and he took up the appeal of my address about the need of everybody helping religion all possible[841] And he was very nice in saying "Can you tell me any way in which I can do more to help the men?" A good man.

Thursday November 2nd 1916, Rouen

A full day – Chaplains meeting – arrangements – a visit to a quaint church built into the rocks, and this evening an overflowing Evangelistic meeting. More tomorrow – thank goodness a mail in the afternoon.

---

840   **Ridley Hall** is a theological college located in Sidgwick Avenue in Cambridge, which trains intending ministers for the Church of England and other churches. It was founded in 1881 and named in memory of Nicholas Ridley, a leading Protestant theologian of the sixteenth century. The first principal was theologian Handley Moule, later Bishop of Durham. Although not part of the University of Cambridge, Ridley Hall maintains close ties with the university and many of its students are awarded qualifications by the university Faculty of Divinity. Ridley Hall teaching tends towards an evangelical theology.

841   Execution of Pte **Elsworth Young** (b.1895 – d.1916) 25th Battalion, Canadian Infantry, born in Halifax (Nova Scotia). Young travelled to France with the battalion in September 1915, serving as an officer's batman. During the major fighting at Courcelette reinforcements were needed and Young was ordered forward to report to his Company Sergeant-Major. However, Young went absent before reporting to his battalion later that evening and answering the evening rollcall. Depite returning, Young went absent again. In September 1916, Young was arrested by the military police some miles behind the front-lines. He was dressed in the uniform of a Corporal in an artillery unit and initially gave false details to the MPs that arrested him. Young was charged with desertion. His court-martial found him guilty and sentenced Young to death. At 06:26 on 29th October 1916, Young was executed by firing squad.

Friday November 3rd 1916, Rouen

The little church was very interesting and is about 8 miles out of the City. Its interior is really a large cave and I enclose a postcard of it[842].

A warm kind of farewell over the Evangelistic meeting – crowded out to the doors, and some came especially evidently. One man I overheard in the dark coming out "he knows how to preach, that fellow!" – better that than criticisms, and it shows that the word tells sometimes when we little expect it.

A message has just come – Friday morning 10.30 a.m. I leave for England tonight.

---

842 Saint Adrien, Rouen. La Chapelle et les Blanches Roches, hermitage in the C16th, present chapel dates from C18th. Enclosed one postcard, the other posted to Eric on 19th November from Brighton.

Postcard to Eric 'Very busy getting ready for a confirmation and the opening of a new church. Thank you for your post card. Very glad of good reports. Lovely weather here: with you too I hope. Much love From Father'

Sunday November 19th 1916, Brighton

SAINT-ADRIEN, près Rouen (Seine-Inf.) — La Chapelle et les Roches

To: E.W.S. Griffiths
St. Andrew's
Southborough,
Tunbridge Wells
As from 4 Belmont, Dyke Road, Brighton[843].
Just a line to show that I have arrived in England alright – though this is a French postcard. I hope to be able to come over some day. Much love from R.G.

---

843 Residence of the Rev Charles Herbert Griffith (b.1859 – d.?) and Alice Sophia (Saumarez) Smith. Alice was the sister of RDG's father-in-law, William Saumarez-Smith, Archbp of Sydney, his wife Margaret's aunt.